D1736279

THE
Leverett Letters

THE Leverett Letters

CORRESPONDENCE OF A SOUTH CAROLINA FAMILY 1851–1868

Edited by Frances Wallace Taylor
Catherine Taylor Matthews
and J. Tracy Power

University of South Carolina Press

/

© 2000 University of South Carolina

Published in Columbia, South Carolina, by the
University of South Carolina Press

Manufactured in the United States of America

04 03 02 01 00   5 4 3 2 1

Library of Congress Cataloging-in-Publication Data

The Leverett letters : correspondence of a South Carolina family,
   1851–1868 / edited by Frances Wallace Taylor, Catherine Taylor Matthews,
   and J. Tracy Power.
      p. cm.
   Includes bibliographical references and index.
   ISBN 1-57003-333-1
   1. Leverett family—Correspondence. 2. South Carolina—Biography.
   3. South Carolina—History—Civil War, 1861–1865—Personal narratives.
   4. United States—History—Civil War, 1861–1865—Personal narratives.
   5. South Carolina—Social life and customs—19th century. I. Taylor,
   Frances Wallace, 1914– II. Matthews, Catherine Taylor, 1954– III. Power,
   J. Tracy.
   CT274.L48 L48 2000
   975.7'03'0922—dc21   99-050784

Contents

Illustrations

Acknowledgments

Many people helped with the preparation of this volume and we are grateful to all of them, especially John Taylor, who worked for years on all phases of the project. We sincerely thank Allen Stokes, director of the South Caroliniana Library at the University of South Carolina, for his advice and encouragement and for permitting us to include a very interesting letter from one of the collections of the library. Patricia Paden Matsen of the Department of French and Classics at the university translated Greek and Latin passages. Grey Minshew Geissler of Beaufort, South Carolina, gave us many papers and letters, some of which we have included. At our request, John Taylor Matthews drew a detailed pencil sketch of the ruins of Sheldon Church. Carolyn R. Harris of Fayetteville, Arkansas, helped us locate the records of Charles Hendee Leverett, who moved to Arkansas in 1867. John Taylor Jr. reviewed the manuscript. We also appreciate the help of the many people who typed letters or assisted in other ways. To each we give our sincere thanks.

Introduction

"It will be an extreme disadvantage to you all your life, not to be able to make easy use of your pen," Mary Maxcy Leverett lectured to one of her sons in May 1863 on the art of letter writing. Milton Maxcy Leverett, a Confederate artilleryman who was stationed in his native South Carolina lowcountry, wrote home less frequently and with less care than his mother thought proper for the college-educated son of an Episcopal clergyman and planter. "So necessary an act is it," she continued, "that every young person should make it their aim to write so freely as to make the habit a sort of second nature to them, and writing a letter become by such means a pleasure, instead of a bore." Her keen interest in the quantity and quality of Milton's letters was much more than an anxious mother's desire for news from her soldier son. Mary and her husband, Rev. Charles Edward Leverett, thought that their children would learn to express themselves effectively by the very act of letter writing, and her emphasis on lively correspondence was the result of a life spent with a large family separated for extended periods. They were a family of well-educated and prolific letter writers who sent and received letters several times a month while residing in McPhersonville; at Canaan, their plantation in Beaufort District; at their house on Bay Street in Beaufort; or at The Farm, outside Columbia. One or more of the Leveretts's four sons—Fred, Edward, Charley, and Milton—was away from home on an almost continuous basis for twenty years. They were at college, in postgraduate study and travel, or serving in the Confederate army, and the family at home expected them to write frequently and at length of their experiences. Replies from both parents and from their sisters, Matilda, Anne, Mary, Julia, and Caroline, often included a brief assessment of their most recent letters and suggestions for improving future ones.

With the exception of Mary Maxcy Leverett's letter to Caroline Pinckney Seabrook of 18 March 1865, which is part of the manuscript collection of the

South Caroliniana Library at the University of South Carolina and is reproduced courtesy of that library, the 230 letters published here are from the Leverett correspondence in a collection of more than 300 letters, documents, and
other papers now (1998) in the possession of Frances Wallace Taylor. The
project of cataloging and transcribing was begun by Frances in 1962, when
she prevented the collection from being burned and assumed its custody. All
but a few of the letters were written by the immediate family, and the rest by
relatives, friends, and business associates. The collection spans over fifty
years and has remarkably few substantive gaps between 1850 and 1868. The
year 1851 was the first year of regular extant correspondence, when three of
the four sons were away in college. Fred's letter to Milton from Harvard in
April 1851 is therefore a natural starting point for this volume, which covers
a period of seventeen years. A few letters from this period were not selected
for publication. These are either fragments of letters, brief notes of little sub-
stance, or repetitive letters whose subjects are covered by others included
here.

One of the most significant of several recurring themes in the Leverett
correspondence is the emphasis on education, both formal and informal, and
the need for continual intellectual growth and development throughout one's
life. "Let not studying be without an object, merely to get through, but study
with an aim in life," Mary Maxcy Leverett advised Milton in a typical letter.
Rev. Charles Leverett tutored his sons and daughters, preparing them for further education. Whether at Harvard, South Carolina College, the Medical
University of Pennsylvania, the Protestant Theological Seminary of Virginia,
the Sorbonne, the University of Heidelberg, or the Barhamville Institute, the
Leverett children were given every opportunity to gain an education that
rivaled any in nineteenth-century America. They were encouraged not only to
pursue structured studies but also to educate themselves by reading, writing,
and traveling.

The family's financial situation is another subject that was often discussed. Rev. Charles Leverett maintained a small plantation with as many as
thirty-four slaves and a house in town with a household of twelve family
members. The plantation was marginally profitable at best, and the expenses
of buildings, livestock, equipment, and crops were frequent topics. Having
three sons in college at the same time, or two of them abroad on an extended
tour, made the Leveretts's situation even more difficult. While in college, the
children were reminded in many letters of the family's financial sacrifices and
were admonished to be frugal. "I do not think you understand the value of
money & the labour of getting it; & I am afraid Tilly & Annie, knowing that
you had 2 suits when one would have been enough, think you, indeed, very

selfish, & too fond of dress," wrote Rev. Charles Leverett to Edward in 1852. Despite their frugality, the Leveretts's financial condition deteriorated rapidly during the war and they struggled financially for many years following.

The letters are usually well structured, and the Leveretts avoided the unimaginative phrasing of so many mid-nineteenth-century correspondents. Many exhibit a narrative rather than the stream-of-consciousness approach common in letter writing. In the best ones, such as Milton's lively transcription of a Confederate officer's conversation with a Federal picket or Mary Leverett's graphic account of the night Columbia burned, the writing is polished and more consciously literary than most correspondence of the period.

The institution of slavery is the one feature of their society that often seems so central to contemporary observers, yet it is discussed only indirectly in these letters. The topic is raised only in reference to discussions with outsiders, as they were in agreement and their views were consistent with others of their time and place. However, they did write about individual slaves. Tales of Ephraim, Hercules, Sary, Lewis, and especially Billy are an integral part of the story told by these letters. The slaves' contact with the Leveretts did not end when they were freed; Hercules and Billy were still with them as late as 1887, over twenty years after the war ended.

This volume was prepared from the original collection and is as faithful to the manuscripts as possible, preserving the spelling, punctuation, and other idiosyncrasies of the originals. Any editorial comments or other minimal alterations within the letters are enclosed in square brackets. Persons, places, events, and significant terms are identified at their first occurrence and only identified thereafter if necessary for clarity. The appendix, entitled "The Leveretts and Their Contemporaries," is included to provide more detailed information than is given in the footnotes. It is especially useful for identifying the almost five hundred people whose names appear on subsequent pages. Place-names are assumed to be in South Carolina unless well known or otherwise noted. All biblical references in the footnotes are to the King James Version.

Even though the letters written from July 1861 to April 1865 comprise over two-thirds of the correspondence in this volume, this is not, strictly speaking, a Civil War book. The wartime letters are not confined to a soldier's view from camp or battlefield but also include a civilian's view of the home front and of the war itself from that vantage point. All of these letters focus on the personal aspects of the conflict as seen by the individual members of the Leverett family rather than on the major events and personalities of the war. The thirty-nine antebellum and twenty-six postbellum letters included here provide context often missing in editions restricted to wartime letters.

Edward Leverett wrote wistfully in the spring of 1858, on the day his sister Anne married Louis McPherson DeSaussure Jr. at Sheldon Church, "I am seated all alone in the wide, wide world . . . thinking of dear Little Canaan every moment, & building pictures of all that is going on there." For nearly twenty years, when they sat down to write the letters in this remarkable collection, all the Leveretts from the eldest to the youngest were thinking of "dear Canaan" and the time when they might be reunited as a family.

I
Boys in College
April 1851–June 1857

You will find yourself in a new world. Take
care it does not get the better of you.

—Rev. Charles E. Leverett

*Charles Edward Leverett, a native of New England and graduate of Trinity College
in Hartford, Connecticut, moved to South Carolina in 1831 to become principal of
Beaufort College, an academy in the town of Beaufort. He married Mary Bull Maxcy
of Beaufort that December. He was made a deacon by Bishop Nathaniel Bowen of
the diocese of South Carolina in late 1832, served briefly as assistant rector of Grace
Church, Greenville, the next year, and was ordained to the priesthood in the spring
of 1834. In 1835 he became rector of Trinity Church, Edisto Island, in Charleston District. After eleven years at Trinity, in 1846, Rev. Charles Leverett accepted a call to
Sheldon Church, Prince William's Parish, near McPhersonville, South Carolina.*

*In the spring of 1851, when the first of these letters was written, Charles and Mary
Leverett, forty-five and forty-three years old, respectively, resided in McPhersonville.
They had a family of nine children, two of whom were adopted. Nineteen-year-old
Frederic Percival, in his junior year at Harvard College, and seventeen-year-old
Charles Hendee, a student at South Carolina College in Columbia,[1] were the sons of
Rev. Charles Leverett's brother Frederic Percival Leverett Sr. (1803–1836) and Ma-
tilda Gorham Leverett (1813–1834). Eighteen-year-old Charles Edward Jr., called
"Edward" to distinguish him from his adopted brother Charles Hendee, was also a
student at South Carolina College. The other children lived with their parents in*

---

1. Now the University of South Carolina.

McPhersonville. Matilda, "Tilly," was sixteen; Anne Heyward, fourteen; Milton Maxcy, "Minny," twelve; Mary Bull, called "Mame," was eleven; Julia Marcelline, five; and Catherine Hamilton, "Kate," the baby, was about to celebrate her first birthday.[2]

Frederic Percival Leverett to his brother Milton

Divinity Hall,[3] April 12<u>th</u> [1851]
Saturday

My dear Min,

Being anxious to pay you a debt long since due, and also to restore your offended dignity to its proper and natural condition, I now commence a letter to you. I will not make a long apology to you for not answering the letters duly received last term, having replied to them during the vacation in persona—Even now that I have taken up my pen I must say that I am rather at loss to find something to interest you. Should I write about shooting I might unluckily mention some unfortunate bird or animal that might cause you to declare "I will not write to Fred as long as he is in college"—should I mention the fugitive slave that has been arrested and sent South I would not hit the right chord then, for it is a subject, about which you know little or nothing, though you are old enough to. However we have had considerable excitement about it, and Mr. Sims, the aforesaid darkey went South this morning. And thus in the opinion of the abolitionists Massachusetts has been eternally disgraced.[4]

Now Min, "in short in a burst of confidence," I find myself run out, it not being lawful to call the Muses to my aid, or to mount the winged Pegasus, while writing in strains prosaic. The reason that I find writing to-night so difficult, is that my steed is sadly jaded, having been hard at work on a theme, today, without accomplishing but little more than nothing; so having found it "no go" to-night I have given it up despondingly. The subject is the generosity of the world. I'm afraid I shall prove it to be as cold as "the snow-clad hills and ice-bound lakes of

---

2. The Leveretts had also lost four children by 1851: Stephen Bull in 1834, Eliza in 1842, William Percival in 1844, and Percival Evelyn in 1849.

3. At Harvard University.

4. Thomas Sims was a bricklayer who had been in Boston only a few weeks when he was arrested under the Fugitive Slave Act of 1850. Lawyers representing James Potter of Savannah claimed that Sims was a fugitive slave, while Sims claimed that he was born free and was in Boston visiting his mother and sister. The case angered many Boston abolitionists, who held meetings protesting Sims's arrest and planned to rescue him from jail, but U.S. Commissioner George T. Curtis ruled that Sims was indeed a slave and ordered him returned to Potter as his rightful owner. *Boston Daily Advertiser*, 4–15 April 1851.

Massachusetts"—I heard from Charly the other day. Tell mother that he said he heard a young lady say, after I left, that the "sun had set"—I really wish I was with him and Ed. I think Columbia the paragon of places. It being after 11 o'clock I must bid you good night—When I commenced writing I felt terribly blue now, however, my spirits are rather better. It is really a pleasure to write home—

Saturday—Dear Min, On reading over the part of the letter written some two weeks since I feel half tempted to burn it, but being decidedly tired and sleepy I believe that I must let it stand. I'm afraid that you will not appreciate some parts of it, and in fact, that none of you will appreciate one of the quotations. I have finished the theme and also a forensic since writing the above; and just to think another theme must be handed in a fortnight from next Thursday and a forensic the week after. Heu me miserum! Vide Latin Grammar.—under Interjections. College life here seems made up of nothing except writing on miserable subjects. I am almost disgusted and very nearly discouraged.

I hope that you are studying so as to give father no trouble. If you try hard I am sure that you will succeed. When you are going to learn a lesson let everything go until it is learnt, and then play as much as you wish to; but always do one thing at a time—some little boys think they can do two, but they are very much mistaken. If I was going over my school days I would study very differently from the way that I did.—Now do try so that the next time I see you I may find you a good scholar and what is still better a good boy.—Try to give father and mother as little trouble as possible. When I was at home the other day I thought that you seemed very much improved and that you did not get put out as easily as formerly—I felt almost obliged to attribute it to us boys being absent. Anyhow I hope next time to see still greater improvement.

Tell father that I tried to get the book for Mr. Gould but could not succeed.[5] I went to 17 bookstores, but it was no where to be found—I dined at Dr. Storer's to-day.[6] He and Mrs. S. are going to Charleston on Tuesday.

I expect you to write me soon and to tell me all about the horses, dogs, cows, pigeons, &c. Goodbye—

Ever yr aff^{ct} brother
Fred^{c} P. Leverett

P.S.
My love to all. Tell Anne that I'll try to write to her soon. You are to write immediately or even a little sooner than that,—but anyhow immediately.

---

5.   Benjamin Apthorp Gould of Boston, a school principal and merchant.
6.   Dr. David Humphreys Storer of Boston, professor at the Tremont Street Medical School and at Harvard College, 1854–1868.

Frederic Percival Leverett to his brother Milton

Boston, Feb. 18th 52.

My dear Min,

As I am somewhat under the impression that one of your letters is as yet unanswered by me I have determined to drop you a few lines hoping thereby to induce you to send me another of your most welcome, most valued and highly entertaining epistles. Your last letter I can assure was the source of very much amusement to me. I took it out to read in the Latin recitation room, but in order to keep from haw-hawing out aloud, I restored it only partially read to my pocket—it recalled to my mind most vividly my own youth (I do not say my youthful letters for I wrote none) I hope that your fowls have commenced supplying you with eggs and that you will be able to make me a present when you write next—"the smallest favor gratefully received"—recollect that and tell the other children so also. You seem to have a much larger number of hens than Mother ever let us keep. You didn't say anything about Mins or Luck I believe—how are they—remember me to them and also tell all the servants howdy'e for me—speaking of Luck recalled Count to mind—how is he? Ed has never mentioned him—did he succeed in learning him to fetch birds?

Today I expected to have gone to New York, but have concluded not to, as Mr. Gould was anxious for me to remain here, so I intend staying with him during the rest of the vacation except a few days which I intend spending in Roxbury at Mrs. Hendee's.[7] I went over there last Saturday and staid until Monday.

Week before last I went to Billerica to see my uncle and staid a few days. While there I went to Lowell and saw a great many of the factories and went over them.

Why has no one at home written to me this vacation? I have been for some time looking out daily for a letter, but as yet there is none of them appearing. If Sister Matilda is at home, give my love to her and tell her I expected, when I wrote to her, that she would have answered my letter before this.

Give my love father and mother and all the children also a kiss to them. Write soon to your most affct Brother

F. P. Leverett —

P.S. If you are unable to understand this letter or find that there are several dozen mistakes, or in fine that there is little [more] than nothing in it, you can easily count for it by this fact that I'm writing in the sitting room with nearly all of Mrs. Gould's family around talking &c &c &c. Goodb'ye. So far this vacation I've had a very pleasant time.

Fred.

---

7.   The wife of Charles I. Hendee, executor of the elder F. P. Leverett's estate.

Fred graduated from Harvard in July 1852 and entered the Medical University of Pennsylvania in Philadelphia.

Charles Edward Leverett to his brother Milton

Banks of the Perkiomen,[8] July 7th 1852

My dear Mintens,

It was with mingled feelings of joy and surprise that a short time before leaving the classic walls of my alma mater[9]—(to meet my other alma mater in Charleston)—that I beheld your well-known handwriting, so <u>often</u> beheld and greeted, with the same feelings, before. With these fond remembrances still clinging to the parietes of my heart, like ivy branches on the broken, tho' still vigorous walls of a dismantled castle, I am pleased to trace with my stilus—like the "pen of a ready-writer"[10]—a few lines to you, my dear boy, containing some brief, graphic, & objective accounts of my travels.

With my heart—and pen also,—thus "inditing of a good matter"[11] I would first invite your attention to the broad expanse of the deep blue sea, where in the words of Byron when leaving his native land—"Once more upon the waters, yet once more"[12]—I stood likewise the second time. The weather was fine, & we had a pleasant time of it—but of all things, I know you would have liked to see sun-set, on the "ocean wave" gilded with the declining rays of Phoebus, just before he gives, as Thomson says "one bright glance, Then total disappears"[13]—the scene, tho' beautiful, is said by travellers, not to be equal to sunrise. We passed several light houses that night—among them one at C. Romain[14]—and in the morning turned into the mouth of C. Fear River,[15] the navigation of which tho' dangerous, is pleasant to those who survey its sandy shores for the first time. We soon after arrived at Wilmington, where we took the cars to Norfolk. Here we took the steamer to Baltimore—Norfolk or Portsmouth, I forget which. Old point Comfort looked as "grand, gloomy, and peculiar," as ever, and the rays of its lighthouse,[16] were shed over the dark waves of the sound, rendering the "darkness of the night

---

8. Perkiomen Creek, a tributary of the Schuylkill River near Philadelphia. Edward and his mother were visiting Mary Maxcy Leverett's sister, Matilda Miltonia Maxcy Fowles.
9. South Carolina College.
10. Ps. 45:1.
11. Ps. 45:1.
12. George Gordon, Lord Byron, *Childe Harold's Pilgrimage*, canto 3 (1816), stanza 2.
13. James Thomson, English poet, *The Seasons—Summer* (1727)
14. Cape Romain, near McClellanville, South Carolina.
15. The Cape Fear River, near Wilmington, North Carolina.
16. Near Fort Monroe and Hampton Roads, Virginia.

more visible." The morning, however, rendered us able to appreciate the beauties of the picturesque shores of the Chesapeake, and the view of retired gentlemans villas, with which the distant land was dotted, combined with the peaceful glid-ing of ships upon the placid bosom of the happy bay, rendered in the words of the Irish Anacreon, "each scene of enchantment more dear."[17] But at the end of the bay, I found in the cars, an end to my enjoyment, until we arrived in Phil^a where of the manner in which I spent my time you all have received some short accounts. The last things we saw, that were of note, were the Aztec children, of whom, without doubt, you have seen, the various accounts, in the papers.[18] There were two of them, a boy and girl, about two feet high, and tho' respectively 16 & 13 yrs. of age, they acted just like little babies. They were copper coloured, had black hair & eyes, and tottled all about after toys. Their history is involved in a maze of mystic conjectures, far more tortuous and intricate, my dear fellow, than the paths of the Cretan Labyrinth. The story of their capture by two Spaniards in Central America, or of there being a city of such diminutive creatures, is undoubt-edly as true, as the rape of Proserpine by the horrible Pluto, or the revelations of Swift's Gulliver—therefore of those tales, as of these Ουκ εσ' [?] ετυμον λογον may well be said.[19]

But here now we are staying in the heart of Pennsylvania environed by some of the most beautiful scenery in the world. From the high hill in front of the house, up which I carried Ma, we, yesterday evening beheld a most beautiful scene—"Low walk'd the sun, and broaden'd by degrees Just over the verge of day,"[20] and while his rays shed a refulgent radiance over the valley of the Perkiomen, illumming its humble hamlets with "fluid gold"—that of the Schuylkill was almost in dark-ness, for as in Childe Harolde, tho', "The moon was up, yet still it was not night, Sunset divides the sky with her."[21] Just so it was with these two vales separated from each other, by a ridge of woody hills. Such scenes cannot be painted, for in them, we see the God of nature reflected in colours, the artist must shrink from imitat-ing; nor can they be easily forgotten—"The last rays of feeling and life shall depart Ere the bloom of that valley shall fade from my heart."[22]

17.   Thomas Moore, Irish poet who translated the *Odes of Anacreon* (1799); this line is from Moore's poem "The Meeting of the Waters."

18.   The Aztec children were actually a dwarf brother and sister from San Salvador, Nicaragua, whom charlatans claimed were from an almost extinct race of Aztec priests and kings. They were placed on public display in Boston in 1850, but authorities quickly closed the exhibi-tion. The children were later displayed to crowds in New York in 1851 and again in Philadel-phia in 1852. *New York Herald*, 4 and 9 July 1852.

19.   Not a true story.

20.   Thomson, *The Seasons—Summer*.

21.   Byron, *Childe Harold's Pilgrimage*, canto 4 (1818), stanza 27.

22.   Moore, "The Meeting of the Waters."

By the time this reaches you, I shall, most probably, be on the way to Cambridge, to see Fred weaned from his foster mother, tho' I am afraid he will always be tied to her apron strings.

I hope you have not forgotten your swimming, or got afraid of the water—you ought to go to the mill pond with Charley or the boys, and see how much you can improve by the time I come. I will bring a book for you that will tell you all about swimming, and show you how to learn all the various attitudes, and methods, of that pastime, so that you will understand not only the science, but the art, of it.

I hope you are getting along well in your studies, and improving so fast that you will be very soon ready for College. And, even if, my dear fellow, you meet anything hard in Geometry or Algebra, (for I suppose you are no tyro, now, in Latin & Greek) you must <u>persevere</u> and you <u>will</u> conquer, for recollect that

"Not for sluggards brow the laurel grows,
Renown is not the child of indolent repose."

—and as Horace says—"vitanda est

Improba <u>siren</u> <u>desidia.</u>"[23] With this constantly imprinted on the tablet of your memory, you will most certainly find the "gradus ad Parnassum"[24] like the descent to Avernus[25] "facilis."[26]

I hope you take good care of the colt, and you must not call it any name till I come, when I will give it a name among the horses of the land.

Tell Charley I hope he is flourishing "bene, apte, et ornate,"[27] among the <u>gentle</u> puella's of the village—ask him how is Miss Goodwyn? & tell him I will write to him next.

Tell Tilly I expect the mail miscarried, for of all the "too-much" letters she ever wrote me, they never reached me.

With my love to Mary, asking for my desk—& Fred's, to you, asking for his desk, Hoping Pa, Grandma,[28] & all the family are well, Believe me

Care frater <u>Minime</u>
semper esse tibi
frater amantissimus[29]
C. Edward Leverett.

---

23. The demoralizing siren, idleness, is to be avoided, Horace; book 2, satire 3, lines 14–15.
24. Climb to Parnassus, a mountain in central Greece sacred in Greek mythology.
25. A lake in southern Italy in the center of an extinct volcano; classical writers believed it was the entrance to Hades.
26. Easy.
27. Well, fit, and elegantly.
28. Mary Bull Maxcy of Beaufort, widow of Milton Maxcy, mother of Mary Maxcy Leverett.
29. Dear Brother Minime always to be to you a most loving brother. The word "Minime," translated as "by no means," is a pun on Milton's nickname, Minnie.

Rev. Charles Edward Leverett to his son Fred

Aug. 10, 1852

My dear Fred.,

To day you have, by the goodness of God, reached your majority. You are the first of our children,—for though a brother's son, I have always considered you in this light,—who has arrived at that important stage of human life. I feel it, therefore, due to you, to say, now that you are passing out of my control, a few words that will be interesting & acceptable to you. I would first assure you of our continued interest in your welfare, & that still for you, with our children, our prayer shall be, that you may have grace to honour the great care that your Mother & myself have put upon you, especially in a true & loving devotion to the God & Father of our Lord Jesus Christ. It is through his goodness, influencing our hearts, that we have been able to do as well by you as we have done. And while I would enjoin on you, now you are free, the warmest affection & respect for those who have been parents to you, particularly to her, you have been taught to call, in the place of your own dear parent, Mother, & who has been truly that, I would above all have you understand your indebtedness to that kind & gracious Saviour whom rightly to know is life everlasting.

When your father died, he left you and Charles, his orphan children to me—his words, and they express a love, gratefully to be remembered by you, were, just before he died, as reported to me "Tell Charles to be kind to my poor boys." You & Charles came to me then—yourself being some 3 or 4 years old & Charles about 2 years younger. Your mother & I have as you know made no distinction between you & our own, & though having a large family to take care of, we have made you share with them, all on the same footing of equality. It is true, I have had to work very hard, but in seeing you & the children, turn out well, especially as we hope in becoming religious, that makes up for all our toils & cares. Your Mother & myself, in the view that you will walk in the ways of holiness, through our instrumentality, instead of repining at the labour & expense & anxiety, are grateful for it. See that you are kind to others, as we have been to you.

Your father when he died was greatly involved. Though he had, with your own mother, something handsome, he contrived, by some speculation, in which some scheming acquaintances induced him to join, to lose it nearly all. Mr Hendee was his executor & settled to the best of his ability his affairs. Among other debts was one to me, with interest, amounting to about $2000. This was money I had reserved out of my salary, when I was Principal of Beaufort College. To free the estate & if possible secure any thing, I signed with the other creditors, a small amount—I am not sure that any thing was paid. However I did not care for that, as I have not needed it. A settlement, however being effected, through Mr Hendee, who has been very kind in this business, I have been able to make an arrangement with Mr Wilkins the Publisher of your father's Lexicon,[30] by which a small sum on each copy has been realized. That amount only began to be paid several years after your father's death. I have rec^{d} it, as your Guardian & carefully husbanded the same; though some of your friends have advised me from time to time to use it instead of defraying your expenses for support & education, out of my own toil. When I took out letters of Guardianship for you & Ch. the Master in Equity gave me to understand that an amount for your support, say your board & clothes & education, could, if the amount was sufficient, be paid to me, as my due. I knew that & had I chosen to avail myself of it, it would have been all spent. But I have not taken one cent & on the contrary have put what I have received including another amount, the balance due on some West India property of your Mother's paid through Mr Hendee, out to interest, and now I have for you as a gift from me, though in the first place, you must feel indebted to your own father & Mother for it, the sum of $4000 or rather that sum, about <u>next February, when the Court</u> will give me a discharge as Guardian. So you will have enough to start with & will, if you can get it out at interest at 7 per cent, have an annual receipt of nearly $300. a year. This with prudence, will release you from being dependent on me, but it must be used with prudence to accomplish that.

This my dear Son, is the gift I have for you, as I told you, if you came out of College to my satisfaction I would do something handsome by you. I trust you will be able to appreciate my feelings & my interest in you & believe me to be as ever your affect^{te} father

C. E. Leverett

P.S. The same amount I have for Charles; but as he cannot have it, until he is of age, perhaps, it is best to say nothing about it, or yours to him. I would advise you not to spend a dollar of the principal but invest it. I will be ready by the time I return, to pay you with permission of the Court, first to be had, a part of the interest; you will however be obliged to go & sign at the Master in Equity's office, in Charleston, my release as your Guardian.

Charles graduated from South Carolina College in December 1852.

---

30.   John Hubbard Wilkins of Boston, publisher of F. P. Leverett's *Lexicon of the Latin Language* (Boston, 1843).

Rev. Charles Edward Leverett to his son Edward

McPh<u>ille</u>.[31] March 25, 1853

My dear Ed<u>d</u>,

 Your letter mentioning that you had been operated on, came today. I am very glad that you have got thro', & so easily, the operation. I trust you will soon have restored eye-sight.

 I felt quite hurt with your letter & the more, as your mother never thinks, I can do enough for you. You intimate that I do not provide sufficiently for you, & that you would "rather leave college" than remain on the present terms. Let us see about it. You wrote me first that your bills &c would be 85 or 90 & I send 85. When in town you say "had you not better make provision for my April bill, which will be 70. & will amt while you are in town to about $100." Supposing that you meant that your bill <u>would be</u> $70, I send $85. presuming that would cover all extras, but I added on sending it, if this is not enough, write & let me know how much is required & you shall have it, or if it is more than enough, credit me with, for your expenses or something of that kind. I thought I was sending sufficient amt. over, especially as I was to pay for your clothes extra, as you wished them to be got in a diff<u>t</u> way. In fact, I thought you meant with the clothes I was to purchase, you would require $100, or rather that I would have to be ready with that amt. That was the reason I sent $85—I was therefore quite surprised to be lectured by you &c. Now the fact is that Mr. P's[32] pocket & mine are two diff<u>t</u> things. He is a rich man & can better afford his son "$24" a month, than I can 1/8 of it, I suppose, & also he is no guide for me, for if I was worth a million, I would do no better by you than I do. I have never seen extravagant boys turn out well & they certainly are not scholars & never very much respected. I am a minister with a salary of $900 per An. & a large expensive family in some respects or rather they have been, seeing I have had at once for some 3 years back 3 boys in college. I have supported my family & educated them by my own dreadful toil, & I have done well by them, for there are few children that appear better or are more respected or respectable than mine. One reason of this is, that I have not failed to train them after my judgment not according to the follies of others. Now if you don't think I do enough for you, when I repeat I will pay all your college bills, buy all your clothes, all necessary books & give you this am<u>t</u> of pocket money, I promised, you must remedy it. You are at liberty to come home & break up your connexion with College. You should be grateful that I am willing to do so much. You will find no father has

---

31. McPhersonville, a town in Prince William's Parish.

32. Rev. William Otis Prentiss, an Episcopal clergyman in Colleton District, whose son Christopher was a member of the class of 1855.

acted the faithful part, I have done. I feel sorry that you all blame me so much, for I do not feel at all to have deserved it.

I send to Fogartie's & DeLand[33] to send you per Allen & M^cC[34] the cloth for pants you wanted. Call at A & M & get the bundle & enclose me the bill, which is in it. When Dr. W.[35] has finished with you get his bill & send to me. Send me also your account. Enclosed is $6 for your gown & $15 over to make up the hundred minus $1. Now let me know how <u>much</u> I owe you for pocket money & you shall have it, when I send to pay Dr. W.

If you determine to leave college, as you cannot appear with so much cash as Prentiss[36] &c, when will you come?

From your letters, when about money, one would think I did not even pay your College bills.

yr. Aff. father
C.

I don't want you to think this is meant for a scolding letter, for I do not so design it.

P.S.

I told Mr. Fogartie to enclose pattern for fancy pants. You can select & send to him & ask him to let them come by McCarter & Allen. Aunt Til is to pay us a visit in April.[37]

As I have told you no news—I suppose you will be disappointed if I do not tell you all.

Mr. Potter came & spent one day & night.[38] He seemed quite surprised, we were so civilized. He is looking out I think for some Beaufort lady. I recommended the elder Miss Hutson's. Dr. Raoul is going away this summer & is to sell his house.[39] Mr. Gregorie & family intend to remove I believe to Ch^n.[40] It will hardly be worth while staying here—but I have no other place & am not likely to get any. Mr. Potter intends going to Europe this summer.

My dear Edward

As I filled up the whole sheet, in an attempt to show that you blamed me unjustly, I add a few lines to say that I do not care any thing about it. You have

---

33. Fogartie & DeLand, a dry goods store in Charleston owned by Arthur Fogartie and Charles W. DeLand.
34. McCarter & Allen, a book and stationery store in Charleston owned by James J. McCarter and Thomas P. Allen.
35. Dr. Alfred Wallace of Columbia.
36. Christopher Prentiss.
37. Matilda Miltonia Maxcy Fowles.
38. Rev. William T. Potter, Episcopal clergyman.
39. Dr. Alfred Raoul.
40. Charleston.

behaved so well, that I always feel sorry to blame you, & I do not mean so much to blame you as to show that you ought not to blame me. But let that go. Write as soon as you can & let me know how your eye is. If you find it troubles you, you must not study. In fact, I would prefer you should not, & will be content with what you have done. I do not think Cuthbert is worth your eye sight nor Middleton either, nor all the honors in the world.[41] So you may as well be easy. I know you will behave well & would try to amend if your health admitted, & that is enough for me.

I am very glad you did not suffer more & I hope you will soon be quite well.

Mr. Mackey[42] has sold his home in the Village to Jno Martin[43] for $7500 & bought his at 500. He proposes to stay at the Point near his house below—& at Jno. M's if it should not prove healthy. Your Ma is better than she was but does not seem very well. We have a buggy here. I bought it for Charles but he did not seem satisfied & I took it. Mr. Heyward[44] wishes to buy Fancy. Do you think she had better be sold. Nero is at home. Mr. H. kept it only for a short time. Would it not be polite in you to present him to Wm Heyward?[45]

With much love yr aff. father
C.

Mary Bull Leverett and Mary Maxcy Leverett to Edward

McPhersonville April 5th 1853

My Dear Brother

Ma received your letter yesterday and was very glad of it but she was very much grieved to think how you have suffured. Ma says she will write to you soon. Aunt Til went on Monday to Beaufort in the steamboat and will remain there a week and then go from there to town and Fred will go with her to study medicine at Philadelphia Tilly will go the same time to town to stay with the Heywards and will remain there a fortnight. Mrs Webb has a daughter born last saturday.

Pa went to town on Monday and expected to stay more than a week because he thinks there will be a great deal of trouble in electing the Bishop.[46] We're going

---

41. Lucius Cuthbert Jr. of St. Helena Parish and John Izard Middleton Jr. of Georgetown District were members of the class of 1853.

42. Probably George C. Mackay Sr.

43. John McLeod Martin (b. 1826).

44. Daniel Heyward (1810–1888), a planter whose first wife was Mary Maxcy Leverett's sister Anne Bull Maxcy.

45. William Milton Heyward (1842–1871), son of Anne Maxcy and Daniel Heyward.

46. Rt. Rev. Thomas F. Davis of Camden was elected bishop of the diocese of South Carolina at the annual convention in May 1853.

to try to send you a box of things by Tilly to town and from there to you. Ma has been hard at work at making up shirts and u[n]der clothes for Fred. Ma's health has been very good she gets up very early in the morning and sews.

Miss Alice Fraser is to be married in June to Mr. Johnson[47] and then to go travelling and her sister is to go with her. Dr. Fraser is visiting Annie Heyward he asked Dan the othe[r day] to go drum fishing with him but he refused.[48] Charlie and Minny went to Mr. Seabrook[49] to spend two or three days and went fishing but the second time he threw out his the hook ran into his thumb and Mr. Seabrook had to cut down to the bone with a lancet, but he has got over it now.

Your affectionate sister, Mary.

My dear Son

It gave me a great deal of pain to find how much you have been suffering. I really thought when the operation was over, you had nothing to do but be careful of your eyes. And, so, you really have to wear spectacles? is it by the advice of the Doctor? poor soul! you have passed through a sharp experience in your short life. Surely the Lord must have seen that you needed continual chastisement to overcome that strong proud spirit of yours. I try often to reconcile myself to the repeated painful trials you have had to endure from your childhood, by remembering that the brightest Christians the world has ever seen, were those whose Christian experience had been one continued series of suffering and sorrow; and so I hope the Lord has good things in store, blessed things, for you and I—for you in making you a Christian Minister, devoted, zealous, holy, meek, winning many souls to Christ, and for me, in permitting me to see it. Oh, that you might have the iron fortitude & endurance, the strong energy, the noble eloquence of St. Paul! What a glorious man was "Paul the Aged"! I am filled with admiration when I read of him.

You suffer, it is true, but remember, even Christ was made "perfect thro' sufferings"[50] and if man wish to partake of his glory, we must first partake of his sufferings.

Remember too, that if we do not improve by his chastisements, he will send us still greater, that is, if we are "sons," & he intends mercifully to save us, otherwise if we do not improve then, he will leave us to our heart's desires and let us perish. Sooner than that, may the will of God be done in you and I suffering when where and how He pleases. Better lose the right eye and right arm too than be lost

47. Alice Louise Fraser of Beaufort District and William Clarkson Johnstone of Georgetown District.
48. Anne Matilda Heyward (b. 1833) and Daniel Cuthbert Heyward (1836–1871), children of Anne Maxcy and Daniel Heyward.
49. Archibald Hamilton Seabrook of St. Helena Parish, a planter.
50. Heb. 2:10.

eternally. Perhaps you think I write a great deal unnecessarily on this point, but the truth is, when I see by one of your letters that you have been suffering, the rest of the letter leaves no impression on me, I see nothing but, that you suffer.

Fred, as Mary tells you, is going, tho' at first when we received from Dr. Morris,[51] thro' Mr. Fowles,[52] the list of what would be his necessary expenses we were fairly scared, & your Father said it would be impossible for him to do it. Your Aunt Til & Father calculated together what all his expenses would amount to and could not make it under $800, & possible $900. the first year. It is enormous, but we will be obliged to do it. Fred's interest money will be $250, & your Father will have to make up the rest. Your Aunt Til offers him a bed in her house, (in Locust St., larger than the one in Filbert St.) he is to take his meals at Mrs Pico's, & study in Dr. Morris' office right opposite. If he does not sleep at your Aunt Til's, it will amount to near $1000.! Your Father feels low spirited at the thought, and I'm afraid will have to look forward to the idea of dying with the harness of schoolkeeping on his back.—Mr Fowles wrote very kindly, and said he had no idea before the expenses of a medical education were so enormous, & offered to do any thing &c. He added if the expenses of a theological profession were as great, few would be able to enter on it.

I have been working very hard on shirts &c. to prevent any extra expense, for any how the expense of his clothing we suppose will be $100 out of $800. Next year Dr Morris says his expenses will be less. It is well that Charlie is employed as he is, as it would be utterly impossible for us to support him at a profession too, this year. If Fred is at it immediately, Dr M. says it will save him a year, continuing at it both summer & winter & not merely attending winter lectures as is generally done, & so he will be thro' in two years which will be a great comfort, as by that time you will need a great deal done for you. If you study for the Ministry, (as I hope & pray God may incline you to, & fit you for,) Your Father will send you on to study with Mr Fowles. He has taken a particular liking to you, I believe because he thinks you remarkably honest and open in your character, (I believe he thinks this a rare & very valuable cast of character!) & your Aunt Til says she's set her heart on having you to spend next winter with her. This however I do not wish. I must have you to myself next winter; & your Father himself wishes you to rest your body & mind both for a while. My own private plan is to keep you at home all winter, send you on & let you travel with Mr Fowles in the summer perhaps to the sea-shore, which will be an improvement to you as well as recruit your health, and then the winter after begin to

---

51. Dr. Caspar Morris of Philadelphia, a member of the Board of Managers, Hospital of the Protestant Episcopal Church in Philadelphia.

52. Rev. James Henry Fowles, rector of the Church of the Epiphany in Philadelphia, husband of Mary Maxcy Leverett's sister Matilda Miltonia Maxcy.

study with Mr Fowles. However we plan, but God alone rules, so we will leave it in his hands.

It is well now that we have agreed to take Dan & Willie, and I would just as leave have them as not, where there is one stranger in the house already. We finish with her the 1st November. So you will be satisfied, as you come home just as the boys go home for the holidays. I know it is very unpleasant to you to have any one in the house, it is equally so to your Father and myself, my son, and instead of chafing over it as you do, you ought to think of it as one of those dispensations of Providence which we can neither avoid nor prevent, and sub-mit to it as cheerfully as we can, believing He has some wise end in view which we know not. It is true, we could have avoided it, by letting you all grow up & live at home together, until we are dead and you gone, but what would become of you all then! because your Father's salary of course would cease with his death, & all I had was $4500. & the interest of that would not be enough even for you all to starve on, & you would have the mortification of seeing your sis-ters become the recipients of the cold charity of relatives while you went to seek your living as best you may. Remember you would not then have had a College education to assist you in taking some stand in life. When Rev. Mr Thomas of Edisto died, he undoubtedly owned more property than the little I mention, yet I know his widow has not only been assisted by the Society in Town but has also been obliged to take young men as boarders (medical students) but even sell milk to get along.[53] And they had only four children, & we have nine.—I men-tion all this because it seems to me that you have always had a sort of lurking feeling in your mind, that we <u>might</u> have done without schoolkeeping, if we chose to. This is a great mistake. It is unnatural to think we would make the sac-rifices we have, without some very strong and powerful motive. I was thinking the other day, was a mercy it was God had put it into our hearts to begin as early as we did, if we had put it off a few years, I certainly would never have had either courage, energy or health, sufficient for the purpose.

Now I think seeing all these things, you ought determinately to make up your mind, not only to bear with, but to help us bear what is unavoidable. Every one in the family circle ought to endeavour to make the burden of life easier by each bearing a part. I hope you are old enough, and have sense enough not to consider this letter as prosy & disagreable, but seriously to examine & see the truth of what I say. You ought to be enough of a man by now, to understand and sympathize with your Father & myself in this matter.

I know you dislike the idea of our having the boys, which is my reason for this writing.

---

53.   Rev. Edward Thomas (1800–1840), Episcopal clergyman.

Friday. I hope you succeeded in your speech last night, my dear child, we all wished to see you, & Fred wanted to go up very much, but we were obliged to think of the expense,

yr aff Mother
Mary Leverett

Dan and Willie came up on Monday, on which day Mr. H. & Annie go to town, & the next day Mary & C. & Lila[54] go down by land, the Wilsons & Hanckels go at the same time.—The Dunwody's are gone on a visit to Alabama.[55] I suppose Fred told you Dr Ed. Jenkins has honoured Prince William['s Parish] by settling here.[56] He is to live at Mrs Chaplin's plantation the winter & I believe the summer with the Mackays

Rev. Charles Edward Leverett to his son Edward

Mcph Ap. 21, 1853.

My dear son,

I have been looking for a letter from you for several weeks, but as you do not write, I will. I enclosed in my last to you twenty dollars, which I suppose & hope you have rec$^{\underline{d}}$, tho' in your statement enclosed in letter to your Grandmother, you do not mention it at all. You should always acknowledge receipts, as it leaves the person (in doubt of the safety of the enclosure) who has transmitted it & it also shows you appreciate a favour, even if it be your due. We are quite anxious to hear about your eyes. I hope you are not using them at all, & trust you will not for all the College honours in the world. Eyesight cannot be put side by side with any such benefits. I would prefer that you should be at home than endanger yourself by study. However anxious I am that you should acquire a good education, I do not think of it in comparison with physical detriment. You must be cautious. I hope your eyes are better than when you wrote.

All at home are well. Mama has not been very well this spring. At present she is at the Hall[57] with Aunt Til. On Tuesday we dined with a tolerably large company at Mr Hanckle's & Yr. Ma & Aunt T. went yesterday to Col. Hamilton's to spend the day.[58] To day the girls & F & C.[59] were invited to a Pic-nic at Mrs. Eustis',[60] but

---

54. Mary Bull Heyward (1835–1898), Charlotte Bull Heyward (1838–1860), and Eliza Barnwell Heyward (b. 1848), children of Anne Maxcy and Daniel Heyward.
55. Rev. James Bulloch Dunwody of McPhersonville, a Presbyterian clergyman.
56. Probably Dr. Edward E. Jenkins of Edisto Island.
57. Heyward Hall, Daniel Heyward's plantation in Prince William's Parish.
58. Col. Paul Hamilton of St. Helena Parish, a planter.
59. Fred and Charley.
60. Patience Wise Blackett Izard Eustis.

as they were to have their contemptible dancing, Ma & myself would not hear to the children going. I told F. who also is at the Hall, what I wished, but told him he was of age & must act for himself. I am afraid his religious views are too unlike mine & too much of the tip top Church order to keep him from what is inconsistent with a religious profession. I wish that he would & we all might give up ourselves more unreservedly to God's service. Those who do not, I fear will do nothing to glorify him whom they profess to serve.

Dan & W. are to stay with us, this summer. Mr. H. seemed so anxious for it, & your Aunt Til & Dan, himself, that I at last consented. It is a great annoyance to me, but for your Ma's sake & their mother's, I have yielded.[61] Dan has really improved. He takes hold in earnest & his conduct is perfectly good. He conforms to all the family rules cheerfully & closely. He requires a great deal of time to be taught, for he has actually learned very little where he has been at school. He has a good Math^{l} turn, & on the whole, I think if he can have much pains taken with him, & be kept from bad associations, will do better than any of us ever thought likely.

I have just finished with Mr Cuthberts Tablet.[62] The whole cost will be over $400—I have got the sub^{ns} & order it next week when I go to town. Mr Wm Heyward[63] Mr Wm Henry Heyward,[64] Col. Keith & Mr D. Heyward subscribe each $70. Nothing as yet has been done about the Church. They have put me on the building Committee, and I am trying to do something. I hope I may succeed. Dr Raoul who was on it goes away this summer & I take his place. He is to be married to Miss Smith, Mrs. Ja^{s} Gregorie's niece.[65] The D^{r} is about to quit McPhersonville altogether. He has offered his house for Sale. Thos Cuthbert, I hear is studying Medicine with Dr Ogier.[66] Mrs Fraser's Alice is to be married to young Johnston of Santee.

You must give our love to Cousin Julia & Cornelia & ask them to come down & pass the summer with us, or as long as they will stay. They can come with you. I wish there was any thing more attractive here. Our best respects to Mrs. Gregg.[67]

---

61. Daniel Cuthbert Heyward was prone to periodic episodes of mental illness caused by the aftereffects of typhoid fever; his mother, Mary Maxcy Leverett's sister Anne Bull Maxcy Heyward, died in 1851.

62. James Cuthbert Jr. was buried at Sheldon Church in 1852. Rev. Charles Leverett officiated at his funeral.

63. Capt. William Heyward (1800–1871), brother of Daniel Heyward.

64. William Henry Heyward, a planter.

65. Cornelia McPherson Smith married Alfred Raoul 22 November 1853; her aunt was Martha McPherson Gregorie.

66. Thomas Fuller Cuthbert of Beaufort District and Dr. Thomas Lewis Ogier of Charleston.

67. Julia deBerniere Gregg (1823–1893), Cornelia Manning Gregg (1826–1896), and their mother, Cornelia Manning Maxcy Gregg of Columbia, who was a first cousin of Mary Maxcy Leverett.

Mrs. Gregorie expects, so she says, to leave McPh<u>lle</u> altogether. My congregⁿ will be still smaller in the pine land & it has been & it has been small enough all along. The Winter Church is doing better.[68] We have quite good congregations there. The music is said to be very acceptable. Anna spent a week some days since at Mrs Midd<u>n</u> Stuart's with Sarah.[69] She had a very pleasant time. Dined one day at Mr Rob<u>t</u> Barnwell's.[70] This week she & Mary are at Mr Mackay's. Tilly, Charles Minny (Miss B[illegible]) Julia, Kate are at home. Minny is to go next week to Pinckney Seabrook's[71] & perhaps the week after to town. Your Ma also thinks of going & Tilly when the girls go down about middle of May.

yr affect^{te} father

C.

Caroline Pinckney Leverett, the last child of the Leveretts, called Carrie, was born at McPhersonville on 21 September 1853.

Rev. Charles Edward Leverett to his son Edward

McPh<u>lle</u>, Nov 23<u>d</u>, 1853

My dear Son,

We saw in Monday's paper the pleasant announcement that you had the 2<u>d</u> honor assigned you at your graduation. I was, tho' I care little for worldly honours, much gratified with the intelligence, for it is a token to me that you have improved your time, & also it is an assurance that you have powers that can be to some purpose used—I hope for <u>Him</u> (whatever be your pursuit) who has given you these. I will add that I have been exceedingly gratified, & what is more that you recognize his hand to whom you owe all things that you enjoy. I pray that as God has blessed you, he will still continue to do so. Be sure you try to realize him as your friend & guide, & in all your ways acknowledge him. Those who honour him, he will honour.

Your letter has just come & one to the girls. I was quite delighted to find that you stood so good & successful examinations. You must really have studied hard to have passed such. I wish I could have witnessed them. Still as it might have embarassed you, I would not, had I been in Columbia, have been present. As to our coming up to Commencement, we would some of us do so, were it not at-

---

68. Sheldon Church.
69. Mary Howe Barnwell Stuart and her daughter Sarah Barnwell Stuart (1838–1918).
70. Robert Woodward Barnwell, U.S. senator, 1851–1860.
71. Cotesworth Pinckney Seabrook, son of Caroline Pinckney and Archibald Hamilton Seabrook.

tended with such great expense & inconvenience, getting from this out of the way place. I will come anyhow, if you wish it & will write to say so. You say you had rather we would not, for fear of your being embarassed. I told your mother, I would prefer to put off going to town until the last week in Nov. & then go up to Colᵃ,⁷² but as she & you both wished me to go earlier in order to get things for house I went. I had to spend a great deal of money, particularly in buying bonnets & dresses for the girls. They are quite pleased with their articles. I would, I think bring Tilly up had we any private place to stay at, but these Hotels charge too much. It will cost $20 each to go up and return.

Mr. Drayton of the Senate spoke of you the other day.⁷³ Said when he went up to Legislature, he would call and see you. He lives in Bluffton & is a very fine man. Get acquainted with him, if he does not call, tho' he volunteered to do so. He is a friend of Col. Hughes, who married our cousin Sallie Maxcy, of Maryland.⁷⁴

If you can get some good chestnuts at a fair rate you h[ad][letter torn] better bring down a peck or so [price in][letter torn] town is $4 bushel; & also a peck of walnuts.

Mr. Fowles, Aunt Til & family are all to come to Hall next week & stay the winter.

You must write soon. I hope you will come off with flying colours. If you wish me to come let me know at once, as soon as you receive this. Will not Cousin Julia come down with you. Ask her

In haste your
gratified & affect<u>te</u>
father C. E. L.

P.S.
A letter from Mʳ Gould came with enclosure

Mary Maxcy Leverett to her son Edward

MᶜPhersonville Nov. 1853⁷⁵

I scarcely need tell you, my beloved son, what joy your success caused the whole house, Grandma is very proud, and Ma very happy, Papa more satisfied and pleased than I have ever seen him since the boys went to College. I hope you have recovered your over-exertion before this, and are now recruiting fast, for as your

---

72. Columbia.
73. Thomas Fenwick Drayton of St. Luke's Parish, state senator, 1853–1856.
74. Col. George Wurtz Hughes and Ann Sarah Maxcy Hughes.
75. The postmark on the envelope is dated 26 November.

mind is now relieved, you ought to begin to improve in body. It causes me deep and heartfelt regret, to think how you have injured your eyes in the struggle, and though that struggle has been successful, it cannot compensate for all the suffering your eyes have occasioned you. I pray that the time may come, when you will be enabled to dedicate yourself, with every faculty of body and soul, to the service of Him who created you. You may not feel like this now, but I trust God will prepare your heart, and make you willing in the day of his power, and so pour the grace of His blessed Spirit upon you as to make you rejoice to be counted worthy to serve before Him.

Your Father, I think, is secretly desirous to come up and hear you speak, but he won't say so, but puts it all on whether you wish him to come or not. I thought he had entirely given up the idea, but, he is constantly talking of it. Your Grandma will pay Tilly's expenses if he will carry her, and really they have such beautiful Bonnets and dresses, that it is a pity for her not to go. He got Mrs Archy Seabrook[76] to assist him in choosing the bonnets—they are rather too gay for a Minister's daughters. He bought two Mazarine blue silk dresses ($1.25 a yd) for Tilly & Annie & also a cherry coloured Merino for each, with trimming to match,—and really, they are in unexceptionably good taste. Grandma does not want them to go, as you express opinion to that effect, and I don't know what to say. Tilly is half dead to go, but your Father thinks the expense will be more than he ought to undertake, so I don't suppose he'll go. They had much better not go sooner than cause you to fail in speaking.

Mr & Mrs John Gregorie are at Richfield[77] living in their kitchen until their house is finished. We called there today. She seemed very much pleased at your invitation to her,—said, all the girls would be jealous of her. She told me I ought to be very proud of you,—both of them appeared to think a great deal of your taking 2d Honour, in fact, it seemed to raise their opinion of you several inches when they heard it. They were at church last Sunday at Sheldon and have taken a pew.

I long to have you back again. Archy wants to send Pinckney here, he found last winter had been such an improvement to him,—his teacher quite praising him up for his improvement.

Every body seems to be coming back to the Parish next week, Dr & Mrs M. Hanckel[78] among them, to spend the winter at Mr W Heywards.

In haste yr. ever aff Mother
Mary Leverett.

---

76. Caroline Pinckney Seabrook of St. Helena Parish.
77. The plantation of John White Gregorie and his wife, Sarah E. Gregorie.
78. Dr. Middleton Stuart Hanckel and Augusta Heyward Hanckel.

Rev. Charles Edward Leverett to his son Fred

McPh<u>lle</u> Dec. 19, 1853

My dear Fred.,

We looked for a letter from you to-day, but suppose you are not fixed yet, & therefore have not written. As you are anxious about Mr. Fowles, I will not wait longer, but send a few lines, tho' nothing very definite can be said. Charles stays with him, & he does not see any improvement. Mr. F. certainly is stronger, but his cough is not at all better. He perspires very freely at night, & very often gets little or no sleep. Many here have no hopes of his recovery, but do not of course tell him so. I have tried to cheer him, & I think he <u>at times</u> feels there is a prospect of improvement & again not.[79] He has every attention possible. The weather has not been so favorable as we would wish. Mr. F. rides out every day & has been out several times horseback. Jimmy is better.[80] He & Aunt Til came up here today. The rest are well.

Edward is at home, but expects to spend Christmas at Grahamville at Parker's who has written to invite him. Tilly & myself attended Commencement & were highly gratified. Ed. carried off the honours of the day. I was quite surprised at his succeeding so admirably. He speaks so beautifully. He was several times applauded during his oration, & as he had several witty things in it, he caused some laughter. He gained more attention & applause than any of the speakers. He spoke twice. His valedictory was quite interesting. His valedictory to the Faculty (not the President)[81] was humorous & caused considerable laughter. The Pres<u>t</u> told me afterward that he was very happy in it. His Valedictory to the ladies caused quite a sensation. The chapel[82] was very full up and down stairs with ladies. In addressing them, he changed to poetry, his own, of course, & it was quite rapturously received. His first Oration was "The Spirit of the Age." He closed one line of his verse by saying "and woman is the spirit of the age." This was received well. His address to his classmates was loudly applauded. He made several happy hits. Among them one in reference to the rebellion—about selling their birthright &c.

Hon. W. C. Preston late Pres<u>t</u>,[83] called him on the stage to him after he had closed & told him it was the best he had ever heard in the Chapel. That was great

---

79. Rev. James Henry Fowles died 5 March 1854.
80. James Henry Fowles (1843–1913), son of Matilda Maxcy and Rev. James Henry Fowles.
81. Rev. James Henley Thornwell of Columbia, president of South Carolina College.
82. In Rutledge College, the first building constructed at South Carolina College.
83. William Campbell Preston of Columbia preceded Thornwell as president of South Carolina College.

praise as Mr Preston was one of our finest orators in Congress. Genl Adams (next Gov. probably)[84] also spoke to him & told him tho' he was pleased with his examinations, he was more pleased with his performances at Com^t. I send you two or three pieces extracted from papers. I do not know who wrote them. By them you will see what strangers think. Dr Thornwell spoke very highly of him & said he wished I would send him some more such lads. Ed. while speaking seemed to me a bright & brilliant boy. You may be sure I was especially delighted also was Tilly. Mama also is gratified & people seeing him praised in Charleston papers frequently congratulate us. If Ed^d had not been so good a speaker & writer I think he would have taken 1st honour. But the 2^d being Valedictory I am almost sure he got it on that account.

I wish you to send back the extracts as I wish to preserve them.

All are quite well here. Mame came up from Hall to-day & Anna is still there. Edward by writing lectures made about $25. just before he left College & is to write more & get some $40. He made a very handsome present of 2 shawls (white crape) to Tilly & Anna & handsome collars.

Charles is up here to night. I wished him to get some rest after being up so much with Mr. F. But I hear him & Ed. & Minny cracking chestnuts round a stove I have put up in the back shed room, & laughing & talking.

Had a letter from Cousin Eliza Haven.[85] When you see them (you had better call some time, as she spoke of you) tell her I rec^d it & am much obliged to her for it.

Make my respects to Dr Morris
& believe me to be
yr affec. father C. E. L.

P.S. I saw on stage com^t day Mr Memminger & Mr Rob. Barnwell,[86] he congratulated me on E's success. Saw also the Gov. (Manning), Judge O'Neall, Jno. Preston, Gov. Means,[87] W. C. Preston, &c &c

The Columbia correspondent of the Charleston Courier, *who attended the commencement exercises on 6 December 1853, noted that the eleven graduates that day were "only the remnant" of the once-large class of 1853. The class lost forty-six members after the*

---

84.   James Hopkins Adams of Richland District, state senator, governor of South Carolina, 1854–1856

85.   Eliza Hall Haven of Massachusetts.

86.   Christopher Gustavus Memminger, of Charleston, and Robert Woodward Barnwell, president of the college, 1835–1841, were members of the Board of Trustees of South Carolina College.

87.   John Laurence Manning of Clarendon District, governor of South Carolina, 1852–1854; Judge John Belton O'Neall of Newberry, president of the South Carolina court of appeals; John Smith Preston of Columbia, member of the Board of Trustees of South Carolina College; and John Hugh Means of Fairfield District, governor of South Carolina, 1850–1852.

"Great Biscuit Rebellion" of 1852, in which 108 students announced their intention to leave school if the college would not let them board and eat at private houses in Columbia rather than in dormitories. When Thornwell and the Board of Trustees refused to give in to their demands, the students withdrew from the college.

John Izard Middleton Jr. won first honor, and Edward Leverett won second honor, which was valedictorian. Edward was the last member of the class to address the crowd gathered in the chapel. His address, "The Spirit of the Age," was described by the correspondent on 7 December as "betraying a play of fancy, a discursiveness of judgment, and a shrewdness of observation, which, in so young a writer, promise rich and noble fruits." His valedictory to his classmates mentioned the "Great Biscuit Rebellion" and commended them for remaining in school. The Columbia Daily South Carolinian of the same day commented of Edward, "he displayed a degree of intellect and versatility of talent of the happiest character, and giving promise of a bright and useful future. Take it all in all, it was one of the best valedictory addresses we have listened to for years."

Soon afterward Edward entered the Protestant Episcopal Theological Seminary of Virginia in Alexandria.

In 1854 Rev. Charles Leverett purchased a Greek Revival house at 1301 Bay Street in Beaufort.

Rev. Charles Edward Leverett to his son Edward

Little Canaan,
Dec. 22, 1855.

My dear Edward,

Your good toned, & good spirited letter came yesterday. All were quite pleased with it, & as all look to you to be the man of the family in these latter days, as Sir John[88] was in former times, I trust you will not disappoint us. Aim high, but always with a trustful dependence on the help of the Almighty & you will be sure of success. I repeat what I have often said before, that I owe all to God's blessing on my toilful labour, & I am certain that your experience will not be unlike my own. You have better chances than I had. I have had to work while bearing a great big load upon my back; you have the results of my arduous endeavors. You can make a name, especially, as you have talents to back your education and my exertions for you. I pray that God will bless you.

We have been looking for a letter from you for some time. The pamphlet of S. H. Tyng[89] came from you, but I had one sent me before. I read it, only to be dis-

---

88.   John Leverett (1616–1679), governor of Massachusetts, 1673–1679, an ancestor of Rev. Charles Leverett.

89.   Rev. Stephen Higginson Tyng of New York, Episcopal clergyman.

gusted with the man's presumption in attacking Bishop Potter[90] & with views, the more confirmed of the Bishop's judgement, <u>adversus</u> the S. S. Union, continue. S. H. Tyng is a man I do not admire or respect, & I hope you will just take the sensible opinion of the Bp. in this matter. I do not notice that he says anything of the expunging charges against the S. S. pub<u>ns</u>.[91] But enough. In this connexion let me say, do not allow the Low Churchmanship of the Virginia School to lull you.[92] Be a solid churchman. Take all the good you can get, but know where to stop.

I regret that you have not seen Cousin Charlotte. You must go & see her on your first visit to V[a]. You will not fail to do so, nor to pay her all the attention you can, when I say, I wish it for various reasons, one of which is that after Ma & the children, I love her more than any person on earth. She & I were kind friends once, & I cannot forget early friendships. Besides, she is the only one almost left of all my early relations. I wonder if she received my letter written shortly before you left. Ask her.

And now you will wish to know about all here. Mama is a great deal better. Her appetite is very <u>remarkably</u> improved. The change has certainly benefitted her. Charley is with us, & is very busy about the place trying to get us out of confusion. But Rome was not built in a day & Canaan with my force is scarcely beginning to be begun. Eph<u>m</u>[93] spent last week nearly in bringing Rafts, & was nearly drowned falling overboard. But for the timely & <u>spirited</u> help of Billy,[94] who caught him when he came up, he thinks we should have seen him no more. I tell him it was lucky as he was unprepared. He thinks I do not know. Lewis[95] & Billy are carting all this week the boards & scantlings & after Christmas, Mr. Arch[d] Seabrook is to hire his carpenters to me. The materials are all at hand, except shingles & then Eph & Lewis go in the holidays to cut at the Pinelands. Eph. has finished the kitchen & it looks quite well. His second house, a double one, back of Sary's[96] is nearly done, only waiting for shingles. I think I told you that Solomon[97] built the chimney & it does very well—quite a good one—the bricks not laid so square as they would be by a professional man, but quite well not withstanding. He is now building a double chimney at the 2[d] house & hopes to finish in two days or so. The houses are now all white

---

90.   Rt. Rev. Horatio Potter, provisional Episcopal bishop of New York.
91.   Sunday School publications.
92.   There were many disputes in the antebellum Episcopal Church between those who favored the High Church, a formal view of the ministry and sacraments, and those who favored the Low Church, a less rigid and somewhat evangelical approach.
93.   Ephraim, a slave.
94.   A slave.
95.   A slave.
96.   A slave. Her husband was Hercules, whose owner was Rev. Benjamin C. Webb. Rev. Charles Leverett performed their wedding ceremony at Sheldon Church on 5 December 1852; in 1856 he purchased Hercules from Webb's estate.
97.   A slave.

washed & look very well. The smoke house is to be moved shortly & when that is done, the yard with the exception of the lumber will appear much better.

I bought a mule (Button) of Mr. A. Seabrook as I told you, I think. He is a nice little fellow. I gave $105. Since then I have bought another larger, but not a great deal & better, out of a drove. The jockey asked 125 but took $115. She (Bullet) is quite a fine animal—ages of both about 3 years. Charles broke her & she is carting with Button "first rate." I do not know if I told you that the Little Giant & Corn Sheller came from Phila. Fred bought them. The Little G. (corn & cob) cost me about $42 out here, in Chn. it would have been $55. It grinds well. Charles & I fixed up the frame. We are quite pleased with it. It grinds just as well as food for the horses. Your horses are quite well & look quite well. I am getting plenty of good Rice Straw from Mrs. Eustis—who by the way sent today a sack full & six turkeys. The other day she called & left a box, which, when opened was found to contain a Talma[98] for your mother & a cap; one Talma for Mary & one for Julia; also sleeves & collars for Tilly & Anna; & a nicely trimmed hat for Julia & a very pretty one for Mary. This was very kind in her to do. The Heywards have been here twice, but Mr. D. H. does not go to Church & we do not speak. Tilly & Anna called there the other day, & that I suppose will close on our part, communications, or our closeness, with them. He has bought Capt. Bacot's negroes. B. goes away in Jan. I hope our loss will be his gain. Bill Elliott[99] has bought his place. Geo. Elliott[100] offers his house in Beaufort for sale, but does not find a purchaser at his price of $11000. He does not go to Church. I believe the excuse is, want of horses & carriage. But he had a carriage & certainly horses, for Mamy who has just come home from Beaufort, says that one of Cousin G.'s horses fell down dead just as he was about to start with it to go somewhere in his carriage. I don't believe a blessing follows the staying from Church to save pew rent. The Heywards say that his "happy go lucky" vessel is a very unfortunate affair, being very leaky & that the owner is very hard pushed for money, having made only a crop of corn this year.

You asked about your horse coming on. I am afraid that you will not find it an easy matter to get it on. I presume that it would cost $40. The best would be to ride it on, if you require it. I think that you will find it a trouble to you. If I could arrange it I would. Perhaps some one might be found, who would like to go horseback to Virginia & would take it for the use. If such a person & trustworthy could be found, he would be the one. But I am sure that it will cost more than I can afford. I will enquire at convention.[101] Perhaps some minister would like to go on that way. I have no objec-

---

98. A woman's long cape, often hooded.

99. William Waight Elliott of Beaufort District.

100. Capt. George Parsons Elliott (1807–1871) of Beaufort, a planter, whose house still stands on Bay Street; brother of Rev. Stephen Elliott (1804–1866).

101. The Annual Convention of the Diocese of South Carolina, held in Charleston in February 1856.

tion to you taking the lessons of which you speak, but I am not in funds at present & you would have to say that I could not conveniently pay before June or July. Would not Spanish be best? I have besides what Fred wants (about 400) between now & Spring to meet the first installment of purchase of Negroes in Jan. & in March for the plant$^{\underline{n}}$, besides house expenses. I will do all in my power for you, you may be sure.

I have engaged Mr. Kent for another year. I am to give him 1/7, though he tried hard to get 1/4. I do not look to make scarcely anything the coming year, as he takes things so cool & easy. I am more the overseer myself than he is & work in every way harder far than he does.

In regard to my study &c. you may be sure that I am as anxious for it, as you could be. Unfortunately <u>for me</u>, I have been forced from circumstances over which I had no control, to be always surrendering my sanctum. And then as for a library, a tithe of the expenditures I have been put to for you children would have given me a library, such as I could improve by. I have been obliged to sacrifice my own pleasure & improvement. Like the Israelites I have had to make bricks without straw. I only wonder that I have done so well. As soon as possible, you will find me in my study—a place very pleasant to me, I assure you. This I hope to have by & by. I do not intend to neglect my duties I beg you to believe.

If I had hands I would put up perhaps, as you suggest a house opposite Mr. K's.—but I have not yet determined. If the carpenters can do it, the addition will be hexagonal at the ends. But I close assuring you of the love of

yr aff. father C.

P.S.
Give Ma's & my love to Cousin Mary Markoe. My respects to Mr. M.[102] My love to Cousin Charlotte.

Lydia Huntley Sigourney to Rev. Charles Edward Leverett

Sachem's Head, Guilford, Conn
August 16th 1856

My dear M[r.] Leverett,
You have sent me a beautiful book,[103] the most interesting, best-written one, of that genealogical class, that I have ever read, for which accept my earnest thanks.

---

102. Mary Maxcy Markoe of Baltimore, first cousin of Mary Maxcy Leverett, and her husband, Francis Markoe Sr.
103. Charles Edward Leverett, *A Memoir, Biographical and Genealogical, of Sir John Leverett, Knt., Governor of Massachusetts, 1673–9; of Hon. John Leverett, F.R.S., Judge of the Supreme Court, and President of Harvard College; and of the Family Generally* (Boston: Crosby, Nichols and Co., 1856).

Your materials have been unusually abundant and precious, and you have wrought among them, with a masters hand. The transcript of your first venerated ancestor (him of trans-atlantic fame, I mean) and that of your talented, and sainted brother, seem to me written wonderfully con-amore.—

This valued memorial, and your kind letter of the 8th reached Hartford after I had left for the sea-shore, and were forwarded to me with other contents of my post-office box, which has occasioned this tardiness of acknowledgement. It may please you to know that your volume is appreciated here, by a variety of good judges, there being quite a proportion of literary gentlemen here, among the throngs that frequent this watering-place.

It would have given me much pleasure to have seen yourself, and your lovely wife, had you decided to take our quiet City on your route. Perhaps, you will write me a few lines, ere you leave New York. Let us do all we can, in our respective spheres, to bind the South and North, together in amity.

I was delighted to gather from your book, the beautiful names of your children, all of which, I had not before known. God make them blessings to their parents, and to the world.

Some time, when you have time, write me a letter, describing them, and also your brother's sons,—will you? In the mean time, with love to Mrs Leverett, & all who are dear to you,

believe me, affectionately your friend
L H Sigourney[104]

Lydia Huntley Sigourney to Rev. Charles Edward Leverett

Hartford, August 26th 1856

My dear Friend,

You can scarcely imagine how much pleasure was imparted by your full & graphic letter, which I found awaiting me on my return from the sea-shore, two or three days since. It seemed to take me into the charmed circle of your joys and hopes & make me more earnestly grateful for the grace that had been vouchsafed for many arduous toils and duties, and the blessing that has so visibly crowned them. I think you know my heart well enough, to believe that I was especially affected by the fidelity and love shown for so many years, by yourself and sweet kindred spirit, to the orphans of your gifted brother. I rejoice in their high promise, as well as that of your own precious children.

I am wishing that you should take with you, some little marks of my remembrance, and since you mention an intention of stopping in Philadelphia, will you

---

104. A popular nineteenth-century author from Connecticut.

have the goodness to call at the store of the Publisher of an octavo edition of my "Illustrated Poems (Parry M. Millan, Chestnut Street)[105]—and request them to deliver you a copy, charging to my account? I will enclose an inscription for the fly-leaf. I should be happy also to present to your children, if they do not possess them, and you think they would be acceptable, "Letters to Young Ladies," "Letters to my Pupils," & "The Faded Hope,"[106]—and if you call at Carter & Brothers, Broadway, they will give them to you at my request. The Harpers have also a book of tales, entitled "Myrtis & others Sketches,"[107] which if you will take the trouble to get from them in the same manner, and distribute with the others, among the members of your family,

[Four lines neatly cut from letter; closing and signature added in pencil]

> with my best love, you write often
> Your affectionate friend
> L. H. Sigourney

Milton entered South Carolina College in 1857 as a member of the class of 1859.

Rev. Charles Edward Leverett to his son Milton

[24 December 1856][108]

My dear Minnie,

Above you have an order for the amt, which you said you would have to pay to the college on 1st of Jan. You will carry it to the treasurer at the Library who will give you a receipt for it. It is the same as money & will be paid when the college sends it. I would have written to you before this, but intending to inclose the amount required, concluded to put it off until this time. As your Ma writes now I will write in a few days & give you all the news. I was delighted to learn that you had entered and now I wait to learn how you succeed. I am sure you will try, as you say, to do well & conduct well. You will find yourself in a new world. Take care it does not get the better of you. Keep on good terms with all the students, but your good sense with your previous habits & training will soon show you whom you are to be intimate with. Behave like a gentleman. Do not be mean & in little

---

105. *Illustrated Poems . . . with Designs by Felix O. C. Darley, Engraved by American Artists* (Philadelphia: Carey and Hart, 1849).

106. *Letters to Young Ladies* (New York: Harper and Brothers, 1842); *Letters to My Pupils: With Narrative and Biographical Sketches* (New York: Robert Carter, 1851); *The Faded Hope* (New York: Robert Carter, 1853).

107. *Myrtis, With Other Etchings and Sketchings* (New York: Harper and Brothers, 1846).

108. An undated letter mailed with the following letter from Mary Maxcy Leverett.

matters act as far as possible with your fellow students. In regard to expenses, be as sparing as possible, but now & then you can give according as the occasion calls. I must leave a good deal to your judgment. But generally be guided by your Bible. You ask about lights. I think you had better use candles. You can buy Adamantion Candles for about 30 cents for 6. Should you buy oil, you can get whale (refined) oil such as we use at home for about $1 a gallon. But you had better try & see which will be cheapest & let me know.

Your aff. father

C.

Mary Maxcy Leverett to her son Milton

Canaan 24 Dec 1856

My beloved Son

We were very glad to receive your letter, which Grandma liked very much and said she wished she had some money to send you. I am very glad you take so much interest in the Legislative debates. It certainly improves a boy in general intelligence, if he takes pleasure in listening to them. I hope one of these days, you will yourself take an honorable station among the debaters, in the meantime, prepare yourself for it, by improving your mind in every possible way. Let not studying be without an object, merely to get through, but study with an aim in life, it will make you twice as efficient in life when you take your stand as a man, to strive for justice, or honour, or patriotism or even or (oh sad come down, it sounds quite common-place) even for a <u>living</u>.

I am glad you are with the kind Greggs. My best love to them all. I wish there was some way of returning their repeated kindnesses. Hutson's boy Anegoes [illegible] Tell Cornelia we all are pained at her not coming, as we expected [illegible] with Charley. Ask if it will suit her better in the spring or if she means to put it off as long as when you come home next summer? Tilly had the room all ready to receive her & Til.

Your Aunt left us two days ago, after staying over a fortnight with Newton, Stevy & Lila & Mary[109] the latter she left with us until the 1st Monday in Jan. She appeared to enjoy herself very much, riding about & dining with the Hamiltons (who also dined with us) Mrs Eustis, Mrs H. Fuller[110] & the Heywards. She went to the wedding and carried Newton & Mary who were invited also. She has gone to Big Island to spend Christmas week.

---

109. John Newton Fowles, Stephen Bull Fowles, Eliza Yallowley Fowles, and Mary Ann Fowles of Columbia, children of Matilda Maxcy and Rev. James Henry Fowles.

110. Mary Barnwell Means of Beaufort, wife of Dr. Henry Middleton Fuller.

We were all so delighted to hear you entered Sophomore. Mr. Hutson told your father at the Steamboat landing and Willie Heyward standing by, heard it and said "I'm so glad Minnie got in." Your father was quite pleased to see how really glad Willie seemed. Dan returned that same day and seemed pleased at your father's speaking with him. They walked in at the [letter torn] with Bell Stuart[111] dropt favour [letter torn] (a bunch of ribbons) [letter torn] groomsmen [letter torn] seated Bell on the sofa & didn't trouble himself about her afterwards. Annie shook hands and made up that night—he told Annie he wanted to make up & Edward that he knew he had behaved wrong. Your father I persuaded to go and just stay to the ceremony to show he had no ill feelings; as I heard that Dr. DeSaussure[112] & T. Hume were both desirous for his going which he did & came home lately. Your Aunt Till went & carried Newton & Mary who had been invited. Our Mary went also with her father, and Louis[113] drove Annie. We had to work very hard to finish their dresses which were of pink organdy over white satin; they both looked quite handsome and from what I heard I think they must have been admired. They got home about two o'clock in the night bitter cold too, it was. Every thing was quite in grand style, splendid supper, band of music &c. Four hundred people were asked, about eighty went. Mr. Potter was there & so very lively that I'm afraid they must have had some reports about him afterward. The bride and bridegroom have been to Canaan since, to see us all, but none of the others from the Hall have come, altho' Charlotte said Dan was coming.

Louis DeSaussure is here three times a week & pays Annie a very long visit. He has given her a very pretty diamond ring. He has brought a new horse & he and Annie are going to ride her tomorrow morning. Charley is pretty well, I really don't see any thing at all the matter with him. I make him drink Porter every day, and as he is indulging himself by not coming out in the morning and often takes breakfast in his room in your house it is to be hoped he will be strong again by Jan. He still insists on going to Virginia, altho' we think the climate will be bad for him in winter.

Sary had a baby a fortnight ago which only lived four days, but she is quite well though.

Christmas day

Dear Min, they are all gone to church & your father said I must not go, it was so cold so you see, my darling, I thought I'd make good use of the time by writing to you. Mrs D^r. Henry Fuller sent your Grandma a boned Turkey for her Christmas dinner. Cousin H. Stuart[114] sent us five Turkeys & five bushels Potatoes last week.

---

111. Isabel Stuart, daughter of Ann Hutson Means and Henry Middleton Stuart Sr.
112. Dr. Louis McPherson DeSaussure Sr. of St. Helena's Parish, a physician.
113. Louis McPherson DeSaussure Jr.
114. Henry Middleton Stuart Sr. (1803–1872) of Beaufort District.

Mr. Hamilton is ginning our Cotton, two bags are packed, and he thinks he will make four hands with it. Primus has only brought one load of oysters since you have been gone, says it is too cold. Our largest four hogs, which used to be in the pen, are all stolen. Our negroes say it is done by the Fuller negroes. So I had two shoats killed, three others are in the pen, the sixth was stolen also.

God help you, my beloved son, and keep you from the evil that is in the world, prays ever

Your affte Mother
Mary Leverett

Take care not to lose the order enclosed to pay the college [letter torn] You have a few candles at present & Pa will send the money. Charly thinks you had better get a few only, as you will have plenty, of borrowers if you do. Should you want a $1 at any time, ask Cous. Julia for it then return it when I send.

By the beginning of 1857 Fred was practicing medicine at the Hospital of the Protestant Episcopal Church in Philadelphia, which opened in 1852 after Rt. Rev. Alonzo Potter, bishop of Pennsylvania, proposed a new hospital to care for the city's poor residents. Rev. James Henry Fowles was a founding member of the hospital's Board of Managers.

Frederic Percival Leverett to his brother Milton

P. E. Hospital, Phil<u>a</u>
Jan. 6<u>th</u> 57.

My dear Min,

I received a letter from Mother, yesterday, saying that you have entered Sophomore. I at once determined to write and would have done so yesterday, had I not then on hand a report of the Hospital, which I had to prepare, and have finished this morning. It kept me up until 2 o'clock this morning.

You have no idea how glad I was to hear that you have safely entered. Be assured that you have my best wishes for your success, my prayers that you may have the Holy Spirit to guide and direct you at all times and in all places. With the new year you have entered on a new scene of duty. Home and home's immediate influences are removed, and college life with its labors are substituted. Enter on those labors, My dear Min, zealously, determined to do your best. Remember that you are a Leverett and that you have a Leverett's reputation to maintain, also that you are a Maxcy. Be daunted by nothing, and if at times your efforts be not crowned with success, let it but instigate you to greater future exertion. Learn well whatever you undertake to, make what you learn your own. In order to do so, study systematically; apportion out your time, as far as possible, and adhere as far as possible to the apportionments. Allow yourself time for sleep, and do not unless absolutely necessary study in the morning before daylight, and any how do not make a practice of doing so. Your eyes are of inestimable value, and in the morning, when you have just waked up, they are especially liable to be injured by artificial light. Take Ed as a warning; his eyes I have no doubt, have been injured by exerting them too much early in the morning. Learn each recitation thoroughly, and those you have the least inclination for, pay most particular attention to. Devote yourself especially to your textbooks and, if you have the time after preparing your recitations, read, and read such books, as, even if not bearing on your studies, will improve and enrich your mind. I need not remind you that you must deport yourself as a christian and a gentleman. Guard well your temper and keep your tongue well reined in. If irritated think twice before you speak.

Excuse my giving you so much sage, paternal advice, My dear Min, but be assured that did not I feel the greatest interest in your welfare and love you far more than you have any idea of, I would not take the trouble. I wish I were able to help you on pecuniarily and in other ways. I hope when you are studying your profession, whatever it may be, that I shall be able.

Do give my love to the Greggs (all of them) especially Cousin Julia. I always liked her very much, but now do so especially on account of her kind care of Mother last spring. Do write & let me know how they are and you are, and all about you. Please also send me one of your Catalogues, when out. Direct to the Episcopal Reading Rooms, no. 146 Walnut St.

yr most aff<u>ct</u> Brother

F. P. Leverett

Rev. Charles Edward Leverett to his son Milton

Little Canaan, Feb. 23, 1857.

My dear Minnie,

Your letters came to-day. Mamma had been worrying for sometime about yr. not writing, but I told her, you probably were very busy with your lessons. I wish however, when I enclose money, that you would always acknowledge the recpt at once. We are pleased with the tone of your letters, & I am sure you will try to acquit yourself well as a scholar & a gentleman. I care more for the last than the first, but at the same time, as it costs me a great deal for you, I think you had better exert yourself somewhat & take a good stand. Besides it will be a great help to you in your after life. I am very glad you were so sensible as to decline making a fool of yourself by joining in the rowdyism of the College. Be sure to keep clear of

such, for there is very little wit & certainly no smartness in it. I should be mortified enough were I to hear that young Leverett was one of the set. Indeed I feel
so certain that you will not commit yourself or me, that I do not worry myself
about your conduct. Try to guide yourself by the Bible & look up to God for help
& you will go on perfectly well. You have not let me know any thing about your
studies—how you are getting on &c. How are you doing in the Mathematics?

We are all well at home. Your Grandmother & Tilly went to Beaufort last
week, & Tilly returned on Friday. Yr. Grandma was tired & wanted a change.
Charles is in Beaufort, studying French & German. Fred. & Edward expect to go
to Europe in April.

We are getting on here, tolerably well. Lewis is ploughing & the others are
making fences. Your Ma has a garden, but I am afraid that between the fowles &
little negroes, she will not do much. Fred sent 8 Japonicas & they are planted in
the little garden. Ephrm is fixing the fences round the yard & they look very well.
The oats planted in Jany in the field are up, but those planted about 10 days ago in
the avenue have nearly overtaken them. They are beginning to look very pretty. I
am having 1/2 the field near the bridge side fenced off, so as to give the cattle a
feeding pasture & have a place to plant various things in. There will be made a lane
from the yard near the corn house, by which the cattle can go down. In addition to
the death of Bates, of which the children informed you, I have to add the death of
the mare. She died about a week ago, never having recovered from the wound she
rec^d. A heavy loss to me. I am thinking of buying a mule of Mr. Tho Elliott,[115] price
$125. All his negroes at Poc^o[116]—were sold the other day, to pay his debts.

We expect to begin to plant in 3 weeks from to-day & I hope we may be successful. My 3 1/2 bags of cotton have gone to town, but I have not heard of the
sale as yet. Thos. Stuart[117] sent me in a bill for 23. which I paid—Pery sent me in
another besides that of Dowling's for 21. Edwd Walker[118] has written to engage our
house in Beaufort. Mr. Wm Heyward bought Huguenin's[119] place for about
$20,000. Mr. Mitchell advertises his plantation for sale. I believe he is going away.
Ma talks of going to the point if Mr. Mackay will move our school house for a residence. Mrs Jenkins is dead.[120]

I believe I have told you all the news.

I expect to go to town next week, 1st March.

I think you have improved in your letter writing & hand.

115. Thomas Rhett Smith Elliott, a planter.
116. Pocotaligo, in Prince William's Parish.
117. Dr. Thomas Middleton Stuart of Charleston, a physician.
118. Rev. Edward Tabb Walker of St. Helena's Parish, Episcopal clergyman.
119. Julius Gillison Huguenin of St. Luke's Parish, a planter.
120. Martha Jenkins (1797–1857).

John Elliott has become a member of the Church & will probably become a minister.[121]

Hope you will try to do & behave well.

I am my dear Son,

yr aff. Father

Charles Edward Leverett Jr. to his sister Mary

Theolog. Seminary

Va. March

1857

My dear Girl—

Your very delightful & enchanting epistle with its complement of news, home talk & chit chat, was really very refreshing & oasis-like to your neglected & Saharah desert-ed brother. There was something new, something budding—about it. I do not mean verdant—& with the exception of a few typographical errors, the printing was excellent!!

Joking aside, it was certainly the best you ever wrote me—(oh! I forgot—this is the first!). I mean the best you ever wrote to anyone. Some of the sentences were very well composed. The following e.g. is even eloquent, though the sentiment is uncharitable—& hurt my feelings, exceedingly! "It seems exactly as if I had you before me, when you receive this letter—that turning up of the nose—that curling of the lip—ejaculating "Stupid"—I would not give two-pence to read it."

Another equally well framed sentence & more truthful runs thus—"If you will look at my writing across the room it looks very well indeed, but just come up close—& the delightful dream is quickly dispelled."

I have quoted these merely to show Tilly & Annie how you are going to out-epistolize them. Just keep on & write a little in a journal to me every day, & I will be as much pleased as you will be improved. Tell me all the little news of home—I love to hear about home—& then about the people of the parish—any of my friends with the measles—or without—the Heywards—give my love to Annie—the dark-eyed Beatrice—or any other subject of dangerous & delightful contemplation.—With such objects as "this, these all"—to write about, you will succeed in writing away many a weary moment for me, & will make a perfect Mdme. de Perigne of and for yourself.

Don't forget to tell me something about yourself too, all. I hope you are as good a girl and better—than ever. That you will remember the advice I gave you

---

121. John Habersham Elliott, son of Ann Hutson Habersham (1813–1843) and Rev. Stephen Elliott (1804–1866).

once before—which reminds me to send you and Annie—some resolutions, which I hope you will both keep in your bibles & read some of them every day. Not skim over <u>lightly</u> & <u>thoughtlessly</u>—but <u>earnestly</u> & <u>prayerfully</u>.

In the same way read your bibles; you should have regular hours, and let nothing impinge on them and pray over every verse—every line—<u>as</u> if it were written to & for <u>you yourself</u>—& no one else.

I know my dearest, <u>you</u> will do as I am telling you—but I am very much distressed to think Annie gives no signs yet of becoming religious.—NOW is the word for all—because that is the <u>only time we can count</u> on. I hope she will remember this therefore, and take it to heart & <u>think</u> & <u>pray</u> over it seriously. I hope you do not forget me in your prayers—All Christians should pray for each other but especially brothers & sisters.

With love to Ma & Pa & the rest believe me my dear sister your ever loving Brother

Edward

Anne Heyward Leverett to her brother Milton

Canaan, May 21st 1856[122]

My dear Minnie,

I hate to write when there is bad news to communicate. Nightmare's colt is dead—we think Tom and Prince must have made it jump the fence and strained the back for it died of spasms—we miss the dear little fellow very much, off the green. Some body—a negro of course, has stolen your boat also—we have sent to tell Primus to keep a look-out in Beaufort, of all the boats that come in and see if he cannot get it back.

Rattle—the new mule—goes splendidly—Pa has not used it in the plough yet—we are in hopes he will not do it either as it will ruin him for the buggy.

Julie is not at all successful with her poultry, what there are of them are dying off one by one, there are so few as that—can't say dying by the dozens for we have not a dozen chickens, ducks, or turkeys.

Ma has a very nice garden—we have a plenty of green peas, turnips and radishes, which latter vegetable we used to be crazy for as children and now Pa is the only who seems to care for them, we are promising ourselves a superabundance of water melons and Cantelopes this summer <u>if</u> Billy does not 'make way' with them. We will also have a quantity of Tomatoes, Okra, Cabbages and Irish potatoes. I am making a plenty of butter. No plums this year, the frost destroyed all.

---

122. 1857.

Don't believe anyone has moved to the Pine lands yet we intend staying until the first of June and then I am packed off to have the house scoured—I will miss you, don't fancy driving the mule up there.

If Pa sends you money again you <u>must</u> keep about five dollars to pay John White's, <u>Solomon</u> he says you didn't do it last summer and it is my impression that you didn't. I have not said anything about it to Pa as I hate worry him about it and I think it but right that you should reserve some of what he sends you for the purpose. I told Solomon to wait until you came as I was not aware of the amount that was due him, and mind now and <u>don't forget this.</u>

Isabella Mackay is not engaged, 'twas merely a report.[123] Benjy Wyman is married! it seems <u>too</u> ridiculous—don't you think so?[124] do tell Big Charley I ask him if <u>he</u> is not engaged yet.

Poor <u>Palmer</u> cried very much at his sister's funeral. I am too sorry for them, they seem so attached to each other. George looks very badly. We are going to have a very dull summer, every body—nearly—will be in mourning. Old Mrs Brailsford is going to keep school for the little children, Matty Davis is to board with them.

The Ladies in Alexandria presented Edward with a handsome rosewood dressing case as a testimonial of their regard for him, he sent it on to us while he is absent, they also sent us his speech, it is a very learned one. I liked it very much and wish I could have heard him deliver it as you can't form a very good opinion of the speech without hearing it spoken.

Charley will be off for Tennesee Springs first of June. Dr Gibbes[125] advised him to go as he thinks his liver affected, gave him medicine and dieted him, told him he must smoke.

Sarah Stuart's wedding take place second of June.[126] Louis is to be one of the groomsmen. Robert Gibbes another.[127] Henrietta & Annie are to be Brides maids, 10 of them.

Louis is quite well, he is in Charleston this week, he was sick a long time with measles, he was very imprudent in coming out too soon.

Don't believe Pinckney has any chum you had better write and ask him to room with you. I invited Annie Gibbes to pay me a visit this summer but her father is afraid for her to come.[128] Henrietta is quite sick.

---

123. Isabella F. Mackay.
124. Benjamin Franklin Wyman of Beaufort District.
125. Dr. Arthur Smith Gibbes (1807–1885) of Beaufort, a physician.
126. Sarah Barnwell Stuart married her first cousin Henry Middleton Stuart Jr. (1835–1915) on 2 June 1857.
127. Robert Reeve Gibbes (1836–1877), son of Phoebe Sarah Campbell and Arthur Smith Gibbes.
128. Ann Reeve Gibbes (1835–1889) and her father, Dr. Arthur Smith Gibbes.

You must burn up my letters and better not let any of ours throw about your room, the students have no scruples about reading them. We are quite well. Katie talks much plainer than she used too.

Canaan is looking very pretty every body admires the trees. Good bye my dear brother and believe me to be your affec^te sister Annie.

Matilda Leverett to her brother Milton

Canaan, June 2nd 1857.

My dear Min,

What in the world is the matter with you, that you are sending messages <u>at</u> me, so continually, when <u>you know</u> that my letters are not fit reading? I begin to suspect that you do it, merely to fill up your letters. I am surprised at your wanting bad ones, when you get good ones, so often. It must be all sham. Do you plead guilty, or no? You do; I am certain you do.

Pa met Willy Martin[129] yesterday, and tried to find out whether you were studying, and what you were doing. But he was not able to get any definite answer, and when he came home, he asked us, whether any-thing was the matter with him. I expect Willy was afraid of him. We all take it for granted, that you <u>are</u> studying.

Annie, Mary, Julie, and Katie are all gone up to the village, and the rest of us follow on Saturday. It is so cool and pleasant down here, that we might easily stay much longer, but Pa prefers being on the safe side. Dr. Hutson[130] said that Ma could remain, without the slightest danger until the first of July.

Her health is a great deal better, and she is very active, and in good spirits. Almost lives in the garden, which is very fine. Has corn 'most as tall as Pa, and sunflowers much taller, musk-melon vines covered with blossoms, and cabbages, tomatoes, okra, Irish-potatoes, and numberless other things "coming on finely." Pa's crops are also looking extremely well. The oats are as superior, as possible, to last year's. I suppose they will be cut in a week or two. The Irish potatoes (of which, he has about half an acre planted) will be fit for digging by the time you get home. I suppose you will come the last week in the month? You must let us know <u>exactly</u> what day you are coming, in order that the buggy may go over the day before. If you come on a Monday, it will have to go over the Saturday previous. So you must let us know in time. The Hutsons are wishing us to join with them, & bring all of you boys over in the stage. It will be cheaper for Pa <u>to send</u> for you, for "Old Ephy" (whom Pa has promised to let go over to see his wife) will

---

129. William Heyward Martin, a member of the class of 1860.
130. Dr. Thomas Woodward Hutson.

carry the mules, and the feed for it to Mr. Ned Webb's yard, where it will stay the night, and bring you home the next day. However, the Hutsons intend sending over to make inquiries, and then Pa will decide. We are all wanting to see you very much. It seems as if you had been away two years, instead of not one year.

Charley was to have gone to the Chick Springs near Greenville, in the upper part of the state, the day before yesterday.[131] Dr. Gibbes' advice. He has been in Beaufort for a week past.

Dr. Tom Cuthbert is to board with Aunt Til this summer. I suppose she needs money, is the reason she agreed to it. Rob Means[132] is growing as fast as "the Bean Stalk." His eye looks very badly still, but the family don't think it bad enough to be fixed. The one that was operated on, looks very well.

Sarah Stuart & Hal were to be married last night. We all received invitations, but declined. Lewis[133] went over to be one of the grooms men. 'Twas a church wedding.

Have not yet heard from Fred and Ed. They must have arrived in England some three weeks ago.

Give my love to all at Aunt Cornelia's, when you see them. Hope they are all well.

Luck is quite well, and in good order.

yr. aff sister
Matilda

Rev. Charles Edward Leverett to his son Milton

Canaan, June 10, 1857.

My dear Minnie,

I have been waiting to hear when you are to be sent for, as I wrote in my last. In Anne's letter you ask her about yr. coming in a hired stage from Walt⁰.[134] I do not know anything about it in particular. You said something about it in a late letter, but then you crossed it out, as if the matter was ended. Mr. Hutson said something about yr. coming that way to the girls, but nothing has been said in particular. Let me now know the day you expect to be in Walt⁰, so that I may send the mule & buggy over the day before & you can leave as soon as the stage arrives. Eph^m will be at Webb's, where his wife is, & you will have to hunt him up, as soon as the stage gets in, tho' I will be sure to charge him to be ready for you. Should

---

131. A popular resort.
132. Robert Means Fuller (1839–1893) of Beaufort.
133. Louis McPherson DeSaussure Jr.
134. Walterboro, in Colleton District.

you be obliged to remain over, you will have to stay a night at the public house. Have the mule driven easily & she will get you over without difficulty. I enclose ____ dollars out of my very poor purse. I did not expect to send any, as you had so much over after paying the College bills. I enclose it, as I fear from what you said, you had got rid of that amt, but if you have not, bring back what I now send, as I am very short of funds.

I am sorry to hear of the College troubles.[135] D͏ͬ DeSaussure told me about it yesterday. I think so far as I can judge that Mr McCay's remark was made in great kindness & that he only spoke in the benevolence of his heart when he said, the young men were sorry. People frequently speak in that way, and if every one's words were fairly criticized, there would be few who would not be convicted of speaking falsely. I feel indignant at the professors & at those boys who are actually badgering a good man for an inadvertent remark. You must put me in his place & then see how you would feel, if they had dealt so with me. I hope you stand up for him. I feel very sorry for him & hope he will yet find some good friends, who will vindicate him from the attack. I hear that Pelham was his friend, but very virtuously gave him up. Pelham is a poor fellow, & should be careful to get the beam out of his own eye, before he attempts to take out the mote of his brother's eye.[136] In reality I think the Faculty & the boys have very thoroughly disgraced themselves in their assault upon the President. I wish I was one of the Trustees, I would stand up for him. If I knew the Pres. I would drop him a kind letter. Should you see him make my respects & tell him, that all are not against him, & that I am sure he will come out aright from this trial.

All are well. The family are at the pine land. I came down with Mamy today. We go up in the evening. Yr. boat, I hear is at Mrs Stuart's near the ferry. The Jenkins & Mackays are at the Point. I suppose you heard that Isabella M. has been addressed by a young Jenkins & that Mr. Mackay has sent him off. Probably you will not be so sorry for Jenkins, as you would be, were it not that you have taken,— I think Mamy said,—some little interest in the young lady herself. You yet have a chance. So cheer up. The crop of corn is looking improvingly. The cotton is backward. We hope to cut oats soon.

yr. aff father,

C.

---

135. South Carolina College president Charles Francis McCay suspended three juniors for disrupting chapel in April 1857. The junior class petitioned the administration to reconsider, but a misunderstanding convinced the students that their honor had been questioned. They refused to attend McCay's lectures, and other students and several faculty members sided with them. On 11 June 1857 the board asked McCay and the entire faculty to resign. A few professors who supported the board and opposed McCay were reappointed.

136. Charles P. Pelham of Columbia, professor at South Carolina College.

2

A Journey through Europe

June 1857–October 1860

So little is it, that man (not woman)
needs while on a voyage. The principal
thing he needs is money.

—Frederic Percival Leverett

*Fred and Edward spent nearly two years in Europe during 1857 and 1858 to further
their education, Edward in theology and Fred in medicine. Edward studied at several
universities, including the Sorbonne in Paris and the University of Heidelberg, and
Fred at several hospitals, most notably the Hôpital Saint-Louis and Hôpital des
Enfants-Malades in Paris. They also took some time off to travel and see Europe.*

Frederic Percival Leverett to his brother Milton

Paris, June 24th 57

My dear Min,

I have been intending to write you for a long time, in fact I intended to before
leaving Phila but regret that until now the intention has not resulted in the thing
intended. It has not been so because I did not appreciate your letter, for there
have been few, if any that I have ever received, that have given me more pleasure.
Before receiving this I hope that you will be safely at home, enjoying yourself
highly and appreciating the pleasures of home after your absence. I hope also that
your examinations that I suppose are going now, perhaps while I am writing this,
will result most favourably and that you will find yourself possessed of a good aver-

age and an excellent stand. Write and let us know all about it, and also how you find all at home. I hope that they will be well, and that this summer will be a pleasant and profitable one to you. Besides studying Mathematics with Father, as you propose, you had much better read, as much as possible, and do so systematically, and if you can make the time write about what you read. It will be of the greatest advantage to you, enabling you to express yourself easily, forming your style &c &c. Another very good thing for you to do during your vacations, will be the keeping up your knowledge of French. We find our schoolboy French now of immense service, and tho' we could not use it at once, we find that it enables us to progress with much more ease than those who came here, as many do, with only their mother tongue to help them. Had we ever realized that we should have used French as we now do, we would have studied it when boys, very differently from the way we did. I tell you this because Ed & I have decided that you will have to come to Paris and Germany when you have studied your profession, whatever it may be—and learn the language. I tell you this, I say so that you may have the advantage over us. I am writing you just after a six o'clock dinner which is a time of Mother's, I find suitable for making good resolutions. I advise you to do as I did this morning, that is not eat any breakfast (I didn't because I had not time until one o'clock, and then concluded to wait until six o'clock, as there by I could save 5 cts. or so) I say wait until six o'clock P.M. then break fast and dine, and read this & I am certain you will be in train for making good resolutions. You have no idea what good resolutions one can make after a full meal—especially what economical resolutions; half after six o'clock is the time Ed & I chose for forming our plans on economy—it is then that we astonish ourselves. We have shortly before astonished Caroline, the waiter at our Table d'hôte, at the amount we are able to eat consecutively for 30 cts a piece. Edward especially amazes her—his appetite is excellent, and far surpasses mine. He outstrips me in eating, I him in talking French. You had better study the mathematics for the coming term—give it a certain amount of time each day and master it. Mathematics conquered will remain with you—thereby you will render your ensuing term much easier and much more profitable. If there is anything else, which you expect to find difficult, study it also. You had better read as much history as you possibly can. It will be of service to you in many ways. Edward [illegible] me [illegible] and says he will be ashamed if you do not come out ahead of [illegible] what he did. He wishes to know if you stand as high in your class as Charley Hutson does in his.[1] Remember that on your shoulders rests the Leverett collegiate reputation—that more is expected of you than there was of us, for you have the benefit of our experience. Read Father's Memoir of the family, and you will realize how much is expected of you, for rec-

---

1.   Charles Woodward Hutson, a member of the class of 1860.

ollect it is the duty of every one of us not to leave the family standing where we find it, but if possible to raise it. I wish Father had written it when we were boys. I think it might [have] been the means of inciting us, me at least, to more vigorous efforts than I made. However much I can do [illegible] now what I might have done I hope that I may do something. At any rate I will try & hope wherever I may settle. I shall be so well prepared in my profession that I shall be able to make my mark. I hope that we shall all make a good mark on the "sands of time".²—Now you <u>commence</u> while in College, and in order to do so, <u>study well</u> this summer. You spoke of my becoming a member of your society & I should like it very much.

Edward and I are still occupying ourselves principally with the study of French, he especially, for I am studying [illegible] hospitals [illegible]. I now understand what is said, for the most part, with comparative ease, & I would like very much to remain in Paris, so much is there to be seen medically, for six months or even a year. This time or more could be passed most profitably, but shall leave here about the middle of August, if not sooner for Germany. You must write to us here. We have received but one letter as yet from home and are looking most anxiously for another. I have written so many home that I am afraid you will be tired of them, especially of the length. This I will make a short one. I wish you to write me word all about the family, the place, everything about Canaan, the crops, the servants, horses, &c. We take as much interest in them while in Europe as we did in America and it does not [illegible] that we are any farther off. I want you to Drive Mother out regularly, and keep her in good health and spirits. Give her my love—the same to all the children—Edward's also.

yr. aff<u>ct</u> Brother,
Fred<u>c</u> P. Leverett.

Charles Edward Leverett Jr. to his mother

Paris, Sep. 24<u>th</u> 1857

Eight weeks have rushed by, my Dearest Mother, & not a word from <u>You</u> and Home! What <u>is</u> the matter? Each mail day, Fred & myself with increasing anxiety, have been waiting & waiting & still waiting, but each day—disappointment, & "hope deferred,"³ behold all! My only translation of the word "Silence" with you is "Sickness," my own, own, Mother, & so I cannot wait any longer, but herewith jot you a few lines of love.

We are at last, after four months, on the point of leaving France for Germany. This time we are in earnest—Fred having improved a great deal in decision of

---

2. Henry Wadsworth Longfellow, "A Psalm of Life," 1839.

3. Prov. 13:12.

character. He does not change his mind now, more than once a day. But you must excuse him: the habit of change is a forceful current, & <u>washing</u> being too dear, to allow it to run in its former channel,—that of <u>shirts</u>—it resulted in the above misfortune. He would have a "clean change" of mind if he could not have it of linen.

I am writing from Nanterre,[4] where my last two months have been spent—& that very pleasantly. Madame Carnet, the lady with whom I am boarding, is a widow with two children—grown, the daughter only is with her & and plays magnificently on the piano. The old lady, whose father had his chateau, horses, & hounds swept away by the Revolution, has seen better days. She is very religious and has treated me with the utmost kindness & attention. She has given me fresh milk for my Cough every morning, & has the table covered with delicacies,—plums, beautiful grapes (on which I have feasted for a month or more) figs, sweetmeats &c &c. I breakfast by myself at 10 o'clock & she sits and talks with me. Indeed has treated me like a mother—& in fact puts me very much in mind of you. We have some long & hot arguments on slavery, & his Holiness the successor of St. Peter. On the former, her ideas are all derived from the Dead Sea Apple of Discord—Uncle Tom's Cabin,[5] which has been translated into French, & goes by the name of—La Case d'Oncle Tom. Plaguey egg of a plaguey crow! On the R. Catholic question—the only point, on which we accord, is the celibacy of the Clergy! She has a kind heart, and our discussions are most amicably & peacefully settled always—I becoming a firmer Protestant—she a Catholic, with the sincere prayer that "one of these days God will enlighten my blinded heart." She often tells me about her mother who was a very pious woman and in return I tell her about <u>you</u>. She spent the whole of this morning making a very pretty green baize cover to a portfolio for me, & while she was sewing, I took out of the portfolio, your last letter you had written to me before leaving America—(I keep that letter always by me, my darling Mother, & read it over & over & pray God to grant all your aspirations for me:—Sometimes I kneel with it in my hands, before His throne, & weep to think how far, far, I am from what you wish,—from what I ought to be—& long to be. Pray for me, that I may go from strength to strength, from grace to grace, till I appear in Zion.)—I took out the letter & read it to Mad. C. in French, & when I finished she exclaimed "what a Mother you have, & how beautifully she writes"!—Yes! I replied—with such a mother I ought to be a good son. "It is so like Saint Monica—the mother of St. Augustine"[6]—

---

4.   A western suburb of Paris.

5.   Harriet Beecher Stowe's *Uncle Tom's Cabin; or, Life among the Lowly,* serialized in 1851–1852 and published in Boston in 1852.

6.   Saint Augustine (354–430), whose mother, Saint Monica, was the subject of a chapter in Lydia H. Sigourney's *Examples of Life and Death* (New York: Charles Scribner, 1852). Sigourney presented an inscribed copy of her book to Rev. Charles Leverett 17 September 1852, and Edward probably read her characterization of Saint Monica there.

she continued, her devotion to & prayers for her son are one of the most remarkable pictures of Ecclesiastical history.—Here she recounted a great deal from the
Confessions of the illustrious Bishop of Hippo.—Do you know—I answered—I
have often thought of that before, & when reading her letters have resembled her
not only to the mother of St. Augustine, but also of St. Chrysostom,[7] & and wished
her son might be as good as <u>theirs:</u> I have never told any one so, but as your
thoughts & mine have coincided so exactly, I can't help expressing myself & in this
connection, there is a practice in your church, at which I am not astonished, &
which can be easily accounted for.—What? asked she. The worship of Saints.—I
returned. I love my mother so intensely, so deeply, so passionately—that if she
were to die before me, which God forbid, I could hardly restrain myself from praying to her in heaven, since she who was my guardian Angel <u>here</u>, would certainly
be so <u>there.</u>—And why not? answered the gentle heart of Rome's implicit child—
No, there is but <u>one</u> Mediator—was my reply, not that I love my <u>Mother less</u>, but
<u>Jesus More.</u>—& here ended our conversation. So you see, tho' far away my well
beloved, from you and Pa—the dearest of earthly ties, I think of you both unceas-
ingly, keeping your names ever in my prayers, your teachings in my practice, &
your love in my heart.

My best of friends, Mrs. Dangerfield, wrote me a delightful letter, not long
since, full of Christian love, & interest for my spiritual welfare. She mentions with
much pleasure, having received your letter. I wish you knew her better. If she had
lived in the time of Diogenes & his lamp, the philosopher would have found something <u>more</u> than a man,—a woman & a Christian Woman.

I have spoken no English for two months now, except when Fred comes to see
me, & even then he speaks French instead usually. We intend remaining together
all winter, & by speaking French to one another, while learning German, will not
forget what we have acquired. One makes some ridiculous mistakes in learning a
language, sometimes. An acquaintance of ours from Va. entered a grocery store, the
other day, & asked for a <u>bijou</u> instead of a <u>bougie:</u> a jewel instead of a candle. A
demoiselle who was studying English, told me once, she desired some <u>sweetmeat</u>
at our English table, & said "I will thank you for some <u>chillblains</u> if you please."
Poor me! I have to tell on myself also that I went into a music store, & innocently
requested some "guitar shoe-strings & I cannot let off Fred either, who came to me
one day looking very traveller-ish & business like, as if he knew all about such
things & said "You had better go and have your passport <u>vis-a-vis</u> <u>a</u>—for vise'd.
Speaking of French, I enclose a copy of a little poem in that tongue, which I wrote
to my little friendship, Meta Hyde. Several French ladies read it, but French ladies
are like all others,—they <u>will</u> say such sweet things, one is bewildered.

---

7.   Patriarch of Constantinople.

How are the crop's? I am anxiously looking forward to the Rhine, Switzerland, Greece, Italy, England, Ireland, Scotland, &c &c—& cannot forbear repeating an epigram I sent Tilly last year, founded on our twelve-labouring Hercules.[8]

> I cannot, dare not think,
> From whence will all the chink
> For such a trip be gotten—
> Pa?—not a cent has he—
> My only hope can be,
> Me—Hercule! from Cotton!

But I must close this prosy missive, My dearest Mother, hoping you are well, yet fearing you are sick. Do take care of yourself. My best love to Pa, hope he is well and in good spirits, he will hear from me on the Rhine. Our address is always the same until you receive Counter directions. We will write as soon as settled at the University,[9] but any letter directed to Hottingues & Co, Paris still will reach us there safely.

Love to Miss Matilda, Miss Annie, & Miss Mary Leverett, and myself to you
Your Edward.

P.S. Fred's changeability was only a joke; really it is the last thing of which he can be accused. He possesses wit, sterling sense, & great weight of character; is gifted with indomitable energy, & is master of his profession. Every morning the whole summer he has risen at 6 o'clock, & walked 3 or 4 miles to St. Louis—the Hospital for children—& in two weeks after his arrival here, knew more about the hospitals of Paris than a good many young doctors here who have been studying two years. He has paid particular attention to Diseases of the Skin, Children & Women, & on these points, I suppose no physician of his age, in America, can lead him. If all the M. D.'s—Men destroyers, possessed his talents, they would not be such "Assassins," as Boileau has termed them.[10] He had better, by all means, settle in Philadelphia; Beaufort is too small for him. In the latter place, the only Talents a man wants, are Friends; in the former, the only Friends he wants, are Talents. Besides a Parisian medical education, he has a Cambridge classical one, and speaks both French & German. Give the young man tether & a Southern wife & he will take the medical world in a sling. I have become completely enamoured of the French method of marrying off the young people. It is a parental Autocracy here, & the only questions asked are—Qu'a-t-il? Qu'a-t-elle? = What has he, what

---

8. "Hercules, a very faithful and excellent servant on his father's place." This note was inserted by Rev. Charles Leverett into an edited version of this letter, which he never published.
9. The University of Heidelberg.
10. Nicolas Boileau-Despreaux (1636–1711), French poet and literary critic.

has she? So I wish you would make a match for the Doctor among your bosom friends not a hundred miles from Canaan. I don't think he will object. I am sure I would not. This thing of Courting, is entirely too troublesome, takes away too much time from ones books, too many shirts from his wardrobe, & tho' one should wear a hundred pair of the most immaculate kids a year, alas! how often is his hand rejected!—You ask—what friends? Happy heart, thou haste 1000,000,000.

> There is a garden on a river's bank
> Where centenarian oak trees grow,
> Bathing their brows in the dews of heav'n,
> Their feet in the Royal flood below.
> Where voices gladden'd with April songs,
> And trilling the sweetest of metres,
> Float softly on in the twilights of Spring,
> With music which speaks of—<u>Mosquitoes.</u>
>
> 2
> Where the happy grey headed Mauma
> In the sunshine basks at her door,
> Sends "T'ankye to Massa & Missis"
> And wonders how soon—she'll get "more."
> Builds Spanish Chateaux—out of bacon,
> Dreams of future—Molasses & past,
> And with faith in—"bacca" unshaken,
> Dies—of Chol'ra <u>Infantum</u>—at last.
>
> 3
> Where the Humming Bird gaily at eve,
> To the Feast of the Flowers doth flee,
> Taking his wine in jessamine cups
> And in "Roses of <u>China</u>" his "<u>Tea.</u>"
> Where flattered, the Peacock for ages,
> Autocrat o'er green velvet has strolled,
> And Shanghai's with plumage of purple
> Strut proudly over bright "<u>Cloths</u> of <u>Gold</u>"
>
> 4
> There—brightest amid brightest of flow'rs,
> All pensively a maiden doth rove,
> Whose mind's a palace of diamond,
> And whose heart is a fortress of love.
> Oh! a lover might feast him forever,

On her eye—such a banquet its glance,
And give to his friends—at the wedding,
Geese fatten'd on the "Glory of France."

5
Ah! tell me could a mortal e'er tire,
In a Park so enchanting as this,
Whose joys are the purest & brightest,
And whose name is the essence of bliss?
Whose Lady & Lord in their Manor,
Tend Pinks of perfection undying,
And the children—little souls—bless them!
And the cats—are never heard crying?

But it is time for my Muse to rest. I hadn't a rhyme in my head, when I commenced this P.S.—Yet there is some truth in it—enough to solve the Riddle: The
happiest plantation has Mosquitoes (as each rose its thorn) & they give decided
piquancy to rhime: the old Mauma—a Southern picture—is peculiarly blessed in
this spot: the flowers—are a palpable fact: the father & mother—your dearest
friends: the children—the best behaved in the world: & as to the cats—I have
seen Gov.—lift a sash with one hand, & with the tongs in the other gently fling a
poor unfortunate out of the window.—Please burn this immediately, for it is written in the greatest haste, & like all improvisational performances fit only for an
Auto-da-fe."
        Once & again you, my dearest mother, to infinity.

                                                              Edward

Charles Edward Leverett Jr. to his father

                                                      Field of Waterloo
                                                      30th Sep. 1857

My dear Father
        I am seated under a tree on the celebrated field of Battle that decided the
destinies of Napoleon—& the World. Did you ever think to get a line from that
spot, & from your own son on that spot? Sergeant Munday—the old guide, who
was in the battle,—has just finished fighting it over for us in theory—and I find it
exciting enough without the powder & bullets. To the poor Frenchmen who listen
it must be galling indeed, but I think from what I have just seen in France if they
ever get a chance, the score will be settled, & with vengeance. The spots where

---

11.   The burning of a heretic during the Inquisition.

Ponsonby fell, Gordon, Shaw—who cut down seven Frenchmen—where Lord Raglan had his arm shot off,[12] the high mound in the centre of the British position (240 ft high) with a lion on the top,[13] the trees where Blucher came up, & where Grouchy did not,[14] the orchard, Belle Alliance[15]—all, were proudly held up to view & commented on by the John Bulls of the party. There is a museum on the ground filled with relics bullets—swords—bayonets—&c&. I brought away a brace of grape shot as mementoes—& as more peaceable tokens, some wild flowers from the orchard—the key of the victory.

Brussels, 26th

We arrived here this morning from Paris, & proceded immediately to Waterloo, in a stage coach—being a distance of 12 miles. On the parting of the coach we were surrounded by a crowd of boys, who to earn a soú, ran alongside turning sommersets & keeping up, with a good deal of agility. Even girls of twelve years performed the same feat. But hard-hearted mortal! I closed my pocket, determined <u>you</u> <u>should</u> see my economy, even at the expense of my charity.

Brussels is a very pretty & neat place, with a beautiful Park,[16] & a Hotel de Ville—of most antique & castle-like aspect.[17] Here Charles V. abdicated.

There is a custom here, which holds also in Paris—of dedicating the stores to some thing, person, object, monkey, dog or saint, E. G.—a la rose du Midi—To the rose of the South—in golden letters over the door. Au bon Pasteur: Au griffon-terrier: A la bonne Mere: A la Sainte Vierge: Au repos des voyageurs: & one I saw at Paris—A la Levrette = to the female greyhound.—We have visited the manufacture of lace here, and found it very curious, but as we had not a thousand dollars to bestow on the poor children at home, we had to deny ourselves the pleasure of buying handkerchiefs for them.

Your & Mary's & Min's letters reached us just as we were leaving Paris. I was delighted to find Ma's appetite restored to its original dimensions of exuberant youth, even at the expense of a famine in the land.—

---

12. These British officers were Maj. Gen. Sir William Ponsonby (1772–1815), mortally wounded; Col. Sir Alexander Gordon (1786–1815), Wellington's aide-de-camp, mortally wounded; Lt. W. C. Shawe of the Blue Royal Horse Guards; and Lt. Col. Lord Fitzroy James Henry Somerset (1788–1855), military secretary to Wellington.

13. The *Butte du Lion*, a man-made hill topped by a large cast-iron lion, was constructed as a memorial to the Netherlanders who fought there.

14. Field Marshal Gen. Gebhart Leberecht von Blücher, prince of Wahlstatt (1742–1819), was a Prussian officer who commanded an army under Wellington; Marshal Marquis Emmanuel de Grouchy (1766–1847) was a French marshal who commanded the right wing of Napoléon's army in the Waterloo campaign.

15. The orchard at the Château of Hougoumont; La Belle Alliance, just south of Waterloo.

16. The nineteenth-century Botanic Garden.

17. Brussels town hall, dates to the fifteenth century.

We left France with less money, but with more knowledge, than we entered it. We entered with English in our mouths, but came out with French, & have passed for Frenchmen with considerable success. I hope you will not accuse us of being imposters.

Antwerp—This interesting old town, we reached yesterday on our way to the Rhine. The principal things of note are the souvenirs of the great Rubens—not to forget Vandyck also. In the Cathedral of Notre Dame[18] is the masterpiece of the former—the Descent from the Cross—prints of which you have seen often. There is nothing, however, like the original, the colouring, draping, & expression &c of which, are worthy of visit all the way from America. The other piece by Rubens—also celebrated—is the Raising of the Cross—I have not yet seen the Galleries of Florence & Rome, but certainly these two paintings excel anything in Paris—not the Louvre excepted.

Cologne, October 2ᵈ. Today finds us, in what ought to be the sweetest of towns, but on the contrary, instead of the streets equalling the "Roses of Gal" in their fragrance & beauty, they are abominable for both the above qualities.—We passed the night & part of this morning at Aix-la-Chapelle[19]—celebrated as the birth place & tomb of Charlemagne. As a curiosity, we ate some eggs boiled in the Sulphur Springs of the place. The water comes out of the ground hot enough for the poor people to cook their dinners. Consequently <u>water</u> is <u>fire</u> there: Strange is it not? to cook by water? If Americans lived in the town they doubtless would introduce some improvement—such as <u>eating</u> by steam &c. I amused Fred very much at Antwerp, by asking our guide who was explaining some statues one of which was David—"whether it was the <u>painter</u> <u>David</u> of France"[20]—This I did with a long and innocent face. Fred stood behind snickering away, & the guide who doubtless thought me a heathen, enlightened me in a benign manner. Passing a storehouse of rice, I was equally ignorant of <u>that</u>, & he kindly explained how it was a grain, to be eaten &c, &c.

I am seated on the deck of a steamboat (The boat not having yet left Cologne) on the Rhine, scribbling away. The morning we spent in rambling about the city (Cologne). The first thing we do always is to visit the Churches, as they contain the best paintings ordinarily & as I am naturally addicted to the Fine Arts, Music, poetry & painting, & am ambitious of being something more than an amateur, I am taking this opportunity of studying the old masters & their <u>homes</u>—the Galleries & Cathedrals of Europe. I wish indeed you could make some money, & let me buy a hundred dollars worth of pictures while I am over here. A few copies of

---

18. The largest church in Belgium, completed in the sixteenth century.
19. A city in Prussia on the Belgian border.
20. Jacques-Louis David. (1748–1825)

some of the choicest works of Rubens, Rembrandt or Raphael could be easily got for that amount. I priced a copy of Rubens' "Descent from the Cross" in the museum of Antwerp; it was about six times the size of this <u>sheet</u> <u>opened</u>—\$20. It depends altogether on the size, so that what would only buy <u>one</u> large picture, will command half a dozen smaller ones. You have two handsome ones already in the drawing room, but I should like to see a few scenes from the life of our Saviour adorn the villa of the Pastor of Sheldon.

You have read Hood's Rhine[21] & will recall the story of Ste. Ursula & the eleven thousand virgins of Cologne. We visited the church where their bones are deposited in fantastic devices around the walls.[22] Their skulls smile as sweetly on the wandering strangers as did that of "poor Yorrick" [illegible line] the size of their shanks led me to think they must have belonged to a strapping set of maidens. Poor creatures! Those horrible Huns ought to have been ashamed of themselves—& so ought the Romish priests. It was bad enough to have been killed but it was adding insult to injury, to hang up to the public gaze a set of <u>scrawny</u> bone lassies. Women are ugly enough when they are thin, but they are frightful when "reduced to skeletons."

Among some curious relics in the same church, were two thorns from the Saviour's crown, a piece of the garment he wore on the cross, a shred of the swathing bands of his infancy—& would you believe it—one of the jars in which he turned water into wine. It is unfortunately not "stone" but of marble, & [illegible] container [illegible] much less "two or three." In the process of time it had become cracked, & so undoubtedly was the Reverend Father who had the audacity to exhibit it.

Credat judicem apud nonego.[23]

I here add, greatly to the relief of sympathising females that the bones of the Virgins have been lately examined by anatomists, who say, they are all <u>men!</u>

Heidelberg, Oct 12<u>th</u>

The Rhine surpasses all the ideas I had ever formed of it. From Drachenfels[24] to Bingen,[25] its bed is between two ranges of mountains, olden time hamlets dot the shores, vineyards climb from the waters' edge up to the clouds, precipices overhang the water, on their summits the ruins of some old castle which in legend [illegible]. I couldn't help sighing over these remnants of feudal days, when

---

21.   Thomas Hood, *Up the Rhine* (New York: Putnam, 1852).
22.   Saint Ursula, Christian martyr put to death at Cologne; the Church of St. Ursula was built in the eleventh century.
23.   Let him believe before a judge, not I.
24.   A castle on the east bank of the Rhine south of Bonn.
25.   A town at the confluence of the Rhine and Nahe Rivers.

thinking how delightful it must have been to have slept in armour, instead of feather beds, to have won maidens with the sword instead of the purse, to have worn gauntlets instead of kids & helmets instead of beavers. Oh there were giants in the land in those days.—Indeed I must say I think the Rhine an exquisite leaf in the Book of Nature—a very poem speaking, living, written by the hand of the Creator, & meant to be read by the World.—

I am at last in Germany at the University of Heidelberg. Long looked for event! Six years have fled, since my mind was made up to come [illegible] if ever there was [illegible]. In fact, this is nothing like "trying," or "having one's own way," owing to the kindness of indulgent fathers & brothers.

I must thank both you & Charley once again. You must excuse this horrible writing—the paper is very thin—& so are the ideas & ink.—But I am paying you & Maim & Minny for your last—we searched half an hour for the beginning—I have not found it yet.

Best love to ma & yourself & all—
from your most affect. Son
Edward

Mary Maxcy Leverett to her son Milton

Canaan,
Nov. 16th, 1857

My dear, my beloved Min

It does indeed seem a great shame that your own Mother should not have written you before,—but God knows it was not from want of love. My heart has often reproached me for not writing and I have daily intended doing so, but when any thing is on my mind and distresses me, I feel as if it was impossible to write to any human being. No doubt it is a wrong feeling, because even when we have nothing pleasant to communicate, an interchange of feeling and opinion is a relief & consolation. When you left Ephraim was off, you know, & from that time my mind was so worried and disturbed that it did [not] seem possible to write without importing my own gloomy feelings. The trouble is at last ended, and Charley now has him safe, and he has at last confessed & told the names of the Fuller negroes engaged in it. And now to tell you all about it. He came home a week after he left, to your Pa in the Pineland, & you ought to have heard his "palaver." (Charley was at Canaan). Pater-familias reproached him with running away. "I didn't run away, sir." "What do you mean, you worthless fellow?" "I <u>went</u> away, sir," responded he, in a softly sort of <u>smoothing</u>-<u>down</u> tone. Did you ever hear such a cool thing, Min? However (to cut short the matter) Pa gave him a ticket, to go down to Charley, telling him not to punish him. This was Saturday. Instead of going there, after eating his dinner in the kitchen, he goes off, and we hear nothing of him for a month, (I much distressed for fear something had happened to him) when D^r DeSaussure sends us a Mercury with an advertisement of Ephraim as a runaway belonging to Mr C Leverett.[26] This was a great pain & mortification to me. The Doctor thought we had better sell him & your father & myself agreed with him, but Charley was very angry, &c. and insisted on his being brought back to him, so Pa wrote,—answer came that he was sick & a Doctor attending him. (This, we feel sure now was a pretense to put off coming, as he looks fatter in the face than I ever saw him.) Next week, he came. Charley shut him secure, as he thought, giving him plenty to eat, but not wishing to punish him, thinking it possible he <u>might</u> have been sick. The fourth morning, the loft window had been burst open & he was gone. Charley of course was enraged as he had treated him kindly, tho' he had told him he should confess. The next day a note came from Mr Copeland, the Chaplin's driver had found him on their place that night & put him in jail, as Mr Copeland called it. Hercules went for him & Charley put off no longer, but had great difficulty in making him confess,—he did at last out with it, and owned to every thing exactly as Billy had described, & the exact names of the Fuller negroes which Billy had already told Charley. Daphne, he described as planning it with him, Lindy helping.[27]—And now, Min, to show you what a hypocrite he is;—when he was brought back from the Chaplins, Charley not being at home (he wouldn't have let me, if he had) I thought it right to go to the back door & have a talk with him, & also let him say whatever he had to say, as every human being, I think, has a right to be heard. It is too long to tell you all,—I told him of his guilt &c. (not scoldingly, mind!). He protested he was as perfectly innocent, and knew no more of it, than a child that had never seen the light, raising his hand upward, and declaring, that as God was living & knew all things, and knew his heart, that what he said was true, and he was perfectly ignorant of the whole matter, begged me to pray for him (which I told him, I had done already) that he was going to lead a new life from henceforth, that he confessed he had killed a goose of Mr Saunders & also a Guinea fowl, but would do such things no longer &c. &c. & begged me to ask Mas Charley not to be hard on him, which I promised. His voice had not the sort of emphatic energy of innocence, but a sort of deceitful, softly sound, so that I did not feel like believing him, and advised him to begin his repentance by confession; when he again protested his innocence. This was in the

---

26. This advertisement appeared in the *Charleston Mercury*, 24 and 31 October 1857: "LODGED AT THE CHARLESTON WORK house, as a runaway, EPHRAIM, who says he belongs to Mr. Charles Leverett, of Beaufort District. He is 5 feet 4 inches high, about 55 years old, and black complexion. W. Withers, M.W.H. October 17."

27. Slaves.

morning Charley got home, and by night time Ephraim had confessed the whole. All of this happened yesterday, and today Charley says, he seems quite cheerful from having made a clean breast of it. Your father is looking forward to a heavy bill from the Work-house, & also the advertisement which they kept in the paper long after we had sent for Ephraim. But enough of this disagreable affair. In the midst of all this trouble, a letter came from Aunt Til, saying she had been sick & Grandma also, who was impatient to come over, & I must come over. So I went & had to stay four days, but returned bringing her with me. She is quite weak, tho' better, but requires some of us to be almost constantly in her room. Add to all this, the moving down, & putting the house to rights, and you may suppose I have had trouble enough. The clouds begin to break now though, and I hope my next letter will be of a happier cast.

Your aunt Til will not be able to go to Columbia this winter, as she has lost heavily by the Bank in Phil. & also because Mr Fielding[28] did not prepare Newton, hearing she was not going. Poor Rob. Fuller has had this cold & fever which every body has had, & it is not now likely he will go to Columbia, as his Mother's uneasiness makes her more inclined to take him to Florida. I send you Edward's last,—don't lose it. God bless you.

My dearest
Ever yr aff Mother
Mary Leverett

I long for you to come down. Mr Coffin[29] has shipped our last year's cotton & credited your father to the amount of $300. on it which is good news.

One of the Camellias is in bloom red & white very pretty. Mame has had a dreadful cold & cough & also fever; so has Kate & Carry & also myself but all are now almost quite well.

Mary Bull Leverett to her brother Milton

Canaan, Nov. 25th. 1857.

My dear Minny,

When I was up in the pinelands I commenced a letter to you, but my desk having been sent down, the news in the letter was so stale, that I burnt it up, and since then I have been half expecting a letter from you. I have been besides unwell, before I came down I had a bad cough and cold, and have it still, although not quite so bad, and Mamma has been dosing me with Salts, Blue pill Castor oil,

---

28. John Fielding of Beaufort, principal of Beaufort College.
29. George Mathews Coffin of Charleston, a cotton factor and partner in the firm of Coffin and Pringle.

and putting mustard plaster on my chest and side, (you ought to have heard me cry) but the latter has done me some good, although I have the pain in my side still, when I cough. I hope that you will not think that I am too egotistic, but I wished to show you why I have not written to you. Tilly has so much housekeeping to do since she has come down here, that she has given the teaching to Annie. You ought to see the school, Annie tells us we must be in at ten as Louis comes at eleven, and she only lets him stay one hour, of course that must be very disagreable to both, for him to take such a long cold ride and stay only one hour, and then it is dreadfull for us to be kept in suspense for so a long time. I have been only a few times to her, not being well enough, but the few times that I went I had such a horrid time that I am going to beg hard (as I will be eighteen in Jan.) to let me study by myself. I will give you a peep at the school-room. Annie is writing, I bring my French reading lesson, and I will sit down there read it and translate it and Annie never looked at it the whole time until I asked her something in the parsing. Charlie went down to Mr. Fripp's last week and bought two tackies for one hundred and twenty dollars. Ever so many people wanted them. They are exactly like Peter Gray, and Charlie has named one Peter and the other Simple. He has finished breaking them already to the buggy, and drove me out yesterday and is going to drive me out to-day. Papa went to town last Monday with a tremendous list. I suppose you know that Mr. Coffin paid him $300. in advance for the cotton, at the rate of 30 cents, and it may sell for a great deal more. It was a great relief to Papa.

Grandma is very unwell and Ma is quite uneasy about her, her memory seems to be failing very fast. She says I must give her love to you and tell you that she can barely keep off the bed. She lies down a good part of the day.[30] She says must tell you she has not forgotten the five dollars, but she has no money now, however she expects some on the 12th of December. I wish I had some cash to send to you, but all of my money except 25 cents I sent to get a riding suit, as I want you to ride with me this winter. Please when you write give me some account of college, and the people you associate with. I suppose you will come very soon, which I am very glad of. By the by Ralph Elliot[31] sent to offer to buy the tackies. Grandma says you must give her love to the Greggs.

Your affectionate sister,

Mary Leverett

P.S. Remember that if you write to me, I will always answer.

---

30. Mary Bull Maxcy died at Canaan on New Year's Eve and was buried at Sheldon Church on 2 January 1858; Rev. Charles Leverett officiated at her funeral.

31. Dr. Ralph Emms Elliott, a physician, son of Rev. Stephen Elliott (1804–1866).

Mary Bull Leverett to her brother Milton

Canaan, Jan. 20th. 1858.

You said my dearest Minny that you intended to write to me, I have looked for a letter ever since, and I have put off from day to day writing to you thinking to myself, well perhaps I may hear from Minny soon, so that then I might write to you, and at the same time answer your letter.

This morning after breakfast, I was sitting in my room reading History, when I heard Tilly exclaim "Ma look what a flock." of course I rushed out also, and saw the largest flock of geese that I have ever seen, you would not believe how much noise they made, I suppose there was about 2 or 3 hundred at least. Mamma said "My how excited Minny and Charlie would have been."

Charlie went to Charleston last Monday to get clothes, more particularly boots, he went to the Store, to see if he could buy any, but they were too large, he therefore determined to go to Town.

Jan. 28th. Do you remember the place that Charlie was talking of getting? Well instead of 12, or 13 dollars an acre as we thought, it was 12 or 13 thousand dollars and Charlie went to see about the terms, as soon as he heard the price he said nothing more about it. Louis also went to see the place, and the houses were in so delapidated a state that he would not trust himself in them, he told us however that he intended to offer 5 and was willing to give 6 thousand, but I do not think that Mr. Chisolm[32] will take it. I have not heard since.

Last Monday Bill Elliot sent a note to Charlie offering his place to him for 6 thousand asking him to come round and look at it. Charlie went round the next day, and went all over it and liked it very much, he says it has been underated. Mr. Davis offered him (Bill) six thousand last summer and he refused it, and is now very sorry. He Mr. Davis is a good planter they say he never would have offered to buy the place unless it was a good one, several of the planters said it only needed draining. Bill said he would make the terms perfectly easy to Charlie, only to pay him 500 dollars now as he was in debt (indeed he only wants to sell because he is in debt) and the rest at his leisure. Charlie is not going to buy it however as he has only seven thousand and he would not have any thing to buy negroes &c.

Daddy Ephraim, Billy, and Carolina[33] went to the Ferry a few days ago and brought 3 rafts, but left the half of another raft which Papa had bought, and which was the principal one, therefore two of the men, E. and Carolina, had to go back last night for it, but they have not come yet. We are very glad the boards have come as Papa can hire the carpenters to finish the house.

---

32. Alexander Robert Chisolm of Coosaw Island, a planter.
33. Slaves.

Charlie has put up the glass door in the parlor, which makes it look much better as well as give much more light. Miss Anne Jenkins spent last night with us and went home this evening, she was very kind also, and carried home plenty of Annie's work, thereby relieving us a great deal. Papa received a letter from Mr. Gould, saying that he had shipped the picture which Papa had bought summer before the last. Mamma and Papa intend going to Town next Monday that is if they can get money. People are owing Pa but do not pay.

I was eighteen last Monday and I do not think that I have spent a more miserable day for a long time, it could not help recurring to my mind, that here I was eighteen years old and was treated more like one of 12. Minny during that whole day not one single one wished me a happy birthday. Ma was saying the other day that she snubbed Julie very often, I could not help thinking that they all snubbed me more than anybody else, Charlie more especially. I can seldom say a word unless

I have had this letter about 3 or 4 weeks, Papa was waiting hear from you, I do not wish to send it now at all, it is so old but Papa says I must.

I am afraid I ought not to have written the above therefore I stopped in the middle of a sentence.

Annie has a beautiful voice and you should have seen how delighted Louis was when he heard her. I can't write any more.

Your affectionate sister
Mary L.

Charles Edward Leverett Jr. to his brother Milton

Heidelberg, April 13$\underline{\text{th}}$
1858.

My dear brother,

You see by the date,[34] how <u>great</u> a day this is in my eyes. Ma's letter to Fred came two & forty hours ago, & I have been counting every minute until the fatal knot is tied.—I am seated all alone in the wide, wide world—Fred at Vienna— you all at home—thinking of dear Little Canaan every moment, & building pictures of all that is going on there. I am wondering if you are all dressed yet, how the cavalcade to Sheldon is arranged, how Annie is dressed, thinking that notwithstanding two years of preparation, all is in a hurry, skurry, flurry.—hearts are beating, dogs are barking, Kate is crying, Carry squalling, guests are coming, horses neighing, pigs squealing, birds singing, fowls cackling, oxen lowing,—all nature &

---

34. This was the date of Anne's wedding to Louis at Sheldon Church.

nature's children lifting their approving voices in favour of the appalling ceremony now about to take place at the moment I am writing. Dear old Sheldon! I do wish I was there! How I envy you all, & how I long for the magic carpet of the Thousand & One Nights to fly across the ocean to home once more! Oh! I never felt so home-sick in my life. This morning I got up feeling desperate (if it had not been so cold would have drowned myself) & determined if I did not have any wedding to go to, I would anyhow put on my Sunday-go-to-meeting clothes & promenade about, & so I did.—I am all dressed up in my best suit writing to you this instant—determined to come near to the thing as possible & celebrate the day after an agreeable and suit-able manner. After finishing this, I will go out about the time you all are enjoying yourselves at table, and buy a piece of cake in commemoration of the sad event. I have also taken holiday, for the day naturally & properly should be spent in as lazy & gentlemanly a mode as possible. But, alas! alas! how can I describe my feelings. The blues choke utterance—Oh! oh! oh! oh! oh! oh! oh! oh! oh! oh! oh! oh! oh! oh! oh!—So now you have an idea of my disconsolation.—Please some of you write & tell me all—every little thing—I do love home more & more every day, & long to be back. If it is possible we wish to have a rendevous of the whole family at Canaan next December at Christmas—Fred & I will do our utmost to be there, & I will study my eyes & talk my tongue out to accomplish it. This last is the worst thing about learning to speak a language. One must talk if one will learn, & that goes against one—I have said so many things in my life already which I ought not to have done, that I am learning to be silent—it is happier—wiser—better. I have visited lately a grand ducal palace & garden not far from Heidelberg.[35] In the gar-den is a mosque, a facsimile of that of St. Sophia of Constantinople.[36] The walls are covered with mottoes from the Koran & among them the following remarkable one: Reden ist Silber und Schweigen ist gold—Speaking is silver and Silence is gold! Learn, my dear fellow, to profit by it now, do not disdain to be taught wis-dom even by a Mohammedan.

I cherish the hope that you may yourself come over here one of these days after you have finished your College course with honor. I feel very ashamed of my college days—& have often wished they could be blotted out. My health it is true was bad, but I know I could have done better, & acted nobler in many things. But I congratulate myself that I have a brother behind me who will wipe out every stain I may have left—one who by manly conduct, upright principles, gentle, but fearless demeanour, studious habits, & religious character—will eclipse by the steadiness of his light, my errors however brilliant, I may have scat-tered in my path.

---

35. The Schloss in the town of Schwetzingen, a few miles southwest of Heidelberg.
36. Saint Sophia (d. after 578), Byzantine empress.

Yes, my brother, I have entered a hundred hopes in you & do not let them be disappointed. You have <u>health</u> (and if you had suffered a little of what I have & do suffer you would prize it above all talent) you have fair abilities—behold the weapons & the strength to wield them! all you want is practice, activity, expertness,—application will give you this—& if you fail 99 times, <u>never be too disappointed to try the 100th</u>! It is not <u>talent</u> or <u>genius</u> which makes the man, it is the <u>man</u> who makes the talent & genius. I have seen & studied much, & am convinced that <u>steady perseverance</u> has made more successful & <u>great men</u> than all the talent of the world put together.—So pluck up heart! If you are not equal to others in mathematics show them you can surpass them in <u>other things</u>. Try to keep on a par in the exact sciences—& <u>far above par</u> in the literae humaniores— you have a taste for these. I abhorred mathematics but such was the course I pursued. Make up your <u>minus quantity in it by your plus quantity in the other brackets</u> that is the secret, & say with Bulwer "in the <u>Lexicon</u> which youth has prepared for a bright manhood, there is no such word as <u>fail</u>"![37]

Among the German students there are some noble looking men particularly those in the Corps, that is the association among which all the fighting is done. The duels are now strictly prohibited by law, but the students go off in carriages with seconds & physicians, & smuggle back the unfortunate ones to their lodgings. My German teacher had lately a Vandal (one of the Society names) boarding with him & he received an awful gash, from the temple through the eyelid—just a half-hair-breadth from cutting the eyeball in two, & cleaving the nose completely asunder—beauty spoiled for life. He was sick on his back—(they always have to be taken on the back for a nose wound) four weeks, & now expecting to be sent to Rachstadt, a fortress-prison for three months—their uniforms are very picturesque & some of their costumes exceedingly singular. I attended a torch light procession, just before this vacation, & sang the "Gaudeamus igitur juvenes,"[38] with all the corps in union. Each man, as all are arranged in a wide [square], flings his torch into the centre, thus making a tremendous bonfire, and the officers, stand in pairs, & clash their swords together, keeping time to the band of music, & singing all the while; the words are beautiful & the melody, & the night gives the whole a thrilling effect.

I don't think the German student, after he enters the university, studies any more than the American, perhaps less indeed than the average of our undergraduates. But the truth is, he has not the need,—he knows already on entering more than most young men in Cambridge, Yale or S.C. College, on leaving their col-

---

37. Edward George Bulwer-Lytton, *Richelieu* (1839), act 2, scene 2.
38. Part of a medieval drinking song often sung in Germany at the funeral of a comrade, "*Gaudeamus igitur juvenes dum sumus*" (Let us rejoice while we are young).

leges. It is before he enters, it is while he is at the Lyceum & Gymnasium, that he
studies—while he is a boy. No whipping in any public school in all the German
Confederation. A prison is attached to each Lyseum, & the delinquent is incar-
cerated without mercy: This however takes place very rarely, for it is a great disgrace, & the parents take great pains to make their children study. Every day in
the streets I see hundreds of little tiny bits of boys scarcely two feet high, or four
years old, with a big knapsack of books—each one—on his back trudging along
like little old dried-up men to school. It is a shame to make the innocent little
wretches "<u>work</u>" so hard. <u>Work</u> is the word—"<u>Arbeiten.</u>" They never use "study"
of children here,—that only of students & professors.————All who are going to
be ministers commence at school to study for that "profession." Theology is only
a profession here, like Law & Blacksmith work, Medicine & Murder, or any other
respectable science across the Atlantic. Besides following the courses of the Professors in Ethics Philosophy, Philology, &c here, I have private teachers. Among
these is a student of Theology who teaches me Hebrew. He is only seventeen
years old, & knows more Greek, Latin & Hebrew than most Professors in America, however so many alphabets of L L D's they tie on to their names, however
many spectacles they keep on their noses, & however many black gowns they
wrap around their ignorance.—I make honorable exception here to the three Professors of Va. Sem.—They are three among thirty thousand—but to some of the
Latin & Greek humbugs "<u>which</u>" (humbugs are not worthy of "<u>who</u>") have hung
like an ironbar over S.C. College I desire this blister immediately to be applied.
My young Hebrew is, as I say, only seventeen & has been studying that tongue
five years, & is really proficient. He knows every note in the grammar by the numbers & will say—"you will find the principle on 44th page, section so & so, a,
b, c.," "there is one exception in section g1, &c."—all by heart. I make my translation in German & whenever the German idiom does not suit the construction,
he turns it immediately into Latin or adduces an example from the vernacular of
Herodotus or Euripides.

The Religion of Germany is very much like the milk—exceedingly diluted—
& that with bad water, & the unprincipled milkmen are the Theologians. There is
preaching enough—& to spare, & in addition to that it is really eloquent preaching—preaching such as is seldom heard by a trans-Atlantic Congregation—always
extensive, fluent, & earnest. But <u>behind</u> the sermon, the Sunday harangue, there
are a thousand fanciful theories & systems of belief, a chiliad of Christologies
which form the esoteric creed of the philosophising Orator, & often totally
opposed to the exoteric harangue effusion directed solely to the hearts & not
heads also, as it should be, of a not always implicit Congregation. Professors must
preach—it is their "business," but it is another question if they <u>believe</u> themselves
all they tell their people to believe! <u>That</u> is the great flaw. A man who is not con-

vinced himself, is not going to convince others. Conviction—the firm unshaken self conviction of the preacher, is for me, the foundation of any sermon. If I didn't feel, believe, "<u>know</u> that my Redeemer liveth,"[39] I could not have the audacity to ask others to do so. Add to that the people of the 19th century are not fools, that they see much farther into the millstone of truth, than the men of a thousand years ago, that they detect "little" inconsistencies very acutely, & think at the same time that the good Shepherd makes the good flock, & the deduction from such premise is immediate that lukewarmness, indifference, coldness, doubting—infidelity <u>must</u> become rife in each community.

A deep thinking & eloquent man here is Schenkel.[40] I heard him preach lately,—quite an orator & he made the whole congregation of Professors & students break into a universal titter by saying, in reference to interpreting the bible by the <u>letter</u>, that of all the persons who held to this system of literal hermeneutics, he had never—in such a precept as "whosoever taketh my cloak, let him take my <u>coat</u>, also"[41]—he had never seen one who had lost his coat!—The wit is good for wit, but it is bad for religion.—I do not believe of the three great clerical wits, who have graced or dis-graced if you will, the English pulpit, Swift, Sterne, S. Smith[42]—one would have taken such a manner of adding a "point" to his sermon. The celebrated Bunsen[43]—lately created Baron, has just published the first volume of his "Bibelwork" & it is intended to be the keystone to his Fame. He lives here at Heidelberg, & is a fine noble looking man of about sixty, Roman features & long white hair. He is what we call decidedly rationalistic but what the Germans term decidedly pious. He is really pious, I believe, after the Teutonic fashion. As his new book is not yet in America & is destined to make great talk among divines, I send you the first three verses of Genesis as he translates them into German, as the difference is marked between it & all other translations since the time of Hieronymus:[44] "Im Anfang, da Gott Himmel und Erde schuf und die Erde würst und Öde war, und Finsterniss über der Flut war, und Gottes Hauch über den Wassern webete, sprach Gott, Es werde Licht und es ward Licht." I send it to you because it will interest theologians of our country & because so great an alteration in the most time honored & sublime passage of the world's literature deserves

---

39. Job 19:25.
40. Rev. Daniel Schenkel (1813–1885), German Protestant theologian, founder of the German Protestant Union.
41. Matt. 5:40.
42. Jonathan Swift (1667–1745), Laurence Sterne (1713–1768), and Sydney Smith (1771–1845), English clergymen and authors.
43. Baron Christian Karl Josias von Bunsen (1791–1860), Prussian diplomat and theologian.
44. Eusebius Hieronymus, or Saint Jerome (d. 420), published the Vulgate, or Latin, edition of the Bible.

notice. Translated it is thus: In the beginning as God created Heaven & Earth & the Earth was empty & desolate, & darkness was upon the Flood & the breath of God brooded over the waters. God said, Let there be light, & there was light. It differs you see as much from the King James style as from the Lutheran & the changes are certainly gratuitous. The objections to, are much greater than the arguments for the innovations Let me cite one or two, deduced from philological & critical grounds. Firstly, whence comes the causative particle "da" as, since, ? It is not in the Hebrew. "Beresheit bara" stands in the original—nothing between them. In a word apply the Law of Parsimony & the intruding guest must fly—he has not on a wedding garment. If it be answered, it is the vav of "vayomer" in the third verse, I reply why transfer a simple vav consecutive of the Imperfect in the third verse to a verb in the Perfect in the first verse? The procedure is groundless & arbitrary. If it be answered it is not the vav of "vayomer" then I beg to be informed what has become of that vav for the translation reads "sprach Gott" not "und sprach Gott" I care not which horn of the dilemma is taken. Secondly, a greater objection founds on Theodoceian & philosophic principles. Namely—Is Moses laying down the axiom of a Cosmogony in which Light is the principle thing, or one in which the world matter—Cosmos is the effect for whose miraculous existence all Philosophy cries "postulate a Cause." Is Light the primary or secondary object of creation? A Cosmogony which says "primary" is a farce, & one badly played. But in Baron Bunsen's rendering, evidently the magnificent & sublime First Truth of First Truths "In the beginning God created the heaven & the earth," loses its preeminence totally. It is cast aside to bring out in powerful relief a secondary object in the picture. Since the days of Sancthoniathe, of Berosus,[45] Confucius, since the Zend-a-vesta,[46] &c have foisted these theories of creation on mankind, we have not lacked in Folly's ideas of Causation. Moses does not wish us to believe the world sprang out of fire, or water, or air, or nothing, or that it was after the Brahmanic philosophy hatched from an egg—No! he tells us simply in contradiction to the mass imbecility, God created all things. Behold the majestic dictum!

As to the [word missing] "Be Light & Light was" (the literal translation) it is sublime enough already, it needs no assistance to increase its effect, it stands alone. Since the heathen Longinus[47] [illegible Greek phrase] has signified it [illegible word] but one person has dared to question it—a French fool & he was "put to reason," as his countrymen term it, by a few caustic touchés of Believers.

Luther's premises—to add no more—it seems to me the learned translator has missed completely the spirit of the most important verse of the Pentateuch.

---

45. Berosus, Babylonian priest and author of the third century B.C.
46. A collection of sacred writings of the Iranian or Persian religion Zoroastrianism, founded in the sixth century B.C.
47. Dionysius Cassius Longinus, Greek philosopher of the third century A.D.

Who can deny but with all this paraphernalia of lore, theory, & higher criticism German Theology must have peculiar & dangerous charms for young men of speculative turn of mind? Who will dare call himself too stable to fall? No one who has seen the system in its practical workings. From some cases which I have met, I could not advise any student of Divinity to come here unless I knew his convictions were rock founded on rock. An American gentleman from N. York, & quite a deeply religious man, has come to my rooms lately & had some long conversations on German Religion. He appears to be completely unsettled—does not know what to believe & what not. He has almost fallen into the common opinion here, that one can hope for salvation after he is dead! He told me examine my Bible & I would find exceedingly little to support the contrary doctrine. I answered, if that was really the case I would fling my Bible in the fire, & cry "carpe diem" for the rest of my days, but that I had fortunately studied the scriptures dogmatically already, & happened to know it was false. Poor young man! to believe in the Apocrypha of DeQuincey,[48] sham-miracles & Coleridge. I do not know where his articles of faith will stop. He sets Wordsworth next to the Bible & says Kant is easy to understand. Poor young man!

Strauss[49]—so noted for his mystical doctrines, also stands among the celebrities who reside at Heidelberg. He married an actress, & of course soon separated from her—it is a scene as to life of all who commit the same folly. But just think—a Divine espousing [letter torn] in a new Divina Comedia.

But I am in a route which is endless—that of great men in Germany—& if one was obliged to combat all the errors of which these "great men" are the fathers he would feel himself very much in the position of Hercules attacking the Lernaean Hydra—for each head he quashes a hundred spring up—so let us bid them adieu.

I do not need to excuse myself for having written you to much theology—you are old enough now to think & read as a <u>man</u> that is seriously, earnestly, deeply. Don't commit the same fault I did—<u>be a boy too long</u>—you will always regret it. Begin to <u>live</u> now. have a high, distinct, noble, christian aim before you in life, & bring everything to it—& it to everything. I think of you often & never forget you in my prayers & hope to live to see you an honor to yourself—your family—your country—& your God.

[Illegible] Please do not let my horses get poor this summer in Beaufort. In my letter to Tillie these two mistakes. I intended to say I studied until 2 o'clock at night— A.M. Ask her to correct it. The other is my address—Hirsch<u>strasse</u>—not <u>gasse</u>. I left my Serma lodging's very peacefully & am now with a French family—

---

48.   Thomas De Quincey (1785–1859), English author.
49.   David Friedrich Strauss (1808–1874), German theologian and philosopher.

a gay couple with two children—Mdme Plau is Protestant & quite pious—it is a pleasure to find a truly religious person over here. My room very pleasant, & I am delighted to be here—shall stay all summer.

Love to Ma & Pa, all the children—write soon & <u>often</u>, you <u>must</u> practice. I my dear brother

Yours truly & ever

ab hoc et ab hac

Edward

The accompanying picture gives <u>no</u> idea of the beauty of Heidelburg or its castle. I live in a house at the foot of the hill beneath the Ruins.[50]

Rev. Charles Edward Leverett to his son Milton

Sat.<u>y</u> May 8, 1858.

My dear Minny,

Your letter to Anne & note to me came this week. The money, I shall endeavor to send in good time. The cotton has been sold but has not paid more than so much corn as we would have gathered from the same number of acres, at about 50 cents a bushel. If I do no better than to make losses instead of profit, I will give up cotton after this & try something else. I am truly unsuccessful. Heard from Ed. He says he cannot return in Sept.—that he must stay longer. But I do not see how he can do it, unless I am likely to be better provided than now seems to be the prospect. The family will probably get ready to go to Beaufort this week & start the week after. It is an unpleasant job to move. I regret to go to B. but would not willingly return to the Pine Land. Anne says she never rec.<u>d</u> that letter, and I hope you will be satisfied about it, unless indeed you had money in it. The cotton is so much injured by the frost, that Ch.[51] wishes to replant, but cannot for want of seed. Every thing looks very beautiful about us, & the weather is charming. Mamma has got well of her cold. Aunt Til left this week. Newton is to get another horse, in addition to that he has. Louis is still with us. He goes almost the same time we do. We have had so many people staying with us, that Tilly is in despair how to find eatables & my poor pocket bemoans the calls it has on its crimped capabilities. Among other items, just think 2 firkins butter about 80 lbs each consumed since November & other things as lavishly. May my right hand forget its cunning, if this does not seem the domicile of a man abounding in flocks & herds & very extensive means, instead of what it is. After the girls we had a pleasant visit from Mrs. Archy Seabrook & family, & while she was with us

---

50.   The Heidelberg Castle, destroyed in 1693.

51.   Charles Hendee Leverett.

Rev. J. B. S.[52] came & spent a night, but we had no room for him but the parlour & there we made his bed. After these had gone, Aunt Til & some of the children came, & now we are still again.

I suppose I may as well tell you the secret, that Ch. went & asked for Hen^a[53] but tho' the Damsel consented, the parents put their veto upon it. Ch. of course like a wise fellow immediately gave up & I believe, altho' he as well as we all were astonished at the result (& they gave no reason), has become consoled—for he plays every day on the flute & I don't think he would if he were deeply gone. I was very glad of it, for from what I saw of H. when last here, I did not fancy her. She is not very pretty, & then she is not much educated & has no accomplishments & is not smart & then her Gr. Pa. was deranged—this you know is her misfortune not her fault. I was quite surprised to hear your sentiments. They quite surprised us all. I only plagued you about her as a joke, nothing more, & I thought you had more sense than to commit yourself to a silly girl. No! let yr. books receive your devotion & not a descendant of Madam Eve—at all events not until you are older & have some means. I was quite amused to hear you speak. It sounded <u>so</u> ridiculous. I hope you will not be sending any note to her, for if Mr. H. objected to C. he would to you. I can't think why he objected unless he wanted a son-in-law wealthy or in business—or unless he thought Ch. rather touchy & perhaps unamiable—but I hear he says he does not wish his daughters to marry at all.

I am glad you are trying to improve—for it costs me enough to have you do so. All well

affy
yr father

Mary Maxcy Leverett to her son Milton

Canaan May 1858

My beloved Son

Perhaps you think "Now Ma's written me to console me:"—far from that my son, I feel much more like being thankful & considering it as a great escape. Tho' often joking you, I had no idea of either you or Charley thinking of such a thing except in jest, until last Christmas I think it was, when at table, you said something about "not standing in Charley's way" when we joked about the lady, & to my surprise, you seemed to look in earnest. It made me feel disagreable, & don't you remember I immediately said something about <u>not wishing</u> it for <u>either</u> of you, on account of derangement getting into our family by it? Don't you recollect? Well

---

52. Rev. Joseph Baynard Seabrook of Edisto Island, Episcopal clergyman.
53. Henrietta Potter Hamilton, daughter of Catharine Percy and Col. Paul Hamilton.

I think <u>that</u> such a very serious objection (& I think you rather assented) that after the hint, I concluded of course both of you had sense enough to see the wisdom of such an objection & would not of course do such a thing. Tilly was perfectly indignant when she found what Charley was going to the house for, & was delighted at the turn the affair took, she considered the connection (for the reason above stated) so decidedly objectionable; moreover, to tell the truth she is not the only one of the family who thinks the lady stupid & uninteresting, even tho' amiable, & not with much sensibility or feeling. I'll tell you more about all this when we meet in Beaufort. Pa thinks it all perfect "fudge & nonsense" & doesn't at all believe in any bones being broken in either you or Charley. Said he had no objection to Charley doing it if he chose to, & was perfectly astonished at the result. Annie was very indignant, she thinks so much of her brothers, & we all conclude it was because a rich son in law was desired.—Other, and more painful things have taken up my attention & I would have written to you before about it, but felt reluctant, as I know you will be sorry. Your Father has resigned,—the Vestry requested him to reconsider it, which he did for a few days & one or two letters passed between them on the subject, but tho' they praised him up in their letter, & did ask him to reconsider it, yet not one of them said "I wish you to stay," or "you had better not go," so Pa concluded to stick to it, & I think he was right. It commenced in this way. An Easter meeting of the Vestry took place—your father sent a letter to them expressing his intention of leaving McPher. as there was no congregation to stay for & requesting to hear from them concerning any arrangements about his going there to preach once a fortnight. They responded, making no mention of what he had asked, but in a polite & courteous manner told him that there was some dissatisfaction about not hearing him distinctly enough & also that his style was such that they found it difficult to understand. Your father thought that "more was meant than met the ear," & heard also that Mr. D.H.[54] had given up his pew & his family stopped going to church, of course making it more difficult to get up the salary,—so he determined he was not going to stay in Church only to be <u>tolerated,</u> & so resigned; in their letter in which they requested him to reconsider it—tho they commenced by praising him, yet they plainly said there was general dissatisfaction for those two faults. Now your father thinks if they had valued him, they would have put up with those, especially as it is caused very much by the reverberation proceeding from the bad shape of the ceiling, which will be remedied in the new church (he had just concluded a contract for it) & that there were probably other little motives actuating some of them,—perhaps our having Canaan &c. Any how the deed is done. I confess it hurt me to think how easily they could part with him. Your father says tell you, it sha'n't affect

54.   Daniel Heyward.

your education that he will continue you in College the same, only be prudent. I write, tho' much fatigued from packing & fixing &c. Tilly, Mame & the two little girls were driven to B.[eaufort] by Pa on Thursday, with the mules in carriage & they gave him great trouble by the way. Dr. H Fuller very kindly lent us his Flat, so all our things went at one load. Cous H. Stuart lent us a man to pilot old Eph. Carolina & Billy in it.

Annie & Louis left us only yesterday evening (Friday) & Pa, myself & Julie are to go the beginning of next week. All the servants gone except Daphne & William. I am sorry to tell you too that Sary lost a baby a week ago. Loney & Beauty have two fine calves. My beloved son, my darling child I long to see you

yr aff. mother
M. L.

In July 1858, a few weeks after his resignation from Sheldon, Rev. Charles Leverett accepted a position as temporary rector of St. Helena's Church, on St. Helena Island, near Beaufort. The church, built in 1756 as a Chapel of Ease for St. Helena's Church, Beaufort, was an independent church by 1812. Though he was asked twice by the vestry to become the permanent rector, he declined, but remained there until July 1859, when Rev. James Theodore Hutchinson took over as permanent rector. Rev. Charles Leverett occasionally preached in other lowcountry churches when asked and frequently held Sunday services at Canaan for his family and his slaves.

Rev. Charles Leverett's account book for the year 1854 is among the papers in this collection. It shows that he held the notes and mortgages, all bearing 7 percent interest, of several planters. The largest of these was that of Rev. Joseph Baynard Seabrook, who owed $7,500 principal amount.

Mary Maxcy Leverett to her son Edward

Beaufort Aug. 26th 1858.

My dear Edward

Your father & myself returned from Atlanta after nearly three weeks stay, which proved beneficial to my health, notwithstanding the intensely hot weather. I enjoyed the fruit there very much—peaches & apples at 10 cts a peck;—in Beaufort they are 12 cts a <u>dozen</u>. Going from home, gives one sometimes an insight into things before unknown,—I think travelling a wonderful quickener of the intellect,—that is if one is disposed to use his intellect at all. I saw there the Episcopal Church, or rather, the <u>Episcopal Ministry</u> under a new phase, and I will tell it [to] you, as it may be of use to enable you before hand to see where the rocks & quicksands of Ministerial life lie, & so be a warning in season. Atlanta has 10,000 inhabitants, 2,000 of whom are children; our church was the <u>first</u> built in the place & has been in existence <u>eleven</u> years;[55] yet thro' the baseness or incapacity of our Ministers, instead of taking the first rank in numbers as well as every thing else, our poor little miserable Episcopal Church is the least flourishing of all. Since its first establishment, 3 Baptist, 3 Methodist & 1 Roman Catholic have grown up under its very nose, & each building I saw looked nearly three times the size of the Episcopal Church. The present Minister, Mr Johnson,[56] has been there four years & is now collecting money to enlarge his charge tho' what for I don't know, for small as the Church is, it is not near filled,—some say he has gone travelling for pleasure, others that he has run from his creditors. I found that he set up there for a great <u>aristocratt</u>, & does not like to visit <u>common people</u>, neglects the middle class (who are the strength of our Church) & takes no interest whatever in the poor, & is unduly complaisant to those he thinks higher than himself, & thro' extravagance & scheming attempts to get rich quicker than God saw fit, is over head & ears in debt. Thus has the Church & its Ministry been brought into ill repute. I was deeply interested there in the wonderful opportunities of doing good there, such as I have never come across before, & all thrown away. Mr Johnson is a great controversialist, and nothing else. His children too are growing up deplorably deficient in religious principle. Altogether the visit made a striking impression on me, showing so plainly the reasons why our church did not succeed & why there was so great a dearth of real religion. Examine yourself, my dear son, & see if you have not the germ of some of these defects in you & root them out in time. I find now I frequently look at Ministers & Churches in reference to what you are going to be & often think to myself "I'll tell Edward to avoid <u>this</u> or to do <u>that</u> or beware of such & such a thing. I am afraid I aim at impossibilities for & in you.

In your & Fred's last letters you allude to Charley & his love affair. I have said nothing about it to you hitherto, as it was so uncertain how it would end, but the coup de grace has now been struck,—Henrietta is engaged to Barney Fuller.[57] I never was more astonished in my life, than the evening Charley sent for me out of the parlor to tell me he was about to set off that moment to address H—. He had never paid her any attention, never even paid a visit to her, & all of a sudden, shows me a note from Annie Gibbes telling him "his dearest hopes could be realized," & urging him to "speak at once"! I was so astonished I could only tell him so—he said "he hadn't wanted us to know before, & was in a great hurry now & only wished to know if I had any objection,—tho' he added it would make no difference, he was going to do it whether any body objected or not." I told him my only objection was the derangement of her grandfather,—that was a serious thing

---

55.   St. Philip's Protestant Episcopal Church in Atlanta, dedicated in 1848.
56.   Rev. Richard Johnson.
57.   Henrietta Potter Hamilton married Robert Barnwell Fuller, 17 February 1859.

"he replied he knew it was, but he didn't care, he <u>would</u> do it any how." Of course
there was no use to say any more. Your father at first seemed rather pleased, until
I suggested that & he agreed with me.

Off Charley posts, late in the evening to Winterdale,[58] speaks to Mrs. H. who did
not object & did not accept, but says she'll inform Col. H. when he returns. Charley
calls the next evening, (or the evening after) sees Col. H.—only talks on in different
subjects instead of what he went for, comes home, & writes a note to ask permission
to address H. The answer from Col. H. is that he was very much astonished as their
intercourse had been so slight & requested that he would let it drop altogether. The
note was short, not a word to soften it. No doubt he was provoked at this suddenness
without the least attention having been paid to his daughter before hand. A. Gibbes
was so alarmed at the result of her romantic note & so afraid of the anger of Col &
Mrs H. that she begs Charley not to tell of her note,—& so matters stood when we
came to Beaufort. The Col & Mrs H & H—all came to see us, & seemed to desire
all intercourse to be on the same footing as before,—Tilly, Annie and Mame were so
provoked that they were very cool to them, but A Gibbes told A. that Mrs. H. & H.
were very much distrest, & wished the match, but the Col. was so incensed he would
not even suffer them to name Charley to him. Of course when a difficulty once
occurs between family, little misunderstandings always follow. Charley in the meanwhile never goes any where but in the country & to church & has never but once
been in the way of speaking to them. Before we came to B. however, there were
rumors about Barney F. & H. which finally ended in his addressing her lately at Bay
Point & her acceptance. Of course the Colonel has no objection to a rich son in law
especially as he is very amiable & very sensible & is said entirely to have reformed
from his drinking habits and is now Candidate for the Legislature. I feel really thankful it has so ended, as I did not wish it on account of the grandfather. But only think
what a risk these two young people are now running. <u>Her</u> grandfather and <u>his</u> grandmother were both deranged, and had to be sent to the North.—I hope if you have
met poor Dan[59] you have been kind to him.

Annie Heyward paid a visit to Beaufort this summer & came to see me & I
made Tilly invite her to tea.

Your father goes over to St Helena every Sunday & returns Monday. I went
with him last Sunday & was quite pleased with the appearance of the two
churches. The winter church was built in old English times, & looks so antique
that I hope it will never be altered, it is of brick, windows curiously shaped, small
paned glass casements opening inwards. The floor is flagged. A very good Organ,
size of Sheldon organ, chancel walls painted & all very neatly finished & fur-

---

58.   The plantation of Catharine Percy and Col. Paul Hamilton, in Prince William's Parish.
59.   Daniel Cuthbert Heyward.

nished.[60] The Village church[61] is quite new, & neat, a beautiful chandelier & two lamps partly the gift of our old friend Mrs Archy Chaplin.[62] The only draw back is, very limited socially, comprised of Fripps, Chaplins, Jenkins, Jenkins, Chaplins, Fripps, & all greatly needing sermons on brotherly love,—added to this, they are considered as heathens by outsiders, who say they have treated their two last Ministers very badly. I say they have not yet had a good chance, a fair trial for <u>who were</u> their ministers but Mr M'Elleran[63] originally an Irish Sailor, who preached neither one thing nor another, a queer character & who boasted in Donner's store that his wine was better than Donner's & brought over a bottle to prove it. The other was Rev Wm Johnson[64] who tho' he had fair abilities preached nothing but the Church. They were extremely kind to him, but he left because his son got in some difficulty & he being a hot tempered man indicted the person who attacked his son. (He now has the Edisto church.) Archy Seabrook, by his letter evidently thinks your father wrong <u>not</u> to accept while many people here evidently consider it as venturing into the lions den <u>to</u> accept, but <u>my</u> feeling is, that I am perfectly willing to try it,—your father is disinclined, & the children give me no credit for wishing to do right, but attribute my willingness to a liking for a change, or going about. Tilly is especially opposed.

Yellow fever is bad in Charleston, so perhaps it would [be] as well for Fred & yourself not to get back before the beginning of Nov., if you only have money to last, for your father has none to send. Neither J. Seabrook or E. Walker have yet paid what they owe, & money matters are only a shade better than last year.[65] Nobody has money, and drouth & rain between them have nearly destroyed the cotton crop, but our provision crop is very promising, the blades are all saved, & much more than last year, & we had potatoes before any body else this summer, & they are turning out well. Our last years corn has lasted until this new crop is made & Charley is now about to sell 30 bushels of the old corn to make room for the new & has kept some besides. Charley is really a capital planter.—Do make a handsome choice in buying Mrs. H's. earrings & brooch, or brooch alone, if the $20 is not enough to buy both. I have not said half that I wanted.

yr ever aff Mother
Mary Leverett

---

60. St. Helena's Church, St. Helena Island. This brick and tabby church was destroyed by a forest fire in the 1880s. Its ruins still stand.
61. The summer chapel at St. Helenaville, the planter's village near the north end of St. Helena Island, is no longer standing.
62. Martha Fripp Chaplin.
63. Rev. David McElheran, rector of St. Helena's Church, St. Helena Island, 1831–1856.
64. Rev. William H. Johnson, rector of St. Helena Church, St. Helena Island, 1856–1858.
65. Rev. Joseph Baynard Seabrook and Rev. Edward Tabb Walker.

Frederic Percival Leverett to his sister Matilda

Venice, Aug. 30<u>th</u> 1857[66]

My dear Tilly,

On going to the banker this morning, I received to my great delight your letter. Such was my joy, my darling, that I sat down at once & read it before leaving the office & how often I have read it since I will not attempt to say. Dont think for a moment that I am sorry to hear the summons for returning home. With your letter was Ma's of the 12<u>th</u> July for Edward. We read that in ascending the St Marcus Tower[67] stopping at the loop holes to read & then hurrying on to rejoin our companions, Mr. & Mrs. Peirce of Boston, with whom we have been making today the tour of Venice. We arrived here Saturday night, and have today done the Island City. How hard it must be for you all to realize that we are here on the classic Adriatic, that we have been wandering in the Palace of the Doges,[68] that we have stood on the "Bridge of Sighs,"[69] a palace & a prison on each hand; that we have been in the chamber of the Inquisition; in the room in which the Council of Ten was held, in fine that we have viewed Venice by moonlight while gliding along in the swift light moving Gondola. I myself can scarce realize it; it seems too like a dream, but nevertheless 'tis true. We arrived here on Saturday, and had most fortunately a charming moonlight night, & availed ourselves of it at once for our Gondola ride. Were you all here it would have been pleasure indeed. As it was, it was delightful. Tomorrow morning at 6 o'clock we leave this quaint, quiet city for Padua, Bologna, Florence, where if all goes right we will be day after tomorrow evening. Thence my wish is Paris, Havre or Liverpool America. Edward argues strong for Rome en route—and who would not? All will depend on letters which we hope to receive at Florence.

I am convinced that there are letters from home to us (?) certainly from us home that have not been received. The letters today were the first for two or three months.

Edward wrote you or rather Ma from Switzerland I dont know if he said anything of his health. It is better now than it was. Had it been good we would have had there a glorious time. We met at Munich, where I found him anything but well. Poor fellow, he had left Heidelberg <u>well</u>, had taken cold in going to Halle and thence continued to Berlin, Dresden etc. rendering himself worse and worse. What nonsense travelling for the health is!—especially such a person as Edward. I have been scolding him almost all the time since we have been together. We commenced

---

66. 1858.
67. St. Mark's Tower, a three-hundred-foot tower that dominates the Venice skyline.
68. The magistrate's palace, *Palazzo Ducale*.
69. The bridge over which prisoners were led on their way to trial.

Switzerland on foot but it was more than Edward was equal to, and he was obliged to make the ascent of mountains for the most part on horse or rather on mule-back. I went on foot, which I found lonely, but very strengthening. It had a most decidedly alterative effect on the appetite, changing the homeopathic appetite of Vienna Hospital creation into one well adapted to do justice to the fine milk, honey, and butter & bread of Switzerland. I astonished everybody by my capacities afoot—the last leg I made forty-two miles in quicker time than the post wagon—I astonished myself. I left Brigne at 1/4 after 4 A.M. while they were putting the horses in the wagon, ascended the Simplon to the Hospice at the Summit[70] by the splendid road of Napoleon, rested there half an hour, and found that it would be yet an hour and a half before the P. would reach the same point, so concluded to advance—to the first village five or six miles further on and thence in like manner to Domo Dossola,[71] where I arrived a little before four o'clock P.M. one half hour before the Post. It was a tremendous route but a glorious one; the scenery magnificently grand.

In the morning the most beautiful of sunrises, guilding superbly the grand the old glaciers—before me the Simplon;—behind me the extensive Aletscker Glacier, and towering above it Monk and the Jungfrau with their eternally snowcapped summits. These with the Rhine valley, and other minor valleys too many to mention, and dashing waterfalls, and beautiful flowers, skirting as Coleridge says the very glaciers presented me with pictures, ever beautiful and interesting.—(I plucked some flowers within four inches of piles of snow, which was melting & bathing the flowers in its icy waters). I eat Huckleberries, which I plucked on the top of the Simplon They were almost <u>tasteless</u>, but <u>otherwise</u> <u>good</u>—But I have not time now to tell you of all the pleasures of that lovely day's journey—not even to describe you the wild defile of ground along which my after noon course lay.

We entered Switzerland from Lake Constance, and as Edward had travelled last winter in the north of S. we passed at once from Linsdau to Rorhschach, St. Gall, Zurich, by its lake to Horgen thence to Zug, Arth, the Rizi, Luzern, its lake with the little chapel of Tell to Fluelen over the St Gotthard to Aisolo, by the pass of St Giacomo to Wald, over the Gries Glacier to München, thence by the pass of Grimsel to Meysinzen to Interlaken, where Edward sent his letter home. Then to Berse, Freiburg, Geneva, Chamaunic where we stayed two days at the foot of Mt. Blanc without seeing the old monarch of E. mountains—thence to Martigny & by the Simplon to Domo Dossola, Lake Maggiore, Lake Como, Mailand, here. I give you our route, perhaps you will find it interesting to study it out. When we come home we will have hundreds of things to tell you of it. Would that we could have hundreds

---

70.   The Simplon is a pass in the Alps with a hospice, founded by Napoléon in 1802, at the summit.

71.   A town in the Piedmont province of northwestern Italy.

of presents to bring you all—but for that your poor brothers are too poor. We have been trying to stock our minds and not our trunk and latterly we have been voyaging for Edward's health. The baggage for both of us in Switzerland, I have been able to carry strapped on my back. I think that if we voyaged for another six months, we would find that our overcoat's pockets would carry all that is requisite—so little is it, that man (not woman) needs while on a voyage. The principal thing he needs is money. Alas, that he needs so much—It is not necessary, is it, for me to say, that I have all along on the route regretted most sincerely that I have been obliged to spend money drawn from the small home coffers, or that I have been and am most grateful to Pa, Ma, all of you that I have had the opportunities which I have had. I hope through life to be able to show my gratitude. I am ready to buckkle on my armour, and I trust, that I will not be otherwise than victorious. If I am able to hold the same position in life as a physician, that I have so far as a student, I have no fear, but that I shall succeed. But why weary you, my dearest Tilly, with talking about myself. You will see your unworthy brothers, in—when we arrive. Beg Pa & Ma to write me most fully all that they think as to where I should settle to Phil<u>a</u>, the old direction. I shall stop there at least several days—and then what I hear from home shall decide me. We will write from Florence and also from Paris.

With much love to you all, I am, my precious,

Your most entirely aff<u>ct</u>
Brother, F. P. Leverett.

P.S. We will see Dan perhaps in Paris. I know Dr. Morton very well. I cannot imagine how the arrangement happened to be made with him.

We are delighted to hear that you all find it so pleasant in Beaufort. Anne seems to have forgotten us.

Rev. Charles Edward Leverett to his son Milton

Beaufort, Wed<u>y</u> Oct. 13, 1858

My dear Minny,

Your 2<u>d</u> letter came today. I have been waiting for it in order to reply to yr. first. In yr. first you said you would again write soon, to let me know the bills. I was in hopes the amount would be less than it is, but nevertheless, I remit the amount so far as I can collect from your scattered items. I cannot see how it is they have raised the board. It must be with the design of getting all possible, thro' the necessities of that much abused class—the parents of students. Price of board should be lower, as articles are reasonable. I enclose a check for one hundred dollars; You will pay at once all yr. bills. Out of debt is out of danger—& debt always makes a person feel like a guilty culprit.

The college bill you say is	$43
Bryan[72]	4.50
Board from Oct. 3 to Dec. 5	
or there about 9 weeks at $4	36
Washing for the term	5
due you	$ 9
	97.50
Pocket money	2.50
	100

with what was
over of the $20
for that.

Have these paid immediately and get receipts.

Mama has been quite unwell with a bad cough & cold since you left. She is now much better. Tilly also was unwell for two or three days: But has quite recovered. And now I am sorry to say that Louis DeSaussure[73] is very ill. He went down fishing last week & had fever. He also overtaxed his strength. Since Sunday he has been quite sick,—his case is so critical that I hardly think he will live out the night. He spits a good deal of blood. This is very sudden & distressing to us all. Your Mama will stay with Anne tonight—Charles with L. I was there this evening & at his request prayed for him. He can only whisper—poor fellow—but he has taken all his sickness in the calmest way possible. I am afraid, I shall have to say before this goes to the office, that he is no more. I suppose it will overwhelm Anne. How melancholy all this is, & how dreadful if we had no Christian hope.

We heard from Fred the other day. As the last funds had not reached them, he staid in Paris & sent home Ed. He was to sail in the North Star 28 Sept., & probably by this time, if the passage has been favorable, has reached N. Y. He will go to Alexandria and remain there for the present.

Ma & Mame & myself were to have gone on Friday to St. Helena to spend a few weeks. This sickness of Louis will prevent it, I suppose.

Julia is still saying lessons to me. She improved very much while with you. I am very glad you taught her, as she required more regular instruction than mine. I do not mind about that you said—which you seemed to regret. I know you are quick, but at the same time am aware, that when you are able to allow yourself cool reflection, you will see that your parents are your best counsellors. But try to

---

72. Bryan and McCarter, a bookstore in Columbia owned by Richard Latham Bryan and his brother-in-law James J. McCarter; now the R. L. Bryan Company.
73. Anne Leverett DeSaussure's husband.

govern your temper—indeed you are bound to do it, unless you would forfeit your Christian name. Make allowances for others & not think that your judgment is never at fault. My own idea is, that it is best to yield often when the matter is of no moment, when we know we are right & find our opponent can't be persuaded. I am certain it is more manly to do so.

I trust you will try to do well in every way. I put great confidence in your integrity & am sure, that with a check upon your wrong points of character, you will be a son of whom we shall be proud. I pray God to bless you.

The election took place yesterday, but I have not heard the result. Probably E. Rhett is elected, but by no large majority.[74]

Charley had the Beef killed yesterday & brought to market. I presume it will not pay much. I have not anything to add at present, that I can think of, except that your mother was to write you & will do so soon.

Your affectionate father
C—

P.S. Thursday about 2 o/c. I have been at D^{r} DeSaussure's about 3 or 4 hours—have just come home. Louis, poor fellow, I am grieved to say is worse. There is very little chance for his recovery—he expectorates so much blood. His father thinks there is very little hope. Your Mamma is staying with Anne, who is greatly affected. She is not staying in the same room now, as it would be bad for L. Last night he was delirious & to-day is wandering. How sad it seems for one so young & with so much to render life attractive, to be struck down. What a sorrowful world it is, & what a very wretched one, without the hopes which the Gospel affords. Poor Anne will be overcome, when she loses Louis.

Write immediately, as I shall wish to learn of yr. getting my check. In case any time of its being taken out of the letter, you must go to the Bk & try to stop the payment of it. I am almost afraid to send by mail, there are so many rogues about opening letters.

Mary Bull Leverett to her brother Milton

Beaufort, Oct. 21st 1858

Your letter my dear Minny came last night, I saw by it that you had not heard about our poor Louis; our letters went last week telling you about his illness. We sent around early Sundy morning to see how he was, & he was the same, Pa and

---

74. Edmund Rhett of St. Helena Parish, state senator, 1858–1863.

I thinking there was no danger went to St. Helena, the next day I was feeling afraid the whole time, that something was the matter & longing yet fearing to hear, before we got half way we heard that he was dead.[75] Oh Minny it seems perfectly dreadful. It seems to me when I look at every thing how he suffered, that "It is all for the best." He was not in his senses for several days before he died. I think if they had not given him so much physic the worst kinds, instead of nourishments as he was weakened by the loss of blood, and the poor fellow had the greatest dread of the physic. Charley would give him something out of one of the tumblers & he would ask him again & again are you sure Charley you sure you did not take it out of that tumbler; pointing to one that had something to nauseate him & then he had taken a great dislike to Ralph Elliot thinking he was going to poison him, asking if they did not take the physic out of Ralph's bottle, Charlie said Ralph seemed to mind it very much, as they had been such great friends, they think the reason why he had this dislike was because he had sat up with him & he was very violent, trying to get out of bed, & you know Ralph is very rough & in putting him back the Dr.'s[76] hand went into his blister (he was covered with blisters an awful one larger than this whole sheet of paper was on his back & this was the one his hand, the Dr.'s, went into) it put him into such agony that he knocked the Dr. flat with the most unnatural strength. Charley said he appeared to be thinking of some horse probably his black one you know I told you about its death in my last, he would say, "Who said anything about my horse beautiful sorrel aint it" Charley answered yes & he was in this way the whole time knowing different people but that was all. There was a great change during Sundy towards evening the Dr.[77] thinking there was nothing to be feared went to lie down (Ma said nobody could have behaved better than the Dr. he was called up at all times of the night, he was sick at the time, he never complained of being worn out but was devoted to Louis I am too sorry for him he minds it dreadfully. Mrs D.[78] behaved extremely well.) Ma & Mr. S. Elliot Mrs T. Fuller were with him[79] & Annie, Charley was there a short time before he died & seeing the change went for Aunt Til. You know Louis never said a bad word, but would say Great peace very often, well Ma said he said this, & then as if he could stand it no longer tryed to get up saying "I must go, I must go." Ma called the Dr & led Annie out of door although she one did not know what for, as the Dr. came in the other, they laid him back, he was entirely overcome & "his Spirit returned to the God who gave it,"[80] those words were his last words, his

---

75.   Louis McPherson DeSaussure Jr. died 17 October 1858.
76.   Dr. Ralph Emms Elliott.
77.   Louis's father, Dr. Louis McPherson DeSaussure Sr.
78.   Louis's stepmother, Jane Hay Hutson DeSaussure.
79.   Rev. Stephen Elliott (1804–1866) and Elizabeth Barnwell Fuller of Beaufort.
80.   Eccles. 12:7.

was a short but painful illness. Ma says he was the most perfect person on a sick bed that she ever saw, although he was suffering so much the whole time he never complained. He was buried on Monday eveing in his Mother's grave,[81] Charley was one of his pall-bearer's; the bell was not tolled because we could not let poor Annie know when it was to be. Poor Annie, sorrow has commenced so soon with her, I think it is one of the most melancholy cases I have ever heard of. She at first had given up all hope but the last one or two days he had seemed better & would only take things from her & seemed pleased to have her wait upon him, this made her feel much better & gave her some hope. She had her wedding wreath buried with him it had a full blown rose, little did I think when we were putting it on her, that it was to be a part of his shroud. Then yesterday was another dreadful day all of their things were brought down just as he had left them. I feel like crying everytime I think of him he was so good & cut off so early. We found some beautiful lines he had written the day Woody H[82] was buried they were <u>very</u> <u>affecting</u> saying how wicked he was compared to W. that he could not account for it, but that God in his mercy had taken W. who was so good & had spared him to repent. It is very pitiful to think that the three chums are all dead one has died each year I believe. We are all so glad to have Annie back again but oh me at what a cost, as Ma says it is hard to let one's child go away to come back in such deep distress, so different from our light hearted Annie. I can't bear the idea of seeing her in a widows' weeds & cap, she has a dear little puppy here that Louis gave her pets it up so it was brought down to day. I can't realize it that he is dead, the poor Dr. looks broken up.

You must write word immediately and let us know if you got Pa's letter with the check, as the papers say that money has been stolen out of the letters from Whippy Swamp to Charleston & from Saltketcher to Charleston & that Mr. G. Saunders has lost several hundred dollars so Pa will be quite uneasy until he has heard from you.[83] I suppose you heard that Edward was to leave in the North Star on the 28th of Sep. because he had not received Pa's letter with money. We saw its arrival in New York, but have not heard from him yet he was to go to the Seminary to be ordained.

I am so glad that you went to tell them good by that night I can't write any more I am afraid you will [find] my letter very much jumbled up.

I remain my dear brother
your affec sister. Mary L.

---

81. Louis's mother, Isabella Harper Means DeSaussure, died in 1844 and is buried at St. Helena's Church, Beaufort.

82. Richard Woodward Hutson Jr. died in 1857.

83. Richard Taylor, postmaster at Whippy Swamp, on the Coosawhatchie River, and James H. Sanders, postmaster at the Salkehatchie Bridge between Beaufort and Colleton Districts, reported the regular theft of mail in the *Charleston Mercury,* 16 October 1858.

On 28 December 1858, two months after the death of her husband, Anne Leverett DeSaussure gave birth to the Leveretts' first grandchild, Louise Isabel.

Mary Maxcy Leverett to her son Milton

Saturday Night Jan 22
1859

My dearest Min

I have been constantly promising myself to write to you, but have been so tired out night & day that I could not. You & Charley little thought the day you left, what dreadful trouble was coming on us,—poor Edward had a hemorrhage that very day, to the dismay and grief of the whole family. He was in the yard when it occurred & they did not tell me (I was in Annie's room) until they had got him to bed. Tilly & Mame cried ready to break their hearts,—I did not shed a tear—I think it was because I had such a strong impression on my mind that he would live,—& I think God gave me that impression to support me under this new affliction. For three or four days & nights we watched him & continually had to wipe the phlegm tinged with blood from his mouth, & just as we were beginning to think he was getting over it, a second hemorrhage came on in the night between three & five o'clock. I was present & called Fred hastily—he spit mouthful after mouthful of blood with a sort of choking cough—Fred gave spoonful after spoonful of salt—then other things—as he laid him gently back on the pillow gasping, with the blood still oozing from his mouth, his eyes raised upward & the cold sweat bursting from his forehead. I felt as if turned to stone & with a feeling almost of dispair at my heart. In a few minutes, he whispered he was that sick at his stomach & must throw up.—Fred begged him to try & keep it down—he said can't help it—must come & asked for the basin,—immediately a stream of water, jelly, phlegm & blood burst from his mouth—It shocked me so I exclaimed "My God!" in horror—Fred hastily caught the basin, examined closely & called out "it is nothing—not from the lungs &c" The first word poor Ed could utter was "I beg your pardon Fred, I couldn't help it"—it seems it had splashed on Freds clothes as it burst from his mouth. I couldn't help think how characteristic. He added that he felt better, & Fred say he was glad it happened, as it would stop the hemorrhage which was the case,—for a day or two we still occasionally wiped bloody phlegm from his mouth, but it soon became nothing but phlegm,—& as Fred would not let him move a finger to help himself for a fortnight, day & night we had to wipe the phlegm from his mouth when he coughed or cleared his throat, & Fred only let him speak in a whisper. Edward thought himself that he would die. He whispered to me as I bent over him "it seemed hard to be cut down just as he had reached the goal

of his hopes and made such severe preparation." I told him I did not think he
would be—he said "oh he didn't expect to live" I answered that "I did not think
he would die—that God had graciously answered my prayers, had given me
back Annie's life, I trusted He would give me his also—that I had a sort of feeling he would live & get over all this"—poor fellow! he still daily expected death
& told me one or two things he wished if he died—I told him when speaking of
some circumstance, that if he felt like repining at any thing, he must always
think of those who were much worse off than he was, he answered "oh no, I
don't repine, I don't repine at <u>any thing</u> now" & then looking upwards adding
"I am trying to set <u>my</u> affections on things <u>above.</u>" You may imagine my dear
Minny, the weight of anxiety & distress that has been [on] our hearts,—if it
hadn't been for Fred's strong, cheerful sustaining spirit, & confident skill in
knowing what to do for Edward, & also the impression on my mind, already
mentioned, that he would live,—it seems to me I would have sunk down in dispair & felt like dying myself. But Fred has been a great blessing and help. He,
Tilly & myself have taken it sitting now for three weeks. The last week I have
given out so much & also Edward being better & my solicitude not so intense,
he & Tilly have taken it almost exclusively,—they could sleep while sitting up,
occasionaly, but I could not & therefore gave out sooner. Mame has had all the
houseking, we would not let her sit up only a few times, because there was so
much housekeeping to do, & so many things to be made & done for the sick as
well as the well. Mame has done admirably. Fred did not go to bed for three
weeks,—only sleeping sometimes on Annie's sofa or floor, or in the rocking chair
in Ed's room. Your father offered over & over to sit up & we tried once, but
found he couldn't hear Ed's whisper, so he could not be any help, but he sits in
the room about two hours every morning after daylight, by which time the person who sits up is tired out & Ed is sleeping. Fred makes Edward take Cod-liver
oil three times a day, & his cough has been very much relieved by gargling with
Alum,—he also makes me rub his chest ribs & back morning & evening with
warm sweet oil. Whenever the weather is cold enough Mame makes ice cream
for Ed. to eat several times a day, jellies also, cream & hominy, milk & biscuit &
every thing that is so nourishing. Even in the night, we feed him, every chance
we can get, by Fred's orders. We have had literally to feed him, for he was too
weak & Fred also did not wish [him] to make the exertion to take any himself.
Oysters too, have been a great help, & now Fred gives him meat also. The three
last good days recently, having improved so much, Fred & myself helped him up
& he sat up several hours. Day before yesterday Fred helped him into Annie's
room, but I thought he seemed afterwards almost knocked up by it. Fred says
his expectoration is not at all consumptive. His is a great deal better since the
last hemorrhage, & in fact he coughs now very little & is beginning to sleep very

well & his back hurts him only a little now, so that, take it for all in all, I begin to hope that perhaps this was the crisis in [the] case, and that if he goes to Aiken or some other place, he may recover his health entirely. This, however, is but a <u>hope</u>, we cannot yet tell what it will be. Fred says the hemorrhage was not from the lungs, but from the bronchial tubes. He has had no fever, & his pulse is good. We did not let Annie know he had a hemorrhage, but told her he was sick in bed, which did not much surprise her, he had been complaining so. Every good day she sends the baby[84] in to see him. Fred has really been nurse to Annie as well as Edward. The burn on her leg is not yet quite well & he has to dress it every day. She is getting so well now that we are no longer uneasy about her, & the baby is quite well. Company now begins to call. Mrs. Eustis sent me four Turkeys & two Geese & Mr Wm Heyward sent me two Turkeys & a quarter of Mutton. Mrs Fraser has sent sausages several times. Mrs Eustis has been to see us again. The Heywards have not been again, but Mary sent repeatedly to ask how Edward is. Nobody sees Dan—he is still somewhat strange—his father carries him up to see Mr W Heyward.[85] He wants to go to the West, they say.

    Tuesday night, Ed's room. I think he is much better today. He has been sitting up a part of the day & lying on the sofa the rest of it & had no coughing & Fred is giving him iron as a tonic today. Find out what would be the price for Ed's staying where your Aunt Til is & eating with her & the children, as tho' he would like Mrs Green's[86] it would suit him better to breakfast at nine with them, than eight with the students, & as he would probably have Nightmare with him, she might be in the stable where Jim's horse is. Edward is in very good spirits. The Bishop was to have ordained him the last Sunday this month in Beaufort,—poor fellow! Dear Min I have got to the end of my paper tho' not to the end of all I had to say. Tell Aunt Til I'll write her very soon & my love. Champion went yesterday. Our cotton has sold at 26 cts. as soon as it got to Town. The baby has many presents. Dr DeSaussure gave it a silver cup. Mrs Eustis gave it a frock. I had a letter from Mrs Markoe[87] lately Still speaks of coming on, but not positively, as they find the expense will be greater than they expected. All well.

Your aff
Mother
Mary Leverett

---

84.   Louise Isabel DeSaussure was almost one month old.
85.   William Heyward.
86.   Elizabeth Green's Boarding House, Columbia; northwest corner of Senate and Marion Streets.
87.   Mary Maxcy Markoe.

Rev. Charles Edward Leverett to his son Milton

Little Canaan, Ap. 12, /59.

My dear Minny,

Your letters 2 to Mamma & me were rec$^{\underline{d}}$ by a late mail. They could have come in one envelope & then one postage would have done. There is no need of wasting postage stamps, even if they do not cost much—so please take notice of my suggestion. We have had Mrs. Markoe, her daughter & son Maxcy a little boy here, for about three weeks. Charles, also came Friday week, but left to-day. The M's yesterday. Yesterday Miss Minnie Washburn dau. of Ex Gov. W.[88] came to pay us a visit. I wrote to invite her. She will remain some days with us. She appears to be a nice girl, about 20, & a great talker. I dare say you would be quite taken with her, & would be very attentive to her, if you were here. Edw$^{\underline{d}}$ is still at home, sometimes better & again not so well. Before long he will go to Col$^{\underline{a}}$. Fred has gone to day over to Ashepoo to Mrs. Eliza Rhett's for Anne, where she has been on a visit of about a week. They have finished planting cotton & much of the corn. It remains to be seen, if we shall make any thing. Sary has a daughter & both appear in good condition. The hen has hatched 40 ducks but they probably will get reduced to 1/3.

The melodeon you lads purchased for the Chapel was very cheap "2.50"—that is two dollars 50 cents. I had the impression it was to cost $250—or two hundred & fifty dollars. How is that?

Edw$^{\underline{d}}$ has had asthma two or three nights & is not near so well. He is to leave to-morrow with Fred for Ch$^{\underline{n}}$[89] on his way to Columbia. Poor fellow! He has a hard time of it. I hope the change of air will benefit him. I suppose you will get this by him. As Mrs. Markoe goes to Aunt Til's, Edw$^{\underline{d}}$ will stay a week or so at Mrs. Green's, probably where you must attend to him all you can. When Mrs. M. goes, he will stay at Aunt Til's.

You don't tell what sort & how large a place is that where she lives—& whether she made a good purchase or not. I suppose not, as she usually fails in her enterprises.

Miss Grimké[90] is to dine here to-morrow & then carry Miss Washburn up to her home to spend a few days with her. She will then return to us & on the Friday after go to Savannah. She plays very handsomely on the piano, but unfortunately does not sing—so that the great charm at music is lost. I do not know that I have anything more to interest you—indeed I do not feel in good spirits

---

88. Emory Washburn, governor of Massachusetts, 1853–1854.
89. Charleston.
90. Mary Augusta Secunda Grimke (1826–1895).

enough to write even this poor scrawl. Yet as I know you like to hear from home I make the effort. Be a good boy.

yr. Aff. father
C.

P.S. You have not sent me the College bill for April—let me know the whole amt. due.

Milton graduated from South Carolina College in December 1859.

Rev. Charles Edward Leverett to his son Milton in Philadelphia

Beaufort, S.C. June 29, 1860

My dear Minny,

I told you, I think, to write me about expenses &c. but your letter contains no statistics, but only the cry of more. I have been waiting to hear from you, but hearing nothing, I send, judging by a note in yr. last, that you had exceeded the am^t given, a check for $30—I wish I had more to let you have, but Charley has not yet let me have the am^t., he spoke of, & so I have not much to meet the constant calls upon me. I also enclose an order on Coffin & Pringle to pay for your leg,[91] should it prove the thing desired. It is written for $140. which I think was what you said it would be after some deduction. If it is more, you can tell him you will send the difference—if less he can pay you the surplus. But I would rather Dr Morris should see about it & also that all is right, for you can not, being unacquainted with business understand these matters. Before it is settled for, you must have a fair trial of it & also get a warranty from him, I suppose—but ask D^r. Morris. Do not give the order until all is arranged & according to agreement. If it does not work well, you are not I suppose to take it. That is what I told you, I believe. Now mind I wish you to advise with Dr Morris about it.

You did not send me any papers to look at, as I told you I wanted.

I suppose you saw a good deal of the Japanese & were delighted with the Niggers. You must write Ma a full account of them.[92]

Campbell Gibbes[93] got out of his situation in town by the dissolution of the firm, he was with & his uncle John Campbell having been applied to for a teacher in Fer-

---

91. Milton was born with one leg shorter than the other.

92. Rev. Charles Leverett is referring to the visit that summer by Japanese diplomats to the United States; large crowds in Philadelphia, excited at the prospect of seeing the first Japanese dignitaries to travel to a foreign country, nearly stampeded the delegation. Some Philadelphians tried to pull the visitors out of their carriages and called them niggers and monkeys. *New York Herald*, 14 and 16 June 1860.

93. John Barnwell Campbell Gibbes (1839–1886), son of Phoebe Sarah Campbell and Arthur Smith Gibbes.

nandina,[94] he got it. He receives board & washing & $300—the 1st year. Among his scholars are young ladies—at least one about 16, his sister says. He teaches Latin, French & I believe soon begins with Greek. Mathematics of course.

The little Fowles Mary and Tilly[95] came from town on Saty to stay with us & yr. mother will write to invite Miss Grimke to-day. Miss Johnston has not yet come. Dan Heyward has been so bad again that yr. Aunt Til was obliged to send him to the Asylum.[96]

Mr. Edgar Fripp has also been very deranged the last month or 6 weeks & died the day before yesterday. Old Mr. Lucius Cuthbert also died.

It is very dull here & monotonous. I really wish I lived in a city at least part of the time.

Heard from Tilly yesterday. Edd was better than when she last wrote. They have hired a house in Aiken & they also write for money. Mr. A. Seabrook has been staying with us—but is now gone. I paid him the bal. due $75—just now the bal due the painter over $30—Send some papers as I wished.

Jno. Barnwell has resigned the company—which paraded yesterday—& S. Elliott hopes to obtain the command.[97]

Robt. Barnwell from Columbia is to be here to-morrow.

I believe I have told you all the news & now close remaining

yr aff. f—C—

P.S. I have concluded to avoid mistakes to make the order payable to Dr C. Morris & so all he will have to do, when he is satisfied that the business is all done, is to endorse it over to Palmer he, P., paying the difference. Palmer can present the bill to him.

The check is also made paybe to Dr Morris he will get the money for it for you.

Charles Chauncy Haven to his nephew Milton Maxcy Leverett

Trenton N Jersey Oct 7th 1860

My dear Nephew,

It is not because "my eye is not dim nor my countenance changed" since your

---

94. Florida.

95. Mary Ann Fowles and Matilda Maxcy Fowles of Columbia, daughters of Matilda Maxcy and Rev. James Henry Fowles.

96. The South Carolina Lunatic Asylum in Columbia, later the South Carolina State Hospital. Dan Heyward was committed to the asylum 14 June 1860, after doctors reported his third attack of insanity; he died there in 1871.

97. John Gibbes Barnwell II (1816–1905) had been captain of the Beaufort Artillery, an antebellum militia company, since 1839; Stephen Elliott Jr. (1830–1866) was captain of the company when it entered Confederate service.

departure that I shall attempt to write you, but because the intimacy of our relations during your Summer trip has communicated to me the cacoethes scribendi[98]
& I act under the influence of that heart-motion which blind love is said to give.
Mr Wood & all the people here were glad to hear of your safe arrival up South &
when you are down upon the North again we shall be glad to have a longer visit
from you!!! what a welcome must that have been when you were almost smoth-
ered with kisses & a delight so much longed for when you were caterwauling
about Trenton! & which you so manfully rejected! How must the little nig[S] have
grinned when Master Milton told them you had no "use for a wife." But home has
a freedom about it that no other place has.

> "O! quid solutis [est] beatius curis
> Cum mens onus reponit
> Ac peregrino labore fessi
> Redimus larem ad nostrum
> Desideratoque requiescimus lecto"[99]

Alas! for my poor memory! After carrying the beautiful lines of Catullus in my
head & heart for forty years, I find myself in fault as to one word, which please
correct. It is venimus instead of redimus. The residue as amended I find correct.
You may find the quotation in Esprullas letters by Southey,[100] an old book of travels in Spain which I read to a fair lady engaged to me when in love with another
chap, forbidden to be her's by a dying father & a guardian brother. She did marry
him nevertheless & resigned me to a much happier lot. N.B. She married a clergyman who still lives without issue. She once told me when I said she should have
a good husband, Pooh! I dont want a good husband! She was not fond of figs, however, by her choice, as it turned out with a barren fig tree.

Ah! master Milton, you see how difficult it is for me to be a grave man, since
you came on here brim full of your Sunny South gaiety! You carry me back, as
Washington Irving said in his letter to me, to my dancing days. But he and they
alas! are gone!

> Full many a lad I loved is dead
> And many a lass grown old!
> And soon must I the dark wave tread
> On nothing earthly can we hold.

---

98. Itch for writing; Decimus Junius Juvenalis (ca. 65–ca. 128), 7.52.

99. "What is happier than cares that have been dissolved, when the mind leaves aside its burden and tired from the labor of travel we come to our home and we rest in our longed for
bed." Gaius Valerius Catullus (ca. 84–ca. 54 B.C.), 31.8.

100. Robert Southey; *Letters from England: By Don Manuel Alvarez Espriella* (1807).

But trusting reverently & faithfully in my ever kind Creator, Preserver & Saviour wisely as well as cheerfully I hope still to spend my appointed time in this world & to do as much as I can to make others wiser, happier & better.

But it is time to say a word about our friends & relations, as well as to joke & moralize about ourselves. It would gratify me at this very moment to step in to your Mothers parlor to see the light of her countenance & exchange a glance of affectionate interest with her & my venerated Nephew! and to be owned & welcomed as a relative by all the young gentle ones who form the happy circle— the olive plants biblically called & to shake hands again with you the <u>wild olive</u>. I was going to say ones more graphed into the parent stock.—But this pleasure is not likely ever to be enjoyed by me. Jersey is my Monumental bound as you know & South Carolina can only be enjoyed by me memoriter & by its agreable souvenirs sent here occasionally. They are always welcome. In turn please remember me & present me most kindly to all your family.

At the cottage I now have your good Cousin Margaret Haven & Mr Wood. They join in compliments to you & Mr & Mrs Risxley & Maria & Charlotte & little Chauncy who dines here today all remember you with interest. So do others too numerous to mention. And now, my dear boy, short metre. The elections are near & all goes on promisingly for all parties as they think—Lincoln & Liberty of course we think are sure to be the peoples choice—but you never need fear emancipation as long as you College élèves, can put us hors de combat! But Heaven save the Union & the Commonwealth & long live the memory of Washington & his comrades.

Farewell! Write again & trust in the affection & friendship of your

fond Uncle
C. C.Haven

Although Rev. Charles Leverett had no permanent church assignment after his resignation as rector of Sheldon, he often assisted other ministers, especially Rev. Joseph Walker of St. Helena's Church in Beaufort. He also became a missionary to slaves on Beaufort Island in November 1860 at the request of Archibald Seabrook, and he held regular services at St. Stephens Chapel every fortnight until the end of May 1861 for more than one hundred slaves of Rest Park and neighboring plantations. His household often attended along with white families from neighboring plantations, and he reported to the diocese of South Carolina that his services drew an average of eighty worshippers.

Part of a memorandum probably written by Mary Maxcy Leverett, from 1856 to 1860.

1856.

before we bought it, but was not large enough for our family, therefore during the year 55 Mr. Leverett had an addition built to it, which is partially finished, and we are now occupying it, tho' but one coat of plaister is yet on it. The servants made a tolerable crop of Corn, tho' the season was so dry, many people lost their crops, and we made scarcely any potatoes, no peas, or rice, and only ___ bags Cotton. In '55 we made about four hundred bushels of Corn. Mr. Kersh, Billy, Sary & Affy (hired) working, and nothing else. This year we made five hundred & fifty bushels. Mr L. bought 2 Mules in '55, & the Oxen we raised are now being very useful. The Mare Betsy Trotwood had a Colt in March '55. The number of Cows & calves now in '56 are 13 head. Number of Sows & pigs 10.

We bought from Mr. Dunwody, who was leaving the Parish, a family of servants who were anxious to belong to us, and if they only perform their duty to us as faithfully as we endeavor to perform ours to them, all will bear well. We also bought Hercules for nearly a thousand dollars, in order to have him with his wife Sary. Names of all our servants

> Daphne and her children
> Sary, her husband, Hercules & their 2 children
>> Paris,   born June 6 1854 d. 1861
>> Hercules   "   1855
>> Phillis   1859   d. 1860
> Billy
> Nanny & her 2 children
>> Gracey   b. 1854
>> Hagar   b. 1856
>> Daphne b. 1860
> Taky
> Sue
> Lindy
> Molly
> Tom
> Ephraim, carpenter
> Cely
> Nancy died 1859
> Marcus, cow minder, 1859

The agriculture and slave schedules of the 1860 U.S. Census supplement Mary Maxcy Leveretts's memorandum and show Canaan to be a fairly typical plantation of its size—one hundred acres improved, with another eighty-five acres unimproved. The Leveretts relied on subsistence crops rather than a single cash crop, growing nine 400-pound bales of cotton, 500 bushels of Indian corn, 450 bushels of sweet potatoes, peas, and, to a lesser extent, hay, rice, and Irish potatoes. Twelve cows produced large quantities of milk and butter, while eight sheep produced a few pounds of wool. Other livestock included six horses, three mules, five oxen, six other cattle, and twenty pigs. Twenty-seven slaves, most of them over the age of fifteen, lived at Canaan in 1860 and worked as field hands or house servants.

3

War and Rumors of War

July 1861–July 1862

> I feel that there is a sacred task before me,
> one fixed object on which my whole
> mind rests . . . fight, fight, fight, fight for
> freedom and for Beaufort.
>
> —Milton Maxcy Leverett

In the spring and summer of 1861 three of Charles and Mary Leverett's four sons entered military service to defend South Carolina and the new Confederate States of America. Milton, the youngest, twenty-two years old, was the first to join. On 12 April, the day Confederate forces commanded by Brig. Gen. P. G. T. Beauregard opened fire on the Federal garrison at Fort Sumter, Milton enlisted at Beaufort as a private in the Beaufort Artillery, an antebellum militia company commanded by Capt. Stephen Elliott Jr. In June 1861 the Beaufort Artillery became Company A of the new Ninth South Carolina Volunteers. Milton was stationed for most of the war on or near the South Carolina coast and spent the first sixteen months of the war in Beaufort District. On 17 July, Charles, a twenty-seven-year-old schoolteacher, enlisted at Columbia as a private in Capt. Thomas Taylor's cavalry company, which became Company D of the Hampton Legion (Cavalry). He went to Virginia immediately but returned to South Carolina by the end of the year. On 7 February 1862, Fred, the oldest, thirty years old, enrolled at Hardeeville as assistant surgeon of the Ninth South Carolina Volunteers, which was reorganized in May as the Eleventh South Carolina Infantry. He spent his first year of service on or near the South Carolina coast. Edward's constant illness prevented him from serving in the Confederate army but he still hoped to be ordained a priest in the Protestant Episcopal Church.

Rev. Charles Leverett continued his service as a missionary at St. Stephen's Chapel on Beaufort Island. During the summer of 1861 he spent a few weeks in Aiken, where his son Edward was convalescing; while there he visited Confederate hospitals and occasionally preached at St. Thaddeus Church. He ended his work on Beaufort Island in November, when Federal forces occupied Beaufort and the neighboring sea islands. From the fall of 1861 through the spring of 1862 he visited and held services at hospitals in the portions of Beaufort District still in Confederate hands, officiated at funerals of Confederate soldiers, and preached at the request of the congregation at Stoney Creek Presbyterian Church in McPhersonville.

Milton Maxcy Leverett to his brother Edward

Bay Point[1] July 29th, 1861

My dear brother

I received Ma's letter yesterday berating me for not writing and must say it has had a beneficial effect not only by being the means of producing this letter but by bringing forcibly before my mind the consciousness of the great guilt I was committing in not writing—a consciousness that I really do not know how I overlooked before unless it be on the principle that "Sinners who grow old in their sins, Are hardened by their crimes." I hope though I am not hardened and will try to prove it. Life down here is not that of prodigality as Ma surmised nor is it one of incessant toil, fatigue, starvation and deprivation of everything that is comfortable. It is the life (I speak as regards the Beaufort Artillery) of <u>Beaufort men</u> who always try to make themselves as comfortable as possible wherever they may be & who in addition to their rations get things from home. We have a plenty to eat (but cannot always thank the commissary) and just tolerable drinking inasmuch as the water is none of the best although it's passable and Ste[2] does not allow the soldiers to have liquor. In writing when you wish to know anything it is always best to put down your questions as perhaps you might like to hear of things that do not appear of any importance to me. Now in regard Ma's queries of how many men &c &c &c. There are some seventy-odd in each company. Ours is the gentlemanly company, the others mostly are Crackers. The Hamilton Guards, Minny Stuart's company from Bluffton are called Goths by us, the Harrison Guards from Wippaw Swamp are called Vandals, Visigoths

---

1.   On Phillips Island, at the entrance to Port Royal Sound opposite Hilton Head Island; the fort built there in the summer of 1861 was named in honor of Confederate Gen. Pierre Gustave Toutant Beauregard.

2.   Capt. Stephen Elliott Jr. (1830–1866) commanded the Beaufort Artillery; son of Rev. Stephen Elliott (1804–1866).

or Philistines.[3] The latter cut a great figure when they first came down, were dressed all sorts of ways, the officers who were of the same type appeared out of their elements, one of them was rigged off in full uniform but unfortunately his pants were too tight and too short and his shoes were too large, and when he emerged from behind a large canal boat (which had been towed there at high water by one of the steamboats, and left high and dry at low water in order that the guns might be taken out more easily) with about a dozen of his men none of them keeping step and all looking like criminals he elicited a general burst of silent admiration, or soft laughter or loud smiling, just as you please. They appeared to be as our drummer expressed it 'the real muffins.' The last sight I unfortunately did not see but heard of it a short while afterwards was, that after being drawn up and formed (the whole company) they marched off in the "most admired disorder" with a fiddle playing at their head and a drum in the rear, the drummer being one of the cracker chaps rapping on the head with his fingers. I wanted Jimmy Stuart to draw them.[4]

30th

We have at present five 32 pndr or 6 in. Columbiads mounted, one of which is spiked and is consequently of no use—supposed to have been so done in the Gosport Navy Yard,[5] as I believe they came originally from there—all our efforts at drilling it or blasting it out have been so far fruitless—four of the same kind not mounted, one 24 pndr mounted, two 4 pndrs, two 6 pndrs, and one 24 pndr howitzer mounted. The four and six pndr pieces are field pieces, the rest are sea coast or ship battery pieces. They are at present mounted on ship carriages (I mean the 32^S) which are very clumsy affairs for siege guns as they take about ten men to man them, while those mounted on siege carriages take five men. The howitzer, the 24 pndr and the 4 and 6 pndrs are all mounted on field carriages. Those on the field carriages are in a line on the beach, those on ship carriages are in a sort of pro tem natural battery made out of one of the sand hills by Mr. Tom Elliott's house leveled off and made ship-shape, in a great measure by myself on a Sunday Morning with 20 negros. So that as a summary you see we have only 4 guns—the 32^S—that can do any effective firing and I am not so certain that they can com-

---

3.   The Hamilton Guards from Bluffton commanded by Capt. Middleton Stuart (1831–1920) became Company E, Ninth South Carolina Volunteers. The Harrison Guards from Whippy Swamp commanded by Capt. John J. Harrison became Company D, Ninth South Carolina Volunteers.

4.   Pvt. James Reeve Stuart studied art in Europe before joining the Beaufort Artillery and became a well-known portrait painter in Wisconsin after the war.

5.   The Gosport Navy Yard at Norfolk, Virginia, was abandoned by Union troops on 20 April 1861. Many ships were scuttled and many heavy guns were left behind by the Federals, who rammed spikes into the vents and muzzles to render them useless.

pete with those of the squadron, the four that are not mounted are of no use as
we have no carriages, and the ninth one is mounted but is spiked. The field pieces
are those which are used generally in combats between armies in the open field
and may be of use to us in a land attack or if they try to land in boats, but in a regular set to bombardment they would be of no use as their calibre is too light.[6] We
do not expect any attack until Fall but we are miserably prepared to resist any such
attack as I noticed was suggested by that extract from the Herald[7] of 25000 men
landing here and marching on Charleston. We have a little more than 200 men
while we ought to have had at least 2000. We are to have (10 in.) 10 in. Columbiads[8] which have not arrived yet but 'are coming.' Our fort which is almost finished
will together with the bastions mount about sixteen guns. Jno Gregorie is attending to the building of the fort, apparently to me with very little energy as he has
had over 200 hands at it for about six weeks.[9] Maj. J. Barnwell is the Confederate
officer who oversees everything in and about the harbour.[10] Neither he nor Gregorie have half the energy or the judgment that Ste has. Ste has only to attend to
the pro tem defence of the island as he is the Senior captain and when the fort is
finished it is to be delivered into his hands. Wm. C. Heyward is our Colonel and
is quite gentlemanly and conversed with me quite affably without ever having
been introduced.[11] He is a small neat looking man. We are having a fort erected at
Hilton Head much larger than the one here.[12] There are at present two companies
there near two hundred men, more are expected.

We have seen one of the squadron sailing pass the bar twice, a large steamer,
through the spy glass men appeared to be running up the masts to take a look at us.

We had almost a fatal accident here yesterday. One of our men F. Talbird[13]
was preparing his gun trying to clear the tube out by snapping the cap and the gun
went off. The shot went through the house into the piazza passed through a sail
and into the head of one of our men (Phillip Murray) but fortunately for the
boards, the sail, the cap and the thick skull it has proved I believe only a scalp
wound. The gun had been loaded with buck shot the day before by some one who

---

6.   Civil War—era cannon were classified according to the weight of the projectile or by the
     diameter of the muzzle. The 4-pounders and 6-pounders were field guns, designed to travel
     with armies, while the 24-pounder, 24-pounder howitzer, 32-pounder, and 34-pounders
     were seacoast guns designed to serve stationary coastal fortifications.

7.   *New York Herald.*

8.   Seacoast guns.

9.   1st Lt. John White Gregorie of the South Carolina state troops.

10. Maj. John Gibbes Barnwell II, inspector of ordnance in the Department of South Carolina.

11. Col. William Cruger Heyward, first commander of the Ninth South Carolina Volunteers.

12. Fort Walker, on the northeastern tip of Hilton Head Island opposite Fort Beauregard, was
     completed in September 1861 and named for Confederate Secretary of War Leroy P. Walker.

13. Pvt. Franklin Talbird of the Beaufort Artillery.

had been hunting, and he not knowing it, was in the room trying to clear the tube in order that he might go that day. He had tried it with the ramrod but it was too short consequently the gun appeared not loaded.

Now as regards myself my duties &c &c. I am fixed off quite comfortably, indeed as much so as I could or ought to wish, have a tent to myself and one other man, sleep on a cot with pillow, sheets, mattress, blankets &c clean clothes to put on, plenty to eat and a plenty to drink. As I was saying to Allan[14] the other day, we have a plenty to eat and a plenty to drink and the wherewithal to be clothed, and what more can a man wish for, and yet human nature does crave for more, but I will forbear philosophizing as it is not now convenient. There are seven in my mess, two of whom are Allan and Jimmy Stuart, most of them are nice men. I am caterer and do very well—try my hands now and then in the desert line and so far have succeeded first rate, indeed one day I made such a nice pudding out of pilot bread that my reputation was almost established by it.

31st.

My duties extend only so far as this. I do not do any parading but am compelled to be there when my name is called or I would be placed on double duty. I do guard duty, that is am compelled to be four or six hours every four days on sentry, my guard squad comes on every four days, the company being divided into so many squads. <u>Whatever</u> manual labour that I can do or Ste thinks I can do that I do, for instance this morning I joined with the rest of the company in dragging up some 42 pndrs (3) which have just come. We cannot mount them yet as the carriages have not arrived. I also drill at the heavy artillery and sometimes at the light. At the heavy artillery there are three prize squads, squads which are to drill and the most perfect is (so it was said) to have some prize or other. Not any or every man is placed on the squads but they are picked men and I am one of them chosen I suppose as being a strong active man. So far my squad has really drilled the best. I expect I must have pleased Ste in it, for he told me confidentially that he intended to give me one of the guns in the fort when it was finished, I was to have command of it or in other words be gunner, and gave me a book to study the drill. As a general thing only corporals or sergeants are gunners. Big Rob[15] is the only one at present who is a gunner without being an officer. If I get that command my ambition in military life is perfectly satisfied. I aim no higher, I just wish to have command of a gun in a fight. I was speaking to Ste of my duties and he said I must not let it worry me that my not marching did not matter as it was not of any consequence (and so it is in an artillery company, which ours is), that he wished he had a hundred men like me, there wouldn't be so much trouble in drilling. Our

---

14. Pvt. Allan Stuart of the Beaufort Artillery.
15. Gunner Sgt. Robert Barnwell Fuller of the Beaufort Artillery.

squads had been racing in the drill one day and the squad on which I was, was a little backward that day although generally victorious, it gave me blues so much that I induced the men in the squad to come and drill until ten that night and Ste having seen the interest I took in it was pleased and thence drew his conclusion. And now my dear brother all that I can recollect of that disagreeable subject Ego has been said. I will try to write to some one of you every week only don't expect it, or be surprised if I do not write, on the contrary be surprised if I do. I will try and write but you must recollect that "there is many a slip between the cup and the lip." I forgot to say that I with the rest of my company and the rest of the companies here have been mustered into the Confederate State Service for the period of one year from the 12th of last April. I signed the paper on the twenty-third (23rd) of July 1861. If any one had told me a year ago that I would have joined a volunteer company in the Confederate State Service or any other service whatever I would have looked on him, her or it as little better than a madman, it seems to me to be perfectly mysterious, I don't understand it. I used to hoot at the very idea when Ma suggested it. I only wish I could have gone on with Charley to Virginia, but I am bound down here now until next April, for that reason Ste told us we had better make ourselves as comfortable as possible, and <u>we are trying so to do</u>.

One of the Harrison Guard from Whippaw Swamp died down here last night from diarrhea, poor fellow I am sorry for him, I am afraid he had very little conveniences for a sick man so far away from home, he was in the hospital but that was not comfortable.[16] Allan used to send him tea and soaked biscuit from our mess. He was sent up to Beaufort this morning.

You cant tell how I wish you were well enough to be down here with me; and to see you perfectly well and gratified in your utmost aim (if laying down my life could do it) I would joyfully and freely lay it down my dear brother.

Your affectionate brother
Milton M. Leverett

Give my love to all. Mr. S. Elliott is our chaplain and preaches for us every Sunday; he has prayer meetings Sunday nights.[17] I never did fancy prayer meetings but what does Pa think, had I better attend them. He comes down every Saturday.

As to my ever having <u>fired a gun,</u> I answer that I never have had the opportunity.

You will recollect that you were trying to find out for your "Pen Ship of State" whether there was any part of the mast of a ship as for instance the extreme top which was so nominated as to afford you two feet so as to correspond with the rest of the verse as "main top" would not do. I inquired while I was guarding <u>the ship</u>

---

16.   Pvt. James Ward of Company D, Ninth South Carolina Volunteers.
17.   Rev. Stephen Elliott (1804–1866).

and found the extreme top was called "main truck," the middle "main top." So that if rhyme would suit you might say "from main truck to keelson."

Charles Edward Leverett Jr. to his brother Milton

Aiken Sep. [1861]

My dear Minnie

Your kind & interesting letter from Bay Point came some time ago. I am much obliged to you for it, & for the brotherly wishes it expressed. I am sure I reciprocate them entirely.

I have been quite sick or would have written long ere this. Even now I am so feeble I can barely drag myself about—& it is a great effort to pen a mere letter.

If there is anything that galls me it is to be so goodfornothing in such grand times as these. Everybody is working or fighting or doing something except me! I feel like Prometheus Vinctus.[18] I am trying to husband the little strength left, in order to come down in Oct. to try and have one shot before I die at those dastardly Yankees on the coast. I wish I could die in battle instead of in bed! I envy you the chance you may have of fighting—of dying for your country. I hope when the time comes you will show all by your coolness & bravery that the heart of the Leveretts is a heart of oak.

Write & let me know soon your state of defence—what Columbiads, what rifled cannon, what range, how many men—everything you have. We are very anxious about Beaufort since the Hatteras affair.[19] There is a storm brewing all along our coast. May God defend the Right! I hear you all are very confident; but 800 men were at Hatteras & they didn't or couldn't even hinder the disembarkation of 300 Yankees, so don't crow too much about "whipping the Yankees" as they did. "Let not him that pulleth on his harness boast but he that putteth it off."[20] How is it about the channels at B. P.?[21] Can vessels of any draught pass anywhere, or are they obliged to come near B. P. or Hilton Head? Write soon & tell me all about everything and everything about all. Letters from home are my

---

18. Prometheus Chained; Prometheus was a Titan in Greek mythology who incurred the wrath of Zeus and was chained to a rock, where an eagle preyed upon him constantly.

19. Cape Hatteras, on the North Carolina coast, was defended by Forts Hatteras and Clark, guarding the main inlet north of Beaufort, North Carolina. On 27–28 August 1861 the Federals forced the small Confederate garrison at Fort Clark to abandon it and move to Fort Hatteras, which surrendered on 29 August.

20. From 1 Kings 20:11.

21. Bay Point.

only amusement. I'm too weak to compose or do anything now & this letter to you, short as it is, costs me great effort. Believe me with much love.

Your aff^ecte^ Brother

P.S.

I have not sent you any advice this time—so you must be doubly grateful.

Mary Maxcy Leverett to her son Milton

[September 1861][22]

My Dear Min

I am so glad to hear thro' Annie that the guns have come for your Fort. I trust you are all hard at work mounting them, for it is not possible to suppose the Yankees are going to pass over South Carolina without paying their respects. Indeed I wouldn't be surprised to hear of a hard and well fought battle in a short time on our coast. I know you will all fight well, but remember your enemies on board ship are much better trained than the land troops—war is their <u>profession</u>, and their lives have been devoted to learning it, so their are not an enemy to be despised. The most intense anxiety will be felt all over the country, and no doubt incessant prayers will be continually offered up. May God give you the victory and shield your head in the day of battle! I hope nothing will be neglected that will insure success, often trifles may cause the loss of a battle. I hope no such disgrace will happen as that on the N. Carolina coast,—I don't see now why they did not attack the enemy (who had landed only over 300 men) in the night, when too it would be more difficult for the ships to fire at them. I hate to think of that whole affair—it seems so disgraceful & badly conducted,—the bravery of the men does not avail if they have Commanders who do not know how to take advantage of circumstances.

You will be glad to hear that during the last few days your brother has been improving, after having suffered for a month the most trying and dreadful attack of Asthma I have ever seen,—I began to fear for the result at last, the difficulty of breathing, the impossibility of lying down, the cough & the sleeplessness, so weakened him that it is wonderful to see how he is now getting over it. His constitution certainly was a splendid one originally, for he has suffered more than any body I have ever seen in my life, and died many deaths I really think in this, nearly three years ill health. He still takes his raw beef & hominy, cod liver oil, bitters, goats milk, rubbing at night with turpentine & morning with flesh brush, chest, back, shoulder & sides, I rub him down like a horse. And I am beginning again to be very hopeful of the result. However he is not yet able to do more than walk his horse

---

22.   This letter was written on the same sheet of paper as the preceding one by Edward.

when he is on horseback. I hear now, that every body here, expected him to have died last year, & consider it as a great recovery or at all events, prolongation of life. But Tillie & myself know enough of what he goes thro' to see that it is still an existence of suffering, or as he once said to me "it is a penance to live. I don't think persons friends ought to wish them to live when they suffer so much," but Tillie & I do wish & hope to see him live many years longer. God bless my dear Minny!

yr aff Mother
Mary

Rev. Charles Edward Leverett to his son Milton

[July–October 1861]
My dear Minny,

Fred is going and I have only time to write a word. Ma & Ed are better & up. I have not been to McP.[23] for a week. I am staying here to try to save what I can from the wreck of ruin, that has come on me. People at Edisto have burnt cotton &c & gone and as many owe me there, I am as Mr. J. Seabrook writes me as well as himself ruined.[24] The cotton that was packed is shipped to the R. R. today. I hope the Yankees yet will not get it, yet how with such a force. But the good Lord reigns.

Goodby
yr. Aff. Father

Charles, in Virginia with the Hampton Legion, was discharged from his company on 9 October "by reason of his duties as Teacher which require his presence in S.C."[25] He resumed teaching on Wadmalaw Island in Colleton District.

Perhaps the single most significant event of 1861, at least in its impact on the Leverett family's future, was the Federal bombardment of Port Royal Sound near Beaufort on 7 November. Flag Officer Samuel F. DuPont of the U.S. Navy, with a fleet of seventy-five ships, steamed into the sound and fired shells into Forts Walker and Beauregard, the Confederate earthworks defending Hilton Head Island and Phillips Island on either side of the entrance to Port Royal Sound. The Beaufort Artillery was part of the garrison at Fort Beauregard and manned thirteen guns there but aban-

---

23. McPhersonville.
24. Joseph Baynard Seabrook
25. Capt. Thomas Taylor, Certificate of Discharge of Pvt. Charles H. Leverett, Taylor's Co., Cavalry Battalion, Hampton Legion, 12 August 1861, Compiled Service Records, South Carolina Department of Archives and History, Columbia (hereafter cited as Compiled Service Records).

doned its position shortly after the outgunned garrison at Fort Walker was forced to withdraw. A correspondent for the Charleston Courier commented, "The Beaufort Artillery deserve credit for the gallant manner in which they defended the fort. Eighty-six men in all, they endured a hard fight for six hours . . . they lost everything but life and honor; they retired in safety, and live to fight another day."[26] The Federal capture of Port Royal Sound, the town of Beaufort, and the South Carolina sea islands gave the U.S. Navy a deepwater port for the South Atlantic Blockading Squadron and the U.S. Army headquarters for its new Department of the South. Most planters in Beaufort District abandoned their plantations just before or just after the bombardment of Port Royal Sound, which many slaves called "the Big Gun Shoot," and the nearby sea islands such as St. Helena, Daufuskie, and Hilton Head became the site of a major experiment in emancipation as the Federal government trained and educated thousands of blacks who were not quite slaves but not yet free.

Edward returned from Aiken to Canaan with his mother in September and died there on 21 December 1861 at the age of twenty-nine. Fred and Milton were stationed within thirty miles of their home at the time and it is probable that the whole family was at home when Edward died.

Milton Maxcy Leverett to his mother

Camp Hardee Feb 5th /62

My dear Mother,

I am sorry to hear that both Lou and yourself are unwell, I wish you would take more exercise and don't think and worry yourself so much, it worries me very much to think of your being unwell, do don't stay in the house and read and sew all day but go out to ride and walk both morning and evening everyday. I hope little Lou's sickness won't be serious and do you or some one else write immediately and let me know how both of you are. Fred will be home shortly, I only wish both of us could come at the same time.

We were both at Camp Drayton at Red Bluff, and we are now at Camp Hardee, about four miles from Red Bluff, having been ordered to fall back some days ago as the post was deemed untenable by the General.[27] During the removal we saw a steamer coming up and the removal soon assumed all the features of a retreat but fortunately the steamer turned off in another direction. As it was we didn't move a bit too soon, for a few days afterward when several others beside myself were on picket duty (some of us were ordered down there to keep guard

26. "Dismounting Guns," *Charleston Courier*, 22 November 1861.
27. Brig. Gen. Thomas F. Drayton commanded the Fifth Military District, Department of South Carolina, with headquarters at Hardeeville, on the Charleston and Savannah Railroad.

every day) down there, two steamers started coming up and commenced shelling the plantations lower down the river, after a while Capt. Elliott who was at Camp Hardee, hearing the firing came down on horseback to see if we were being fired on, and when he came down he ordered us to leave the fort (it had been disman-tled before) and not too soon for we had to leave the fort and go across a wide field before we could get to the woods, before we got across the steamer had got a good ways up, about a mile and a half from us and at that instant Nenny[28] who was with us said "they have fired" and I looked around and saw a white puff of smoke from the side of the boat, and in a second heard the boom of the gun, then in another second I heard the singing of the shell in the air high up describing its curve, as it was coming at us, I was behind all the others and it came more directly at me, and as I looked up and heard it rushing down thought I, it will hit me right on my forehead and I ought to dodge, but in the first place it was in a bare open field and I could only dodge it by laying down flat but it was coming so direct that I thought it would hit me, if I laid down and somehow or other I couldn't bend my body to lay down, I don't know why, but I felt fascinated, charmed to the spot, I believe in that instant I uttered a prayer and providentially the ball dropped before it reached me, ploughed up the ground and rolled within twenty or twenty-five feet of me and did not burst, otherwise some of us (there were five altogether including myself) would have been killed. The Capt. told us to hurry up for the woods and indeed we didn't need any injunction for we all started in a run so as to get to the woods before they could fire on us again, he jumped off his horse and told me to take it, I told him I preferred his keeping it but he ordered me to take it and I jumped on and we all got safe to the woods, where I got my horse which I had hitched in the woods some distance, so as to be safe from the shot. It was a beau-tiful rifle shell, and the fuse had providentially not taken fire in coming out of the gun. Nenny and myself went back that night and got it. After that the Capt. made our pickets & those of the other companies fall back about a mile and a half into a place of safety, as the enemy were shelling our empty fort, as well as the woods. I was then placed in command of the pickets and the Capt. went back to bring his company, so as to be ready in case of necessity. He ordered me also when I heard the cannonade cease to go back and reconnoitre. When it had cleared I gal-loped back on Bella, hitched her in the woods, then climbed a tree on the edge and could see the villains at work on a boom formed of pieces of timber fastened on a large anchor chain, which had been placed across the river just below the fort, and was meant only to resist barges, they were cutting it away with axes and had the steamer hitched to it tugging it away, when they got through and came steaming up to the bluff on which the fort was, at the same time I could hear them

---

28. Sgt. Henry Middleton Fuller of the Beaufort Artillery.

sounding and crying out the number of feet, then letting go of the anchor, then put out the gangway, and I saw them going to and fro from the boat to the fort, I then came down from the tree, where I was afraid they would either see me and fire on me or would come on and rake the woods with shells. (I was above the fort at the time) and then jumped on my horse galloped through the woods to a nearer point, where I could see they had built fires and were burning up our old palmetto houses and the woodwork of our fort, and where I saw the steamer much nearer, just about then I heard a pistol shot then a cannon and a shell went singing through the woods, on which thinking perhaps it was a prelude I left and went back to our station, giving the Capt. in my report. I found out afterwards that the pistol had been fired off by a little Guerard fellow[29] who had gone down there and fired off his pistol just at the smoke of their fire which he had taken for the smoke of a cannon. I told him he was wrong in doing it as we wished everything as quiet as possible. Nenny and myself went back that evening, found the enemy had left, and we got our shell. The enemy since then have been coming back every day. I think they will send troops up here after awhile and make a demonstration here on Savannah. And now that is all my news and the end of my first scouting expedition my dear Mother I hope all may end happily.

Your Aff<u>ct</u> son
Milton M. Leverett

P.S.
Do write early to me and let me know how you all are. Love to all.

Frederic Percival Leverett to his brother Milton

Camp Lee Hardeeville, Feb. 14th, 1862.

My dear Minny,

I hoped to have heard from you today or yesterday, as a letter from home passed through here for you a day or two since. I went home last week & spent the morning on Wednesday. I found all well. Lou looking pale after her attack of Scarlet Fever—Ma passably well—Pa very cheerful—all glad to see me, & I very glad to see all of them, only two sorry to stay so short a time. After getting back here at about 10 o'clock that night I received orders to go to Charleston the next morning to attend my examination. It was altogether unexpected & came like a thunder clap. I went down & got through, I hope pretty well. On Friday afternoon as I was going into the Mills House[30] I met Charley just from Cheraw. We came

---

29. 2d Lt. Jacob J. Guerard of Company C, Ninth South Carolina Volunteers.

30. A Charleston hotel that is still in operation today at the corner of Meeting and Queen Streets.

up together as far as Pocotaligo, where Pa met us. I had expected to go home
that afternoon & spend the night and had written for the buggy to meet me. In
Charleston I heard that Burnett[31] was to be examined on Monday, so Charley
went home instead of myself. Burnett is now back & I hope to come down &
see you early next week. I send you by wagon a bag of Corn. I sent one last week
or the week before, but never heard if you got it; nor have I received the bag.
Write me by the first opportunity & send it.

yr. Aff<u>ct</u> brother,

F. P. Leverett.

Milton Maxcy Leverett to his sister Matilda

Camp Elliott

Feb 15<u>th</u> /'62

My dear sister!

How long isn't it since I have headed a letter of mine with these three
words! <u>those</u> <u>three</u> <u>words,</u> "My dear sister"! ah, what numberless various vary-
ing thoughts does it not call up to my minds eye! but chief o'er all these
thoughts, there is <u>one</u> that stands forth in bold relief, and that is <u>how often</u> has
that "dear sister" headed her letters with these three words "My dear Minny"!
<u>Thought</u> rises up and says "only four times,"—"only four times"! only think. But
I won't moralize for it will do no good, you are incorrigible, it is a melancholy
fact.

I would certainly have answered your letter, but I didn't notice or didn't recollect that your name was signed to the letter which came with the candy, and
on receiving Ma's letter stating it I got the letter out of my knapsack and found
it was a <u>real</u> <u>fact,</u> <u>you</u> <u>had</u> <u>written</u> <u>a</u> <u>letter</u> <u>to</u> <u>me.</u>

The camp which we are at now is not Camp Hardee as I said, but Camp
Elliott. There is no news very exciting or even very interesting now, but there
is no doubt but that there will be some soon. Savannah's day I am afraid is
drawing nigh, the enemy are concentrating their forces towards that point and
soon there will be a roar there, she won't die without a kick that's certain. I
hear that a great many cannon have been placed in position on the Savannah
river and that five rafts etc. have been prepared for the warm reception of the
enemy. Nevertheless, for all that, I am afraid the city will be shelled unless
the channel of the river has been stopped up, which (I do not know whether
it has been or not) and as the forts that are on the river are only barbette forts,

---

31. Assistant surgeon Andrew William Burnet of the Ninth South Carolina Volunteers.

like Fort Beauregard at Bay Point, and not casement like Pulaski and Sumter.[32] I understand also that there are guns stationed in the city on the banks of the river. Genl Lee[33] I hear has twenty-five thousand men in and about Savannah so that if the forts can do their share I think there will be [no] danger as regards the land attack. The question whether we had not better offer our company to man Fort Jackson[34] (as it is believed that they are in want of artillerists)—is being discussed amongst us. Some favour it and others do not, while if a formal request would be made to us I think the whole company would volunteer. Our terms of service only pledge us to serve in the State of Carolina. Our company is being armed with a Siege Train of cannon, we now have five and will soon have six guns.[35] I was delighted to hear that Fred has passed his examination. None of you have written to tell me how Lou is, and whether the Scarlet Fever has spread or not. How is Ma, Pa and all of you? As regards the prayer meeting you ask me of, nothing of the kind can be done here, Episcopalians are too few and too lukewarm. I spoke to Jimmy about it but it didn't seem to interest him, he does not go to the Baptist prayer meetings, or very seldom. Besides him there are only two others who are members of the Episcopal Church, two Chaplins, who are not men of the energetic character necessary for such a purpose. Consequently nothing of the sort can be got up, I have my own prayers, and read out my own prayer book night and morning, and attend the other prayer meetings regularly, have only missed once, I do not take any "lead" but only join in.

You ask me about I. Middleton and the bible, I wrote some time ago to Ma or Anne that I had told him about it, and that he requested that it might stay at our house for the present. I will stop for awhile as I hear a cannonading going on and although it is raining yet I will have my horse saddled and ride down to Red Bluff to see if I can see the fight which I think is at Fort Jackson.

Tuesday, 18<u>th</u> /62

I haven't had a chance of writing this letter out until today as I had to shovel dirt on Monday—making a breastwork. The firing on Saturday that I spoke of ceased before I went, but heard that it was only some of the enemy's boats trying to cut off the Ida from the city she having gone down to Pulaski.[36] She got back

32. Fort Pulaski, on Cockspur Island, near Savannah, Georgia, at the mouth of the Savannah River; Fort Sumter is on a man-made island in Charleston Harbor.
33. Gen. Robert E. Lee commanded the Department of South Carolina and Georgia November 1861–March 1862.
34. Fort Jackson, brick masonry fort on the south side of the Savannah River, three miles south of Savannah.
35. A siege train was an arrangement of field guns of differing types and caliber intended to serve in various combat situations.
36. On 13 February 1862 Federal batteries on Jones Island, in the Savannah River between Forts Jackson and Pulaski, fired on the Confederate steamer *Ida* but did little damage. The *Ida* made it to Fort Pulaski and returned to Savannah three days later.

safe in the end. Our company is detached from the 9th Regt. now and another company will have to be raised to fill the vacancy.

I would like for Charley's sake, to go and see him married, as it is a pity that circumstances prevent any of us from being there; they prevent me most effectually inasmuch as I have not yet received my pay, for almost four months, and also I don't believe I could get leave of absence as we are expecting a battle to come off every day, which we may possibly have something to do with. From your letter you seem to think I see Fred very often, you have seen him since I have,—I have not seen him since I left home about six weeks ago.

And now here is my lecture to you all, and especially to my darling Ma, tell her and do please all of you notice especially, Never allow my letters to be read by any one but those of you there at home—my own immediate family—for reasons which you are all perfectly conscious of. I in the innocency and simplicity of my disposition, express in my letter certain wishes, meant only for the private eye, about an officer of the Staff—which you all quite innocently give to almost the very person to read. If that's to be the case, my letters will have to be curtailed to that certain point which declares only my health whereabout &c. I would much rather write to Coz. Maxcy[37] than have any letters given to him to read.

Tell Ma she needn't be afraid about that "Implement of the Devil" which she speaks of as Nenny has it, has taken out the powder and sent it to his parents, I think I shall waive my ownership in it as I expect to have enough of them before the war is out. Tell Mame I am very much obliged to her for the candy, it was very nice.

I am out of paper, envelopes, pen and ink consequently you needn't look for any letters immediately. I saw Pa's advertisement of his Algebra out. I thought it was quite a fitting notice. I read also his hymn which was very pretty.

Love to all

Your affct brother
Milton M. Leverett

P.S.

I think all of our prayers are needed now for our country. Stuart Gibbes[38] says I must remember him to the family. And [a] piece of advice all of you must recollect, always put down the whole date of your letter and your name perhaps ought to be in full, but I lay great stress on the date, especially in these times as historical records. Yours was correct but Ma and Anne seldom put down the date and

---

37. Brig. Gen. Maxcy Gregg, son of Cornelia Maxcy and James Gregg (1787–1852), commanded a South Carolina brigade in the Confederate Army of the Potomac.

38. Cpl. James Stuart Gibbes of the Beaufort Artillery, brother of Anne Reeve Gibbes and John Barnwell Campbell Gibbes.

Ma has in several letters to me put down the year <u>1863</u> for 1862. It is a natural mistake and one I have made too. Do keep the newspapers for me, I seldom have a chance of reading them and I think in after years I would like to read them if I live till then. Do keep the reports especially of the Battle of Port Royal for me. N.B. It is a mistake about our company being detached. Capt. Elliott wouldn't allow it. Fred has come today (Wednesday) to see me and tells me Charlie is to be married tomorrow, earlier than I expected.[39]

Mary Maxcy Leverett to her son Milton

McPhersonville Feb 24th, 1862

Now my dear Min, I intend to write you a long letter and tell you all the news to be had in this part of the world. Tilly received your letter and put it up, as I also do, as a sort of memento or record of the times we are passing through. Perhaps some son, or rather <u>daughter</u>, of yours may hereafter be interested in reading them,—I say <u>daughter</u> because they care much more for such relics of the past than boys ever do who are always taken up with the present and practical. Julie says Annie Rhett tells her, that Stuart wrote word you were the most popular man in the whole company,[40] (which we were quite pleased to hear,) and added that she thought you were "so cheerful and good tempered!" so you must take this last opinion and <u>be</u> what she thinks you & seems to like you for.—Dr. Hutson, Sen has lost two children with scarlet fever, and his wife was so worn out & exhausted by all she had gone through added to previous bad health, that day before yesterday she was not expected to live & all yesterday was under the influence of morphine. The last child that died suffered so intensely it did nothing but scream the two last days of its life & it was this that affected the poor mother so.[41] Their next door neighbor Mrs. W. F. Hutson[42] has scarletina—she assisted to nurse them as well as other ladies, and it will probably go thro' the village,—Annie's Nancy had it last week, but luckily got well thro' it, tho' it was during all that rainy weather, & Carry after complaining of a headache one or two days broke out with an eruption all over day before yesterday but it was not a very deep colour like real scarlet fever, it was paler yesterday & today has almost disappeared. She seems so per-

---

39.   Charles Hendee Leverett and Julia Blanche Jenkins were married at Westmoreland, the Chesterfield District plantation of Col. Allan Macfarlan near Cheraw, on 20 February 1862.

40.   Ann Stuart Rhett (1846–1918) and her brother Pvt. Thomas Middleton Stuart Rhett (b. 1844) of the Beaufort Artillery; children of Mary Williamson Stuart and Edmund Rhett.

41.   Dr. Thomas Woodward Hutson and his wife, Eliza Ferguson Bacot. The children were Louis DeSaussure Hutson (1856–10 Jan 1862) and Eliza Ferguson Hutson (1859–20 Feb 1862).

42.   Sophronia Lucia Palmer Hutson.

fectly well, no fever, and excellent appetite that I have not so much as given one dose of medicine, but made her gargle as her throat was red.—We concluded not to let Charley send the colt, and have sent it to Capt. A. Haskell[43] to break, as he offered repeatedly to do, said he had a right to draw Confederate rations for it, so I willingly sent it down Saturday. The wagon came up with cotton seed, blades &c. on Saturday, we kept Hercules during Sunday on account of his family, & today sent down by him a present of a basket with a fat goose, large loaf bread, a nice pat of butter, & some groundnuts;—I will try my best to return some of the many kindnesses his family have shown me and mine. Tomorrow we are going to get up a basket to send you and Fred.

Maxcy and his aids scour the country in every direction to see how the land lies & know the cut offs, &c. They are all expecting an attack daily. The General was to have had a Review for our girls last Monday & the girls had invited other girls & intended to carry a nice luncheon, but the weather disappointed their whole plan. I make Sary feed the five calves every day with a quart bottle of gruel <u>each</u>, and they have kept in good condition & the family have had butter enough for table use all winter. The ladies are quite taken up at present in the village with establishing a "Ladies Kitchen;" it has proved an excellent idea—two ladies go each day to the little kitchen (which has been built for them in front of Fraser Gregorie's)[44] which contains a little cooking stove, and large closet containing stores and contributions, and there cook whatever the Doctor prescribes for the sick patients as gruel, mush, chicken broth, custard, &c., they have a recess of two hours when they go home to dinner & back again afterwards. All day the nurses go with slips of paper on which is written what is required, so the poor fellows can get their food hot now, instead of different people sending from often away across the village. Our girls take their turn also; and the Kitchen is the meeting place of all the ladies in the village.—another larger kitchen is also in operation for all the men who are well enough to walk thru to their meals. The Presbyterian church bell rings a few times and you see them all assembling from the different hospitals. Negro cooks are in that kitchen & the Superintendant Adams sees after it & I am told it is kept beautifully clean. Our sick have lessened,—the Presbyterian church has been cleaned and fixed again for church & we went there yesterday to hear Mr. Axson.[45] Mr. Reed went back to Flat Rock last week, not very well, and in pretty bad spirits about the state of affairs in our poor Confederacy. I won't give up,— and still trust to see "the goodness of the Lord in the land of the living"[46] for our beloved State and country. Your father attends the Hospital daily, and has service for them Sundays also. There are no sick in Mr. Mitchells house now.

---

43. Capt. Alexander Cheves Haskell of Brig. Gen. Maxcy Gregg's staff.
44. Alexander Fraser Gregorie.
45. Rev. Edward Axson, minister at Stoney Creek Presbyterian Church, McPhersonville.
46. Ps. 27:13.

I have just had a note from your Aunt Til,—she has been so sick with cold & cough for a month that she has been mostly in her chamber, and is worn out with anxiety about her sons,—Newton still sick at Charlottesville & Jim has great hardships to go thro',[47]—they recently had to march all night in a pelting rain & lie down on the wet ground without even straw, the consequence of which was only twelve out of 60 were well & they had to do the guard & picket duty for the 60.—The Cavalry cannot drill at all for the <u>mud</u>, and the horses are starving. An encouraging state of things truly! The Rev. Dr. Howe of the Pres. Seminary went on to bring the body of his son back to Columbia, & was shocked at the privations the <u>well</u> soldiers even had to go thro' on the Potomac.[48] He found his son lying on straw, not even a pillow, died of Typhoid fever.—Annie Hanckel[49] had chill & fever at your Aunt Til's Farm & has gone back to Charleston, but keeps her trunks packed ready to fly. Col. Hampton[50] got discharges for the College students but Jim thinks it will be a shame for them to come home as so many men are on furlough from there,—but your Aunt Til has written to tell him to come home.[51]—Your father gave Charley the silver teapot and waiter for his wedding present—Fred, you know will have the splendid earrings & broach when he is ready. How little those three boys knew, when looking forward in life, under what circumstances the first wedding of the three would take place, & that one of the three would then be in his grave! Ah me, how little did I know it. I find constant need to pray continually for the presence of the Holy Comforter in my heart. But I will not damp your energies with moans & complaints, you have need now of all the energy, & strength & resolution which these trying times require & I hope and pray you will be equal to the emergency. I hear that Gen. Lee says that Savannah is now so well fortified that it will be <u>almost</u> <u>impossible</u> for the enemy to take it. He sent for Gen. Pemberton[52] day before yesterday to have his opinion & <u>he</u> gave it as his, that it could not be, if <u>Lee could depend on his men.</u> <u>This</u> seems to be the question now making anxious all hearts I am ashamed to say— for it is asserted that our men at Roanoke Island <u>did not fight</u>.[53]—It was reported yes-

---

47. Pvt. John Newton Fowles of Company D and Pvt. James Henry Fowles of Company A, both of Hampton Legion (Cavalry).

48. Rev. George Howe; his son was 1st Sgt. William Howe of Company C, Second South Carolina Infantry.

49. Ann Matilda Heyward Hanckel of Charleston.

50. Col. Wade Hampton III commanded an infantry brigade of Georgians, North Carolinians, and South Carolinians in the Confederate Army of the Potomac.

51. James Henry Fowles was discharged from his company on 24 February 1862 because he was a student at South Carolina College.

52. Maj. Gen. John C. Pemberton commanded the Department of South Carolina and Georgia.

53. On 7 February 1862 a Federal expedition landed on Roanoke Island, North Carolina, and flanked most of the Confederate defenders, who offered minimal resistance. The entire Confederate garrison surrendered the next day.

terday that the Generals had all consulted together, & agreed to determine that every body must move higher up the country & give up the low country, so as to draw the enemy on. But no orders have yet been given but I think they have set the report going in order to prepare us. It was positively asserted last night that the Merrimac (which has been altered into an iron-clad Ram I believe) is a complete success[54] & Newport News was to be attacked by us with its aid & if successful our forces were to go on to Washington! great news, if true. Old Com. Tatnall[55] considers the Merrimac such a success that he says he would be willing to attack even Fortress Monroe with it. Monday was the day fixed for it, but I don't know if it was yesterday that was meant or next Monday, any how it is not to be in the papers.—Lou is quite well & in fine spirits. Annie & Tillie often ride to the Depot, on horseback, & we use Rena in the carriage to the Depot & I think using has improved her, she goes perfectly well. Miss Grimke often comes to take me to ride in her phaeton. Because of having promised you I take exercise so regularly that I am now able sometimes to take two walks & one drive in the course of the day without minding it, we are all much more out of doors walking than usual, the girls following my example.

Your aff mother

Mary L.

You & Fred must divide what is in the basket between you—he must dine with you to get some Turkey, I wish [we] could send two.

Milton Maxcy Leverett to his mother

Camp Sturgeon Feb. 26th [1862]

My dear Mother,

I have not heard from home for some time but through Fred's letters and from which I heard news that worried me, that about our occupation of Wm Fuller's house.[56] I am very sorry for it as I occupy at present very pleasant relations with Rob and Nenny Fuller and I wish that if any letters pass, they might be worded in as inoffensive language as possible. I have no doubt that Dr. Henry,[57] consid-

---

54. The U.S.S. *Merrimac,* was scuttled by Federals when they abandoned Norfolk and was raised, fitted with iron plating, and rechristened the C.S.S. *Virginia.* The new ironclad fought its famous battle in Hampton Roads, Virginia, with its Federal counterpart, the U.S.S. *Monitor,* on 9 March 1862.

55. Comdr. Josiah Tattnall of the Confederate navy commanded the naval defenses of Virginia at Hampton Roads, with the C.S.S. *Virginia* as his flagship.

56. Dr. William Hazzard Fuller, physician.

57. Dr. Henry Middleton Fuller Sr. of Beaufort, physician.

ered that after Wm Fuller loaned him the house, it was <u>his house</u> essentially
and that after <u>he</u> loaned it out, it was still his house essentially, and that consequently there was on his part this mental reservation, <u>that if ever he should</u>
<u>need it he would be able to require it of us</u>, precisely as if it were his building
<u>bona fide</u>. To be sure, I consider that he has no right, or perhaps is not just in
requiring it of us, although I daresay that <u>legally</u> he might demand it. I do wish
he could find a house somewhere else. There is always a <u>mental</u> <u>reservation</u> on
the part of selfish people, and the F's are very selfish. Perhaps you might write
and let them know how very inconvenient it would be for us to move, and if
they still persisted in it, then I think Pa had better sell out his corn to the Quartermaster with the condition of transportation included, then sell out every
horse mule [letter torn] and keep two cows perhaps, then go up and keep
house with Aunt Til. Columbia, he would find much pleasanter, on account of
the College library,[58] in his writings. In selling out horses, sell all except Dora,
she will be easily kept. Don't let him worry himself about his plough animals
and horses being sold, for after the war horses will be cheap as dirt, while he
can sell those that he has now to advantage. This <u>I know</u> from seeing horses
bought for cavalry and artillery purposes. Either Fred or myself could sell them.
Horses are being bought now for our company. So now Ma do don't Pa and
yourself worry yourselves, I expect all to be right yet. I am well and hearty, and
hopeful, and hope you all are so. As regards the war we, soldiers, are too much
more hopeful than those at home are. We have suffered some reverses, but I
think with God's assistance we will conquer yet, and establish our Confederacy. My motto is now more than ever "Spes intra, Deus supra,"[59] I feel that
there is a sacred task before me, one fixed object on which my whole mind
rests, my weapons I feel to be as it were consecrated to that object, and the
embodiment of the whole is fight, fight, fight, fight for freedom and for Beaufort. That is my doctrine and I am ready to bear it out not only by words but by
deeds. To that end I have volunteered again,—to serve in the Confederacy, and
for any number of years, which will be of course for the war. I have thus volunteered unconditionally, and my trust is in God that "<u>unconditionally</u>" won't
come hard on me. Our time of service for the State is almost out and we are
being reenlisted for the war, or for two years. Some have reenlisted and some
have not. I am ashamed to see how late members of the company are in reenlisting. They all want a holiday first. I think all will be right yet. Several of us
wished to volunteer our services for the fight to come off in Savannah, but our

---

58. The first separate college library building in the United States; now the South Caroliniana
      Library at the University of South Carolina.
59. Hope within, God above.

company officer will not agree to it. I mean our services as a company. If we are requested, as we can't be compelled, we will volunteer. I will be able I expect to come and see you by the middle of April.

Your affectionate son
Milton M. Leverett

[Portion of postscript illegible] We are living near Purysburg now, hence the name Camp Sturgeon, we are shovelling.

Milton Maxcy Leverett to his mother

Camp Sturgeon Feb 7th /62[60]

My dear mother,

I do not write to impart news, because I have none to impart, in the first place, and in the next, I think that that should be only a secondary object in letter writing, the main object should be that of being able to converse easily with one's friends by pen, therefore as Adam intends going to McPhersonville tomorrow to see his wife I thought I would send a letter by him. You wrote me a very nice long letter, just the kind I like to receive, and it deserves in answer two such little epistles as this. I am afraid that you showed me in it only the bright side of things, as the letters to Fred seemed to indicate, you mustn't mind mentioning everything. I am very thankful to see that the Scarlet Fever has not been severe at home, and I am very sorry for poor Mrs. Dr. Hutson, she has really had a miserable life of it. I am delighted to hear you are well enough to take so much exercise and hope you will continue to. How is Pa? I wrote to him long ago and haven't received any answer that I remember. I hope none of you despond at our late reverses, I do not, we have only more to do and [a] little harder to fight, we can't be conquered, it's an impossibility. I scorn those persons who think of succumbing on account of a few reverses, and I am determined rather than submit, to satisfy myself with five feet six inches of land for my home in the Southern Confederacy; or if God wills otherwise I will migrate to some far off Utopia, in the west or the east, where the sight of a Yankee will never come across my vision; and I know both Pa and yourself will agree with me. We have been digging earthworks for the last three weeks now and I begin to think that I can handle the shovel as good as an Irishman.

I wish I could come home to see you all for awhile but we can get no furloughs. In my last letter I sent you a twenty dollar bill, hoping it would be of use in case you had to move, if you won't need it that way I wish you would subscribe

---

60.   Penciled note on the envelope written by Milton at a later date gives the date as 27 February.

to the gunboat "Palmetto State," I will try and let you have more shortly as I am in no need of it. The gunboat idea is a capital one and war will not be finished until we can cope with the enemy by sea as well as land.[61]

I have heard that the Yankees are preparing to plant cotton on Beaufort Island, that they are compelling the negroes to work, and the consequence is that a great many have taken to the woods and the Yankees are afraid to follow. I have heard also that they are trying to come back to the mainland, that a flat boat tried to land at the Mackay's Point but that the pickets drove them back, that they are building rafts to cross over with. I do not know whether the reports are true but I prophesy two things, that the Yankees will make no cotton and that the negroes will have a tough time of it. I doubt if Carolina is gone over to the Island yet but I think he is lurking about trying to find the means of crossing.

I am very much obliged to you for the basket of things. Tell Mame they are very nice indeed. The turkey unfortunately I had for dinner on fast day and as I seldom see turkey, and had Fred to dine with me, all my premeditated ideas of fasting were unfortunately knocked in the head, but I went to church that day though. I hope all the girls at home <u>fasted</u> <u>well</u>, enough for <u>themselves</u> and <u>myself</u> <u>too</u>. I hope Aunt Til is not seriously sick. I think Jim ought to come home to her.

Love to all and hope all are well.

Your aff'<u>ct</u> son
Milton M. Leverett

Subscribe the whole ($20) bill to the gunboat unless you will need it for anything else. I have money now and will have more shortly.

Frederic Percival Leverett to his mother

Camp Jones
near Hardeeville, S.C.
8th Apr /62

My dear Mother,

Soon after getting home last Friday evening our Regiment was ordered to pack up & march to this place some five miles below Hardeeville, as the Pickets brought up word that the Yankees were coming up to Buckingham Landing in two or three gunboats & a number of barges. I don't know how it is, but we have seen nothing & heard no more of them yet, so we are quietly encamped here; the Col. staff all now living in Tents. My tent is occupied by Sancho & myself; he keeping

---

61. The *Palmetto State*, an ironclad ram built by the state of South Carolina with funds raised by subscription, was known as the *Ladies' Gunboat*; it was launched in October 1862 and commanded by 1st Lt. John Rutledge of the Confederate States Navy.

watchful care over every thing, barking furiously if any negro, except Jake, attempts to raise even the side of the tent. I never saw a less troublesome dog— he never gets on my bed, & if my clothes are on the ground he is satisfied to be by them not on them. Ever since getting here until yesterday I have been busy with those intolerable monthly & quarterly reports which are the bugbears of an officer's life, especially a surgeons. They are, however, finished for this time & happily three months must elapse before another quarterly report is to be made.

Minny arrived safely last Saturday & passed the night with me—his company is about a mile and a half below here. I visit it almost every day, having now medical charge of it. I was glad to hear of your safe arrival & that you are in a measure comfortable. Minny found the articles that were missing at the Depot in Charleston & sent them on. I don't know how they happened to be left, as when I left Charleston, Charley was then very busy in seeing after every thing's being moved from one depot to the other. Col. Heyward said nothing against my having gone to Charleston, every one thought I was right. Mr. Fripp sent the colt to the depot to meet me & I brought her on with me. I have found her very useful. She could have been of no use in Columbia, as I found her hardly bridle-wise. She was only half broken & had in the days she was not ridden forgotten a great deal of what she had been taught. I am taking a great deal of pains with her & she will make, I hope a very fine pony. What name does Anne wish given to her? Tell her not to call it Sippy, anyhow.

Minny tells me you have been unable to buy a cow. Do if one is found no matter what the price is buy her out of $100.00 I sent Pa which he said he intended depositing in the bank, & take her as a present to yourself from me. I wish also you would take $20.00 of it & buy the sow Minny tells me of. If you don't raise some pigs &c. this summer I don't know what is to become of the family, as respects meat, next winter. Do have also every attention payed to the poultry, & try to raise some of every kind. Do buy some guinea fowls at no matter what price. They will pay for themselves, & their eggs can be set throughout the summer. Do also buy beef regularly from market. I will be able to let you have money again before long. I hope your garden is coming on well & that you will have a full supply of vegetables. I wish I could be there to enjoy them, but of that there is no chance this summer, unless the old 9$\underline{\text{th}}$ now the 11$\underline{\text{th}}$ is not reorganized, & of that I fear there is great danger.[62] Not more than half the men have as yet revolun-

---

62. The Ninth South Carolina Volunteers was being reorganized into the Eleventh Carolina Infantry and was holding elections for company and regimental officers. This was a common practice in the Confederate army early in the war, as many units that had originally enlisted for one-year terms of service when the war began reenlisted. The Beaufort Artillery, originally Company A, became an independent artillery battery and was permanently detached from the rest of the regiment in September 1863.

teered. The Government has issued an order retracting all furloughs and forbidding any more to be given; which the men consider to be virtually a breaking of the pledge to give furloughs, if they would reenlist. All are highly pleased at the news from the West & were it not for the death of Johnston there would be an universal hurrah.[63]

Do give love to all & tell Maum Daphne [that] Jacob and Billy[64] are well. Minny was in excellent health & spirits yesterday & had a very nice box of things, which he had brought with him. I don't know when I have tasted such butter.

I hope Hercules & Lewis are getting on well with the planting, every grain possible of corn ought to be planted, & also peas.

With much love,
Ever your aff<u>ct</u> son,
F. P. Leverett.
Surg. <u>11</u> Reg S.C.V.
Hardeeville,
S.C.

Milton Maxcy Leverett to his mother

New River Bridge April 8th 1862

My dear mother,

I arrived at Hardeeville safe on Saturday evening and got a seat from there in Fred's wagon (one given him by government and for which he is responsible) to where the regiment was stationed, stayed with Fred that night and came here next morning about a mile and a half on Bella and am settled here until the Yankees and General Drayton see fit to remove us. I was very loath to leave you all but it couldn't be helped. I could not and would not stay at home now any longer than a few weeks, in such times as these. While in Charleston I looked after the melodeon and other things, carried the note to Haines office and gave his clerk twenty-five cents to have the things carted to the other depot. The melodeon and leaves of the table were all I could find in the freight house, the former was standing up on end, I had it placed properly, it had been left standing on the wharf, so

---

63. Gen. Albert Sidney Johnston, commanding the Confederate Army of Mississippi, was mortally wounded and died at the battle of Shiloh, Tennessee, on 6 April 1862. The Confederates surprised a Federal army commanded by Maj. Gen. Ulysses S. Grant and drove a portion of it back, but they were unable to press their advantage before Johnston's death and before Federal reinforcements arrived. Johnston was succeeded in command by P. G. T. Beauregard, who was forced to withdraw on the night of 7 April.

64. Maum Daphne, Jacob, and Billy were slaves.

I understand from one of the freight house keepers, who had brought it in. The other things I suppose were stolen in some such manner either by being left out there, or by the wagoners themselves. Fred said Charlie came around to see after the things and didn't understand how anything had been left. The country down here is far advanced into the spring, and all the trees look beautifully reminding me so forcibly of byegone spring times. I am almost led to think that the low country when the woods are all in full bloom is much prettier than the up country.

10th 1862

Old Pocotaligo looked quite desolate when I passed and saw so few familiar faces—almost as it were expecting to see our own carriage there. I have Billy with me, so far doing very well, somewhat <u>deliberate</u> though in his movements, he cooks sometimes, waits on table, makes up our beds, cleans our shoes, and attends to my horse, also a pair of the cannon horses which I have to attend to, washing he does also, the latter he does very well and appears to like it very well inasmuch as it takes him away or he takes it away to a neighboring plantation where with his usual aptitude he has managed to make some acquaintances among the "<u>ladies</u>" got the washing done by one of them, staid and took dinner and brought my clothes back done very nicely. When I asked him if he intended to court the one he appeared to take a fancy to, he said "<u>donno</u> sir don't tink I will hab time." Only Ste. Barnwell[65] and myself with a fellow named Glover[66] from Walterboro are here now. Stuart Gibbes and Nat Fuller having gone home, we have two boys in the mess consequently neither of them have a great deal to do. Nat got a furlough on account of his father having died somewhat unexpectedly,[67] Stuart Gibbes got off on account of being unwell for sometime, and all furloughs having been suspended and revoked I was very fortunate in getting mine when I did.

I hope you apologised to the Greggs and Aunt Til for my not having been round to bid them good bye as I wouldn't like being rude at all to any of them. I created quite a sensation in camp with my new clothes, new shirts and cleanly shaved face, everything looked so horribly rough that I really felt somewhat out of place, my clothes were very much admired as also my shirts and with my beard off some fellows declared I looked ten years younger. A great many wanted to know how much they cost, and Wm Elliott wanted to know if he could buy such a suit said they were worth thirty dollars, and intended trying to raise some money from his factors (on the strength of his two negros which are all that he has left

65. Sgt. Stephen Elliott Barnwell (1842–1890) of the Beaufort Artillery, son of Emma Gibbes Elliott and Maj. John Gibbes Barnwell II.
66. Pvt. L. H. Glover of the Beaufort Artillery.
67. Pvt. Nathaniel Barnwell Fuller (1837–1910) of the Beaufort Artillery and his father, Dr. Thomas Fuller (1788–1862).

from the Yankees) in order to purchase clothes. It was agreed on all sides that I mustn't keep on those clothes in camp.

How is your garden getting on, and the planting generally, tell me everything about it, whether the fields are being manured or not. Pa mustn't worry himself too much about things, there is no necessity for it, I think our affairs are very encouraging much more so than a great many others—and the affairs of the country are much more encouraging than lately. Do purchase beef, butter &c &c, as Fred said he sent up enough money, health is the first thing and without good food you may bid good bye to good health, good temper etc., with good food and after a good dinner especially we acquire good spirits and good temper, the most "crooked things are made straight"[68] and all the little mountains in our path of life are smoothed down and turn out to be nothing but sand hills which shift with every passing gale or are blown away entirely.

There is some very heavy firing going on now, the enemy may be attacking Pulaski with their mortars, and although we are at New River Bridge with many a plantation intervening and some twenty miles distant we can see the shells as they burst in the air showing the white puff of smoke, evidently fired by mortars, as guns could hardly throw them so perpendicularly in the air so as to be seen at such a distance.

I am very anxious to join the Navy if I can obtain a Lieutenancy which I do not think is doubtful if I only knew to whom to apply to. My reasons for thinking that I might obtain a position there is because it is a new thing just being established, we have no Naval School consequently won't be expected to be naval officers all at once, the navy that is being established will require a great amount of men, and I will of course be in a subordinate position,—it is also the true and proper place for me, I feel every day that I am not where I can do my duty most effectually.

When I opened my box I found the candy it had been put in evidently at the last moment—I suppose some of it was abstracted first. The box—poor box! is most gone I've kept open house and open box and the contents are fast flying.

Haines or his clerk or whosoever it was said he would write to Pa and tell him the things would be sent. Pa's note to Peake[69] I gave to the omnibus driver to give to him as he said he would have an opportunity and I had tried several means of getting to him and couldn't—the Ticket office was closed and that was my last resort. I would write more punctually but haven't pens or ink convenient, do look in my box in the outer closet and get some pens in a little box and send by letter to me.

Love to all, and hope all are well.

Your aff^{ct}

son Milton M. Leverett

---

68. Isa. 40:4.
69. Henry T. Peake of Charleston, superintendent of the South Carolina Railroad.

Do tear up when read. I hope the pictures and everything are fixed up. I hear Natalie Heyward is engaged to W<u>m</u> Taylor, is it true?[70] I think it must be so, it occasioned quite a commotion in our little circle down here. Tell Maum Daphne [that] Jake and Billy are well and hearty. I send you a little key that I found when I was in Columbia in the furniture car.

In April 1862 the Confederacy, beginning the second year of a war few expected to last that long, instituted the first military draft in American history. This draft, which covered men between the ages of eighteen and thirty-five, spurred the voluntary enlistment or reenlistment of many of its soldiers who were unwilling to be stigmatized as "conscripts." Charles Hendee Leverett, who was teaching school in Colleton District, reenlisted on 16 April at Adams Run, in Charleston District, as a private in the Rebel Troop, Company I of the Third South Carolina Cavalry.

Milton Maxcy Leverett to his father

Camp Elliott Apr. 22nd /62

My dear father,

I have been from home about three weeks, and have not heard at all how you are all getting on—what is the reason? I have written to Ma and certainly expected a letter by now. The fall of Pulaski[71] must have paralyzed you, that is the only reason I can muster up, you mustn't allow such little <u>fortunes</u> of <u>war</u> to affect you or your correspondence. If I didn't see Fred's letters I am afraid I should be pretty ignorant of affairs at home.

The fall of Pulaski really did surprise us all and I have and will insist on laying it down to the score of treachery or cowardice. I think and it is thought by a good many that the fall of Savannah is now only a question of time. If the city is attacked by the fleet in all likelihood they will be beaten off, but the enemy will certainly erect mortar batteries along the banks of the river in the marsh and with their superior guns will easily shell out Fort Jackson and the other batteries, with no protection above, consequently the mortars,—which differ from guns in that they are very short and can be shot at almost any degree, and which can throw shells almost perpendicularly, so as to be able as it were to drop out of the clouds upon the object aimed at very much like a monkey dropping a cocoanut out of the

---

70. Nathalie Heyward (1841–1913); William Hayne Taylor (1838–1862), a Confederate soldier, died of disease eight days later.

71. On 10 April 1862 a Federal expedition bombarded Fort Pulaski with Parrott rifles, a particularly accurate type of field artillery; the fort was reduced to near rubble and surrendered the next day.

tree on the ground in order to burst it—will be able easily to shell out our forts and then Savannah, unless we are able to prevent their erecting those mortar batteries which some think we can and some that we cannot—the fleet will of course cooperate in the attack, but only act in a secondary manner. Some of the Savannah people think the city can be taken and others that it cannot. Ste Elliott went down to take a look at the batteries and concluded that a fleet could be beaten off but that slow approaches of these mortar batteries along the river banks will be fatal to Savannah. There is an island down there which if we are able so it is said, to keep possession of and prevent the enemy from erecting batteries will save Savannah,—this island it is said will be held by us at any hazard.

We are all getting on very well only it is so dull and wearisome—this miserable soldier's life. Our company is divided into two squads, one is at New River Bridge, alias Camp Alligator the other at Mr Hardee's place Camp Elliott, on the road to Savannah. I am with the last squad and have as a portion of my duties a pair of horses to take care of and am one of the riders, a position that I do not like at all for several reasons, although the one for which I am most fitted and if I saw any chance of my getting a position in the Navy I would leave right off. I am very anxious for such a position as I could serve my country and my family both much more effectually than in the Army. I would hate to request any one to make an application for me as it would be one of delicacy to the person, and of all, Cos Robert,[72] I would not ask; Cos Maxcy is the only man of whom I would request an application to Secry Mallory,[73] and I am afraid he would think it one of delicate consideration to himself. I wish you would see if there are any works on the Navy in the bookstores of Columbia, describing the duties of officers, men &c&c.

Today is the twenty second of April, exactly a year ago I joined the Army, and what a busy teeming year it has been, it is the sign post and the turning point I think of my life. Three weeks before the twenty second of April 1861 I hadn't the slightest idea of what I would do and least of all the thought never entered my head that the Army was my destination, and although it was my very great desire to be there still I thought that I was entirely too incapacitated for such a life to be accepted, and probably would <u>never</u> have applied if Ma and sister and brother had not urged me to it, I thank them for it, and believe it was the dispensation of Providence entirely, the whole thing from beginning to end is a perfect mystery to me. Ever since I graduated I have been planning and devising and attempting to find some means of making an honorable living, but every attempt failed and here am I at last making my living as a private in the Confederate Army, the last means

---

72. Robert Woodward Barnwell, member of the Confederate Senate, 1861–1865.
73. Stephen R. Mallory, Confederate secretary of the navy.

under the sun I would ever have dreamt of resorting to, I believe it has been entirely God's direction and hope and pray he will continue so to do.

I am delighted to hear you have got a cow and it will turn out a fine one. We have one also down here—my mess being a different one from that at the other camp. I was taken from the other camp to this one and had to unite with another for the present as my old didn't come along with us. At present my mess consists of Jimmy Stuart, Stuart Rhett, Heyward Barnwell[74] and Stephen Barnwell (Major John's son) and Mr. Hardee's cows being allowed to run loose with danger of being killed we took up one of them and finding old pea hams and cotton seed here we are feeding it and milking it; we get about two quarts at a milking, and find it a great help to us as really we were feeling miserably down in the mouth and stomach from our hard fare. Remember [me] to all the Greggs, and love to all at home as well as Aunt Til.

Your aff<u>ct</u> son
Milton M. Leverett

P.S. How are you managing about blades?

In the spring of 1862 the Leveretts left McPhersonville and moved the family, includ-ing Anne and her baby, to The Farm, a sixty-four-acre tract near the northern bound-ary of Columbia. The Leverett's new home, a one-story frame house on a hill overlooking the city, was one-half mile northeast of the South Carolina Lunatic Asy-lum and about one and a half miles from the State House at the center of the city. They remained there for the rest of the war. Rev. Charles Leverett preached occa-sionally at Trinity and Christ Churches in Columbia, at the Church of the Nativity in Union, the Church of the Advent in Spartanburg, and at St. Mark's Church in Chester. He also held regular services at the South Carolina Female Collegiate Insti-tute, often referred to as the Barhamville Institute, in Richland District near Colum-bia. In addition he continued to hold Sunday services for his family and slaves.

Rev. Charles Edward Leverett to his son Milton

Columbia, May 3, 1862

My dear Minny,

Your letter to me came a few days ago. The same day I put in a letter for you from Ma, and so I delayed sending until a few days had elapsed. I think I wrote to you sometime back, but may not have done so, tho' intended to. I have not been very particular in writing, as your Mother takes it upon herself to be scribe to you,

---

74.   Pvt. Nathaniel Heyward Barnwell (1844–1910) of the Beaufort Artillery; son of Edward Barnwell (1813–1885).

& she does it so much better than I, that I know you prefer it. I have been very busy about my books but from present appearances of the times, fear it may be useless labor. Nevertheless we don't know & so I choose to be prepared, if the sun shines out again upon us. It is a very dark time now. The villainous Yankees have so far as the Sea Coast goes, as we expected, got the upperhand. They are a rascally set from Lincoln down. I feel ashamed to have been born in New England & denounce the people as the meanest criminals that ever disgraced humanity. Liars, thieves, robbers, adulterers—villains generally. They have not a redeeming qualification. My only wonder is that such wretches have been allowed to pollute the land so long. But patience—the day of retribution will arrive, & God will strike with a vengeance suited to their criminal career. We are living in hope, but hope deferred maketh the heart sick.

You speak about a Lieut.ᵞ in the Navy, that could hardly be without going through the preliminary office of midshipman. Probably you are too old for that, tho' I do not know if the service is organized. If Mr. Barnwell comes here, as they say the government is to be removed to this place, I could speak to him, & get his views.[75] A letter from Ste Elliott mentioning you as one of his soldiers, might be of service & a letter from Drayton (tell him I ask him to give you one) might be of use. But I would if I were you, prefer a private life. Officers are seldom satisfied with their condition.

I suppose before long, Savannah will be attacked & then the fate of N. O.[76] I look daily for an attack on Chⁿ & burning of the city by the unscrupulous Yankee rogues. You will perhaps be engaged, but I hope will not suffer. Still you may, but God be praised if we have hope in Christ, the change from earth will be a joyous one. Those who have lived as long as I can not with my sad experiences care much for earth. It is a sad trying place, & but for these females to look after, I would hardly wish to live.

Everything is dreadfully expensive here. Bacon I paid $4 nearly for a piece which in common time would be bought for less than a dollar. Salt is not to be had at all. I have bought peas for 1.25 but they were short in measure, as to be about $1.40. I bought 500 wt. blades the other day at $2 hundred & I suppose I will have to buy more. I have also bought 20 additional bushels corn @ 1.25. Sugar worth 5 cents cost 16 & 8 cent sugar 20 & 25 cts. Beef is 30 cents. We are living very slim—almost keeping a constant fast. I don't care for myself. Butter is 60 cents. Our cow is no great thing. We get from it about 6 quarts a day, but do not make a sufficiency of butter for the family; I am sorry I could not have got a better cow. I bought Aunt Til's 2 for $50 & have sent them to Hampton's place for a while. I also bought a sow & pigs from Dr. Parker.[77] He charged $30, the sow ought

---

75. Robert Woodward Barnwell.
76. New Orleans, which had surrendered to a Federal naval fleet on 28 April.
77. Dr. John W. Parker of Columbia, superintendent and chief medical officer of the South Carolina Lunatic Asylum.

to have been sold for $12, but extortion rules the day. I am sorry Hercules did not bring poor Ball. I am sorry for poor Columbus. It is sad to think about leaving our homes & everything. I look for complete ruin & consider myself as nearly bankrupt. I have property in Savannah, if the city is taken that is lost. What a rascally war & what a rascally set the Yankees have shown themselves to be. I dislike them from my very heart. There is nothing to tell you that is interesting. Hercules & Lewis are still working at ploughing & planting. This place is too small for so many hands & too poor to make anything. Ask Fred if his buggy could be sold if he wishes to sell it & what would be the price. Somebody was asking about it & I said I would write & see. Our carriage is in a very shabby condition. I have very little to add. I hope if you are in a battle you will fight bravely. "Trust in God keep your powder dry"[78] & aim low. It is well in ordinary life to aim high but where you have a low set to contend with you must aim low. Besides some of their braves wear shirts of mail, but their legs are not cased, for if they were they could not run. I would aim for their heel as there, Archilles like, they are vulnerable. I wish you would try to maintain a spirit of religion. A camp is a wretched place for it, & therefore the greater the necessity for you to keep your heart clean & spirit right. Pray to God for daily help & protecting care. I am very much worried at times. Constant occupation keeps in a measure off sad & gloomy thoughts.

Have you heard of my colt. Trusty has come & has a nice colt, which will be an iron grey.

Give my love to Fred & believe me to be your affectionate father,

All are well.

Frederic Percival Leverett to his mother

Camp Allen near Hardeeville,
11th regiment S.C.V.
5th May 1862

My dear Mother,

As you will see by tonight's Mercury our regiment has been reorganized (<u>disorganized</u>) and our good old Colonel, whom all intimately associated with him loved and admired, has been discarded, & Col. Ellis, the Whippyswamp politician has been put in his place. Along with Col. Heyward all the field officers & almost every company officer that was worth having have been thrown out.[79] I am so sad

---

78. Valentine Blacker (1778–1823), Irish poet, "Oliver's Advice, An Orange Ballad."
79. On 5 May 1862, Col. William Cruger Heyward, Lt. Col. Robert Campbell, and Maj. Benjamin Burgh Smith were replaced by Col. Daniel Hix Ellis, Lt. Col. Frederick Hay Gantt, and Maj. John J. Harrison. Eighteen out of thirty of the officers in the regiment were replaced.

I can hardly write. The men vowed that they would not have gentlemen over them & so in exercising their right to vote rejected all who had any pretensions to being considered gentlemen; they elected men of their own stamp—not with reference to their qualifications & fitness for office, but such as they supposed would be lenient, & could be imposed upon. The result is that one of the best officered and best disciplined regiments in the service is virtually demoralized, and will soon be not worth the powder and shot it would take to kill the men. This election has utterly disgusted me with democracy. I never was much of a democrat, and henceforth will be less of one. I never wish again to see a vote polled. The miserable low lived scoundrels—The idea of turning out such a man as Col. Heyward for a good for nothing drunken, fiddling politician—When Col. Heyward and his officers left today I felt like crying. I feel myself now disgraced in being here. I have applied for a transfer. If it is not granted, I do not know what to do. Write & advise me. If I should resign, I would have to change my present pay for that of a private, which I do not like to do, because I can help to make all of you comfortable, a matter that may be of more importance henceforth, than it now is, for where this is to end none can tell. If I do resign, I will join a partizan corp.

The B. Artillery is virtually detached from the Regiment. It took no part in the recent election. It will receive its battery in about six weeks. I saw Minny today. He is perfectly well, and as disgusted as myself.

Last Saturday I went down to Canaan—borrowed a horse at Pocotaligo from Joe Wilkie.[80] It was a sad visit every thing was so terribly desolate. Every room and closet in the house was open—every thing thoroughly ransacked. I did not know what was left by you, & so could not tell what had been carried off. All the books from upstairs were gone except 3 copies of Homer, a Latin Dictionary & a Caesar, all my medicines were gone—Annie's wardrobe smashed. The storeroom window had been broken open & every thing taken out—the stable had been evidently used for the picket's horses—blades being in the racks—a few handfuls still in the loft—the cotton house for a wonder had not been broken into. The garden fences were somewhat delapidated. One bed of Peas was litterally covered with peas; the strawberries were bearing pretty abundantly. I think several quarts could have been gathered. The Quince trees had a good many quinces on them; the apple trees were in bloom, & undoubtedly would bear this year. That was the case in both gardens. The Japonicas surprized me—they had grown so much this spring. The largest orange tree by the house was as tall as the roof. The place looked as pretty as ever but desolate. I looked around for the cattle—& saw near the orchard a cow of the color of Dolly, I rode up to see if she might not have strayed back to her old range, but it was some one's stray ox. I went over too to Sheldon, where

---

80. Joseph B. Wilkie of Charleston, a merchant.

all was quiet and still—I then went down through Mr. Daniel Heyward's to the cars. This visit decided me not to send Ephy[81] back to Canaan—He could be of no use there—he was sick in McPhersonville, with Rheumatism, so I did not see him—I sent down today by Bill Elliott[82] a ticket for him to go to Walterboro & thence to Columbia. I also sent money to pay his fare on the cars. There were no seeds at Canaan except some watermelon seeds & most of those were eaten by the rats. I sent to Town yesterday by Dr. Burnet for some seed, which I hope you will receive this week by express. I had them merely directed to Columbia, so you must look out for them.

The fire at Canaan had caught from a fire in the parlor chimney & had been put out without doing much damage by tearing down the mantlepiece.

By the late disgusting election Minny Stuart has been thrown out of office; his wife & his four children were absolutely dependent on his pay.[83] Bill Elliott was also discarded. Ben Wyman was put in his place. If all the Regiments in the service were to be reorganized, I would despair of our cause. The new Col. has not yet arrived— The Lt. Col. one of the slowest of slow thinkers is in command. If this Regiment were to be carried into action now, the men would run like sheep. Some of the company officers can hardly write their own names. In as much as requisitions for supplies have to be made out in the most exact manner & sent to Hardeeville eight miles off & in as much as they will not be honored if not exactly correct, I hope some of the democratic soldiers will suffer from hunger before many days through the incompetency of the officers. Drayton takes this election, I hear, very much to heart.

With much love to one & all,

Ever yr. most affectionate

Son

F. P. Leverett

P.S.

If Pa does not need the Buggy, beg him to sell it for anything he can get & use the money—It ought to be worth 50\underline{^{00}}$ or 60\underline{^{00}}$/ fifty or sixty dollars.

P.S.

Mr. D. H.[84] has sent me an order for the last $50.00 he owed me. I will send it to you when I get it cashed & you had better pay Aunt Til with it for her cows, if you do not need it for anything else—Do write me soon.

I enclose a $10.00

---

81.   Ephraim.

82.   Capt. William Waight Elliott of Company F, Ninth South Carolina Volunteers.

83.   Middleton Stuart's wife was Emma Barnwell Stoney; their children were Middleton, Sarah, Emily, and John, a baby who died several weeks earlier.

84.   Daniel Heyward.

Mary Maxcy Leverett to her son Fred

The Farm, Columbia,
May 9 1862

My dear Fred

Your letter arrived last night with enclosed $10 for which I thank you, as it is very convenient to feel that one has money, even if they don't spend it, but you have sent so often lately that I am a little uneasy lest you should need some yourself. However it is just as well for you to send, as I think it is the only way we will be able to make you keep money in your pocket, for we will put up for you whatever it is not really necessary to spend for the family. Why your first X is not finished yet! Your natural impulse is to scatter abroad, so I hope one day you will get a wife who will teach you to restrain your hand sometimes. Apropos of this—I wish you would if you have opportunities for so doing, call in M^cP. at Capt. George's[85] to see the ladies. The girls & myself were quite pleased with what we saw of Helen B.[86]—she is pretty & pleasing, amiable & kind hearted a good housekeeper & with sense enough too.—Next to the choice I once made for you, I think there is a greater chance of your happiness being secured in this direction than in any other I know of. She is both young & pretty also which is an additional advantage.—I wouldn't be surprized if you had been disappointed for your own good in the end.

And now about the matter most important to you at present— I am decidedly of the opinion that you had better not resign at present, & on an uncertainty. At least try your present position some time first, it would [be] most judicious & prudent. A certain support is a very important thing in these days, & I very much fear you will not find many regiments with so many gentlemen in it, as your late regiment had judging by all accounts. It made me feel grave to read your account of what had taken place, for I think it augurs bad for the country that such a spirit should be abroad, and it is to be feared that though often not openly shown, it is very extensively shared in, among the uneducated and poorer class of people, & in this stage of our country's trials & peril, if it gets the upper hand, much mischief will be done. I expect we will have to end by a near approach to a limited monarchy. So dangerous is it, to be governed by Tom Dick & Harry, I would much prefer a government like that of England. I wonder how much crime has been committed in the land, in consequence of juries composed of Tom, Dick & Harry. I am truly sorry for all this on your account as it must be extremely unpleasant to

---

85.   George Parsons Elliott.
86.   Helen Barnwell (1839–1879) daughter of Eliza Zubly Smith and Capt. Edward Barnwell (1785–1860).

you, & the loss of such a Colonel as Colonel Heyward is really a misfortune to the Regiment. I am truly sorry for Mid. Stuart too. But I cannot but think Benj. Wyman is far superior in character to Bill Elliott—his standing is respectable, father a physician, & he married a Miss Edwards[87] of Walterboro, cousin to the DeSaussure's. I never heard anything against Wyman all the years he was in [illegible passage, the letter is torn]. His fault will probably be, too easy and yielding to his men. How is it about the transfer? are you sure of getting among gentlemen? & will you not be liable to be sent out of the State? I tell you plainly what I think, my dear Fred, but I do not wish you to go by that, but had better weigh the for and against as impartially as you can, & make up your mind accordingly.

Your Aunt Til had a telegram yesterday evening, merely that Jim & Newton were well. They were at Williamsburg & she supposes they were in the battle or at least Jim as two of Jim's messmates were wounded one was Mr. Thornwell's son.[88] Columbia is full. A thousand women & children from Charleston passed through day before yesterday, to the up country—& people are coming every day. Geo Coffin & family have taken a house & are come. Your father found Mr Kemper yesterday hunting in every direction for a lodging for his wife whom he came to bring up, none could he find. The poor McKee's[89] have lost two children at one blow of Scarlet fever, & today Professor Rivers eldest little boy died of the same disease.[90]

O Canaan, poor Canaan, how desolate it must have looked! Was your father's Secretary in the living room disturbed? it had any quantity of [letter torn] sort of things, papers, books &c. I am sorry to hear of Annie's wardrobe—her washstand was left also.—is that gone? I brought up a part of your medicines & all of your instruments. Did you see your father's picture frame? in unpacking and putting up the pictures & frames, we found that was not among them. I suppose it must unknowingly been left in the up stairs where all of them had been hid—I am very sorry, as we are now unable to put it up. I wish we could have eaten some of our own fruit this year—it was what for so many years I had been looking forward to, and now it seems as far off as ever. But it is useless greatly to desire any earthly thing—there is no rest here—for so much as the sole of one's foot, and one must try willingly to wait for it until all things earthly have faded from our eyes. "Love not the world, neither the things that are in the world"[91] is a most difficult lesson to learn. I have been learning it these many years, and am just as stupid a scholar as ever. To be sure houses & lands & gardens & cotton fields are not the things

---

87.   Mary N. Edwards Wyman.
88.   Pvt. Gillespie Thornwell of Company D, Hampton Legion (Cavalry).
89.   Jane Monroe Bold and Henry McKee of St. Helena Parish, refugees in Columbia.
90.   William James Rivers. His eldest son was William James Rivers Jr.
91.   From 1 John 2:15.

that move me—in fact they seem little to me,—heart-pangs for the loved whom we can see no longer, who are, tho' "lost to sight, to memory dear" are what move me. These thoughts & feelings are a daily crucifixion of the flesh to me, and I am only comforted in looking forward to the glorious Meeting that Eternity I hope will bring me. It is well however that he, my beloved is not here now.—the desperate condition of the country would have been too much for him. He is in a better land, and I would long to be there too, but for those I love and still have here.

Does Minny get our letters I wonder? he always seems to write as if he didn't, & I have written very regularly with the exception of the two first weeks after he left when we had so much to do, & got so little done that I did not like to write discouragingly. We are all well satisfied, & I think in spite of the hard times & hard fare of the servants, that I have never seen Hercules so cheerful & satisfied looking. He is always in good humour, & seems to be interested in the farm as he is the only person to manage it,—Annie & myself often talk with him about it. The potatoes are coming up & the corn looks very well—Hercules says he will be well contented if it will continue looking so. Daphne asks Minny about some Georgia money which she says she sent by him to Jake to change for her. Where is Milton to be fixed? I hope not far from you.

y^r affte
Mother Mary

Milton Maxcy Leverett to his mother

Camp Elliott, May 10th/62

My dear mother,

I received your two letters and was very glad to see them, indeed in the words of one of those letters, "If you are as glad to get my letters as I am to get yours you would write often." I took a trip to Savannah about two weeks ago with Stuart Rhett and made a few purchases,—carried Billy along with a basket to bring along the parcels, gave him money to spend, with which he purchased something for his wife; he seemed quite fond of gazing in the toy shops, looking with admiration at the round jolly figure and laughing quizzical face of some paste or wooden imitation of humanity. The Savannah people seem to me to be quite laggard in their operation of defense and quite confident in their ability to ward off the threatened blow. The gunboat that was being built was laid aside unfinished and all the work was being placed on a large floating battery which when covered with a sufficiency of iron I think will be a very nice affair, but the work was being carried on very slowly. I heard that yesterday a flag of truce had been sent up by the enemy for what purpose has not as yet transpired, some think to demand the surrender of the city, others that perhaps it was to bring the wounded of Pulaski up.

We are presently doing nothing but simply waiting and waiting, both for the enemy and our long expected battery. As regards my going into the Navy, say no more about it and don't mention to Cos. Robert Barnwell any desire of mine or any one else for a recommendation, as <u>I know positively</u> that he dislikes giving recommendations, especially for men to get into office when he has two sons and so many nephews and other kinsmen privates in the ranks. To be sure, <u>the office of Lieutenancy</u> in the Navy was entirely secondary with me, my chief idea being that my duty to my country could be performed much more effectually there than in the Army. It would have been a situation much more pleasant to me corporeally, or rather physically (<u>no great mental satisfaction</u> for I abhor the Navy) than the position of private in an Artillery Company, although a company composed to a great extent of gentlemen. The chief mental satisfaction was that of being in a position pleasing to my parents, but since Pa has acknowledged his preferences to my present position, my own wishes shall be entirely secondary. There are other reasons also why I have taken this determination.

I killed a beautiful wild gobbler the other day, had Fred round with me and had a big feast off him. Sometimes our fare is quite dry, very often nothing but biscuits and water for supper. We had some cows up for awhile, but the overseer having carried them off we had to come down to first principles—water—we have been trying since then to get up some more cows out of the woods, but didn't succeed, but today a little tame one with a little calf came up and the mess has declared its intentions of keeping it <u>vi et armis</u> which being interpreted means in spite of the overseer and all he can do.

You have heard of the lamentable election of officers in the 11<u>th</u>; most of the gentlemen have been thrown out; our company didn't vote as we wish to be detached. Don't direct to me any more as in the 11<u>th</u> Reg. but simply Beaufort V. Artillery, Hardeeville.

Your aff'<u>ct</u> son
Milton M. Leverett

The flag of truce was to treat for the exchange of prisoners. Ask Annie to see if she can find any Denham cloth with one side blue and the other leaden colour and send it round to a tailor and have an overcoat of the same style as the winter one I have, with a cape to it, only I wish it a little shorter. I expect she knows the kind, about Pa's size but shorter. I wish the lead colour outside but if that can't be obtained get the blue. Do have the edges of the cape and down the front of the coat trimmed with a red cord.[92] I'll write to Pa and Julie next. Fred & I always show each other our letters from home. Tell Julie she must write again. Have you got the pictures up

---

92. Confederate uniform regulations prescribed different colored trim and facings for each branch of the service. Red was the color for artillerymen's uniforms.

in the parlour? There is a report here that the Yankees are on the Main as far as Mr. Rhodes—Mr. Adams saw them.

Mr. Rhett is here on a visit to Stuart.

Tell Annie never mind to worry about the coat.

Mary Maxcy Leverett to her son Milton

The Farm Columbia May 20th 1862

My dear <u>Milton</u>, <u>Min</u> or <u>Minny</u> is certainly too feminine for such a brigand looking war like, & masculine specimen of human nature as you are in these days, so I really must begin to give you your real name <u>Milton</u> which sounds much better. You must be tired of camp life truly when there seems to be nothing to do but move from one place to another. I suppose the girls told you of Newton's narrow escape—his head must have been too hard but it must have been but a slight wound, as he rode fifty miles to Richmond that night to carry dispatches. He generally acts as Courier, because he likes that best. His horse went off full tilt to the Yankees, with his saddle bags containing all he had, also a bible Tillie had given him & Mary & Ste's last letters to him. He got a Yankee horse, however, but with nothing but an old greatcoat tied to it. I didn't hear that he <u>killed</u> anybody, but Thornwell has the satisfaction (what a commentary on the times that a woman should talk of the <u>satisfaction</u> of killing any human being) of knowing that he killed his adversary; he has also, several other wounds it is said, and arrived here on Saturday with his father, who had gone on for him.—he was sufficiently recovered to walk from the carriage into the house when he got home. It is said he behaved bravely. Your poor Aunt Til had the trouble & expense of having to get up another outfit for Newton. I believe it is <u>three</u> times now at least that she has had to do that. But she is so pleased at their being unhurt in the first encounter they have been in, that it makes up to her. Tillie Fowles came here with a shirt to make up for him in a hurry & got our girls to help, as it was to go next night by Clarkson's servant. The shirt was fancy, made out of part of a pretty worsted dress of Tillies, with an inside lining of white, so making it double for strength,—he rides often without a coat. It is a very good idea, for some of the girls dresses would make very pretty ones, & the young men of the B. V. A,[93] had better suggest it to their sisters. I suspect it is very extensively done in these days of hard times & high prices. Would you like one or two? for I have already spoken to your sister for a pretty one of hers, if you wish it.—I feel so incensed about the news nowadays, that I can scarce write with patience.—We are doing nothing but giving up men,

---

93.   Beaufort Volunteer Artillery.

forts & towns. If half our public men were hanged, or put in pillory, it would be good for the country. Ripley deserves to be cashiered & the Charleston people were geese for insisting on his being made General.[94] Only think of the Planter![95] Mr. McKee told your father one of the negroes was his. When I read of N. Orleans I can scarce keep from crying. It is said the Government were offered money & mechanics to finish the iron Ram more quickly there & refused saying they needed no help, one citizen alone offered a thousand dollars to the foreman if they would work at night & he wouldn't—they went on in the most leisurely manner & you see how it all ended. The man who had the building of it was brother in law to <u>Mallory</u>, & I feel afraid that <u>he</u> is not sound now, & that the slowness was purposely designed. The principal mechanic also was a Maine man. Oh that I could lift up my voice and blow a trumpet blast in the ears of the President & Secretary Benjamin[96] & that Mallory! wouldn't I give it to them & make them shake in their shoes, especially the two latter. I feel like boxing Ripley's ears too. In fact the whole generation, lock, stock & barrel, need a thorough rousing, and if I had them all by the nape of the neck I'd shake them into their senses. I am disgusted with men, since this war began. They are not half as honest as women are slow and stupid, a drinking, swearing, good for nothing set, selfish & unpatriotic. How I hate 'em! Luckily to save the sex from absolute infamy, & to give one something to swear by, (take your affidavit, I mean!) there are some few splendid specimens of courage, sense, manliness & patriotism still left, who act as the salt to keep the rest from putrifying. Were it not that these give me some hope of the country yet, & that there is a God to whom I can still plead & appeal, I would forswear my country & go off to some other land—yes, and but for one other tie— that grave, that dear grave in old Sheldon Churchyard—I can never leave that.[97] The women are ready to do & suffer any thing,—it is the men who are at fault in this war. I don't know what has made me write so, dear Min, for I never intended to indulge in <u>politicals</u>, when I commenced writing, but out of the fulness of the heart the pen writeth, I suppose.

May 22^d. We were delighted yesterday at the confirmation of the news of Jackson's complete victory in Western Virginia over Milroy & Cox.—he has swept

---

94. Brig. Gen. Roswell S. Ripley commanded the District of South Carolina in the Department of South Carolina and Georgia in the fall of 1861.

95. The capture of the Confederate harbor steamer *Planter* near Beaufort on 23 May 1862 by crew member Robert Smalls, a slave. Smalls and the other slaves aboard the *Planter* took the vessel while the Confederate crew was ashore and delivered it to the South Atlantic Blockading Squadron of the U.S. Navy; Smalls later served as pilot of the U.S.S. *Keokuk* and then as captain of the *Planter*.

96. Judah P. Benjamin, Confederate secretary of war September 1861–March 1862.

97. Edward's grave.

every thing before him, & it is said McDowell had hurried back to Washington fearing we are going to attack the Capitol.[98] Another good piece of news also was Gen. Gregg has written word to his mother, & she sent me word to me yesterday, that we will certainly beat them, that there is not a doubt on his mind as to the result, & that his mother must not be at all uneasy or even in the slightest degree depressed, <u>that we will have peace very soon</u>! Now Maxcy has not said as much as this once yet, & hitherto has believed the war would be <u>long</u>, & something he must know there lately to induce him to speak with certainty of peace, so I entirely believe it, for he never says anything without having good grounds for it. He writes very often, sometimes they get two letters at once. Cornelia says it is really a strange thing,—that Maxcy never hears of an alarm & hurries off to get into a "scrimmage," but what the enemy is sure to disappear & clear off.

Old Ephy has just come, & looks very well—your father will try & hire him to some salt petre works that are being established on Dr Parker's farm between this & Columbia on the other side of the road. I am sorry to hear too nobody is minding W. Fuller's house,—Eph. says that Henry Fuller & Dr M. Hanckel had a sort of fight about it, that H F carried his negroes up & put them <u>in the house</u>, Capt. Hanckel asked him what right he had to do it when <u>he</u> had hired the house, H F wrote to W F to ask if he had hired out his house when he knew that <u>he</u> needed one, W F said no, he hadn't, so H F thereupon went to fisticuffs & words with Capt. H & then neither would take the house, & he brought his negroes up the country.—Tell Fred the garden seeds came yesterday but no Rutabaga were among them. I only laid stress on getting them now, because if we put off until time to plant, soon as people begin to inquire for a thing the price is raised, they say they have not got it, 'wait a while & then produce it' at a high price. Thank Fred for the seed. Annie & I work hard in the garden every day, & it is encouraging to see things improving. Cely set out over a hundred cabbage plants. Our <u>animal</u> family are doing well in Tillie's hands she has increased the feed of Betsey the cow & yesterday she gave nearly 9 quarts of milk. I am glad you went to Savannah & wonder you men don't go there to church. I hear Fred's is not the only Regiment that has served its officers so badly. The troop Charley was in in Virginia turned out their Captain too & many others have done the same. Your father is busy at his History day & night, & reads us a few chapters every other night for me to criticize, the intervening night he reads the newspaper to us aloud. On the whole we are having a quiet & pleasant life, very little cast down considering we

---

98. Maj. Gen. Thomas J. "Stonewall" Jackson, commanding the Confederate Army of the Valley in the Shenandoah Valley of Virginia, defeated a Federal army under Brig. Gen. Robert H. Milroy at McDowell on 8 May 1862; Brig. Gen. Jacob D. Cox, commander of a Federal brigade in western Virginia, was not at the battle. Maj. Gen. Irvin McDowell commanded a corps at Washington, D.C.

are refugees. You gave some directions to Annie in your last to me, about a great-coat & then marked it out, but why did you mark it out? don't you want it? I'll do my best for you. Let me know.

> Love to Fred.
> yr aff Mother
> Mary

Mary Bull Leverett to her brother Fred

Columbia, May 29th /62

My dear Fred,

You are very long in writing but I suppose you are in Minnie's fix; having noth-ing to say, was his excuse for not writing us for more than a month, we know every one in his company anyhow, so he could even mention them; Ma has just come in my room & is at present helping rub Lou dry, with a towel & sundry scolds at Nanny for not being quick enough. She says there is a large bottle belonging to you, that came in the china from Canaan, she wishes to know if you wish it, and what is it. I think it is varnish but she, the spirits of turpentine. We were so sorry to hear yesterday evening of Mary Elliott's death, they have been in Aiken for sometime but we have not heard any particulars.[99] You must have heard of Cousin Ann Stuart's death, they are in Flat Rock, she died of dropsy, it is so sad to think how many of the Beaufort people have died since leaving there.[100] Cos Henry has a farm near Flat Rock, given up the one in Edgefield, or wherever they were before. Miss Annie Cuthbert is dead too. Cousin Liz has a son, she passed through last week on her way to Pendleton, they think of hiring a farm there; Mary Heyward was with her still. Aunt Til says Mary and her father have quarrelled, Mary was in the wrong I believe, she spoke rudely to him & Annie reproved her, so she got vexed with Annie and they don't speak, and Mary intends living with Cousin Liz. Lila came to see us last week, Julie is going there very soon. Miss Mary Rhett and Lila speak to Pa. We have not seen them; yes! I saw Miss Rhett once, she bowed, so I returned it. Natalie asked Mary Fowles if <u>Mary Heyward</u> was <u>not crazy</u>!. and so many other impertinent questions, that Mary is very shy of her now. Natalie is simple and don't know any better, I suppose; but I do wish Mary H would behave herself, for it certainly looks strange, before they left Charleston she remained in bed some weeks complaining! Eliza DeSaussure spent one night with us, she has been in Columbia for a long time now and leaves

---

99. Mary Barnwell Fuller (1835–1862) died 23 May, wife of John Habersham Elliott.
100. Ann Hutson Means, wife of Henry Middleton Stuart Sr.

this week for Cheraw, as her father has taken a house some miles from the village.[101] Mary Fowles and Sue Maxcy walked out yesterday evening, the former looks very well; Aunt Til and Ste walked out on Saturday. We carried them back in the carriage in the evening. Some of them are coming out tomorrow to spend the day with Mattie Cornish.[102] We have not invited her here yet and she leaves very soon for Aiken, and we wish to pay her some attention.

I am so hoarse, I can hardly speak, Ma's, Tillie's, and my cough are hanging on still, we are the only ones in the house that have had it and we have taken paregoric, nitre, flax seed tea, and hore hound candy, until we are tired, but it seems to do no good. Ma was in bed for three days, hers & Tillie's cough are better today. We have so much rainy weather here and the climate is so chilly that all of the down country people are suffering from colds and complaining of Columbia's unhealthiness.

I have just been out to feed the horses & little turkies, two turkeys hatched out 40, at present there are 34, 6 were mashed & killed by geese & gobler, these are quite bright and a very pretty sight, one turkey is carrying them, the other I have set again, two more turkeys will hatch soon too; cannot buy guinea hens or eggs; the hen that carried the chickens, has laid and is now <u>hatching</u>, she never lost one of the 24 chickens, I brought up here, every now & then I kill one for Ma. They are very fine, fat chickens, 6 or 7 pullets I will keep, for there is no buying any, a poor-woman brought some to sell—a very fine hen & 6 chickens, I gave 40 cts for the hen, 25 cts for the chickens, one was very small so they threw that in for good measure, two are very fine pullets, which I will keep, so I have a very fine set to increase my stock with. I have more out, not many though, about 25, 10 have been killed in different ways, there are still three hens to hatch. Hercules & Lewis made a nice large poultry house yesterday, the others were too small & low, made with rails too, so the hens were continually getting out. Only two goslings hatched and a rat eat one.

The corn behind the garden is very fine. The old man says, it is the best crop that he has ever seen on the place; the rice has come up beautifully. Mr. Vaughn, the gentleman who bought the field in front of Aunt Til's, took the liberty of walking over the fields, where H. & L.[103] were, he told them, it was a fine stand of corn; the fodder peas looks very fine, potatoes also they are running, if everything could only continue as they are now, Hercules & myself will be satisfied, but we are afraid everything will burn up. The cow gives 8 qrts & a pint nearly every day, both cow & calf are in good order.

---

101. Eliza Ford DeSaussure and her father, Dr. Louis McPherson DeSaussure Sr.
102. Martha Sarah Jenkins Cornish of Aiken.
103. Hercules and Lewis.

What is the joke about the willow root? You have taken such a time to write, have you determined to continue in the same regiment? Do write soon & let me know. Miss Grimke said her father[104] intended to ask Col. Heyward to spend the summer with them. Old Ephy came to hand last Thursday, he said nearly every one had left the pinelands; he is hired out at the Salt petre works not far from us. Prof. LeConte[105] is at the head of it. Ephm's wages are $9 a month, and $1 and a half for allowance, this is what he says, but I told Pa he ought to have given a ticket and told Ephy to bring back whatever he was hired for, written down, but Pa doesn't seem to think he will have any trouble. Well you must be tired out with this long epistle.

Cousin Maxcy is now ten miles from Richmond, and the two armies now are facing each other.[106] Every one expects to hear terrible news before long. Cos. Julia has not been well. She is <u>always</u> <u>out</u> at prayer meetings and takes something like opium to make her sleep. I would not be surprised any time to hear of her being crazy. She is as thin as a lath and nervous as possible. She has had a valise packed ever since Cos. Maxcy has been in Va., to go to him right off, if he should get wounded. Ma and the girls all send love, Lou in particular, cried because Katie said she would too.

Your aff^{ct} sister

Mary Maxcy Leverett to her son Fred

The Farm, Columbia, June 17 1862

My dear Fred

At the last moment Annie tells me her letter is not ready, and as the bundle of shirts &c. for you is ready, I will not keep them a day for her letter, as you may need them quickly & time is precious. We have worked every day since your letter came in order to send as soon as possible. Everything is very dear however & I do not know if they will suit your expectations. The socks are English & cheap at 45 cts pair—it is cheaper some say than to knit, as yarn is now so expensive that I saw coarse knitted socks at <u>60</u> cts. the same place where I bought these. The cloth for drawers was 45 cts. & the shirts stripe 55 cts per yard. Your old cap Min

---

104. Mary Augusta Secunda Grimke and her stepfather, William Heyward, brother of Daniel Heyward.
105. John LeConte, superintendent of the Confederate States Niter and Mining District No. 6 1/2 in Columbia.
106. The Confederate Army of the Potomac, commanded by Gen. Joseph E. Johnston, was on the outskirts of Richmond facing the Federal Army of the Potomac, commanded by Maj. Gen. George B. McClellan.

carried off long ago for Billy—as he had none, Min's cap we gave Tom, so Tom has sent one he made himself for Jacob. What is the reason neither of you answer the question so often asked by Daphne, of where is the Georgia money she sent by Minny to Jacob to get changed? We had two satisfactory letters from Milton, but he does not mention a word about the people of McPhersonville, who is there & who gone. We had an interesting letter from Miss Grimke also lately. It shows how necessary it is for people to write minutely & distinctly, it was not until we got Milton's letter that we could clearly make out where the fight had really been, tho' we read all the newspaper accounts, as well as Miss Grimke's & your letters. I think some able man, who is known to have a ready pen, ought always be required by the company or regiment to write a minute & graphic account for the newspapers, whenever a fight takes place. You have no idea how superior the Richmond papers are in that respect, as well as in editorials, to our two poor Charleston ones. Your father buys them occasionally. I feel quite incensed to think of the Yankees being allowed to retreat so leisurely instead of our cutting them off by the Green Pond Way. Where was Gen Pem.'s head?[107] He must be nervously afraid of everything. Oh, that we had a General that was afraid of nothing! When asked the reason, they say he answered "he didn't know the country"!! O that we had a General that <u>did</u> know the country & the people too! The Governor[108] telegraphed to him by no means to let the Yankees land on James Island, but he <u>would</u>, & I'm told, that after they landed, he burst into tears "because he had been such a fool as to let them land!" he said. Now, I want our Generals to <u>fight</u>, <u>we</u> can do the crying, no fear of that. I hear also, that when Gen. Smith[109] arrived he ordered a battery to [be] fixed in a certain post in the harbour, Pemberton forbid it, Smith told him any one who gave up such a post as that for defense was a <u>coward</u>! Pemberton asked if he knew who he was speaking to, he said <u>yes</u>, Gen <u>Pemberton</u>. And Pemberton had him arrested. Today I hear that Evans is to command,[110] Pemberton is unwilling to undertake the defense of the city. If Charleston is surrendered without a great and ever-to-be remembered struggle, I'll forswear my country, for the men have turned cowards. We, South Carolina commenced this struggle, and it is our duty and <u>ought</u> to be our glory and our pride, to bear the brunt of it. We have suffered only a little yet, I consider it, & ought to be willing to bear ten times as much again. It would be too contemptible after all the talk & bluster, to sneak out of the fight like a little puppy dog with the tail between the legs.

---

107. John C. Pemberton.
108. Francis W. Pickens, governor of South Carolina December 1860–December 1862.
109. Brig. Gen. William D. Smith commanded the District of South Carolina in the Department of South Carolina and Georgia.
110. Brig. Gen. Nathan G. Evans commanded a South Carolina brigade in the Confederate Army of the Potomac.

I'm so sorry you have lost Nightmare. What <u>will</u> you do for a good horse?

Julia had a letter from Charley day before yesterday, a satisfactory one for him.

In great haste

yr. af mother
Mary

Frederic Percival Leverett to his sister Mary

Camp Lee, Hardeeville.
18<u>th</u> June, 1862.

My dear Mary,

I received yours of the 11th Inst. last week and was very much obliged to you for it. I was getting quite uneasy, it had been so long, since I had heard from any of you. I hope this will reach you, before you send the bundle of things, I told Ma of, in my last. I wish Anne would put a pocket on the left side in front of each of the shirts. I hope they will be made nicely & will be of neat material. I want the pockets large enough to put a handkerchief in. Beg her to sew on the buttons twice as strong as usual. It will not matter about the stockings as I got to Savannah for a night last week & bought some there. I also bought some India Rubber cloth for myself & a piece large enough for Minny, which I sent him, so if we have any exposure at night, we will have it on the ground under our bedding. I bought a pound of Turnip seed (Globe, not Rutabaga) none of the latter are to be had in Savannah or Charleston. I will send them in the box. I will send it as soon as I receive the things from Columbia. Do put into the bundle the bit & curb, which are on my bridle; it is the one with yellow leathers. Tilly had it to ride with, when I was at home. I will send in the box a bit that will answer as well. I hope some of you will certainly attend to this for me.

I never see nor hear anything of Minny now—not a word since he went to McPhersonville.

I am glad you found the money useful. I enclose another check for $30.95. Ask Pa to get it cashed & to give $10.00 of it to Anne for housekeeping, $5.00 to Tilly & yourself each, & $10.00 to Ma to buy things for Julia, Kate & Carry; and the 95 cts. beg him to buy postage stamps with & you all write me at least once a week.

I am very sorry to hear of the accidents to Anne's poultry. If she has not yet succeeded in rescuing them from the rats, tell her the only chance will be to have a box fixed off of the ground, well aired & at the same time so close that rats cannot get in, & have the young poultry put in every night. She must not despair about raising them, even if she has to set eggs later than this. If I had not made

Sary set eggs through last summer, you would have had very few guinea fowls, turkies &c last fall. Hens do not stand setting in summer well, but turkies do. In the latter part of September & October chickens can be hatched & raised almost as well as in the Spring. Tell Anne that is worth remembering.

Do tell Pa I did not send Mr. Heyward's order. I used it in paying one or two bills. I sent $28.00 about three weeks since to Miss H. Fuller[111] for Isaac's services but have not heard if she received it. I am afraid it is lost, as I wrote to Dr. Henry & begged him to acknowledge it.

I am getting more and more lonely here. Burnett my assistant has been ordered to Grahamville, & a Dr. Dan Tucker here in his place.[112] He has not come, but I did not like his appearance, when I saw him. Burnett & I have got on well together & I am very sorry to lose him. Our new Col. & most of the new officers are even poorer & more distasteful than we had anticipated them to be. They at once dislike & are afraid of me. The one that gives out feed for the horses, the other day, did not wish to give out feed to Jacob, as he had not been there exactly at the right moment. Jacob told him he would come to me then. He asked Jacob if I was much of a fighter. He was answered <u>yes</u>. He at once gave out the feed, remarking that he wanted to have nothing to do with the Dr. as he looked & talked like a <u>bruiser</u>. Such then is my character. Not one can say I do not attend to my duties, or that I do not do everything in my power to make men & officers keep the camp in the best order. Jacob will send Maum Daphne's money in the box. If you can spare some let her have it & I will see that you get it.

Love to all,
Ever yr. aff<u>ct</u> brother
F. P. Leverett

P.S. Did Pa ever get my account book?

Milton Maxcy Leverett to his sister Anne Leverett DeSaussure

McPhersonville June 20<u>th</u> /62

My dear Anne,

We are now encamped in this village on Mr Jenkins' lot and have been here for a week or so. I would have written before and blame myself, but my time has been very much occupied. The manner in which we came to get here was this. When we were encamped below Hardeeville about five miles or so, the report came, that the enemy were within a mile and a half of the railroad on which we

---

111. Harriet Barnwell Fuller (1791–1864) lived with her brother Dr. Henry Middleton Fuller and his family.

112. Assistant Surgeon Daniel Tucker of the Eleventh South Carolina Infantry.

were immediately ordered off to Pocotaligo;[113] all of our guns got off, except the one to which I was attached because there was no ammunition for it, and I was consequently compelled to remain until Sunday at Hardeeville, and our camp, when the rest of us went on to Pocotaligo. Our company did not get in the fight as the enemy who were as far as Mr. Tom Elliott's saw the cars coming up with troops and with artillery and before everything could be got out in marching order they had commenced to retreat and couldn't be caught up with. The little fight that had taken place was just the other side of Old Pocotaligo, our men (the Rutledge Mounted Men[114] and another company) about thirty eight altogether were stationed among the live oaks and about the edge of the bushes, firing across at the enemy who were stationed near Mr. Screven's big canal and the bridge over it near the other oaks on the causeway which forks off from the one leading to Saltketcher just after you leave Pocotaligo. Some of our men had been stationed over along the dam in Mr. Screven's ricefield[115] but had fallen back to Old Pocotaligo. The enemy would rush up to the bridge and try to get over under cover of the causeway, at the same time attempting to pull up the bridge, they could be heard cursing and damning at their men and trying to incite them on but 'twasn't any go, at last a fine large looking fellow a captain rushed up on the dam right by the floodgate when a ball took him through the chin and came out at the back of the head and he dropped as they all ought to.[116] Our men kept them back for a long while until the enemy from their superiority of numbers were beginning to flank them and their ammunition was giving out when they retreated as far as Mr. Tom Elliott's place and the enemy came on as far as the spring and rested. They could easily have taken the railroad then but they seem to have been afraid, they were there at least two hours before the cars came up with reinforcements. The prisoner taken said if they had had three or four hundred more men they could have beaten us while in reality they had twelve or fifteen hundred men fighting against

---

113. On 29 May 1862 a Federal force commanded by Col. Benjamin C. Christ of the Fiftieth Pennsylvania advanced from Beaufort toward Pocotaligo in a reconnaissance toward the Charleston and Savannah Railroad. The Confederate force ordered to meet this advance, commanded by Col. William S. Walker of the Third Military District, included Company A of the Rutledge Mounted Riflemen, Companies A and D, First Battalion South Carolina Cavalry, the Beaufort Artillery, and Companies I and F, Eleventh South Carolina Infantry. Federal losses were two killed and five wounded. Confederate losses were two killed, five wounded, and one missing.

114. Two independent cavalry companies raised in Charleston District, with Capt. W. L. Trenholm commanding Company A and Capt. T. J. Magee commanding Company B. They later became Companies B and G, respectively, of the Seventh South Carolina Cavalry when that regiment was organized in May 1864.

115. John Henry Screven's Old Brass plantation in Prince William's Parish.

116. Capt. Charles H. Parker of Company H, Eighth Michigan Infantry.

thirty eight or forty. Later in the day we had some twenty five hundred men in the field and pursued the enemy until they crossed over into Beaufort. They seem to have taken the retreat from some accounts quite leisurely, as one of Mrs Eustis' men told me they had rested there about two hours there, others say they appeared quite fagged out. They stole all along the way, horses mules, negroes, &^c &^c went into Mr D. Heyward's and made Charles give them liquor, the best of which he had hidden, stole Mr H's guns and took a shot at him as he came up towards his house. One prisoner was taken—by Nat Fuller and Heyward Barnwell, he was found sleeping at Dr. H. Fuller's right among our company— was either drunk or overcome by fatigue. He had been sleeping there all night, they supposing it was some man out of another company when their suspicions being aroused they took away his arms, woke him up and on asking him found that he belonged to the Michigan Regt. and he asking them found out that they belonged to the B. Artillery—he then said "I suppose I may as well give up" and gave up.[117] Only one man was killed on our side and he was killed while on picket duty, they shooting him down like a dog, just after you leave Garden's Corner near the turn off to Sheldon, two others were wounded.[118] We killed about half a dozen of theirs, (as Mr. D. Heyward's Josy said he helped to put that many in the cart and cover them over with bushes) and took one prisoner. They took a prisoner or two from us, Mr. Codding[119] one of them, he was sitting in the piazza at Dr. H. Fuller's when the enemy came up and he taking them for some of our men invited them to take seats, and on inquiring found out who they were, when they informed him that he was their prisoner. The trees at Pocotaligo are shot up with a good many balls.

I wish that you all could be staying here now if it was perfectly safe, but think you are much better off there than here. Miss Ann Jenkins wrote a very kind note to me offering to do anything for me that I wished and asking me to come and see her. Mike is in our company and is quite kind and affable. Fred asked me to be kind and polite to him. Fred told me he had got an invitation to the office of Surgeon in Jenkin's Regt.[120] but I don't know whether he has got it as I haven't heard from him.

One of the Yankees said he knew all about the country had shot many a snipe at Mrs Eustis' and at Mr D Heyward's and dined many a time at Mr Wm Hey-

---

117. Cpl. Frederick Bishop of Company H, Eighth Michigan Infantry, a native of Germany.

118. These three Confederates, members of Capt. W. L. Trenholm's Company A, Rutledge Mounted Riflemen, were Pvt. Peter Cuttino Goddard, killed; Pvt. G. C. Hughes, wounded and captured; and Pvt. J. Charles Lawton, wounded.

119. Elisha Codding, a civilian and overseer.

120. Jenkins's regiment was the Palmetto Sharpshooters, South Carolina Infantry, organized in April 1862 and commanded by Col. Micah Jenkins.

ward's that they would take the railroad next time and might probably come on to McPhersonville. He told Mrs. Eustis' Henry so. Direct my letters to McPhersonville now.

Love to all and hope all are well.

Your affectionate brother,
Milton M. Leverett

P.S. Do have three pair of drawers (coarse cloth, homespun will do) made for me. I'll also be much obliged to Mary if she will knit some stockings for me. I am very much in need of drawers and stockings. They could be sent to me by Express, just direct Beaufort Artillery Care of Capt. Elliott. As regards those outside shirts Ma spoke of I would like one or two, but not if they are fancy and flashy. I don't like anything especially conspicuous. As regards the direction for making a cloak that Ma inquired of in one of her letters and which I had scratched out, I have had a tailor to attend to that. Do have the drawers made with full legs, with good tape strings for the stockings and with loops to button with. Always date your letters when you write.

Milton Maxcy Leverett to his mother

McPhersonville
June 20th /62

My dear Mother,

I have not written to you since your infamous Philippic against, or great Denunciatory Address of the powers that be. Cease my dear mother and don't indulge in any more of those warlike demonstrations of shaking the Executive in their shoes, boxing their ears and making the poor devils tremble to their very toe nails. Mr. Davis I consider a good and a capable man and am willing to leave things in his charge, Mr. Benjamin is an able man, Mr. Mallory may have been injudicious, but we can't judge with certainty of things until we know all circumstances. So cease my dear Mother don't turn Rhettite[121] as I shan't, all that I can allow you to indulge in is the trumpet blast you speak of, in case though you can't get a trumpet, get a cow horn and get Da' Ephraim to fix so it will blow well and you can give a good blast on it—all day if you would like it, only Pa might be disturbed by it.

Seriously speaking though there have been a great many mistakes throughout the present war and the Executive although not free from blame are not to be blamed altogether, for my part I don't excuse the <u>Sovereign People</u> altogether.

---

121. Milton is referring to criticism of the Davis administration by Robert Barnwell Rhett Jr., editor of the *Charleston Mercury,* and his father, Robert Barnwell Rhett.

I haven't much to mention in this letter as Annie's contains the most information or news that I have acquired. One little episode in my military I have to
mention, one not altogether devoid of amusement and laughter although to the
actors in it at one time it had a serious aspect. The Capt. all along has been wishing to make some excursion against the Yankees especially on Beaufort Island, so
he got up one the other day to go over to the other side of the Ferry and burn
Mingo's house, destroy the flats and boats on that side, and if possible to capture
or kill the Yankee pickets stationed there. He picked out twenty men, men especially for that purpose, among the first of whom I was one, these were to proceed
in a boat from Mr Rhodes' place and were to make the attack, while two pieces of
our artillery with some infantry out of Izard's company[122] were to be stationed on
our side of the ferry and cover our retreat in case we should meet superior numbers. The boat had been at our place in the canal and I had been there with two
others all that day fixing it up, it was then to proceed from the bridge around to
Mr. Rhodes' and I was to go around on horseback. There was a cavalry company
stationed at Mr. Rhodes acting as pickets for that part of the country. When our
boat went around with seven or eight men in it, their pickets whom we thought
knew that we were coming by water fired off two barrels as an alarm. I was then
near Mr. Rhodes' gate and hearing the reports I galloped around up to the house
fearing that they had fired on our men and intending to prevent a repetition of it,
when I got there I found them (the cavalry company) in the greatest alarm crying
out the "Yankees are coming," the "Yankees are coming," "a boat load of Yankees
coming" and they were saddling up and hurrying out of the way as fast as possible and after hollooing after them for awhile got them to listen and to understand
that they were our men. The poor fellow who gave the alarm had run off leaving
canteen and biscuits right where they were, on the latter of which our men I
among them being rather hungry pounced. We slept there until one o'clock then
got in the boat and started on our expedition to the ferry.

Before we had proceeded far Ste told us his plans. We were to land between
Rest Park[123] and the Ferry causeway then go around and come down on the causeway so as to take the pickets prisoners, he was if necessary to talk negro lingo to
them and on the given signal to fire. The given signal was a sentence in which
General Stevens name was.[124] If this plan had been followed it might not have
been as hazardous as the one circumstances compelled us to take. The circum-

---

122. Capt. Allan C. Izard's Company I, Eleventh South Carolina Infantry, organized in early 1862
     from the disbanded companies of the Ninth South Carolina Volunteers that did not enlist
     for Confederate service after their one-year term of enlistment expired.
123. Archibald Hamilton Seabrook's plantation in St. Helena Parish.
124. Brig. Gen. Isaac I. Stevens commanded a Federal brigade in the Northern District, Depart-
     ment of the South, headquartered at Beaufort.

stances were these. Ste lost his exact route and instead of going right across towards the place where he intended landing, he found himself several hundred yards off in the river from Mingo's without his knowing and we received the command "Halt" from the Yankees without knowing that we were so near them. We were rather surprised but Ste immediately sung out "Mossa Mossa da me sir—da bring nigger ober" (and then we edged up our boat nearer as we were beyond the range of our double barreled guns while their guns could hit us) they saw us coming closer and cried out again "Halt," we halted and Ste commenced the palaver again, one of them asked "Are there any white people in that boat" with a clear Yankee twang, and evidently thinking he was talking to negroes, Ste answered No sir, da was all niggers, da bring ober bote man and ooman bote, and at the same time we edged closer Ste saying, Pull up da right han oar Jukkup, Jim you pull up da lef han oar now bote oars pull togedder. They saw we were coming closer and ordered us to "Halt" again, they then asked how many were in the boat. Ste told them "bout twelve sir" the sentinel seemed surprised at there being so few and evidently was counting us. We held down our heads so our faces couldn't be seen then he said "Hold on there," as if he intended asking his officer what was to be done with us. By this time we were within range having been edging up all the time, then Ste hollooed out to him "Mossa kin you tell me bout a wite man named General Stevens where he da;" at that signal our boat was a blaze of light and bang, bang, bang, from every part of the boat, my gun among the number, and the poor fellow uttered a cry, some say he cried out O God O God and then the fellows could be seen going it pell mell up the causeway and our fellows popping at them like deer. We didn't find any dead when we went ashore although from the cry we heard and the crowd of balls we threw among them no doubt is entertained of one or two being killed or perhaps all wounded. We put a pile of blades in Mingo's house and set it fire but unfortunately it didn't burn down; we also brought off the boats and flats tied there and carried them up near Periclear's and cut them up; that was the principal aim of the expedition. The cannon we also had playing on the head of the opposite causeway. Col Walker[125] who was in command carried the cannon off too soon so that we couldn't go up the causeway and find the dead or wounded men we suspected to have fallen on the causeway, he said that he was perfectly satisfied with what we had done. His first question was whether any of us was hurt. I never felt the slightest qualm at shooting at a man any more than if he was a post. The reason we didn't kill dead was that we used double barrelled guns with buckshot instead of balls so as to make sure of hitting. When we were palavering with the Yankees the degree of excitement was of the

---

125. Col. William S. Walker commanded the Third Military District of the Department of South Carolina and Georgia.

most intense kind because the slightest slip in this lingo would have sent several balls crossing through our boat and we were so thick a great many of us would have been killed. As far as I could judge there were about five of them and they being on land had the advantage of us.[126]

Do send me a blanket or two; if you have any calico to cover them over with do do it for me. I'm in a hurry and won't have time to put the quotation marks necessary for the lingo in here and beg you to do or consider it done.

Your aff^{ct} son

Milton M. Leverett

Let me know how everything is getting on, and love to all. Remember me to the Greggs.

Your aff<u>ct</u>. son

Milton M. Leverett

Whom do I owe letters to now? Tell them put in their claims as the stock on hand now is flush.

Anne Leverett DeSaussure to her brother Fred

Columbia, June 22nd [1862]

My dear Fred,

Your letter and check arrived safely on Saturday evening, we were right glad to hear from you and Lou perfectly delighted with her note, she made me read it again to her this morning, <u>every</u> <u>time</u> I leave the house to go in town, she begs me to bring 'Fedda' back, and on my return rushes out & asks immediately, if you had come & then calls me 'mean,' on finding I have not brought you too, it is strange how often she talks of you, & says I must tell you she eat some <u>squash</u>, she is a funny little thing, she took some rhubarb the other day, when she had finished, said right off, 'tell Fedda, have dinna.' I am so sorry you missed my letter for 'twas a long one telling about everything. I am so disgusted with the poultry, I don't know what to do, out of a hundred chickens, only thirty-seven left, it is too discouraging, five hens are setting now, but it seems useless, only 16 turkeys left, and eggs over 40^{cts} a <u>dozen</u>; everything is enormous, shanks are gone up a <u>dollar</u>; the Middletons told Pa they bought as little as possible at the market & that they

---

126. This expedition took place 6 June 1862, and Capt. Stephen Elliott Jr. described his conversation with the Federal pickets: "the pickets hailed us and I replied representing myself as one of a party of contrabands and getting up in this manner conversing with them and giving directions to the crew until we got within 50 yds . . . I <u>am</u> pleased at having taken a boat load of men up to a picket without being fired on." Elliott to his wife, Charlotte, 7 June 1862, Elliott Family Papers, South Caroliniana Library.

found it very hard to get on, we only send once a week—Pa bought a box of salt beef, cost $12.⁰⁰, 126 lbs, for the servants, they were very glad of it, they boil their hominy with it, it is so salt. Old Ephy's wages are raised to $12.00, Dr Gibbes wanted a jobbing carpenter for fences, Pa offered at the above mentioned price, he immediately said he would take him, & Ephy told the superintendent of the nitre works he was to leave & what wages he would have, so rather than lose him they raised the wages; he is to be paid on Monday, hope 'twill all come right. The field looks very well, in two places it is very hard to get a good stand of corn, Hercules thinks the rice splendid. I am afraid the heat will burn up the hill corn; the fodder peas is not ready for cutting; the horses are having no fodder. Tony cuts a little grass every evening, not much tho; it is fortunate the drive to town is short, or they could not stand it; we think Lewis uses them on Sundays while we are in church, sometimes they are covered with perspiration, when the evening is not at all hot & go so badly, it looks very suspicious, he has found some cousins up here formerly belonged to the Dunwoody's so I have no doubt he takes them riding, as it is done up here sometimes by coachmen. Sary has grown very impertinent since she has been up here, wish we had not brought Mauma. Hercules looks more contented than I have ever seen him, we could not get on without him.

Julie has a little fever, looks rather badly, green plum attack, I don't let Lou touch a plum, the little thing walks with me through the orchard, & never even asks for one, we have not had many plums tho', the negroes took their good share.

If you wish to be transferred why don't you write to Dr. Kinloch,[127] as it must be very disagreeable to you to be where you are and we don't like to think of it. How was it that you were disappointed about Jenkins' regiment, maybe your telegram was not received. The hospital here is very badly conducted, Aunt Til with Mrs DeVeau, Mrs Albert Rhett's sister go there every Friday, as the Doctors don't stay long & only see the patients, prescribe, & leave, don't pretend to see if they get nourishment, it was nearly 9 o'clock the first time Aunt Til went, the sick soldiers had not had a mouthful to eat, & they were so hungry, some told her they never got their medicine. Mʳ McKee is steward of the Hospital, & we are very glad of it.[128] Mʳˢ McKee & Eliza[129] make $40.⁰⁰ a month cutting bank bills, a good many

---

127. Surgeon R. A. Kinloch, medical director of the Department of South Carolina and Georgia.

128. The women of Columbia established a Soldiers' Hospital at the old State Fair Grounds in September 1861. The Confederate government took over the administration of the hospital in 1862, and by late June the hospital moved to the campus of South Carolina College. The hospital remained open until the end of the war even though the college closed.

129. Eliza Mathews Coffin (1843–1919), daughter of George Mathews Coffin. Her signature appears on five dollar bills dated 17 February 1864.

other refugees also,[130] amongst them, Gov. Wise's[131] brother's wife & daughters. We sent a letter of Cos. Maxcy's yesterday, he had a little brush with the enemy, he & McClellan are not far apart, he was going to try shooting at the balloon, they are going up every evening, this one had the United States flag, a bust of Gen. Jackson[132] & McClellan painted on it, he saw it through his telescope.[133] Minnie never mentioned a word about one single person in McPhersonville. We were sorry your letter came too late about the pockets you wished in your shirts. Julie is the only one sick, Scarlet fever at the Pringles.

Your affect. Sister.

We are making three homespun twilled drawers for Minnie. Charlie wrote to Julie, said Pa would have to send the negroes clothes, bacon & molasses, homespun is the only thing to be had, at 20^{cts} a yd. Bacon & molasses it is impossible to buy, they will have to go without. We have not given these any, they seem to understand it very well, for they have not asked for any clothes; what ought to be done.

We heard Mr Bull was mortally wounded, stabbed by someone, he was laughing at a particular company & a soldier present told him he belonged to it, & he should not speak so of it. Mr. Bull slapped him in the face, the other drew a knife & cut him up terribly, we don't know if it is true.

Milton Maxcy Leverett to his brother Fred

McPhersonville June 23rd /62

My dear Fred,

This is about the first opportunity I have had of writing since I have known positively that you were in Hardeeville. I would have written by Capt. Elliott but did not know until too late that he was going to H. I am very much obliged to you for the enamelled cloth you sent me as it was the very thing I was wishing for and trying to get. I suppose you have heard of our expedition to the other side of the ferry and being halted and Ste's deceiving them by talking negro lingo and at the

---

130. The Confederate Department of the Treasury created a Treasury Note Division to superintend the production of notes, and the office in Columbia was in charge of the printing and preparation, including cutting large sheets of bills into individual notes before they were sent to Richmond.

131. Henry A. Wise, governor of Virginia, 1856–1859.

132. Andrew Jackson.

133. One of Col. Thaddeus S. C. Lowe's seven observation balloons (the *Intrepid* and the *Constitution* were the best known) which operated with the Federal Army of the Potomac during the Seven Days' Campaign in late June to early July 1862.

given signal our pouring in a volley. We had double barrelled guns loaded with buckshot and we were very much surprised not to see any dead on the ground when we landed but the distance may have been greater than we think and buckshot is much more easily carried off than ball. I think though that one at least if not two were killed and dropped higher up the causeway as one man uttered a cry when we fired and we picked up a straw hat with a buckshot hole through it. We captured two nice oilcloths, a blanket, some pots, a box of nice pilot biscuits,—much better than ours—some pots, a musket and a straw hat.

Since then we have been on another excursion and killed one Yankee (certain this time as the fellows took him up to bring him off but left him), and scared the others. I was in the artillery part of this excursion to cover the retreat, if necessary. In the other, I was in the boat part of the expedition and had a shot but can't say whether I hit or not.

Have you got Sancho back for when I left Hardeeville I left him there apparently with no one. You ought to teach him to follow none but yourself. I am sorry you are having such a dull time with those Yahoo officers. There is nothing of any interest transpiring here at present, the old village is the same and its few inhabitants, none of whom I have visited yet except at Capt. G. Elliott's. Mrs. Hutson, Miss Ann Jenkins, Miss Grimke, and Mr Wm. Heyward all have been polite in their offers of assistance to me in anything. I shall pay them each a visit.

Your affct brother

Milton M. Leverett

Mary Maxcy Leverett to her son Milton

The Farm June 24th, 1862

My dear Milton

As soon as we received your two letters which were very interesting to us, I went to Town and bought some Graniteville cloth[134] for your drawers, and will probably send a parcel containing them tomorrow or the day after. I would have made your drawers out of the same excellent strong white cloth that I bought for Fred's if your letters had come a little earlier, but when I went back to Kerrison's[135] to get it, every particle was gone & no more expected so I had to get this which was only five cts. less (40 cts. per yard.) Every thing is enormously dear. The fancy shirts I thought of making, the girls advise me to put off until near the fall, as they

---

134. Cotton cloth produced at William Gregg's textile mill at Graniteville in Aiken District.

135. Edwin Lane Kerrison of Columbia, a lawyer, operated a warehouse that furnished clothing and other necessities to South Carolina Confederates through the Central Committee for Soldiers' Relief.

would be too warm now being lined inside with white cloth and being worsted also, but if you think the contrary, I will make up two now & send in another parcel. I feel very sorry not to make up some eatables to send to you and Fred, the necessaries of life are now so high (much higher than when you were here) as to put it out of the question for even rich people to indulge in what they are commonly accustomed to. Eggs are 35 to 45 cts. dozen, sugar the <u>cheapest</u> 30 cts., flour 12 $ a bushel & every thing in proportion. Mrs. Oliver Middleton, & her two daughters Mrs. Reid (Mary) and Matilda (Susan) came to see us yesterday evening.[136] She kissed me really affectionately, and I was more glad to see them than any body else in all Columbia, except of course my own relatives. They asked after each of the family and mentioned that Jack Middleton had told them something about you being so brave and gallant.[137] You really seem to have made yourself known very extensively. They have lost a great deal, in fact everything, as all their Edisto furniture & even a bale of cotton bagging (<u>which cost $700.</u>) had been taken to Charleston to save from the Yankees, & all was burnt, family pictures & every thing except the silver. She says she walking out of their burning house at 4 o'clock in the morning with literally nothing but her spectacles in her hand and added smiling, "and even that was without its case." Only think Mr. J<u>no</u> Izard Middleton (Jack's father) lost everything also in their house & what they valued most of all "<u>family pictures</u>," they said which can never be replaced for one was a full length picture Jack M's mother when young painted by the great painter Washington Allston (who is dead) & another painted by the celebrated Sully (also dead) as well as many others.[138] Such things can never be replaced. The Izard Middleton's lost also, as you saw by the papers, at their plantation Santee, their rice mill worth twenty-five thousand dollars, as well as all their rice which he was busy getting out to send up to Darlington, where he had sent his family & negroes; he was getting out the rice to send up to feed the negroes as they find it impossible to get corn. The people in this up country are behaving too bad shamefully, I think,—they are asking $1.50 cts a bushel for corn & some are keeping it back hoping to get $2. I hope they'll be disappointed. Mrs. Middleton said Helen Middleton & her sister had to go thro' most dreadful difficulties and hardships in escaping from the Yankees. May the Lord reward these men according to their doings!—Poor Charley Hutson! Jim Fowles writes word that the last that was seen of him he was lying on his back, within a short distance of the enemy battery, with a

---

136. Susan Matilda Harriet Chisolm Middleton of Charleston and her daughters Mary Julia Middleton Read (1828–1904) and Susan Matilda Middleton (1830–1880).

137. 1st Lt. John Izard Middleton Jr. of Brig. Gen. Thomas F. Drayton's staff.

138. Washington Allston (1779–1843), native South Carolinian, and Thomas Sully (1783–1872), American painters.

dreadful wound.[139] So they think he is dead, poor fellow! I am so sorry for his parents and the old Captain! Oh, that the Lord would stretch out his mighty arm and deliver us from these cruel enemies! We are being sorely put it now. I think the Lord is permitting many things to happen to us because of the wickedness of our own soldiers.—Julia had a letter from Charley not long ago; I was very glad to find how honourably he had been made Commissary,—that is it was pressed upon him by the Captain & his men, and he agreed to it on one or two conditions, the honorable one was that he was to be permitted to go on every expedition and be in every fight. I doubt if another Commissary in our army has had the spirit of honour sufficiently alive in him, to do thus.—Julie is sick in bed with fever—We think it likely to have been caused by eating half green plums, as she has been every day in the orchard as well as Carrie, and says herself, that she was more fond of the half ripe ones. The little negroes were so constantly in the plum orchard that the fact is the plums of which were not as numerous as usual and had very little chance of becoming fully ripe; she probably would not have wanted the half ripe, if she could have got enough of the fully ripe ones, & I did not know until she had fever that she had eaten half ripe ones. However she has no pain in the stomach at all, & therefore it was not overeating that has made her sick. I gave her castor oil at first, & then next day as she still had fever gave her a blue pill at night & then next morning a tea spoonful of oil & have been writing this in her room. She sends the enclosed note.

Mrs. Pringle is sick with dysentery & Clara her little girl with scarlet fever.[140] Your Aunt Til has sent her children to board next door, except Tilly, to keep them from it. I think many people are now made sick by the bad diet they live on—every body is living hard. Mrs Middleton says they seldom venture to send to market, & would only be too thankful to get vegetables. I sent a nice basket of them (they have no garden to the house they hire. We are having a plenty of Irish potatoes & snap beans & some squashes also, & Annie & I feel fully rewarded for our hard work.

Willie Heyward is up here sick with fever,—had a relapse—I had an affecting letter from Mrs. Gregorie, she says they feel so gloomy & lonesome. Do go and see them, for she mentions she saw you at church, looking well, but that you had not been to see them. Do go for my sake.

I was glad (all of us were) at your being in that expedition to the Ferry, & think it was a very critical & well managed affair. Now would be a capital time to contrive attacks on the forces over there, for I've no doubt all nearly have gone to James Island, & no doubt the naval force also. If no more than one Gunboat was

---

139. Pvt. Charles Woodward Hutson of Company A, Hampton Legion (Infantry), wounded and captured at Seven Pines (Fair Oaks), Virginia, 31 May 1862.

140. Jane Edwards Ford Pringle, wife of Rev. James Maxwell Pringle, and her daughter Clara Alexandria.

left in Beaufort (which is possible, I think) I should think our Military men could arrange to make an attack by boarding at night, while a land force attacked those on land & also those negroes who may have taken up arms. I heard thro' the Middleton's that another expedition was on foot but had not succeeded. Ella Middleton's husband, Capt. Rutledge,[141] being of the number is the way they knew, Ste Elliott's company was to be a part, they said.

We were very much interested in your two letters. What is the reason you never mention any of the Artillery? We know them all & you ought to mention something of each of them now & then. Ask James Stuart if he could not make a slight sketch of the Bay Point battle, so as to show what an imposing number of vessels came against our small forts,—an outline sketch merely would do.[142] Let him put a price on it too, as a mans talents are his capital. If he were to paint a picture of it when the war is over I think Pa would buy it. Your father is making a very interesting & excellent book of his "Sketches of the War," I think, & will go to England as soon as the port of Charleston is opened, which I hope will be not long hence.—Maxcy Gregg has been put right opposite McLellan's headquarters. Your Aunt Cornelia read me quite an interesting letter from him the other day. He had just opened a battery of two guns of long range on them that day (23d I believe) one of the guns was "Long Tom," taken at the battle of Manasses,[143] & he put them on an elevated position, overlooking McLellan's quarters, a mile & a half between the two parties, the Chickahominy flowing between; he scattered the Yankees in every direction, a perfect stampede taking place among soldiers, wagons, ambulances &c. A balloon had been sent up by the Yankees the day before, with the American Eagle & old Gen A. Jacksons bust painted on it (Maxcy saw it plainly thro' his telescope) & he has ordered his men to keep a look out & if it is again visible, he means to try "Long Tom's" powers on it.

Thursday June 26th. I sent for Dr Fair to Julie on the fourth day of her fever, not feeling easy about her.[144] He said give nothing but sweet spirits nitre, a little soda, benne leaves in the water she drinks & mild diet, her tongue looking red. Followed his advice & think & hope she is better; today being the sixth day & fever still

---

141. Capt. Benjamin Huger Rutledge of the Charleston Light Dragoons, an independent cavalry company that became Company K of the Fourth South Carolina Cavalry in December 1862.

142. A pen-and-ink sketch depicting the Beaufort Artillery flying a flag bearing the initials B.V.A. and firing at ships from Fort Beauregard on Bay Point during the battle of 7 November 1861. Perhaps drawn by James Reeve Stuart, this sketch is among the Leverett papers and is reproduced in the illustrations.

143. A 30–pounder Parrott rifle captured by the Confederates at First Manassas (Bull Run), 21 July 1861.

144. Dr. Samuel Fair of Columbia, chief surgeon at the Soldiers' Hospital in 1861–62.

there I sent again for him & he says she is threatened with typhoid fever & continued the same prescriptions. But he is so careless in his talk, he mentioned some girl just Julie's age, he said & like her, & she died of the same disease &c. Of course, it scared Julie so, that she had a long cry after he was gone, & of course it has been no benefit to her. She seemed much better (having had an excellent night's rest) when he <u>came</u>, but since that looks distressed & dull, tho not nervous as I feared she would be. Send this letter to Fred—I wish he could get a furlough & come up. He said he had not heard from you since you went to McPhersonville.—Is it possible?

Your affte Mother

Mary Leverett

P.S. Julie having taken up my attention & time, your parcel cannot go until tomorrow, 27th u[ltimo].

P.S.[145] Tilly and I rode this evening & saw the Greggs. It is said that Cousin Maxcy has the finest brigade in the army.[146] He is in the centre now of the Grand Army just where he wanted to be. Long Tom had silenced six guns, unluckily the balloon did not go up near enough after Long Tom was mounted.

Gov. Pickens received a dispatch yesterday saying "The crisis is at hand, there is no doubt but we will get the victory." Jackson was to have attacked them in the rear yesterday morning at day light, but there was some detention & the battle did not commence until 3 o'clock—it lasted until 5, we having the better of them, it recommenced this morning, of course Aunt Cornelia is feeling very badly Cousin Maxcy being in the midst of the fighting. Jim wrote word that the last that was seen of Charley H. was he was lying flat on the ground ten yards from before a battery. I am so sorry for his poor mother. What is the reason you don't mention anybody in the pinelands. Mrs. G. in her letter said you had not been to see her. Is Helen B. & the Elliotts still there if so do give my love to Helen. We send two pair of stockings. I knit one pair & one foot, finding we would not have time to finish 3 pairs, Annie finished the foot she was knitting & put it with mine. I hope they will last until I knit some more. Mrs. A. Haskell died yesterday, leaving a baby a week old.[147]

You did not say if you had received the long letter from your aff<u>cte</u> sister Mary.

---

145. A postscript written crosswise at the top of the letter by Milton's sister Mary.

146. Gregg's brigade consisted of the First South Carolina Infantry (Gregg's), First (Orr's) South Carolina Rifles, and the Twelfth, Thirteenth, and Fourteenth South Carolina Infantry.

147. Rebecca Singleton Haskell of Abbeville died in Columbia 26 June 1862; her daughter, Rebecca Singleton Haskell, was born 20 June.

Rev. Charles Edward Leverett to his son Milton

Sat. morng. 29th June [1862]

My dear Miny

I write a line as this is the last day of cheap postage. After this you will only hear and I suppose write occasionally perhaps once a fortnight. All is still here. We have just heard that a victory has been had over the Yankees but know nothing about it.[148] I am going into town directly. Julia has been & is still sick with fever; she is better to day. Dr Fair has been here twice to see her. Lewis is sick with dysentery from drinking ditch water like a goose. We had a splendid rain yesterday, which was greatly needed for the crops. The fodder peas, I think can be cut by the middle of next week for the horses & I hope will supply them till blades come in. The corn looks pretty well. Ephraim is hiring at the Salt-petre works & I would hire two or three hands at 9 or $10 a month if I had them here. I could also hire some women at the hospital as nurses I suppose as I see an advertisement for them. Eph^m this month gets $13. Every thing is gone up flour is at $16. Sugar is so dear that I don't use it at all. We live very poorly. We get Irish potatoes out of our garden & shall soon have corn & by & by okra and tomatos &c. I myself am very busy writing my history. I have a volume & a half done & your mother likes it. I shall if the blockade is raised go to England (D. V.)[149] at once. Your mother so advises. Fred's box came yesterday & yr letter to him in it. Can't Ste. Elliott go to Beaufort, & rout those negros out of our houses? I should think there could not be a large force of Yankees stationed there. I hear they are withdrawing troops from James Island to send to Richmond. Pemberton is very unpopular I hear. I dare say very justly. I never liked him from the first time I saw him. Draw me a sketch if you can of the Port Royal fight &c. I wish to get some cuts for my book. I shall if published, probably not put my name to it. Give my love to Fred when you write. I hope you may be protected in all dangers. Put your trust in God & don't forget him amid the turmoil of the camp.

yr. aff. father

Milton Maxcy Leverett to his mother

McPhersonville July 5th 1862

My dear mother,

I expect to send Billy up to Columbia on Monday next by Express and not knowing whether he can be delivered at the farm wish Pa would be on the look-

---

148. On 27 June 1862, in the second major battle of the Seven Days', or Peninsular, Campaign, elements of Lee's Army of Northern Virginia defeated elements of McClellan's Army of the Potomac at Gaines' Mill, near Richmond.

149. *Deo volente* (God willing).

out for him. I will telegraph to you when I send him that you may be on the look-out for him. The reason I send him is that he bothers me very much going off to see his wife; not satisfied with once a week he dodges off every possible chance he can get and when I do let him go which is every Saturday evening, to return on Monday morning, he stays until Tuesday midday and not withstanding my punishing him and absolutely forbidding him to go he still persists in it. My determination was at last fixed in sending him from his staying a day over the time allowed him and my punishing him (although to be sure not very severely) and forbidding his going off for a certain time and then just after going to bed that very night my being called up to a boy of mine that was taken by the pickets near Pocotaligo. I didn't know who it could be thought perhaps it was Carolina but on going out found it was my precious boy Billy with a bag of grist, flour, and some biscuits going off to see his wife and expecting to be back in the morning. Didn't do anything more to him than just tie him give him a blanket and put him under the care of the sentinel until morning then let him go thinking that perhaps that would be admonition enough to him as he appeared quite scared. But on Friday (he had been taken up on Wednesday night) the Fourth we all went off on an expedition to the Ferry and Pages Point to burn Mingo's house, and fire at the enemy's pickets there and at Rest Park, and thus to celebrate that day, we carried one boy as far as the Corner to wait on us and left the other (Billy) with positive orders to remain at camp and take care of things until we returned and by no means to leave, and even told him that even if he did go to Sheldon as we were down that part of the country we would be able to find out whether he was there or not. Notwithstanding all of that, as we were returning that day just about night fall, we saw Dr. Fuller's cart with several persons in it and as I thought I saw a figure stretched out in the bottom looking like Billy's I immediately halted my cannon jumped off and ran to the cart and ordered my precious valet out who was lying on his face among the other negroes hoping that he might pass unrecognized. I made him trot by my horses to Pineland and then let him go; if he doesn't leave before Monday I will send him then. His idea isn't to run off to Beaufort as he can't do that unaided, he hasn't head enough, can't paddle a boat and would be very apt to be shot by the pickets, but it is simply infatuation after his wife. I think his conduct is somewhat redeemable and may be palliated on that score somewhat, but I can't keep him here he is too great nuisance to me whereas he might be a great convenience. I wish Pa would hire him out and let me have the wages to hire another boy, if one could be hired up there and sent down to me. I would prefer it as I need one very much, although I would rather do without one than keep Billy. Do write and let me know as soon as possible after receiving him (if you do). So far for Billy.

We could hear the Yankees celebrating the Fourth in Beaufort beating their drums and firing a salute. We succeeded in burning Mingo's house and running off the enemy's pickets both at the Ferry and at Rest Park. Just after we got out of ammunition a part of the Yankee artillery came down to engage our first section but we couldn't of course; the section on which I was went to Pages Point. From Pages Point there appeared to be a first rate crop of corn at Rest Point. Can't write anymore as I am in a great hurry.

Your aff<u>ct</u> son
Milton M. Leverett

Milton Maxcy Leverett to his father

McPhersonville July 8th /62

My dear father,

I am writing rather oftener lately than I had intended but it has been on account of Billy. I shant send him as yet for a week perhaps, or perhaps not at all, as I have punished him and if he behaves better there will be no use to send him at all, at any rate I shall telegraph on to let you know first. You could though find out if it is not inconvenient whether he could be hired to any advantage, and whether there may be any boy whom I might hire in his place, as I can't say as yet what will be his future conduct. I don't think I could hire a boy down here under $13.00 per month.

The Yankees took a few shot with their artillery at ours the other day (the 4th of July) but as ours had shot out their ammunition before the enemy battery had arrived they had to leave. We succeeded in burning Mingo's house inside of which the Yankees had dug a pit and knocked down the upper half of the chimney so as to be able to fire at our men the better. I was in the party that went to Pages Point. Tell ma the bundle came safely and am much obliged for the drawers, the cloth is plenty good enough and quite strong. Tell her never mind for the fancy shirts as yet and don't worry herself about eatables for me as I am well aware what is the condition of things the blockade has forced on us. They have stopped giving us sugar now I believe. Charley Hutson is a prisoner and none of the others were injured [in] the late battles.

I hope Julie is better now. I went to see Mrs. Gregorie as Ma requests, she seemed quite low spirited, saw Miss G. and Mr. Wm Heyward there also. I had been round to see them but they were not at home; I expect to go again. I see them driving about the pinelands, & by our camp very often, once they passed right by our eating shed made out of pine boughs and called to me to give me some peaches they had with them. I was rigged out in a loose red flannel shirt, a leather belt round my waist and hat way back on my head and looked altogether beautiful, but I don't mind those kind of things now at all. All the week I look like a jockey but on Sundays like a gentleman; so different that some of our men "had to look twice to see if it was the same fellow." The fact is to have to attend to horses and harness, to grease to the latter clean the former and hitch them up at any time, water three times a day, feed ditto, it is impossible to look neatly, so on Sundays I reward myself with dressing neatly and going to church, and hearing Mr Axson preach when he was here, but as he has left now, Mr Norton a Baptist minister in our company preaches in the church every morning.[150]

As to our expedition "not having succeeded," it is not so, it succeeded in a great measure although not entirely. I think the "Charleston Dragoons" are not willing to allow that our expeditions succeed through jealousy and because it increases the <u>danger of their picket duty</u> down at the ferry. And as regards our company "<u>taking a part</u>" in the expedition, it took the lead, it (the expedition) emanated from our company and <u>no other company</u> had a share in it but a portion of Izard's which being an infantry company is attached to ours to protect the guns and even when the firing commenced they turned round and went back to the shore. The Charleston Dragoons didn't have a man in the expedition.

Ma asks the reason why I never mention any of the company. I suppose the reason must be because I am in daily contact with them and unless anything remarkable happens dont think of them. Campbell Gibbes was wounded in the side fortunately I believe not seriously, got shot while he was laying down.[151] So Jim or Newton or Pinckney informed? I am much obliged to Mame and Anne for the stockings as I was in need of them. Tell Mame and Anne, Helen Barnwell has gone to Roswell Georgia.

I am delighted at the succession of victories that are taking place and think that it's only the beginning of the end, I don't think the end will be as yet. Some how or other I think there will be a heavy battle in S. Carolina before the war is closed or that I will be in one. Our place is the post that all the mounted companies use as their headquarters when they go on picket duty. I wont be able to write in a hurry again as I am now about out of paper and haven't been paid up yet and having no stamps is why I am obliged to put on it Soldiers letter.

Your aff<u>ct</u> son Milton M. Leverett

All the low country below the railroad is one scene of desolation, only one or two places being now occupied. Going about the different plantations you see poor cats half starved and mewing after you so glad to see any human being; dogs you see here and there starting life on their responsibility, risking their all through starvation and drawing on the woods for rabbits etc. and as a finale at night time are

---

150. Pvt. R. W. Norton of the Beaufort Artillery.
151. Pvt. John Barnwell Campbell Gibbes of the Washington Light Infantry, Company A, Twenty-fifth South Carolina Infantry, wounded at Secessionville on James Island, 16 June 1862.

heard howling their sad solemn requiem over the ashes of the old homesteads and the <u>spirits</u> of their <u>departed</u> <u>masters</u>. Columbus I have not seen at all, would not be surprised if he started life on <u>his</u> <u>own</u> responsibility but <u>failed</u>. Alice I suppose ditto. Terror more wisely is loafing on his friends at Dr. H. Fuller's being a refugee with not a rag to his back and feeling I suppose doubtful of supplying himself.

I think more notice ought to have been taken of Mattie Cornish than was. Remember me to all the Greggs, love to Aunt Til. How is Willie Heyward?

July 9th

I went to see Ferguson Hutson's[152] family yesterday evening and also Mrs J. White Gregorie. In the course of conversation the latter said she had been told that the Yankees had sent word to you that your property should not be injured; O heu mores! when will this lying world be content with its own affairs and speak the truth. People must be in a horrible state who lie so unconscionably. I hooted at it and told her there was not a word of truth in it. She added that the person who told her said it must be a mistake as you were one of the hottest secessionists about. You had been told your property would not be injured by some near relatives that you had in the Yankee army. It needn't worry you as your character as a secessionist and a fighting man are too well known.

Caroline Pinckney Leverett to her brother, probably Milton

Columbia July [1862]

Dear Brother

I hope you are well and I hope to see you soon. Deanna has a fine calf It is fortnite old. I thank you for your story pa is going to fix it down in his reading book. the cat had kittens and some thing eat them up. One day I went to town to spend the day with Aunt Till Mr. [illegible] tried to kiss me but I jumped down the steps [illegible] he catch so got away

Your [illegible] sister

Mary Maxcy Leverett to her son Milton

The Farm Columbia
Sunday evening July [1862]

My dear Milton

As Mr. Shand[153] is to go down tomorrow to Pocotaligo, I thought it so direct an opportunity, I would write, hoping he may see you. Your father is to preach for

---

152. William Ferguson Hutson.
153. Rev. Peter Johnson Shand, rector of Trinity Episcopal Church in Columbia.

him next Sunday. The Bishop is here & held Confirmation today (Sunday) at both churches.[154] Mary & Susy Heyward were confirmed at Mr. Pringle's[155] & Cornelia Gregg at Mr. Shand's church. I feel uneasy all the time about you. The other blanket I intended sending you had to be washed before it was lined with Calico, & unluckily the washer did not get it done in time for me to get ready yesterday, so I will either send it by Express if you say so, or wait for another opportunity. The Greggs are in the greatest uneasiness & excitement of feeling about Maxcy—he is in the thickest of the fight every where balls falling all around him, a spent ball struck him on his knee, only hurting him slightly, another struck right at his feet dashing up the sand & dirt over his face & a third (a shell) fell near by without bursting, providentially. This is the last they heard & are dreadfully uneasy, because he has for sometime past written during all the first days of the battle, telegraphed them every day, but now they have not heard for several days. But I think it is only because they are getting too far off from Richmond in their pursuit of the foe. Our men have behaved grandly, nobly. Such bravery is wonderful. We hear all the dispatches, public & private, the girls or your father go in every day, & Gov. Pickens gets dispatches up to 10 or 11 o clock at night. Surely a Mighty God is fighting for us & blessing us & causing us to prevail. Let us give Him the glory. I had a letter from Caroline Seabrook, the Capt. of Pinck's Company[156] has prayers in his tent every day. O that all Captains were like him!

Did you get the parcel I sent you?—Your father attended Mr G. Coffin's funeral yesterday—the body was afterwards carried on to Charleston. He went on to nurse his son who was wounded.[157] We are so sorry he was such a good man. You will be glad to hear Julie is well again after ten days sickness—indeed it may have been <u>fifteen</u> days, for she was complaining several days before she took to her bed. She looks quite pale & has lost flesh, but her appetite is beginning to revive & I hope she will soon look like herself again. Annie complains of vertigo very often & nausea too. I wish Fred could prescribe for her, does not look badly, except her complexion rather dark.—No time for more.

Your Aff^{te} Mother
Mary Leverett

---

154. Rt. Rev. Thomas F. Davis.
155. Rev. James Maxwell Pringle, rector of Christ Episcopal Church, Columbia.
156. Capt. William Thomson Haskell of Company H, First South Carolina Infantry (Gregg's).
157. George Mathews Coffin became ill while bringing his wounded son home. His son Pvt. Ebenezer Coffin of the Washington Light Infantry, Company A, Hampton Legion Infantry, was wounded at Seven Pines, Virginia, 31 May 1862.

Milton Maxcy Leverett to his mother

McPhersonville
July 24<u>th</u> /62

My dear mother,

I received your letter several days ago when I was on my way down to Poco-taligo in a wagon <u>for a load of marsh for the horses</u>; the blanket also came the same day for which I am much obliged, it looks quite nicely. Your letter seemed to intimate great fear as regards Fred's health, you needn't worry yourself as I saw him a short time before your letter came, on the occasion of an alarm when his regiment was ordered to Pocotaligo, he was then perfectly well and has received all the letters written as I believe I have them now, he having sent them to me. I suppose you know Burnett the assistant surgeon got out of the regiment into a cavalry squadron which he dislikes very much and intends getting out of that. Poor Fred is quite lonesome and solitary, he has been up here twice to see me. His pres-ent assistant surgeon I don't believe bids fair to be as pleasant as Burnett. I didn't know until yesterday Evans had been ordered to Virginia, I suppose Charlie must have gone with him although I don't know, I conclude so though from Fred's hav-ing gone on to Greenpond the other day, which I afterwards heard of.

Billy has behaved very well latterly, that is has not troubled me about going continually to see his wife, his usual dilatoriness exists still of course, that I bear beautifully as patient as Job and almost as meek as Moses. I have paid several vis-its to persons about here since I have been living here, one was to Miss Grimke and Mr. W<u>m</u> Heyward, there I found Mr. D. Heyward who was quite affable, they expected me and had after the regular supper a fruit supper at neither of which did I pretend to do my self justice whereas if I had just had it laid on my table in camp I would have "<u>knocked</u> it cold." One of the best times I have had was tak-ing breakfast one morning with Mrs. John White Gregorie. I was watering my horses at the branch on the way to the Swamp leading one and riding the other when on returning I met her riding out to carry the cooking house key to Miss Ann Jenkins whom and Sarah I had just passed on the road coming for it, I bowed and told her that I would rather ride with her than water my horses, she says, "come on then let's take a ride" I gave my other horse to Caesar who was following and we took a short ride, she then says "Minny I have a first rate breakfast this morn-ing come over and breakfast with me," says I, "all right but I look very shabby" and indeed you could hardly have found a more thorough looking knight of the cur-rycomb than your <u>excellent son</u> at that time, she says, "Oh it don't matter—you can basin and water there" so when I went she brought a basin, towel, soap, brush and comb and a big looking-glass (one of a such a calibre I hadn't seen for many a day), well, there I performed my morning ablutions, and soon as breakfast was ready went in and sat down at the head of the table, and presided with all the dignity of a gentleman, and eat the very nice breakfast with all the gusto of a soldier who didn't see a good one very often. My costume was a blue check shirt, rolled up at the sleeves when we met, rolled down afterwards, blue Denham pants, hat fixed on jauntily and no cravat, altogether my <u>tout ensemble</u> was diabolical for a gentleman but beautiful for a cannon driver or horse boy. Miss Grimke sent me a nice basket of vegetables and three watermelons on Saturday and on Sunday Mr Wm H. drove by and left me another basket of them and a nice leg and loin of mutton. I had so many vegetables that I sent them around to a great many messes.

I am very glad and thankful Julie has got well, and will write to her by and bye. Do follow out Dr Fair's prescription for Katie, persevere.

Your aff<u>ct</u> son
M. M. Leverett

Frederic Percival Leverett to his brother Milton

Camp Jackson,
Hardeeville,
25th July 1862

My dear Minny,

I have not heard a word from home since the letters I sent you by Mr. Porteous. I have been thinking for sometime of getting a furlough—sick one, having not been very well of late, and going to Columbia for a week, but have now given up the idea, being somewhat better. On Monday however, I am going to Charleston, D. V. to return the next day, in order to make some purchases. If you can get off, you had better join me, & go down; if not & you wish to send for anything meet me at the depot, only writing down on a piece of paper before hand what you want, in case you do not have time to tell me.

I suppose Charley is off for Virginia. I have heard first one account & then another. Mr. Graham who came down from Yorkville night before last, says the Rebel Troop[158] was in Columbia in route for Va. when he passed—that Evans carried them in spite of Pemberton. Drayton is gone and a splendid brigade he will have. I hope he will be able to wipe out Port Royal. It is much more disagreeable for me here, since Drayton & his staff have left. They have promised to do all in their power to get me away from here. Drayton has been very kind indeed to me,

---

158. An independent company of South Carolina cavalry raised in Charleston District and commanded by Capt. John Jenkins; later Company F, Third South Carolina Cavalry.

& expressed just before leaving his regrets at my being obliged to stay. Were a Staff surgeon allowed him, he would have taken me. He knows the Surgeon Gen. well & will try to get him to remove me.[159]

The way in which matters are conducted here now is really a farce on the Military. I hope Walker will be up here soon & try to straighten up matters. Brig. Gen. Col. E. is a failure.[160]

I went down to Adams Run last Sunday & returned the same day. I wanted to see Charley before he went on to Va. but he was off on a furlough.

Ever yr. aff<u>ct</u> brother,
F. P. Leverett.

Caroline Pinckney Leverett to her brother, probably Milton

Columba July 30 1862

Dear Brother

I hope you are well and I hope to see you soon. You asked me if Sister ever gave me any popping no no she does not she has not given one since I have been learning French. Kate says I must give her love to you. Watermellons are in. We got two small ones out of the garden hurry and come in town they are five and ten the smallest is one dollar acording to their size they are very scarse. Ma says that she intends to send a box of Irish potatoes and a misquitonet on the 29 of july which was yesterday but that she felt so sure that you were coming that she did not. I hope you don't come out bareheaded in the hot sumer. Cant write any more.

I hope to see you soon.

Your
affectionate sister
Carrie

---

159. Confederate Surgeon General Samuel Preston Moore.
160. Nathan G. Evans.

The ruins of Sheldon Church in 1997.
From a pencil drawing by John Taylor Matthews.

Fort Sumter after the Civil War.
From a watercolor by Matilda Leverett.

The interior of the South Carolina College Library
(now the South Caroliniana Library).
From a watercolor by Matilda Leverett.

A gun at Fort Beauregard.
From a sketch by either James Reeves Stuart or Milton Maxcy Leverett.

Milton Maxcy Leverett at his twentieth
college class reunion.

Rev. Charles Edward Leverett.

Mary Maxcy Leverett.

Mary Bull Leverett, age eighteen.

Caroline Pinckney Leverett
Adams.

Anne Heyward Leverett DeSaussure.

Charles Edward Leverett Jr., age fourteen.

Frederic Percival Leverett.

Charles Hendee Leverett.

State of South Carolina

Know all men by these presents that I, Mary M. Webb, executrix of the last will and testament of Benjamin C. Webb, under and by virtue of the power and authority to me given in and by the said last will and testament and in consideration of the sum of nine hundred and fifty dollars to me in hand paid by Charles E. Leverett, at and before the sealing and delivery of these presents (the receipt whereof is hereby acknowledged), have bargained and sold, and by these presents do bargain, sell and deliver to the said Charles E. Leverett a certain negro slave named Hercules, to have and to hold the said negro slave Hercules unto the said Charles E. Leverett, his executors, administrators and assigns, to his and their only proper use and behoof forever.

In testimony whereof I have hereunto set my hand and seal this eighteenth day of February in the year eighteen hundred and fifty-six, and in the eightieth year of the Independence of the United States of America

Signed, sealed and delivered
in the presence of
Wm. Cursell

Mary M. Webb

Bill of sale for Hercules, a slave.

The Leverett House at 1301 Bay Street in Beaufort.

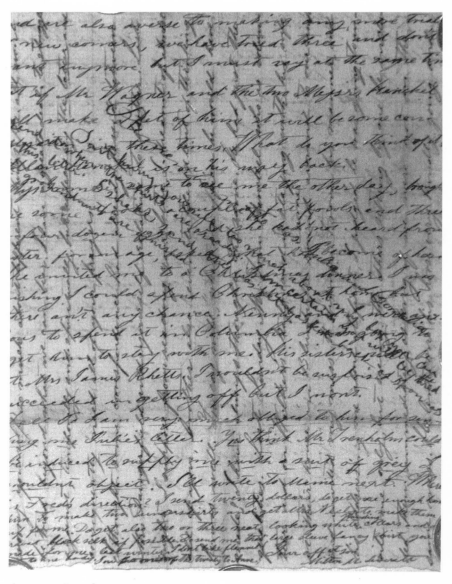

A cross-written letter.

4

Sons on Two Fronts

August 1862–August 1863

> I am keeping passably well, though still
> far from being really so. Camp fare
> is not benefiting me.
>
> —Frederic Percival Leverett

During this period Milton remained near McPhersonville with the Beaufort Artillery, but Fred was transferred out of the Eleventh South Carolina Infantry and away from the South Carolina lowcountry for service in Virginia. Special Orders No. 177, issued July 1862 by the Adjutant and Inspector General's Office, Confederate States Army, in Richmond, read: "Surgeon F.P. Leverett is relieved from duty with the 11th Regiment South Carolina Volunteers, and will report to the Surgeon General in this city."[1] Fred examined conscripts in the Twelfth Congressional District of Virginia until the spring of 1863.

Frederic Percival Leverett to his brother Milton

Hardeeville, S.C. 5th Aug. 1862

My dear Minny,

I was notified yesterday that orders have been sent from Richmond for me to report forthwith in Va. to Gen. Drayton, but that I was not to say to whom I was to go. Cannot you come up this evening or at any rate tomorrow & to spend the night with me before I go. I wish to see you.

---

1. Compiled Service Record of Surgeon Frederic Percival Leverett.

All were well in Columbia last week. I brought a basket for you & left it with Miller at Pocotaligo.

I intend going by way of Columbia & stopping a day.

In haste, ever yr aff^{ct}

brother,

F. P. Leverett

Milton Maxcy Leverett to his sister Mary

McPhersonville Aug. 8th /62

My dear Mary,

I am much obliged to you for the basket of peaches, and to all the rest for the different things sent in the <u>basket</u>. I have sent back a few things in the basket which I wish you would have put in my trunk. The pants being severely wounded in the seat has received an indefinite furlough or rather a dismissal from the army, the coat has received a furlough to stay at home until needed, the boots and shoes Pa may take if he wishes, they are of no use to me and are of strong English make, the books put also in my trunk with the leathers etc. that I have sent; letters of mine will be found in the leg to one of the boots put those also in my trunk.

I am much obliged to Anne and yourself for the stockings and wish you would make them a little longer in the toes and calves. I wish if you send any bundle down to me again you would include a white pants my longest and best. The handkerchiefs that came were very unique, but not exactly the kind that I wished, which were a couple or so of large white ones. I wish if you can that you would purchase some letters for my cap (B.V.A.);[2] perhaps they may be obtained from the bookstores.

We have three Yankee prisoners in McPhersonville; they were taken some where near Pinckney Island by the pickets down there and were sent here to Col. Walker, they were out fishing and came too close the shore, when they were ordered in. They say that they are sick of the war that they came to see Dixie and had seen enough of it, that they were fighting for the <u>damned</u> Union &^c &^c &^c.[3]

I wish you would sew some shirt buttons together as Anne did for me, only not too close and a little larger than those she sewed, one of which I send in this letter. Enclosed I send ten dollars $10.00 to be used for anything or anybody. Love

---

2. Beaufort Volunteer Artillery.

3. On 6 August 1862, three Federals of Company H, Third New Hampshire Infantry deserted to the Confederate lines from picket duty on Pinckney Island.

to Ma, Pa and all. Remember me to the Greggs and Aunt Til. About six sets of the buttons will do.

Your aff'ᶜᵗ brother
Milton M. Leverett

9ᵗʰ

Miss Grimke and Mr Heyward are very kind they send me quite frequently vegetables and mutton. She brought me yesterday evening some muskmelons, a watermelon, and beans and tomatoes, besides a note which I will answer shortly. No more to say only sick of my probationary life as a private and wish I had some honourable position in the Army. But there is nothing like "pushing ahead," a thing which I have not done and consequently have not obtained any position. Only think of little Bob Chisolm being a Captain in the Sharpshooters, and Minny Stuart a Lieutenant.[4] The former is a pusher ahead, and refused on Bay Point to fight in the fort with his own schoolfellows, kinsmen and fellow townsmen, although men were needed to fight three guns and Ste Elliott offered him the chance.[5] He preferred the inglorious position of being a volunteer aid to Col Dunovant,[6] where no aid was needed, and yet that fellow will brag of being in the fight. If you can make me a small black silk cravat I wish you would.

Milton Maxcy Leverett to his sister Julia

MᶜPhersonville Aug. 8ᵗʰ /62
Dear Julie,

I am glad to see that you are well again and have nothing more to fear in the shape of misery in the stomach as plums have long since gone and peaches fast following. Indeed I think that Ma oughtn't to let you range so freely over Miss Smith's Orchard as misery in the stomach may take place again. You really must learn to restrain that green fruit affection and only take the ripe as that won't hurt you, while there is no telling what bitter feelings and sad experiences green fruit is productive of.

As regards your poetic effusion which you request my opinion of, I tell you plainly that the sentiment (so far as I remember, I haven't it before me now) was good but it lacked rhythym—the measure wasn't good, and to produce harmony

---

4. Capt. Robert Chisolm of Company A, First Battalion South Carolina Sharpshooters, and Lt. Middleton Stuart of the Beaufort Artillery.
5. During the bombardment of Forts Walker and Beauregard on 7 November 1861.
6. Col. Richard Gill Mills Dunovant of the Twelfth South Carolina Infantry commanded the Confederate force at Bay Point.

there must be concert of action in the feet, each line must have a certain number of feet to correspond with some other line in the stanzas to which that line belongs. Your mistakes may have been perhaps due to the internal agony and misery of stomach which you were then enduring. Get Pa to help you on until you're able to go it smoothly, and then strike out for yourself.

You seem to think that there was a great breach of etiquette in N. H's[7] requesting Mary to make a pair of gloves for her, I myself see no such breach inasmuch as she did not specify according to your letter, for whom she wished them, she may have wished them for her father and not being able to manufacture them herself, she acknowledged Mary's superiority in the art, by requesting her to make them. If she <u>had</u> <u>said</u> she wished them for such and such a young man <u>I</u> would think Mary very wrong to agree to make them for her. Mary is presumed to know nothing of what is intended to be done with them. Tell Mary and Annie I am much obliged for the stockings, but they ought to be a little longer in the calves and feet. Tell Carrie I am exceedingly gratified to find that she can hem so nicely and that <u>she</u> has taken to that which <u>you</u> never did, tell her I wish I had her here to sew for me. I have a whole sleeve to put in a shirt which I will have to make Billy sew up, as he is my seamstress. I have Bella with me now and will either sell her or turn her loose in Mr Wm Heyward's pasture as I have his permission. Mr. Ben Palmer[8] is here and preached in our company the other night, ladies and all attending. I brought Mrs J. W. Gregorie she having sent her little sons around to ask me to call for her. I wish some of you would see if you can get me a red cord half as large round as my little finger with two rather large tassels to it to tie around my hat. I bid Fred goodbye yesterday on his way to Virginia, hope he will get on well.

Your aff'<u>ct</u> brother

Milton M. Leverett

I wish this letter burnt.

Milton Maxcy Leverett to his brother Fred

McPhersonville Aug /62

My dear Fred,

I received the basket the other day and am much obliged to you for it. I did not know what day you would pass but guessed at the day on which you did pass,

---

7.   Nathalie Heyward.
8.   Rev. Benjamin Morgan Palmer Jr. of New Orleans, minister of First Presbyterian Church, Columbia, 1843–1855.

and tried to come down on that <u>day</u> but didn't succeed. Everything here remains in <u>status quo</u> the same monotonous routine to undergo, with little to see, hear or do. I am getting to be comfortably fixed although I don't know how long it will be. We are going to have two of those revolving rifles or young cannon whatever they are. Capt. Elliott saw Gen'l. Jenkins to whom they had been given and got them from him. They shoot fifty times a minute and very correctly. They are being fixed up and when finished will be sent on to us. Jenkins had come on to get conscripts and we were cut out of the supply that was expected for our company.[9] We are having miserably rainy times now, if it were not for that oil cloth you sent me my things in my tent would be in poor plight, as my tent leaks all about. I was thinking of joining with Nat. F.[10] and getting a wall tent but we are in doubt whether we will be allowed to carry it to Va. as they are so many private tents in our company, although I am tolerably comfortable where I am, as Stephen B. and Stuart G.[11] have got a wall tent and I have the whole of the army tent to myself. I saw Mr Wm. Heyward about what you wished as regards Bella and he was perfectly willing. He asked me if she could take care of herself, meaning, if she was a tackey and was accustomed to feed herself. I told him she could. He said that he had his horses divided into two sets, one set pastured down towards the end of his place near the railroad, the other up about the pinelands around him. He asked me which set you wished her to go with as she might stray off from that by the railroad, while she wouldn't be able to stray off from the pineland set. I suggested the pineland set, although I think she would fare better with the plantation squad as the pasture would be ten per cent better, though she would be safer with the other. His two sets of horses must be his yard or pineland squad, and his plantation animal squad.

Enclosed you will find two dollars and a half ($2.50) that I owe Mr White-head (Stephen E. Whitehead) for corn and rice straw. I tried to pay him in Hardeeville before but he couldn't make change, and since then I had forgotten it, do pay him. Have you heard from Charlie, whether he is gone to Va. or not?

Your aff<u>ct</u> brother,
Milton M. Leverett

---

9. Brig. Gen. Micah Jenkins, commander of a South Carolina brigade consisting of the Fourth South Carolina Battalion (Infantry), Fifth, Sixth South Carolina Infantry, Palmetto Sharp-shooters, and Second South Carolina Rifles, was at home in South Carolina recruiting volunteers and enrolling conscripts.

10. Nathaniel Barnwell Fuller.

11. Stephen Elliott Barnwell and James Stuart Gibbes.

Frederic Percival Leverett to his sister Mary

Raleigh, No. Ca. 14th Aug.
Thursday 1862

My dear Mary,

When I left Columbia last Monday, I thought that by this time at least, I should be in Richmond, but when one travels with a horse, he can make no plans, likely to be carried out. Here I am in Raleigh, where I have been since last evening & where I shall remain, until tomorrow morning.

On Monday night about 12 o'clock when we had gotten some 8 miles beyond Chesterville & most, in the cars, were sound asleep, we were aroused by a tremendous thumping, bumping, jarring & sudden stopping of the train. The front axletree of the front freight car had broken, and as a consequence the running parts of three freight & baggage cars were knocked out & broken, making an almost complete smash resulting providentially in the injury of no one. The car in which the colt was, was knocked off of its wheels and the floor was smashed in, up to just where she was standing. Had the cars not been stopped so quickly her legs would certainly have broken. It was a most fortunate thing that I had no other horse, for if I had had, one would have been certainly ruined. As it was the colt escaped with a few scratches & bruises. In consequence of the accident instead of proceeding on the journey and reaching Charlotte on Tuesday before daylight, I early that morning rode back to Chester to telegraph for a car to be sent from Columbia to carry on the horse. About 12 M. the train arrived & we were once more underway, and in the evening we reached Charlotte safely. Now vexations really commenced. The connection train was then ready to start for this place; the R. R. Agent however said the horse could not go, she would have to proceed by the freight train. What to do I did not know. I could not bear the idea of travelling by freight train, and so at last concluded to stay at Charlotte that night, start by the morning passenger train, and have Jacob to come on a few hours later with the horse. They reached here safely before dinner today both looking rather the worse for bad travelling. Jacob will again start tonight for Petersburg, which I hope he will reach safely tomorrow night. I myself will leave in the morning & hope to get there tomorrow evening. The next day, if nothing prevents we will push on for Richmond. I never knew before the annoyances of travelling. It is a comfort, however, to think, that I am making $5.40 per day, and am to draw mileage for the route.

Do tell Ma that there was not a drop of water on the cars yesterday from Charlotte to Raleigh. The country through which this road lies is very picturesque and all along were numbers of peach and apple trees laden with fruit, strange to say far fewer in proportion to the number of travellers were offered for sale than are on the C. & S. R. R.[12]

With much love to all
Ever yr. aff<u>ct</u> brother
F. P. Leverett

P.S. Tell Pa wheat is selling at $3.00 per bushel, and Corn at $1.00 in Chester. Freight is 8 cts. Had I had money, I would have bought & sent down. I was told that if they had rain in a few days Corn would be very cheap. Crops along the road are suffering very much. I have not been able to find any cheap homespun. It is everywhere at 45 to 50 cts. per yard.

Milton Maxcy Leverett to his mother

M<u>c</u>Phersonville Aug. 23<u>rd</u> 1862

My dear mother,

I received your letter some days ago telling of the sad death of Aunt Cornelia but did not answer before having nothing very particular to speak of. Do try and be as kind and attentive as possible to the Greggs, as they have done the same by us in our troubles and afflictions before; I can hardly think how Coz. Maxcy could have taken it, he must have minded it very much indeed.

Have you heard from Fred yet? Burnett told me that his commission was Senior Surgeon of Drayton's Brigade,[13] a position I am delighted at his obtaining if it be true. I wish he would write to me and let me know his direction. He is very bad off for horses and ought to have a larger and stronger horse than the colt; he left Bella with me to put in Mr W<u>m</u> Heyward's pasture, as he had given permission to do it, but she died a day and a half after he left her with me, in great agony. I can't say positively, what was the matter, but think I can guess; it was something internal. We have been on another expedition as you may see by the newspapers, one which involved more danger and was more successful than any yet. We went to Pinckney Island, and all but annihilated a New Hampshire company we found there. Providence as usual spared our company any loss.[14] We left here about day-

---

12. Charleston and Savannah Railroad.

13. Drayton's Brigade, in Brig. Gen. David R. Jones's Division, Right Wing (Maj. Gen. James Longstreet's Command), was composed of the Fiftieth, Fifty-first Georgia Infantry, Fifteenth South Carolina Infantry, and Phillips's Georgia Legion (Infantry).

14. Early on 21 August 1862, about 120 Confederates, detachments from the Eleventh South Carolina Infantry and the Beaufort Artillery, in an expedition commanded by Capt. Stephen Elliott Jr., surprised the pickets of Company H, Third New Hampshire Infantry. During a brief action, Lt. Joseph C. Wiggin and three Federal privates were killed and seven non-commissioned officers and twenty-nine privates captured. Confederate losses were eight men wounded, six of them by their own men in the confusion of the predawn action.

break on Tuesday morning with about forty-five men from our company and trav-elled by wagons to Boyd's Landing where we launched six boats about seven o'clock that evening. From there we were to row to Foote Point that night, but hav-ing missed the way by going up a wrong creek (Hazzard's I believe) we were com-pelled to stop on a little hammock, that you could almost jump across, about 2 o'clock that night, where the men slept on the wet ground. I slept in the boat I was rowing, with nothing but my overcoat over me in a hard rain, half sitting down, doubled up in as small a space as possible with my head bent and my over-coat hauled over me so as to protect myself and my firearms as much as possible. I was so hungry then that I took a knife and hauled a dirty piece of bacon out of the bag I carried with me, cut off one or two slices and eat them raw with as much gusto as if I was eating wild duck. You have no idea how nice raw bacon is. We had rowed about twenty miles or more that night, and after a sleep of two hours we were waked about four o'clock next morning and rowed down the river behind Simon Island to Foote Point about five miles or more, the greater part of the time we were able to see the enemy's fleet at anchor in the bay off Hilton Head and Bay Point. About seventeen were counted. After resting awhile the boats were car-ried across the Foote Point neck of land to Chas. Colcock's[15] landing where sev-eral other boats with men from the 11th Regt. met us. That occupied us until nearly dark, when having cooked we went to sleep and were aroused about 12 oclock that night to prepare the boats and ourselves for starting which kept us until quite late, but being ready we jumped in and rowed to Pinckney Island at which place we arrived just about day-dawn, one boat landing before the sentry discovering it. The rest then coming up he discovered them and immediately began shouting out "Boat ahoy," "boat ahoy," without halting us, we didn't answer but bending to our oars run the boat up on the beach and made the men jump out and run up. In a second or so we heard a few shots then a whole volley and then scattering shots, after which the air seemed rent with the pitiful moans and groans of the wounded and dying. The affair was concluded in fifteen or twenty minutes. Four oarsmen were ordered to remain with each boat, so that in case of defeat they would be able to run down and jump in the boats and put right off, on account of this order a great many of the crack men of the company were left on the beach. I was not in the shooting part of the affair but did my duty where I had been placed for I had at the end of the journey rowed (30) thirty miles without being relieved by any one, and as the Captain said we must not mind being left with the boats as it required cool men and good oarsmen and that we acted as necessary a part and had as much credit as the other portion of men, which was very true as the fighting was the least part of the affair, the enemy being almost

15.   Charles Jones Colcock.

entirely unarmed and just routed out of beds were shot down easily, like rabbits. There were not more than five shots from the enemy. Another reason why I was not in the fighting portion was that I had understood we would have had to march two miles which I knew I couldn't do, but it turned out to be only a few hundred yards from shore, at which distance we could easily hear the poor fellows groaning after being shot. I do not regret very much not having killed a man, for although I know I would have shot them unarmed or not but still it would have been disagreeable to me. I felt perfectly satisfied throughout the whole that I was doing my duty in the position I had been placed and if a man can go through life with the satisfaction of knowing that he has done his duty <u>through life</u> he has done not only moderately well but superlatively well. We captured thirty-six, eight of whom were wounded and sick, a great many dead and wounded were left on the field around the house. We could have brought off a plenty of arms and clothes &c but two gunboats were steaming up from Hilton Head to the rescue and we had to ply our oars to get back to the main land safe.

Your aff^{ct} son
Milton M. Leverett

We passed through Grahamville and fared and slept well there that night (Wednesday) and came on home next day. The prisoners said that if we came that far to capture them we <u>must</u> be fond of expeditions.

There were several men of the 11<u>th</u> Regt wounded by their own men in the affair, one of whom has died since. The papers are very wrong in saying that the day had been carried by the two first boats; the first six boats at least if not all contributed most thoroughly to the success of the enterprise and the enemy were not captured by the two first boats alone.

Love to all and hope all are well. Remember me to the Greggs, Aunt Til &c.

Frederic Percival Leverett to his sister Anne Leverett DeSaussure

Orange Court House[16]
23rd August, 62
Saturday

My dear Nan,

I did not get off from Richmond before yesterday, owing to the Rail Road being occupied in transporting troops to points between Richmond and Gordonsville and hence not going to Gordonsville yesterday however I started, reached G in safety and found almost the whole army advanced, came on here,

---

16. Virginia.

where Ripley's Brigade[17] [letter damaged] & passed the night on a settee of a house from which the whites had fled some weeks since on the approach of the Yankees. I am still some thirty miles in the rear of Drayton's & do not know yet [letter damaged] course [letter damaged] horse, and have my saddle & baggage which are too bulky for me to carry, though I have brought as [letter damaged, missing line] Dr Hoyt, whose address is Richmond, (General Hospital No. 13)[18] Do direct to his care, not to the address I gave Ma in my last. I am as you may imagine in a very unpleasant position, but trust it will all come out right, as I have got on so far safely. I find it exceedingly expensive, and will be pretty low in funds, if I do not reach Drayton before long. It seems strange but it appears that all the trouble I have had could have been avoided, had I stopped but one day in Columbia.

The Yankees retreat before our army and we cannot press on more rapidly owning to the difficulty of carrying commissary stores. Jackson is in advance, and there is a constant capturing of prisoners.

I hope I will be able to hear from you sometime though it be [letter damaged] With much love to all & many a kiss to my Lou.

F. P. Leverett

P.S. I have left two or three of your ginger cakes on hand and wish I had a bushel & could carry them. It is hard to get anything to eat now. [letter damaged] but none were to be had.

Frederic Percival Leverett to his father

Culpeper Court House, Va. 25th Aug. 1862

My dear Father,

I wrote Anne a note from Orange C. H. on Saturday whence I walked in company with Rev. Mr. Stewart of Alexandria, who is a chaplain in a N. Carolina Regiment.[19] I have found him very kind and useful. He stopped and I with him at Mrs. Col. Taliaferro (pronounced Toliver) on Saturday in the middle of the day, after crossing the Rapidan, & found her all politeness & hospitality. We afterwards came on here & stopped at Rev. Mr. Coles' the Episcopal Minister, who is a most

---

17. Brig. Gen. Roswell S. Ripley's Brigade, in Maj. Gen. D. H. Hill's Division, was composed of two North Carolina and two Georgia regiments in the fall of 1862 but was not with the Army of Northern Virginia in the Second Manassas (Bull Run) Campaign.

18. Assistant Surgeon William D. Hoyt was the surgeon in charge of General Hospital No. 13 at Richmond, which included Federal prisoners as patients. It was also known as Castle Thunder Hospital, Eastern District Military Prison Hospital, and Lunatic Hospital.

19. Rev. Kinsey Johns Stewart, chaplain of the Sixth North Carolina Infantry.

excellent man.[20] He and Mrs. C. are regular hospitable Virginians. I found yester-day that our wounded are being brought in from the Rappahannock. An artillery engagement took place there on Saturday. We dislodged them from their positions on this side the river, when they retreated across, and destroyed the bridge.[21] They command the ford with their artillery, so that, as the river is high, it is not known what will be done. Immense fires were made, it is said by Pope[22] on Saturday across the river; some were judged by the smoke to be of bacon, so it is supposed that he was destroying his commissary stores. Stewart[23] on Saturday night made a dash down to near Manassas & captured Pope's immense baggage train & de-stroyed it, bringing off some 300 horses, among them Pope's own horse & trap-pings, sword & new uniform, & considerable amt of specie.[24]

The Yankees proved themselves veritable fiends here, stealing everything they could lay hands on; in fact ravaging the country; they left over 100 of their wounded, many of whom they might have removed, and carried off hundreds of negros, they even stole little negro children from their mothers that would not go with them. The Yankees are hated with a detestation that is extraordinary by chil-dren who are hardly more than infants.

I will push on tomorrow after the army in the first train of wagons that come up, when I hope I may reach it safely & not be again separated.

Our poor wounded fellows here are anything but comfortable yet, though the ladies are exerting themselves to their utmost for them. Stripped as they are of almost all that they had, it is really extraordinary how much they are doing. A num-ber of prisoners are just coming in I hear, so goodby with much love to all.

> Ever yr aff<u>ct</u> & ob<u>ent</u> Son
>
> F. P. Leverett

20. Rev. John Cole of St Mark's Parish, Culpeper County, Virginia.

21. A preliminary action in the Second Manassas Campaign on 23 August 1862, as Confeder-ates attempted to force their way across the Rappahannock River near Culpeper, Virginia. Though Federals destroyed the railroad trestle Jackson's engineers completed a bridge that night and the Confederates crossed the next morning.

22. Maj. Gen. John Pope commanded the Federal Army of Virginia in the Second Manassas Campaign.

23. Maj. Gen. James Ewell Brown "Jeb" Stuart commanded the cavalry of the Army of North-ern Virginia.

24. A Confederate cavalry raid on 22 August against Catlett Station, on the Orange and Alexan-dria Railroad, in which Stuart captured several hundred Federal prisoners, five hundred horses, and Pope's headquarters wagon, including the Federal commander's dress uniform coat.

Milton Maxcy Leverett to his mother

McPhersonville Sept. 16<u>th</u>/62

My dear mother,

I received the hat you sent me last Friday and am very much obliged to you for it, it was entirely unexpected and consequently took me by surprise and very agreeably for I am or was in great need of a hat, and I expect if I waited for my uniform hat to come it would be when winter was half past. The cord and tassels are very pretty and far beyond what I expected, every one has admired them very much. The price was pretty high though,—how much did the hat cost? Are any more such tassels to be found where you obtained that one? I am sorry you had so much trouble in obtaining it. Who fixed it on the hat? You I suppose. Tell Anne I am very much obliged for the stockings. I am glad the wool sold so well and think it's a capital way of doing, I suppose cotton will supply its place very well. I haven't heard from Fred at all since he has gone, and haven't written as I don't know his direction. I wish he could get me a position with Cos. Maxcy or even if I could get a commission under Genl Stuart I would be delighted. I am perfectly delighted with the news we receive now, and the only damper to it, one which always qualifies the news to me in a measure, is that <u>I am not in that army</u>.[25] I am very anxious to be there, to be one of the Invaders of the North, to pay my northern friends another visit would be pleasant in the extreme.

Stephen Elliott lost his eldest son (Steevy) here the other day from diptheria,[26] they buried him at Sheldon, a good many of us attended; Mr James Elliott[27] was telegraphed for to perform the ceremony but didn't receive the telegram time enough, consequently Mr. Norton acted, using our prayer book. Since then James Creighton of the Dragoons has died[28]—of dysentery at Mr. James Gregorie's.

I received that letter Pa sent by Mr Hanckel, it had come when I was up with you in Columbia. I am glad Mame's teeth have been fixed. Do pay the dentist with the enclosed $5.00, for my teeth. Nothing stirring here at present.

Your aff'<u>ct</u> son

Milton M. Leverett

The hat fits very nicely, may be a little too small, but nothing of any importance. The same man has had the making of our company hats ever since the middle of

---

25. The Army of Northern Virginia.
26. Stephen Habersham Elliott (1856–1862) died 8 September; son of Charlotte Stuart and Stephen Elliott Jr.
27. Rev. James Habersham Elliott (1819–1877) of Charleston, Episcopal clergyman; uncle of Stephen Elliott Jr.
28. Pvt. James Creighton of the Charleston Light Dragoons died 15 September.

the summer, and we haven't seen them yet. Love to all. Tell Anne, Stuart says he didn't know she had such a poor idea of him before as to think him a "sort of infidel," and is quite sorry to think so. He seems to like to talk of the nice times he and Anne and all the rest have had at Bay Point. Thinks I am very much like Anne and both of us the two most mischievous persons in creation, a quality that I have eschewed pretty much of latter years, although it will show itself sometimes, being Pa's son. I find that our hats have arrived, but with no ornament whatsoever.

Milton Maxcy Leverett to his father

McPhersonville Oct. 1st /62

My dear father,

There is either a miscarriage in the mails or all at home write very seldom, perhaps both are at fault. I went around yesterday to see Mr Wm H. and Miss Grimke, they were not at home, but Mr D. Heyward was and I went in, and sat a little while, but they not returning I left, and met them on the way, she told me she had just received a letter dated the 20th from sister, in which she requested Miss Grimke to discover what was the reason I had not written, and in a postscript added that a letter had just been received from me. Now the reason of that delay I can't understand, unless it be the fault of the mail master either here or in Columbia, for I had written that letter about two weeks ago. I am very much worried by a statement of Mr D. H's that he had just received a letter from Columbia saying that Carrie was taken down with the scarlet fever, is it so? or is it serious? Do write immediately and let me know. I think if it is so I would have heard by mail or telegraph.

We have lost three men from our company, the first since we have been in service. They went on a scout to Beaufort Island, not knowing the portion of the island to which they were going and have not been heard from since. They volunteered, and were not ordered. I heard that Col. Walker intended trying to bring about an exchange for them, of three that we have in Hardeeville, of the first crowd we had captured at Pinckney Island, and who were in the hospital. Mr. George Elliott has lost all his negroes but one, they went off very suddenly and left the crop not yet harvested, everything was put exactly in its place, keys left in the doors, and their allowance already drawn left as it was drawn.

W. Heyward, D. Heyward's nephew lost his own also, they carried the boat from under a Mr Glover's house hitched behind a buggy and dragged it right past the camp of the Beaufort District Troop[29] (I believe) at night and made off. There

---

29.   The Beaufort District Troop, originally an independent cavalry company commanded by Capt. Thomas E. Screven, and after August 1862 Company B, Second South Carolina Cavalry.

was a report here that a telegram had been sent to Beauregard to look out for an attack on Charleston in ten days, and that was some days ago. There was also a report here yesterday that the enemy were landing at Bluffton, don't know whether it is true though. Have you heard from Fred, he must be very busy as I haven't heard yet. I heard that there was a rumor in Columbia that all of Drayton's staff had been killed or captured. Have you heard anything of it?

Write soon and let me know how all are as I am very anxious to hear. Edward Cuthbert has been exchanged and is now in our company.[30]

Your aff'<u>ct</u> son
Milton M. Leverett
Love to all.

Matilda Leverett to her brother Milton

Columbia, Oct 4, 1862

We have all been so disappointed at your writing so seldom, My dear Minny, that we had begun to think you did not care to get any letters—but your last letter has just come, and shows that you do care somewhat, so I answer immediately.

Carrie was taken down last Sunday with the scarlet fever and on Tuesday, Mame with fever and sore throat, and on Thursday, Katie, in like manner. The doctor said that Mame's was catarrhal fever, and not scarlet—he prescribed for her and she is now out again, but weak and pale. Carrie is also out, having got over it wonderfully, having been thickly covered with the eruption—which is always a good sign. She was as red as a boiled crab. Katie is the one we feel uneasy about. It is evidently scarlet fever with her. The eruption is not as much as we would wish, and her throat is ulcerated and mouth very sore. If she only gets over it as well as Carrie has so far, we will be very glad that they have had it. Carrie is in excellent spirits with an excellent appetite. Lou, I hope is exempt, having had scarlatina in the Pinelands last spring.

As to Fred—Pa received a note from Jack Middleton, dated Winchester, saying that Fred had requested him to write and let us know that at the battle of Boonesboro[31] there had been a great many wounded, and that he was one of the

---

30. Pvt. Edward Barnwell Cuthbert (1828–1878) of the Beaufort Artillery was captured on Ladies Island shortly after the battle of Port Royal and imprisoned at Fort Lafayette, New York; after his exchange in May 1862 he reenlisted at McPhersonville 25 September 1862.

31. A portion of the fighting at South Mountain, Maryland, 14 September 1862. This was a prelude to the bloodiest single day of the war at Sharpsburg (Antietam), Maryland, on 17 September, in which Lee's Army of Northern Virginia fought McClellan's Army of the Potomac to a draw on the battlefield but was forced to end its invasion of the North and retreat back across the Potomac River into Virginia.

Surgeons who staid with them, so that on our army falling back, they all fell into the hands of the enemy. Mr. Middleton said he did not think there was any occasion for uneasiness, and that he hoped to see Fred back in a few days, for that Surgeons were allowed to return as soon as their duty was performed. We do not feel uneasy—and are only too thankful to know that he has not been killed. No mention was made of any one else. What has become of Jacob we can't imagine. Fred's last letter to us, dated Hagerstown, said that the colt had broken so entirely just with the journey into Maryland that he could not use it, and had left it with a farmer in Maryland, hardly expecting to see it again. He had bought an ambulance and an old horse to use instead. He was quite disappointed at their reception in Maryland, but was told that they were in the wrong part of it, for secession sympathy—that there were mostly Unionists in that part of the State. I think "My Maryland" has turned out quite a humbug.[32]

I am afraid that we will have hot work on our coast this winter. A dispatch came last week to Beauregard from Richmond saying that he must work night and day on the fortifications as the President had received information that Charleston would soon be attacked. It is said that the President has determined that Charleston shall be held at all hazards, that he says <u>it shall not be given up</u>.[33]

Pa saw Mr. Joe Seabrook in Columbia two or three days ago. He said that he had just been in Charleston, and that while there, Charley had got him to go with him to Dr. Ogier to get a discharge from the service—he, Mr S. being acquainted with Dr. O. who is now on the board of Surgeons appointed by government. Dr. O. would not give him one however, but told him he must be contented with two months furlough. Charley wrote word to Julie a few weeks ago that his health was so bad that the Surgeon of the Regiment said that he would have to be discharged.[34] We have also heard through other sources that his health is bad, and that he was very imprudent. We feel very sorry about it.[35]

Pa sent for Hagar, Prince, Nanny and big Toney[36] two weeks ago. Charley sent them, but in the place of Toney, he sent <u>Peter, as he had been</u> married to Nanny four months ago. Pa has got places for them all—Hagar as cook at 8 dollars a month and Prince at two dollars, in the same yard, he having to bring water, and

---

32. Many Confederates hoped that Lee's invasion would inspire Marylanders to support their cause, and the Army of Northern Virginia crossed the Potomac River on its way north singing James Ryder Randall's popular song "Maryland, My Maryland."

33. Beauregard, after sixteen months in Virginia, Tennessee, and Mississippi, returned to Charleston in September, replacing Pemberton—who had been widely criticized for his indifference to the fate of the city—as commander of the Department of South Carolina and Georgia.

34. Assistant Surgeon Henry Woodbury Moore (1831–1902) of the Hampton Legion (Cavalry).

35. Charley's discharge from the Hampton Legion (Cavalry) was approved 9 October 1862.

36. Slaves.

sweep up the yard. Nanny's place also, as cook and washer, is eight dollars. Peter at present is helping take in the crop (which is not amounting to much). There are three places open which he can get, the one at the Charlotte Depot at eleven dollars a month, being the one he will probably be sent to. Old Quash's family had also been sent for. I hope none of them will take it into their heads to make off down the country to Beaufort. I am very sorry for the George Elliotts. It was a great mistake keeping their people so near the Yankees.

Have you seen Mrs. Gregorie lately? How are Liz and her little daughter? Fred's last direction was Drayton's Brigade, Surgeon care of Adjutant General Cooper, Richmond.[37] That was before the advance of the army into Maryland— How it would be now I don't know. The children caught the Scarlet fever from the Fowles', Mary, & Ste and also Mrs. Pringle's youngest died having had it about two months ago.

from Your affec sister
Matilda

Milton Maxcy Leverett to his mother

McPhersonville
Oct 25th /62

My dear mother,

I can only write these few lines to say that I am quite well not having received a scratch.[38] It was quite a heavy fight, the balls were almost like hailstones. One of my mess, (Nat Fuller) was wounded in the arm not dangerously. We had fifteen wounded in our company and one killed, Edmund Fripp of St. Helena, who died after he got to McPhersonville.[39] One of my horses was killed, my saddle horse, shot

---

37. Gen. Samuel Cooper, adjutant and inspector general, was the ranking officer in the Confederate States Army.

38. During the battle of Pocotaligo (Coosawhatchie), 22 October 1862. An expedition of over 4,400 Federals commanded by Brig. Gen. John M. Brannan of the Department of the South landed at Mackay's Point, near Pocotaligo, intending to cut the Charleston and Savannah Railroad. The Federals were met by a force of some 475 Confederates commanded by Col. William S. Walker at Pocotaligo and some 200 Confederates commanded by Col. Charles Jones Colcock of the Third South Carolina Cavalry at the Pocotaligo Bridge over the Coosawhatchie River. After sharp clashes at both Pocotaligo and the Coosawhatchie, Brannan withdrew to Hilton Head with losses of 43 killed, 294 wounded, and 3 missing; Walker's and Colcock's combined losses were 21 killed, 121 wounded, and 18 missing. "Those who went through the first Manassas say they never experienced such a rain of bullets." *Charleston Mercury*, 27 October 1862.

39. Pvt. J. Edmund Fripp.

when I was off him, the other one really seems to mind it very much. I can't help feeling that God has been very kind to me again, and the whole company readily admit that a special Providence has been taking care of us throughout the war.

I will write more in detail shortly and am quite sorry you haven't heard from me before.

your aff<u>ct</u> son
Milton M. Leverett
P.S.
The Beaufort Artillery behaved worthy of its antecedents. Hope you are all well.

Rev. Charles Edward Leverett to his son Milton

[October–November 1862]
My dear Minny

I am very glad to learn that you escaped in the battle without harm after I presume a gallant fight with the desperate scamps, who invaded our sacred soil. You seem to have been providentially protected and I hope will continue to be unto the end. I should like to have some particulars. Let me have them from the time you first heard of the landing of the enemy. I am glad to know that you were in the fight. I wish that I had been. I suppose there will be enough more until we get our vessels from England[40] & then I think we shall [have] peace with the villains. I am writing in great hurry being just on the eve of going to town on business. Every thing is high here & consequently very worrying to us. I wish we might have good times once more. Fred is here. The children are better & so is Mamma. Remember me to my friends in the pine land—particularly to Miss G. our especial friend & Mr. W. H.[41]

Hoping you will still be protected & in the surety that you acted boldly & bravely

I remain
y aff. f.

---

40. Though the British government was officially neutral, Confederate agents convinced private contractors in England to build cruisers for the Confederate navy, including the C.S.S. *Florida* and the C.S.S. *Georgia*. Many of the most successful blockade runners were owned by British firms and manned by British crews running goods into ports such as Charleston and Wilmington.

41. Mary Augusta Secunda Grimke and William Heyward.

Frederic Percival Leverett to his brother Milton

Columbia, 5<u>th</u> Oct.[42]

1862

My dear Minny,

I sent word to you by Rob Means' boy to meet me today, as I expected to pay you a visit. Yesterday afternoon I went into Columbia prepared to start for Charleston, but found it so dusty, raw & uncomfortable, & withal such a crowd going down, & moreover that the fare had been doubled since I left here. Taking all these things into consideration I remounted the horse, & very wisely, I think returned to the Farm. I paid for my ride by coughing the better portion of the night, which fortunately Ma did not hear me do. I regretted very much not going down, as I wanted very much to see you.

Your long letter to Ma giving the acct. of the battle[43] arrived on Monday; we were all very glad of it & much interested by it, as the paper descriptions of it were so indistinct that we could make hardly head or tail of it. I was truly thankful that your company was so protected, & that you escaped unscathed. The fight must have been much hotter than I had any idea that it was. I was very sorry to see that D. Campbell of Izard's Co. was killed.[44] He was a young man of very pleasing manners & very gentlemanly. He died like a man & a soldier. Where was Izard's Company in the fight? I am glad he is now to be Major but was truly sorry Harrison was killed.[45] I hear his death was caused by mismanagement. I exclaimed, as I read the account—so much for a fool[46] being in command. So fell the best field officer of the 11<u>th</u> Reg. I am glad Izard is to be Major & hope it may be the precursor of other changes.

Often while in Virginia previous to the battle of Manassas I wished the Beaufort Artillery there.[47] That however satisfied me. I then realized what a battle field really was & was truly glad that your company & the Rebel Troup were safe on the coast. I joined Drayton's Brigade the night before the battle of Thorough Fare Gap,[48] which took place the day before that of Manassas. I sat high up in the mountain with Gen. Jones, who ordered all the movements of our troops from a position where every movement of the enemy could be seen. It was a beautiful

---

42. November.
43. Not found in this collection.
44. Pvt. Daniel P. Campbell of Company I, Eleventh South Carolina Infantry, killed 22 October.
45. Capt. Allen C. Izard of Company I, Eleventh South Carolina Infantry, succeeded Maj. John J. Harrison, who was killed 22 October.
46. Col. Daniel H. Ellis of the Eleventh South Carolina Infantry.
47. Second Manassas, Virginia, 29–30 August 1862.
48. Thoroughfare Gap, Virginia, 28 August 1862.

sight to see them in the plain below deploy their columns, moving them in various directions; again to see them moving their artillery to the most favorable positions, from which they literally raked the gap, so that we were unable to use our
artillery at all. The position of the Yankees was very strong, so much so that we
were all astonished when about [dusk] they retreated, leaving all the dead that
were in our immediate neighborhood. Our loss was comparatively slight. When
we reached the Gap, it was raked by the enemy's artillery & the mountains on
either side were held in a measure by their sharpshooters. These were driven out
completely by our sharpshooters before dusk. Our men behaved splendidly. A
Capt. Patten of Ga. who fell two days after at Manassas[49] killed three Yankees
there with his pistol. This fight was but a small affair in reality, but was most
important in its results, for had the Yankees held the field until the next day,
Longstreet's Corps could not have reached Manassas Plains by two o'clock the
next day, in time to support Jackson who, we knew, was fighting the Yankees all
the time that we were stopped at the Gap. Well we reached the plains the next
day, Aug. 29th, as I said, in time for us to join in the fight. The van of the Corps
went in at once, while the rest avant of it was so deployed, I believe, as to prevent
the enemy flanking us. The battle raged until night put an end to it, we capturing
several peices of Artillery, & quite a number of prisoners, & driving in the enemies'
lines at various points. The next morning the fight was resumed in the distance
the enemy having fallen back during the night. From 9 or 10 o'clock A.M. until dark
the cannonading was incessant, & the firing of Musketry constantly going on. The
Yankees were driven from hill to hill, leaving their dead & wounded & frequently
cannon behind them. Drayton's Brigade was kept all that day, as on the afternoon
& night previous, until late in the evening guarding a point on our right, where it
was supposed an advance would be made on us. Late in the evening he was
ordered to advance his brigade to where the battle was raging, then three miles
off. All started off in splendid style at the double quick. When they had gone
about a mile a cavalry picket came dashing up with orders for Drayton to return
to his old position, as the enemy were advancing. No sooner had they got back
there than orders came from Gen. Jones, the Division Commander for Drayton to
leave one Regiment there & come with the remainder of his brigade at once, as
his troops were much needed. By this time all the other pickets had come in &
reported that it was our own men that had been seen by the pickets. That news
being received off the brigade started again; this time to reach the scene of action,
when so near dark that they themselves could hardly participate in it. The enemy
were in full retreat across Bull Run for Centreville. Thus was fought the second
battle of Manassas, to which the first was but a skirmish. Both terminated in a

---

49.   Capt. John G. Patton, Company F, First Georgia Regulars, killed 30 August.

Bull Run Stampede; the first having been far more an utter rout than the second. The ground was left strewn with knapsacks, blankets, haversacks, canteens, & arms of all kinds. Some of the hills were literally covered with dead & wounded. Some of the latter were not removed from the spots where they fell five days after the battle, and but few of the Yankee dead were then, if ever buried. This was the case, though every privilege was allowed them for removing their wounded & burying their wounded [dead].[50] All of [our] wounded[51] were in before the night after the fight & the most of the dead buried. I was left behind with other surgeons to see to our wounded, who were carried to Warrenton[52] as rapidly as possible. After being kept there for about a week by which time the place had become offensive in the extreme, I started off half sick, with some others to hunt up the army. We crossed the Potomac on Sunday, 7th Sep. & joined Longstreet's Corps that evening at Frederick City,[53] as it went into camp. Here all remained two days recruiting. The afternoon before starting again Jacob joined me with the colt. He had brought her around with some wagons from Richmond. She was completely knocked by starvation & the long march. Seeing that she could go no further, I left her with a farmer, who promised to take good care of her, she died as I afterward heard in about ten days. So I have been unfortunate in horses during this war. From Frederick we were marched to Hagerstown, & on the following Sunday were brought back to Boonsboro, where we found the Yankees, in great force pressing D. H. Hill's Division, our rear guard. Just out of Town we met the enemy, & fought the battle of South Mountain, which would have resulted in our overthrow the foe being in such force as to flank us right & left, had not night opportunely come on. Our army retreated during the night to Sharpsburg. A large proportion of our wounded were left in Boonsboro Guild, Lee's Med. Director[54] selected me to remain in charge, an unpleasant compliment I then thought it. He left with me one Surgeon & seven Assistants—all for the most part pleasant and gentlemanly men. The people of Maryland proved unboundedly kind, doing for us every thing that was in their power, supplying us with clothing & every thing that we needed. I have a complete winter outfit, drawers, stockings, undershirts, overshirts & a suit of clothes, & a travelling bag &c. &c. as presents from them. I never saw such kindness as they exhibited. The best portion of Maryland is hotly secession. It had however no chance to rise, while our army was there. But my letter is getting too spun out. I was sick before going into Maryland with a cough & Diar-

---

50. The word *dead* has been inserted in pencil above, probably by Milton Leverett after the war.
51. The word *our* has been inserted in pencil before *wounded*, probably by Milton Leverett after the war.
52. Virginia.
53. Maryland.
54. Surgeon Lafayette Guild, Medical Director of the Army of Northern Virginia.

rhea & got worse there. On my return to Richmond—we were sent via Fortress Monroe. I applied for a furlough of thirty days, which was granted me. I came home & have improved since doing so, but am by no means well. My cough is better, but almost every thing disagrees with me & I have an exhausting Diarrhea. I have lost thirty lbs. in weight. All the family is pretty well. Kate & Carry improving. Charley came down since I commenced this & spent two days with me. He is looking very well & is much better for his furlough. Tell Stuart I saw Campbell[55] a few days before the battle of Manassas, going to join his Reg. but have not heard of his being wounded. The old sow has ten more pigs—pretty good twenty in six months & one half. Do write me as soon as you receive this, as I probably leave for Va. on the 19th inst.

Ever yr aff^ct brother,
F. P. Leverett

The cow bought from Aunt Til has a heifer calf, so the family will do very well for milk. I intend applying for a transfer South on account of my health, as soon as I return to Va.

Milton Maxcy Leverett to his mother

Pocotaligo Dec. 8th /62

My dear mother,

I have been and perhaps am surprised at your long silence, I having been a month without receiving any correspondence from home, until Julia's letter came, and then the things you sent me with your letter within. I had supposed that Fred had returned to Virginia by the tenor of the letters that were written to me sometime ago, and do not account now for his not having returned except on the grounds that his furlough must have been extended. Ask him what is the row between Drayton and his staff, why, is it that Middleton[56] is Quartermaster in DeSaussure's regiment[57] &^c &^c. If Fred can get a transfer to the Southern Dept. it would be very good for all parties concerned, especially to himself as cold weather is increasing. Everything that you sent has arrived safe and I am very much obliged for all the trouble you took as well as the groundnuts & apples &c. Tell Mary I am much obliged for the candy, it was very nice. The shirt is quite a nice shirt only the buttons are not strong enough; I won't object

---

55. John Barnwell Campbell Gibbes.
56. John Izard Middleton Jr.
57. The Fifteenth South Carolina Infantry, commanded by Col. Wilmot Davie DeSaussure.

to the match to it you speak of, if it is not too much trouble to make, or too fancy for me to wear.

Don't worry yourself about my being comfortable, as I am as much so as it is possible, having just finished building (Ste Barnwell and myself with some help from our boys) a very nice small loghouse with a board top, (the boards we purchased a little ways up the country) and a nice clay chimney, which I made myself, and it is indeed very comfortable, the most comfortable house "on the hill." We have a nice black (jet black) cat named Jezabel which purrs itself into a soft comfortable slumber on our hearth while we all sit around in the most approved and comfortable positions and postures that the human race has yet managed to discover, discussing the meanwhile the topics of the day, camp rumors &^{c} or jibing or jeering one another, perhaps about his <u>dulce</u>, or else reading novels and such light literature, conning newspapers, discussing women, the rates of interest due on the stock after the war, whether the market would be brisk or dull low or lively, with other interesting topics such as horses, dogs, cats &^{c} &^{c} including all creation generally and finally dropping off to our several tents to bed. So don't worry yourself about me at all as I am quite comfortable, only needing a pillow to make me perfectly so, so far as camp life goes. A pillow I think would make me dream. If the inner man was as well off as the outer man I might be happy, if there could be happiness in this world, and especially in camp, but I regret to say that the inner man is not as well off as the outer, our larder being often in a woeful state and as I am getting <u>rather old</u> now find it hard to manage the beef, but on the whole we manage to get on tol lol [tolerably].

I am glad to hear of the cow and sow abiding so faithfully and rigidly by the doctrine of increase and multiply, the latter I esteem especially as a most worthy old sow, and to both I say "go on and prosper," and wish them "many happy returns." The price of pork down here is 15 cts cleaned, not in the gross.

Kiss Katie, Carrie and Lou for me and tell them I will come home first chance I get. Tell Mary I never received any letter from her that I recollect of.

I will return the basket you sent me, in a few days, with some of my summer clothes and a few other articles I would like to send home. Tell Julie I received her letter and will answer it shortly.

Miss Grimke called on me a short time ago and very kindly brought me two large packages of old novels, reviews, magazines &c to read and circulate. Quite a prize in camp, one that the reading camp public was quite eager after. I told her that I was very much obliged to her for them and extremely flattered at her call. Love to Pa and all the rest, and memory to all friends.

Your aff'^{ct} son
Milton M. Leverett

Milton Maxcy Leverett to his sister Julia

Pocotaligo Dec. 15<u>th</u> /62

My dear Julia,

In the basket that I send are some of my clothes which I do not now want besides a few other articles. I send a few Yankee balls and pieces of shells, also a couple of collars got off two of their artillery horses, besides a few other articles, that may be useful. The rope[58] with the iron pin in one end belongs I think to the engineer's branch, and is used I dare say in marking out distances &c &c but I got it especially for Ma to survey her garden alleys with, so as to make them straight. There are one or two other things also that I have but couldn't send as there was not room enough in the basket. I got a bridle which I use myself, as well as a small saddle, which being too small for any one but a little boy I gave it to Lieutenant Rhodes,[59] for his little son.

I wish you would look up my lectures on Dr Jno LeConte and Jos. LeConte,[60] the first is on Mechanics coming under the head of Nat. Philosophy, the other is on Chemistry, in the old blank book you gave me, also send Davies Bourdon if you can find it, and the key, with all the sums worked out. If you can find these books send them to me, but if you are not able to find them, or they are too much trouble, don't worry yourself. I dont wish them myself, but to loan out,—to Mr Porteous who is studying for a position.[61]

I have just received Anne's letter this evening, and am quite surprised to hear that Fred hadn't received my letter, having answered his the day after I received it. I wrote that and another to some one of you, and waited so long for an answer that I got quite uneasy. I think it is always best that we should acknowledge the receipt of letters. Have any of you been around to see Miss Eliza Trescott yet? I sat up with her brother Bocquet[62] when he was wounded and staying at Bill Elliott's house, several nights. I there renewed my acquaintance with his sister and think that she is a very fine girl indeed.

---

58. A pencil note was inserted by Milton after the war: "The rope I speak of was meant for tethering out horses to graze. 1899 M. L."
59. Second Lt. John Jenkins Rhodes of the Beaufort Artillery.
60. Joseph LeConte, professor of physics at South Carolina College and chemist for the Niter and Mining District No. 6 1/2, headquartered in Columbia.
61. Pvt. John F. Porteous Jr. of the Beaufort Artillery was commissioned a lieutenant of artillery and assigned to ordnance duty at the Charleston Arsenal in February 1863.
62. Pvt. Edward Boquet Trescot of the Beaufort Artillery was severely wounded in the leg at Pocotaligo.

I am truly sorry to see by to-days papers that Cos. Maxcy is killed,[63] it must be dreadful to Cousins Julia and Cornelia. I wouldn't be at all surprised if it killed the former, or seriously affected her. I hope all of you will be as attentive as possible.

If you have a copy of brothers' Sunshine,[64]—copied neatly, send it.

Tell Ma not to worry herself about Billy's clothes as he seems to be very well off in that line,—he is a most valuable boy on that score, always having a plenty of clothes, and very good too considering the times. I only wrote to Ma about it because I wanted to be on the safe side. Tell Ma the sleeves to my shirt she sent the other day are too long & large round. You did not send my gun punch the other day to cut wads with. How is Pa getting on? When you write to him next do give my love to him. With love to all, I remain

Your aff'ct brother
Milton M. Leverett

Rev. Charles Edward Leverett to his son Milton

Col.[65] Dec. 17, 1862

My dear Minnie,

I write a line by Miss Bet Elliott, who leaves tomorrow morning. You have heard of the death of Cousin Maxcy and have seen his noble message to Gov. Pickens.[66] His loss we greatly deplore for a man like him could ill be spared. He was one of the luminaries of the State & his character was second to none. We expect his body this evening. The carriage will be sent for Julia & Cornelia who went on but too late to see him. It will be a dreadful loss to them. I hardly know how they can support such a shock. But God, I trust, will out of his store house, give them grace suited to the day. How many sad calamities these days have shown. What a heavy retribution must, in the nature of things, fall upon the North.

---

63. Maxcy Gregg was wounded in the Confederate victory at Fredericksburg, Virginia, 13 December 1862, and died two days later. His South Carolina brigade helped repulse the only substantial Federal success of the day; the battle is known for a series of futile Federal assaults against a strongly entrenched Confederate position on Marye's Heights.

64. Edward's melancholy poem "Sunshine" was written in Aiken in March 1861 and published in the *Southern Episcopalian,* the journal of the diocese of South Carolina, in May. "There's sunshine in the woodland glen / On every leaf and tree, / There's sunshine lavished on the world, / But none of it for me!" Edward wrote in the first stanza and ended with the fourth and final stanza, "But when the gentle hand of death / Shall set my spirit free, / In heav'n I'll find that God has made / Some sunshine too for me!"

65. Columbia.

66. Maxcy Gregg dictated a telegram to Francis W. Pickens, governor of South Carolina, 1860–1862, which ended, "If I am to die now, I give my life cheerfully for the independence of South Carolina, and I trust you will live to see our cause triumph completely." *Charleston Courier,* 18 December 1862.

We are all well but having colds. Fred has gone to Richmond and on temporary service to the battle field. There is nothing new. Every thing proceeds in the usual humdrum way. Charles has bought Annie's servants for which I am glad. I mean to try and sell Marcus soon. I still employ myself in writing & hope to go to England as soon as the blockade is up, if it can be accomplished to publish there.

You ask about the use of the words expect and suspect—and which of the sentences is most correct. "I expect him to come tomorrow" and "I suspect him to come tomorrow" &c. &c. The last sentence is nonsense and can not be parsed. The former can be used but is less to my mind, English, than the following, of which you ask, "I expect that he will come." You could say, "I suspect that he will come," for the reason that the word implies a suspicion of the event. According to Webster, whose work is before me and is good authority, expect always in its legitimate sense refers to a future event, as we expect a visit that has been promised. (The common phrase "I expect it was" is both vulgar and improper.) It is therefore proper to say I expect him to come or I am expecting him to come tomorrow.

It is also proper to say, "I suspect that he will come," because suspect means conjecture, though generally the word implies mistrust, and doubt as we suspect the truth of a story or the veracity of a person.

You can say then "I suspect that he will or may come tomorrow"—and "I expect him to come" or "I expect that he will come tomorrow." But you cannot say "I suspect him to come." That is perfectly ungrammatical.

As to the parsing, him is governed by the transitive verb expect; which also the infinitive is governed by nouns, pronouns &c preceding. In the phrase "I expect or suspect that he will come" if I had the phrase in Latin, I would of course employ the Latin rule "the infinitive mode has an accusative before it,"—as siunt regem adventare in English "they say the king is coming," <u>that</u> being understood.

I have no books to consult except the dict^y but the thing is plain enough without.

I hope you are doing well & will not forget your duty to yourself, your country and above all to God. My love to the friend who is so kind to you.

your aff father

P.S. If this is not satisfying, I can hunt up some books, but it is hardly necessary. Sorry to have nothing to send, but we are out of everything nearly.

Frederic Percival Leverett to his mother

Camp near Fredericksburg Va.
19th Dec. 1862

I am quietly domiciled here for the present, partaking of Capt. Middleton's hospitality. He has a tent to himself being Quartermaster, & kindly invited me to share it with him. To be sent to an army as I have been is anything but pleasant. I am attached to no Regiment or Brigade but am merely assigned to McClaw's Division[67] as a Supernumerary Surgeon, who has no duties whatsoever to perform, unless there be an engagement. Were it not that my friends have sheltered & fed me I don't know what I would have done. For two or three days I imposed myself on Dr. James Surg. of the 15th Reg. S.C. Vols[68] but he was crowded & I did not like to stay longer, then Chas. Hanckel,[69] Gen. Jenkins & Middleton all kindly invited me to stay with them. I chose the last, as he was by himself & was in the Division to which I had been assigned. I don't know how long my stay here is to be. I hope not much longer, as I have come up without a single change of clothing, & it will be a week to night since I have undressed. Guild the Medical Director, has promised to send me back to Richmond to the Surgeon General, so that he may assign me to Hospital duty for the winter, if possible, as I am hardly well enough to stand the exposure of the camp this winter. The weather is cold & freezing & I am now writing to you under difficulties, which cause the letter to be much more highly valued than its intrinsic merits would set it at. I am sitting as near to a log fire as I can draw myself, with my overcoat thrown over me to assist in keeping me warm. I am using my knee with a small book on it as my desk, & have my inkstand on one end of a log that is in the fire, so as to keep the ink from freezing.

I wrote to Pa on Sunday after getting up here. It was then supposed that the Yankees would give us battle again before retreating across the river. I then said that I could see no reason why they should do so, for they had on the day before suffered a disastrous repulse at all points, & our positions were so strong that they could not hope to carry them. During Sunday & Monday there was an occasional cannonading going on on both sides & the Yankees in large numbers were drawn up across the river as if about to come over & give battle which as you know they did not do. On Monday night the most of those that were on this side effected their escape across the river on their pontoon bridges, carrying off their wounded and leaving their dead or many of them unburied. They also left several hundred stragglers in the town who were taken prisoner. Some of these wanted to know of our men, if we did not think Burnsides[70] a fool, & said that if we did not, they did. The reason that we were not again attacked was, we hear, because the men refused to fight. Capt. Cutts brother-in-law of Stephen Douglas & aid of Burnsides,[71] who came over with

---

67. Maj. Gen. Lafayette McLaws commanded a division of Georgians, South Carolinians, and Mississippians in the First Corps, Army of Northern Virginia.

68. Surgeon Joseph A. James.

69. Charles Frances Hanckel of Charleston, an attorney; husband of Anne Matilda Heyward.

70. Maj. Gen. Ambrose E. Burnside commanded the Federal Army of the Potomac at Fredericksburg.

71. Capt. J. M. Cutts of the Eleventh United States Infantry.

the flag of truce told Col DeSaussure that "their victory consisted in their getting themselves out of their unfortunate position." Had Lee known how they were situated, he would have doubtless shelled Fredericksburg on Monday, which would have necessitated the surrender of every Yankee on this side. Some one of the officers who came over under the flag of truce said that he considered their escape from this side the greatest misfortune that could have befallen, at the present time, the Southern Confederacy. We have, however, unbounded reason to be thankful. We have obtained a signal victory over the foe that had determined to go to Richmond, no matter what the obstacles, were he obliged to advance at a not more rapid rate than one mile a day. We have routed, nay almost demoralized an army on which the whole North was looking with breathless anticipation; and this army is the one that they say defeated us at Scharpsburg; the one that has needed over three months to rally after a claimed victory sufficiently to be able to advance. How long will that army require to rally after what cannot but be admitted to be a defeat? The North, it seems to me may now well begin to think of making peace; though I fear they are yet too hard hearted & stiffnecked. We may indeed say "The Lord of Hosts is with us, the God of Jacob is our refuge."[72]

On Tuesday evening Lee sent over a flag of truce & offered to allow the Yankees to bury their dead. All the next day & yesterday they were accordingly busy covering their dead out of sight. On Wednesday I rode over the field and through the city. I never saw the dead lie so thick before. A portion of the field was almost covered with the disgusting objects. At one place an embankment had been thrown up & dead bodies were used to make it, they being laid in regular layers & dirt then heaped upon them, this they made for their men to fight behind. Some of the citizens who remained in the city say that hundreds of the bodies were hauled to the river & thrown in. I went into several houses & in only one did I not find dead bodies. The dead lay every where in chambers, parlors, cellars, scattered over yards & almost literally covering portions of the fields. In some of the houses there were wounded left, who have been carried to Richmond. I saw yesterday one of their papers giving an account of their advance and entrance the first day in Fredericksburg, where they took a few of our men prisoners. Those taken this paper says "were treated without much mercy," a sentence which to my mind speaks volumes. What is to be thought of the humanity of a people to whom such a telegram as the above should be sent. This is the people who used to boast of the advancement of the 19th century, & who considered themselves as exemplifiers of all that is humane, generous & religious. Thank God that we have the truthful & modest Lee, & the high toned & humane Jackson, as our leaders & examples.

---

72. Pss. 46:7, 46:11.

I have heard but little of the end of Gen. Gregg. When I arrived here Sunday, I was told that he was dead. He did not die, however, until the next evening. I was very sorry that I did not know of it, as I might have seen him. He was five or six miles from where I was assigned to duty. He told the Surgeon who was with him to tell the Haskels[73] that he loved them both very much—that if he had ever spoken to them harshly, they must not remember it, but must think only of his kind feelings to them—that he esteemed them too much to feel harshly even if he had so spoken. A sterling, noblehearted, polished man & valiant soldier has fallen. Gen Jackson visited him on Monday. I do not know if he was then conscious.

I am keeping passably well, though still far from being really so. Camp fare is not benefiting me.—I wish whenever Jacob comes you would send by him a moderate sized warm comfort for me. I need one very much, for the nights are very cold. Do send me also if possible a comforter to put around my neck. The weather looks as if about to change & by tomorrow, I fear, we may have snow. The soldiers are, as far as I have seen, now for the most part clad & shod, though their clothes look far too thin. The Government has, I heard in Richmond 500 men at work there making shoes, and is now paying far more attention to the preservation of hides. The health of the men generally seems good & their spirits are as high as possible over their recent victory. In a few days I hope to send for Jacob. Do see that his clothing is warm & that he has warm covering. Do have the children all vaccinated. It is of the highest importance now. Smallpox bad in Richmond & may be so elsewhere.

I hear a New York Brigadier told Burnsides when ordered to advance "Gen. I hold the commission of Brigadier from my state, but before I will lead my men into that slaughter pen, I will rend my commission in pieces & offer myself on my country's altar."[74] I wish they would all come to that conclusion & go home.

I find it very inconvenient being here without a horse. The one I had was during my absence claimed by a Virginian, as having been stolen from his father by the Yankees.

With very much love to all, ever yr. aff<u>ct</u> son

F. P. Leverett

P.S. Write me care of Dr. Hoyt, Richmond.

Fred's stay with McLaws's Division in the field lasted only a few days. He was not assigned to hospital duty in Richmond, as he expected, but was instead ordered to

---

73.   Alexander Cheves Haskell and his brother, Maj. John Cheves Haskell; the former was severely wounded on 13 December 1862.

74.   This rumor, almost certainly apocryphal, had its roots in a council of war Burnside held on the night of 13 December, when he proposed another advance against the Confederates, but his generals quickly convinced him that such an assault would be disastrous.

Brookhaven, Mississippi, in the Confederate Department of Mississippi and East Louisiana, and assigned to duty examining conscripts at the large Confederate conscript camp.

Mary Maxcy Leverett to her son Milton

Farm, Columbia Jan. 14th, 1863

My dear Son

You will be surprised to hear that Fred has again been at home, and is also off again—and this time to <u>Mississippi</u>, to my great aggravation. He came unexpectedly on Saturday evening by the Charlotte train, & left this (Wednesday) morning to go by the way of Augusta to Brookhaven, Mississippi,[75] to examine Conscripts, but expects to be ordered somewhere else shortly. His health is much better & looks well but thin, but says he is not well, & applied to be relieved from field duty, so I suppose that is why he is sent South, not being as rigorous a climate as Virginia. He says he wishes you Beaufort men could be sent to the Army of the Potomac for a while,[76] just to learn what hardships really are, only he wouldn't wish you all to get killed. He says you all have a ridiculous number of clothes,—that he has learned to do with very little more than what he can carry on his back. He stayed with Middleton in his tent and both of them slept on the <u>ground</u> in all the bitter freezing weather & a large gap in the tent at his feet. It was so cold when he wrote me from there he was sitting on a log, one end of which was burning in the fire & on which end he had to put his inkstand to keep the ink from freezing. Middleton tho' <u>Quartermaster</u>, to his honor be it said, lived just as roughly as the rest. Corn bread, and parched corn with boiled water poured on it, was their meat and drink, the latter, he says is the best tasted substitute for coffee, he has met with.

You must have been shocked as we all were to hear of poor Paul Hamilton's death, just too when he had returned to the army full of hope & spirits, after having distinguished himself.[77] I have written to his poor Mother. I am very sorry for poor Margaret Smith.

Your father wants to know if he went to England soon, whether you could not come home and take care of the family. He has strong intentions of going shortly whether the blockade is broken or not.

---

75. In southwestern Mississippi, south of Jackson.
76. The common name for the Army of Northern Virginia before Lee took command 1 June 1862.
77. Capt. Paul Hamilton of Brig. Gen. Stephen D. Lee's staff in the Army of Tennessee, killed at Chickasaw Bayou, Mississippi, near Vicksburg, 29 December 1862. He was the brother of Henrietta Potter Hamilton Fuller.

I had an interesting letter from Pinckney, on the occasion of the death of Gen. Gregg lately, and intend to publish a part of it in the Columbia Guardian & will send a copy to you; also Dr Palmer's Address is to be published,[78] with a letter from Gen Lee to Gov. Pickens, & one from Gov. Pickens to your cousin Julia, all on the same subject.[79] His funeral was a grand one, but as I suppose some of the girls have described it to you, I will spare you. The coffin was covered with laurel wreaths and hot house flowers which ladies sent for the purpose.[80] We felt so sorry for the forlorn state of Julia and Cornelia that your father told me to invite them to live with us, which I gladly did, and they have been staying with us ever since, except that [they] take it by turns to go in, for several days at a time to attend to packing up & putting away & sending many articles of furniture here for themselves and us also, as we are gradually sending in Aunt Tils things, she expecting soon to move to her own house. Julia and Cornelia were very much overwhelmed at first & tho' Cornelia has cheered up since she has been out here (we brought her out the evening of the funeral) yet it will take a long time for Julia to get over it. She was in bed four days, with all the windows shut, after she got out here.

Julie can't find your other book, we suppose it may be in a box of our books left in Wm Fuller's room, neither have we got Bourdon. I will send the only book found by Express, as also a fancy shirt for you & a worsted cap Mary knitted for you. Fred wears his at night to sleep in, & some use them in smoking—many ladies are now knitting them, but it is very difficult & expensive now to get worsted.

In haste

yr aff mother
Mary Leverett

---

78. Benjamin M. Palmer, *Address delivered at the funeral of General Maxcy Gregg, in the Presbyterian Church, Columbia, S.C., December 20, 1862* (Columbia: Southern Guardian Steam-Power Press, 1863).

79. Lee wrote Pickens: "The death of such a man is a costly sacrifice. . . . Among those of his State who will proudly read the history of his deeds, may many be found to imitate his noble example"; 18 December 1862, *Official Records of the Union and Confederate Armies,* ser. 1, vol. 21, 1067. Pickens wrote Julia Gregg: "He fell where he would have chosen to meet death, in the front rank, pressing hard on the enemy, surrounded by the troops he loved so well, with the shout of victory in his ear. Peace be to his noble ashes!" 28 December 1862, Maxcy Gregg Papers, South Caroliniana Library, University of South Carolina, Columbia.

80. Gregg's funeral was at the First Presbyterian Church, Columbia; he was buried in Elmwood Cemetery.

Milton Maxcy Leverett to his sister Mary

Pocotaligo Thursday 15$\underline{th}$ Jan. /63

My dear Mary,

I received a letter from Fred some days ago, he seems to be having a very hard time, not having been appointed to any distinct command but only acting as a generally operating surgeon. He requested me to send his love to all at home, and that I should write oftener home than I did when he was there, a request totally unnecessary, it being the chief thing Ma looks to, my not writing often, otherwise she would be worrying herself perpetually.

I saw Miss Grimke yesterday, she comes around every now and then and pays me a call, she told me that some naval officers (English) that were expected up here were going to stay at Capt George Elliotts in McPhersonville and that he had been collecting beds all about for them. Capt Trenholm[81] I believe is to furnish provender; they are to have a big hunt. I told Miss G. that I had expected that they would have put up with her father and that I had no doubt that she would perform the duties of hostess well. Oh! said she the times would not admit of it.

Since writing the above they have arrived and I understand are a very yea nay looking set, they were carried up to the village in a four mule wagon.

I received the package by Express from home today and am much obliged to you for the sleeping cap, it being the very thing I wished and a very nice one. Tell Ma I am very much obliged to her for the shirt, it isn't too fancy for me, she mustn't worry herself about my welfare in camp as I am amply supplied with everything; tell Julie I am much obliged to her for the books. I have also received Ma's letter for which I am much obliged to her; I do love to receive them they are such nice chunky looking little letters, so compact and with generally so much in them. Pa asks in Ma's letter if I wouldn't be able to come home in case he went to England, tell him I would gladly gratify him if I could but I wouldn't be able to come home to stay unless I got a <u>discharge</u> and that I wouldn't like to do, although I am almost disgusted with the life of a private soldier, but if he thinks it absolutely necessary I will do anything he wishes.

Ask him if he has sent in his bill to the Confederate Government for losses incurred in the war &^{c} &^{c}? If so he should send in one for the injury picket companies have done to Canaan. One of the japonicas that was about to be destroyed by horses Dr Manigault saved and put it in a box and carried it up to his camp and let me know of it so that I might recover it if I wished, but as I think he wants it I will let him have it for his thoughtfulness and gentlemanliness. It is seldom or never nowadays you meet with such gentlemanly acts in like situations. I don't

---

81. Probably Capt. William Lee Trenholm.

wish Pa to sell the Farm, at any rate not immediately, or rather don't be in a hurry, as I think Columbia will grow and then it will be very valuable, also Canaan must be perfectly settled before the family returns, God willing that our lives be all spared.

There has been one case of smallpox in the Pineland but that has been moved up the road somewhere.

Our scouts that were taken prisoners have all returned, they say the houses of Beaufort are occupied by negroes, some by officers, and some few white families, they have a negro school in the Baptist Church,[82] and the little wretches were going all about the streets with satchels on their shoulders and saying "Good he catch em." There are a few omnibuses there. Mr. Melvin Sams house is used as a negro hospital.[83] Some of the negroes wished to return and others didn't. I haven't time or space for more. Miss Ann Jenkins sends her love to Ma.

Your aff.<u>ct</u> brother

M. M. Leverett

Haven't any stamps, so I must put Soldier's letter.

P.S. Please send me the clothes at once. Don't lose a minute more than possible in getting them off.

The Rebel Troop is on James Island.[84] Charlie is commissary of his company— he is thereby relieved of guard duty & other irksome duties.[85] I hear from him indirectly every now & then, & believe he is well. The Rebel Troop are having now I hear very hard times, much exposure, no tents, & few servants—since the move to the island.

An excursion party sent by Drayton to Clarence Kirk Is. saved about 700 bu. corn & 80 head of fine cattle.

Frederic Percival Leverett to his father

Brookhaven 28<u>th</u> Jan. 1863

My dear Father,

I have been now a week with nothing to do. It seems to be my fate nowadays to be in this position. The other Surgeons have now arrived, & still we cannot be

---

82. The Baptist Church of Beaufort still stands on Charles Street.
83. Dr. Melvin Melius Sams's house, built by his father, Dr. Berners Barnwell Sams, still stands on New Street.
84. Capt. John Lawton Seabrook's Company I, Third South Carolina Cavalry, formerly an independent cavalry company.
85. Charles was detailed to commissary duty in August 1862, but is listed as absent on sick furlough on the company muster rolls from September to December 1862.

assigned yet to duty. The plan ordered for the assembling and examination of Conscripts by [letter badly damaged; two lines missing] told us, we must wait until he can hear from the Sec. of War before he can give us any orders.[86] So we will be yet ten or fifteen days without any work. Major Clark told us he would give us furloughs for that length of time if we wished it.[87] How glad I would be could I spend it at home. Two or three of us anticipate going to Vicksburg on a visit of a day or two.[88] The Yankees seem to be about again to attack that place with redoubled force. I trust this assault may prove as futile as their previous ones.[89] The people out here seem confident that the place will be held. Joe Johnson has inspired the utmost confidence. I understand the state of feeling here now is far different from what it was previous to his arrival & Davis' visit.[90] Before that all were exceedingly despondent, very little confidence being had in hardly any of the commanding generals. Bragg was regarded as more of a tyrant than anything else,[91] so destitute of judgement that one day he would fight an army with a handful of men, & another he would retreat from the same force while [letter badly damaged; several words missing] if not quite equal his. Affairs are not as bright for us here as we would like them, consequently the prospects of peace are not at present good. If Vicksburg falls the war will be indefinitely prolonged & its final result will be exceedingly dubious. The accounts in today's paper just arrived are not pleasant. I trust a Gracious Providence will watch over us & help out of this difficulty as he has so often done. The prayers of the whole country should be offered up to him now. This is now the turning point of our destiny.

I hope in your Book you will give a good account of Wheeler's exploits.[92] He certainly during the Battle of Murfreesboro & since has been achieving feats that surpass anything of kind performed in this war or any previous one. I hope

---

86. James A. Seddon was appointed the fifth Confederate secretary of war in November 1862.
87. Maj. Henry M. Clark, adjutant and inspector general on the staff of Maj. Gen. Sterling Price in the Department of Mississippi and East Louisiana.
88. A strategically vital city, the key to Confederate control of the Mississippi River.
89. After the first phase of his Vicksburg Campaign stalled in mid-December 1862 Grant attacked Pemberton's Confederates at Chickasaw Bluffs north of Vicksburg. After three days of fighting, from 27 to 29 December, Federal losses numbered seventeen hundred men, while Confederate losses were only about two hundred.
90. In November 1862, after recovering from a wound received at Seven Pines, Johnston was ordered to take command of the Confederate Department of the West, including territory from northwestern South Carolina to Louisiana. Davis traveled to Mississippi in December to meet with Johnston and addressed the state legislature.
91. General Braxton Bragg commanded the Confederate Army of Tennessee at the battle of Stones River (Murfreesboro), Tennessee, 31 December 1862–2 January 1863.
92. Brig. Gen. Joseph Wheeler commanded the Cavalry Corps in the Army of Tennessee.

too you will [give] Magruder full credit for his Galveston affair.[93] He is the first one to show gun boats can be boarded. I am keeping some of the Western papers which may be of use to you. I saw a notice the other day of a volume of official reports of battles having been issued.[94] You ought certainly to get it so as to correct many of the accounts you have. I saw a day or two since some ladies from New Orleans among [illegible] Mrs. Cushman & Miss Screven, nieces of Mrs. [illegible]. They had been in the city since before the arrival of Butler, & were allowed last week by Banks to come out with a number of others.[95] They represent Banks as conducting himself comparatively well. They say he and Butler both have treated those who refused to take the oath with much [more] respect than those who did. He is allowing all those to leave the city who wish to—at least all non-combatants, thus increasing the number of consumers but not fighting material in the Confederacy. They said the negroes of the Creoles have all remained with their owners & that they have been surprised to see how many have proved faithful. They say those who have gone to the Yankees are suffering very much—death from starvation being a daily occurrence in N. Orleans. That the Yankees & Negro Soldiery[96] are having constant fights together and that it was a perfect relief to get out of the City. A short time since some of the troops were to be sent from New Orleans to Baton Rouge when they refused a [missing line] taken out to arrest our men & they [missing word] be forced on at the point of the bayonet.

I expect you will find much difficulty in reading this letter, so poor is the paper & pale the ink—It is written moreover in greatest bustle and confusion, several people being in the room interrupting constantly.

With much love to all
Ever yr. aff^ct son
F. P. Leverett

P.S. I wrote to Julia last week. I hope soon to hear from home.

---

93. Maj. Gen. John Bankhead Magruder commanded the Confederate District of Texas and recaptured Galveston from the Federals on New Year's Day 1863.

94. Confederate States War Department, *Official Reports of Battles. Published by Order of Congress* (Richmond: Enquirer, Book and Job Press, 1862).

95. Maj. Gen. Benjamin Franklin Butler commanded the Federal Department of the Gulf and was military governor of Louisiana with headquarters in New Orleans from April to December 1862. Maj. Gen. Nathaniel Prentiss Banks, who succeeded Butler, was commander of the Department of the Gulf from December 1862 to September 1864.

96. Three regiments of free black soldiers from Federal-occupied New Orleans—the First, Second, and Third Louisiana Native Guards—mustered into the U.S. Army in the fall of 1862, respectively. They were later redesignated the Seventy-third, Seventy-fourth, and Seventy-fifth United States Colored Troops.

Frederic Percival Leverett to his brother Milton

Brookhaven, Miss. 3$^{\underline{rd}}$ Feb. 63.

My dear Minny,

I am rather badly off for paper, so I write you on half sheets to your last received a few days since, sent here from Richmond. You have heard before this from home of my being out here in the West, sent to examine Conscripts—a most delectable employment to say the least of it—Five of us, Surgeons & Assts. were sent on to this place by the War Department to report to the Commandant of Conscripts at this place. He was ordered to form contracts with ten physicians two of whom should act with each of us to form boards of examination. We were then to be sent to different Congressional Districts to make the grand round of inspections. We were to travel the best way we could, after the fashion of Methodist ministers, except that we would probably go on broken down government hacks, from county to county & village to village, announcing by every available means ten days before hand the day of our intended visit. We, the Surgeons arrived here safely after very arduous, fatiguing & expensive journeys, & reported ourselves to Major Clark. We have found him very polite & obliging, but unable to give us anything to do. He cannot get a single physician to act with us & has written to that effect to Richmond. We have all written to beg to be ordered to some other service. I have been here a fortnight tomorrow, doing absolutely nothing. If I were well the situation would be intolerable. As it is, I am hardly fit for anything but to attend to myself—in fact not fit for that. I stopped at home a few days, when coming on here. I was feeling then remarkably well for me these times, and all thought me well. The result may prove far different. I cannot get rid of this miserable diarrhea which I have now had for months, & which has reduced my flesh & strength & ruined my spirits. In addition to this I have a troublesome cough, which I had in Maryland, got over when at home, & which has come back since getting on here. What is to be the result of this long attack God only knows & in his hands I am satisfied to leave it. I am using remedies now that I trust may prove beneficial, & am following a strict course of diet. I am following the directions of Dr. Maury, Surgeon of the hospital here—he was formerly colleague of Edmund Walker at Bellevue Hospital & a great friend of his.[97] If I get worse than I now am I will be obliged to get another furlough & perhaps resign. Where to go then I do not know. It is of no use for me to go to Columbia & I almost dread the idea of going there again sick. I wish I could get to Beaufort. Salt air would be

---

97. Surgeon Richard B. Maury of Mississippi, surgeon in charge of the General Hospital at Brookhaven. Surgeon Edmund Rhett Walker of South Carolina, surgeon in charge of the South Carolina Hospital at Petersburg, Virginia.

more beneficial to me than anything else. But that cannot be had. Don't say a single word about what I have now said in writing home. If we continue to hold Vicksburg & prevent the Yankees using the Canal, should they suc. in getting the water through, some of us may be in Beaufort this summer.[98] The good news from Charleston reached us on Sunday & caused general rejoicing. I trust we may keep the blockade now raised there & long to hear that Port Royal has been retaken. Three cheers for Ingraham, the Palmetto State & Chichora.[99] I wish the blockade could be raised in the same way at Mobile, but unfortunately nothing has been constructed there with which it can be effected. I saw there two very good Gunboats & a Ram the last apparently of no account except to butt, & it looked as if it would not be able to do much at that. The prow was iron sheathed, but the stern was perfectly open—unprotected. At Montgomery & Selma three or four Gunboats are being built, but not near finished. At Richmond two more ironclads are underway. Our fleet is gradually increasing much to the annoyance of the Yankees. Wheeler & his cavalry out here perform wonders. Railroads, wagon trains, transports & gunboats all dread him. His exploits have surpassed those of all other cavalry officers in the West, though Morgan & Forrest are not far behind.[100] Everyone here is all anxiety for the result of the attempts now being made on Vicksburg. People talk confidently of the failure of the Yankees, but I think they privately fear their ingenuity & perseverance may succeed in opening the Canal to their transports. If so, & if we have not the means to prevent them using it (which no one seems to know anything of) the general impression [is that] the attempt to open the Mississippi will be a success. But our Generals must have guarded against such a disaster. I look forward hopefully. If we hold the Mississippi the war will not last long. The Northwest is now in a ferment & the Democrats, though now talking of prosecuting the war, will when they come into power, if we do not previously meet with any reverses show themselves a peace party. They have not yet given up the idea of restoration of the Union, but if we prove firm & act as men, they will soon drop that.

I am truly sorry to hear of the condition of the houses at Canaan. Our soldiers ought really to be ashamed of themselves. I long to be there & engaged in

---

98. Grant's Federals made a second unsuccessful attempt early in 1863 to dig a canal across the peninsula created by a bend in the Mississippi River opposite Vicksburg.

99. The C.S.S. *Palmetto State* and *Chicora*, both commanded by Flag Officer N. Duncan Ingraham of the Confederate States Navy, engaged the Federal blockading squadron in the Charleston Harbor early on the morning of 31 January, badly damaging the U.S.S. *Mercedita* and *Keystone State*, although both Federal ships escaped and the blockade continued. The *Chicora*, sister ship of the *Palmetto State*, was an ironclad ram commissioned in September 1862. It was commanded by Lt. John Randolph Tucker of the Confederate States Navy.

100. Brig. Gen. John Hunt Morgan and Brig. Gen. Nathan Bedford Forrest commanded Confederate cavalry brigades in the Army of Tennessee.

having the place fixed up. If my life is spared I think I shall go back to Beaufort to practice & as it will be sometime after the war ceases, before anything can be done there, I hope to spend that in getting Canaan fixed up. I think if the depredations committed at Canaan were represented to Gen. Walker, he would authorize his Quarter Master to pay fully for the damages. That ought to be done & done soon, or at any rate Gen. Walker ought to be notified of the fact that it will be done. Ask Ste or someone about it. Tell Ste I told you to. Wherever our troops were encamped in Va. or Md. Lee had all damages paid for. Of course the money does not often pay for the losses, but it assists to replace. I wish Pa could get his Cotton off to England now. I had the first set of pigs altered when at home in Nov. & had two of the young sows killed & sold as pork. They brought over $22.00. They proved to be both young with pigs. There are three young sows left, which I thought might also be with pigs. After they have them, they ought to be spayed, as they will then make fine bacon for next year, much larger than they otherwise would. There are four boar pigs of the second litter which ought to be altered as soon as the weather becomes moderate. Attend to this, whenever you go home. If you can purchase a bull calf at Hampton's (brahmin)—do so on my account.

Remember me to all your company. I wish I were with them.

Your aff^{ct} brother
F. P. Leverett

This place is a little R. R. town sixty miles S. of Jackson on way to N. Orleans. I am boarding at a little hotel, & have Jacob with me, a great expense but comfort.

P.S.

If well enough I hope in a day or so to visit Vicksburg.

I am living now on eggs, milk, wheat bread, & rice—all which articles except the last not being furnished by the Hotel, I have to buy them as extras, it makes my board or pension—eggs 50 to 75 cts per doz. Fortunately I am paid here as if in Hospital, a little over $200.00 per mo. Last month is $215.50 & about $150.00 to pay for my journey on here. Lately I have hardly paid expensive [expenses]. They have kept me moving so much.

Charles, who had been absent on sick furlough for most of his service with the Rebel Troop since April, was discharged from the company at Adams Run on 10 February 1863. "I think he is totally unfit for the duties of a soldier, in any branch of the service," Capt. John L. Seabrook wrote on the certificate of disability. Assistant Surgeon William S. Cannon granted the discharge based on "total debility from chronic diar-

rhoea of five months duration & structural disease of the right lung" and concluded that Charles was "unfit for duty in any department of the government."[101]

Milton Maxcy Leverett to his mother

Pocotaligo Feb. 18th /63

My dear mother,

    I have heard from Fred since my return, he seems to have a pretty rough time of it, notwithstanding the comfortable salary of $200.00 per month which he draws. He has not got over his sickness or his indisposition if you may so style it as yet, and seems as if he would like to be in old Beaufort again. His letter was quite pleasant and interesting; his chief desire being to fix Canaan all to rights again.

    My valise arrived here safely under my protection, <u>notwithstanding</u> your maternal care of placard and tacks. The basket though was inadvertently detained in Charleston and did not arrive here until next day when I got Carr[102] to send it up by Express. Ed. Barnwell's[103] cap which I had to carry down was also detained in town by my wanton forgetfulness and did not arrive here until the Sunday after when it was brought up to me by Willie Cuthbert,[104] I having previously written to Carr asking him to send it by Express. When at the Mills House I had placed it under the charge of Carr who is the clerk for safe keeping and next morning I jumped in the bus and went off without thinking of it. I ascribe my forgetting it in a great measure to worry of mind about my basket of cake etc. which I had not been able to obtain the night before from the car on account of the quantity of baggage on it, and the baggage wagon which I sent for it next morning did not arrive time enough before I left. I had written to Pa thinking he was at the Planters' Hotel[105] to attend to the missing articles for me, but didn't receive any answer so I suppose he could not have put up there. Any how alls well that ends well and it all ended well especially the cake and candy which I am very much obliged to Mame for, and which we all 'knocked cold' in less than no time.

    I saw Dr Manigault the other day, he came up and introduced himself to me, and told me of his having the japonica, and also that it was blossoming, that if I

---

101. Capt. John L. Seabrook, Certificate of Disability of Charles H. Leverett, 4 February 1863, and Assistant Surgeon William S. Cannon, Endorsement, 10 February 1863, Compiled Service Records.

102. W. S. Carr of Charleston.

103. 1st Lt. Edward H. Barnwell, assistant adjutant general on the staff of Brig. Gen. William S. Walker; son of Rev. William Hazzard Wigg Barnwell.

104. William Henry Cuthbert.

105. The Planters' Hotel, at the corner of Church and Queen Streets in Charleston.

wished it I could obtain it by sending to his camp for it. I felt very much like sending for it when he told me it was blossoming, and taking care of it for you, but I wouldn't, and thanked him for his thoughtfulness, and said I would be happy if he would keep it. He said he was glad of it being somewhat of a flower fancier &c &c. He said the pickets had ruined a great many fine ones at Mrs Frazer's.

I received quite a pleasant letter from Mr. A. H. Seabrook, in his usual nice friendly, hearty, style, giving me full leave and license to sell his carriage, the existence of which had slipped his memory. He begs me in the name of a man tired of expatriation to relieve the wearisome monotony of his exile life by sending him all the floating gossip &c &c of Beaufort and the Main.

We are all on the qui vive for an attack down here. It may happen at any moment, the enemy from all I can understand seem to be collecting their forces, land and naval, on Hilton Head, and in the harbour. A Miss Jenks an exiled Floridian from St. Augustine was sent over by flag of truce from Beaufort the other day. She is a relative of Gen'l Walker's wife and must have some spirit, as I understand she demanded to be sent over and declared if she was refused she would find some means of communication, which hint they took and sent her over blindfolded. A Yankee picket was captured on H. Head the other day. I understand that the river from Beaufort to the harbour is crammed with vessels, the ironclads, transports, &c being collected there. The Yankee picket said that they had 30 regiments on H. Head.[106] A lady and child have been lately sent by flag of truce boat to Savannah, and I understand that she overheard some officers conversing of Charleston's being about to be attacked next Sunday with fifty thousand men. I wouldn't be surprised if it was a dodge and Savannah be the point. At any rate I expect they will try to cut the railroad again and all of your prayers will be needed for the cause, and some for myself. If they don't come in too overwhelming a force we will beat them back, but I do despise fighting five or six thousand men with three or four hundred. This we will have to do unless they give us more troops of which there seems to be some conflicting rumours. The reserves have all gone home, and we have only our original force with the exception of a few of them who have been drafted into the different companies about here. We have in our company fifteen involuntary, rough looking old chaps who have been forced in, and henceforth the 'Volunteer' applies only to a portion. One of them complained of not having seen his wife and children for six weeks! I heard that we were to have three regiments sent here to us but it is not certain. We have been practicing with our guns and marking the distances at Pocotaligo so that when the enemy

---

106. The detachment of the Federal X Corps stationed on Hilton Head in early 1863 consisted of four infantry regiments, an artillery regiment and an additional battery, a regiment of engineers, and a cavalry company.

appears we may know the right distances and the exact time to burst our shells. I am only afraid of their marching right through Inverness and flanking us and thus taking the railroad, as the defenses there are not very great, unless we have more troops sent us. I went up with Nat Fuller yester-evening, paid Rob. Means' wife a visit[107] (she is staying at Randolph's) and then went over to Buncombeville next to Bluntville[108] to see a set of Tableaux got up by the ladies of the said villages, at a dollar admittance, in behalf of the sick soldiers of the McPhersonville Hospital. I would write of it more at length but haven't space. Tell Coz. Julia I delivered her message and the book to Miss G. myself, she having called around for it. Love to Cozs. Julia and Cornelia and all the rest.

Your Aff'ct son

M. M. Leverett

I suppose you all have heard of Mr Edmund Rhett's sudden death.[109] He came down a part of the way on the same train with me, and from what I saw of him appeared perfectly well.

Has Lindy made her appearance yet. I am <u>getting on</u> quite <u>swimmingly</u> and <u>pleasantly</u> as you will be glad to hear. Tell Pa if I have a chance I intend to sell all the old iron at Canaan as a man has written to me about it. I haven't stamps always so you must look out for A 'Soldier's Letter.' I saw Ralph Elliott here the other day perfectly well, and is now on his way back. I received a paper the other day from Shelbyville Tenn. (The Daily Rebel Banner) with an account of the disasters in Savage's Regt at the battle of Murfreesboro sent by him I suppose.[110] His brother Lieut Col. Savage was severely wounded.[111] The direction was simply Parson Leverett Pocotaligo. I will send it. His reputation down here as a man and gentleman I find is not much although no question is entertained of his bravery.

Morning of the 19<u>th</u>. Some troops arrived here for us last night.

---

107. Josephine Rogers Walker Fuller.

108. Bluntville, or Blountville, was a settlement in Prince William's Parish just north of present-day Yemassee.

109. Edmund Rhett died in Spartanburg on 15 December 1863.

110. Col. John Huston Savage of the Sixteenth Tennessee Infantry, whose regiment lost 207 out of 402 troops engaged at Stones River on 31 December.

111. Capt. L. N. Savage of the Sixteenth Tennessee Infantry was acting lieutenant colonel and mortally wounded at Stones River.

Milton Maxcy Leverett to his brother Fred

Pocotaligo Feb. 20th 1863

My dear Fred,

We are all on the lookout for an attack down here now, the enemy seem to be making preparations for an advance either on Charleston or Savannah. Beaufort River from the town to H. Head I hear is filled with their vessels, iron clads &^c and a large force is thought to be on Hilton Head. A Yankee picket was captured there the other day and he reports 30 regts there, although some reports make out fifty thousand, seventy thousand &^c. A lady (a Miss Jenks) some connection of the General's, was sent across the Ferry a few days ago by flag of truce, the first that has crossed the ferry since the hurried flight of the fair Beaufort birds after the battle of Port Royal.

I hope we will be able to hold our own in the expected battle or battles along this portion of the coast, we have some reinforcements at this post but not a great many. I am afraid the enemy will advance the next time right through Mr Wm Heyward's, passing by Pocotaligo which we have fortified quite extensively. The space of country from the Pocotaligo to the Tulifinny[112] is comparatively unprotected and in their last attack if they had had any gumption they could have taken the road and flogged us, they may have learnt their mistake and may do it this time, the obstructions to their passage being only a few pits, fences etc. unless we are able to have troops enough. I despise fighting such odds, it discourages a man.

Feb. 23rd

Three regiments have arrived since writing the above, and the men are more cheerful now. I feel so myself and I know that N. Fuller had the blues and was as nervous as possible until their arrival. It is a certain thing that men get discouraged in fighting against odds even if they are victorious for their numbers few as they are get thinned more certainly. I should hate to fight the battle of Pocotaligo over with the same odds. I suppose you have seen by this time that the injury done the Yankee fleet at Charleston was pretty much nominal. The fate of the Mercedita seems still doubtful though.[113] The Yankee account of the battle report her as having escaped through deception and got to Port Royal, although the officers of the French war vessel Milan say she is not there. Ingraham is thought to have acted not quite as bravely as he might have. I wouldn't speak of it publicly, if I were you, let it be a state affair, and don't let citizens of other states think the affair

---

112. The Tulifinny River.
113. The U.S.S. *Mercedita*, commanded by Comdr. Henry Stellwagen, was badly damaged by a shot from the C.S.S. *Palmetto State* but managed to make her way back to Port Royal.

was a failure, and that like the Yankee eagle we sing too soon. I believe it is going to be tried over. The Isaac Smith was nothing but a cattle boat on the Hudson once, and fitted up as a gunboat.[114]

I have been home since you were there but couldn't attend to the pigs as you wished on account of its being very cold, so much so as to sleet. They all seemed very well, better than when I was there before.

I am very sorry indeed my dear fellow to hear of your ill health and hope it is not so bad as you think. I would hate for you to resign but if your health requires it resign immediately, if you cannot get a transfer to another department. Health is the first thing and I consider it criminal to neglect it. You had better try to get a transfer to the department of Charleston, or somewhere on the coast, and if you cannot stand active duty get in a hospital. I think you might be able to get an <u>unlimited</u> furlough on the plea of ill health. They are given sometimes I believe. I know that Washington Chaplin[115] in my company had a sick furlough of about six or seven months, with the same sickness as yours, chronic diarrhoea. It was even expected that he would have had to get a discharge. The consequence was, that with a decent furlough and proper treatment he was able to return to the company with health perfectly restored. The great thing is to begin in time, and I would advise you to try and obtain a furlough now. I think you had better try to obtain both the transfer and the furlough before you think of resigning, if you fail to obtain either, then resign and come home.

We have been having a series of Tableaux, given by the Buncombeville and Bluntville young ladies, a dollar admittance, the proceeds to be devoted to the sick soldiers. I went the first night and got full four dollars worth. It was much better than I expected but on the whole rather insipid, nothing very dramatic. The soft style prevailed such as 'The Fatal Secret,' 'The Rivals,' 'Womans Curiosity,' 'The Sleeping Beauty,' &c &c. The last was the most popular and occasioned numerous remarks from the numerous soldiery there such as 'Wake her up,' 'O God she's dead,' 'Beautiful' 'B-ea-uti-ful' etc.

Do you hear from Charlie?

Aff'ct brother
M. M. Leverett

P.S.

A mulatto fellow sent over to Beaufort some two months ago by Gen'l Walker has just returned with files of the latest newspapers. He says we are to be attacked between now and Saturday. He was recognized over there by a Dutchman who

---

114. The U.S.S. *Isaac Smith*, a Federal gunboat, was captured on the Stono River on 30 January 1863 after being fired upon by the South Carolina Siege Train.
115. Pvt. Washington A. Chaplin.

said he was a spy and he was put in jail but he declared that he was not. The Dutchman said he knew that he had a good master and that he would not have left him except as a spy, but he answered that his master had sold him and he didn't like it. The Dutchman said he knew his master would not have sold him for $3000.00. Still he got off and after staying there two months, he dodged off, paying another negro to row him over. The negroes have the idea that they will be shot if they return.

Frederic Percival Leverett to his sister Mary

Cooper's Well, Miss.[116]
6<u>th</u> Febry. [March] 1863.

My dear Mary,

I was truly glad to receive your letter night before last. In fact I felt that I could not thank you enough for it. The only other one received since I left home was the one from Ma of which you asked me, & in which was one from Julia. I did not think Anne would have let me be from home two months without writing, even if others did. I have written home each week but one since I came out here, at least one letter, & once or twice more. I had hoped Minny would have written me when at home, but was disappointed in his not doing it. Do when you write tell me of everything on the place—how each thing is getting on. Tell Ma in a day or so I will send her by Express some Green Peas & other seed. They will be given by an old gentleman who lives near this place, whose acquaintance I have made. I was at his house yesterday afternoon & he and his wife took me over their garden & showed me everything in it. It is true there was little to be seen except an abundance of onions & seed just coming up, but it was evident that if nothing happens they would in due time have an abundance of vegetables. I wish Ma had such a promising garden. How I wish I were at home helping with it & everything else instead of being out here virtually doing nothing. I hope Ma is planting a plenty of vegetables & that her strawberry bed is in good condition. I think Sary had much better be at work in it than anywhere else. I hope Ma calls on Hercules to work it as often as necessary. I hope too Tilly has had the hogs, her special pets well attended during the winter & that they have grown well. Tell Hercules he ought to keep their pens well littered, and while I remember it, that it is time he had the potatoes "<u>banked out</u>" to sprout. Tell him out here they do not dig a hole & put the potatoes into it but raise a large bank with dirt and plenty of manure & put the potatoes out in it and plant the sprouts as they come. If there is room to

116. A popular mineral spring west of Jackson.

spare in the garden he might make his bank there. I suppose Anne hardly has any chickens out yet. Mrs. Parker at whose house I was yesterday has already about forty in the yard. She is a regular managing old lady, full of energy & seemingly very kind hearted. Her husband, Col. Parker has offered me the use of his riding horse to exercise on at any time I may wish it while here. I intend to avail myself of his kind offer. Their daughter is a widow of a Mr. Spann of Sumter, So. Ca., a cousin probably of Mr. Spann of Beaufort. Tell Ma she ought to plant a plenty of mustard, & set out her Thyme and get if possible a plenty of Sage plants. Also plant a plenty of Turnips, Squashes & such things as will be useful for cows and hogs—by all means a plenty of "Red Peppers" to season soups with. I have not found the last article used as freely anywhere in the Confederacy as at home, and that was due to my buying them in Market. The Spring out here this season is exceedingly backward, owning to the almost constant rains, & the consequent cool weather. In fact were it not for a few spring flowers, especially violets and the merry singing of the Mockingbird, one would not suppose the time for Spring were even approaching. People here are exceedingly behind hand this year in preparations for planting. They are all unsettled by the Yankees anticipated attack on Vicksburg. It has been now so long postponed that many doubt whether any attack will be made. Should it fall this portion of the country will be abandoned. The next month or two must decide our destiny, it seems. We have, however, so often before thought a short period would settle everything & have been so often disappointed that perhaps even now when we are apparently so near our goal, we may be almost as far off as ever.

I see by the papers that Mr. Edmund Rhett is dead. I am truly sorry for it. He will be truly a great loss to Beaufort. Death has indeed revelled in South Carolina.

I wish Pa would write me with reference to his plans in case the blockade is raised. Everything seems to indicate that in the course of a few weeks something will be done. If Charleston be attacked & does not fall, Louis Napoleon[117] will not remain much longer inactive. When he hears of the insult offered by Seward to Mercier,[118] I would not be surprized, if he acted forthwith. He has been shrewd enough to put off all action until after the 4$\underline{\text{th}}$ of this month, whereby he may compel his majesty Lincoln to summon his new Congress. This very month I look for decisive news, if Charleston does not fall. I seize the papers eagerly each day to learn the news from there. If the port should be opened I suppose Pa would go abroad at once in which case I would know nothing of it, until after he is gone. Do beg him to write me fully of his plans. I suppose he has made no arrangement

---

117. Napoléon III, emperor of France, 1852–1871.

118. Henri Mercier, French minister to the United States, proposed that representatives of the United States and the Confederate States meet on neutral soil to negotiate a peace settlement. Secretary of State William Henry Seward refused.

for sending some of the Hands to Canaan in case it be practicable. I think he had much better do it. I am sorry the carriage is broken, as it will hardly be possible to purchase but at great disadvantage, & Pa will probably be unable to get anything in which our horses will look much larger than goats, or which will not be for them horse killers.

Much love to all.

Ever your aff<u>ct</u> brother,
F. P. Leverett

P.S. Col. Parker has brought me the seeds & last night I have them put up in a cigar box with some papers for Pa & some old letters & papers sealed up in an envelope, which I wish Anne would put away for me in my trunk. Tell her I beg her to see whether the clothes in it have tobacco enough in them to keep off moths.

Milton Maxcy Leverett to his father

Pocotaligo March 16<u>th</u>/63

My dear father,

In my last letter I wrote to ask whether you would like me to send in a report to the Gen'l, of the injury done to Canaan, but as usual when I write home making inquiries, or desiring information, unless the particular query is brought forward in the most conspicuous manner it is not ever noticed. Wouldn't the report interfere with that you have already sent in? wouldn't you have to write and have that report curtailed. If I do send in a report, present indemnification may be obtained, while the other would of necessity be postponed to some distant future day. Besides the corn house and a portion of the bower being demolished as well as the McCarthy gin itself carried off Lewis' and Hagar's house has been razed, floor taken out of Quash's as well as other houses. Only three trees have been cut down, the two in front of Sary's house and a medium oak in the corner of the front part of the yard, near Eliza's house. The shed that has been punched through in the dwelling is not fortunately over the drawing room, parlour, company room, and the dark room, but over the partition between the main body of the house and the long entry from Ma's to Anne's room, and over the front piazza. I told you while home pretty much the rest of the injuries. There are some very nice ploughs in the garret. What do you mean by Brown's lending you one? The scouts that went to St. Helena have just returned and report forty thousand men there, so an attack is certainly meant some day or other. Those that had gone to Port Royal Island and Hilton Head had reported only about eight regiments on both Islands, the scout to H. Head had seen them on dress parade and heard what he supposed since must have been the groans for Hunter.[119] We are having ten inch shells filled with powder with sensitive tubes attached, and buried on the principal expected routes of attack, so that when the enemy pass over them they will burst. The pressure of a quarter of a pound will explode them.[120] The prisoners that were captured by Mickler[121] <u>I believe</u> said that an attack might be looked for at any moment. Ste Elliott's wife is staying at Bluntville with Tom Hanckel,[122] and Rob Means' is staying with R. I am in McPhersonville.

Your aff.'<u>ct</u> son
M. M. Leverett

I wish you would destroy all papers of mine you come across with boyish effusions on them. Love to the Greggs.

Rev. Charles Edward Leverett to his son Milton

Col<u>a</u>, March 26, 1863.

My dear Minny,

Your basket & letter came for which I paid $2. Had you paid previously. I wish you would prepay your letters as they go into Mr. Middleton's box & I have to go through some trouble to pay them. Yr. mother will send some stamps. I had written to you before yr. letter came about presenting an account to Col. Walker. It would not be in the way of the presenting of the account to the Confederate States as if Col. W. made any allowance it could be deducted in the final settlement. But the paper has not been adjusted at all: The Auditor not having sent in his queries. You had better ask Mr Wm Heyward or Mr Ja^s Gregorie to affix a value & then present it to Gen. Walker. In making up the estimate there should be considered not merely the damages done but cost of labor & too the increased difficulty there will be of obtaining hands. The oak tree they cut down I would not have taken $500 for. Also should be taken into consideration, future injuries likely to be done by the same troops. I understand that all the walls are ruined. I doubt if $2,500 will cover the damages done or what would cost me to replace things to their original status. You can advise with Mr. Heyward, however.

---

119. Maj. Gen. David Hunter commanded the Federal X Corps in the Department of the South.

120. The Confederate employment of land torpedoes or mines was quite controversial during the war; some observers on both sides considered them an uncivilized form of warfare.

121. Capt. John H. Mickler commanded the Hamilton Guards, Company E, Eleventh South Carolina Infantry.

122. Charlotte Stuart Elliott, daughter of Henry Middleton Stuart Sr.; Thomas Middleton Hanckel of Prince Williams Parish, an attorney.

There is nothing new at home. I live in constant anxiety about being able to find provisions a little later for so large a family. These times are a halter about my neck. I am dreadfully worried. How I am to get corn I don't know, if the war goes on. We are planting, but if we make anything, it can go only a little way. I am waiting on the coming fight to get out. I can't publish here. The cost is 7 or 8 times the common cost. In common times a page cost about 75 cents now about 5.50 or $6.

I did not sell Trusty. B. S. afterwards offered $180 & then again $200 but I was told she & the colt were worth 350. If I could keep them I would not sell them at all, but what I am to do for corn I cannot say. If it was my pleasure I would not have one animal in the yard in these times. Times look dark for us. The Yankees are preparing to come down with a heavy hand. I trust they will get enough when they do try it to silence them forever.

Cousin Julia is away at present but Cornelia is here and Mary Fowles. Lewis had Mr. Brown's plough again yesterday and the corn had not come after all. Hercules went in for it. He is planting now. Heard from Charley the other day. Also Fred regularly. I sold Marcus for $500 but if I had kept him till next day could have got 700. He was put up at the board for that by the man who bought him & was knocked off at 700. The man said his age was 35. He grew young in a month's time. Negroes are selling very dear. Charley got those he bought of A.[123] very low. They would bring twice that. Are any shoes about N° 7 1/2 to be had at a low rate down your way—as I am badly off for them. Mine having given out.

yr. Aff. Father

P.S. I hope if you have a battle that you will be protected & will also cover yourself with glory. I always hear you well spoken of. If I have to send a hand down to work on the forts I shall want Billy to go. They will want him for 3 or 4 weeks. I will try to get off if possible as I worked before. Edmund Walker is married and is in town with his bride. Julie will tell you all the news. Charley had a school in Camden offered him $1500 a year. I don't know if he will take it.

If I have to take Billy, you can have the pay.
I enclose a note to Gen. Walker, which you can read.

Milton Maxcy Leverett to his mother

Camp Beaufort March 27$^{\underline{th}}$ /63

My dear mother,
I received your very nice letter some time ago and <u>hasten</u> to answer it. The fight has been put off much longer than I expected, there seems to be some sort

---

123. Anne Leverett DeSaussure.

of delay among the Yankees, but I suppose April will be the fighting month, if not there will be none or very little here after that. Torpedoes are the mania now, and there are going to be vigorous attempts in Charleston, made for destroying the enemies' fleet with them.[124] There have been collected a great number of row boats, to the prows of which are to be affixed some long projection with a torpedo at the end, the boat is driven in the night silently against the side of the gunboat, it then explodes and knocks the vessel to flinders without any injury to the row boat. Capt. Elliott has just invented one which he tried yesterday in Pocotaligo creek on a flat and raft, which it broke up, it succeeded very well. It is allowed to drift down held by a long rope, on the object intended to be destroyed. Personne[125] was down there when the preparations were being made to test it. He is a nice looking little fellow with a tolerably thick brown beard, a delicate and intellectual face, with just a trace perhaps of conceit or selfsatisfaction on it. His next letter will of course be from Pocotaligo.

I am very glad to hear of the addition to the family public of calves, pigs and poultry, as well as the hopeful condition of the young offshoots and limbs of Marrowfat Peas, Early Corn, Big Squashes and Squash head Turnips etc. The carriage ought not to have been painted and varnished at home but by a regular painter and it would have looked as well again. I am very glad the children are learning French, hope sincerely they will be able to read and speak it fluently.

I did not succeed in selling the carriage for Mr. Seabrook as the person who wanted it had gone up the country when I returned and when I went down to look at the carriage I found some one just as I had anticipated had abstracted the two hind wheels, and as regards the selling of the old iron, the man who wanted it, did not meet me according to appointment. The "suggestion in the papers" of soldiers planting gardens is a perfect humbug when men don't know if they will be in any one place two months at a time, and when they don't winter and summer at the same camping ground.[126] For instance if we planted gardens where we are now staying, it would go for nothing as in six weeks or so we move perhaps to McPhersonville, and also Jno Gregorie who is planting the field we are in will need the ground.

---

124. Civil War–era naval torpedoes were actually mines—either kegs lying just below the surface of the water or spar torpedoes attached to long booms on the bows of ships, which rammed enemy vessels.

125. Felix Gregory DeFontaine, writing under the pen name of Personne, was editor of the *Columbia Daily South Carolinian* and an army correspondent in Virginia; his dispatches were later published as *Marginalia; or, Gleanings from an Army Note-Book* (Columbia: Steam-Power Press of F. G. DeFontaine and Co., 1864).

126. A reader of the *Charleston Courier* claimed that two men working two hours a day could cultivate an acre, which could then produce enough vegetables for a company. With encouragement from the editors, some citizens donated seeds for the soldiers to be forwarded to Confederates on or near the coast. *Charleston Courier*, 7, 12, 25 March 1863.

Miss Grimke came to see me the other day with a Miss Barry from Wheeling[127] in the "Pan Handle," some connection I believe of the Healys. She brought me a supply of magazines, and a bottle of milk for Mr Webb who is very sick. How is Mr Pringle? I hope he will soon recover.

You mustn't worry yourself about me, as it just worries me to know that you are fretting yourself for fear I would get killed. I must and will fight as long as I can and if I get killed I won't be the first man who has been killed in battle, nor you the first mother who has mourned in this war. So you must cheer yourself up when you hear the fighting has commenced trust in God yourself and trust me to him.

You ask after Canaan and your Orchard. I have already written about them. Didn't my letter arrive and has Pa received my inquiry of sending an account of the injury done to Canaan in to the General.

Your aff<u>ct</u> son

M. M. Leverett

P.S.

I won't be able to write as often as I have being doing as I am entirely out of envelopes and nearly so out of paper. I will try to keep you informed of my whereabouts and health. Love to all. Remember me to the Greggs. None of you have answered <u>my query</u> as regards Mr Seabrook's direction.

Frederic Percival Leverett to his brother Milton

Brookhaven, Miss. 28<u>th</u> March 1863.

My dear Minny,

I received yours of 20th February a fortnight since, and right glad was I to get, though I must confess myself disappointed at its not being longer & fuller. I was truly glad to hear of the arrival of reinforcements at Pocotaligo. I can fully realize how depressing it must be to look forward to a fight with such disparity of numbers as you had in the last engagement there. May God continue his protecting care to you & your company, & may the enemy meet if they decide to come as decided a repulse as they did last Fall! The Yankees have indeed shown great respect to the Carolina main land, and appear verily as if wanting stomach for the fight there. I trust that the attack on Charleston will prove a disastrous failure. It would be a good thing for us, if they would do whatever they are going to there at once, for we are sadly in want elsewhere of the troops now necessarily kept on the coast for the defense of Charleston & Savannah—15000 to 20000 men added to

---

127. **West Virginia.**

Bragg's army would enable Johnston to redeem Tennessee, a matter of the utmost importance to us. The Yankees hold so much of our grain growing country, that we have to fear starvation more than anything else. As it is, there are many who fear Johnston will be compelled to fall back to Chattanooga, as it is thought Rosencranz will be able to flank him.[128] I trust not as that would surrender Eastern Tenn. to the vandals to be ravaged. The wretches destroy everything out here now that they can lay hands on. They have a particular spite, it seems, against all farming utensils, & exhibit a diabolical determination to prevent crops being raised, wherever they may, unless they feel pretty sure they will be able to remain. They have recently met with two or three repulses that must be very disheartening to them. Banks' attack on Port Hudson resulting in the destruction of the Mississippi & the passage of two of his vessels was, though pronounced by him a complete success a perfect failure.[129] Farragut is now between Port Hudson & Vicksburg. If he attempts to pass Vicksburg he will have to stem the current & meet almost certain destruction. If on the other hand he attempts to go down he will have not only the batteries at Port Hudson to meet, but before getting there he has to run the gauntlet of heavy guns at Grand Gulf,[130] which Pemberton has had mounted, since he went up. When he passed up there were only a few small field pieces there. Add to these difficulties our gunboats are preparing to attack the rear admiral. I wish one of them could succeed in planting a shell in his rear. Truly he is in an unhappy position. He certainly will not attempt to pass Vicksburg after after the disastrous failure of the four boats that tried to come to his aid two or three days since—One passed crippled; one was sunk & two driven back. Their attack on the Yazoo, which they confidently thought, must be a success, proved also a failure.[131] "They," to use the words of one of their letter writers, "did not give the rebels credit for sufficient gullibility to suppose they would make an attack with such a force in such an unlikely position." But alas for them Loring[132] was there & Fort Pemberton's guns were too heavy for them. Disaster there would have been worse for us than failure at Charleston & Savannah. Vicksburg would have fallen & the Mississippi been opened before long. I hope if we continue to repulse them whenever

---

128. Maj. Gen. William Starke Rosecrans commanded the Federal Army of the Cumberland.

129. On 14 March 1863, while Banks's Federal Army of the Gulf made a demonstration on land near Port Hudson, Louisiana, Rear Adm. David Glasgow Farragut of the United States Navy's West Gulf Blockading Squadron steamed two ships past the Confederate batteries.

130. In southwestern Mississippi.

131. A Federal naval and land expedition on the Yazoo River peninsula in which Lt. Comdr. Watson Smith of the United States Navy attempted to run a flotilla of ironclads and transports past the Confederate defenses at Fort Pemberton. By 20 March the Federals admitted defeat and withdrew.

132. Maj. Gen. William Wing Loring commanded the First Corps of the Confederate Army of Mississippi.

they advance we will have peace before many months, especially if we get the war vessels which we are assured are being built in Europe. I understand the reason why they have not been finished long is the difficulty the Confederacy has had in obtaining money abroad. That trouble is now, it seems, done away with—loans of large amounts having been recently contracted. We are having gunboats constructed out here at various points; on the Alabama, Yazoo & Red Rivers. On the Yazoo there is one, if not two very large & powerful rams constructing. There is great difficulty in getting ironplating for them, & on that account it is said they will not be finished for twelve months. Could one of them be completed and brought down on the Yazoo fleet above Vicksburg, it good [would] do good work. In fact we might almost go down & take New Orleans. But enough of warlike matters. I heard day before yesterday from home. I get a letter about once in three weeks on an average, & write home once a week. The enclosed advertisement will show my whereabouts next month. Write me here. I am somewhat better than when I wrote you last, but by no means well. I have applied for a transfer to Hospital service, but have no hopes of it being granted. I hope you are well & that I shall soon hear from you. If I were in Carolina, I would take my colt from Mr. Simms' & break her. She is three years old next month, & I fear will be ruined by the negros. Were she not Nightmare's colt, I would sell her, situated as I am, but will risk her loss rather than part with her. Wm Fuller wrote me last Fall that she had filled out, was looking well, and would not be large. He promised me to try & keep her from getting with foal. I hope our pickets have not cut down the trees at Canaan. I fear the place will hardly be worth going back to. The land however will be improved by the rest.

Remember me to all

Ever yr. aff^{ct} brother,
F. P. Leverett

P.S. I received a letter from Anne this evening & one from Blanche, with a note from Charley; She writes a very pleasant letter. She says Charley has been obliged to get a discharge on account of his health; that since returning to Cheraw he has had an offer of a school at Camden, 15 scholars, at $1600.00 a year. He had written to accept it, much to her joy. But he agreed to take it only for a year or the war, & did not know if it would be given him on that ground, but thought it would. Charley was obliged to sell my mare, & got $280 for her. I suppose it is the best thing could be done considering everything, though I regret very much that I shall never again cross her. I am sorry Charley has been obliged to resign, but think it far better for him to have done so than to remain in service constantly sick. Blanche says that one week after returning to his company from a four months furlough he was sick in bed. He was employing himself fishing & killing turkeys.

A few days before she wrote he went out & brought in three turkeys. Anne tells me a hospital is about being established in Greenville. I wish I could be put in charge of it. I fear there is no chance though. Col. R. Barnwell[133] might get me assigned to it—he is the only person I know of who could. Anne says it was thought Ingraham would make another attempt on the Yankee blockaders about the time she wrote. I wish he could have with prospects of good success.

Julia Marcelline Leverett to her brother Milton

Saturday 28th [March 1863]

My dear Minnie,

I suppose I ought to thank you for your letter, at least Ma would say so, but really instead of thanks, are you not ashamed to write such a letter? It was not philosophical for once, but it did not have any news. That anecdote about the alligator was quite amusing; who got up the scheme? You were at the bottom of it I know. Quite a number of marriages seem to be going to take place up here in April. Anderson Clarkson was married on Wednesday to Miss Brice.[134] The "happy couple" went off the same day to Alabama where they will just get today, travelling day and night. Mr. Jenkins is to be made "happy" on the 30th of April; to be married at twelve o'clock and to set off forthwith, for Charleston. Speaking of marriages, I suppose you will be quite astonished at Edmund Walker's own. The bride is a Miss Perkins of Suffolk Virginia. We have not seen her yet. They have been engaged ever since November. Brother Fred will quite envy him, wont he? In his last letter, some time this week, he mentioned having received your letter. He has bought 100 pounds of sugar. He will send them to us by express I suppose. He has also sent some garden seeds to Ma that he obtained from a Mr. & Mrs. Porter whose acquaintance he struck up while at Cooper's Wells. He says they (the surgeons) are to travel through the country to examine conscripts. Brother Charlie has had the offer of a school in Camden, but as the first person (a Mr. Middleton) to whom the school was offered has decided to take it, I am afraid he won't get it. Blanche wants him to go to Camden with a view to a permanent residence, which shows her sense. I was <u>seventeen</u> a week ago today. I am so ugly, stupid and different to what other girls of seventeen are. But mind, this is strictly confidential and if you breathe a word of it to anyone I will hunt for your "Jessie Bxxxxx" and never cease plaguing you about it.

---

133. Robert Woodward Barnwell (1831–23 June 1863), son of William Hazzard Wigg Barnwell, was chairman of the executive committee of the South Carolina Hospital Association and was in charge of all hospitals for the South Carolina troops.

134. William Anderson Clarkson married Sallie Bryce.

Mary Fowles says she hasn't got any letter from you and you needn't think she is going to write until she does. She evidently knows that you are "artful" but you wouldn't "come it" this time. Can't you buy a pair of soldiers shoes for me to have them exchanged for ladies shoes. I am in dreadful want of every day shoes. I will send the money. Sister made me a very nice pair of gaiters but they don't do for every day. Carrie sends her love. Cousin Cornelia sends her love & says she hopes you are "getting on finely."

Ever your affectionate sister
Julie.

Thank you for looking for my Jessamine. I am sorry to hear it is "wanting."

Frederic Percival Leverett to his mother

Port Gibson, Miss,[135] 11th April, 63

My dear Mother,

I left Brookhaven on the 1st & have since been engaged in making my conscription tour. My first place for examination was Bovina not far from Vicksburg. While en route there I had to stop at Jackson, and there saw Gen. Drayton, who is there on the Lovel Court of Inquiry.[136] He took me to see Dr Crowell of So. Ca. who had just been ordered to Charleston as Medical Director to Beauregard's Army.[137] Dr. C. very kindly promised to use his influence to get me transferred to that Department when I get through the work I am now engaged in. It will indeed give me much pleasure to have the transfer obtained. I wish it could have been accomplished prior to the attack on Charleston. Night before last the news reached us of the failure of the assault on the 7th It was indeed glorious, and I trust with the blessing of the Almighty we may continue successful.[138] We have heard as yet of no renewal of the attack, but are constantly expecting news. Not

---

135. In southwestern Mississippi.

136. Maj. Gen. Mansfield Lovell, Confederate commander of New Orleans when it fell in April 1862, was so widely blamed that he requested an official court of inquiry; although the court acquitted him of any blame, his reputation was ruined.

137. Surgeon Nathaniel S. Crowell, medical director of the Department of Mississippi and East Louisiana, was assigned medical director of the Department of South Carolina, Georgia, and Florida.

138. The attack by Rear Adm. Samuel F. DuPont of the U.S. Navy with seven monitors and the ironclads U.S.S. *Keokuk* and *New Ironsides* opened at noon on 7 April 1863 and was answered by seventy-seven Confederate guns from the batteries surrounding the Charleston Harbor. DuPont's ships were battered and forced to withdraw; the *Keokuk* sank during the night; and DuPont was removed from command. This action began the Federal siege of Charleston, which lasted until February 1865.

one word as to any attempt to move by land. The dispatches are very meagre, and I long for a full account, for which unless we get it today or tomorrow I will have to wait, until we reach Natchez next Friday or perhaps until we get back to Brookhaven week after next. We hear that the Keokuk was sunk, and that our men behaved gallantly. I long to hear from the B.V.A. especially of Minny. I trust that he & that company may be protected in the day of battle.

My trip so far has been much pleasanter than I could have expected. I have been very fortunate in my associates and in the District to which we were assigned. The Yankees hold the disagreeable portion of it, so that we are unable to visit it. This part of the State compares to the other portions in wealth &c., I think, as our Seacoast does to the up country. I travel with my enrolling officer Lt. Jones, in his buggy, so that we move about very comfortably. The first night after leaving Bovina we spent at a Mr. Blount's, who entertained us very hospitably. The next Sunday & most of that day & of Monday we stopped at Lt. Jones' Grandmothers, Mrs. Robertson in Utica. She was the impersonation of kindness, & seemed determined to kill us with good things. Our next appointment was at Gallatin on Tuesday, and as we knew accommodations would be poor there for man & beast, and would at the same time be very expensive, we drove that evening to within a few miles of town & stopped at a Mr. Dillard's. He made us very comfortable, and refused the next morning to let us pay anything. He was originally from So. Ca. I constantly meet with people from our State settled out here. Tuesday night we spent not so comfortably at a small Hotel in Gallatin. On Wednesday evening we were invited by a Mr. Jones to go out & spend the night at his place some sixteen miles on the way to Port Gibson where we were to go the next day. To that afternoon we have to look back for our chapter of accidents & providential escapes. When a few miles on our route, we came to a bridge over a creek, which like most creeks out here was fortunately nearly dry. The bridge was pretty steep & on our reaching the top we found a wide crack between two of the planks. The horse seeing the crack stopped and commenced backing. There were no railings to the bridge so I saw in a second that the buggy was certainly going to be thrown off, & jumped out in time to escape the fall. Lt. Jones also leaped out just in time to save himself. Over went the buggy & after it the horse, they having a fall of about eight feet. The buggy was turned upside down, the horse partly on top of it. We thought of course there would be no further travelling in that buggy nor with that horse. To our astonishment on getting the horse loosed from the buggy we found him only scraped and bruised; otherwise not at all injured. We then went to work on the buggy. After working a long while, we succeeded in turning it up, & drew it out into the road—both shafts were broken off near the axletree, the dash board was broken and bent and one spoke to a front wheel was cracked, but otherwise with the exception of a few scratches and some pieces of iron bent the buggy was uninjured. We tied on the shafts & started again hoping to reach Mr. Jones safely, though it would necessarily be very late. We had gone about four or five miles further, & it was just about dusk, when as we were descending a long & rather steep hill one of the breeching straps broke, & the buggy ran into the horse. He at once commenced running as rapidly as possible & at the same time kicking. The buggy had no back to it to lean against & our overcoats were spread on the seat for us to sit on, so that my position was very insecure, & the situation of both of us was very alarming. Lt. Jones succeeded at first in drawing in the horse, but he was so alarmed that he continued kicking & to prevent his knocking everything to pieces, he had to let him out again. The jerking backward & forward toppled me out & away I went over the back of the buggy, striking the wheel with my shoulder & lighting on the back of my head. I picked myself up rather stunned, but with no bones broken, only a bruised & sprained shoulder, fortunately the left arm. I have to carry that arm for the present in a sling & hence find writing rather inconvenient. The Lt. stopped the horse at the foot of the hill. We had passed at the top of the hill a very comfortable looking settlement to which we returned and asked if we could be accommodated for the night. The answer was certainly & we soon found ourselves in the most comfortably and handsomely furnished house I had seen in Mississippi. It belonged to Mr. H. Taliaferro who with his family received us very kindly & entertained us very hospitably. They as every one I have seen were living very plainly. The planters I have met seem determined to live within themselves. They use no coffee or tea, or wheat flower. Milk, butter, ham and corn meal bread are found & everywhere that we have been in the country, & with those certainly anyone can be satisfied. Every one is planting corn, & potatoes almost exclusively—next to no cotton—hardly enough for seed; they are also paying great attention to hogs. They unfortunately find that the hogs for the last year & a half are frequently dying of some kind of distemper, for which they as yet have found no remedy.

Thursday morning Mr. Taliaferro made his blacksmiths mend up the buggy for us, so that we were able in the afternoon to start for this place, where we had to be yesterday & today. We came to within a few miles of Port Gibson & stopped for the night at a Mr. Humphrey's, an acquaintance of Lt. Jones, where we were really handsomely entertained. He insisted on our returning last night & spending the night, which we did. He also invited us to do so again tonight, but we do not wish to trespass too much, & so shall not accept the invitation. I would like to stop either here in town or somewhere nearby so as to go to the Episcopal Church tomorrow. We have two or three invitations in the country, but the Lt. wishes to ride some twenty odd miles out of the way to make a visit to his wife & spend Sunday with her. If he goes, I must also, as we have on Monday to go on to Fayette to meet on Tuesday our appointment there. It would be the first opportunity I have had to attend the Episcopal Church since leaving home in January.

We have made but very few conscripts, but few present themselves for examination, & the most of those are sure of getting exemption papers. We have some rather amusing scenes taking those, who have thought themselves certain of not being conscripted.

With much love to all

Ever your affectionate Son,
F. P. Leverett

Rev. Charles Leverett and Charley were delegates to the first General Convention of the Teachers of the Confederate States, held in Columbia on 28 April 1863 with Robert Wilson Gibbes as chairman. Charley attended as principal of Cheraw School, Cheraw, and his father as a delegate from Columbia.

Mary Maxcy Leverett to her son Milton

The Farm, Columbia, May 2$\underline{d}$ 1863

My dearest Son

You will be surprised to hear that Charley has come and gone within the last two days, carrying Annie's beauty, Nancy,[139] back with him,—she looked rather blank at the transfer, but I am very glad, as she gave Annie unbounded trouble. Charley says in three years she shall be a tip-top servant,—no doubt, but it will be owing to her training by Annie, quite as much as his discipline. He did not look well, but had a cough, although scarce able to walk for large boils, which he has been suffering from all the time for a year I think he said, ever since he commenced a camp life. He had <u>seven</u> on him & could only walk with pain & difficulty, but is quite cheerful, & is in hopes, probably, that they may carry off from his system the tubercular disease, which the physician in Cheraw, Dr Kollock,[140] said one lung was affected with. Your father gave him all his papers, which he now has in his own hands to conduct his business himself. We hear from Fred about once a week—he sets you an example in this which I am very desirous you should follow. It will be an extreme disadvantage to you all your life, not to be able to make easy use of your pen. So necessary an act is it, that every young person should make it their aim to write so freely as to make the habit a sort of second nature to them, and writing a letter become by such

139. A slave.
140. Dr. Cornelius Kollock.

means a pleasure, instead of a bore, as some ill-educated or lazy young men choose to call it.

I read with much pleasure your account of the gunboat expedition in Coosaw river. Several letters appeared in the Columbia papers, very good, describing it,—one must have been written by a Fripp or Chaplin, as he mentioned "brother Marion" in it; I liked it very much. A letter about an expedition is always far more interesting and readable if it is in the first person, and has occasional personalities in it one reads it with twice as much zest, even when unacquainted with the individuals. I am glad you young men of the company are getting awake to the fact that you must tell your own deeds, or the public generally will never know them. If your account of the battle of Pocotaligo had been written in this way I would have published it tho', of course, as these were, without the name at the end. But you confined yourself to generalities (which belong to history) instead of personalities, which belong to letter writing. You scarcely mentioned yourself, nor where you were, nor the men around you, nor any anecdote connected with individuals, all of which would have enlivened it, and made it more graphic. If any of the young men of the Company had the spirit and sense, as well as the tact and policy to have written an account of the battle of Port Royal, as it was fought from Fort Beauregard immediately after it occurred, you would all have stood far better justified in the eyes of the world, than you have been. I hope it will yet be done, even if it is after the war is closed.—Charley in the course of conversation, mentioned so much of the exalted terms in which Ste Elliott spoke to him of you formerly, that I cannot help feeling grieved at the thought of your not being on good terms, and hope it is all blown over. You have failings yourself, and must not be surprised to see them in others, for all are human, and we are told in the best of books, to bear with each others infirmities, remembering each must give his own account to the Judge of all, & after all, perhaps the beam in one's own eye, is of a worse kind than the mote in our brother's. So "bear and forbear in love, forgiving one another, if any man have a quarrel against any."[141] When however I say "bear with the infirmities of others" I don't mean be tolerant of vices, that is a totally different thing. I should rather say and wish you to flee from and abhor them & condemn them. But I can put up with a man's failings, even if they are disagreable and unpleasant to me, if he have not vices. As this is not the case with Ste, I hope you will have the good sense and forbearance to be on the same terms as formerly.

Your father has nominated Cos. H. Stuart[142] for Senator in Edmund Rhett's place, but nobody except Cos. Henry himself knows who it was that nominated him, your father having requested him not to mention it. He did not care to have

---

141. Col. 3:13.
142. Henry Middleton Stuart Sr.

it known as he was a Minister & it might seem like meddling in politics, & because it would probably get the ill will of Pope[143] & Co. and he does not wish to get the enmity of any one just as he is going to publish books. So don't mention who nominated cos. Henry, but electioneer all you can in a quiet way for him. He is pleased at being nominated and would like to be elected, as he says he has nothing to occupy his time, and as he has for years taken interest in our political affairs and often written for the papers & is far superior to Pope in character and patriotism. I want him to be elected very much. The family are going to move down to Columbia in the fall as he is sick & tired of the mountains, being so far out of the way.

Cornelia left us last Wednesday to join Julia in Charleston where she is on a visit to her friend Miss Toomer. They are not to return until June, when they will stop with us for a short time, then go to Cheraw for a month or two, & then up the country higher. They have appreciated so much what we have done & seemed to have felt so deeply our inviting them to make our house their home, that I am more glad than ever I did it. Never were there two better persons to stay one's house, so quiet, giving no trouble that they could avoid, and above all so grateful to be able to look to our house as their home.

Your Aunt Til spent a night here lately. She is going to Pendleton where she has hired a house for six months at only $120, & hired out her house here for $425 to Mr. Sharp who superintends some government concern,—he says "he'll contrive to get out old Bryce, leave it to him," which is just what Til wants. Things in Pendleton are much cheaper than Columbia.

When do you think you can [get] a furlough? I would like you to apply for one as soon as your father is able to get off. He wants to go in the course of this month if he can, as he has now got thro' the battle of Charleston harbor. But I am still unwilling for him to run the blockade and daily live in hopes that "something will turn up" so that he can go in safety. Did you see D^r DeSaussure? He came to see Annie and Lou, & brought her a pound of candy, & a sq yds muslin, which must have cost a sweet sum, for candy is $3 a lb. & muslin is $3.50 a yard. We have many visitors. Miss Izard came to see me lately with Miss Lucy. Miss Preston called on the girls also. We are getting acquainted with and visiting several Charleston people besides the Middletons. Can't you become acquainted with some Charleston men? why not with young Oliver M.[144] He is backward

---

143. This name, which appears twice in this paragraph, was erased, probably by Milton Leverett, sometime after the letter was first read.

144. Pvt. Oliver Hering Middleton Jr. of the Charleston Light Dragoons, Company K, Fourth South Carolina Cavalry.

and bashful & inclined to melancholy, I hear, & I wish you would ask him to your camp.

Ever your affectionate Mother
M. Leverett

Fred left Mississippi in mid-May to report to Surgeon General Samuel Preston Moore in Richmond, and was assigned to duty on 20 May 1863 as an assistant surgeon in General Hospital No. 12.

Frederic Percival Leverett to his mother

Richmond, Va.
20th May 1863

My dear Mother,

I arrived here safely Sunday morning early, having met with no accident by the way except a detention of half a night at Raleigh, where I had the pleasure of seeing my old friend, Collins. On Monday morning I reported to our old tyrant, the Surgeon General. He was wonderfully mild & told me I would receive orders the next day to report to Medical Director Carrington[145] of this place, which meant that I would be assigned to Hospital duty in this Department—that was almost incredible good fortune. To have charge of a Hospital in Richmond is considered the most desirable situation medically in the Confederacy. I would not allow myself to believe such good luck was to be mine. Fortunately for me I did not. I received my orders yesterday & reported to Dr. Carrington, who informed me that he had already more Surgeons than he could find posts for & that he was sorry he would have to assign me to a Hospital already in charge of a Surgeon to fill the post of an Assistant. It was rather a bitter pill for me, but there is no use kicking against the pricks. Behold me in charge of two wards in Dr. Thom's Hospital.[146] The situation is an irksome one to me. To have some one, however competent he may be, telling me to do this & to do that, directing what treatment I shall use, overseeing all that I do and being obliged to remain in this Hospital every 3rd day for the twenty four hours is not agreeable. My pay will be so long as I am kept here a great deal larger than it ever before has been, but my expenses will be heavy. Everything cost enormously here. I stopped two days & a half at the Hotel. Bill was $21.00. I had not had a single thing extra. I am rooming now with my old

---

145. Surgeon William A. Carrington of Virginia, medical director of Confederate general hospitals in Virginia.

146. Surgeon William Alexander Thom of Virginia, surgeon in charge of General Hospital No. 12, Richmond, January–July 1863.

roommate at the Episcopal Hospital, Dr. Hopkins. In that respect I am very comfortable. Mrs. Irvin, Dr. H.'s cousin with whom we board keeps a capital table, a far too good a one for the times. Dont say anything about the position I have here, except you can say I have charge of wards in Hospital No. 12 in Richmond, or am on Hospital duty here. It is rather humiliating to be so situated, but I suppose it is all for the best. Had I a home to go to where I could practice medicine I would resign. The fact is there are more Surgeons in the Confederacy than they know what to do with, yet they continue to make them daily. How lucky it is I was not sent as Asst. to Edmund Walker's Hospital. I must thank my good luck for that at least.

I will deliver Pa's letter to Mr. M.[147] tomorrow. I tried to see him day before yesterday, but could not. Pa had better hire out Jacob. Do ask him to do it so that I can get him at any time should I be sent to the field, which may happen almost at any moment.

With much love to all,

Your aff^{ct} Son,
F. P. Leverett

P.S. Do tell Jacob to be certain not to lose his knapsack, oil cloth or anything that he will need again when with me. I may soon need him. I hope you have had rain before this. The prospects of wheat along the road were good. Miss Ella Izard & her mother came on here with me from Columbia.[148] I took charge of their baggage most of the way. Do write me soon & direct me Hospital no. 12 Richmond, Va.

P.S. I am sorry to send you such an irregularly written note.[149] You must look at the numbers of the pages. Do tell Julie I brought her knife with me by a mistake.

Frederic Percival Leverett to his father

Richmond, 29th May, 1863.
General Hospital, no. 12.

My dear Father,

I saw Mr. Memminger & he told me he would send you the letters you desired. He said he would have sent them before, but you had written to the President direct requesting letters & he supposed you preferred them from <u>him</u> (Davis). The Pres. referred your letter to Mr. M. & he recommended that the letters

---

147. Christopher Gustavus Memminger of Charleston, first Confederate secretary of the Treasury.
148. Ella Elizabeth Izard (b. 1840) and her mother, Rosetta Ella Pinckney Izard.
149. This letter was written on a long narrow sheet of paper and folded horizontally; its pages were not numbered in the order one would expect.

be furnished you. He asked if you had not received the letters from the Pres. I told him, no. He said the Pres. must have forgotten it in the press of business, especially as for sometime past his health has suffered very much. I met yesterday a Mrs. Weston, a lady of this place, whose husband is now in England on government business. She said he gives glowing accounts of the attentions he has received. He says the people of England are overwhelmingly for us, & that the government must change its course eventually. He says he would prefer to be a rebel agent in London than a live lord. He says we have a fleet undoubtedly in course of construction there. He visited a few days before writing one of the vessels that was soon to sail, & says she was a splendid craft. I hear two of vessels recently sailed from some English port on the same day, just in time to escape being stopped. I wish you could get an appointment as bearer of dispatches. Mrs. Weston says she hears about every month from Mr. W. He has sent over things & they arrived safely.

The siege of Vicksburg is progressing. Last night's accounts were very hopeful. I understand that at the War Department the utmost confidence is felt in our holding our own there. Joe Johnston & Pemberton have been much pressed by superior numbers, but all seem to think the enemy will fail in taking our stronghold. I really trust so, for much, very much depends on that. Lee, it is generally supposed, will before long make an advance, Stuart preceeding him on a grand raid. If he could get as near to Washington, as Stoneman was to Richmond,[150] & could find it in the same condition, he would raze it to the ground. The Stoneman party could have destroyed Richmond as easily as not.

I have not heard yet from home. With much love to all,

Ever yr. aff<u>ct</u> Son
F. P. Leverett

P.S. My duties here are arduous & not very agreeable. I have been treated badly to say the least. Had Drayton proved himself capable & been promoted I would now have been Division Surgeon instead of serving as Assistant Surgeon in a Hospital.

Frederic Percival Leverett to his father

Richmond, 8<u>th</u> June 1863
Hospital no. 12

My dear Father,

I received your & Anne's letters yesterday & truly glad was I of them. I hope this may reach you before you leave. I will not feel easy now until I hear of your

---

150. Maj. Gen. George Stoneman, commanding the cavalry corps in the Federal Army of the Potomac, conducted an ineffective cavalry raid during the Chancellorsville Campaign.

having arrived safely abroad. I really wish the fate of Vicksburg could be decided before you leave. I do not feel at all sure about the result. Pemberton will I am sure do his best, but the place must fall, unless Grant be compelled to raise the siege either by Johnston, or by scarcity of water or owing to the sickliness of the country. How fickle is popular feeling! The papers commence now to speak of the gallant Pemberton! His two addresses to the troops are certainly of the right stamp. His proclamation was very much after the order of Lee's. If he only succeeds in holding Vicksburg, & should be killed just as the siege is raised he will have as bright place in our history as any general in our army. Lee's army is supposed to be in motion. His supposed plan is to cross the Potomac & to get in the rear of Hooker if possible—between him & Acquia,[151] or if not to do that to fight Hooker again on the Manasseh Plains & then to move into Md. & onward. While he makes these moves he leaves a considerable force at Fredericksburg to prevent Hooker's moving in this direction. I trust that we are to have a bright summer's campaign, a series of successes. I trust that God in his mercy, may let us this Fall see the end of the war. I am sick of it, heartily so. The surgeon experiences only the heart rending portion of warfare. I am almost wishing to be in the field again, so disgusted am I with my present position. My pay is here $110.00 higher than in field per month, but money goes no great ways in Richmond. The price of every thing is enormous. I was in Market the other day & saw a calf tied in a wagon & asked its price. It was about as large as the little red calf was at home when I was there. I was answered $130.00—(one hundred & thirty dollars). It actually gave me the blues.

You have about $200.00 to $300.00 of mine in bank. I wish you would take it with you & use it if want it. I will have no need for it.—If you do not need yourself, I wish you would take it & invest it in any way you see fit. I think you would do well to take all your Confederate bonds and sell them in England—for gold. I understand cotton bonds are selling in England for gold at 65 cents on the dollar & they are worth here about 60 premium, while gold is worth $5.50 premium. I wish if it will not put you to too much trouble that you would buy two woolen undershirts (gray), two nice English travelling overshirts, & a half dozen overshirts (white plain) also some stockings (gray) & a pair of strong heavy gaiters & some handkerchiefs. I wish also you would get me, if it will not cost too much an overcoat of light gray English cloth impervious to the water—also a pair of pants made of very strong gray cloth. If you find it will put you to too much trouble to get these articles or if they will cost too much, or put you to too much trouble, I hope you will not trouble yourself. A white shirt here cost $15.00. I really trust you may have a successful trip, & that God may be with you, protecting you from all the dan-

---

151. Aquia Creek, on the lower Potomac River in northern Virginia.

gers to which you will be exposed, & that he will bless your undertaking & bring you home in safety. I wish I could be stationed somewhere near home during your absence. Gen. Jenkins is stationed on the Blackwater this summer or at least for the present, so I suppose he will have poor chance for distinguishing himself.

Trusting, my dear father, that before long you may be once more safely at home. I am

Ever your aff^{ct} Son,

F. P. Leverett

Fred was at General Hospital No. 12 in Richmond for only two weeks. On 9 June he was ordered to take charge of the General Hospital at Palmyra, Fluvanna County, between Richmond and Charlottesville and remained there most of the summer of 1863.

Frederic Percival Leverett to his mother

Palmyra, Fluvanna County, Va.

17th June, 1863

My dear Mother,

I wrote Mary a few lines before leaving Richmond telling her of my being sent up to take charge of this Hospital. My situation is not by any means a desirable one, for the locality is a very out of the way one, and why selected as a site for a Hospital I cannot see, unless it be because it could afford healthy country air. The buildings could not well be less calculated for the purposes, for which used, than they are—a contracted church, two diminutive boarding houses, and two or three small stores constitute the Hospital. On the whole I do not think my position an enviable one. I have all the pecuniary responsibility &c. of a large Hospital and have charge of an illarranged infirmary devoted principally to incurables. About six miles from here is a large female Institute now closed, well adapted for a Hospital and pleasantly situated. I expect to go to Richmond next week & then intend applying to have the Hospital transferred to the Institute. If declined I shall apply to be assigned elsewhere or to be sent to the field. I have no idea of having charge of an Institution I would be ashamed to show a visitor. My pay here is no larger than if in the field. The only advantage for me to be here is my being unexposed and not being obliged to purchase a horse, which would cost now from $600 to $900.00 & over. I am anxious however to be with Lee in his advance into Md. or Pa. which I doubt not is now being made. I suppose by this time Pa is off for Europe if he decided to go at this time. I pray & trust he may be preserved from all accidents or mishaps & that his undertaking may be abundantly blessed. I would be truly glad to be stationed near home now, but that good fortune cannot be vouchsafed me. I try very hard to feel satisfied with my strange positions, but I do not succeed well. I certainly have had no lack of variety. A constant change has been my luck—a complete rolling stone—consequently gathering no moss. Somehow of late I have not been bettered in my changes. In Richmond while not having a pleasant professional position, which annoyed me beyond measure, I was delightfully situated as to my accommodations, & was just being introduced pleasantly into society. Hopkins knew every one & was related to many of the very best. Here I have next to no society, and am not comfortable as to room or meals. In the neighborhood is a Dr. Sneed, I hear, an old acquaintance of mine, my successor at the Phil^a Dyspensary, who has, they tell me, a very beautiful sister. I have not yet met them, but I think I shall be obliged to fall in love with her, if kept here for want of something better to do. How gladly would I try and fall in love with Anne's favorite if I could see her. My heart seems however, steeled against the sex. Somehow none make any impression on me now.

My predecessor at this Hospital was a Dr. Pinkard, a Virginian, resident of this place. He resigned rather than go before the Board for examination. He lives in this place and has been very polite to me. To succeed the resident of a little Country town, in his own town, when he remains in it, & is of course injured by being relieved of charge of Institution, which he established is not a very pleasant piece of business. I have found it a very awkward matter. Dr. P.'s mother had acted as matron of the Hospital, & of course would not serve under me, which made it yet more disagreeable. Fortunately the Hospital Steward is a very capable and gentlemanly man, and I try to make him as far as possible relieve me of what is unpleasant. The organization and arrangement of this Hospital has shown me how perfectly absurd it is for men who have not had Hospital experience to be appointed to such positions. Everything is in a slip shod style, destitute of method, with scarce any pretense to comfort. The beds are raised but about ten inches from the floor and act as admirable secretors of dirt. The coverlets are mostly made of white cloth and quilted, and have been used about ten months. You can easily imagine how clean they are. It would not grieve me to wake up some night & see a fire spreading from building to building. It would be hard work though for it to do so, they are so scattered. There are but few patients here.

I hope all of you are well and doing well, and that everything is progressing favorably. I wish Minny had written me while at home. If he has not yet left, do tell him I beg him to—and to write particularly about all farm matters. I hope good care is being taken of the hogs, and that Anne is succeeding well with the poultry. She ought to set through the summer every guinea & hen egg she can & raise as many as possible. Tell Hercules I hope he and Lewis are succeeding well with the crop. Tell Jacob howd'ye and that I miss him very much. He must not forget the way on to Richmond as I may have to send for him almost any day. Very much love to all. A kiss for Lou. Do tell Tilly I anxiously look for a letter from her. Do mention in your next the address of Jim & Newton.

Ever yr. aff<u>ct</u> Son,

F. P. Leverett

P.S. Let the negroes know how the Yankees put the negro soldiers in the front at Port Hudson, when nearly a whole Reg. was killed.[152]

Frederic Percival Leverett to Mrs. Sarah McGough

Gen. Hospital, Palmyra Va.

29<u>th</u> June 1863

Mrs. Sarah McGeough,

Cardsville,

Jones Co. Ga.[153]

Madam,

It was my painful duty to have charge for the most of the time of the Ward in the Hospital in Richmond in which your late husband was.[154] Almost as soon, as assigned to duty there, I was attracted to Mr. McGeough by the patient & I may say cheerful manner with which he bore his severe injury. So buoyant & elastic were his spirits that to within a few days of his death I felt that he really must recover, and I tried frequently to cheer him up with the prospect of his being before long restored to you. But that such was not the will of the Lord at last became apparent, and I advised his kind brother, who had nursed him indefatigably to make him aware of his true condition (two or three days before his death). Shortly before his decease I asked him if he was aware that he was fast sinking & if there was anything I could do for him. He replied that he knew he was dying & that he felt prepared and that he would be glad for me to write you & tell you how he had been, & that you must meet him in Heaven.

I feel, Madam, that the words of a perfect stranger must appear to you cold at such a time; but I would fain express my sympathy with you, for I feel assured

---

152. On 27 May 1863, at Port Hudson, Louisiana, the first major engagement in which black Federal soldiers participated, the First and Third Louisiana Native Guards charged a strong Confederate position several times and were repulsed with heavy casualties.

153. Fred's copy of his letter of condolence to Sarah McGough.

154. Pvt. James H. McGough of the Byars Volunteers, Company I of the Forty-fifth Georgia Infantry, was mortally wounded in the shoulder and chest at Fredericksburg on 13 December 1862, and his arm was amputated at the shoulder joint; he died in General Hospital No. 12, Richmond, 3 June 1863.

that the Confederacy lost in Mr. McGeough a brave & noble soldier, and you a true & faithful husband. Every thing was done for him that could be done, (I think). He had constant & kind attendance; his brother ever at his side, and Mrs. Turner, the warm hearted Ward matron always by trying to minister to his comfort. He is now, I trust, in Heaven enjoying the bliss of the souls made perfect through Christ. May it be your happy lot Madam to rejoin him there.

Very respectfully,

yr. obd^t Servant,

F. P. Leverett

Surgeon C.S.A.

Milton Maxcy Leverett to his brother Fred

Columbia June 29th /63

My dear Fred,

I have been at home a long time, over five weeks, as busy as a bee and intend leaving by this evening's train. I would have written before but I have been at work steady every day on a thing to which I was totally unaccustomed and about which I was worried fearing I would not succeed, and anxious that when I should write to you I might say that I had succeeded which I trust I can now say. I have been using it over two days and although it is not lighter than the other, which is only due to my want of practice and want of material, i.e. the right kind of leather, as the wood I believe is the right sort although I am not exactly satisfied on that score. I must try other kinds first, the willow especially. When I first came home I went around to Hopson the harness maker, offered him a hundred dollars to fix one for me showed him of course the old one and desired improvements which I was to show him, but he seemed totally devoid of enterprise and like to a man knocking about in the dark, and withal possessed of a vacuity of mind, which I ascribe to ignorance of that sort of work, to such an extent that I felt the utter inutility and hopelessness of applying to any one but myself. I felt sure that I understood the manufacture as clearly as any body, but I felt at the same time aghast at the magnitude of the task being entirely unaccustomed to such work and fearing it would take me an age, but I fell to 'like a good fellow' first fixed a new spring to the old one, then worked incessantly on the new one until it was completed. The chief thing I mistrust about it is the spring which belongs to the old one and was broken but I mended it again and placed it in the one I made. I had wire enough but just as I was in the midst of making it, the wire broke there being a flaw in it. I think my boot (I have made it almost precisely like a boot, I draw it on as you would a boot) may be more serviceable than the other as I had made it waterproof, and made it shorter than the other i.e. the leg portion so that I might be able to ride much easier, the other projecting too much against the saddle. I have not tried this yet on horseback but am in great hopes it will succeed.

If you ever see any <u>brass</u> wire about the size of cotton bagging twine or any catgut about the size of a lead pencil, do get some for me. The wire was very cheap before the war, but catgut is very dear I believe. They both are generally obtained in hardware stores. A yard or two of either will do me or as much as you can <u>conveniently</u> get.

I was very sorry when I returned home and found you had just gone the night before. Ste Elliott told me I had a perfect right to demand a furlough. Since then Hal[155] who is now captain sent word that it was usual to send certificates, and telling me I ought to send one stating the reasons of my protracted absence. I sent word I was under no surgeon's care and could send none, but would be ready to be in camp at such and such a day. I told him I could get a discharge any moment I wished but would reject any such act as totally contrary to my wishes &c. The enemy have made a negro raid on Combahee ruined a great many plantations,[156] among them Col. Wm C. Heyward's, he has gone on to Richmond to get a position in the army. Since then I see by the papers they were attempting another raid when they were discovered and were compelled to return. I wish very much we could make a raid on Beaufort Island. There was a rumor of one being intended.

yr affct brother
M. M. Leverett

We have been having abundant rains, rather more now than we want. Hercules seems very well satisfied with the corn, but grass is growing so fast that five or six hands could be employed. Oats and wheat have been cut and stacked long ago, the former we have been using steadily, but we have not had a chance of threshing the latter on account of the rains. Watermelons and green corn are about coming in. I will just miss them. Potatoes look very nicely, & the peas are improving.

If you can help it don't marry in Virginia, get a wife from the State you intend staying in, don't marry anybody, be very particular about that I believe in blood. There are some first rate girls down here, I am quite pleased with the Rutledge girls Maria and Julia both I think quite intelligent and the latter would make you a first rate wife.[157] I like her very much what I saw of her. If they don't suit you try

---

155. Henry Middleton Stuart Jr. (1835–1915).

156. A Federal raid on the Combahee River on 2 June 1863, commanded by Col. James Montgomery of the Second South Carolina Volunteers (Colored), destroyed property, burned houses and mills, and captured over seven hundred slaves from seven rice plantations, including Cypress, owned by Col. William Cruger Heyward.

157. Maria (b. 1834) and Julia Rose Rutledge (1841–1899) of Charleston.

into the Middleton family, just make up your mind to marry in the best family, and in a South Carolina family. If I had your advantages I would certainly. As it is <u>I will have to wait</u> until I can see my way clear and get enough money to back me, and then if I don't pluck one of the best blossoms off one of the best trees I shall have been blindfolded. I will have to make my match by diplomacy. If I don't marry into a good family I shan't marry at all. Begin to lay aside a monthly portion of your salary as you must get married, it is now time, and money is the hinge, on which the world turns.

Julie was confirmed yesterday. I have had Billy hired out since I have been here so as to make money enough for my return transportation.

Jacob and myself have employed ourselves making shoes since I have been here for Ma and the girls, we did very well. I've done a great deal of shoemaker sewing lately, had a great deal to do on my boot.

yr. aff<u>ct</u>
M. M. Leverett

Direct next letter to Pocotaligo.

Frederic Percival Leverett to his sister Julia

General Hospital, Palmyra Va.
8<u>th</u> July, 1863

My dear Julia,

I have for some days been intending to write you, but it has been so dull here I have not been able to get up sufficient animation to do so. We hear that last Friday the Yankees made a raid or an advance in force, as some say, on the Central Rail Road, and since then we have been without Papers. A thousand and one rumors are in circulation. Some person or other sees a paper, while off in the country or sees someone who has read a recent paper or has seen someone who has heard one read, and he brings the news with his own emendations and improvements. According to our reporters reliable and unreliable, New Orleans has been retaken by Magruder, Grant has been demolished by Pemberton & Johnston; Hooker has been superseded by Meade,[158] & he defeated by Longstreet or somebody, & Lee is ploying wild work around Baltimore, causing old Abe to quake and tremble, and to look anxiously after his cap & plaid.[159] Seward also has grown

---

158. Maj. Gen. George G. Meade succeeded Hooker as commander of the Federal Army of the Potomac in June 1863.

159. In February 1861 president-elect Lincoln, in the face of death threats, took a night train to Baltimore wearing a soft cap and his overcoat over his shoulders, a ruse which was transformed by a *New York Times* story into a Scotch plaid cap and military coat.

nervous, wishes to resign & slip off to Europe before the crash. Add to all this, Rumor says the Yankees are advancing 30000—some say 50000—strong in this direction—a monstrous & incredible tale! In the meanwhile it rains on almost incessantly. It really seems that the fountains of Heaven are opened and that the land is to be deluged. It has rained now almost every day, and mostly nearly all day & night for about three weeks. The rains are doing much good to the high land oats & grass & corn crops but are damaging beyond calculation the wheat. Thousands & thousands of bushels will be lost. Along the rivers where it had been just cut whole fields of it will be washed away. Great quantities of it will be destroyed by sprouting.

I was very glad to hear from Minny that you had been confirmed, & hope you may have the blessing of the Almighty in your efforts to lead a new life. Write me soon and let me hear about yourself and everything. Give the enclosed to Lou.

I have absolutely nothing to do here—some eight or ten patients with whom nothing much is the matter and for whom as I have an Assistant, Dr. Talbot of Ky.,[160] a much older physician than myself, I do nothing. Yesterday I sent off nearly the whole Hospital by way of the Canal to Richmond to assist in the defense of Richmond. They were a motley crew, a set of Hospital birds whom nothing will cure but Peace. They will do very well, however, to fight in the entrenchments. They do not stay in Hospitals complaining of imaginary pains and aches because they are afraid to fight, but to escape marching and the fatigues incident to Camp life. On Sunday as soon as they heard they were to go one or two who had been previously well commenced complaining, but it did no good. On Monday we went around to see how many we could send, and came to the foot of the bed of one who has been up ever since I have been here. I woke him up & took him so by surprise that he said he was very well. I told him then to get up & be ready to go to Richmond the next day. Yesterday I had him marched to Columbia[161] 12 miles then sent to Richmond. If it does not rain tomorrow I am going down myself on business connected with the Institution. It would not surprise me much should a party of Yankees ride in here any day, & capture the Hospital, much good it would do them however. Every thing is so shabby, I would be ashamed for them to come. They would not say to me as they did to Maury in Brookhaven "This Hospital is as good as ours" in a tone of surprize as if we could not have anything as good as they. I am afraid I would feel inclined to apologize for the appearance of everything. The people about here have suffered less than most others in Va. and they are decidedly the most grasping. They charge for every thing. I gave the other day

---

160. Probably Assistant Surgeon John P. Talbot, who was not officially appointed until February 1865.
161. Virginia.

$138.00 for a calf—a pig as large as the smallest ones at home when I was there would cost $30.00. They sell their sweet milk, their butter, their buttermilk and their calves. Cows are valuable animals. With a half dozen one could make a fortune in a few weeks.

Dr. Talbot has just come in & told me one of the men who is to go to Richmond tomorrow is complaining of every conceivable malady. He says he has been doing so each time for months, when on the point of being sent off. I have ordered that he be made sick of himself—the next time I wish him to go he will be glad to go. Some men are like Billy. The only way to get on with them is to be kind, and strict, never to allow them to humbug you.

Much love to all.

Ever yr. aff<u>ct</u> brother
F. P. Leverett

Frederic Percival Leverett to his mother

Palmyra Hospital,
14<u>th</u> July 1863.

My dear Mother,

Since the fall of Vicksburg & Lee's semiunsuccessful battle in Penn<u>a</u> have been announced, I have been so melancholy, that I have hardly smiled.[162] All my calculations have been based on the "if we continue to hold Vicksburg." It has now fallen, (I am so foolish as to sometimes half think it will prove a mistake) and I cannot see the slightest prospect of the war's ever ending through anything we can do. I now look longingly and hopefully for interference from France. Napoleon has succeeded in Mexico.[163] The North is not favorable to his designs in that country, and could she crush us would overwhelm him. It is for his interest to have an ally in this country & to have the North and South separated. If he will assist us, and enable us to conquer a peace, never did a nation have such an ally as we would be to France. On the other hand, if Napoleon allows us to be overwhelmed which I do not fear will ever be the case, never did any nation

---

162. Pemberton surrendered Vicksburg to Grant after a six-week siege on 4 July 1863. On the same day, Lee retreated after a three-day battle at Gettysburg, Pennsylvania, in which he gained an early advantage over the Army of the Potomac but was unable to exploit it in heavy fighting and failed to break the center of the Federal lines in the assault known as Pickett's Charge.

163. Napoléon III had supported a military expedition in Mexico by Archduke Ferdinand Maximilian Joseph (1832–1867) of Austria since 1861. Maximilian was made emperor of Mexico in 1864 but was captured and executed in 1867 after the United States government refused to recognize him.

have such a foe, as we will be to him. On France throwing herself in the balance, do I now rest my hope for a termination of the war. I am truly glad Pa did not get off for Europe.

I went down to Richmond last week and returned yesterday. I had to walk ten miles of the way back, my ambulance not meeting me at the depot. I found my friend Hopkins very ill with the Diphtheria. I disliked exceedingly leaving him & returning here to do nothing except to attend to business matters. You would be astonished to see what an amount of business a Surgeon in charge of even a small Hospital, especially one in the Country has on his hands. The Medical Director told me if Lee's Army remained where it is, this Hospital would be broken up—also all others similarly situated—that would probably necessitate my being sent to the field, a work I am hardly equal to. Where money is to come from to buy a horse I do not know. I have with me or in Richmond some $500.00 but that would be hardly more than half enough. I had one offered me today for $1500.00 that was worth about 250.00. I suppose you all can hardly spare Jacob again. I wish you would send on to me to the South Carolina Agency, Richmond my saddle & trappings. Do tell Jacob to be certain to put in everything. Send it by Express, or perhaps Dr. Laborde may be sending on.[164] Do have a waistcoat made for me out of my blue coat & send it at the same time. Jackson has my measure—also another Tailor on Main St. Anne knows the one. They will say the cloth is too short, but it is long enough if pieced in two places—neither of which will injure it. I enclose a rough diagram, the marks indicate where the pieces are to be put in. Please attend to it without delay. I hope Nan has had my clothes aired at times to keep out moths.

I heard from Min last week written the day he was going to start for Pocotaligo. I long to hear the attack on Charleston is over. It was said in Richmond that the Yankees had withdrawn, but nothing definite was known. If Beauregard be successful there this time, he ought to have some more prominent position given him. He ought now to be in command of Bragg's army.

Do send me some stockings with the saddle & waistcoat. I have some, one or two prs, if I recollect aright in my trunk.

With very much love, & with earnest prayers in which all should join that God may enable us soon to see the end of our terrible contest, I am,

Ever yr most aff^{ct} Son,

F. P. Leverett

---

164. Dr. Maximilian LaBorde of Columbia, physician, chairman of the Central Association for the Relief of South Carolina Soldiers.

Frederic Percival Leverett to his mother

Palmyra, Va. 31st
July, 1863

My dear Mother,

Yesterday on returning from Richmond, whither I had gone two days before on Hospital business I received your & Mary's most welcome letters, together with one from July,[165] containing one from Tilly to her. Your account of the siege was far more interesting than the one in the papers, and made me realize most fully how much we all are interested in what is there going on. May God save Charleston from that Vandal horde. How I wish I were there. Here I am doing nothing but making out reports & writing. I have had my pen in hand nearly the whole day long. You would be astonished to see what a mass of matter is mailed from a Hospital. From a small one just as much goes as from a large one. The more particular a Surgeon is the more exacting those in authority are. I have been amused at several things, in that respect, since having in charge here. My predecessor let everything go on as it chose, and no one found fault with him. I have been as exact as possible, & more than once my accounts have been sent back disallowed & I referred to Army regulations, in very short style. It has not been intimated to me yet where I shall go or what do. I shall leave here next Monday, D. V. & hope never to be obliged to see the place again. The people are the shabbiest Virginians I ever saw—eaten up by extortion. I am ashamed of them. I do not know how to tell you to write me.

With very much love to all, I am

As ever yr. most aff^{ct} son
F. P. Leverett

I hope Hercules will succeed with everything as you say he has with Watermelons.

Mary Bull Leverett to her brother Milton

Columbia, August 1st, 1863

My dear Minny,

Here is my letter, at last to you, however I believe in that old adage "Better late than never"; besides Fred had written to me some time before so I wrote to him first. In his last letter, he said that he had been ordered to shut up that hos-

---

165. Julie.

pital & would go to Richmond in a few days (the dear old fellow is very fond of going to R; the last time, he paid very dearly for it, his ambulance did not meet him & he had to walk 10 miles!) so we must not write to him as he did not know where he would be next. He seems to think that he had been tossed about a good deal & really, I think before the war is ended Fred will have traversed every foot of ground in the Confederacy. He told us a very amusing anecdote, what one of the assistants of the Surgeon General said. He has had so many applications in every direction about Fred, even from Charleston, that I expect he not only had taken a dislike to him, but thinks he is the most discontented person in the world. Fred's friends in Richmond did not like his being sent to Palmyra at all & spoke of it, & this assistant said "I declare I don't believe we will have any peace until Leverett is housed"! There was a young man at church on Sunday, Lieutenant Procter,[166] nephew of Beauregard, who had been under Fred's charge in Vir. His leg was cut of[f] below the knee, he was in the highest spirits, said he intended entering either the cavalry or artillery. Mamma spoke to him & he told her Fred was [in] Richmond trying to get some hospital. He went off to walk with one of the girls, on his <u>crutches</u>! The female Lieutenant passed through here not long ago, she was dressed in a Lieutenant's uniform. I believe it was about a year ago, that she heard that her husband had joined the Northern Army. She immediately entered ours & has fought very gallantly, was taken prisoner in New Orleans put in prison, & her husband who was there tried to persuade her to join him, she would not have anything to do with him, however he got her out of the prison, when she immediately came over to us, & went to Richmond. Col. Preston said her papers were perfectly good, he said she was a very respectable looking sort of somebody, talked very well. The conductor on board of the cars was impertinent to her & she gave him a good whipping, & the little negroes at the Wayside hospital were not very attentive to her that she took a stick & beat them all.

Our society meets in the morning now, & we stay two hours & work, our tongues do quite as much work as our needles, the Report came out in the paper & it seems that we have done so much work, that all of us girls are astonished.[167] Did you see Timrod's last piece called the two Armies, the ladies & the men? it is quite pretty.[168] The Middletons took tea with us the other evening. I think they had a pleasant time. Miss Matilda plays beautifully on the piano. Emma plays well

166. 2d Lt. James T. Proctor of Company C, First South Carolina Infantry (Gregg's), acting as staff officer, was severely wounded in the right leg at Chancellorsville, 3 May 1863, and his right foot was amputated. In July 1863 he was assigned to Charleston as an ordnance officer with heavy artillery in the Department of South Carolina, Georgia, and Florida.

167. Mary and Anne were members of the Young Ladies' Hospital Association of Columbia.

168. Henry Timrod of Charleston, poet; "The Two Armies" was published in the *Southern Illustrated News* of Richmond, 30 May 1863.

too. They wish us to come soon & spend the evening with them. Olivia told me she expected soon to have a horse brought from the plantation, & then we could commence our rides again.

We were very much worried at the beginning of the week, as we expected to hear of the fall of Fort Wagner,[169] as at one time every gun had been dismounted, however, we are getting heavier guns every day from Richmond & people are very hopeful. Everyone blames Beauregard, but I do not think he is to be blamed so much as I heard that he has been sending on to Richmond begging for guns, but the answer always was "wait until September," they did not think the Yankees would come until then & so he said what was the use for him to throw up fortifications, just for the enemy to take them as he had no guns to defend them.

We are getting plenty of watermelons. Annie made some very nice syrup out of the juice. Julie is coming next Wednesday, Mary Heyward will come with her & stay with us a few days. Julie said she had had a letter from Charley. He says Blanche is a perfect shadow of her former self, he is in pretty much the same condition, the baby is better. He says next year he will try & get a school somewhere else that it was dreadful living in such a crowd. Ma says must give her love to you & tell you she has ever so much to say, & is sorry paper is so scarce. Tillie says she hopes you have not given up the French. That was a capital letter you wrote to me, by the by do tell Nat. I hope he does not think I can only make cake & bread. I don't care to have any one think that I can only cook. If I could only hear of any opportunity, I would send something to you. Tillie says you must send plenty of wire grass when you send the Palmetto. If you are not tired of this letter I will write another next week.

Your aff^ate sister
Mary Leverett

Frederic Percival Leverett to his mother

Petersburg. 11th July, 1863.[170]

My dear Mother,

Last night I arrived here having had the pleasure of Charlie's company from Richmond. Monday was my birthday & as a present I had a visit from Charlie—

---

169. Fort Wagner, also called Battery Wagner, on the northern end of Morris Island near Charleston, had been under siege by Federal forces commanded by Brig. Gen. Quincy A. Gillmore since 10 July 1863. Two major frontal assaults on 10 July and 18 July—the second with Col. Robert Gould Shaw's Fifty-fourth Massachusetts Infantry (Colored) at the head of Brig. Gen. George C. Strong's Brigade of the X Corps—failed to dislodge the Confederate defenders. Gillmore then shelled Wagner with his artillery and the naval guns of the South Atlantic Blockading Squadron.

170. The month should be August.

a pleasure I had not dreampt of having. On the same day also I saw Newton & Jim—the latter in Hospital but doing well. He will, by next week, I hope, be able to go home. Charlie will I suppose see you before you receive this & will have told you of my having been ordered to this place in July. My address is "General Hospital, Petersburg." I am not the Senior Surgeon, so I am not the Surgeon in charge. My senior seems to be a gentleman, & I trust will, as he appears disposed to, make everything agreeable—I am not yet settled, but hope to be so tomorrow. Please write me at once & do send me by Express the things I asked you to send me. I wish it were possible for you to send me some shirts & collars. I will be obliged to dress neatly here, but am aghast at the price of everything. Jenkins' Brigade is here, encamped about a quarter of mile from the Hospital I will be at. His Brigade is in magnificent condition & is universally admired. It was sent to Richmond a short time since & the people were enthusiastic in their admiration of him & his men. He requested Pres. Davis to send him to Charleston to dislodge the enemy from Morris Island with his Brigade shortly after they made their foothold, & offered a plan to him which the Pres. considered feasible, & which he said he thought Jenkins' men were the men to carry out & Jenkins the man to lead them, but that he could not spare them from Richmond. Jenkins said he wanted to fight one battle in So. Ca. & he wanted the old State to see what men it had to be proud of. He says he is sure he could have massacred or captured the whole force of the enemy—that it ought have cost from 600 to 1200 of his men, but that he would have given them & himself to have accomplished the result. I wish he could have been allowed to undertake it, for now I fear exceedingly for Charleston. It has come now to heavy artillery, the enemy cannot be dislodged & I fear she must eventually fall. The people's ceasing to be uneasy makes me fearful. Our poor country is in a sad condition. Were the men at home of the same spirit & determination as the soldiers, all would be well, and that ere long. One of the Surgeons in the Hospital says he never saw any thing like the applications made to be returned to their commands, men who are not fit for duty and begging to be sent. They say Old Lee wants them & they wish to go. I have seen men who have made money by the war, who are at home & have done nothing for the Government except demand outrageous prices say we cannot succeed, so we might as well stop. Such men, I hear, are also to be found in So. Ca. There are some I hear, who are saying if Charleston must fall, it ought not to be burnt. Poor fools, too shortsighted to realize that if we are subdued we are ruined irretrievably, as a people & as individuals. The recent successes of the enemy have induced the wretched Yankees to bravadoe over us in a manner they have never before done. What would they not do, did they have us firmly in their clutches. The Yankees have conducted this war as savages. Could they conquer us, they would act as demons. May God, in his mercy, help the right.

I sent home by Charlie a package of white sugar, & some turnip & cabbage seed, for you. I also sent $615.00—Six hundred and fifteen dollars—$500.00 are seven per cent notes, which I wish Pa would have put away for me. The $115.00 I sent for you and the girls, $20.00 for you, Tilly, Anne, Mary, & Julia each, & $5.00 for Kate, Carry & Lou each. Do take it & use in buying something for each of you & dont let me hear anything about your not wishing to take it. I want you each to have it & shall feel really hurt if any of you refuse.

Do make Hercules plant a plenty of turnips & everything of that kind. He ought to sow enough for the house, servants, cows & hogs & if possible some to sell. Sow all the seed you can get, also Cabbages & Collards. Tell him I say cure all the tops of the corn—also as much grass as possible—also all pea vines, potato vines & groundnut bushes. Everything will help in winter & may save you from purchasing fodder.

Edmund Walker has been ordered to the field, and Dr. Peyre Porcher has his hospital.[171] It would be pleasanter for me, were he here, except that he would be Surgeon in Charge of a Hospital & I acting as assistant in another much smaller. So it is well as it is. It must have been a hard trial for him to go. He gave I hear general satisfaction. Petersburg seems a very pleasant, quiet place. In winter my old friend Dunn lives here, so I shall have the pleasure of his society, if kept here so long, though I do not expect to be, so constantly am I moved. My frequent changes I believe do not arise fortunately from my not giving satisfaction. If I remain here, I shall need my trunk. If it will not cost too much do get me some neat check cloth, or calico & make me two shirts, after pattern of old one (Paris shirt) in trunk, except neck band not so wide & wrist band not so large & send them with other articles. I wish my colt was here. I wanted Charley to take her, but it will cost me too much—about $300.00 a year to feed her.

With much love to all,

Ever yr. most aff.ct son,

F. P. Leverett

P.S. If you make the shirt, don't cut the cloth bias for the sleeves, as you did last time. They stretch too much.

P.S. The ladies of Va. will spoil Jenkins with their attentions, if he is to be thus injured. They go into raptures about him. If he were not married he could select from the state. One seemed much disappointed on my telling her he had a wife & four children.[172]

---

171. Surgeon Francis Peyre Porcher succeeded Walker as surgeon in charge of the South Carolina Hospital at Petersburg.

172. Jenkins's wife was Caroline Harper Jamison Jenkins of Orangeburg District; their children were Micah John, Robert Flavel, William Edward, and Whitemarsh LaRoche.

Mary Maxcy Leverett to her son Milton

Farm Aug 11th 1863.

My dear Milton
    Your last very welcome letter contained a good deal of information which we were all much interested in. The newspapers say some of those negroes were Mr Trescot's.[173] How I wish some of poor Mr. Seabrook's had been taken. I have just received a letter from Caroline who seems sad, tho' resigned. The Rev. Cotesworth Pinckney preached here on Sunday.[174] He says his father and mother, cannot get over Pinckney's death, the spirits of both of them have been very much depressed ever since.[175] He made one remark which struck me, as I had never thought of poor Pinck's death in that connection;—it was, that his loss was peculiarly lamentable, as <u>there were so many looking to him</u>. And so it is, for poor Mr. Seabrooks is lame, sickly and helpless, and nearly all the children more or less weakly, as well as young. The whole family indeed looked up to him as one who was to be their stay and protector, and his grandparents felt him to be their prop and pride. Poor old Miss Harriet Pinckney is dreadfully distressed, and grieves to see, as she says, "all the young people taken, and she, at <u>ninety</u> years of age still left, of no use to anybody." She is up here, in Columbia, again until the fate of Charleston is decided.
    Charley came very unexpectedly this week with a budget of papers to go on to Richmond and get off Mr James LaRoche[176] from the Conscription act which calls out all men between forty and forty five,[177] and as he is absolutely necessary there to keep the negroes in order, as well as take care of the ladies & children, they all got Charley to go on to try and get him excused, especially as the neighbors say they will run off the negroes from there, if Mr LaRoche does not stay to keep them in order. He (Charley) says he will stop here on his return. We had a letter recently from Fred, the last he hopes to write from Palmyra; he was to go to Richmond to know where he was to be sent. I sent your message about the horse to him, by Charley, who left here the evening of the same day he came. I feel very

---

173. William Henry Trescot, attorney and diplomat.
174. Rev. Charles Cotesworth Pinckney III (1812–1898) of Charleston, Episcopal clergyman, brother of Caroline Pinckney Seabrook.
175. Charles Cotesworth Pinckney II (1789–1865) and his wife, Phoebe Caroline Elliott of Abbeville District, were the grandparents of Cotesworth Pinckney Seabrook, who was killed at Chancellorsville, 3 May 1863.
176. James LaRoche (1823–1899), uncle of Julia Blanche Jenkins Leverett.
177. A revision of the Conscription Act, passed by the Confederate Congress in September 1862, raised the upper age limit to forty-five; an Exemption Act passed a few days later, however, provided for a wide range of exemptions, including one for overseers responsible for plantations with over twenty slaves.

much indebted to Mrs. Gregorie for her kindness to you, and told Julie to say so in a letter she recently undertook to write to Mr Gregorie.

Aug 13th Charley came back from Richmond yesterday having by his energy accomplished his business and succeeded in it. He met Fred in Richmond, and came on in the cars with him as far as Petersburg, where Fred has been ordered to report to the Senior Surgeon. What his position is to be there we do not yet know, neither does he, so say nothing of it until I hear from Fred himself. It seems, Edmund Walker has been ordered to the field, no doubt to his great disgust,—the crusty old Surgeon General having been heard to remark, on hearing that Edmund was married, "that the man who married in these times deserves to be sent to the field." Charley says Fred looks extremely well, though he says he isn't, and ate heartily, tho he says he hasn't any appetite. He said to himself, when he got to Richmond, "well I'll be sure to find Fred in an ice cream shop," he did not however at the time, but met D[r] Michel[178] who told him that he had met Fred in an ice cream shop the night before! The Doctor said he and Fred were great friends. Fred sent the girls and myself each twenty dollars (making a hundred dollars) and Carry & Kate each five. If Fred prospers truly his whole family will prosper, for his hand is open as the day. He is getting very handsome pay; and what rejoiced me much was, that he sent $500.00 for his father to put up for him—which is a step in the right direction, as it is high time he commenced laying by something for himself, as the girls said, to get married on. Charley said he didn't believe it was any "to get married but, to get a horse on." I suppose in his next letter he will say something about it. I did not scruple to accept what he sent, for I know it would not only hurt his feelings, but he would just throw it away or waste it, if we did not, and Charley says he is not denying himself anything. C. left at twelve today for Cheraw. The girls sent Blanche each, a present for the baby. Julia sent a little white bonnet she had made while in Pendleton for it, Annie a white Talma,—Charley said he had heard Blanche wishing for exactly the two things and couldn't get them, & Tillie sent a beautifully worked frock. Mary had already sent a pair of socks.

Julie returned last night from Pendleton, having had "a splendid time" as she says, and coming very near, as she confesses, making herself sick with the fruit she ate all day, Charley having written to her there sending a five dollar bill to spend, she had no scruples about indulging her taste that way. She was a month at your Aunt Til's, who is living well, things being so much cheaper there than here. She wrote word before coming that Mary Heyward was going on a visit to Camden to see the Miss Moultrie's and did not know where to stop the night she

---

178. Surgeon William Middleton Michel of South Carolina, surgeon in charge of the South Carolina Hospital in Richmond.

would have to spend in Columbia, so she invited her to stop with us—Of course Tillie wrote to repeat the invitation which Mary accepted and came down with Julie and Lila Heyward who was also on a visit at Aunt Til's. Mary seemed delighted to see us, and Tillie rode down in our carriage to the Depot next morning. Annie Hanckel and Lila came round and took tea with us the evening Mary was here. I am glad I have been the means of bringing them together again. It is a long time since the two have met, and when I found Mary accepted our invitation, I went round to Mr Heywards to see Annie & told her she must come while Mary was there. She seemed pleased and immediately accepted and came according to appointment. She brought old Mom Sary[179] to see Mary (who had sent word for mom Sary to come and see, without sending any message to her sister Annie) and Mary put her arms around her old Mauma and shed tears. I was glad to see her show some feeling. The sisters kissed each other and I think the hearts of both are somewhat lightened by the reconciliation. It affected me much, for my heart was full of recollections of former times and love for their Mother, your poor Aunt Ann.[180] Mary is to spend some time with us, when on her return.

We were all highly amused with your account of Billy carrying out pears. I am glad you are getting into the habit of writing more freely to us than you formerly did. I like to have a minute account of everything. This seems to be a time of gloom in the Confederacy; a day of darkness to try mens souls, and many are disheartened, feeling despondant about every thing. But such are the times which will show what metal men are made of. I wouldn't give a brass button for the man who is ready to give up the moment any untoward event happens. I would not give up so long as the breath is in my body, and I consider that man a sneak, a coward and a traitor who talks of such a thing. We are a proud, vain, boastful people, and deserve to have some hard knocks, for we Southern people have too often "done the thing which we ought not to have done, and left undone that which we ought to have done,"[181] but I do not think God will forsake us altogether, but after chastening and humbling us expect and trust yet that He will turn again and deliver us. If our men will not get tired of fighting for us, we will yet conquer. My greatest fear is that our armies have suffered and are still suffering so much, that their spirits may get cast down, from so long continued and severe strain on all their faculties, and such sad losses. If prayers can keep them up they will never fall. I doubt not the people of God in this Confederacy are praying day & night for the army, for it is the army alone of earthly things that will save us, and not diplomacy. I pray day and night, & no doubt other women do the same, for a blessing on our

179. A Heyward slave.
180. Anne Maxcy Heyward.
181. The Book of Common Prayer.

poor men and our cause. Yes in the dead of the night and in the dark when I fear anything special for them, I get up and kneel to cry to God for mercy for them. And you my dear Son are never forgotten you may be sure.

Your ever affectionate

Mother

Mary Leverett

Fred was relieved from duty as the surgeon in charge of the General Hospital at Palmyra on 19 August and assigned temporarily to the Medical Examining Board at Petersburg. He was ordered to Dublin, Virginia, 26 August to serve as the examining surgeon for the Camp of Instruction.

Frederic Percival Leverett to his sister Anne Leverett DeSaussure

Petersburg, Va.

25th Aug. 1863.

My dear Nan,

I received just now a letter from Ma, which I welcomed no one knows how gladly. It had been an age since I had heard a word from home, and I am half crazy to hear every day, now. I hardly think of anything but Charleston, and our poor men there. I cannot imagine any situation more forlorn than that of Rhett[182] & the men in Sumter. To have a fort they have so long guarded and of which all are so proud knocked down around their heads, and they unable to fire hardly a gun. Poor fellows! Dr. Hitt, one of the Asst. Surgeons here has just got a letter from one of his brothers, who is on Morris Island,[183] which says they all expect Sumter to fall, but that not one of the men thinks on that account Charleston will be taken—that with the sand batteries they can resist all Lincoln's armada. God grant it—for the fall of Charleston would have a fearfully depressing effect.

I wrote Ma a letter last week, which I hope she received in time to prevent her sending on the things I wrote for. I am looking every day to be ordered to the field, Jenkins' Brigade. In that case I shall I hope to get a furlough of a few days, and I will be obliged to draw on Pa for the $500.00 sent on by Charley to buy a horse. I hate to do so, no one knows how much, but if sent to the field there will be no helping it. Once in Jenkins' Brigade, if my health lasts, I will not be likely

---

182. Col. Alfred Moore Rhett (1829–1889) of the First South Carolina Artillery commanded Fort Sumter from April to September 1863. He was the son of Elizabeth Washington Burnet and Robert Barnwell Rhett (1800–1876).

183. Assistant Surgeon Virginius G. Hitt of Georgia and either 4th Cpl. William M. Hitt or Pvt. R. G. Hitt of Company F, Twelfth Battalion Georgia Light Artillery.

to be removed, which will be one comfort. As it is I am tossed hither and thither without my comfort or taste being consulted. I decided, when sent to the General Hospital this place, to remain as contentedly as possible if kept to the end of the war. When lo, and behold, I was not there but one week, when I was relieved from duty, and put on the Board for furloughing &c.

I have nothing of interest to write you of here. A flag of truce boat arrived yesterday & brought up some three hundred of our wounded Gettysburg prisoners. All that I have seen are doing finely. They were treated in Baltimore. They say that for some days they were kept in Penn$\underline{a}$ and while there were treated with the greatest kindness by Baltimoreans, who ran the blockade and carried them all kinds of things, but when taken to Baltimore the citizens were not allowed to visit them at all. The people would sometimes collect in front of their Hospital & the Yankee guards would drive them back at the point of the bayonet. They say the Baltimore ladies proved themselves very adept in smuggling clothes into the Hospitals for them, while they were near Gettysburg, by concealing them under their dresses. These prisoners represent themselves as having been well treated by the Yankees, such is not the case with those that go to Fort Delaware.[184] They come looking like beggarly skeletons. They are really pitiable objects.

Ma's letter had very little about home in it except of Sibby's being so sick. I trust she is now better. I wish I were stationed near you all instead of being so far away. Is Minny still at Pocotaligo?

I cannot help thinking frequently of how providential it was that Pa did not succeed in getting off to Europe. All things work together for the best for them that serve God.[185]

I hope all of you are well. Do write me as soon as you get this. Much love to yourself & all—A kiss to Lou.

Ever yr. aff$\underline{ct}$ brother,
F. P. Leverett

P.S.
Tell Mr. Pringle I say he had better try quinine for the pain Jim [has] if he suffers from his arm. To give five grains three or four times a day for several days, & I am sure he will experience relief.

I hope Pa will not hire out Jacob for a week or so. I will pay for him whatever he will be able to get & will insist on his letting me do so, if sent to the field.

---

184. **Fort Delaware**, on Pea Patch Island in the Delaware River, was a military prison housing about seven thousand Confederate prisoners in mid-1863.

185. Rom. 8:28.

5
The War Drags On
August 1863–May 1864

> I see not any prospect of the war closing.
>
> —Rev. Charles E. Leverett.

Milton remained with the Beaufort Artillery at Camp Sturgeon near McPhersonville, while Fred assumed his duties as examining officer at the Camp of Instruction at Dublin, Virginia.

Milton Maxcy Leverett to his mother

Sunday August 27th /63

My dear Mother,

I tried to send the basket yesterday but it couldn't go as no Express was running. I have had two letters to send to sister and Julie ready to send some time, but didn't as I was going to send them in the basket, and not having stamps also at the time, but as the basket can't go I will send them by mail. They will find them somewhat 'behind the times' but that won't make much difference tell them to <u>take</u> <u>them</u> <u>and</u> <u>be</u> <u>thankful</u>. The enemy have fired into Charleston nine out of twenty shell, one went into the grocery store of a Mr. G. W. Williams,[1] and one as far as the Newbridge so it is said.[2] I was very dull before that (having just heard

---

1. George Walton Williams of Charleston, banker and merchant.
2. The bridge on the Charleston and Savannah Railroad, crossing the Ashley River, was built in 1857.

from Bill Elliott how Sumter had been smashed up by their powerful guns) but as soon as that news came I felt almost joyous, felt almost like shouting. I said immediately Charleston is safe, or at least the ground on which it is built, now <u>the women and children will have to run out of the city</u> and there is a chance now of the city being fought street by street. Before that the inhabitants were sort of infatuated but now they see 'what's what' and they will have to leave. I had come to the conclusion that the city would have been surrendered if the monitors had come in and held their own in the harbour for a day, but now they not having come in the citizens would rather run than be shelled to death at a distance, especially <u>that class</u> who would have liked the Yankees to have got possession. Bill went to Fort Sumter and it is almost literally a mass of ruins. There is but one portion (the seaside)[3] standing of any importance, on that there are about ten heavy guns mounted, in a position only to fight the monitors; when he was there they tried to come in but Rhett opened a heavy gun on them and they turned round and ran evidently very much afraid of the fort. The fort is perfectly silent, indeed not being able to fire at any thing but the boats all the other guns having being either taken away or covered with the rubbish. The fort of course is not level, only a great portion is down. I hear this evening that the monitors tried to come in again; they came within 100 yards of Sumter and both Moultrie and herself opened, in fifteen minutes they all ran, some of them evidently injured.[4] I hear also the Yankees have given 48 hours to remove women and children from the city and will open tomorrow night on it.[5] I'll try and write again. I am expecting to go down to Huspa creek tomorrow with several others to draw the seine over the bridge.[6]

Your aff'[ct] son

M. M. Leverett

---

3. This note was added by Milton Leverett after the war: "Also side towards town pretty good order. 1900 M. L."

4. Before sunrise on 23 August Adm. John A. Dahlgren sent five monitors—the U.S.S. *Montauk, Nahant, Passaic, Patapsco,* and *Weehawken*—to test the guns of Fort Sumter at close range. Many of the fort's guns were out of commission and its defenders fired only a few shots; heavy fire from Fort Moultrie forced the monitors to withdraw.

5. Brig. Gen. Quincy A. Gillmore, commander of the Federal Department of the South, wrote Gen. P. G. T. Beauregard, commander of the Confederate Department of South Carolina, Georgia, and Florida, on 21 August, demanding the immediate evacuation of Morris Island and Fort Sumter and threatening to shell Charleston if the Confederates did not comply. When Beauregard objected that Gillmore had not given noncombatants enough notice, Gillmore answered that he would postpone his bombardment for forty-eight hours. This was part of a seven-day bombardment of Forts Sumter and Moultrie and Battery Wagner, 17–23 August. On 22 August the Swamp Angel, a Federal battery built in the marsh between Morris and James Islands, fired sixteen shells into the city. The gun exploded during the next night's bombardment after firing thirty-six shells into Charleston over two days.

6. Huspah Creek, a branch of the Coosaw River, near Sheldon.

Julia Marcelline Leverett to her brother Milton

Columbia August 28th

My dear Minny,

I intend to treat all that part of your letter referring to my writing with silent contempt, except that you must allow me to say that you have an extraordinary amount of brass in your composition. And also you say "other people write once a week;" as you don't mention whether they are <u>brothers</u> or sisters who do so, I presume therefore that the brothers take their part in writing as well as the sisters. Well when you write once a week, it will be time to speak of my doing so. I wish I had favorable accounts to give you of Aunt Til's family, but Tillie poor Tillie is still very sick with typhoid fever and dyptheria together. Oh Minny, if anything happens to Tillie what will I do, I care more about Tillie than any other of my friends. Mary came down on Wednesday to attend to Jim. He, poor fellow suffers excruciatingly sometimes. And yet Mr. Pringle seems to think his wound is coming on very well. We want Jim to change and go into your company. It is what he wanted to do himself but since his horse has been killed I'm afraid he won't be able to as he would have to give his horse to the person who exchanged with him. He said he wanted to go into the company because you're there. Do write a kind letter to him and tell him you can get a horse for him.

We are quite pleased at the way our wheat has turned out. We got a barrel of white flour, a bushel and half of middling, and about a barrel of bran. Ma says 'tis very sweet-tasting wheat. It is so good to have wheat again after having corn so long. Brother Fred sent each of us twenty dollars by Brother Charlie and five to each of the children. I sent up to Pendleton and got a pair of shoes for $15.00. I can lend you a little money if you want some. Only think since January I have had $45.00. Brother Fred has been moved again. After having been at Petersburg a week, he has been placed on the "Board of Furloughs" and is going to try and get one himself. Jim says that 'tis a splendid post—nothing to do. The Doctor isn't getting on at all in the line in which you and I want him to walk. Indeed I heard that some <u>Mazyck</u> had got the priority of him but I don't know if 'tis true. I don't know how he is getting on [in] Virginia. Ma predicts that if he is stationed in Richmond he will be a great beau. I think he has an inclination that way. By the way, if you are so anxious to get married, there's a very favorable opening for you or any one of you in Miss E. B.'s sickness. You can commence by sending a message to inquire how she is, with a bunch of flowers (I dare say you can find some "partridge peas" and "bachelor's buttons") which little attentions will soften her heart and all the rest will be quite easy. I hope Ma told you all about Brother Charlie's coming home. He only paid a mean flying visit as usual. We sent some things to the baby. I sent a hat that I made. He succeeded in exempting Mr. LaRoche. His address is Cheraw. I don't know that there's any use in your sending Jake's letter as I have written two for him since I have been home. It is perfectly ridiculous Minny. I write all the sentimental parts. Yesterday he sent in for me to write a letter for him by Mauma Cely.[7] After having given me messages and a gold watch key in the shape of a cross, he said I knew what else to write. So yesterday I sat down and made up a beautifully affectionate letter and then read it to him in the evening. I believe it satisfied him. He is hiring out at the saltpetre works now but Brother Fred seemed to think that if he came home he would want to carry him back if we could spare him. Daddy Ephraim has been to Walterboro and come back so I haven't told him about the letter. You will be sorry to hear that the old hog is dead. It had been unwell for some time, seemed to have a sort of fever. It is a great loss. One of the second set is sick now.

Madame Togn[8] wrote to Pa to ask him to preach there every Sunday & to teach there two or three days in the week and to let her know his terms. Pa decided to preach there but has not determined about the teaching and asked her to make an offer. Since then we haven't heard from her. Ma thinks it would be a very good thing as Pa has nothing to do now. She is only to have a limited number of scholars and all grown up girls. You must write sooner than you did if you want me to write again.

Your affect. sister
Julie

I have made some envelopes but how should I send them down. Mame made some too.

Milton Maxcy Leverett to his mother

McPhersonville Sept. 9th /63

My dear Mother,

It is a long time since I have written home, but there is nothing of any importance to mention in this place. Affairs around Charleston worry me very much, I always said that the city would fall and it is certain to fall. It is said that Gillmore wrote a pert note to Beauregard, telling him that he had heard that he was the best engineer in the Confederacy, but that he had got the key to Charleston and intended keeping it. Beauregard, I think was out generaled from the start. Now,

---

7. A slave.
8. Madame Acelie Togno, principal of the South Carolina Female Collegiate Institute (Barhamville Institute) in Richland District near Columbia.

all of Morris' Island, with Wagner and Cummings Point gone[9] and Fort Sumter one mass of ruins I can't see how the enemy can miss getting the city. Major Elliott is in command of the Ruins of Fort Sumter, and I understand captured about two hundred Yankees who attacked him last night, our gunboats assisting.[10] I must say that our defence of Charleston so far has been worthy of Carolina and the silent defence of Sumter splendid, but the great mistake was made at the start. The Yankees ought never to have been allowed to obtain a position on Folly Island. In the attack on Charleston it is not the fleet that I fear but those abominable parallel approaches and the superior artillery of the enemy, which they are able to obtain so much easier than ourselves. We have a couple of guns, I understand, presented by Mr. Trenholm to the Government, that are heavier and better than anything yet made in that line. One of them is mounted on the Battery in Charleston.[11] It is warranted to crush through any ironclad in the world at 6000 yds. and I believe throws a ball five miles. The weight of the shot is between 650 lbs & 700 lbs. There was a rumor also that there was a still heavier gun of the kind just made in Richmond and coming down South, but I conclude it's all report. We may get heavy guns but as soon as they are worn out or burst there's an end of them, while the Yankees can replenish themselves. Our western campaign is worrying me, Bragg had better not move anymore if he wishes to save himself and the country, he has already done too much of that for the good of both.[12] Why didn't you write and let me know Fred was at home, after coming as far as Charleston he might have come on to see me. What is he doing and what is his position? I hope he has arranged affairs at home somewhat. I hope you are all well and living better than at last accounts. I have been quite unwell, but am now up and knocking about again. Mrs. Gregorie and Mrs. Tom Elliot have been very kind to me.

---

9.   The Confederates evacuated Morris Island 7 September 1863.

10.   With all but one of Fort Sumter's guns dismounted by the Federal bombardment, Beauregard ordered the First South Carolina Artillery out of the fort on 4 September 1863. The artillerists were replaced by an infantry garrison—the First South Carolina Battalion (Charleston Battalion)—under the overall command of Maj. Stephen Elliott Jr. On 8 September the 300-man force, supported by fire from the C.S.S. *Chicora* and batteries at Forts Moultrie and Johnson, repulsed an attack by 500 Federal sailors and marines who attempted an amphibious landing. The Confederates suffered no casualties; the Federals had 127.

11.   Two 600-pounder Blakely guns came through the blockade via Wilmington, North Carolina, as a gift from Fraser, Trenholm and Company of Liverpool. One of the guns burst while it was being tested, but the other was mounted at the corner of East Battery and South Battery Streets.

12.   Bragg, commander of the Confederate Army of Tennessee, evacuated Chattanooga, Tennessee, on 5 September and withdrew into Georgia; Maj. Gen. William S. Rosecrans's Federal Army of the Cumberland immediately occupied Chattanooga.

They send me things everyday. Mrs. Gregorie generally attends to my meals sending me what I ought to eat, while Mrs. Elliot sends me whole baskets of nice things, a great many of which I can't and oughtn't to eat. Do write to both and thank them for their kindness to me. I haven't reported for duty yet and shant until I feel positively strong enough. I had what the doctor calls Bilious Remittent Fever, but it was much more like Congestive Fever. My whole system was at first feverish and my head felt almost like bursting open, that was relieved by salts, after which the pain went to my bowels and a swinging hot fever went there too. To relieve that I took a small dose of caster oil, then Oh ye Furies did I suffer the torments. But after awhile that passed off to a great extent, only it left me very weak and the doctor (a Doctor Adams of the Rutledge Rifles,[13] our surgeon was ordered to Charleston sometime ago) had to use stimulants to make my pulse act more vigorously, which it did after awhile. After that I got well rapidly, just being careful with my diet and taking only those things that would strengthen me. I was most sick on Thursday. I received Julie's letter then the 3rd but was too unwell to read it until the next day. Pa's little slip inside made me feel quite down in the mouth. He spoke of your living so hard, although I am glad to see you have new flour; when will your syrup be ready for use? Write soon and tell me everything. All of you had better write and purchase a supply of butter. When Charleston falls things will be much higher.

Your aff^{ct} son
Milton M. Leverett

My sickness I think was caused by my seine expedition when I staid in the river about seven hours until two o'clock at night, from the evening, attending to seine which didn't succeed very well. It was at Huspah.

Frederic Percival Leverett to his brother Milton

Direct to me as Surgeon of Camp of Instruction

Dublin Station, T.
& Va R. R[14] Va
16th Sep^{br} 1863

My dear Minny;

You have doubtless heard from various sources that I have been at home. I intended while there to write you, but my time was so very short, I was unable. I suppose Rob Fuller or Bill Elliot told you of my meeting them in Charleston. I

13. Probably Pvt. Lawrence A. Adams of the Rutledge Mounted Rifles, later Company B, Seventh South Carolina Cavalry.
14. The Virginia and Tennessee Railroad.

went down one night, spent a day, & returned that night. I wanted to see the old city once more. I fear I never shall again. The visit was one of the most melancholy I ever made to any place. It was a visit to an almost deserted city. The streets were such as one sees on a rainy Sunday, but the sun was shining brightly. Nearly every house closed; hardly a female to be seen, and few men but soldiers. I saw the big gun which is a monster, and I trust will do good work. I confidently expect the city to be destroyed, but trust the Yankees will never get it.

I wish I could have had time to visit you, but it was impossible. On the 29th Aug. I received orders relieving me of duty in Petersburg and ordering me to report here for duty. This was on a Saturday. On Monday I went to Richmond & applied to the Surgeon General for a leave of absence of ten days. He granted it. I started at once for home, & reached there on Wednesday. I remained one week and then came back, and arrived here on Sunday 13th Inst. I found everything in commotion here— a Yankee raid momentarily expected, here or rather in the neighborhood. The consequence was that I found myself a stranger in a strange place without an acquaintance, no hotel to stop at and much at a loss what to do. I hunted around and at last got lodging at a neighboring farmer's. I stopped there two days, and am now settled down as Surgeon of the Camp of Instruction, of which Maj. Dorman is the Commandant.[15] My duties will be light in the extreme and very unimproving. An easier or more comfortable berth cannot be found in the Army, unless it were the one I last had—Junior Member of the board for Furloughs & Discharges at Petersburg. There I was indeed in clover. I have gotten so in the habit of being moved about I never consider it worth my while to make myself comfortable. In fact I cannot stand the expense. I ought now to have a horse and servant, but a horse would cost me $1000.00 and whence will the money come? I must try & get the Quarter Master to furnish me with a horse, and I must secure the services of some one's servant. That as you know, from experience, is not the most convenient mode of living. I expect to pass my time as much as possible reading. I have brought one or two German & French works with me & intend brushing up those languages, which have been growing rather rusty of late. Camp life is well adapted to making a man rough in every respect. You should guard against that effect. Situated as you are in a village in which you have acquaintances, some of whom have libraries, you should avail yourself as much as possible of the advantages they offer. I wish you would apply for a position in the Ordnance Department. It is to be gotten by standing an examination and I am sure you are able to do that. Allan Stuart or some of those who have obtained appointments can let you know how to get an invitation to apply. If you pass & are assigned to a Post or to some General's staff, your position will be far pleasanter and more lucrative than it now is.

---

15. Maj. James Baldwin Dorman of the Third Virginia Artillery, Local Defense Troops.

This place is a small R. R. village in Southwestern Va. in Pulaski County, not far from the various Sulphur Springs, but too far for me to visit them. It is the Hd. Qrs. of Maj. Gen. Jones, Commandant of this Department which extends into Tenn.[16] The recent fall of Cumberland Gap has thrown this part of the Country open to the advances of the enemy, who I fear, will advance in heavy force to seize the Salt & Iron Works, which are in the neighboring counties. If they do so, they will inflict a serious blow on the Confederacy. The principal iron mines of Va. are in the adjoining County. A portion of Pickets Division[17] passed here last night, going to reinforce Gen. Jones. Backing Bragg has been, we hear, again at work, evacuating Chattanooga. If something is not done to stop him, he will evacuate the Confederacy. I hope Johnston will have command in the fight with Rosencranz, which ought soon to come off.

While coming on last week I met train after train of Longstreet's Corps going on to reinforce the Army of Tenn. I hope they may not be too late.[18] At Petersburg I met Jenkins about starting. He sent in an urgent application to the Surgeon General to have me assigned to his Brigade at once. I do not think the request will be granted, but hope it may, as it would lend far more to my future advantage to be associated with men of the State in which I, of course, expect to live & it would be better for me to make a reputation & get a stand among them, than to be tossed about the Confederacy as I have been for the last year. My experience has certainly been a varied one.

I am very anxious to hear some news from Charleston. Not one word since last Thursday's dispatches & today is Tuesday. I trust Ste may continue fortunate at Sumter. I would like much now to be stationed in So. Car.

With kind remembrances to all. Write soon

Ever yr aff[t] brother
F. P. Leverett

Everything at home was going on much as usual. The family were well except Lou. I left her with fever. She was about taking the Hooping Cough. I am anxious about her. Julia had improved considerably. She was about going to school. Mme _____ Mary was looking wonderfully well. We spent one very pleasant evening at the Middleton's. Mary Heyward was on a visit at our house. She has improved very much. Pa while I was at home made arrangements with a Mr. Patterson to

---

16. Maj. Gen. William E. "Grumble" Jones commanded the Confederate Department of Southwest Virginia and East Tennessee.

17. Maj. Gen. George E. Pickett commanded a division in the First Corps, Army of Northern Virginia.

18. Two divisions of Lt. Gen. James Longstreet's First Corps, Army of Northern Virginia, contributed to Bragg's victory over Rosecrans at Chickamauga, Georgia, on 19–20 September.

publish some of his books.[19] If the man be honest, he will doubtless do well. He will anyhow have no risk of losing by the operation. The horses were well, but thin. Your colt had grown but needs pasturing badly. The two hogs promise well for bacon. The old sow was dead.

Julia Marcelline Leverett to her brother Milton

Columbia, Oct 6th

My dear Min

I really have been so busy since going to school that I have had time for nothing scarcely. I like school very much only 'tis a little tiresome to have to walk over there every day. Madame thinks me very childish. Indeed she told Pa so. I like all of them, Madame, Miss Acelie, Mr. Torriani the music teacher[20] and Miss Carter the English teacher. Those are all the teachers. There are some very nice girls over there. Leila Barnwell is coming over there too.[21] I tell you Min, I am <u>rather</u> afraid of Madame. She can be pretty sharp, and wo to the unlucky girl who thwarts her.

But that is enough of myself for the present. You will be so sorry to hear the doctors judged it necessary, last week, to amputate poor Jim's arm in order to <u>save his life</u>. So last Friday they cut it out from the <u>very</u> <u>socket</u> and had to scrape it out for the disease had got as far as that. He is getting on very well now, and the doctor says the wound looks more healthy. But he is not yet out of danger. I do hope he will be out of it soon. One of us goes in every day to stay with him and he has some one to sit up every night. Poor fellow! Mr. Heyward says he couldn't have lived under the operation if they had not given him chloroform. Newton has gone on to Virginia. Aunt Til says that Jim's arm has decided her to buy a farm even if it cost $10,000, but of course she doesn't know yet whether she will remain here this winter or not.

Brother Fred is to be removed again. This time he is to go to Jenkins's Brigade, so we will see him again soon I expect. We can however never see you boys too often. Indeed, I wish the war would stop so you all can be at home again. Min don't you wish Brother Fred would get engaged for really he never seems to get up to the point. He wrote word some thing about some young lady

---

19. James T. Paterson of Richmond moved to Columbia and then to Augusta, Georgia, during the war, first as a printer of Confederate notes and later as a publisher.

20. Madame Acelie Togno; her daughter Acelie; and Eugenio Torriani, an Italian opera singer stranded in the South, professor of music at Barhamville Institute.

21. Eliza Woodward Barnwell (1829–1887), daughter of Eliza Barnwell and Robert Woodward Barnwell.

who asked him if he wasn't very young to be a Surgeon. He asked her how old she thought him. She said "24" then he told her "not exactly" and then she said 25. It must have quite pleased him. What do you think of the affairs out at the West? We hear that all the army is quarelling. Bragg never does seem to be perfectly successful. They have been pressing at a great rate up here. Yesterday they pressed 100. Old Mrs. Ball's horses were pressed and the old lady had to walk home. We took fifty pieces of artillery in the West[22] and the horses were killed so that they have to press to supply their place. Your wretched cat brought in all four of the kittens to-day and we have been surrounded by cats to-day. I should think six cats were almost too many for this little place. We have made about half a barrel of molasses up to this present time but we have some trouble about the grinding. Dr. Parkers old man doesn't seem willing to grind for us and he seems to lead Doctor Parker. The syrup is very good, but it blackens the teeth not permanently of course but still that is not very agreeable anyhow. Dr. Parker's own did the same last year.

I send you the advertisement of Pa's Arithmetic.[23] It is quite famous. Pa did not put it in himself, the publisher wrote it. Three dollars is pretty don't you think so?

I hope you have got well again. Miss Grimke said you were quite pulled down. I should think 'twas enough to make anyone sick to stay in the water seven hours.

You never told me how to send down the envelopes to you. They are still somewhere about the house. I believe you owe me a letter too so you may wait three months for another one.

Write soon

Your affectionate sister
Julia

---

22. The Army of Tennessee captured fifty-one pieces of Federal artillery at Chickamauga.

23. This advertisement appeared in the *Charleston Courier* 6–16 October 1863: "IN PRESS. LEVERETT'S ARITHMETIC. . . . COMPLETE ACADEMICAL ARITHMETIC, prepared for the use of Schools and Academies in the Confederate States, by the popular and successful Southern teacher, Prof. C. E. Leverett, of South Carolina. This work, prepared with great care by one who has an experience of twenty years as a teacher, has been submitted to the examination of teachers and others of known judgement, and it has received their favorable notice, and has been pronounced to be 'the best school arithmetic in the Confederacy.'" The book was *The Southern Confederacy Arithmetic for Common Schools and Academies, with a Practical System of Book-keeping by Single Entry* . . . (Augusta: J. T. Paterson and Co., 1862).

Milton Maxcy Leverett to his mother

McPhersonville
Oct. 10th 1863

My dear mother,

I think that I have waited long enough to hear from home so I write to see what is the matter. Is anybody sick? or perhaps you are waiting for me to write first, if so it is a bad habit to get into for I generally wait to hear from <u>you</u> first. Winter is coming on rapidly, we are now preparing our future camping ground preparatory to our move. It will take at least a month to get it ready and will be in the neighborhood of Jno. Gregorie's plantation near the field we camped in before in the pine woods on a hill toward Buncombeville. Mr & Mrs. Jno. G. have made such a fuss about the Beaufort Artillery injuring their place that we wouldn't camp in their place this time, they can't bother us outside. We would reap the whirlwind if we camp inside, we sowed the wind last year or I think they did rather. Mrs. G. sort of came the whirlwind at me one day about the injury done to her place by our company. I laughed at her and told her she had better wait until she got a house burnt down before she said anything, but I believe I have already told you all about it.

We have had another expedition to Big Island which was quite pleasant. Some forty odd of us volunteered to go over there in charge of a sergeant—Stephen Barnwell—to capture twenty or thirty Yankees that were said to come over every day in charge of hands to get in the crop. A portion of us were detached to hunt up all the prog and put them on the boats, after which this squad was to go on and join the ambuscading party. You would have been amused to have seen the zest with which we rushed to the poultry houses jerked open the doors pulled the roosters, ducks and hens off roost and not, without any regard whatever to their feelings about being waked up two o'clock at night, the windows of other houses knocked open the fellows rush in, run hither and thither, looking in this corner and that corner, in this cupboard and that barrel, this box and that tub, looking here and there, smelling this jug and shaking that bottle, hauling out from their corners box, barrels, cupboards, tubs and all overturning and examining their contents with every now and then an exclamation of "Ha, see what I've got," "I've found so and so, a net or a coat or a chair as the case may be, or "look at what the villains have here." then "let us look in this room, it is locked" with perhaps an admonitory question implying doubt as to whether anybody might or ought not be inside with a gun "say squire can I come in there without waiting for leave break open the door and drag out its contents. We obtained in this manner a good many things which are quite useful in camp. There were some hogs in pens but we didn't trouble them as their squealing would have defeated the object of the expedition, besides they were so poor, as poor as the poorest hog you or I, or anybody else, ever saw that they were not worth killing, although if we could have brought them off alive we might have fattened them. After the progging was over this squad joined the ambuscading party about two miles off, watching the road leading from a landing the enemy were expected to advance by, but through some mischance or other no enemy came. We afterward learned from a negro we took that the flat they were accustomed to come over in had been broken. But so it turned out a negro who happened to be on the island hiding about saw some of our men coming to the landing where the boats were, to cook our breakfast, and gave the alarm by firing three guns, when after awhile a couple of boats were seen coming ashore from Little Island. Four or five of our men who had been sent off in that direction to scout for the negro went to meet them and found that there was but one Yankee, all the rest were negroes. The Yankee was shot down by one man, while another went at the negroes some of who aimed and snapped their guns, while one went off, hurting no one, the negroes all then (with the exception of two, a man and a boy, who came up and surrendered themselves) threw themselves back on their boats upturning them, several being drowned while the rest swam and bogged over to Little Island. As we were discovered now and nothing more could be done we returned to the main land.

Your aff^ct son
M. M. Leverett

The crop over there appeared very good rice & corn we found here and there in different houses pumpkins also. I dug some ground nuts and eat them, also tried the potato crop but they seemed very poor. The negroes that had guns were not in the army but were exempts, who had muskets given them to protect the different plantations. The two captured belong to Dr. Rose[24] and Mr. Trescott. I asked after Mr. Seabrook's property. The plantation was still worked, house rather rickety, Peg was at the place, George had a little cake and lemonade shop in Beaufort. Sam & Charleston were working in the town, Sam's wife Charlotte was also working there. Abram died last May and some of the people were working at the Half Way House.[25] The day after we got back to camp we had a raffling off of all the prog. It was quite ridiculous and laughable. The prog all in all was not very valuable and to be divided among forty men made it still less so. There would be a shout of laughter as one man wd. draw an old piggin almost in pieces or an old pot that couldn't hold anything or anything of the sort. Nenny drew an old saw & hoe. I drew a large oven without a top. In an overcoat that I found I got between fifteen and sixteen dollars in Greenbacks Shinplasters and

---

24. Dr. Arthur Barnwell Rose, physician.
25. Archibald Hamilton Seabrook's slaves.

silver.[26] I send up a couple of the greenbacks and a shinplaster for you to see. Do keep them as objects of curiosity. The rest I have given away with the exception of the silver. The latter is only two dollars and a quarter. Some of our men have gone to Charleston on a torpedo expedition the object being to blow up the Ironsides.[27] I hardly think it will succeed. Barnwell Rhett and Ayr[28] spoke at our camp last Friday. By the bye, I have written this letter by instalments, today is Tuesday the thirteenth. Rhett is decidedly the man of the two to represent us. Ayr follows him about wherever he goes to speak in order to speak also and thus nullify the effects of Rhett's speeches, but he ruins his prospects by that very act as he cannot compare with Mr Rhett either in his carriage as a gentleman or as a speaker, his delivery is miserable, like some clumsy schoolboy. Sometimes they get at repartee and expartee, and the consequence is that Ayr generally gets used up. Mr Rhett came out boldly, denied that he was a factionist, declared that if they sent him they would have to take him as he was, that he was too old a man to change, and besides that he would be the tool of no man, that his opinions should not be guided by those of President Davis. Proved by certain Resolutions of Congress which Davis had vetoed that the President was headstrong and sometimes to blame, said that the position he took was not one as against him but for the country, and declared that he saw what we did not see, illustrating it by the allusion to the anecdote of Cardinal Fiesch[29] and Napoleon the First. The former was trying to argue Napoleon out of some act but could not when Napoleon seizing him by the arm and carrying him into the balcony asked him if he saw a certain star, the Cardinal answered in the negative and Napoleon turning on his heel said "I do" and walked away. Rhett is far superior to Ayr and I shall vote for him. Our Congress has too many slow old fogies, we want some pushing men, there is a plenty of intellect there but they are all too slow and timid. Jeff has them under his thumb. When the speeches were ended, Rhett was applauded, while Ayr was not.

I received Julie's letter on Saturday and was quite sorry to hear of poor Jim's arm, there must have some bad attendance somewhere. None of you as usual

---

26. Greenbacks were U.S. Treasury notes, authorized in 1862 as a war measure and printed in green ink; shinplasters were notes issued in denominations less than a dollar.

27. On 5 October the C.S.S. *David*, manned by Lt. William T. Glassell of the Confederate States Navy and a three-man crew, left Charleston Harbor carrying a torpedo and attempted to sink the U.S.S. *New Ironsides*, off Morris Island. The torpedo was detonated and the Federal ship was badly damaged but did not sink. Glassell and one crewman were captured when the Confederates abandoned the vessel but the other two crewmen returned safely to port.

28. Lewis Malone Ayer Jr. of Barnwell District ran for reelection to the Confederate Congress against Robert Barnwell Rhett Sr.

29. Cardinal Joseph Fesch (1763–1839), French ambassador to the Vatican, uncle of Napoléon Bonaparte.

have ever mentioned what arm or in what battle he was shot. His friends in the company appear quite concerned for him—Stuart Rhett chiefly. Almost everybody speaks well of Jim, but you don't hear a word for Newton. We have had a couple of bad accidents lately in our company. One A man, Branch[30] of Beaufort, in jumping out of a wagon when the mules were running away broke his leg just above the ancle, the small bone stuck through the pants. The other accident was the shooting of a little fellow, a mere boy, who had just joined our company, Richard Reynolds of Beaufort, by Henry Elliot.[31] Henry was playing with a pistol and pointing it at this fellow and said he was going to shoot him not knowing that the barrel was loaded, when pulling the trigger the pistol went off, little Reynolds walked on for a second then clapping his hands to his chest cried out and fell, and died in a few minutes. Henry minded it very much. The Reynolds family have had a sad fatality attending it, that makes four or five since leaving Beaufort. Miss Sallie Reynolds died just lately, she was teaching in the Up Country and just lately turned both deaf and blind.[32] Little Richard Reynolds, we had taken in the company out of kindness, in order that he might do something for himself.

I will send up my basket shortly if the enemy dont destroy Charleston. I wish you would get Julie to send me Davie's Bourdon and Smith's Arithmetic[33] and I also send some money to purchase an "Ordnance Manual." It will cost about five dollars. If the Bourdon has to be purchased, purchase it, get both at any price. Perhaps the Fowles may have a Bourdon. Do get Julia to overhaul all the old newspapers and find a number containing the Examination programme for application to the Ordnance Department.

I wouldn't be surprised if Dora and Rena were impressed soon. If you can, Rena had better be substituted for Dora. If Anne would like it Dora might be kept in our company by one of our officers. I would rather do it if I were she than lose her. Mrs T. Elliott always inquires after all of you at home. This letter is long enough for you isn't it.

Fred was given a temporary appointment as surgeon of the Palmetto Sharpshooters, in Brig. Gen. Micah Jenkins's South Carolina brigade, on 22 October. Jenkins's Brigade

---

30. Pvt. W. S. Branch, an artilleryman.
31. Pvt. Richard M. Reynolds enlisted at Camp Coosaw near McPhersonville on 3 October 1863 and was killed on 5 October. Pvt. Henry DeSaussure Elliott (1848–1906) was the son of Sarah Gibbes DeSaussure and Rev. Stephen Elliott (1804–1866).
32. Sallie Reynolds died in Spartanburg on 14 September.
33. Charles Davies, *Elements of Algebra, Translated from the French of M. Bourdon. Revised and Adapted to the Courses of Mathematical Instruction in the United States* (New York: Wiley & Long, 1836), and Francis H. Smith, *An Elementary Treatise on Analytical Geometry Translated from the French of J. B. Biot, for the Use of the Cadets of the Virginia Military Institute, at Lexington Va.* (New York & London: Wiley and Putnam, 1840).

belonged to Hood's Division, one of two divisions of Lt. Gen. James Longstreet's First Corps, Army of Northern Virginia, which had been ordered to Tennessee in September. Longstreet reinforced Gen. Braxton Bragg's Army of Tennessee during the Chickamauga Campaign and then took command of the Department of East Tennessee in an attempt to capture Knoxville. Fred joined the Palmetto Sharpshooters just before the Knoxville Campaign began in November.

Frederic Percival Leverett to his sister Julia

Junction of East Tenn. & Ga
R. R. Tenn. 7th Nov. 63.

My dear Julie,

We are here awaiting our turn to be taken off on the cars whither we do not exactly know except that is somewhere towards Knoxville to meet we believe, Burnsides.[34] We all hope we are to go to a more fruitful country than we are leaving, one less worn out than this is,—& we trust it will be removed from the supervision of Bragg, Commissary Bragg, as he is called. We hope we will go where he will have nothing to do with rations. Our supplies have been of late deplorably short & disappointing. Longstreet is said to have proposed the following Conundrum, "What is the difference between Gens. Lee & Bragg?" Answer.—The one gains a victory and beheads his enemy's Gens. The other gains it & decapitates his own Gens. D. H. Hill, Polk,[35] & I don't know how many more.[36] Since the above was given he also decapitated his enemy, Rosencranz.

D. H. Hill on being removed from here is said to have written to Bragg to demand the reasons, why it was done. He received an answer, they say, as follows—"You asked the President to remove me. He refused. I asked the President to remove you. He did." Longstreet will command us, where we are going.[37] Our men are in fine spirits & I trust will do good service. Heaven grant that we may wipe out Burnsides. By so doing we may possibly in conjunction with other move-

---

34. Maj. Gen. Ambrose E. Burnside commanded the Federal Army of the Ohio in eastern Tennessee.

35. Lt. Gen. Daniel Harvey Hill, commander of a corps in the Army of Tennessee, was relieved on 15 October. Lt. Gen. Leonidas Polk, Episcopal bishop of Louisiana, commander of the right wing, was suspended in September and reassigned to the Department of Mississippi and East Louisiana.

36. Many of Bragg's subordinates were so frustrated at his failure to pursue the Federals after Chickamauga that they petitioned Jefferson Davis, asking him to replace Bragg. Davis visited the Army of Tennessee to investigate the matter but left Bragg in command.

37. Longstreet was appointed commander of the Department of East Tennessee on 4 November and ordered to oppose Burnside at Knoxville.

ments compel the evacuation of Chattanooga & relieve Tenn. The season is so far advanced & transportation is so small that I doubt if we go much further than Knoxville, if we succeed in getting there. We are to go some 60 miles by R. R. & sent on our horses yesterday. Mine is a miserable old mare nearly as large as Mr. Heywards carriage horses. She does as well as any other will to starve & maltreat. If I can get a chance, I will trade her off for some small artillery horse suitable for riding. I hope no attempt will be made to press Dora. If there is, tell Annie to recollect that she is my <u>reserve horse</u>—kept at home to be sent for as soon as needed. I don't know how A. Rhett[38] succeeded in protecting his sister's horses. He as Capt. is entitled to but 2 horses & doubtless has that many of his own. I received Mary's letter yesterday & was very glad of it. It had a great deal in it—I will write her as soon as I can conveniently. You also I must thank for your letter. It was the best I ever got from you. I hope you will make decided improvement at Mme. Tognio's. Your next letter must be in French, though I will agree to reply to it in that language. Before long I must try & write to Lou as it seems she wants to hear from her Fedda. I often think of my little darling. I never see a little child without my little Puss being recalled to me. My best love to my darling.

I hope all of you are getting on well, and that some means may be found for feeding the family, negros & all. I hoped before this to have heard from Tilly & certainly expected to from Anne, but suppose the latter has been too much worried by household duties, & that the former is too busy with the negros and stockings. I am glad Tilly has taken the matter in hand & hope she may succeed in so getting the negros to work as to cease giving her trouble. I wish I were at home to assist her in so doing.

Last night I slept under a tree with Col. Walker & Staff.[39] It was pretty cold. I had only my buggy blanket & overcoat—having sent my other blankets on with my horse yesterday. I am very much afraid I have lost my valise & all its contents. If so I will be in most unhappy condition. It is hard to get on the field now with anything beyond saddlebags. I wish I could have gotten the ones sent by Charlie.

Much love to all. I wrote Ma night before last. I had to direct the letter with lead pencil.

Ever yr aff<u>ct</u> brother
F. P. Leverett

---

38. Capt. Albert Moore Rhett (1834–1911), Quartermaster Department, brother of Elizabeth Barnwell Rhett Heyward and Mary Barnwell Rhett (1824–1896).

39. Col. Joseph Walker of the Palmetto Sharpshooters. His staff included 1st Lt. Henry Thomas Hughes, ensign; Adj. James M. McFall; Capt. John William McLure, regimental quartermaster; Q.M. Sgt. Augustus John Sitton; and Chaplain James McDowell.

Milton Maxcy Leverett to his mother

Nov. 9th 1863

My dear mother,

    Please don't insist on my writing so many times a week, it will just be a regular annoyance to you and all; I am a very considerate son, I don't wish to worry you is of course one reason why I don't worry you with my letters. If I had been in the bad habit of writing five times a week to you, you would have fretted yourself awfully at not receiving any letters when I was sick, you would have found it out, and thus plagued yourself, but through my good habit of not writing often you never found out I was sick until I was well. That's a conclusive argument. I don't like the principle of selling Greenbacks, it is in a manner depreciating or at least continuing the depreciation of our currency. I have a great deal more faith in our currency than that of the Yankees. I send up a box and basket with some of my things that I don't wish in my way in case the enemy attack us. The basket can be emptied and the things put aside if you might need it to use. The bottle of wine I send for you. The things in the box can be taken out with the exception of my boot which I leave there in order that you might return it in the box anytime I may need it, the books can remain there also, my coat do have put oneside carefully, my blue pants do have mended, the other pair one of the boys can have. According to the regulations of the road I have to put the value on the articles sent by Express, they won't take pay here, require it to be paid for at the place to which it is sent. I enclose the money to pay the freight, do let me know if it is enough. Do see that my things are attended to yourself. I am in want of envelopes and writing paper but you needn't send much as it might induce me to write often. They could be sent when Mame sends the basket back with my pants and other things. Don't make the mistake that we belong to the 11th Regt; now; it has been arranged. I am surprised at rice birds being killed up there. We have service every now and then, it has been pretty regular, every Sunday, morning and night, and one night every week. How is Pa getting on with his books. Love to him and all.

Your affectionate son
Milton M. Leverett

Tell Julie I promise to write to her one of these days. I wish all of you at home could remember to answer questions that are asked in letters, henceforth I shant write until they are answered, it is very provoking. I have had a great many persons to ask me in what arm and what fight Jim was wounded. I am compelled to say 'I don't know,' notwithstanding repeated letters inquiring. That is only one instance of numerous questions. I received the Ordnance Manual safe, it is a very nice one much nicer than I expected,[40] I wanted the one in pamphlet form which is an abridgment of that and cost only five dollars,[41] the arithmetic also came safe; could you not get a <u>Bourdon</u>, I thought the Fowles' might have had one? How about the newspaper that I wanted Julia to look up for me, none of you mentioned whether it could be found or not, it is one of last year's, one of the winter months I think, it has the advertisement of the Examination for the Ordnance Department. You needn't count on my studying for it, I am rather taken aback at the magnitude of the task, and studying in camp is really so difficult.

Mary Maxcy Leverett to her son Milton

My dear Min,

I am fixing a basket for you which is to go the same time as this letter, so inquire of the Express immediately. Your two white pants you sent must have got wet (probably in a rain from the Depot to the Express office in Columbia) & have two large spots of mildew on them as big as my hand, I wonder if the Express will pay damages? I had them washed, but it won't come out. Every thing in the box was safe. I have turned your pants and taken a great deal of pains with them and hope they will suit you, as I did every stitch with my own hands. The basket will be full of groundnuts, and cake which Mame took great pleasure and pains in making for you, it is <u>all</u> made with our own syrup, as we had no sugar. She & I looked over a quantity of Couriers[42] but have not yet been able to find what you want, & I shall find out who is in the Ordnance Dpt. here and ask about it for you. You must be mistaken in supposing it requires such a great amount of knowledge for the Mrs Rowan[43] who hired Molly last summer was here last week to try and hire Lewis, and accidentally in the course of conversation she happened to mention, her step-son who had lost an arm in the service, had got an excellent place in the Ord. Dpt. in Columbia & was receiving $1200 a year, as well as $400 a year for his pay, (for he would not take a discharge purposely). Now, I know this young man certainly has never had so good an education, or such advantages as you have had, & I doubt if he is half as fit for it as you are now. The reason your father

---

40. *The Ordnance Manual for the Use of the Officers of the Confederate States Army. Prepared under the Direction of Col. J. Gorgas, Chief of Ordnance, and Approved by the Secretary of War* (Richmond: West and Johnston, 1863). Milton's copy is inscribed on the inside cover and flyleaf "Milton Leverett Fort Sumter, C.S.A. 1864."

41. *The Field Manual for the Use of the Officers on Ordnance Duty. Prepared by the Ordnance Bureau.* (Richmond: Ritchie & Dunovant, 1862).

42. *Charleston Courier*, one of two daily Charleston newspapers.

43. Sallie A. Rowan of Columbia.

bought so expensive an Ord. Man. (it was your own money) was none other was to be had. Books are now held at enormous prices. You say we have not yet told you at what battle & what arm Jim lost. I am sure it has been told you once or twice, but I am pretty sure you only glance at our letters <u>once</u> & don't read them again & then tear them up. I'll tell you again however it was at one of the Cavalry battles (of which several took place at the same Station) at Brandy Station,[44] and it is his left arm. He is coming to dine here today with his Mother poor fellow, and we are to give him roast pig for his dinner, but Ben will have to cut it up for him. Ben has made him a very good nurse, and sleeps in his room every night. The wound is almost well, yet abscesses continually form and burst on and about his shoulder, which give great pain, and D[r] Chisolm says it will be the case a good part of the winter.[45] Fred's dressing gown is the only thing he can wear (Fred gave it [to] him, for he had nothing to put on) and he had to wear it even when the Trenholm's sent their carriage to take him out there to lunch the other day. Ben comes for our carriage once or twice a week & the Heywards' send theirs also so that he may get exercise enough, but his knees are so weak Ben has to lift up his foot & put it on the step of the carriage and then help raise him up bodily. D[r] C. says his knees will be the last part of him to improve. It was not the amputation that made him weak however, but the anguish he went thro for two months before that, so that when the operation was performed it became a relief to him. It was a surprise, a pleasant surprise I may say to me, to find how little he suffered afterwards, and what a relief it was for the arm to be taken off. He is in very good spirits, & is going up to Pendleton to see his sisters sometime this week.

I thank you for the wine, my dear son, which is quite a treasure to me, good as medicine, and far pleasanter. The pants are quite a treasure to be altered for Toney, but I do not see how you can spare so good a pair. Every thing here is at fabulous prices, and I have ceased going to stores, or asking the prices of any thing. The homespun dress I have on cost $3. a yard, one Julie wears to school $2 75c. If it were not for the stocking work that I have put the four servants at, I do not see how we could live at all. The pay is so good that they make me $70 a month, and seventy dollars is not to be sneezed at in these times, especially when there is not a grain of corn left in the corn house, and we have to give the servants money instead of corn, & it takes twelve dollars a week for the grown negroes only. Sue's wages also are $12 a month, which makes over eighty dollars. To do this, tho', I keep no seamstress, so that we each do our own work, as well as your fathers &

44. The battle at Brandy Station, near Culpeper, Virginia, on 9 June 1863, was the largest cavalry battle of the war.
45. Dr. Julian John Chisolm, surgeon in the Wayside Hospital in Columbia. He was the author of *A Manual of Military Surgery for the Use of Surgeons in the Confederate Army* (Richmond: West and Johnston, 1861–1864).

the children's. Your father finds that Annie & I have managed so wisely that he leaves every thing to our management now, & is only too thankful that we do not consult him. We have bought rye & planted & it is up & looking well. We also bought wheat, & (purchased manure also) it is planted & now coming up, & Annie is having the ground prepared now for oats, which we did not have to buy.

I could not succeed in getting a Bourdon for you, but have written to the Fowles' to ask if they are using it up there, as it is not here & the Greggs have none. The Greggs have helped us out in many things. Julia insisted on contributing $180 dollars to the housek[eep]ing & said she would not stay without. Would you believe it Charles Hanckel contributes to Mrs D Heyward to the amount of <u>a hundred dollars a month</u> for his family. Mr H. did object but C. H. insisted & Mrs Heyward agreed to it. Annie H. has another daughter Charles H. says it makes him feel "grey." Cousin Henry Stuart & Mrs Sarah Fuller are engaged![46] & to be married tomorrow at Mrs James Rhetts.[47] It is a very good thing for both, tho' people profess to be shocked at it. I think Annie Stuart[48] probably made the match, thro' fear that her father might "turn fool" as so many old men do, & marry some unsuitable young girl, for they are all extremely fond of their Aunt Sarah. I am glad of it, for it is a most convenient match for both sides; since Rob. married & has <u>two</u> children now,[49] she was certainly more alone in the world, & I know the Stuarts will be delighted to have her with them, for they have felt very lonely since their Mothers'[50] death & Annie herself was very sick indeed last spring. I have so much to tell you always that I am sure you get tired of my long letters, and that is the reason you write so seldom. Were it not that I have such an amount of work to do, I would like to write to you every week, for it makes me feel as if I was talking to you and had you nearer to me than Pocotaligo, but there is an immense amount of mending now for us all to do, & your sister has to work for Julie also (who has not a moment to herself now) to teach Kate & Carry, & see after the servants stocking work (otherwise it is done badly) carefully, to take music lessons also, as well as do all her own work, & has knitted a nice pair of black worsted gloves for me (gloves are too dear now) & is now knitting <u>one</u> glove for poor Jim, who sent to beg her to do one for him, & intends knitting a pair for her father & another for you when she has time. She taught Matilda Middleton (who came out here several times and spent the whole morning) how to knit a pair for <u>her</u> father, & she really seemed grateful to Tillie for showing her. Our family is so large that

46. On 2 December 1863 Henry Middleton Stuart Sr. married Sarah Barnwell Means, widow of Thomas Fuller (1813–1845).

47. Charlotte Haskell Rhett (1794–1871), widow of James Smith Rhett (1797–1855).

48. Ann Means Stuart (1827–1905).

49. Robert Means Fuller and his children Phoebe (1860–1886) and Ellen (b. 1863).

50. Ann Hutson Means Stuart (1808–1862), sister of Sarah Barnwell Means Fuller (1816–1879).

Annie has as much as she can do in attending to the house keeping & farm concerns, sewing for Lou & herself & taking music lessons also, Mame has more time than any, tho' even she has enough to do in studying her French lessons & music lessons to keep her also fully occupied, especially as they all walk in to their lessons on account of the horses being so poorly fed and attended to now, Lewis not half cleaning them. We <u>all</u> knit all the stockings we wear also. So you see, this minute account of the family will show you how very full our hands are. But there is no excuse for your writing so seldom, notwithstanding your <u>ingenious plea</u>.

We did not make more than eighty bushels of corn this year, & had to commence using it the last of August. The fences were so bad that cows from Town got in and destroyed a good deal, and I am certain Daphne sold green corn in Town also, from what I heard. But we did very well with potatoes, have been using them freely from the 1<u>st</u> Aug. and have in banks about 30 bushels still. We gave out one or two full allowance to the servants at first, and then determined to keep the rest for the house during the winter. We made but little rice, but of groundnuts about 1 tierce & a half, so groundnuts are a standing article of supply in the house.

I have a letter from your poor brothers kind Virginia friend lately, Mrs Daingerfield, and it unintentionally gave me great pain, for she had heard thro' some one that your brother had preached in Chester (it was your father) not long ago & she wrote to ask which report was true, for her nephews Capt. Jacquelin & Clifton Smith[51] had told her they heard he was no more & so between conflicting accounts she did not know what to believe, I wrote to her, of course, but it gave me exquisite pain.

Paper is scarce and dear now, that I am writing now only on pieces. You must promise to read this over three times.

Your Gen Walker & Col. Rutledge won't get any "golden opinions" from the public if they continue managing no better than they have hitherto done. When the Yankees can steal every piece of property from people, under their very noses and this wonderful General & Colonel can't stop it. What inefficient ignoramuses! I hear Col. R. didn't even know the way to Cunningham's bluff. An expensive army is kept there for nothing. Where were the pickets? I haven't seen Mr Heyward, but hear that outwardly he bears it very well, only shrugs his shoulders and says "Well it can't be helped." I am ashamed of our country producing such lazy specimens of officers. Oh! What an officer your brother would have made! I fear for my country greatly—affairs look gloomy & no great man arises to deliver the

---

51.   Capt. LaRoche Jacquelin Smith, assistant chief of artillery and ordnance in the Department of South Carolina, Georgia, and Florida, and his brother Capt. Clifton Hewitt Smith, assistant adjutant general on the staff of Gen. P. G. T. Beauregard in the same department.

country either in diplomatic affairs or in fighting ones. We miss Stonewall Jacksons <u>prayers</u>, as well as his fighting.[52]

Fred was near Knoxville when he last wrote, & you will see his letter, for since I commenced writing this I find your father has made a great mistake & <u>directed</u> a letter (which Julie had written to Blanche who had asked Julie by Charlie & her wishes, to name the child & to be godmother, it not having been yet baptized) <u>to you</u>, instead of to "Mrs Charles H. Leverett," so you will have the benefit of it, & Julie will be horror-struck at the contre-temps; You must enclose it immediately after reading Fred's letter, to Blanche at Cheraw. Charley sent word he was coming to see us the second week in Dec.

Your Aunt Til & Jim are come so good bye.

yr aff Mother
Mary Leverett

P.S.

Mr. Trenholm has made Jim a present of a suit of clothes (grey) which would have cost $200. The tailor Walker ask $75 to make it up.[53] I send you a letter of Fred's to read, older than the one in Blanche's letter.

Katy sends her love to you.

Rev. Charles Edward Leverett to his son Milton

30th Nov.

My dear Minny,

I wrote to you the other day, when Mamy sent, but she forgot to put in my note & I write now as your Ma has a letter to go. There is nothing new here, but all is dark & gloomy. It is very hard to get along, as we have no corn & there is none to be had from other places than the cheating shopkeepers & farmers who generally ask about 5 or 6 dollars a bushels. With such a large family & so many servants & horses to feed you may suppose it is discouraging. And then the expense of shoes is so great, & cloth. I feel quite in despair. The unjust tax on me because I had a few bales of cotton of nearly a thousand dollars has made me you may suppose very short of means. The tax on my cotton alone when it ought to have been about $100 & would have been, if it had been sold, was alone about $750. The tax next year is to be worse than before from present appearances.

---

52. Jackson died 10 May 1863 after being accidentally wounded by Confederate troops at Chancellorsville on 2 May.

53. W. W. Walker, a tailor in Columbia.

It seems we have been defeated out west after all our hopes of success.[54] Bragg ought to be in an inferior position, though to be sure Lee was unsuccessful in Penn^a.[55]

You are to be attacked I see below. I hope the troops there will be able to beat the wretches that are pressing on us at all points. If you we had a better General than Walker who I think is a poor inefficient character, something might be done. Nevertheless, try to whip the villains, for they deserve it. I hope you will be protected in the strife, but all is known to him with whom we have to do & all I suppose will turn out right at last.

What a poor affair that was to let 5 Yankees come & take D. H's negroes.[56] All the leading soldiers down there ought to know all the cuts & byways of the coast so as to be ready for such raids. It does not say much for the parties who had control of things.

I see not any prospect of the war closing. The Yankees with their numbers seem certain of beating us, but I would prefer death to be conquered by the rogues. Now that England has seized our vessels like a mean thief & France withholds recognition, as it was supposed she would extend it, we have nothing to look to but home & heaven.[57]

Fortunately we are on the right side & we cannot believe that a just God will allow such villains to succeed, except temporarily. The arithmetic is not out yet, tho' it will be in a few weeks. What its success will be, remains to be proved. I am not very confident, as it has to be sold on account of cost of paper &c at so high a rate.

With much love Yr. Aff. f.

P.S. I hope you thanked Capt. H. for the wine.
Remember me kindly to him & Miss G. when you see them.[58]

---

54. In three battles around Chattanooga, Tennessee, Bragg's Army of Tennessee was defeated by Grant's combined Army of the Cumberland and Army of the Tennessee at Orchard Knob on 23 November, Lookout Mountain on 24 November, and Missionary Ridge on 25 November. After the last battle, in which the Confederates were driven from their entrenched position, Bragg asked to be relieved and Jefferson Davis appointed Gen. Joseph E. Johnston to replace him.

55. At Gettysburg, 1–3 July 1863.

56. Daniel Heyward.

57. Though neutral, Great Britain allowed the Confederacy to contract with English shipyards to build blockade runners and other vessels. Among the ships being constructed in 1863 at the shipyard of John Laird and Son were the Laird Rams, ships with iron prows designed to ram enemy vessels, intended to be the C.S.S. *North Carolina* and *Mississippi*. On 5 September 1863 the British government seized the two ships for violating its neutrality. Neither the British nor the French ever recognized the Confederate States of America as a legitimate nation.

58. William Heyward and his stepdaughter Mary Augusta Secunda Grimke.

Mary Maxcy Leverett to her son Milton

Friday morning

My dear Min

I send you by Willie (who paid us a long morning visit & offered several times to carry a bundle or anything we wished) 3 shirts, two of which I bought ready made and had them dyed at home by Cely; (the opportunity was so good a one I would not keep you waiting while I made them) calico is <u>eight</u> dollars a yard, too dear to purchase now. Your sister sends a pair of gloves which she commenced as soon as Willie told us of his going, and nearly worked her fingers off to finish them in time, knitting the pair in two days. I send one handkerchief which I hastily ran up for present necessities,—I hear that a store is to be opened by the Bee Importing Co.[59] which is intended to lower prices by selling at <u>half</u> the price the other stores up here ask (& they say they will make money at it then) when it goes into operation I will get some handkerchiefs for you. Let me know if the shirts will do. I have a letter from Mrs Gregorie condoling with me on our house at Canaan being burnt down—is it? we had or Julie rather, a note from you by the same mail & you make no mention of it. Pa groans out that he never expected any thing better. Corn is 7 dollars a bushel here, you may know how all poor refugees are pushed. We heard of one family who live on <u>cow peas</u> for breakfast, dinner & supper, being a little cheaper than corn. We have not heard of Fred's whereabouts for some time. He sent us a package of beautiful Chamois leather which he got out of a Yankee wagon we captured. Did not you tell me you wanted some when you were making your boot?

Every body is in the dumps about our late disasters. I do not despair. Col. Elliott of Sumter will have a world-wide celebrity. What a pity you ever had that <u>tiff</u> with him. You[r] company is & will be noted also, for having been <u>his</u> Company,—but he himself will live in History long after <u>we</u> are all dead and forgotten, no matter what disagreabilities may have been about him. He has made a splendid defense of it & I admire him for it.—Mr Edward Means,[60] at Sarah Fullers marriage, told Annie he had been to see you after your sickness &c. and said you were the most popular man in the Company and the most cheerful, adding something also about your being brave. You never mentioned his coming to see you. We all got more ideas of every thing & every body & how things are working down there, than we get out of you for months, by pumping Willie.

---

59.   The Importing and Exporting Company of South Carolina, a blockade-running firm in Charleston operated by William C. Bee and Charles T. Mitchel, was a rival of John Fraser and Company, owned by John Fraser and George A. Trenholm.

60.   Edward Barnwell Means.

I don't think there will be any attack down there, I don't believe a word they have men enough.

Do see if you can find out if the "Peg" you heard of at Rest Park was not <u>Peggy</u> their old cook, for Caroline[61] writes me she does not see how Peg can be there if George was in Beaufort. If you can find out let me know at <u>once</u>. She was so sorry to hear about Abram's death (which you mentioned) that she would not tell Archy as she knew he would mind it too much. Do notice my questions, and never tear up my letters until you have answered them & put them before when you write home.— Your father's Arith. is not out yet but they are at it & he is now doing the key.

yr. ever affte Mother
Mary Leverett

Matilda Leverett to her brother Milton

Columbia, Dec 10th, 1863

My dear Minny,

I hope you have received your basket safely—if your last letter had only come a little sooner we might have sent you the things you wanted, in it. Willie came round to see us a few days ago, and told us he would take anything down to you that we wished—that he intended leaving on the 11th I immediately set to work on a pair of gloves for you, and have at length finished them, and hope they will suit and fit you—Mame got the shirts, ready made, from the society (it is frequently done) can't tell at what price yet. She looked for the handkerchiefs in a great many stores, but could find none—however next week a store is to be opened up here by Wm C. Bee & Co. to sell goods brought over by their vessels, at cost prices, and we hope to get some for you then. I would have made gloves for you long ago, if I had known you wanted them—you ought always to write and say when you want anything—if these don't suit I will make another pair, only you must let me know.

What is all this about the house at Canaan being burnt? Mrs. Gregorie writes to Ma about it, but does not know the extent of the fire—your note to Julie came at the same time and yet you say nothing of it. Willie said he heard it was very much pulled to pieces.

Julie was quite provoked at your note; we thought it did very well—she wrote a different one to Blanche after this one had been sent to you by mistake. We are expecting Charley everyday.

Fred's last letter was dated the 20th Nov. and came through to us by a Mr. Easel father of one of the serjeants in the Sharp Shooters, Fred's regiment.[62] Fred

---

61. Caroline Pinckney Seabrook.

62. John S. Ezell of Spartanburg District was a farmer; his son was Sgt. Landrum C. Ezell of Company H, Palmetto Sharpshooters.

sent to us by him a chamois skin taken by him from one of the Yankee Surgeon's chests. It is beautiful, perfectly white, and looks like thick kid skin. He thought it would make good shoes for us girls, and we intend trying it, putting blacking on them after they are made. The shoemakers asked $15.00 merely for sewing of the shoes—and 30, 40, and 50 when they supply the materials.

When Fred wrote he was near Knoxville—since then, the report is that they have retreated to Morristown, and entrenched themselves, there. We think Davis' appointment of Johnston to the head of the Tennessee army, and Bragg his chief of staff, excellent.

Pa sold Trusty this morning—for how much do you think? I know you won't want to believe me—for one thousand dollars; 750 paid in cash this morning, the remainder to be paid tomorrow—what do you think of it? The man said he would give that for your colt now, that it was worth it—but that he wanted a working animal for his family, as he is soon to go into the army himself, and wanted to have them a steady creature to use. I think Fred will open his eyes when he hears of it. Almost all of it however has to go right off for corn—we are giving 6 dollars a bushel for it; in Columbia it is selling at $7.00. The Association has not yet gone into operation.

Ma and Mame have been looking for the Paper you wished, but have not been able to find it. Pa has tried to find out from the ordnance officer up here, all about it—but cannot find out who the officer is.

Rob Means' mother and Mr. Henry Stuart were married last week, Annie was at the wedding—she was the only one invited except Aunt Til. We hear that the Means family do not like it at all. How the Stuarts like it remains to be seen. A great many weddings & engagements are taking place up here—Dr. Huot's marriage to a Miss Horsey took place a short time ago.[63] We are very glad that you are quite well again.

yr. Affect. sister
Matilda.

Milton Maxcy Leverett to his father

Camp Wilderness Dec. 11th /63

My dear father,

I received your onceinawhile letter the other day and would have answered that as well as Ma's and Anne's before but have been so very busy building a log cabin, which is much larger than the ordinary run of them that I couldn't get the time. Today happening to be a rainy day just suits me in that respect. I am quite

---

63.   Louis V. Huot, a native of France, a physician, and a partner of Dr. Samuel Fair, married Lizzie
      F. Horsey of Charleston at Trinity Episcopal Church, Abbeville, on 17 November 1863.

sorry to see how gloomy you are by your note, I suppose that caused your sickness the other day, you mustn't let these things worry you so, as Fred says in one of his letters he "has a firm trust in Providence that all things are ordered well, and even if, we be tried beyond what we can bear, else he would be in despair." I am very sorry things are so high but somehow or other I think they have reached or almost reached the crisis, and there will soon be a cheering change in the aspect of our internal affairs, not that the war will stop, for I do not think it will yet, but that the depreciation of our currency and the high rate of necessary articles of life have attained their climax, and some change for the better must now take place. Pity you had not sold your cotton before that unequal tax, taxing one half of the nation for the other or rather for both halves. Is it to late to sell it, before any more such foolish laws come out, or do you prefer keeping it. Somehow or other I entertain a glimmering hope that France and England will see their folly about our ironclads and will yet let us have them, if so we can soon raise the blockade here and there, and I am certain, say what they please, that that will help our finances. About that late raid down here, all I may say in exculpation of the Department is that in such an extended coast as ours with so few troops it is very hard to prevent such things especially when the country below is so entirely uninhabited. Canaan has been the picket headquarters until last Friday night when through some carelessness of theirs I believe, the house caught fire by one of the chimneys, on the inside so they say, and it was burnt down. I heard that they lost some of their guns and pistols, so unexpected was it. A Captain Foster was in command down there at the time, the same man whose company should have been up with the Yankees in their retreat the other day and was not.[64] Picket headquarters are now at Mrs Chaplins, "Riverside."[65] The artillery are also picketing now, one of our guns is now at Wm Fullers.

Your affe^ct son
Milton M. Leverett

You mustn't let that worry you, many a person has suffered worse in this war than you. A great many have had their houses burnt down here. Mr Henry Stuart you recollect is one and it isn't as if you had no other house, fortunately you have. Knowing your objection to cross written[66] letters I must stop. I hope you will succeed with your Arithmetic and other books. I will write more at length by and bye. I see from Ma's letter that all of you are very busy so that accounts for the slender correspondence.

---

64.   Capt. John Cantzon Foster of Company H, Fourth South Carolina Cavalry.
65.   Isabella Field Baker owned Riverside, a plantation on St. Helena Island; her second husband was Saxby Chaplin. This plantation was sometimes called the Baker Place after she married Robert Little Baker in 1843.
66.   From this point on this letter was cross written.

Monday 14th I received the bundle sent by Willie all safe, am much obliged to sister for the gloves which are capital, and her letter which I will answer as soon as possible. The shirts I am very glad of and are very good, only I would have preferred them not dyed as I wished them for undershirts but now they shall answer both purposes. The Bourdon I am much obliged for. Don't worry yourself about the Ordnance Examination. I don't care about your ascertaining concerning it. I didn't know when I last wrote that Canaan house had been burnt. Tell sister the chamois skin won't last for shoes two weeks that my canvass bag will be twice as enduring. Tell Ma I wish she would try and find out at what price that new store will sell nice officer's grey cloth, enough to make a full suit, if reasonable I will try and put aside some more money and send it up to her to get it for me. I am sorry you sold Trusty for <u>some</u> reasons although I suppose you couldn't help it. It was an enormous price. Tell Ma never mind about those shirts since this bundle came, only pay the Society girls for them and find out <u>which of the girls made them for me</u>. Do let me know the price of things in that Bee store.

Milton Maxcy Leverett to his mother

Camp Wilderness Dec 11th /63

My darling mother,

I write in bed—with all my clothes on—not that I am sick, but on the contrary perfectly well, only the day being rainy and raw and I having purposed to devote it to writing thought that I could do so more comfortably in this manner, not yet having my house finished but living still in an army tent. I have already finished two, one to Pa and one to Anne, and hope to make this a third. I am much obliged for your nice long letter which I have read three times and expect to go over a fourth. You make a mistake in supposing that I "<u>tear</u> up any letters after only <u>once glancing over them</u>," I <u>always</u> read letters written to me <u>twice</u> at least and have them open by me when I answer. I always thus answer any questions propounded. My letters I almost always weed keeping those with the least mistakes and my dear mother I <u>always</u> keep yours and am always glad to get them and wish you <u>would write</u> <u>every week</u> or oftener. Nor do I <u>get tired</u> of your long letters. Don't worry yourself about my white pants, I don't expect to wear them again as pants, perhaps I may as drawers or have them cut up into something. I am very much obliged to you for the blue pants, they were done very nicely and I am sorry <u>you</u> had the trouble. The basket with the cake and groundnuts came safe, for which I am very much obliged to both Mame and yourself. We, that is my mess ate them quite happily i.e. the cake, the groundnuts are not yet gone. I have just had a pan of parched ones eating them. One of us would say "who says Basket & another would say, you Nat, didn't you? then Nat would say Leverett, and Leverett would say Stuart and it would end by all of us agreeing that "Basket" ought to have been said if no one did say it and we would all go to it and sit down around it and eat. I think I can see sister as she says how foolish and laughing says, "just like hogs"! but that makes no difference, it all went. Today being rainy I still continue my letter as you may see by the date. I am much obliged to Mame and yourself for looking over the Couriers for the notice of the Ordnance Examination, it is in one of them under the Official notices I believe unless they have been torn up, a winter or spring number. The person you speak of in the Ordnance Office of Columbia is evidently only a private, and merely a clerk, as I judge from the salary, which is made up by commutations &c to its amount, he must be a detailed private. I suppose if I had tried I could have got such a position also but I don't like the position of private anywhere else but in the ranks. To be a non fighting officer (i.e. a commissary, quartermaster or some such thing) is bad enough but a non fighting private, i.e. a clerk is still worse. Ordnance officers may also in general be styled non fighting, but not always, their clerks though always. I wished Charlie to get one of the two positions which he could easily do. If he was not ambitious he could pretty easily have got a detail into the Ordnance Dept as a clerk and draw a good salary, instead of getting a discharge, he would have found the duties quite light. Or if he preferred and it is not too late he could perfectly easily stand an Ordnance Examination and get a Captaincy or a lieutenantcy. He could easily do it as he has just been teaching school and arithmetic and mathematics are fresh in his mind, ten thousand times more so than in mine, indeed I am certain he would succeed. That I suggested before as much easier for him than to be plodding away and wearing out his life as a school teacher. Give him my advice when he comes. If I was as certain as he of getting such a position I would be thankful. The salary counting in commutations and perquisites is very good. As regards myself my dear mother I am somewhat in doubt whether I will be able to stay in the Army at all, although I shall keep in as long as I can. My boot is getting out of order and I shall be compelled to get you to send back the other by Express for me. Send it in the same box carefully packed and particularly marked to me, have the box nailed properly. Why I say mark it carefully is because the box has other directions on it already and a mistake might occur. This is one reason why I am in doubt whether I shall undertake studying for that Examination, as I wouldn't like to take a position the duties of which I would be in doubt as regards my being able to fill. It has caused me some thought but no despair. That word I underline as a word that ought to be banned by us, and why? Yesterday I read three letters from different members of our family and I was very much amused to see the same word in each letter. Our word is Hope and I venture to say that if you look over my letters of a year you won't find such a word, except perhaps in a deprecatory tone. The three letters to which I refer were all "almost in despair." Yours was not one of them. And my dear mother you will see by the above that I have <u>my</u> <u>troubles</u> also, only no one knows of it but myself, yes not even you. So don't let Pa and yourself be in <u>despair</u> or worry yourself so much about different things. We all won't be tried beyond what we can bear. I have a great deal to struggle against, temporally and spiritually, but <u>especially</u> the <u>latter</u>, and consequently need all of your prayers.

I thought some correspondence had already passed between Mrs. Daingerfield and yourself relative to brother. Last night, I suppose from reading your letter, I dreamt of almost all of you, brother also even to the extent of thinking he was well. You say well, "what an officer he would have made." I have always thought the same. He had just the qualities. Last Sunday Mr. Tom Hanckel who is volunteer aid on Walker's Staff and is staying with his wife at their house in Bluntville came around to our camp and invited my mess to dinner.[67] From his manner, and his addressing me alone at first, I judged he was going to invite me only, but seeing the others sitting by me he included them immediately asking if we were not in the same mess. He lent me his horse very kindly going and coming. He had quite a nice dinner, turkey & jowl &c. Mrs. Tom was there in all her blooming splendour of rotundity, fat! geewoolokins, don't talk, her eyes are almost shut, and I believe she was dozing half the time we were there, for she would keep her eyes down half the time as if she was meditating and Nat said she was sleeping. She is a regular show. If I was Mr. Tom I would have some cut off or do as Big Rob said he would have done "make her trot a mile every day." I think the invitation had something ulterior in view, for in the course of conversation I discovered that he had a nephew named Tom, son I believe of Mr. Jno Hanckel who wished to join our company, and of course the mess he should get in was an object, for Mrs. Tom said whatever mess he got in would be lucky as he was a great pet of his grandfather's and a nephew I believe of Mr. Wagner's who would be continually sending him things. She over did her part, it was too plain. She said he was quite weak and sickly and didn't know whether he could stand camp life. Now we have found out that a small mess is the best in camp and are also averse to making any more trials of new comers, we have tried three and I don't want any more, but I must say at the same time that if Mr. Wagner and the two Messrs Hanckel will make a pet of him it will be some consideration in these times. What do you think of it? Allan Hanckel is on his way back.[68]

Miss Grimke came to see me the other day, brought me some books, a couple of fat fowls and three or four dozen eggs. Said she had not heard from sister

---

67. Thomas Middleton Hanckel and his wife, Sarah Thomas Heyward.
68. Allan Stuart Hanckel, husband of Charlotte Bull Heyward (1838–1860).

for an age, asked what had become of her. She invited me to a Christmas dinner. I was wishing I could spend Christmas at home but there an't any chance. Nenny and I were anxious to spend it in Columbia, I was going to get him to stay with me. His sisters will be at Mrs. James Rhetts. I wouldn't be surprised if he succeeded in getting off but I won't. Tell Pa <u>I am very much obliged to him for sending me Julie's letter</u>. <u>You think Mr. Trenholm could be induced to supply me with a suit of grey</u>. <u>I wouldn't</u> <u>object</u>. I'll write to Mame next. Where is Fred's direction? I send twenty dollars to get me enough homespun to make two undershirts and get Mrs. Neely to make them up for me. Do get also two or three neat looking white standing collars and a cravat, black silk if possible. Do send me that large sleeve fancy shirt you made for me last winter. I don't like flannel next to my body. I owe some of the twenty to Anne.

> Your aff<u>ct</u> son, Milton M. Leverett

Remember me to Cos. Julia and Cornelia.

Don't hurry yourself too much about my box. You can send it when the shirts are ready. I am certain you will be tired of this letter. I shall send the basket back as soon as the groundnuts are finished.

There are a plenty of ducks and game down here but I have no shot, powder, or gun.

Milton Maxcy Leverett to his mother

> Pocotaligo Jan'y 5th 1864

My dear mother

I am about answering a series of little notes from you now, and Julie or Mary perhaps may also come in for a share. I am getting wiser, I find that it is best to answer all my letters from home in one envelope instead of answering each separate correspondent apart. I am doing as you all do. You make a mistake in supposing that Mr. Edw. Means had called purposely to see me when I was sick, he only happened to be passing my tent with some of the officers and they all seeing me in bed in my tent came up to speak to me. Also my dear mother don't try to flatter yourself or me that I am popular and the most cheerful man in the company that may have been once but it is not so now and I am not so blind that I can't see. The fact is, not being or ever expecting to be an office seeker depending upon popularity I can laugh in the faces of the people, as the empty traveller in the face of the robber. I am pretty certain that the "Peg" I wrote about was George's wife, I am under the impression although it is a long time now that I particularized by calling her "the Driver's wife." I think it not at all unlikely that the Yankees compelled George being a driver to stay in Beaufort and not at plantation fearing that he would communicate with us if left on the place, and I suppose Peg was compelled to stay on the plantation with the other women to work, women and old men being now the chief hands used by them in planting. The negroes from whom I received this information have succeeded in getting back to the Yankees. A small boy from Big Island was the one that gave me the information. It is a mistake that a section of our company was on picket at our place and it was not Captain Pinckney I believe but Captain Foster, I will ascertain positively shortly. I had a very nice Christmas dinner at Mr Wm Heyward's. There was no other guest there except Henry Hamilton of Bluffton, a clerk under Middleton Hanckel.[69] Middleton Hanckel and his family were there also. We didn't have a very jolly Christmas in camp but some of the cavalry companies had the usual pranks being practiced such as climbing the greasy pole, a furlough and fifty dollars being on the top for the winner, gander pulling, this joke consisting in men running by and tugging at the poor creatures neck until it is pulled off, the puller off being the winner of the goose, and catching or pulling the pig, the pig in this case was killed and buried, the tail being shaved clean and greased, it is then buried only the tail left out and then the men run by and try to pull it out of the hole by the tail, the winner getting the pig, this species of joke is conducted in different manners, the pig being alive sometimes and run down by a party. All of them are games adapted I think to a very barbarous stage of society, the only passable one being the greasy pole. Is my colt worth while keeping, does he look promising? do you [think] a thousand could be got for him? if so let me know. I suppose Charlie didn't come because his wife couldn't, pity you couldn't have invited both. My box came last Monday safe, I'm much obliged to you for your trouble as well as for the groundnuts, and to Mame for the groundnut cake which was very nice and always acceptable. Tell Mame I am much obliged for the cravat and the gloves and am afraid she deprived herself of the latter, indeed I know it as none of the girls hands could have fitted mine so nearly. Was Henry Fuller or any of the girls around at our house at all. Miss Harriet Fuller died the other day, she has been unwell for some time and was losing her mind. I suppose you have seen poor Allan Stuart's Obituary.[70] Jimmy Stuart had been up there but came down and a week or so afterwards he died, he had been suffering great pain, couldn't eat a mouthful without groaning loud enough to be heard over the whole house. The real cause of his death was a sore throat which he didn't take in hand time enough.

69. Pvt. Henry C. Hamilton of Company H, Third South Carolina Cavalry, and Capt. Middleton Stuart Hanckel, quartmaster at Pocotaligo.

70. After serving in Alabama, Allan Stuart died in Aiken on 2 January 1864 from a wound he received at Port Royal in November 1861. "He had served his country faithfully as a Christian soldier and patriot having only left his post . . . to be cheered and cared for in his last hours by those he loved." *Charleston Courier*, 6 January 1864.

There were other contingent causes also but his sore throat was the more immediate and positive cause. You speak of my "tiff" with Col. Elliott as if something
serious, I assure it isn't so serious as you suppose, it was only in the line of company matters and therefore not of such a personal cast as you suppose, I still
esteem him as an officer but never as a man, nor does anyone else. His notoriety
in History will never help me as he has many others more closely connected with
him than I am and I never expect to be a military man.

Your Aff'ᶜᵗ. son
Milton M. Leverett

Frederic Percival Leverett to his brother Milton

Camp near Morristown,
Tenn. 15ᵗʰ Janry. 1864.

My dear Minny,

It is a long time since I have written, and a still longer since I have heard from
you. Reverse the above sentence, and it will be what I should have written, for I
recollect now having received of you the day after we started from Lookout Mountain the letter you wrote me while I was stationed at Dublin, Va. So here is to you
in reply, and once for all let me beg you to write me oftener than you have done
& not think it always incumbent on you to await an answer before sending me
another letter. I am always truly glad to get a letter from you & wish you would
always let me hear of my old friends of the Artillery. I never hear from Charley
except occasionally through Blanche. Let not the same be true of you. What a varied time I have had of it during this war. Constant changing has been my lot. I
have been until lately since being out Surgeon of Jenkins' old Reg. the Palmetto
Sharp Shooters, but on 2nd Jan. was relieved from duty with it & ordered to take
charge of Hood's Div.[71] Hospital to be established, for the winter we suppose, in
Morristown. It is not yet opened, so that I have not yet entered on my new field
of duty. My experience with the Sharp Shooters has been rough but not unpleasant. We have passed through an active winter campaign, been subjected to great
exposure & many hardships, but there has been little complaint except that it has
been so resultless. Why so it is hard to say. There are many reasons given, but I
doubt whether the real ones are assigned. I don't know what the papers have said,
as we hardly ever see one. I have not seen but two or three in the last two
months—not a dozen since coming out West. We all inquire from each one

---

71. The division of South Carolinians, Texans, Alabamians, and Georgians commanded by
    Micah Jenkins, formerly commanded by Maj. Gen. John Bell Hood in the First Corps,
    Army of Northern Virginia.

returning from home the news, first from Charleston, and then from each point of the compass, then what is Congress doing. From you I wish to hear what are you doing? What the B.V.A.? Is it reenlisting? Here the men are very willing to do so, if a furlough of 30 days be granted at once. I wish you to lead off your Company again, unless you have a chance for some better position. I wish Charley could give up his school, & go again into the field. No one should be at home now except those who are absolutely obliged to. Our struggle is a desperate one and every man is needed. If I had the strength I formerly had, I would resign my position & take my place in the ranks. But that is out of the question. I have never gotten over that miserable Diarrhea & I am delicate & generally half sick. So I shall try & "discharge my duty in the station in which it has pleased God to place me." For the last three weeks I have been having a most uncomfortable time with boils on my neck. I have had a regular siege with them & am still suffering. On the whole I have borne the fatigues & hardships of the campaign wonderfully well. We were almost every night without tents & were obliged to have the heavens as our canopy raining or shining. The cold at times was very severe, and we were obliged to sleep almost in the fire at times. One night my time honoured buggy blanket came near being burnt up. It was seriously injured, and I sincerely regretted it. I have spent but one night in a house in bed since leaving home 15th Oct. & that was the night I was detained in Atlanta while en route to Chattanooga. I have slept in stables, corn cribs, barns, and in almost every conceivable situation. I have kept while doing so remarkably free from colds, and that, though I have had no flannel undershirts.

P.S.

Friday 29th

I received letters from home, a great treat, one had been sent me while near Knoxville, also a letter from Blanche & a P.S. from Charley.

1st Febry. Hood's Div. Hospital
Morristown, Tenn.

I had written the previous portion of this letter, when the long roll was beaten, my dear Min, for the Reg. to fall in to move to the front. I was not obliged to go, as I had been relieved for Hospital duty; I am suffering with Boils on my neck; the weather was very inclement, a warm rain was melting the snow and in that had been on the ground for a week or ten days, rendering locomotion very disagreeable to say the least. I hesitated about volunteering to go, but finally decided to & off I went, folding up your letter which has [not] been resumed until now. We marched some six or seven miles & camped for the night. In the evening the rain cleared off, & it became bitterly cold. We had no tents & were obliged to bivouac in the open air. About midnight orders came for me to go back to Morristown to

attend to some business for the Div. there, and when completed the next day to
return to the command. I can assure that that was a ride to be remembered. I
jumped on my horse, and never put her out of a walk until I reached my destination, except once when half frozen I dismounted to warm by a guard fire. Part of
the way the road was so slippery my horse almost [had] to creep along.—then
again she would slide. At 1/2 past 5 a.m. I was glad enough to get to my tent and
go to bed. Jacob gave me a comfortable breakfast at 8 o'clock. I attended to the
business, started off, & joined the command about dark that evening. (It had
advanced several miles) One of our Brigades had been in a skirmish that evening
and the Yanks had retreated. Much fatigued I spent a most delightful night by a
large camp fire in the open air. The next day was Sunday, 17$\underline{th}$ Janry. We started
in the morning & advanced toward Dandridge. In the afternoon we came up with
the Yankees, & had a warm (yes hot) skirmish with them.[72] The Hampton Legion
was principally engaged. The Yankees did not wait for a general engagement, but
retreated pellmell, badly worsted. They left us over one hundred prisoners, some
few horses, & some booty. We principally engage out here mounted infantry. They
are armed generally with Burnside's breech loader, which has a long range, fires
with much force, & can be discharged with great rapidity.[73] They avail themselves
to the full of their advantages. They choose a good position, fire away on us as rapidly as possible, and as soon as pressed by us they retreat to choose a new position. They of course have their horses close in the rear, which offers great
advantages in a retreat. Had our cavalry been as good as our Infantry, we would
that day have taken about 1000 horses. We had them (our cavalry had) for a while
in our possession, and while the Yankees were pressed in one direction by our
infantry, some Yankees came up & rescued their horses & got off. That night they
cleared out toward Knoxville, & our Div. started back on Monday. That night we
had a sharp snow storm, and we woke up in the morning to find our covering
made very heavy by the snow. I was ordered to hurry on to Morristown to take care
of our wounded, so leaving the others to come on, I started off early Tuesday
morning & arrived here safely. Since here I have been very busy taking care of the
wounded, and getting my hospital organized. I have had forty odd wounded, some
very severe cases & so far (a fortnight has passed) have lost but two cases, and
those two from comparatively slight wounds. So often does it happen that men die
from scarcely more than a scratch, and again survive the severest injuries. I fear

---

72. Jenkins's Brigade, along with elements of dismounted cavalry, attacked a Federal force of
   infantry and dismounted cavalry near Dandridge and drove it from its position. Casualties
   were estimated at one hundred on each side.

73. The Burnside carbine, a .54 caliber breech-loading rifle patented by Ambrose E. Burnside
   in Bristol, Rhode Island, in 1856, was popular with the Federal cavalry; over fifty-five thousand were produced during the war.

however for the future. I have four men shot through the chest, three of which will probably get well, one not only through Lung but Liver, also another one shot thro' Liver getting well.—I am not by any means as well now as when I left the Reg. My old complaint is becoming troublesome & I suffer still from boils on my neck. They have tormented me now for nearly six weeks. There was a great deal I wanted to say to you but time & paper are both getting exhausted. What do you think I had best do with my colt now at W$^{\underline{m}}$ Fuller's. He wrote me sometime since that she is a chuncky, thickset pony, pretty & would probably prove of good endurance. She will be four yrs. old in April. I wrote lately back home to have her broken to the saddle this winter, and spoke of having her put with some good horse in the Spring, if there were a good one in the neighborhood. Second thoughts make me think the latter part of plan bad. She is so young, she will be just ruined by breeding and made dull and sluggish & have her shape spoiled. I have been thinking she might be of service to you. I do not wish to part with her. If you can keep her & she can be of use do send for her. If not she had better remain where she is at any rate until I come home. I intend to try and get off in March for a furlough.

Write me when you get this.

Ever yr. aff$^{\underline{ct}}$ brother
F. P. Leverett

Mary Maxcy Leverett to her son Milton

Farm Columbia Jan 25$^{\underline{th}}$ 1864

My dear Min

Mame received a letter from you on Sunday. Very true, you have written very often lately and it has pleased me so much, as well as all the others. When you only write now & then it looks as if you did not care about us, or home, and it is very gratifying to my feelings to hear frequently. I do not think, indeed that you are half conscious of the comfortable feeling of satisfaction it gives me to be in constant communication with you, and know all you are doing and feeling and seeing and thinking. I write now however on a business matter. I have had another kind & excellent letter from Mr. Prentiss, to whom after his first answer, I had sent down eleven bags per Express, and he writes that he will ship them as soon as I send word to whose care in Chars$^{\underline{ton}}$ they must be consigned in order to be transferred to the S.C.R. Road, that if he finds any friend of his going he will try to get him to do it, but if not what shall he do? I have just written a letter to send by the same mail which takes this, to say to him that I will write to you to see if you can get a furlough for a day or so, and if you can he is to let you know what day he will send it, so that you can get on the cars, go down and have it transferred to S.C.R.R. to come up here. You must write to him as soon as you can get the furlough, so that he may know. If you do not succeed I do not know what upon earth we shall do. We are in actual distress for want of corn for servants & horses, the latter and the mule have been looking ready to die, tho' they have had fodder, but I am doubtful if in cold or bad weather Lewis takes the trouble to give it them. You can have no idea how horribly they looked after all the freezing weather we had, I was shocked & am sure it was his neglect. We have not used them for ever so long, yet Dora has lost a foal, & looks miserably. Mr. Prentiss does not think he will be able to get more than this quantity through unless I can get an order from Beauregard which I am determined to do if possible, and shall write to him myself.

Mr. Prentiss' letter yesterday was so warm and so kind that it touched my heart. I should like you to see his two letters. In this last one he gives me a Cow & calf, and says I must not be so foolish as to refuse! and I will take him at his word, so as soon as possible I will send Hercules & one of the boys to drive it up. You must remember in writing to him that his name is spelt tiss, not tice. We had to give $9 for a bushel of corn last week, you may suppose how we are put to it. The Mutual Supply Association never has enough to let us have it, we have only been able to get three bushels of grist from it so far at all.[74] It won't be necessary to go to Mr. Prentiss, write instead. You will be glad to hear that Fred has been appointed to a Hospital just established for Hood's Division at Morristown, Tenn. I was very glad, as he will be so much more comfortable. Direct to him Richmond Va. Your father came home from Augusta blank with despair at all of his cotton being burnt up in this great fire, and it is only too true, but you will be glad to hear that he met Mr. James R Pringle today who told him he had ordered it insured (as your father had told him) but of course not at its full value, but to the amount of $600. a bale, so if the Insurance Companies do not break, at such an immense loss to them, we will have that much, so that the 16 bales will still come to something handsome. Their real value would have been, more than a thousand dollars a bale. We still have five bales left in Camden. Your father feels quite relieved since meeting Mr. Pringle, as he had feared M^r P had neglected to insure them. He feels encouraged also about his Arithmetic, it is almost finished & Patterson very hopeful of its success & Townsend, the bookseller here told him this morning that he wanted 500 now, instead of the 200 copies he first spoke for. No doubt you will like the trip to Town, you ought to take the opportunity of seeing all you

---

74. The Columbia Mutual Supply Association, created in November 1863, was established to aid citizens as prices rose and food and other supplies became more scarce. Stockholders could purchase from the association store at reduced rates and others could buy at or near cost.

can of the damage to the Town and the Forts. It will cost you something to carry the bags from one depot to the other but I won't be able to send the money down to you until next week, so borrow if you can. You must try hard for this short furlough be pushing as you can. Try your best.

In great haste

yr ever aff^te Mother
Mary Leverett

You had better when you send your basket put in some more wire grass for Tillie.

Frederic Percival Leverett to his sister Matilda

Hood's Div. Hospital,
Morristown, Tenn.
1st. Febry. 1864.

My dear Tilly,

Last Friday night was a happy one for me, as a letter came to me from you, also one from Nan, and one from Blanche with a P.S. from Charlie. I have read and reread them until I know their contents almost verbatim. I have not time to write you a letter now but drop you a line, so as to let you know those letters have been most gladly received, and that others are anxiously expected. You all do not treat me rightly. None of you except Nan will write unless you hear your letter has been received. It takes often a long time in the army for a letter to come, but it generally arrives at last. Do write me frequently & let your letters have even one half as much as the last and it will be most acceptable. If I wrote only when a letter arrives, it would be very seldom. You all have no idea what a treat a letter is in camp. Since our fight near Dandridge on 17th ultimo I have been busy enough. The Hospital has been pretty full of sick and wounded. The Hampton Legion was most heavily engaged. It was quite a brilliant little affair, resulting in giving us over 100 prisoners, some horses and booty, and driving the Yankees away from our frontage ground, which they were trying to occupy. I have forty odd wounded of which as yet but two have died, & these from very slight wounds. I fear for the future however. It is really strange to see how severe injuries men can survive, and again what little things can kill. Among the wounded I have four men shot each through a lung—one also through his liver and a fifth also thro' the liver. Only one of these will probably die. Again I have one with a slight wound of the thigh who will scarcely get well. I am tired of attending sick and wounded soldiers, especially when having so little to make them comfortable. Flour meat & salt are a poor pabulum for wounded men. I have a man to make purchases in the country, but so little transportation is furnished, he does not get me much. He succeeded a short time since in buying me a fine cow for $200.00 which helps me very much. I ought to have three or four. I have some coffee, but no sugar. The poor Confederate soldier does not see much of comfort whether well or sick. He bears up, however, cheerfully through all. I have 6 Yankees in the Hospital. I hate the sight of them, but have to treat them well. I am feeling decidedly the effects of having charge of a field Hospital & intend applying for a furlough in March or early in April. Write me as soon as you get this. Give much love to all.

Ever yr. aff^{ct} brother
F. P. Leverett

P.S. I was much amused at Lou's remark on getting into my shirt. What has become of Pa's arithmetic? Charley writes me you are all fat.

I went down to the fight near Dandridge. We were exposed to severely cold weather with no tents. The last night we had a snow storm on us. One night I was ordered out at midnight to ride six miles by myself. It was a fearfully cold night—the ground so frozen & smooth I could not go out of a walk—sometimes hardly at that—my horse sliding about most unpleasantly.

Mary Maxcy Leverett to her son Milton

Farm, Columbia, Feb. 4, 1864

My dear Min,

Your letter came last night. No need to trouble yourself any further, as the business is settled by Mr Prentiss having the kindness to go to Green Pond and prevail on the Quartermaster Melton[75] to receive 50 bushels of corn there, while he wrote to me to get the Quartermaster up here to pay the same quantity over to us, which we hope now to get, as I sent down his paper signifying his willingness to accede to the proposition to Mr Prentiss to day. Tho' Major Rhett had declined doing so when your father requested it a short time ago, & so your father would not ask him again, but got Annie to speak to James Rhett who immediately promised to get it done.[76] So we hope now to get it in a day or two. I have asked Mr Prentiss to do the same with peas. In one of his letters he said he was afraid that was all the corn he would be able to get for us, so if he is not able to get more, I think it would be well for you to make inquiries in time so as to get it at the price you mention $3 a bushel. Perhaps you had better inquire at once of Quartermas-

---

75. Maj. George W. Melton, quartermaster, became temporary provost marshal of the Second Military District of South Carolina and commander of the Confederate post at Green Pond in early 1864.

76. Maj. Roland Smith Rhett (1830–1898), quartermaster, and his brother James Moore Rhett (1820–1888), sons of Charlotte Haskell and James Smith Rhett.

ter Hanckel or whoever acts at Pocotaligo, of their willingness to receive two hundred bushels of corn if you purchase it down there, and then let me know so that I could ask the Quartermaster here if he will be willing. That is, do it as soon as I find out whether Mr Prentiss can get any more. I am very glad to save you the trouble of seeing to the transportation & feel very grateful to Mr Prentiss for all the pains he has taken about it, especially as it saves us freight. The horses are improving somewhat, as Annie makes Lewis bring them up and clean them by her window, giving also a little scrap of corn. You would be surprised to see how much better your colt looks than the horses do, it is in very good condition, and as tall as Dora.

Annie received a letter from Mrs J G. last week saying she would be in Columbia Friday, to shop unless she should stop in Charleston, & asking Annie to meet her at Nickersons Hotel[77] to go shopping with her, of course as the letter only came a day or two before Friday she could not answer it; but went at the appointed time to meet her intending to invite her to stay with us, if she could put up with our fare & share her chamber, but no Mrs J G. was to be seen or found as she must have altered her mind.—You think it would have been better to have sent down one of the horses to you than have them starve, but I think not, the expense of sending down would have been great and then too, you forget both Nightmare & Bella died under your charge, and I would not like again to trust one to the tender mercies of the camp boys who no doubt rode those two to death. Nevermind, they will soon improve more. Julie and Mame will go to see Anne Elliott immediately, and as soon as the horses look fit for it, will bring her out on a visit or pay any other attention they can. I shall always be grateful to Mrs Elliott for the attention she paid you.[78] You must be a pretty steady visitor at Bethel by your own confession, eh? Rob must go as a sort of blind? I'm willing if you are!— About what you suggest in the shoe and leather line,—we will join with you in buying a hide, and it would be a prize if you could teach Billy how to make shoes for the servants; I suppose it would take a whole hide for that though. As regards ourselves, the girls are learning to make shoes. Annie has made two capital pair of boots for herself, and Tilly has bought a last & intends to begin also. She mended a pair of shoes for Julie, and the day your father was to go to Camden, she got up in the night and mended his shoes, putting in a patch so nicely with an awl & your shoe thread that your father was astonished when at two o'clock in the night she knocked at the door and handed it in, for he was to leave at past three. What other girl would have done so? I am rejoiced that you are beginning to tan. If you Beaufort men would take the trouble you might help your families much as regards salt

77.   Operated by T. S. Nickerson in Columbia.
78.   Anne Barnwell Elliott and her stepmother, Sarah Gibbes DeSaussure Elliott, who was the wife of Rev. Stephen Elliott (1804–1866).

& leather both. People in the up-country will sell corn & such things for salt sooner than for money. I am very glad you have got at the leather. Jake did a great deal of mending, & so has Tom, as well as the girls themselves so I fear you will find your shoe thread much gone down, but we can buy some here to send you. Mr Henning, a very gentlemanly head of a shoe store on Main St.[79] showed Annie & Tillie & made his foreman show them all about shoemaking, he gave Annie a ball of shoe thread far better than yours which they showed him and he said it was rotten and would require six strands to make it strong enough to use.

Fred did not ask for the appointment, he was <u>ordered</u> to it. He was so well pleased with his field position, that he did not wish to change. His Asst. D[r] Bedon he found a very pleasant companion & they occupied a tent together.[80] He seemed to have an orderly also, as he several times mentioned sending off his "Orderly" to forage for him & his bringing wild ducks &c. They had a hard time on their march to Tennessee, as sometimes the rations were only 1/2 # beef, & 2 ears of corn, which they had to parch, & this was for officers, of course the privates must have had only the two ears of corn.

I do wish, my beloved son that you had a brother in the army with you to be a mutual help and consolation to each other. I hope you spend Sunday suitably. You cannot hope to prosper spiritually unless you do. Pray, pray, my dear son for body & soul both.

yr Aff Mother
Mary

Annie's boots only cost $10 each, in consequence of her making them herself, but she found the double soled one very troublesome to make. As soon as you get the hide or hides let me know exactly what to send & I will send it, if nothing more is required than what I see in your letter, perhaps I had better get them at once. Our old sow skin which we sent to the tan yard is not done yet, and when it is, will only be fit for saddles. The girls went to the tan-yard lately and bought a hide at $10 a pound. I think it came to $80. Cornelia joined with them & bought a kid skin for upper leather. A man in Columbia makes lasts for $2 50 cents, & says he has earned some thousands of dollars lately by making them, so many ladies are beginning to make their own shoes. Tillie is to try and make Carrie's shoes.

---

79.   Robert Henning.

80.   Assistant Surgeon William Z. Bedon of the Palmetto Sharpshooters.

Frederic Percival Leverett to his mother

Hood's Division Hospital,
Morristown, Tenn.
13<u>th</u> Febry, 1864

My dear Mother,

I received a day or two since Pa's letter from Augusta mentioning the heavy loss he had met with by the fire in Columbia. It was what I had always feared. The day before I had seen a Charleston Paper, the first since my leaving home in which it was said a severe fire had occurred in Columbia, and much cotton had been burnt. I felt at once well Pa's cotton is gone. The loss is indeed a serious one the family could not well bear, but it is not a crushing one, as I fear Pa felt it at first. His letter made me truly sad, so much so I have not had heart to write him since. I had been thinking for some time past of making application for leave of absence. I did so at once, for I felt that I wanted to be with you all to assist in making some provision for you. The application has been disapproved by Gen. Jenkins, so I cannot come, and must do the next best thing to coming—that is write to you. I wish I were able to be with you, for then I could assist you in getting in supplies, which I feel sure can be had. I have two or three hundred dollars on hand, which as I cannot come I will send you by first opportunity. I really hate to think of what hard times you all are having. You and Pa have indeed had your share of troubles. What a comfort it is, however, to think it is a Father's hand that inflict them, and that they are sent in mercy. The present loss is more to be minded, however, for its effect on the future than for any immediate result. Pa did not intend to use the cotton now, and therefore it need not affect any present plans. It may interfere with his publishing, but depend upon it some way will be opened for that. Let us but whip the Yankees and get an honorable peace, and if our lives be but spared, we will do well yet. "God will help us, and that right early." "Though He slay me, I will trust in him."[81] I trust that the time is not far distant when we shall be once more reunited at home in peace and safety, and then I hope that the days of prosperity will commence. But for the present, what had better be done? I suppose the working on the stockings feeds the negroes—at least I trust it does. Louis and Bullet ought to have been feeding themselves and the carriage horses in Columbia all the winter. If they can do that they would [be] doing as good a work as they could be engaged at. I hate to think of Dora and Renas being starved The former ought to be fed anyhow. The latter if she cannot be ought to be sold. The colt should be sold by all means or gotten into some ones pasture. Have you all of the cattle at home this winter? I should think they must suffer. When I sit

---

81. Ps. 46:5 and Job 13:15, respectively.

down to my bountiful but badly served meals I often think what a feast you would make of the same materials at home. In a Hospital a Surgeon situated as I am here, can always have a super abundance. Enough is thrown away here to feast a family. I do not enjoy myself near as much as in the field; there my appetite is better and also my health. A Hospital of this kind is not like a well organized General Hospital. Here we have an abundance of the things essential to life, but no means of preparing nicely what is furnished. Everything is rough and makeshift. The amount of trouble to the surgeon is very great. He is obliged to wage war incessantly with Quartermasters & Commissaries in order to get his rights. I have [been] much amused to see how good an effect a little real or well counterfeited anger has. It is necessary almost to swear sometimes in order to make them do for the sick and wounded what will put them to any trouble. They will put a Surgeon off with the most paltry excuses, until they see his patience is about gone and then yield, when they might just as well have done so at first. Longstreet and the whole Command have gone on towards the front. It is supposed that there is to be a move on Knoxville, or in that direction, before long. We have had since the fight of 17$\underline{th}$ Jan. near Dandridge most charming weather almost continuously. Hood's Div. has been nearly the whole time bivouacking. If a forward move is made, it is supposed that this Hospital will be closed, and I will be once more afloat—then I fear not in Jenkins' Brigd.—as all Reg. are supplied, unless he is promoted, which is not thought probable unless if it be true that Kershaw has been made a Maj. Gen.[82] Whenever this Hospital is closed, I intend to try and get a leave of absence so as to go home. How soon that time comes I do not care. I wish in the meanwhile I could get some letters from some of you. I hear very seldom, though I write often.

    With very much love to all and hope that you all are not feeling so sad as I do here, I am, my dearest Mother

                                                    ever yr. most aff$\underline{ct}$ son
                                                    F. P. Leverett

P.S. Jack Middleton starts home next week on furlough.

In early 1864 Rev. Charles Leverett's The Southern Confederacy Arithmetic, for Common Schools and Academies, *intended to be the first in a series of arithmetic textbooks for use in the Confederacy, was published by J. T. Paterson of Augusta. Leverett wrote in his preface, "it will be a source of the deepest gratification to him [the author], if, through his humble agency, any text book of the section, which has developed the most*

---

82. Brig. Gen. Joseph B. Kershaw commanded McLaws's Division in McLaws's absence during the winter of 1863–64 and was promoted to major general in May after McLaws was reassigned following his poor performance in the East Tennessee Campaign.

*malignant principles and exhibits the cruelest practice, should be forever excluded from a Southern school." The problems had an occasional Confederate slant; for example, "South Carolina passed the ordinance of secession, December, 1860; how many years is that era from the discovery of America in 1492?" Paterson's advertisement on the back cover promised "*LEVERETT'S*Arithmetical Series. Prepared for the use of the Schools and Academies—Male and Female—of the Confederate States," in six volumes ranging from "Leverett's Primary Arithmetic" to "Leverett's Academical Algebra" and "Leverett's Plane Geometry," but* The Southern Confederacy Arithmetic *was the only volume published.*

Mary Maxcy Leverett to her son Milton

Farm, Columbia, March 2 1864

My dear Min,

I am glad to say that yesterday Major Rhett sent the fifty bushels corn to us, for the fifty Mr. Prentiss delivered to Major Melton at Green Pond. So, for the present we are easy. But we will be glad to hear if you can succeed in getting more for us. You have no idea what a perfect relief it was to get this fifty bushels in hand, instead of paying $10 for every bushel & spending twenty or thirty dollars every week for so little corn, or sending Hercules perpetually from his work to see if we could get grist at the Mutual Supply Ass. which is $6. but for which there are such crowds of claimants that half the time we never succeeded in obtaining it. Corn has now risen to $12 a bushel in Columbia & what it may be before the next crop comes in, none can say, as it is $25 in Greenville now. I wrote to Mr Prentiss to see if he could now get us peas & rough rice, as anything will be better than an empty corn house. He has really been kind. I wrote word to him to know the amount to be paid & your father would send it, & he merely wrote in pencil on the back of the transfer papers "keep the money until called for," by which I am sure he does not intend to let us pay; however your father enclosed an order on Mr Pringle with a blank amount for him to fill up as he pleased. He has small pox on his place & proposes, instead of my sending for the cow & calf (which would be dangerous) this plan,—that a Capt. Gregg[83] encamped on his place is willing to buy my cow & we had best buy one here, which the said Captain will pay for. I would be very glad to do so, but there is not much prospect of it, as they are scarce & poor & high priced too, & your father wouldn't think of riding about to hunt up one, so I fear we will remain in statu quo, until the cows are obliging

83.   Capt. Thomas E. Gregg commanded Company C, Manigault's Battalion, South Carolina Artillery (Siege Train), at Battery Pringle, a large earthwork overlooking the Stono River on James Island.

enough to have calves.—Charley is here again—came yesterday unexpectedly, as usual, bringing Nancy to hire, because he couldn't stand her, (& Major Jenkins has given him another prime young woman also)[84] & he also had a great deal to purchase for Maj. Jenkins at the Bee store. The girls & Charley have gone there this morning. The former have been several times already, as their father gave each of them a hundred dollars of Trusty's money, to purchase what they were in need of, for it was a long time since they had bought any articles of clothing. Confederate grey is $40 a yd.—if I succeed in putting by money enough I will buy a suit for you, tell me how much it will take? Are not you going to try for the Ord. Dept.? you know I want you to do so, & <u>do not</u> wish you to go to Tenn. if ordered there. Think of Charley Pinckney from a private in Marion Artillery, entering Ord. Dept. as Capt. through three weeks hard study (but I think it was thro' <u>favour</u>) and he has done nothing to deserve it, you have done ten times as much. Virginia was his Mothers birth place & home, and to me it seems very strange that he has kept himself safe out of harm's way all the war, instead of fighting in Virginia.[85] Mr Seabrook & Mary his daughter were here all of last week, on their way to Sumter & Grahamville. We all spent a very happy week together, it was so long since we had met, & Archy really seemed to enjoy it. He examined your father's Arithmetic said it was worth fifty thousand dollars & got your father to read some of his History to him, & it is so seldom your father has any one to sympathise in his pursuits & tastes (except his own family) that it was gratifying to him, for Archy evidently took a real interest in it for your father's sake.—They had purchases to make at the Bee store too, so the horses wretchedly as they looked had to be used nearly every day, as he could not walk, & Mary couldn't walk very far. Poor Carrie's[86] death was a relief to the family as well as herself, it seems, her mind was almost entirely gone except when speaking of religion. Archy said, Pinckney's death was to him, as tho some tremendous great sledgehammer had suddenly fallen on and crushed him. ah! we will all never forget these last few years! We have suffered so much. Old Mr. C. Pinckney had to bring thirty negroes down to sell the other day, in order to feed the rest.[87] He only made <u>fifteen</u> bushels of corn last year, and the expenses of moving them, losing some, & supporting the rest amounted to <u>$10,000</u>! they are all now at Cokesbury[88] Seabrooks & Pinckneys both.

---

84.   Richard Henry Jenkins (1812–1868), father of Julia Blanche Jenkins Leverett.

85.   Capt. Charles Cotesworth Pinckney (1839–1909), ordnance officer of the First Military District of South Carolina, assigned to the Charleston Arsenal. His mother was Anne Randolph McKenna, wife of Rev. Charles Cotesworth Pinckney (1812–1898).

86.   Phoebe Caroline Seabrook died in Flat Rock, North Carolina, at the age of seventeen on 1 January 1864.

87.   Charles Cotesworth Pinckney II (1789–1865), of Charleston, father of Caroline Pinckney Seabrook.

88.   In Abbeville District on the Greenville and Columbia Railroad.

Charley seems in very blue spirits, sure he is going to die, dreams of Edward all the time, no dream is ever without him in it. It is strange that Fred also is forever dreaming of Edward.

Write to Fred, he is constantly asking after you, and wanting you to write to him. His direction is still "Richmond Surgeon of Hood's Division Hospital, Morristown, Tenn." I never saw any one long so for letters from home as he does. His last was in bad spirits so sorry for us and your father, about Canaan & the cotton being burnt. Said his appetite was bad since he had charge of the Hospital had 40 wounded in his charge. We hear that Longstreet's Corps is on the move so, he must be with them, as he expected his Hospital to be closed if they advanced.

Capt Middleton (Jack) who passed thro' Columbia sent us word he thought Fred would be on in a few days, that when he got his furlough he rode over to Fred's Hospital to see if they could fix to come on together, searched the Hospital from top to bottom, & waited six hours to see him, but could not find him, nor hear where he was, so had to leave. We do not expect Fred however, for he wrote us that Jenkins would not give him a furlough. No doubt Jenkins knew they were soon to be on the move & may be in a fight, so of course, he would want him at his post.[89]

Milton Maxcy Leverett to his mother

Camp March 4th 1864

My dear Mother,

I haven't answered Anne's and your letters before because I was trying to find some one who had the corn but have not as yet heard from the person—I had inquired of several others previously. Mr Wm Heyward said that he would like to let Pa have some but didn't seem certain how to act as he wanted to know how his crop, I believe, would turn out, and said he could let me know a little later in the season. Major Screven[90] who is Quartermaster down here now, Hanckel having been ordered to another post, was perfectly willing to make the transfer as soon as I could get the corn which I hope may yet be obtained. He was quite polite about it. I went round to Captain Foster of Rutledge's Regt. Fourth S.C. Cavalry and got him to give me a certificate stating that Canaan house was burnt down while in the service of the Government, he being in command there at the

---

89. The last paragraph was written on the top of the page of Fred's letter of 8 March to Milton. The two letters were folded together as if they were written at the same time. Mary Maxcy Leverett never closed her letter and it appears that Fred came home and continued writing on the same paper.

90. Maj. John H. Screven, quartermaster at Pocotaligo.

time. I wish also to have it signed by Col. Rutledge and then by the General.[91] There is an expedition on foot (not the Laurel Bay affair) but one requiring more nerve, I am going to volunteer (although I don't know that I will be allowed to go,) I know that you would like your son to show spirit, and not give in when an extra touch is needed. I have been through a good many expeditions, trusted in God in each one and came out safe and will try and have the same trust still and leave the result in his hands. I know that I have Pa's and your prayers always. Be mum now and don't let the cat out of the bag, secrecy is a great item.

My leather is getting on very well, I hope to supply all of you with enough after awhile. Has Fred written that he would get his furlough and when? Several of our men got furloughs by taking up deserters, a great many from the 11th regt. having jumped off the cars when it was passing here to carry them to the fight in Florida.[92] I rode a great deal one day about the country above Saltketcher to see if I couldn't take up some but failed. Twenty days is given here for every deserter or skulker taken up.[93] Any quantity of dwelling houses & plantations have been destroyed down the country by fire. The whole country was on fire, the carelessness I suppose of pickets. The fire would just burn through the country destroying everything in its route.

Your aff^{ct} son
Milton Maxcy Leverett

P.S. Don't know when the expedition will take place, may not come off for days or weeks, as preparation is needed. I will go and see Mrs Gregorie or Mrs Screven this evening I expect.

Monday 7th I paid Mrs Gregorie the visit, saw Mrs Dr. G. and herself, she begged to give her love to you when I wrote again. I think that we can get corn a few

---

91.   The certificate, dated 4 March 1864, is in Charles Leverett's file in "Claims for Property Loss Due to the Enemy, 1862–64," in the State Auditor's Papers, Records of the Comptroller General, South Carolina Department of Archives and History, Columbia. On 27 January Henry McKee filed a claim on behalf of Rev. Charles Leverett, estimating the house and other property in Beaufort at $9,700 and Canaan and its outbuildings, fences, and landscaping at $17,500, for a total of $27,200. Capt. John C. Foster of Company H, Fourth South Carolina Cavalry, Col. Benjamin Huger Rutledge, commander of the regiment, and Brig. Gen. William S. Walker, commander of the Third Military District, all attested to the losses at Canaan while occupied by Foster's company.

92.   The Eleventh South Carolina Infantry was one of four regiments ordered to leave South Carolina for Florida to reinforce Brig. Gen. Joseph Finegan, commander of the District of East Florida. The fight Milton refers to is the battle of Olustee (Ocean Pond), 20 February 1864, in which Finegan (without the units sent from Charleston, which did not arrive in time) defeated a Federal invasion of northern Florida.

93.   By 1864 a twenty-day furlough was offered to any soldier capturing anyone avoiding the draft, absent without leave, or deserting his command.

weeks later perhaps cheaper & easier. The Quartermaster Sergeant (Chas Wilcox)[94] of this company will be able to obtain it up the country and do the transportation down here for me. He forages for our company and will find it just as easy to get the corn that we would buy, and hand it over, to our company for Gov. use as he would in buying corn for the Gov. itself, only he won't be able to attend to it for some weeks. That I think is the best way for Pa to get the corn. Wilcox will do it for he has told [me] he would, but cannot now as he has corn on hand. He can buy it for Pa, as he is all the time foraging all over the country.

yr. aff^ct son M. M. Leverett

Frederic Percival Leverett to his brother Milton

Home, 8th March/64

My dear Minny,

I am at home once more, arrived here safely last Friday and found all well. I rode thro' from Bulls Gap, some seventeen miles below Greenville, Tenn. to Spartanburg. I then took the cars & sent Jacob on with my horses. He reached here on Sunday night without accident except that the horses were badly galled & somewhat jaded. I have three of them, none extra animals. One is a six year old sorrel, long legged, slim in flesh, but well gaited & were he in good condition would be very desirable—I gave $300.00 & would sell him could I get $600 for him. The second is a mare, chestnut sorrel, that will match Dora very well. She had her back badly hurt on the trip. She has one defective eye & one leg swollen from a severe & protracted attack of scrapies. I gave $250.00 for her. She is seven years old and reminds me more of Nightmare under the saddle than any horse I ever rode. She fidgets and frets incessantly. I drove her today in the carriage with Rena & moved gently & well. I want to sell Rena & leave her for the family to use. She will be far more useful than Rena & more easily kept. My third is a little bay mare I bought just before leaving Camp to bring my baggage on. I gave $250 for her. I ought to be able to make $100 on her. I draw feed from the Q. M. here so am not worried on that score. I brought some forty lbs. wool with me with which I hope to buy some clothes. I have nothing here with me except a very common pair of blue pants & a jacket. I sent on my valise by Dr. Bedon a week before I started and have not yet received it. So you may imagine I am slimly off & look very very shabby. I am moreover hard up for money, fortunately perhaps I cannot go about much in consequence of a bad boil on the back of the neck from [which] I am suffering night & day. It is hard to have my furlough thus ruined. I want you

---

94. Q.M. Sgt. Charles H. Willcox.

to get a furlough and come home as soon as you can, that I may see you. I will be here a fortnight or so. Be certain to come. I am sorry to say they are having pretty hard times at home, & I fear will see harder. I have been trying to buy a cow ever since I came. Today I decided to take one at $490.00 and went in to get her, but she was sold a half hour before I arrived. She was a pretty good cow, but nothing extraordinary. High prices have almost astounded me. Horses & negros have fallen; everything I wish to get is fearfully high. Everything to eat is awful. The cows at home look as though they will be in no hurry to calve, & the family is living on Anne's Bl.[95] Rice & the two hogs which are growing less & less. Do, if you possibly can buy corn, buy as much as you can; rice also I should say if possible. I wish very much I could come down to see you. Instead of that you must come & see me. Remember me to all. What did you do about my colt? I left Hood's Div. now Buckner's[96] at Bull's Gap. The remainder of Longstreets Corps lying from there to Greenville. Pa asks if you have received the letter paper he sent. Ma says she has a ball of thread for you & will keep it until you come.

Love yr. aff[ct] brother

F. P. Leverett

Milton Maxcy Leverett to his mother

Pocotaligo March 9th, 1864

My darling Mother,

I write a line to allay your looked for worrying. I have not gone and don't expect to go on the expedition I wrote about. It has been postponed indefinitely by the General which I take for granted is equivalent to being knocked in the head entirely.[97] The expedition was (although you had better not speak much of it) to assault a blockader off the Combahee and Ashepoo rivers in the Sound. We had got about sixty men, in three boats, and were to go with muffled oars as quietly as possible and throw up grapnels on deck and hold on with boathooks, then perhaps have a hand to hand fight in which we expected to come out best, although thinking we could hardly get through without having at least somebody killed. If we could succeed in getting on board we would in all probability succeed. (Commodore Tatnall said if we could get six men on deck the boat would be ours) but if they were able to repel us while climbing up or discovered us before our boats touched the ship and then opened on us with grape and canister we would have

---

95. Boiled.

96. Maj. Gen. Simon Bolivar Buckner.

97. Brig. Gen. William S. Walker proposed taking a boat from St. Helena Sound out to Otter Island, at the mouth of the Ashepoo River, to capture the Federal blockader.

had a hard tale to tell, however it has been indefinitely postponed although I think we could have captured it, and had made up my mind to the job. I think though if some of my friends had got killed, I wouldn't have felt repayed. The men were from different companies who were to attack it. This expedition has been cast aside and the first one resumed, the Laurel Bay one which we expect to go on tomorrow, and will carry a large ten oared boat with us to bring back the prog. There is a company of the enemy picketing there, I think that they are blacks, because every time our scouts have been there they have seen nothing but negros, & we deferred this expedition before in the hopes that a white company would take their place as we didn't wish to kill up the blacks,[98] but now I hear Beauregard has sent orders from Florida to make attacks on the island consequently we are going to Laurel Bay. I intend to join and row there at least, although I hope to have a share in it, nevertheless I feel doubtful about shooting the ignorant negroes right and left. I'll try and let you hear as soon as possible of the success of the affair although it maybe a full week or more before you can hear so don't worry, it isn't much to worry about, nothing like the other affair. Love to all. I can't get stamps here now so I write "Soldier's letter."

Your aff<u>ct</u> son.
Milton M. Leverett

I hope Pa is in good spirits. I think everything is looking better and better and expect the war to end in a year's time although everybody here is looking for it to end this fall. I have just got two small calf hides which I fixed up myself and will do very well for shoes for all of you. If nothing prevents I intend trying my luck at catching deserters and skulkers again so that I can get a furlough to come up and see you all. I know of one down the country dodging about, Mr. Rich<u>d</u> Johnson's son, Smith Johnson, a very poor shoat indeed.

yr. aff<u>ct</u> son
M. M. Leverett

Frederic Percival Leverett to his brother Milton

Columbia, S.C.
10<u>th</u> March 1864

My dear Minny,

I received your note last night. We were all glad to hear you were safely back & regretted the expedition was a failure. Ma says she considered very providential

---

98. The black Union regiments in the vicinity, headquartered on Port Royal Island, Hilton Head Island, and St. Helena Island, were the Twenty-ninth Connecticut Infantry (Colored), Twenty-sixth United States Colored Troops, Thirty-third United States (the old First South Carolina Volunteers, Colored), Company G, First Michigan Infantry (Colored), and Company B, Ninth United States Colored Troops.

that the boat stuck, & she is very thankful for it, & says it was quite Stuart like to miss the tide. We hear the force you were to have met was far greater than your own. Ma says Ste Elliott's lead must have been missed.

I wish very much you could get a furlough & come up while I am here. I shall leave on Monday 28th Inst. The two lasts in package are Mary's & Carry's. The former answers for Julia also & the latter for Kate. They are all very anxious for shoes, Tilly for leather. She wishes you to send or bring up one of your Calf Skins. All are passably well. I am still in search of a cow.

In much haste,

yr. ever aff^ct brother, F. P. Leverett.

Within a month Fred made his last transfer of the war from his temporary assignment as surgeon of the Palmetto Sharpshooters. Since another officer had a prior claim on the position and there was no permanent vacancy in the Sharpshooters or the other regiments of Jenkins's Brigade, Fred was given his choice of vacancies in several brigades of the First Corps and chose the Fifth Texas Infantry, in the same division. He was appointed surgeon of the regiment on 10 April 1864.

Mary Maxcy Leverett to her son Milton

Farm, Columbia, April 14, 1864

My dear Min,

Annie and I walked into Town to see your aunt Til day before yesterday. Stevy was in bed with measles. Til asked me to stay to dinner, but I did not, & in walking out we sent in to the Middleton's for letters, & got yours which (as I had no spectacles in my pocket) Annie read aloud to me while walking out. You may suppose how startled, how pleased, how uneasy, in short, how great a variety of sensations it excited in us both, but especially in your loving ever-uneasy Mother. All of the family are pleased at the prospect of your leaving the ranks, even for no higher position than Sargeant, and that too in the historic and ever memorable and far famed Sumter! the girls console and quiet my fears, by predicting that no more fighting will probably be done there. But I don't know, that's quite uncertain. Still, I see by the paper today, that Beauregard is about to take up his quarters in Savannah,—so he must regard it as pretty sure that Charleston is not to be attacked. No telegram came up from Col. Elliott—your father went to the Telegraph office this morning. No letter has come from Major John[99]—very likely he is not in Charleston. If you do get the appointment what are you going to do with

---

99. John Gibbes Barnwell II.

Billy? carry him with you, or what? I wish he was a more sensible and useful servant to you. You had better get Cornelia's shoes done as soon as possible, for Julia
Gregg, we hear, arrived at Mrs Green's yesterday, & it would be a great opportunity to get them to her. Old Mrs. Green died very recently, and Julia has come to
see Lucy Green.[100] I scarcely slept the night of the day I got your letter. I am glad
you saw about the corn so soon—we are truly in want of it. We spent $60 for
allowance for servants last week, & will have to do the same every week I fear
unless you succeed in getting corn or rice for us, & to add to our difficulties in the
household the tierce of rice Annie bought is all but gone, we have had to live so
entirely on it for so long. We expect to be paid for the stocking work, however, on
Saturday, which will amount to $90, & they have found no fault with the work this
week, and sent more for them to do. Annie had to give $5 today for a peck of
peas.—Mary Heyward left today for Camden on a visit to the Miss Moultries'. Mr.
& Mrs. D. Heyward called on us a few days ago. He offered to carry your knife
down, so we sent it by him. If you can, you had better go and see Willie before
you leave,—I mean of course if you get the appointment. Intercourse is resumed
between the families & it is well that bygones should be bygones. Mary Heyward
& Mary Fowles dined with us yesterday,—Mary H. told your Aunt Til they had a
very pleasant time.—A Concert took place in Town night before last for the Young
Ladies Hos. Ass.[101] The performers were all Amateur & not professional. Dr Taber
& his sister sang, separately & together, Mrs Dr Chisolm[102] & Miss Chisolm, Mr.
Ancrum, as he is called here, better know[n] as Jemmy Ancrum in Beaufort,[103]
Miss Kelly of New Orleans & several others played & sang, and the Hampton
Legion Band "made the air vocal" at intervals—tickets $5! proceeds $3000!! My
Mame went with Mary & Jim Fowles & the Miss Boyd Mary has been staying
with. Mame was delighted, being the first she had ever been at, & spent the night
at Aunt Tils. Opinions differ, some people say it was humbug, others it was
delightful.

Friday April 15. Dear Min,
If you succeed about the corn, send the transfer paper which the Quartermaster
gives, to us, so that <u>we</u> may send it to Major Rhett,—for the transfer receipt paper
makes no mention at all of the name of any person, but only that so much & so
much has been delivered into his hands. It really takes a great deal of Hercules'
time to go in so often for a bushel of corn or of grist at a time.—The weather is

100. Lucy Pride Jones Green (d. 6 April 1864) and her granddaughter.
101. Mary Bull Leverett and Anne Leverett DeSaussure were members of the Young Ladies'
     Hospital Association of Columbia.
102. Mary Edings Chisolm of Columbia, wife of Dr. Julian John Chisolm.
103. Pvt. James K. Douglas Ancrum of Company K, Second South Carolina Cavalry.

exceedingly chilly & unpleasant still day after day. My Irish potatoes are coming up beautifully—the peas are recovering from the devastations of the rabbits, squashes are up, & we have had radishes for breakfast three mornings, so things look a little more promising. I hear Willie Heyward has a capital garden—he persuaded his father to let him have old Toby down there, & the servant he had there is now driving the Heyward's carriage. Toby was so often complaining of Rheumatism & deafness that I expect Mr. Heyward was very willing to make the exchange & no doubt Toby is delighted.

Mr. Fielding has written a first-rate recommendation for your father's Arith. giving the highest possible praise. He says that "during thirty years of my life devoted to the instruction of youth, I have never met any treatise on the science of Arith. which gives the pupil so clear and simple a view of the subject; nor do I know any work of the kind in which the principles of Arithmetic are laid down with so much brevity and perspicuity," &c. Do write as soon as you know about Sumter, or the corn. Kate sends her love.

Your aff^ate Mother
Mary Leverett

Frederic Percival Leverett to his brother Milton

Camp near Zollicoffer, Tenn.
16th April, 1864.

My dear Minny,

You are, I suppose, long before this once more in camp. I hope you have succeeded in getting some corn & peas & have sent receipts for it home. It worries me very much to think what trouble and straights all at home, especially Nan will be put to if you do not succeed. A Mr. Brown, formerly my clerk at Morristown is soon to go home on furlough.[104] He thinks he can buy corn & peas for himself of a friend at Gov. prices or less not very far from Columbia—up the country somewhere, & turn them over to a Q. M. He has kindly promised, if he succeeds in doing so for himself, he will do these [letter damaged] or rather he [letter damaged] from [letter damaged] to stop & see Pa on the subject. I really trust [letter damaged] also assist the family to weather the summer.

[Letter damaged] may be more successful planting this summer than last for though the place cannot feed all, it ought to make an approximation to doing so. I hope you have done something about your colt. Have you been able to do anything about mine? If not, before asking, you had better drop Fuller a line (Direc-

---

104. Probably Pvt. Samuel G. Brown, Company E, Palmetto Sharpshooters.

tion, Midway S.C.) & find out that the animal is in statu quo. I have succeeded in purchasing a horse since arriving here—a young [letter damaged] gelding—bay, six years old this spring, a fast pacer; consider him a fine [letter damaged] I do not like a pacer. He [letter damaged] and strong but in very [letter damaged] condition & has a ugly wart inside of his mouth. I am to give $500.00 for him, when the [letter damaged] money to pay me. It was the best I could do & by trading [letter damaged]. This summer I may possibly get suited for the $500.00. [letter damaged] of my other horses will not be a bad affair. I have sent [letter damaged] and Jacob on to Charlottesville with the wagons. Today is the is the fourth day since they left. They have a journey of about 300 miles. We start for the same destination as soon as the cars can take us, possibly some time next week. We go to reinforce Lee against Grant in his great "on to Richmond."[105] That is to be, I think the decisive battle of the war. I cannot & willnot think of anything but success with it. May God graciously give us an overwhelming success! Then will the end be not far distant. Such result will, I feel confident, crush out Grant, destroy the North's last hope, and discourage them too much to attempt raising another army. On the other hand our soldiers will soon be in condition to push forward and the way will be open before them. The summer too will open upon us & we will have a good chance for a long and, I trust, brilliant & decisive campaign. The fall may see negotiations for peace. The men here are all determined, but very serious on the subject of the return to Va. They seem to fully realize that the work they are going to is one of the greatest importance, & they are resolved it shall not be their fault if it be not [letter damaged] done. We hear that troops are being hurried on from the [letter damaged] from every direction. The [letter damaged] not appear probably to great advantage with [letter damaged] They have been so exposed to hardships this winter [letter damaged] are out in great measure at knee and elbow. I [letter damaged] company will be left on the coast. It can do as good service there as anywhere else, and is thoroughly acquainted with locale & accustomed to the climate.

I am now Surgeon of the "5$^{\underline{th}}$ Texas Reg. Gregg's Brgd. Field's Division, Longstreet Corp."[106] That is my direction. No need to specify a locality, unless you chose to add via Richmond. I am altogether among strangers, & find it pretty lonely. There was no vacancy in Jenkins' Brgd. & I was obliged to go into another. Had he [letter damaged] then, he might, I think, have arranged to keep me. As it was I was

---

105. The Overland Campaign, which included the battles of the Wilderness (5–6 May), Spotsylvania Court House (8–20 May), North Anna (23–25 May), and Cold Harbor (1–3 June), began with Lee's Army of Northern Virginia and Grant's Army of the Potomac in northern Virginia and ended a month later on the outskirts of Richmond and cost fifty thousand Federal and thirty thousand Confederate casualties.

106. The Fifth Texas Infantry was one of four regiments in the old Texas Brigade, commanded by Brig. Gen. John Gregg of Texas.

given the choice of [letter damaged] in Humphrey's Miss. Brgd.[107] [letter damaged] McLaw's Div. or [letter damaged] Anderson[108] or Benning's[109] Ga. Brgd. or this in Hood's [letter damaged] Brgd.[110] I chose the last as being next desirable after [letter damaged] and as being nearest akin to So. Car. I find a great many [letter damaged] own state and great kindliness of feeling to kin. The men [went] through there last fall en route to Ga. They were better treated than anywhere else. The ladies were kinder in bringing and giving supplies, and that they saw fewer young & able bodied men at the depots. It of course gratifies me to hear them talk so, as very often our [letter damaged] is much decried.

Gen. Field, our new Div. Commander will, it is thought, be quite popular.[111] He is a Kentuckian, West Pointer, quiet & business like. I stopped two or three days at Hd. Qrs. with Parker whom he has appointed Div. Surgeon.[112] I thus made the acquaintance of the General and his Staff. I took quite a fancy to Maj. Mason, Commissary & Captain Mason[113] one of the aides. They are Virginians, refugees from Fredericksburg.

I had a tiresome journey on here. As far as Richmond I travelled with Middleton. We arrived on Sunday morning early. He went on in the afternoon. I stopped over on account of Sunday & because\I had some old Hospital business to settle up. I stopped until Tuesday afternoon & then came on. By skillful maneuvering & delicate engineering the ladies cars were secured all the way. Soon after [letter damaged] Columbia Middleton succeeded in slipping himself [letter damaged]. I shortly after seeing some people slipping in [letter damaged] with them. That took us in comparative comfort [letter damaged]. Then, when about starting, in a lucky moment, we [letter damaged] two ladies without escorts. I went to buy our tickets & deputed Middleton to offer our services. On my return I found him comfortably seated & I told the Sentinel I was of that party & [letter damaged] me pass. At Raleigh the guard very properly had respect [letter damaged] our stars & bars & did not attempt to stop us—at Wel-

---

107. Brig. Gen. Benjamin Grubb Humphreys, whose Mississippi brigade in McLaws's Division consisted of the Thirteenth, Seventeenth, Eighteenth, and Twenty-first Mississippi Infantry regiments.

108. Brig. Gen. George Thomas Anderson, whose Georgia brigade in Hood's old division consisted of the Seventh, Eighth, Ninth, Eleventh, and Fifty-ninth Georgia Infantry regiments.

109. Brig. Gen. Henry Lewis Benning, whose Georgia brigade in Hood's old division consisted of the Second, Fifteenth, Seventeenth, and Twentieth Georgia Infantry regiments.

110. Hood's Texas Brigade, one of the most renowned units in the Confederate army, consisted of the First, Fourth, and Fifth Texas, and Third Arkansas Infantry regiments.

111. Maj. Gen. Charles William Field.

112. Surgeon Francis LeJau Parker, surgeon of the Hampton Legion (Infantry) was promoted to surgeon of Field's Division.

113. Maj. Julien Jacquelin Mason and his brother Capt. W. Roy Mason Jr. of Field's staff.

don[114] the sentinel was obdurate. "Nobody, officer or no officer gets on without a lady. Them's my orders & I shall obey them, if the car goes empty." [Letter damaged] a mental row. But we would ride in no other coach but this one—Middleton went off & got some subordinate of the Conductor [letter damaged] & pass us in. When he arrived he found so many waiting at [letter damaged] that he himself found subterfuge necessary. He merely [letter damaged] Middleton & myself. You two gentlemen wish to go in together. We took the hint & replied certainly & were let in. At Petersburg Middleton hunting for me and I for him. After that I do not know how M. succeeded. At Richmond I was almost in [letter damaged] when I saw two middle aged ladies without visible escorts. I tendered them myself as escort. They were only going to Amelia. I was going further. They saw the object of my politeness & kindly accepted my offer. I got in. At Burkesville we had to change cars. I looked around to find some one to attach myself to. I could only see an Irishwoman encumbered with sundry carpet bags. Help her or go in the crowded soldiers cars. I chose the lesser evil of course. Her answer was "I will be moighty thankful, Mister." I went out to see if the cars from Petersburg, which we were to take, had arrived. They had not. At last they came. Mrs. Paddy did not more than half trust me, for she took her baggage along herself, & would not let me help her in that respect at all. It was all the same to me. I got a seat & slept most of the way to Lynchburg. There we were detained by missing connections a day & a night. Next morning the cars were crowded. I was certain I must now go with soldiers. At last I espied two ladies without gentlemen. I asked if they were provided. They said yes we have an escort! Have you two? if not please allow me to pass myself with you. We are only going a little way & the car is very full. If you are not going far, so much the better as there will be more room when you get out. They had no answer to that. I pushed off to the Conductor who after hesitating a good deal let me pass. Thus I worked my way. Traveling is very expensive now a days & it costs almost as much for [letter damaged] as for the master.

Remember me kindly to the [letter damaged] to Hal Stuart, Jno Rhodes, Rob Means, Barney, Nat & Nenny [letter damaged] Gibbes & many others. Don't pause in your exertion to get peas for home use. With much love to yourself.

Ever yr. most aff<u>ct</u> brother
F. P. Leverett

P.S. Do write me soon. The weather here is awful especially [letter damaged] who have been home—it has rained every day except three since I left home & those were not clear. Today the sun has shone two or three times [letter damaged] has rained, hailed, snowed, sleeted, & is very cold. This is 16<u>th</u> April weather. We are rather high up a mountainous region.—Goodbye [letter damaged]

---

114. On the Weldon Railroad in northeastern North Carolina.

Milton Maxcy Leverett to his mother

Pocotaligo April 26th 1864

My dear mother,

I am still here not having received as yet notification when I am to leave, indeed I am afraid something has turned up to put a stop to it. I am quite surprised at not having heard from home since my last letter (I received some time ago one from you,) with the certificate for the corn; I had expected that you would have acknowledged the receipt of the same; if you had done so immediately it would have saved me some worry, and I hope nothing more. Tell Pa that the parties from whom the corn was obtained wouldn't take anything but the new currency or the old at the discount,[115] consequently I had to write to Mr. Pringle asking him to fill the order to the same, the fives wouldn't be received neither were they willing to take the order.

Tell Anne the lunch she gave me did me good service as well as Fred's did him, it lasted me until I got here although Albert Rhett[116] and Thom. Lowndes[117] helped me with it. Any quantity of troops are passing here all the time. Gen'l Walker has left us, and also a pleasant little note to the B.V.A. in which he begs Capt. Stuart to assure the gentlemen of the B. Vol. Artillery that "during my continuance with their command they have been linked to me by <u>ties</u> which I hope may never be <u>broken</u> and connected with me by associations which I <u>trust</u> will never be <u>forgotten</u>." He shed tears the morning he was leaving.[118] He had told Hal so I hear that he would have liked to have carried us with him but that he thought really that we were of more importance where we were. We are having theatric shows etc. in our company by the "Thespian Corps." Some of our men being the actors and actresses. They have done very well indeed, acted the "Lady of Lyons"[119] in which Johnny DeTreville[120] represented Pauline so well that a great many men said she was the prettiest girl there that night (thirty-six ladies were present, the

---

115. The new currency authorized by the Confederate Congress on 17 February 1864 replaced the old authorized in 1863; the 1864 issue was conservatively estimated at two billion dollars or more in face value before the end of the war.

116. Cpl. Albert Rhett (1833–1895) of the Beaufort Artillery, brother of Roland Smith Rhett and James Moore Rhett.

117. Cpl. Thomas Pinckney Lowndes of the Marion Artillery (Capt. E. L. Parker's Company, South Carolina Artillery), on detached service with the Signal Corps in Charleston.

118. Walker was relieved from command of the Third Military District of South Carolina 19 April 1864 and ordered to North Carolina to command the South Carolina brigade of Brig. Gen. Nathan G. Evans in the Department of North Carolina and Southern Virginia.

119. Edward Bulwer-Lytton, *The Lady of Lyons, or, Love and Pride: A Play in Five Acts* (1838).

120. Pvt. John L. DeTreville of the Beaufort Artillery.

public generally had been invited, the General also was there). Girls came from Grahamville to it, the Gregories, Mrs. M. Hanckel was there, Miss G. didn't come that night. I daresay she thought it would be a failure as I had told her I thought it wouldn't be worth looking at. Henry Elliott acted old Mrs. Des Chapelles, didn't have on any hoops and looked just like one of the old Sand-hillian women with a light colored calico frock on, when he pursed up his mouth he looked precisely like Nancy Elliott; he performed his part capitally though, Robt. Gibbes[121] of Aiken took the part of Mrs. Melnotte an old lady and did first rate. There was also a farce called the "Conscript" written by Mr. Durban[122] which was acted, it took very well, the audience were quite amused, there was also some negro minstrelsy performed which was very good. On the whole it was capitally "got up" and I think is a very good thing for camp, the General was all in for it, encouraged the members of it and thought it was a firstrate thing for the soldiers. I think it has a refining influence on the men, makes them more willing to seem like gentlemen and less uncivilized by bringing ladies in camp, everything was perfectly decorous. The camp looked firstrate on each side of the street between the houses there were lamps for a hundred yards, one for every two houses, nineteen in all, and the camp is always clean as a penny, so that when all were lit up that night it looked firstrate. We will have more by and bye. I am very glad to hear your garden is getting on well. Why you must be coming out to walk all the way into town. Beauregard has gone to meet Burnside.[123] I am glad to hear that Mr. Fielding has given such a recommendation to Pa's Arithmetic. Why don't Pa get one from Ben Stuart and also some of the Columbia school teachers.[124] I wish he would send me a hundred dollars of my watch money, direct to here. I have two pairs of cards one for cotton and the other for wool, cost ($18) eighteen for the two, if you wish them at home, let me know, if not I can get rid of them here. I have got that certificate for the destruction of our house signed by both Rutledge and Walker and send it within. I may send Billy up for my colt and perhaps for that bull calf to put on Nat's place. I am having the shoes made now. Love to all, Major Jno. B. is in Augusta.

Your aff^{ct} son
Milton M. Leverett

---

121. Pvt. Robert M. Gibbes of the Beaufort Artillery.
122. Pvt. E. E. Durban of the Beaufort Artillery.
123. Beauregard was assigned to command the Department of North Carolina and Southern Virginia, with headquarters at Petersburg, Virginia, on 15 April 1864.
124. Benjamin Rhett Stuart (1835–1904), son of Claudia Smith and John Allan Stuart.

John Gibbes Barnwell to Milton Leverett

Head Quarters, Department of So. Ca., Ga. & Fla.
Ordnance Office,
Charleston, S.C. Apl 28, 1864

To
Milton Leverett Esq.
Columbia, So. Ca.

Dear Sir:

Your letter reached Charleston during my absence from the city on duty at another post in the Department.

Regret to inform you that no appointments are now made in the Ordnance Corp, as the Com'd'g Col reports too many on duty.

It would have given me much pleasure in obtaining a place for you—Perhaps you might get an appointment in the Signal Corps.

Yours most Respectfully
Jno G. Barnwell
Maj Corps Arty. C.S.A.

Mary Maxcy Leverett to her son Milton Leverett

Farm Columbia May 10, 1864

My dear Milton,

We started Billy off yesterday with the colt and hope he will get safe down to you. Your father sent Hercules through Columbia to convoy Billy safe thro' the dangers of the town, having a slight suspicion that the eight dollars he gave him in small bills might not last beyond the precincts of the town, left to the tender mercies of Billy's conscience, so Hercules saw him safe over the bridge, and Billy with the most superlative confidence in his own abilities, was certain that there was no danger of any trouble if he only got the colt thro' the Town. Hercules says <u>if he had the money he'd give a dinner</u> (for joy) <u>in honor of the departure of the colt</u>, it gave them so much trouble.

I hope my dear Min you are not too downcast at your disappointment, for I suppose of course it is a disappointment, as we see by the paper & heard thro' the Barnwell's of Col. Elliot's appointment as Col. of the Holcombe Legion,[125] so your

---

125. Maj. Stephen Elliott Jr. was relieved of duty in South Carolina and appointed colonel of Holcombe's Legion (Infantry) in Walker's Brigade, Department of North Carolina and Southern Virginia.

promotion is probably at an end. It is very much smoothed to me by knowing that you are thereby more safe, having to remain in the same position in the Artillery. Ste Barnwell was very much worried, his sister[126] said, he did not know what he was going to do, as according to military rule, he had no right to the position he was holding any how. I dare say you will get some other post sometime, so don't be discontented and consider it as the alotting of God, only continue patiently to do your duty until something points the way to a different position. Columbia is crowded with soldiers coming & going all the time. The ladies are going to have a grand Fete tomorrow in the Park, Annie and Mary have been very busy preparing things for the table they are to serve at Mrs. Fisher's. We were greatly relieved at getting the corn at last from Major Rhett. Everybody is waiting on everybody up here for the new currency to come out, which has been much delayed by moving the ladies to Columbia, (who sign the bills) from Richmond.

Billy brought your skins & leather safe. Charley who has just paid us one of his flying visits, said it was excellent leather. Mame has already been glad to get hold of some of it to new sole her shoes, which had worn out. I believe you know already that Fred is in Greggs Texas Brigade, Fields Div. Longstreets Corps. He said he had not known a well day since getting back to the Army. Hard & uncertain fare Fred can't stand.

Wednesday 11th

We are just beginning to cut some rye for the horses, it has headed better than we expected considering the calves were on it all winter—the wheat looks beautifully and so does the oats, but both garden & field need rain badly. We picked six quarts strawberries yesterday to give to Mrs. Fisher's table at the Fete today. The whole house intends going. I mean to take Kate & Carrie after dinner, so there has been a great doing up of clothes. Kate is to stay in the carriage where she can look on, your sister will stay in the carriage with her some of the time & I the other, Cely is to be along also—poor little thing, she is delighted at the idea, if she had shoes I would have walked with her about the park, but the old ones are too worn out. Your cousin Julia is going on Monday next, I hope Cornelia's shoes will come before then, as she has sent to ask for them. Julia has stayed at Lucy Green's a short time, the Maxcy's some of the time at work for Sue, and with us frequently at dinner while looking over papers & putting to rights in their rooms, but has not spent the night. She dined here yesterday –

What delightful news we are getting, and how thankful we should be! and what a righteous nation we ought to be for all time to come! I wish we could become more of a God fearing people. We are all so grieved about Gen. Jenkins' death & by the hands of the unfortunate Brigade that shot Stonewall Jackson, that

---

126. Isabel Barnwell (1841–1867).

one's to die by the hands of friends is dreadful.[127] We have lost so many valuable men that way. Would you believe it, John Haskell who lost his arm is again in these battles near Richmond.[128] Captain A. Haskell has been made a Colonel.[129] We were quite amused at your camp theatrical. Henry Elliott must have looked very funny. I hear Ben Stuart has been conscripted and was very indignant, immediately took some additional <u>girls</u>, not having boys enough to complete the number of scholars requisite to exempt a teacher. Your father intends sending his <u>Arith.</u> to him & some other teachers whenever it comes out but it is taking a long time because the presses are conscripted for Government.

Charley has taken the school two miles from where he lives as he finds it more convenient than Cheraw; & he has just as many scholars, some following him from Cheraw & boarding out. He looked much better than last time he was here.

Write soon dear Min.

Your affte Mother
Mary Leverett

---

127. Micah Jenkins was mortally wounded in the Wilderness, 6 May 1864, when Brig. Gen. William Mahone's Virginia brigade accidentally fired into a group of Confederate officers including Lt. Gen. James Longstreet. Troops of Brig. Gen. James H. Lane's North Carolina brigade, not Mahone's, accidentally wounded Stonewall Jackson at Chancellorsville in May 1863.

128. Maj. John Cheves Haskell commanded Haskell's Battalion, First Corps Artillery, Army of Northern Virginia.

129. Alexander Cheves Haskell was appointed colonel of the new Seventh South Carolina Cavalry in April 1864.

6

A Year of Sorrow

May 1864–April 1865

O will this cruel war never be over!
It seems to me that the Almighty will
surely send some awful judgment on this
execrable Yankee nation for their unjust,
brutal cruel conduct during this war.

—Mary Maxcy Leverett

Milton was appointed as ordnance sergeant with the Beaufort Artillery on 4 May 1864 and reported for duty at Fort Sumter shortly thereafter. Fred continued as surgeon of the Fifth Texas Infantry in northern Virginia.

Milton Maxcy Leverett to his mother

Pocotaligo May 10th /64

My dear Mother,

We are preparing our summer camp now,—in McPhersonville on the road to Mr Wm Heyward's, to the rear of Fergurson Hutson's yard. It will be some time before we can move up there are so many houses to be built, it will be a long time before mine will be ready. I don't feel a bit like work, especially handling pine logs. I am so sorry you had so much trouble about the corn, and had to trouble the Quartermaster so much, although I know that you couldn't help it.

May 11

I received my appointment to Fort Sumter yesterday when I was writing here quite unexpectedly. I am not so glad now, since Col. Elliott has left and there will be nobody there whom I know.

I have tried to get fodder and peas but see no chance although I make another effort before I leave. I will be able to get more corn by and bye.

Major John's note wasn't as satisfactory as I would have liked. He misunderstood me, I didn't ask whether appointments were being made in the Dept where he is but whether examinations were still instituted through out the <u>Confederacy</u> for applicants. And as regards the Signal Corps, I wouldn't think of it. As regards the danger in Fort Sumter you needn't worry yourself, as the danger there is pretty much nominal now the actual siege is about over. I am rather sorry that I couldn't have been there when there was a true <u>bona fide</u> siege. Don't worry yourself about money for me, you need all at home, besides I shall draw better pay now. I have Cos. Cornelia's shoes and Anne's ready, but don't know whether to send such a small parcel by the Express or not. I will have the others done after a while.

We have had another theatric exhibition which came off capitally. Some of the men say Pauline was prettier than any of the audience. We were all quiet amused in the dressing them (Pauline & the other ladies) for the exhibition, their crinoline would sometimes consist of sundry blankets, one old lady, Mrs. Milnotte had my blanket for a coat and looked first rate too, perfectly natural. The costumes were all very good, Bill Elliott gave the "Corps" some, and Mrs Tom Elliott lent us some of the "girls fixings." For the sake of the girls I'll give them an inventory of Pauline's dress. She had first, or last, don't know which you call it, call it first, <u>lots and cords</u> of coats, scolloped and starched to boot corsets (borrowed from Christiana Jackson) laced till she could "<u>scarcely breeve</u>," besides other jigamarees and thingumbobs which made her look <u>perfectly natural</u> just like a "<u>gurl</u>." So much for the <u>inner man</u> now for the outer. For a dress she had a nice light coloured silk pink skirt which being too short had to be let down before her waist and pinned to her coat, then around her waist to hide that defect she had a light thin gauze scarf I believe which extended over and around her waist half way down the skirt and was looped on one side with a bunch of evergreens looking very pretty, then for a body, she had a light thin lace bodice, chemisette, shirt vest or something which met the thin scarf at the waist and then a long light coloured satin ribbon made into a bow and pined to the waist and hung down in front. Then she had for a headdress a nice scarlet coloured silk net with a silver coloured sort of band running around her forehead under the net and which sparkled in the light very prettily. Altogether she looked "<u>stunning</u>." Her dress really looked first rate. She was in short sleeves and low neck. Her neck and arms were as fair as any girl's I ever saw. Glad I've finished that—won't write the description of another dress long as I live. Suffice it to say that blankets very generally act the part of crinoline. I send you a programme, it was very much altered after it was first made out. All the characters in Fortunes Frolic are not designated.

We have bought boards enough to make a permanent theater when we move up. Don't let the cards go but for what I gave for them, you may <u>exchange</u> them at the Mutual Supply Association though in what manner you see most proper. Tell sister I won't hear of her obtaining a position in the Money Bureau, she has to get my sanction before she does anything of the sort, and that I never will give, although I know that some of the first families of the Confederacy (the F.F.V.'s)[1] have relatives there, still I don't like it. I will leave for Fort Sumter Saturday or Monday I expect. I anticipate a dull time.

Your ever affectionate son
Milton M. Leverett

Mary Maxcy Leverett to her son Milton

The Farm Columbia
May 20th 1864

And so you are in reality and truth in that far famed and world renowned Fort Sumter? my dear boy congratulate yourself; your children's children will be proud that their father's father was one of the heros in Fort Sumter during the bombardment, and the Roll of Honour of Fort Sumter will be equal in glory to the Battle Abbey Roll of Honour of Old England! You will say "but I was not there at its commencement and during the greatest bombardment that has ever been?" nevertheless you are there now, and the end is not yet, perchance you may live to see greater things than have yet taken place there. Oh! how gratified, how proud your brother would have been to say "I have a brother in Fort Sumter." I know exactly how he would look, just as he did when, very much gratified by hearing from several persons how gallantly you had behaved at the Battle of Port Royal, he turned with a bright pleased smile to us and said, "and so we have a Hero in our family!" I see him before me now and the expression of delight on his countenance I can never forget, and to this day I feel grateful to you for having put that drop of pleasure in his bitter cup. It was not a passing feeling either, but an abiding source of satisfaction to him, & he often spoke of it to me in the Pineland, as a lasting cause of thankfulness. He felt as though he had lifted the family with one hand and you with the other, and so each had done their part to establish the family name.— Your father we can all see is secretly proud of it, tho' he tries not to seem so. He says the fame of Sumter is historic and will never be forgotten, and he thinks it an honour for all time to come, to have been even one of the <u>commonest</u> <u>men</u> in Sumter! and you know when he praises anything it means much. It is true you must find it trying to leave a set of companions who really seem to be so kindly attached to you, and it must be equally as trying to give up the open air & skies for such a dark dismal cave of a room, if it can be called such, and the girls and

---

1. First Families of Virginia.

myself feel a great deal of sympathy for you on both causes. It must be severely trying to one's spirits to live in a hole that has to be lighted by a lamp night and day, but courage, my boy, you won't live there forever, and it is the highest wisdom to bear unavoidable evils well, and with a steadfast will to patiently endure the hardships and trials which lie in the path of duty. I must confess that dark and lonely cell would be more intolerable to me than anything I ever read of, not that I am afraid in the dark, I am not at all so, nature & early education have made me more fearless in the dark than any one I ever knew of, but the <u>loneliness</u> ah, that's the rub, that is hard to bear after such a cheerful mess as you had in the B.V.A. But I'll admire you all the more if you prove capable of enduring it with an equable spirit. So courage brave heart, you have fought your fight well so far, don't be tempted to throw away the advantages you may have it in your power to gain, because of the first step upward proving disagreable & difficult. Remember too, God is present everywhere, and I knelt to Him in the dead of the night, to beseech him to lighten up your dark cavern with his presence and loving countenance, and preserve you by night & by day from all assaults of your spiritual and temporal foes. Your letter came last evening and caused some commotion, being the first from Sumter:—the girls wanted to hear it read the moment it came, but your father called to me to say (from the chamber) that I must not read it out until he came in, so when he appeared, I read it aloud to the assembled family, amid their various comments and exclamations. When I saw by the papers the Monitors had been at their game again & the land batteries also, I said then I was afraid you were in Sumter, sure enough you were, but you do not seem to be as much impressed with the terribleness of an attack as I expected. Why the papers say, it was a very hot attack. I trust you will have sense enough not to expose yourself unnecessarily. It was kind of Ste Elliott to mention you favorably to Capt. John-son, in some sort, helping you to make a friend.[2] Of course I know you deserved it. I am sorry he is not there, but never a man seldom has the option in this life, of living only where his friends are, and if he does, he is apt to become narrow & contracted in his ideas, from coming in contact with nothing beyond his little world of friends. It does one's intellect good to go beyond this, the mind becomes more expanded, and knowledge comes to him even from contact with others, without much effort of his own, of course, the advantages are doubled if the man in addition, strives himself for improvement. I have no doubt you will soon make friends. When you first went to the B.V.A. do you remember how few you really knew, and how doubtful you were how you would stand, & whether you would get along at all, & see how differently you feel now, & how infinitely pleasanter you found it than you expected, & what a number of real friends you have! So, it will

---

2.   Capt. John Johnson of the Engineer Corps, chief engineer at Fort Sumter.

be in this step I am confident. Depend upon it, "the first step is the most difficult" in this, as in many other cases.

What a pity it is you did not send up Cornelia's shoes at once, as I especially
requested in both of my last letters, for Julia Gregg has now gone. I particularly
begged you to send them, as she was to go the next Monday after I wrote, she went
on Tuesday, but no shoes came, tho' she had been in Columbia a month or more.
Cornelia wrote to her to bring them, & I know of no other opportunity & almost
begin not to expect to see them at all. I dare say you hadn't the funds to send them
by Express, I would much rather have paid for them after they got up here, than
have to keep them all summer as I will probably have to do, tho' I have no money to
be sure, as every body is waiting still for the new currency to pay in. You never wrote
by Billy, but as he said he was to stay until Monday, so we did not send him until
that day. I was in hopes he would get there before you left, but I am glad that you
heard some certain news of him before you left. I asked him if he would like to go
to Fort Sumter, to my surprise he said "he would like it first rate!" Write me word as
minutely as you can, all your arrangements. How do you all manage about water,
surely such an important thing as water is not left to the uncertain contingencies
attending transportation from Charleston as it was at Fort Wagner? An artesian well
could surely be bored there as well as elsewhere. Do ask if it is practicable.

When I last heard from Fred it was before all of these battles in Virginia, just
before, and he was sick and said he was too unwell to be of any service to himself
or any one else. I feel very uneasy about him, as that was sometime ago, when Lee
was about to Review Longstreets Corps previous to any fight.[3] Perhaps he is too
busy & communication is very much cut off.

We are having quantities of strawberries which we send to our many friends
in Columbia, but we don't care so very much for them as we have no sugar.

In great haste

yr. aff. Mother
Mary Leverett

Rev. Charles Edward Leverett to his son Milton

[20 May 1864]

My dear Minny,

I intended to write by this opportunity, and send to-morrow but as yr. Ma has
concluded to send this evening I drop a line only & will write in a day or two.

---

3.   Lee reviewed the First Corps at Gordonsville on 29 April 1864, just before the opening of
the Wilderness Campaign on 5 May.

Mr. Pringle has the money to pay for the corn, but can't pay till the new currency is out, which we look for daily. Let me know how to direct him to send & to whom & what amount. You had better destroy the order on Confed^e treasury for $160. Let me know if you have done so.

I hope you will keep a bold heart in your new office & place and I trust & pray God will protect you.

yr. aff. father

Anne Leverett DeSaussure to her brother Milton

May 23^d /64.

My dear Min,

Right sorry am I that you have left Pocotaligo, it seems so useless to run into danger, 'twon't do to look back now however, you will have to fight it out and I am afraid 'scratch' it out also, for Jim tells us he hears the place is very lively—You will not find it so dull after a while, make acquaintances, what a pity you have not a cat and Billy too, what a heavy loss the latter is, if he arrives at Pocotaligo, safely with your colt, he will have redeemed his character for laziness, if nothing else for Hercules expected him to take <u>three</u> weeks at the least. I was rejoiced to get rid of the animal, Hercules likewise—I overheard him telling Lewis if he "could only afford it, he would give a big dinner the day the colt left."—I was very much obliged to you for Lou's shoes, they fit her exactly and came in time for her to dine at Aunt Eliza's with me, she behaved very well, got over her shyness very much as she had a little maid to play with, was laughing and running all about the house. She says give her "love to you and tell you howdy and a kiss too." Carrie and Kate too. I hope my shoes are not too small if the man knows how true to measure a foot he can not go wrong. Mine is No. 2, measured by a shoe maker; wish I had the money to send for them but I have not been paid Peter's wages for some time now. Provisions have gone down now a little, corn $8 at the Association, flour 60^cts, sugar $6.00, wish I had money to get some of the latter as I wish to preserve some strawberries; we are getting a good many of them only wish you and Fred were here to enjoy them. We have not heard from Fred for a long time now and feel very uneasy, he was not feeling well when he last wrote, I do wish he would write, he always writes so we can't help feeling uneasy, however we may be mistaken. The corn will be out very soon, in two weeks time, to my great sorrow, for if the corn was $1.00, we could not buy it without money, and the wages from the servants are used every week to pay for what we get at the Association, if you could only get some more corn, there would be nothing to worry about for we are getting on better now in the way of milk & butter, and I am making beautiful butter.

My chickens are getting on finely, having only lost two, have <u>40</u> with two turkeys & keep them out in the woods. Guinea hens are laying too, set some of their eggs today: no turkeys hatched yet; have about 74 eggs, turkeys, duck & guinea & hen setting. I am trying my very best without every thing, if I fail 'twill not be that I have neither prayed or tried. I have just succeeded at last in making beautiful soap and am very proud of it. I will write soon again.

Your affect sister
Anne DeSaussure.

Rev. Charles Edward Leverett to his son Milton

Columbia, May 23, 1864

My dear Minny,

I hope you received your Mother's letter & my small package of letter paper & envelopes. I am sorry that you have not Ste Elliott as the presence of a friend or acquaintance, would greatly relieve the tedium of your very monotonous life. You are in a very important station and as it came to you without seeking, I hope you may be able to make it instrumental to some good end. It must be tiresome, but will probably become less so the longer you stay. I would try to get the good opinion of the Captain and others, which if you secure, you can perhaps at no very remote day, use for advancement. I would look at the position as a step to that, and if I were in your place, I should try hard in every honorable way to obtain my end. Patience is generally rewarded and I will hope you will have that. Accomplish yourself in your humble department. Nearly all distinguished men have risen from humble beginnings, and you at least [are] in the way for rising which you were not in the Artillery. As for being homesick, I have known in my time what that was, but like every thing else that has its end. When you write let us know what you have to do, & how you are getting on. I would, if it were possible, change with you to beat back the villainous enemies of our country; & I would do it to get away from the enormous pressure every now & then upon my mind. This constant worry about providing the wherewithal to eat, drink & to be clothed, is a weight enough to drive a man distracted.

I have not succeeded yet in selling your watch. I have put it in the hands of an auctioneer, but whether it is because money is scarce or not, I don't know. I hope Billy got down safely with the colt, which promises to be a fine & handsome animal. Billy had better be sent up here to be hired out, but it will not do to tell him so, as he may choose not to be found at the time of departure. You ask about corn. We shall be out soon, & if you can't aid us, I don't know what upon earth to do,—except pray. Do see if you can get any transferred. The money, Mr. Pringle writes is ready to be paid over, or rather will be as soon as the new currency is out, which we daily look for. Let me know to whom I shall direct Mr. Pringle to send & what is the amount. The order on Confed. St. for $160, destroy as I will get Mr. P. to collect it & <u>let me know</u> if you have done so. I heard nothing and did not expect to hear anything from that man, Fred wrote about. Do write & see about the corn at once & say the money for any bought is only waiting for the new issue, as the factor writes. Let me hear from you as soon as possible.

Poor Jenkins' (the General) body was brought here, but it simply was detained a day & was not taken out of the outer box. I went up to the arsenal to see the remains of the gallant fellow, but was disappointed. What a dreadful blow to his family. His mother died a month or so ago.[4] He was there to see her.

The accounts of the Virginia battles are very confused.[5] I hope we shall be able to beat the Yankee wretches, but they are going to struggle hard & to beat them I fear will be like drawing sound teeth. But they must come out, even if we break the whole jaw. Our cause is good, & for me I will lift up mine eyes to the hills from whence cometh my help.[6]

Anne did not send any measure for herself or Lou.

As everything is uncertain I hope you, my dear son, will ever keep in mind that Almighty One. At all times, we should do, but especially at such a time as this, should men have their hopes centered in Christ. But how very few have this trust. Let it not be so with you. Be always ready to die & then you are always to live. I pray God to take care of you, & bless you for Jesus' sake.

yr. aff father
C. E. L.

Milton Maxcy Leverett to his mother

Fort Sumter May 24th 1864

My dear mother,

I received your very very welcome letter last Sunday night and was delighted to see it. I was in bed, being sick at the time and was quite dull therefore was very glad to see it. When letters come to me from home they seem to me just like familiar companions talking to me and you may believe I always read them quite eagerly especially now when I am so dull and lonely. Don't be frightened about my sickness for I am out and well again attending to my duties. It was an attack somewhat like my last summer's bout only on not so extensive a scale but I suf-

---

4. Elizabeth Clark, widow of John Jenkins.
5. The battles of the Wilderness, 5–6 May, and Spotsylvania, 8–20 May.
6. Ps. 121:1.

fered exceedingly for about eight or nine hours way down in my dark cave out of reach of anyone, I groaned and groaned and called for the sentinel posted at the entrance to my vault but he either was sleep or wouldn't hear, and there being no other person within possible hearing distance I had to grin and groan and bear. It was congestion of the bowels with a touch of fever, anyhow fever I know was inside. I stood this until ten or eleven next morning when the boy whom I had been hiring to wait on me came in, when I sent him for the doctor—a Dr Geiger[7]—from near Columbia who gave me some blue pill, and a mustard plaster to put on my stomach, and some quinine pills to take every three or four hours. Next morning or so I got over it but was pretty weak afterwards. I had been over a hundred hours without seeing any more day light than I could by taking a peep up the length of my bombproof from my bed now and then at what little chanced to come through my door at the end and other crevices. I believe it was nothing but the fare, the "blues" and the complete change in my system of life that made me sick. I get plenty enough to eat but it is so distasteful to me that I don't eat except when I have to. No fresh meat but plenty of bacon, loaf bread, but I would much rather have wheat flour and make fried bread of it, unless I had butter and then it would do but loafbread is very little better than shavings as brother used to say, hard tack, these hard biscuits which have always been to my mind and to my experience the most indigestible kind of food, and rice the best article of food in the whole world for the soldier scarcely any only a little now and then—all that is to save water I suppose which they get up the river somewhere near Wappoo Cut and bring it in a steamboat here when they need it, you get enough of that for drinking purposes but not enough for washing—you get your washing done in the city and have it sent down to you by the row boats which come every night. I have not arranged about mine as yet, don't know exactly how to, fortunately I have a pretty good supply of clean clothes on hand—molasses, you can take a couple of gills in place of your bacon ration every day if you wish, I generally alternate coffee, they have just commenced giving us a little, but no sugar consequently it is not very interesting—salt, a wee bit now & then—soap a bit or so now and then. I am messing by myself and one of the hands through the kindness of Captain Johnson cooks for me and attended to me when I was sick. When I first came I used to eat my hard tack and raw bacon just so. I am compelled to have Billy here, my life for the last week has satisfied me on that score, besides he will run much less risk than I do, comparatively none unless he gets sick and their are liabilities in every phase of life and I will let him have a furlough now and then when I think he needs it, and above all things I want a frying pan and a pot. I haven't a cooking utensil, except an oven in camp, which Billy is to bring. Have you any such

---

7.   Assistant Surgeon Franklin J. Geiger of South Carolina, on duty at Fort Sumter.

things to spare. If you ever send me anything by Express direct it care of Lieut. Swinton Transportation Agent, Ft. Sumter.[8] Billy is in camp, arrived I believe the Sunday after he started. A basket won't do to send down here, a box nailed strong is the only thing, the soldiers steal too freely. Nenny Fuller was coming to Charleston the first of next month and promised to come over and see me. I expect Billy and other fixings I have left behind to come with him.

My dear mother, I have just reread your letter preparing to answering the <u>pros</u> and <u>cons</u> and can't help feeling pleased, <u>sadly pleased</u> I may say to see how little satisfies you, just my being in Fort Sumter—a non-commissioned officer. I do really wish it was more than that if it were only for Pa's and your sakes. I had told Hal Stuart before I left to keep open my place in the company for a couple of weeks or so, so that in case I did not like my situation here I could resign and go back, but since I find how little pleases you and know how little I have ever done to please either Pa or yourself I won't leave again and promise you D. V. and if the war lasts any length of time to get a commission or it shan't be my fault. Don't mention Port Royal to me.[9] I always feel chagrined at not having obtained what I considered my right and bounden meed of distinction there. I must say that I always entertain a sort of lurking feeling of being wronged. The flag was shot off with a shell I was the first man on the parapet had raised it and was proceeding to tie it on the staff (Big Rob. Fuller had sprung up <u>after</u> me and was by my side) when some men in the fort halloed to me to let it alone, that it was that that was drawing the enemy's fire so accurately on us, then Rob. jumped down and returned to his gun and I left the flag alone in a sort of undefined feeling that Kaimes himself couldn't analyze.[10] After the battle my friends all congratulated me on having distinguished myself. Nenny came up and congratulated me on the name I had won for myself, and so did long Ralph, for "being one of the bravest little men he ever saw" and men throughout the company generally threw out hints, innuendoes and congratulations and all—my dear Mother—after all, my dear mother's hopes (for I thought of you and all the rest at the time) have turned like Dead Sea apples to ashes on my lips. Since then I have learned that glory is not to be won by a private; there have been too many flag protectors since then, many and more worthy than myself, and what have the poor fellows got, nothing more perhaps than that their bodies should be left rotting on the ground or that they themselves should be forgotten entirely after the first casual notice in the papers. I grieved that poor brother's words didn't turn out as accurate as he wished, and I am only glad that he never knew of the disappointment.

---

8. First Lt. Thomas L. Swinton of Company B, Twenty-third South Carolina Infantry, on detached duty at Fort Sumter.

9. The battle of Port Royal, 7 November 1861.

10. Henry Home, Lord Kames (1696–1782), Scottish philosopher, author of *Introduction to the Art of Thinking* (1781).

I wish that I could be on a furlough, I feel as if I could almost scream for joy if I could now be on the cars rushing home, breathing the free air of heaven and being in its pure sunshine.

I believe it is midday now or somewhere in the neighborhood about four or five perhaps and here I am writing by my lamp. I can easily conceive of prisoners being shut up in a dark cell and turning crazy or idiotic for want of light. It is a sort of longing hankering feeling.

I don't know to what attack of the Monitors you allude whether to the one that happened the day I was coming down or the one that has happened since this Monday or Tuesday I don't know which. I believe I had written to you before it came off, no I must have written the very day it came off. I was sitting here a portion of the time at my desk writing while it was going on and a portion of the time I was outside looking and listening. Everything and everybody gets as much out of the way almost as possible when the large fifteen in. shells come roaring in, fortunately our bombproof are excellent and Sullivan's Island dont let the Monitors have it entirely their own way or Fort Sumter might and would be in a much worse condition. I can scarcely say which we hate the most the Monitors with their big shells, the Parrott shell or the mortar shells. I am inclined to think the mortar are worst because they go almost straight up in the air and drop almost anywhere perhaps right in front of your door but they travel slowly and you have time to get out of the way, but the Monitors with their fifteen in. and the Parrott shells describe a sweeping parabola and you can get behind a wall or traverse when they come but at the same time they travel quite quick, the Parrott shell so quick indeed that the sentinel can scarcely cry "Look out" before the shell has come. I have got almost indifferent to them and generally am in more fear of the bricks than the shells. Not that I don't respect the shells but the danger from the bricks is generally more immediate and imminent perhaps. The Monitors got the worst of it that time, Sullivan's Island batteries were too much for them. Ripley had just mounted two heavy guns especially for them and one had her turret pilot house knocked off when she raised the white red and white pennant and left for Hilton Head, the other came up and took her place and soon raised the same pennant and also left.[11] All the batteries are giving us rest now. The barges came up two nights in succession, I believe trying to tap the wire between Sumter and Fort Johnson, the first time we fired on them with a howitzer which they impertinently returned with their boat howitzers, the next night they came up a portion of the way then went back, both nights. I was sick but the second I got up although quite weak determining to get a musket and go on a parapet and repel them with the rest, my

---

11.   On 16 May the U.S.S. *Nahant* opened fire on the fort with another Federal monitor and were answered by Confederate batteries on Sullivan's Island. After an hour the pilothouse of the *Nahant* was badly damaged and both monitors withdrew.

ordnance duties were being then performed by the ordnance sergeant but as the barges went back I returned to bed. When I know the officers better I'll describe them.

You never sent me measure for any of your shoes although I asked particularly, it may have slipped your memory though, send them by the next letter, I didn't send Cos. Cornelias because I am afraid in going by express they may get stolen and I had no other way. I left them with Fickling who will send them by the first opportunity, he will have more of them than I will.

Your ever affectionate son
Milton M. Leverett

Mary Bull Leverett to her brother Milton

Columbia May 30<u>th</u> 1864

My dear Minnie

I am so sorry you are so uncomfortably situated, nevermind, I <u>know</u> all will turn out for the best. I wouldn't like you to leave for it would look as if you were afraid, & <u>we know</u> that is not so. I think men in these days think too much of their own honour & preferment instead of God's & their country's, if they could only think less of the former two & more of the latter two things would have turned out much better for us, & them, & when they perform a <u>good</u> & a <u>brave</u> action, instead of looking to the world for praise & reward, they ought to remember that God sees & knows it and although the <u>world</u> forgets them, <u>He</u> does not. This doesn't mean that I wouldn't like you to be honored & prefered above all others for <u>nothing could delight & please me</u> <u>more</u>, but I wish you try & be contented wherever God places you. Heigh-ho! here I am trying to persuade my dearest brother to be contented, when, to my shame be it spoken, I am the most discontented person in the world, however Minny, let us try together, & pray to God to bless our endeavours. I am sorry I express my thoughts—feelings & wishes so clumsily. I went to Mrs. Pringle's[12] last week to get her to help me cut out my dress, the rain caught & kept me there nearly two days, & then I went to Aunt Til's & it kept me another two days, altogether, I spent a very pleasant time. I cannot help loving Mrs. Pringle she is so good, & she seems to have taken a fancy for me, why, I cannot imagine, & shows her affection by giving me all sorts of religious books to read, which I am sorry to say, have not done me one bit of good.

Tillie Fowles has come down & looks very pretty with her short curly hair, she plays & sings very sweetly, all of them sing together & you have no idea how very

---

12. Jane Edwards Ford Pringle.

pleasant it is to hear them. After tea we went into the drawing-room, & when they had finished singing plenty of songs of which they know any number, Johnny Elliott, who was spending the night at Aunt Til's, had gone out to pay a visit; we commenced dancing. Jim & Ste figured together in a Polka, of course it was very hard for the poor fellow to dance with one arm, but you cannot imagine what strength he has in that arm, after & while twirling Ste about, he suddenly gave him a little kick & catching him by the seat of his pantaloons—danced him all around the room backwards & forwards, Ste pawing the floor meanwhile, he landed him on the sofa, if you could only have seen that child's face as he raised himself in an upright position, such an insulted & indignant look I have not seen for a long time, it was long before we could stop laughing. Mr. Elliott says Rosa Stuart[13] has grown perfectly lovely, that living in Flat Rock has done them all good. Dr. DeSaussure is practising medicine in Camden, Annie has not heard from him for a long time. I dare say he did not like her selling those negroes.

Yankee prisoners & our wounded have been arriving every day, we were at the depot on Friday to meet our wounded, ever so many ladies were there, plenty ladened with good things for them, carts, carriages, wagons were there to carry them to the Hospitals, the Wayside Home, a splendid supper was waiting for them at the latter place. The fine fellows were in the highest spirits, one that we were talking to, said he had not been wounded until after six days fighting, there were only 30 in the Company & 18 had been wounded, one died. He said (pointing to the cars the tops of which were covered with the prisonners thick as black birds) the ground was covered just as thick as that with Yankees, you could not walk without walking on them. It was so, Col. Wallace writing to Mrs. W. says the ground is strewn with <u>tens</u> of thousands dead & wounded Yankees, & he is not a man to exaggerate.[14] Only those that are slightly wounded have come on. We have really cause to be thankful our army has been so signally blessed.

There is a good joke against Mr. J. Elliott & the people of Anderson; it seems to be the custom there to send egg rubbed up with sugar to the minister either between or after the services.[15] Mr. Pringle said he could not imagine what was meant when a lady up there asked him if he would have an egg he found out afterwards.[16] It seems that some lady made some custard & told the servant he was to put it into Mr. Elliott's own hands. Well, the servant carries it to Mr. E.'s house, they told him he was at church, what does the goose do, but carry it <u>there</u> & was proceeding up the <u>aisle</u>, when, I believe someone stopped him, this is the least

13.   Rosa Stuart (1843–1926), daughter of Henry Middleton Stuart Sr.
14.   Col. William Wallace of the Second South Carolina Infantry and his wife, Victoria C. McLemore of Columbia.
15.   Rev. John Habersham Elliott of Grace Episcopal Church, Anderson.
16.   Rev James Maxwell Pringle.

exaggerated of all the stories, & I suppose it must have some foundation. I wanted to ask him so badly if there was any truth in it & laugh at him a little. It is enough to turn his head, the ladies make so much of him, so stupid in them. I am afraid I won't have room enough to tell you about the Fete. The ladies gave it to get up money for the Hospitals. They made over $17000. We helped a great deal, not only in making all sorts of things, eatables &c. but I almost knocked up myself selling things. Haven't you received 4 foolscap pages from Julie telling you of the large saucer of ice cream she got "only for a dollar." I wish so much you could have been there you would have enjoyed it so much; as soon as peaches are ripe they will have another & you must try & come up to it. I made a homespun baby & dressed it up in uniform, cut off some of the hair off that deer hide, you sent up & made a long moustache & beard, & Papa drew one of his very handsome faces on it, I made also an Artillery cap with plumes in it, printed on the haversack, One of Hampton's Cavalry (at which one of the girls who had a brother in it was quite indignant) & really it was a most <u>natural</u>, outrageously ugly & ridiculous looking object, ones risibles were excited every time they looked at it. It attracted crowds, some laughed so I thought they would have fallen down, all of them agreed in saying it was the image of an Adjutant Ball who was walking about the ground.

Eliza Coffin is in the Treasury Department, Bet Barnwell is trying to get in but has not succeeded yet, plenty of others that we know are in it also.[17] I expect we will send a box to you tomorrow, I am going directly to try & make some cake for you. I am so glad things are going down, I mean prices, we will be able to send things oftener to you.

Your affectionate sister
Mary Leverett

Frederic Percival Leverett to his sister Mary

Camp near Gaines Mill, Va.
3<u>rd</u> June, 1864

My dear Mary,

Yours are the oldest letters unanswered. You must take this, tho' it will be a short one as an answer to both of your long ones. I was glad to hear you all had been enjoying yourself so much in Columbia, while we had been having such hard times here. Today is the thirtieth day we have been fighting. The So. Ca. braves have suffered heavily. Many of the bright young men who were so recently engaged in the festivities in Columbia are now tossing with wounds in the Hos-

---

17.   Elizabeth Barnwell (1837–1916), daughter of Rev. William Hazzard Wigg Barnwell.

pitals of Va. Many a one is in the hands of the hated enemy, and many a one is lying under the cold sod occupying the soldier's grave. The Charleston L. Dragoons have been in several engagements & much cut up.[18] The men have behaved well. They brought with them here two Lts. Nowell & O'Hear. Both were killed last Saturday.[19] Our Cavalry was thrown against an overwhelming force. They stood their ground until flanked right & left & then gave back leaving their killed & wounded in the hands of the enemy—also some of their men were taken prisoners. Among others was my old friend Josiah Bedon formerly Cap. of the old 11th.[20] I saw day before yesterday Boyle[21] a great friend of Bedon's. He told me he was believed to have been taken unwounded. He was quite lame from an old wound in the foot.[22] He told me Oliver Middleton also was missing, whether wounded or not was unknown. I trust for his mother's sake if nothing else he may prove uninjured.[23] There has, I fear, been some gross mismanagement of the new Cavalry Regs. from the result. I don't know with whom it lies. I suppose it is with their Brigadier. Day before yesterday Ralph Elliott was I fear mortally wounded—shot in the head. I sat by him yesterday evening for a long while & doing what I could to make him comfortable. He was perfectly unconscious & could not be aroused. I saw him again this morning & found him in the same condition. I wrote to Col. Barnwell yesterday to tell him of his condition & asked him to acquaint his friends with the facts. I went to see him as soon as I heard of his being wounded. He had been conscious prior to my seeing him. Some one told him of Ste's having been made Brigadier & they said a smile played over his face. Poor fellow. It is too sad for one to fall after having been in so many engagements. There were a great many around & passing in & out of the passage, where he lay, but I prayed for him as I leaned over him attending him.[24]

---

18.   Charleston Light Dragoons, Company K, Fourth South Carolina Cavalry.

19.   1st Lt. Lionel Chalmers Nowell and 2d Lt. James W. O'Hear of the Charleston Light Dragoons, Company K, Fourth South Carolina Cavalry; O'Hear, acting as regimental adjutant, was killed in a sharp action at Haw's (Hawe's) Shop, Virginia, on 28 May 1864, in which the regiment lost some eighty officers and men and the Charleston Light Dragoons lost twenty-one out of forty-seven officers and men. Nowell was not killed at Haw's Shop but was captured at Cold Harbor on 30 May; his wife, Anne Heyward Barnwell (b. 1838) died two months earlier.

20.   Pvt. Josiah Bedon of the Charleston Light Dragoons was the first captain of the Summerville Guards, Company C, Ninth (later Eleventh) South Carolina. He later served as a lieutenant in the Second South Carolina Battalion before enlisting as a private in the Charleston Light Dragoons.

21.   Pvt. W. A. Boyle of the Charleston Light Dragoons.

22.   Bedon, who was severely wounded at Seven Pines, Virginia, in 1862, was either killed or mortally wounded and captured at Haw's Shop.

23.   Pvt. Oliver Hering Middleton Jr. of the Charleston Light Dragoons was wounded at Cold Harbor on 30 May and died the next day.

24.   Capt. Ralph Emms Elliott of Company I, Second South Carolina Infantry, brother of Stephen Elliott Jr., was wounded at Cold Harbor 1 June 1864 and died five days later.

Ste Elliott's promotion has been very rapid & shows in what high estimation he must be held.[25] He will be compelled now to be dashing in the extreme & untiring in the discharge of his duties to sustain himself. Let him succeed therein & give satisfaction to his subordinates & he will if his life be spared be, before very long, what Jenkins so aspired to be Maj. Gen. I saw yesterday evening Col. Keitt's remains about being sent to Richmond.[26] He had been here two days—a short career in Va. The old 11th Reg. is not far from here in the trenches. All concur in saying it has behaved well since being out here & suffered much in the battles near Petersburg.[27] Our losses are nothing in comparison with those of the Yankees. Today there has been heavy fighting & we have slain the foe by hundreds. Everything is progressing well.

When you write, let your letters be in part of home. Much love to all. I am a little better.

Ever yr. most aff^{ct} brother
F. P. Leverett

P.S. 4th Saturday
Everything is progressing favorably. Yesterday the enemy suffered heavily.

Frederic Percival Leverett to his sister Julia

Camp Texas Brigd.
9th June 1864.

My dear Julia,

I have been writing home so often of late, that I suspect you all will get quite tired of hearing. One thing is certain since I've begun writing, all at home have ceased sending me letters in return. This may be due, however, to derangement in the mail. Nearly all the clerks in the Post Office in Richmond have been sent out into various military Companies. It is said that ladies have offered to take their places in the P. O. but the Post Master General thinks they do not or cannot understand the work & accordingly keeps the Country deprived in great measure of the Mail.[28]

---

25. Stephen Elliott Jr. was promoted to brigadier general 24 May 1864 to command Nathan G. Evans's old brigade in the Department of North Carolina and Southern Virginia, consisting of the Seventeenth, Eighteenth, Twenty-second, Twenty-third, and Twenty-sixth South Carolina Infantry regiments.

26. Col. Lawrence Massillon Keitt of the Twentieth South Carolina Infantry, whose regiment was transferred from the Department of South Carolina, Georgia, and Florida to Kershaw's Brigade in the Army of Northern Virginia, took command of the brigade on 30 May 1864; he was wounded at Cold Harbor 1 June and died the next day.

27. The battles of Port Walthall Junction, 6–7 May; Swift Creek, 10 May; and Drewry's Bluff, 16 May.

28. Postmaster general of the Confederate States, John H. Reagan of Texas.

We are lying here quietly awaiting the movements, we suppose of Gen. Grant. He has so far virtually accomplished nothing, but has sent most unblushingly false telegrams to his government. He has done that to effect the Baltimore Convention.[29] Our troops, notwithstanding their many hardships, are in fine condition & spirits. All are anxious for Grant to advance & give them another opportunity to butcher his myrmidons. The men have been better fed since being about Richmond. We have Bacon & Corn Meal & salt, occasionally flour; sometimes Coffee & Sugar & once to our Brgd. Onions. I am sorry to say, however, that on this diet I cannot fatten but am still very thin—I long for the fights about here to be over as then I would leave the army & recruit. At present, I feel that it is incumbent on every one to be at his Post, if possible. This afternoon I went to sleep & dreamed I was at home. Pa was about the first person I saw & I had hardly sat down before he told me one of the negroes was sick, & that <u>he</u> had prescribed two or three doses of Calomel. I was so much surprised that I woke up at once— much to my chagrin.

Goodbye. With much love to each and all.

Ever yr. afft. brother
F. P. Leverett

Milton Maxcy Leverett to his father

Fort Sumter June 11<u>th</u> /64

My dear Father,

I received your letter a week or two ago and was quite gratified at receiving it, it had been such a long time since I had received a letter from you, a couple of years or so, for I don't call your little notes letters. I am quite pleased with your gratification at my being here but think and indeed know that you lay more stress on it than it deserves. It is indeed a very humble position that I occupy and nothing but a consciousness that I was acting right and that I was in a really right path for preferment would have caused me to have taken or to keep in such a position. It is true to a certain extent that the man honours the place and not the place the man for I have already raised the dignity of my position much higher than the former incumbent had it. I associate with all the officers and gentlemen and mess now with nothing but the regular army officers. There are two messes of standing in the fort, one of them Mitchel's[30] composed of, besides himself, several other

---

29. The National Union Convention of 1864 was held in Baltimore 7–8 June and unanimously nominated Lincoln for a second term.

30. Capt. John C. Mitchel Jr. of the First South Carolina Artillery succeeded Stephen Elliott Jr. as commander of Fort Sumter.

officers and some of the Signal Corps Men while the other is composed of different officers, principally from the two regular regiments, who are sent over here
on detached duty relieving one another every fifteen or thirty days. This is called
the Artillery Mess and is the one I am in.[31] I consequently will see any quantity of
officers and expect to know all round about here on the islands if I stay here any
length of time. There used to be a week ago but one mess but it was so large it
was divided in two. Stuart Rhett is here on duty now and is in our mess, it was
through him in a great measure that I got in this mess. Henry Stuart was here just
before him, before the original mess was divided.[32] All of my friends seem to think
I took a wrong or rather an unnecessary step, in taking an isolated position as it
were among strangers, and one perhaps not exactly in accordance with my position as a gentleman. I am sorry to see the Senate vetoed the President's recommendation for an increase of Ordnance Officers. I don't know when I will get out
of this then but hope it will all turn out right yet. I wish that I had an arithmetic
here to do some studying. You ask what do I have to do; I have a great deal to do,
more than two thirds of the Commissioned Ordnance Officers. I have eight magazines & closets of different sizes to attend to between five and six thousand lbs
of cannon powder, between twenty and thirty thousand rounds of small arm car-
tridges besides shell shot hand grenades, fuses, friction tubes caps muskets, rock-
ets, blue lights, some dozen pieces of artillery their equipments, accoutrements,
besides even buckets, brooms, lanterns, things wise and otherwise and what not
I can't tell you to keep account of, make out a monthly Return of things
Expended, Received and Remaining on hand, besides a Quarterly Return also of
the same, overlooking Invoices, receiving Orders, signing receipts and last but not
least always being on hand on the wharf at night no matter what hour to receive
anything that may come for the Dep't. You see I have more to do than a commissioned Ordnance Officer because he has his clerk or Ordnance Sergeant to do
just what I am doing and only has the signing of his name to put to Returns Requisitions &c &c. I collected the $150 in the new issue the other day to pay Will-
cox for the corn. I went to the city and saw Mr. Pringle. I send off a letter tonight
to Willcox to see if he can let me have any more corn. I wish you could succeed
in selling my watch and sending me some of the money as I am in great need of
it now. I am almost totally out of shoes and don't see any chance of getting any
immediately as there is none in the Quartermaster Dep't. My expenses are much
higher here than they were; my washing has to be done in Charleston as we don't
have water enough here and that I am afraid will cost me a sweet sum. Clothing

31. Milton added this note after the war: "The Signal Corps men were in my mess also. M. L.
     Dec 20/99."
32. Henry Middleton Stuart (1841–1865).

costs more. I am almost out of pants, I drew one the other day and just to have it cut down to my size and made up will cost me twenty-two dollars and then it won't be done unless I pay cash. My pay isn't more than twenty-five and of that I owe two months already. Take it all in all I am about bankrupt almost ready to "go up the spout." I direct soldier's letter as I have no stamps having used my only one to write to Willcox about corn and couldn't get any in town. Will write to the girls when I get some but that must not keep them from writing to me. Have you heard from Fred yet and how is he?

Love to Ma and all the rest.

Your aff'^{ct} son
Milton M. Leverett

Robert Barnwell Fuller to Milton Maxcy Leverett

McPhersonville June 16th [1864]

Dear Minnie

Nat has gone off on a scout leaving several jobs unattended to that I will take in hand for him. Amongst others the disposition to be made of your boy Billy. I was under the impression that he had gone down to you ever since last Wednesday 8th inst when to my surprise he presented himself a few days ago saying he was to have gone that morning but that the cars left him. Not knowing how soon Nat would be back nor what understanding there was between yourself & him I have waited for him until now to attend to it but he is still away and as you must miss the service of a servant in your grim old hole I will wait no longer but write to know what must be done about him. If you wish him sent to you—I think it would be advisable to appoint a day far enough ahead to avoid all possibilities of disappointment by reason of your letter miscarrying or Billy being out of the way—say three days after you mail your letter or telegraph.

I see by the papers that a Bill has passed both houses of Congress to increase the number of Ordnance Officers. I suppose the method will be the same as that adopted Spring before the last by examination. Why don't you avail yourself of the chance. I suppose you must have plenty of time for study where you are and your position would give you an advantage in experience in the practical details of an Ordnance Office. Your knowledge of the value of x and the extraction of a square root could be easily brushed up and you might get letters of recommendation from both Hal & Mitchell if you found any difficulty about the moral character part— I would stretch a point and give you one myself, provided I don't hear that the temptations of Fort Sumter were too much for you.

Our encampment here is on a magnificent scale comprising I don't know how many square miles. Communication is kept up between the sentinels and the main body of the encampment by signal stations, so also between the captain's log palace and his bureau Offices. The encampment is most picturesque and the battery going to the dogs.

We have just heard of the death of Ralph Elliott in Virginia. He must have been killed on the 3rd. He had passed through so many dangers that I had hoped he would be one of the very few of the original Army of Va. to survive the War. But it was ordered otherwise—and so we go—the best and the noblest filling with their life blood the measure of their Country's sacrifice.—There is no local news at all except that our men have to do outpost duty—filling six picket posts for forty-eight hours when they are relieved by Bachman.[33]—Nat has been away ever since last Saturday and I am a little uneasy about him. He went to Port Royal with Woodie Barnwell.[34]

Believe me dear Minnie

yrs very truly
R. B. Fuller

Fred wrote a tribute to his friend Micah Jenkins, which was published in the Columbia Daily South Carolinian *on 18 June 1864. He saw Jenkins on the morning of 6 May, "his face not beaming with smiles, as it usually did on such occasions, but it wore a sad and* determined *expression . . . Poor fellow! When I next saw him he was lying in his tent unconscious, with a ball buried in his brain." Fred commented on Jenkins's death: "His old brigade thinks their loss irreparable, and it is indeed so. In him the country has lost a firm and gallant officer, a noble soldier, whose courage and dash in action won the admiration of all. Our State has lost a polished and elegant gentleman and a high-toned Christian. . . . May God in his mercy sustain his widow and fatherless boys, to whom he was most devotedly attached. I hope his sons may prove worthy of their sire."*

Mary Maxcy Leverett to her son Milton

(Exiles Retreat)[35] Columbia
June 20th 1864

My dearest Son

I have waited in vain to hear of the receipt of the box I took so much pleasure in packing for you with my own hands, a box which was a veritable Noah's Ark for

---

33. Capt. William K. Bachman's German Light Artillery, an independent South Carolina artillery battery that served with the Army of Northern Virginia before being transferred to the Department of South Carolina, Georgia, and Florida in 1863.

34. Pvt. Woodward Barnwell (1838–1927), an independent scout in the Third Military District in the Department of South Carolina, Georgia, and Florida; son of Eliza Zubly Smith and Capt. Edward Barnwell (1785–1860).

35. The Farm.

the multiplicity, if not value, of the things therein deposited, not counting a letter & note from your respected Mamma, and a curiosity of a note and package from his ingenious sister Caroline, and paper enough from both for him to indite his answer acknowledging the contents of said box. It must have been lost in that unlucky steamer which the Yankees (how I <u>bless</u> them!) shelled to death, and whose fate you never even mentioned, nor did the paper say if it was going to, or coming from Sumter. I know your hands must be full, judging by the last letter to your father, who was <u>quite</u> <u>encouraged</u> to find how much you had to do, especially in the business line of writing, receipting &c &c. It always gratifies him to hear that his sons have a plenty to do, and he says it will make a business man of you. I was also surprised, not having an idea before of what the duties really were, except that it was some powder & shot concern, and rather pleased than otherwise to find you had a great deal to do in the way of writing. It will improve your hand, and that is much, for if the mechanical part of a letter is easy to a person they are apt to improve in their endeavours to express their ideas, without too frequent a repetition of the same words. For instance, instead of saying "You asked what do I have to do," you will say "You asked what my duties are," which expressed the same meaning but in a better form or shape.—Now, darling, I see plainly by your enumeration of the variety and number of offices you have to perform, that your hands must be full, and you must have but little time to yourself, therefore, it will be excusable, and indeed commendable in you to write to me and any of the family on <u>Sundays</u>; an act which I have always discouraged and forbidden hitherto either to myself or my children, as unsuitable and wrong, believing that holy day ought to be employed solely in acts of devotion, reading the Bible & other good books, & reflection, but the exigencies of the times demands a relaxation of these rules, so that writing to a Parent, may now be deemed as an act of piety & necessity, inasmuch, as man was not made for the Sabbath, but the Sabbath for man, and both for God and we are serving him in it in performing the duties according to His Commandment in loving & honouring our Parents in times so awful and uncertain that no Mother and Son now writing to each other ever can know whether another letter will ever pass between them. I am glad you are in Sumter; comparatively safe, instead of Virginia being slaughtered as they have done the poor Charleston Light Dragoons. Poor fellows, only a short time ago they were in Columbia at parties, balls &c. and now numbers of them are in the cold earth. I hear that Gen. Hampton reprimanded Gen. M. C. Butler severely for it.[36] It seems the reputation the Dragoons had of leading too easy a life, & being too much of gentlemen soldiers, did them a harm. They were sneered at & laughed at, and Gen. Butler (<u>upcountry man</u>) who, it appears had command over them treated them shamefully

---

36. Brig. Gen. Matthew Calbraith Butler commanded a South Carolina brigade in Hampton's Division, Cavalry Corps, Army of Northern Virginia.

cursing & swearing at them, calling them "silk stockings" & other names & it is thought he purposely to give them a taste of war, and make them see what the soldiers in Virg. have had to undergo, ordered them to charge an overwhelming number (a <u>Division</u>, it is said) of the enemy when any prudent Commander would have known it could only result in immense slaughter & no good. Other troops who went in with them having experience soon they saw the immense odds, immediately retreated, but these poor men knew no better, heard no orders to retreat & were ashamed to fall back as they had been so sneered at & spoken of as if they were cowards, so they held their ground, until surrounded, and the consequence is they were fearfully slaughtered. Many are missing, to the agony of their relatives, among them poor Oliver Middleton, whose parents are suffering acutely. This morning we hear a report that he is a prisoner, the family would be only too thankful if he is, they are so fearful of hearing he is dead. Poor Mrs. Middleton had such a nervous attack lately, from distress, that the Doctor had to be sent for in the night, & poor Mr. Middleton seems as if scarce able to refrain from tears. After the battle only fifteen men answered the roll, Col. Rutledge in the next letter said thirty were left, & his wife[37] has not heard since but believes him to be with Hampton somewhere, always on the move. Many of them are suffering from sickness, from change of diet, water &c. the Col. himself is sick all the while, tho' still in the saddle.—What a shocking murder is that of poor Mr. Andrew Johnstone, & how bravely his fifteen year old son acted![38] Mr. Seabrook & Margaret[39] were living next door, that is, they were the nearest neighbors, & he wrote an account of it for the Carolinian.[40] I can't think how any one can wish to live in such an unpatriotic community—Mary Seabrook[41] writes Mary that four letters were sent to them by different [people] to inform them that Capt. Tom Pinckney was "dead" or mortally wounded &c. and behold they have just had a letter from himself "<u>a prisoner</u>, but very well."[42] It was a great relief. His mother has been very ill, but is better.

---

37.   Col. Benjamin Huger Rutledge; his wife, Eleanor Maria Middleton, was a sister of Oliver Hering Middleton Jr.

38.   Andrew Johnstone was murdered at Beaumont, his Flat Rock, North Carolina plantation on 10 June 1864. Six men claiming to be Confederate soldiers entered Beaumont when the Johnstone family was at the dinner table and demanded money and valuables. When the leader of the group shot Andrew Johnstone in the chest, mortally wounding him, Johnstone's young son William Elliott killed two of the group and wounded a third.

39.   Margaret Hamilton Seabrook.

40.   Archibald Hamilton Seabrook's account, "The Murder of Andrew Johnstone, Esq.," appeared in the *Columbia Daily South Carolinian* on 18 June 1864. "This war has developed untold evils; but no deed, I think, more atrocious than the one I am about to relate." Seabrook concluded, "Farewell, my noble, generous friend!"

41.   Mary E. Seabrook, daughter of Caroline Pinckney and Archibald Hamilton Seabrook.

42.   Capt. Thomas Pinckney, commander of Company D, Fourth South Carolina Cavalry, brother of Caroline Pinckney Seabrook, was captured in May at Haw's Shop, Virginia, and exchanged in December.

I am so glad you are in the officers mess, and think it a very good omen for you. It quite relieves my feelings, so much did I sympathise with your lonely, unwholesome, disconsolate, solitary meals. Is there any way of helping you in your new mess by sending things? but if that box is lost, I fear the whole family will oppose sending another "only to be lost or stolen." I had it tightly nailed, & Mary wrote to you the day before to inform you of its coming. I got your father to write as soon as your letter to him came and begged him to send you a check on Mr. Pringle, which he agreed to without demur, surely you have received that, & I hope it will help you out. Do you know that even the Middletons frequently (generally I expect) go without meat. Matilda[43] told Tillie so. We ourselves are half the time without it, but we have a plenty of Irish potatoes, & they really seem to make up for it. We had cucumbers today for the first time. The oats & wheat look beautiful, we are to commence reaping sometime this week. Annie went to Mr. Geigers & bought 200 of blades for $24 last week, & oats will soon help out the horses; Dora has improved, Fred's Fanny looks badly, but he told us himself to plough her, so she ploughs whenever poor Bullet takes a fit of the sulks. Nobody would recognize the latter animal, she is such a shadow, except that she still has good spirits. Corn is now $25 a bushel,—the stocking workers just make enough for allowance money, & tho' Sue's wages are now $30 a month (Mrs. Keating is still quite pleased with her) yet the heavy prices seem to swallow up every thing. Were it not for the cows & garden, we really would not be much short of starving, but as it is I believe we are doing better than most people. Annie even gave us a Chicken pie, the other day, chicken of her own raising, tho according to present prices the cost of the pie would have been $15! if we had bought the chickens. I hope you went to Town about your shoes & clothes as soon as you received the check. Do you want any shirts or any of your things, sent you? You haven't said anything about Billy, surely you have him to wait on you? Your father is trying Mordecai now in selling your watch, as Lance did not succeed. As soon as any more money is paid in I will send you money to pay Fickling for the shoes, which I wish he would hurry up, as I want to take Carrie to church very much.

Miss Trenholm is to be married to Capt. Hazzard this week.[44] Jim, Mary & Tillie are invited to the Reception the night after from "9 to 12 o'clock at night" the card said. It is to be a great affair, everything from Nassau. Old Mr. Trescot stays at your Aunt Tils, as well as Mary Heyward. The old gentleman walked out to see us the other day.

Poor Ralph Elliott came to before he died, so as to recognize persons & send messages. Rev John Elliott passed thro' Columbia lately he asked Mame whom he

---

43. Susan Matilda Middleton.
44. Emily St. Pierre Trenholm and Capt. William Miles Hazzard were married at DeGreffin plantation near Columbia 21 June 1864.

met at your Aunt Tils, to say to Fred how deeply grateful he felt to him for his kindness to Ralph.[45]

God bless & protect my beloved son, prays his aff^{et} Mother

Mary

Fred was admitted to General Hospital No. 9 (Wayside Hospital) in Richmond on 14 June suffering from chronic diarrhea and emaciation.

Caroline Pinckney Leverett to her brother Milton

Columbia
20 June 1864

Dear Brother

I hope you got the box which Mama sent you. I sent some of my trash in it to you, and five sheets of writing paper. Jezebel is equal to her name. She has cleared the house of rats but the other kitten is two bad for it kiled two of Sister Annes chickens and my pet chicken.

yr. aff^{ct} Caroline

Milton Maxcy Leverett to his sister Anne Leverett DeSaussure

Fort Sumter June 21st 1864

My dear Anne,

I suppose you are tired waiting for an answer by now. I have several others to answer but as yours is the longest unanswered that comes next. Tell Julie I thought I owed her one before anybody else but on looking over all my letters I can't see any of hers that I have not answered, consequently she had better hurry up and write if she wants a letter. Mary and Sister and Pa also Carrie and Ma come next. I didn't get my box until some eight or ten days, I expect after it was sent, and all the vegetables, the milk, the eggs and the plate of biscuits were ruined, the cake was good and the butter kept admirably, the salt or the rag over it seemed to give it character of being hermetically sealed, for it is very nice, the potatoes were perfectly good. I am very glad Ma's garden is doing so well. I am very much obliged for everything and am sorry they didn't arrive sooner but I take the blame upon myself as I ought to have told you to direct care of Maj. M. A. Pringle Q. M.[46] but I didn't know it in time

---

45. Rev. John Habersham Elliott and his brother Ralph Emms Elliott.
46. Maj. Jacob Motte Alston Pringle (1827–1886), post quartermaster at Charleston in the Department of South Carolina, Georgia, and Florida.

myself how things were to be arranged. Some of you ought to let me know positively when I was to look for it. Mame's letter only said they expected to send on the next day. But notwithstanding from that time I always inquired for it, but it wasn't until I received Sis' letter saying Ma had sent it that I was certain it had been sent and took steps to look it up and got Stuart Rhett to call at the Express Office when he went to Charleston where he found it. It was all my fault. I am much obliged for the sundries, some of which were just what I wanted—the cake Stuart Rhett and myself eat. Tell Carrie I am very much obliged for her little package and will write to her. You said truly I must fight it out as well as scratch it out, the latter is especially the most prominent feature of Fort Sumter, the fleas are dreadful all over the whole fort, even as I write they are <u>crawling</u> up me. I have just a few minutes ago caught one off my hand as I was writing that must have crawled up from the floor, they almost run me crazy, I don't exaggerate a bit when I say they are dreadful. I will be able in all probability to show any <u>quantity of scars after this war</u>. Fleas are the only type I have seen of that insect tribe. Tell Lou <u>I kratch werry much</u>. Your soap is beautiful, ten per cent better than what we draw here, it washes delightfully and only needs a little firmness. The soap we draw here has too much rosin in it.

Our flag was shot down yesterday, afterward put up by a Lieut. Clayburne, a Marylander and another man,[47] the enemy meanwhile blazing away at them, I happened to be trying to sleep in my room on my bed at that time or might have tried the same game. It is a miracle they were not shot down. He had been a private in the 1st S.C. Infantry and had been promoted to a Lieutenancy from the ranks for gallantry. There is here or in Savannah a Lieut. Markoe on the Signal Corps, who is he?[48] We heard a report yesterday that Ste Elliott had been killed by a cannon ball, but hope it is a mistake. Think poor Ralph's death must have caused a mistake. I will go to town to night to see if I can't draw some money from Mr. Pringle. I am very sorry to do it but I am dreadfully in want of shoes although the Government owes me two pair—but they have none on hand. I am expecting every day to hear about the corn. I long more and more for peace and wish I could be at home. Tell Sis, if she will, she must do as she sees fit but I am very sorry if she is compelled to, although I do and have heard other young men say the same thing, think very highly of the ladies who are acting so praiseworthy and inde-

---

47. 2d Lt. Charles Harrison Claiborne of Company K, First South Carolina Regulars, Sgt. N. F. Devereaux of the Engineer Corps and Pvt. Barney Brannon, Company G, Eighteenth South Carolina Infantry, detailed as a carpenter at Fort Sumter, were cited for their bravery in General Orders of 30 June 1864, by Maj. Gen. Samuel Jones, commander of the Department of South Carolina, Georgia, and Florida.

48. 2d Lt. Francis Markoe Jr. of Baltimore, son of Mary Maxcy Leverett's first cousin Mary Maxcy Markoe, was an officer in the Signal Corps.

pendently. My mess at present consists of a Lieut Boag and Whitridge[49] (one who was the tutor in Mr. Wm. Cuthbert's family) of the Gist Guards, Lieuts Ainsworth and Clayburne and Stuart Rhett of the 1st S.C. Infantry but they will soon be relieved and others will take their places. It can't compare with my former mess. How are the horses looking? Do hope you will succeed with your poultry. Love to Ma and Pa and everybody. The Blockade runners come and go now and then.

Your Affct brother
Milton M. Leverett

Fred, his condition worsening, was transferred to a private residence in Richmond on 22 June. He was scheduled to be furloughed for forty days to Columbia but was too ill to travel.

Julia Marcelline Leverett to her brother Milton

"The cot beside the hill."[50]
June 27th 1864

My dear Min,

It is a perfect shame in you to say that you cannot find any of my letters unanswered. It is because you <u>don't</u> want to find any for if you had chosen to you could easily have remembered that I wrote to you before you left Pocotaligo. But I won't say any more for if I do it will make you imagine that I think it a great thing to receive one of <u>your</u> letters. We have not heard from Brother Fred for a long time but I suppose he is very busy. Some people think we are in a very precarious situation now for if Petersburg is taken supplies will be cut off from Richmond and flour is even now $500 per bbl there, but I think the Yanks will find it a "hard road to travel" before they reach that delectable city.[51] The two Mrs. Wallaces (William and Alfred)[52] were out here on Saturday and they were telling us what Col. W. and a Mr. Kershaw had told them. They say our own men fight as they never fought before, that they are desperate. Every man down to the vulgarest and commonest in the army feels that they cannot be beaten and that <u>he</u> himself cannot be over-

---

49. 1st Lt. Theodore G. Boag and 2d Lt. Alonzo C. Whitridge of the Gist Guards, Company E, Manigault's Battalion, South Carolina Siege Train.

50. The Farm.

51. John R. Thompson's "Richmond Is a Hard Road to Travel," a song published in 1863, made fun of the numerous Federal attempts to take Richmond; a parody of Daniel Decatur Emmett's minstrel song "Jordan Is a Hard Road to Travel."

52. Victoria McLemore Wallace and Sarah Burroughs Wallace, respectively, the wives of Col. William Wallace and Dr. Alfred Wallace of Columbia.

come. Col. Wallace had not undressed for three weeks and there are some in the army who have not done so for six weeks; he was living in the trenches, sometimes when the firing is very hot the servant cannot bring them their suppers. We hear that our men are so tired out that they have no appetite at all. Both of the armies are at Petersburg. We think the great battle will take place there. So much for army news, now for home gossip and chat. Annie and Mame went to see Phoebe and Annie the other day. Annie says you are a mean fellow; she intends giving you "bringers" (to use your own elegant expression) when she sees you for trying on her pink saque. She is a perfect little Roman Catholic, says all their prayers etc. etc. Phoebe does not like it as well as Annie and does not intend returning. Annie had a piece of holy wax which she said thirty-six of our generals wore to protect them, and she was going to send it on to Willie to wear. Mame asked her whether she really believed it would save the generals. "Well" she said, "if <u>they believe</u>." It is my opinion that Annie doesn't believe any more than you or I do. Our Annie went to the "Commencement" of the Convent,[53] they only let her in because her name was DeSaussure and the old Lawyer DeSaussure had done them some kindness.[54] The reason they would not let any more of us in was that everybody behaved so outrageously last year that it quite mortified them, so this year pupils were allowed to have only two tickets and Phoebe and Annie had given theirs to their father and brother, They were both mentioned "with honor" and some of Phoebe's paintings were exhibited. They were the prettiest girls in the room. Gov. Bonham[55] gave out the wreaths and crowned the girls and from what Annie says the old gentleman must have done it awkwardly enough too. But I expect you are getting tired of the Ursuline now. Ma says you must ask Lieutenant Claiborn (she thinks his name is spelt so and not Clayburn, she has seen his name in the paper) whether it is true that Maxcy Hughes is killed and whether Mrs. Hughes is now living at Baltimore if he knows.[56] Cousin Cornelia wrote word that some young lady who knew them had told her that he is killed and that Frank Markoe who has been in the Signal Corps had now gone West. We hear that he is considered as something of a "puppy" at Charleston.

By the way—before I forget it, let me tell you that Ma says you are mistaken in supposing that the number of ordnance officers in artillery is not increased. She

53. An academy for girls at the Ursuline Convent, Columbia; run by nuns from the Ursuline Convent, Black Rock, County Cork, Ireland.

54. One of Dr. Louis McPherson DeSaussure Sr.'s brothers, Henry Alexander DeSaussure (1788–1865) or William Ford DeSaussure (1792–1870).

55. Milledge Luke Bonham, governor of South Carolina, 1862–1864.

56. 1st Lt. Maxcy G. Hughes, assistant ordnance officer in the District of Texas, New Mexico, and Arizona, died in Houston on 12 November 1863. His mother was Ann Sarah Maxcy Hughes, first cousin of Mary Maxcy Leverett.

says that she saw in the paper that it was, and think you had better consult with your captain about making an application. We are very anxious to see our "soldier boy" rise, but I wish you would do so without applying. Any how we feel assured that the fault will not be in you if you fail in it. I believe I could pray for it if it was a thing that we ought to pray for, but I suppose we must be contented with your staying there at least a while longer, and trust that the other will will come in good time.

Now let me tell you about the much-discussed subject—the Trenholm's reception to which Mary, Tillie and Jim were invited. If the account is meager do not blame me but them. Mame had as she said "to dig it out." As they had no other mode of conveyance it was determined that they should go out in our old carriage, with Jim's horse and Dora to draw and Hercules to drive it. The eventful night being come they got into the carriage and drove off. The horses however did not anticipate much pleasure and determined to rebel. The carriage assisted them by running something in the way our old cart used to do—zig-zag. So the horses ran away and our party was obliged to dismount at Mr. Pringle's. Luckily Mr. Pringle had room in his carriage and he carried them out. The girls had a very nice time but Jim found it rather stiff. Only one or two sets were danced as Mr. Trenholm did not wish to have it. The supper dashed to the ground many hopes about ice-cream etc. for strange to say on the very night when there was the greatest number of people and they ought to have had a splendid supper, they only had cake, wine and candy sugar plums etc. That would have been very well for other people but for Mr. T. it disappointed people. The night before they had a splendid supper, bananas, ice-cream, and every sort of thing but only a few people were invited.

Ma's garden is supporting us now. We live on Irish potatoes, some of them are very fine. I hope you will get a furlough about watermelon time. I am afraid we won't have very many of them. Hercules has been cutting the wheat which is very fine, and last but not least Diana has a fine calf. Those are the home items. I have not been to town for three weeks for want of shoes. I gave a pair to a man in town to make for me a month ago, and the wretched creature has not sent them home yet. If we have sent or been there once we have done it about twenty times. "Solitude and reflection are good for the mind" but really I am getting too much of them. I suppose you will leave this letter unanswered for two months and then you "cannot find any unanswered."

Never mind my boy if you don't write to me others do, and so I won't pine about it.

Your affec^{ate} sister
Julie

P.S.
I hope you don't wear those horrid whiskers now. If you do I'll have to disclaim all resemblance to you.

Milton Maxcy Leverett to his mother

Fort Sumter June 29$^{\underline{th}}$ 1864

My dear Mother,

I received your delightfully long letter last Friday, coming here from Charleston. I had expected to have gone a day or two before but put off until Thursday night so that I might meet Billy whom I expected on Friday. I have hadn't him with me until then for several reasons, first I let him go to see his wife for a little while after having brought my colt down, then Nat was to send him to me but Billy let the cars leave him and I expect he must have gone then to Robertville[57] for Nat just then went off on a scout and didn't come back for some time, in the mean time I wrote to Nat and Barney answered whom it seems was under the impression that Billy had reached me. He sent him to me and I went down to meet him at the cars but they arrived before I got there when I went to the Express Office and there found him just getting into a wagon to go to Major Motte Pringle preparatory to reaching the fort. Barney had arranged so that he couldn't miss me. He is here now cooking for my mess. He said when he first came that he wanted to be with me, didn't like Pocotaligo but before the next day was out the Yankees commenced throwing their shells (one man was struck down not far from Billy's kitchen another time) and I suppose Stuart Rhett's boy must have been expatiating on the dangers that he had undergone by "flood and field" (he had been in the Etiwan when she ran aground)[58] to him for he told me on my inquiring how he liked his change of life that he did not like um didn't expect it to be that kind of thing. Every time a gun fires when Billy happens to be out of doors you see him gazing in the sky to try and ascertain where the shell is going to and looking a little wild preparatory to making a rush for cover if it is coming for the fort.

I am still very busy my dear mother but am not so always or I would have written to you last Sunday but if there is a chance of its continuing I shall not hesitate to write to you on that day. I have now you will be glad to hear, a man under me, a temporary assistant Ordnance Sergt who is a very great assistance to me, is very willing to work and has been Ord. Sergt before consequently knows what he is about, I make him attend to the manual labour and tedious business details especially, while I keep the accounts assisting also of course in other work whenever it is necessary and taking the responsibility generally. We had an alarm the other night, false though; we were all busy eating cake, and drinking whiskey

---

57.   Billy's wife lived in Robertville, a town in Beaufort District.
58.   The C.S.S. *Etiwan*, a Confederate side-wheeler used as a transport ship, drifted over obstructions in Charleston Harbor near Fort Johnson on 7 June 1864 and was caught. Confederate artillerymen in Battery Gregg, on Morris Island, fired on the wreck and sank it.

punch—hot, (don't include me among the latter <u>wes</u> of course) when we heard
the little bell ting-a-ling &^c, however, as you wish to know as brother styled it
"everything about all and all about everything" I'll commence. Well it was Saturday night and I had been up till near midnight waiting for the steamer to get the
mail as well as to look out for Ordnance Stores, was sleepy and tired and had just
returned to my inhospitable looking cave, was half undressed, reading the newspaper and almost ready to get into bed when the Captain's Orderly comes and
says, "Sergeant the Captain wants to see you." "All right" says I, but soliloquizing,
"I do wish Capt Mitchel, could let me alone, let me rest some, he might have
known that at this time of the night I was in bed or about to get in" however as
there was no help for it, I slung on my coat and went down grumbling and revolving in my mind, Ordnance Stores, Requisitions, Reports, Invoices, Receipts and
even perhaps a <u>Reprimand</u> for some imaginary fault, but on stepping in the Captains Quarters met the Adjutant (Percival Elliott of Savannah, brother to Carrie
Elliott)[59] who gave me a polite military salute sweeping and pleasant (which I
returned in the same spirit) and on my inquiring the commands, pointed to a table
with several plates of cake and a bowl of hot whisky punch the concoction of
which was just being finished, I in an agreeably pleasant surprise saw immediately
how matters stood, <u>that it was a "Treat"</u> and asked him if Peace Times had come
again. Capt. Mitchel began to hand round the punch which I of course refused,
to his surprise, while all began to help themselves generally to the cake and
punch, while I made a vigorous attack on the cake and a cup of water. Says some
one "just to think if we have an alarm now"—all of us lounging around and helping ourselves promiscuously, newcomers stepping in as the feast progressed, says
another, "Suppose an alarm was to happen now" and the words were scarcely out
of his mouth when the little bell rung and everybody pitched up and rushed off to
the ramparts, some carrying their punch with them while others made a dive into
the cake plates among the latter of whom include me, and off I went thinking I
could manage my cake before the enemy could make much of a fight, but as
usual, the alarm turned out to be merely a Yankee picket boat firing at one of ours
and after awhile all returned but myself and I went to bed thinking it was too near
Sunday for any more carousing. You must know we have little bells ranged
throughout the bombproofs all around the whole fort, so arranged as to have ropes
extending up to the parapet and on an alarm up there the different ropes are
pulled by the corporals of the guard and it is taken up by guards at the successive
bells in the bombproofs and thus an alarm is run around the whole fort without

---

59.   Adj. Percival Elliott of the Savannah Volunteer Guards, Company B, Eighteenth Georgia
      Battalion, on detached service in Fort Sumter, and his sister Caroline Elliott; first cousins
      of Gen. Stephen Elliott Jr.

the enemy scarcely imaging that we know of their approach. You will be glad to hear that I have now different quarters much pleasanter in some respects than the others, being able now to write without a lamp, this letter being the first for many a day that I have written by the light of the day. You have heard by this time of the box which I regret so much not having reached me in season, there were many little things in it though that could not be injured and were just precisely what I wanted. It was not on the Etiwan—she ran aground going back to Charleston and was riddled up by the enemy who fired on her day and night for several days. Is it true that Mrs. O'Hear, wife of Lt. O'Hear of the Dragoons has become insane since her husband's death. As it is dark I will have to stop. This letter you must understand I am writing by instalments.

Saturday 2<u>nd</u>

This is the third day that I have been writing this letter, having been very busy lately. Tell Pa I saw Mr. Pringle who let me have a hundred ($100) but it was on his own account on the State Bank. I was in great need of it, my shoes being worn out and the Government not being punctual in delivering supplies, it owing me now two pairs of shoes. I bought a pair from the Bee Store for forty dollars. The cheapest from other stores were a hundred dollars a pair. I am very much obliged to Pa for it. I couldn't help thinking well of Mr. Pringle, he had young Coffin (the deaf and dumb one) as his clerk instructing him by signs in his business. I am in some need of summer clothes but will try to manage. I will get my clothes washed by Billy I expect after a manner by saving water. I have done so already but didn't have any smoothing iron.

Your aff<u>ct</u> son
M. M. Leverett

Milton Maxcy Leverett to his sister Matilda

Fort Sumter July 4<u>th</u> /64

Dear Sis,

You will have to excuse the brevity of my letter but I have been doing a great deal of writing laterly and still have so much to do that I am compelled to curtail my letters which you must all admit generally err on the other side. I saw a beautiful defeat yesterday from the parapet of Fort Sumter, unfortunately I only saw the last half as I didn't know a fight was progressing. The enemy attacked Forts Johnson and Simkins and failed entirely from want of pluck, the hindmost boats failing to come up to the scratch. You may imagine with what delight and glee I stood upon the walls of Sumter and saw the miserably scared jaded flogged wretches rowing back with all their might to get out of the way while all of our batteries from different portions of the harbour blazed away at them, I'm sorry to say with very little effect as it was so early in the morning and so misty that they could not see where to fire. If Fort Sumter only had had parapet guns or guns bearing on that quarter of the harbour we could have ruined them. I couldn't help wishing that Pa and Ma and all of you girls could have seen it, (we being safe, the enemy only popping at us now and then which we easily dodged) and knowing how delighted you would have been at seeing some little of the tragic part of war i.e. of the fighting, I could imagine Pa's glee at seeing them pulling back defeated.[60] If they had been Confederates they would have run over half a dozen such forts. I hear there was an attack at Adams Run. There has been yesterday and all today fighting going on on James Island toward Secessionville. Foster seems determined to wake us up.[61] We are prepared for an attack on this fort at any time but could easily flog them off, it being much harder than Fort Johnson to capture. The enemy fired from their works today which are quite close to us, a Fourth of July salute which I observed from the parapet. Tell Anne I received her last note yesterday and have written tonight that the shoes that are finished should be sent, one pair is Cos. Cornelia's. Do as you see fit my dear sis in the step that you have taken, I hope you will succeed. Do any of you know the whereabouts of Ste Elliott? Tell Julie she certainly will have to write another letter to me before she can expect any from me especially as I am very busy. The fleas and mosquitoes are horrible especially the former. Where is Fred's direction?

yr. aff^{ct} brother M. M. Leverett.

Mary Maxcy Leverett to her son Milton

The Farm Columbia July 11, 1864

My dear Son

We are all so glad you have an assistant Sergt. to help you out with the drudgery, it must be quite a relief to you. Your letter came about dark, as I knelt in front of the lightwood fire to read it, Pater-familias, who, hot & dusty had gone into the chamber to refresh and cool off, calls out "don't read 'til I come," so behold me waiting expectant (not impatiently tho', for I took the opportunity of running my eye over the valued "word from the absent") the girls and children ditto all assem-

---

60. An amphibious assault against Fort Johnson and Battery Simkins, on James Island, was launched on the night of 2–3 July by one thousand Federals in rowboats; but the boats withdrew as soon as the Federals landed and the Confederate defenders discovered them. The Federals lost 119 killed and wounded and another 139 captured, including Col. Henry M. Hoyt of the Fifty-second Pennsylvania Infantry, commander of the expedition.

61. Maj. Gen. John Gray Foster commanded the Federal Department of the South.

bled around me, when the signal being given by Pater's appearance, I read, to the delectation and amusement of the assembled family. The various comments approbatory, congratulatory, and exclamatory I need not mention, but you can readily imagine, especially the last; all laughed at Billy, were glad of the Surprise "Treat"; and your declining the punch capped the climax, exclamations of pleasure and approval ran around the circle, and as I cast my eye over my shoulder to catch the smile which I knew by intuition was beaming on the countenance of the Pater, it was there sure enough, as the words "oh, thats right, thats right!" expressed his gratification. It is "wisest, virtuousist, discretest, best" in you, to avoid drinking, as you are in the highest health and drinking is not advisable except for pale, weak persons. Where it is pursued as a <u>habit</u>, it inflames the blood, and finally makes a man like a beast in his conduct. I am glad, and deeply thankful there never has been reason for me ever to have a fear for you on this score. You don't know what interest every thing and every body in Fort Sumter, animate and inanimate have in my eyes, since you have been there, added indeed, to all the interesting that were connected with it previously. You can't be too minute in detailing every thing that happens, however trifling you may think it. Let me know how often you have preaching, and if you benefit by it, which I trust you do, unless your prevailing temptation, sleep, overcomes you. I have a good way to prevent this infirmity from stealing away all the good I may get by sermons on Sundays, & that is to sleep <u>before</u> you go to church, if time allows. You never said in your two letters to Tillie and Mame, a day or two ago, how you liked Bishop Lay & his sermon.[62] I hope you still keep up regular reading in your Bible, praying to your Heavenly Father to enlighten your understanding and make the truth "as it is in Jesus" more plain and clear to you. The wisest need thus to pray, how much more you, who, with so many others in these perilous times, have to live as it were, with their lives in their hands, and know not what a day may bring forth?—You ask about Mrs O'Hear, she went distracted for awhile, I don't consider it as insanity, & on recovering the shock, her friends persuaded he was a prisoner & not killed, & when last I heard, she was hopeful it was so, as it has been the case with several who were reported dead & who proved since to be prisoners. But poor Oliver Middleton is really killed. His parents are wo-worn. His father has been so wrapped up in him ever since he was born, that they were like shadows to each other, so constantly together were they, & it goes hard with him.[63] Your father went to see them. Capt. Trenholm[64] (who is wounded) had been there & told them all he

---

62. The Rev. Henry Champlin Lay, Episcopal bishop of Arkansas, whose sermon was "Letters to a Man Bewildered among Many Counsellors" (Charlotte, N.C.: Protestant Episcopal Church Publishing Association, 1864).
63. Oliver Hering Middleton Sr.
64. Capt. William Lee Trenholm of the Rutledge Mounted Rifles, later Company B, Seventh South Carolina Cavalry, was wounded near Cold Harbor, Virginia, 30 May 1864.

knew. It seems, Dr Isaac Gregorie went to a house not far from the battle-field where Oliver had been carried, desperately wounded, & the women there told Dr G. all relating to him, for by the time a clue was found to know where to look for him, he was dead & buried near a church not far off.[65] They said he sent his watch & pencil, after writing with it to his family, and a message, the purport of which was that "he died a Middleton, a true out and out Middleton." He meant that he died like a brave man, such as a Middleton ought to be. Some of the family, indeed all of them I believe both of the John Izard & Oliver Middleton's are much mortified that John Middleton[66] (your brother's friend) is Quartermaster, & would rather he should be in the ranks than that, but he, though very anxious to be something else than Quartermaster, is yet reluctant to go into the ranks as private. He would gladly change his position, but not for a lower rank, his sister told me he & they had tried their best to get him another position, but had not succeeded. Drayton's mishap has been an injury to all under him. Matilda Middleton has very just & exalted views of a man's duty in these times, which "try men's souls" & she holds that it is infinitely more honorable to be in the ranks than to be Quartermaster.

I will send you a piece of mosquito netting, as well as your facenet & a smoothing iron as soon as I can get a box to suit. Had I not better send you a bro. Holland coat you have? & any other summer thing I can pick up?

I do not wonder at your delight at seeing the Yankees beaten off in their barges.—I hope you are all well prepared for an attack "prevention is better than cure,"—if the Yankees think you thoroughly prepared, perhaps it may hinder the attack. We hear that Capt. Mitchell himself was on the watch that night, and that he says he cannot imagine how they could have passed unseen by him. If the attack had been successful at Fort Johnson, I should suppose this would effectually prevent his promotion, for it is said that the barges had to pass near Fort Sumter (which ought to have given the alarm) & failed to do so. What sort of a man is Mitchell?

Your father told me he couldn't think why Mr. Pringle used his own funds for you, as you mentioned, as he has funds of his own in Mr. Pringle's hands. The only way I can account for it is this, that I know Factors sometimes make use, either for themselves or others of any persons funds they happen to have in hand, sometimes to accommodate a friend, or to speculate, the Factor being accountable is bound to hand it to him whenever called for, but in the interim they often make a good sum. Archy Seabrook seemed to think it very kind in Mr Pringle, who offered to relieve him of some money of the old issue which Archy had some time ago, saying he had use for it at that time. Archy was thankful, for if kept by him, it would have been in a short time valueless.

---

65.   Dr. Isaac McPherson Gregorie of Prince William's Parish.
66.   John Izard Middleton Jr.

I suppose you heard of poor Nat Barnwell being missing & his horse being found killed in the same battle with poor Oliver. His father & mother are greatly distressed.[67] Old Mrs. Pinckney is dead[68] & Carrie P. is very ill at Pendleton. The Seabrooks are gone up to Flat Rock. No doubt you heard of Mr Andrew Johnstone's murder,—his son, only fifteen wounded the whole six murderers by repeated discharges of buckshot from his gun, which he went into his room and loaded, thinking there was something suspicious in the behaviour. Two were killed; all of the others wounded by this brave boy, who after wounding the first two (mortally) ran after them all as they took to their heels, & fired as fast as he could get near enough, so enraged was he at his father's death. Now, see what odds—six to one! Yet they fled from that one! What a mercy that God sometimes puts a sort of dread or fear into the wicked, which makes them fly even when there is but one to oppose them as in this instance. They intended to rob, A. Seabrook wrote us, but not finding Mr. J. as compliant as some of the other gentleman up there had been, they shot him, but soon as they found they were resisted, they ran. There is a great charm in an undaunted manner. If that boy had been scared and ran as some would have done, perhaps the whole family would have been robbed & then murdered.

We hear that Helen Barnwell is engaged to a Dr Gieger of Maryland, a wealthy man.[69] Perhaps it's the same Dr Gieger who attended you. Capt George is quite indignant rumor says.[70] I daresay Capt. George has seen this old Gieger here in the Legislature.

I think our war affairs look encouraging and hope this year will end the war and our privations. Charley has been here for a day or two on business. He sent us a large ham, it was partly not sound, but the rest of it very good. He had been paid by some in provisions. We have been suffering terribly for want of rain, everything is burning up in the garden & field, but we had some rain last night, which I hope will save the crop, but it was not enough. We are thrashing wheat now, and have made an excellent crop of it, no red at all. I don't know what we would have done if the wheat had failed. I think it will be enough to last until the end of the year at least. The Irish potatoes from the garden have been a wonderful help. We

---

67. Pvt. Nathaniel Berners Barnwell (1845–1883) of the Rutledge Mounted Rifles, Company B, Seventh South Carolina Cavalry was captured while on a scout at Hanover Station, Virginia, 27 May 1864, but was exchanged in September. He was the son of Eliza Barnwell and Robert Woodward Barnwell.

68. Phoebe Caroline Elliott Pinckney died 20 June 1864, mother of Caroline Pinckney Seabrook.

69. Helen Barnwell of Beaufort District married Dr. Charles Atwood Geiger of Roswell, Georgia, before the war ended.

70. George Parsons Elliott; his wife, Mary Bower Barnwell, was a half sister of Helen Barnwell.

even have them for <u>breakfast</u> to help out. Corn is $\underline{26}$ a bushel, so we seldom buy it, & get rough rice instead for the servants & ourselves, which is $12 a bushel, & give them a peck & a half allowance.

Annie & Lou have been invited by D^r DeSaussure to pay them a visit & are going the last of this month.

God bless my son prays

yr aff Mother
Mary Leverett

Milton Maxcy Leverett to his mother

Fort Sumter, July 15$^{\underline{th}}$ /64

My dear mother,

It is sometime since I have written to you or you to me but I have been quite busy, not only in my duties, but also in writing to persons in my company to whom I owed letters. I will have to beg you all to be content hereafter for awhile with hearing from me only casually, taking one letter for all as I wish to do a little studying, and may not perhaps be able to meet all my engagements, but don't let it stop any of my home letters; the children will be certain to slack off their letters at this intimation, but if they do I may stop my studying. Nat Fuller wrote and asked me why I didn't study for the Ordnance Examination soon to come off? It is hard to bring oneself to it and I feel so diffident that I half doubt myself. I wish you could have seen the Fort Johnson attack, I know you would have been delighted to have seen the mean wretches going back discomforted. It was on a Sunday morning just about the break of day when they made the assault. I didn't see the first portions of it as I didn't know what was going on but I found out and got up there time enough to see the retreat. They failed from want of courage, the rear guard failing to support the front party. Fort Simkins the work next to Fort Johnson being between the two and a smaller work was silent. The enemy could easily have captured it but pluck was wanting. Confederates would have walked over half a dozen Fort Johnsons and Simkinses in the same space of time. The enemy evidently intended to try to take Fort Sumter from it, but that having failed are now trying a different plan, are bombarding us with their heavy guns and then after having made a sufficient breach will in all probably assault us. We all expect to beat them easily at that as Fort Sumter is ten times harder to be taken by an assault than Fort Johnson. I have a good supply of incendiary and other infernal machines ready for them when they try it. They have thrown between two and three thousand shells and shot at us during the last week and had breached my main magazine or rather, the room next to it which is a portion of it, my dark room, but I had evacuated it some days previous and had moved all ammunition to different portions of the

Fort where it would be more secure. The enemy didn't know that they had breached it and stopped about long enough for us to fix it. When they thought they had breached it they commenced firing their horrid smelling incendiary shells to try and blow it up but they found that was no go. Very few persons have been injured by their firing, but the wall has been very much damaged. They had yesterday I believe a jollification on Morris Island—saw in the Fleet a beautiful white steamer evidently from Hilton Head with the pic-nic party—saw the ladies they had with them showing them around the forts and exhibiting the accuracy of their fire and their bravery over us poor defenseless wretches. I understand they even let some of the women pull the lanyards. It seems to me I wouldn't hesitate to shoot women in such a case if I could i.e. give them a flesh wound with a Minnie Ball. They have been trying yesterday for a long while to shoot our sentinel whom we have on the lookout, and whose business it is to give the garrison notice every time they fired so that protection might be obtained, and at last succeeded in burying him in dirt with a three hundred pound shot but without injuring him. As the place was thought too dangerous the sentinel was transferred to another point and the officer of the day taking a piece of wood put a hat on it and placed it in the old sentinel station, the Yankees thinking it was a bona fide sentinel took a shot at it with one of their Parrotts and popped him over first shot. They were all delighted. The officer clapped his hands and all rushed up on the embankment to take a look. Every time they fire they examine with their glasses what damage is done. My life is much more pleasant than it was. Love to Pa and all. Tell Julie to look out for a letter.

Your aff$^{\underline{ct}}$ son,
Milton M. Leverett

Rev. Charles Edward Leverett to his wife

Richmond Monday 18 July/64

My dearest wife,

After a delay of 12 hours on the road in consequence of the break in the Danville road, I reached here last night about 8 o/clock. I found Fred better than I expected, & the D^r says he is better than he was a week ago. He is however quite sick, but I trust not hopelessly so. He seems to have brightened up considerably & talks of getting home by & by, though at present he is too weak to walk across the room, without the aid of Jacob, who is here and attending to him. F. has lost so much flesh that a part of his body looks very poor indeed. The D^{rs} here are very kind & attentive & I hope he will yet rally. He staid entirely too long in the camp after he was sick. I shall know later to-day if the D^r thinks him improved since yesterday.

The break in the R. R. was finished Saturday night & that is the reason I arrived so much earlier than I expected. About 50 miles we had to ride in grain cars & there was a prospect that we would have been obliged to walk from five to ten miles which with my carpet bag was a very discouraging view.

I have to board at the South Carolina Home, near by, where the price is $15 a day, which is much cheaper than any other place, although every thing is coarse & suited to rough & terrible times. I do not know what you would have done, had you come on. It is fortunate you did not. There is no living here & your money goes like snow before a hot sun. Fred gives for each pd. chicken that he gets $10 a piece. Of course money is literally worth nothing.

The first letter sent was without knowledge of F, then afterwards he reported to Fred also telegraphed to Charley to come on. I believe he did not expect me.

If F gets any better, & Charley comes, I will return home, as I am really of little or no use. I intend sending a telegraph today which you will of course receive before this.

On Saturday night I staid at Mr. Dame's the Ep. M.[71] at Danville, to whom I was introduced, at the cars on my arrival. He asked me to stop with him should I be detained on my return.

Being a clergyman, I think it likely, I shall be charged less at the place where I sleep & take an occasional meal. Anne's biscuit will last me two or three days.

Fred sends his love to all. He dreamt he saw you all in distress & that you lifted up yr. hands saying O my son, what is the matter? He says tell you he feels a little better, tho still weak & his bad symptoms have disappeared.

My love to all with especial love to you.

Ever yr. own affectionate C.

P.S.

Stuart Barnwell died about a week since.[72]

Fred tells me to say, he hopes to be with you after a time, but how soon, is impossible to say.

Julia Marcelline Leverett to her brother Milton

"Cot beside the Hill" July 20th [1864]

My dear Min,

Ma has been giving me such bitter reproaches (with the greatest injustice) about writing to you that I am fain to sit down and commence forthwith. She has

---

71. Episcopal minister; Rev. George Dame (1812–1895) of Danville, Virginia.

72. Pvt. James Stuart Barnwell of the Rutledge Mounted Rifles, Company B, Seventh South Carolina Cavalry, died from typhoid fever in Richmond 9 July 1864.

been writing to Pa or else doubtless would take my place. You will of course inquire where is Pa. I answer in Richmond. Last Friday he received a letter from Dr Hopkins[73] saying that Brother Fred was very ill with Chronic Diarrhea and he had better come on at once. This threw us into the greatest distress and Pa went on that evening. I would have written to you then but they thought I had better wait. We telegraphed on Saturday but received not a word until yesterday when Mrs. Watie's servant rode out here to tell us there was a dispatch come for us saying that he was better now. Minny you may imagine what a load was taken from our hearts and how thankful we were. We hope and pray that he will get better and then be brought home safe again. How thankful we ought to be that we are spared this heavy blow. If prayers could protect you boys, you would never be hurt through want of them. Which is the worse, pencil or pen.[74] The pencil for you, the pen for me. However as I received a french letter written in pencil from Sallie Stuart[75] the other day, and as I read it I think you may very well read an english written in the same. By the way, I hear Sallie is engaged to our friend Charlie DeSaussure.[76] I don't believe it exactly however for she does not speak at all flatteringly of his beauty in her letters but it may be so. I think his relations would like it very much as well they may for she is as nice a girl as ever I knew. I mean to plague her about it in my next letter. And so you have at last had the pleasure of seeing Brother Jonathan beaten on his own element. I dare say many a thought of Bay Point was in your heart at that time. Good for them. I hope they got enough. A Mr Starke was wounded in one of the fights on the islands.[77] Jim says he says the negro troops were screaming aloud (those that were wounded) but that their officers behaved admirably. Are they white or coloured?[78] He was wounded by a negro. I think I should hate that of all things the worst. They were three thousand against three hundred. But I suppose you know this already so I will stop especially as I have finished what I have to tell about that battle.

July 22nd.

There really seems to be something almost providential about our receiving that telegram. Just the day after, we received another letter 4 days older than the

---

73. Probably Dr. A. Hopkins, appointed acting assistant surgeon at Howard's Grove Hospital, Richmond, in June 1864.

74. Julia's letter was written in both pencil and ink.

75. Sarah Means Stuart daughter of Henry Middleton Stuart Sr.

76. Pvt. Charles Alfred DeSaussure of the Beaufort Artillery, son of Dr. Louis McPherson DeSaussure Sr.

77. On 7 July 1864, the Twenty-sixth United States Colored Troops attacked a Confederate position on John's Island, incurring and inflicting moderate casualties.

78. All commissioned officers of United States Colored Troops were white until early 1865, when the first blacks won their commissions near the end of the war.

telegram from Dr. Hopkins saying that Brother Fred was desperately ill, that it would
be almost a miracle if he got over it, that he had telegraphed to Brother Charlie to
come and carry him home but he was afraid the only home he would go to would
be one beyond the sky. Oh Minny! think what despair we would have been in without that telegram. Yesterday we received a letter from Pa written the same day as the
telegram, saying he had got there Sunday night and had found Brother Fred better
than he was a week ago, his bad symptoms have disappeared and he seems cheered
up. Says he has lost a great deal of flesh and cannot cross the room without Jake's
assistance though. He says he dreamt he saw us all in distress and that Ma lifted up
her hands and said "Oh my son, my son!" He will come on as soon as he can if
Brother Charlie (who came here this morning) were able to go, he might I suppose,
come on very soon, but Brother Charlie looked miserably and said he is afraid he
will get sick at some of those stations.

What a dreadful thing it is about poor Captain Mitchell.[79] How dreadfully you
all must feel. We are so sorry. Do Minny, take care of yourself and don't expose yourself at all. But we trust in a higher Power to take care of you and bring you home safe
again.

What a dreadful shock Stuart Barnwell's death must have been to his family. I
suppose you saw his obituary in the paper. Nat is a prisoner at Point Lookout or somewhere.[80]

The shoes came out yesterday but only two pair, one for Cousin Cornelia, one
for Annie and they are entirely too small. Ma is wearing Annie's, they fit her very
well. You had better write to Mr. Ficklin and tell him he must not make the others
so small as they won't fit. I have got mine at last but not before Pa threatened to have
the man taken up for stealing. Then he finished them. Mame is sadly in want of her
shoes. I wish Mr. Ficklin would finish them. I am glad you admire my name that I
have given this place. Isn't it pretty? Yours is almost as pretty as mine. But the others don't agree in my choice. Pa would like something high sounding. What do you
think of "Ilderton Manor"? Pa got to Richmond very quickly; he left here Friday
night and reached there Sunday night. Brother Fred receives every attention that
kind friends can offer. He is staying at the hospital in Dr. Hopkins' room, sleeping
in Dr. Hoyts' bed. I think South Carolinians have reason to bless the Virginians for
their kindness to our friends and relations. Pa is staying at the South Carolina Home
paying $15.00 a day taking an occasional meal there. I am afraid he'll starve himself
but if Brother Fred will only get better it will do him good to go there. He made the
acquaintance of a Mr. Daniels[81] an Episcopal minister at Danville who asked him

79. Capt. John C. Mitchel Jr. was wounded by a shell during a bombardment of Fort Sumter
    on 20 July 1864 and died the same day.
80. The Federal military prison at Point Lookout, Maryland.
81. George Dame.

to stay with him on his return if he were retained. He hopes that being a minister they will charge him less.

Mr. Lance[82] sold our melodeon for $600 the other day so that is some help. Jim has obtained another place through Mr. Chas. Hanckel in the Treasury which pays him $3600 now. Poor Cousin Annie[83] lost her youngest daughter yesterday, a sweet little baby. It died very suddenly. She is in great distress. Be sure and take good care of yourself. I won't ask you to write to me, it flatters you too much.

Your affectionate sister
Julie

Rev. Charles Edward Leverett to his wife

Richmond Wed. July 20, 1864

My dearest Mary,

I send a few lines today to let you know how Fred is & also to give a direction to Julia about the key. F. is no better so far as I can see after being here two days & I am very apprehensive although my fears may be unreasonable. Dr Hopkins told me this morning that he was no better, but still that he might get well. His disease continues unchecked & he has very little strength. He has had a very acute ear ache & Dr Campbell says such is critical. The result may be for the better or the worse. I am endeavoring to prepare myself for the worst, although that may not come. Dr H. says Fred ought to have left last May. At that time, he advised him to do so, but he would not. F thinks he may not get well & told me this morning if he did not, he wished to be buried by the side of Edward. Still, he said I may have many years. He asks me every day to read the Bible to him & have prayers and asks me to repeat hymns to him. Dr. Woodbridge who visits him, called Monday & administered the communion.[84] There is a Mrs. Bryant in the house from Charleston. She helped Dr Campbell in the Hospitals at one time. Her sister is Mrs. Byrd who lives at Smith's near us. She is very kind and attentive. I stay with F. all the time except at night, when I have to go to my lodging. The price for a bed is $3 a night. So far I have taken only one meal, & try to shuffle along on such poor fare as four or five biscuits a day—those, which Anne made. I took breakfast yesterday morning but not this. They had coffee, biscuit, bread, hominy & ham but no milk or butter. The price of each meal is $5 which would be a week $105 or $420 a month. Such living is not very agreeable, but somehow I am called to bear very many disagreeable things. It is not very pleas-

---

82. Probably William S. Lance of St. Luke's Parish.
83. Anne Matilda Heyward Hanckel.
84. Rev. George Woodbridge, rector of Monumental Episcopal Church in Richmond.

ant apart from the sad thoughts of losing one, who, I thought was to take my place & see after you all. I hope I may stand up under all the trial and anxiety & I am very well. Fred's legs at the upper part have shrunken to about the size of your arms, but his voice is strong. Jake is very attentive and is a very good nurse. He is in constant requisition. I will leave off now, so as to write a few lines tomorrow. Charley has not come & I suppose it will be very difficult for him to leave. Fred told me this morning he wished he was at home.

I had not intended to send this before to-morrow, but Fred, who knew of my writing, said I must send it to-day & write again tomorrow & every day, which I may or may not. Fred is very dictatorial & I yield to him out of consideration to the poor fellow's state. I thought yesterday he was better as he was so exacting about this & that. I wish he were so, but I am afraid he is not. While I am writing Mrs. B. is sitting by the bed, with a bunch of feathers.

I hope you are all contriving to get on. Fred says the condition of the people where the soldiers lines were was bad enough. Everything destroyed & the women & little children digging to get some corn in the ground, depending on the army to advance, for protection. The times are sad indeed. I hope we may get along but feel sometimes very doubtful. If the miserable Yankees take Atlanta, I am afraid there are to be sadder times than any had.[85]

My love to all the children. I wish I was at home but of course I shall remain until we see how things are going or until Charley comes, when it will be of no use for me to stay. When you have anything to write about let me hear from you. I hope Milton is safe and well.

I am any thing but agreeably fixed here you may judge.

Your affectionate husband.

Rev. Charles Edward Leverett to his wife

Richmond, Friday, July 22, 1864

My dearest Mary,

This is one of the darkest hours & weeks of my life. I have been in a sick room continuously for about five days, & the prospect is sad enough for earthly hopes. I wrote you day before yesterday to say that poor Fred was no better, & I have now to add that he is evidently worse. There is one bright aspect in the case. Thanks to our early care & training, he is right on the most important point and is not troubled by

---

85. Rev. Charles Leverett was writing on the same day as the battle of Peachtree Creek, the first of three major battles in the vicinity of Atlanta in late July 1864 between the combined Federal armies of the Cumberland, the Tennessee and the Ohio under Maj. Gen. William T. Sherman and the Confederate Army of Tennessee under Gen. John B. Hood.

fears. His hope is in Christ & when he goes hence, I have all confidence that it will be a translation from earth to heaven. This takes away the gloom of death. Now all we have to grieve for is our loss. That is sad enough, you may believe & must feel.

Fred was apparently better yesterday forenoon. But in the afternoon after a pretty bad operation, he immediately became wandering & with very few lucid intervals continuing in the same condition. I was apprehensive lest he would be taken last night & determined to stay with him, but he would have me leave him, though I did not leave the house. This morning he is still wandering, but with short lucid intervals. The D^{rs} all think there is very little if any hope. I told him yesterday afternoon I was going to write to you & asked him what message he would send. He told me that he could not collect his thoughts to send any at that time. I said shall I give your best love to Ma & Tilly & Anne & Mary & Julie. He said yes! Afterwards he said tell Ma (he was still wandering somewhat) that the reason I did not come home before was on account of the Rail Roads but that, I will be back in about two months or two months and a half. When he would have me leave him about 9 or 10 o/c last night, thinking that I might not see him again, I said, remember, my son, you have a good Saviour to trust in & to take care of you. He said, yes, I know that, & it is my only strong hold and consolation. About an hour before he asked me to read a psalm to him & to pray & asked that I would not make it long. He has called on me every day to read & to pray with him & to repeat hymns. Last evening, I asked him to say with me, "Jesus, Saviour of my Soul." He did, a part of it, but stopped after a while & said he could not go on. His mind a part of the time is on Charley, whom he thinks has come. Yesterday evening he said, pa, call Charley, he is in that (pantry) closet, isn't he? This morning he is lying quite still, now & then talking at random. He asked me to go to the Confed. Apothecaries for flax seed & a bottle of medicine a while ago as he wished the flax seed at once. I went. Mrs. Bryant, who is in the room a good deal, has just put on two poultices on his face, which is much swollen. I am to go directly to the surgeon general's office for a permit for brandy for him. I thought Charley would have been here by today and sincerely wish he would come, though he can do nothing for him now unless there should be a most wonderful change which I don't expect.

You may suppose how sad it is to see the one on whom I was relying to take my place in the family so reduced & so near his apparent end. I trust that we may be supported under this great bereavement & in the triumph of a lively hope, may be willing to give up one, so dear to us all, to the Almighty Giver.

Love to all

yr. ever affecte h.

Friday 1 o/c

I have a poultice, by Dr Campbell's direction on my eye, so that I do not see very well to write.

Poor Fred is quite calm & has been quite himself again. Speaking of Milton just now he said he had the deepest affection for him & that he loved you all from the bottom of his heart. I have written a memorandum for him, in which, in the event of his not getting back, he says he wants whatever money belongs to him to be divided among his six sisters, with the exception of one sixth to Milton to give him a start with. His gold watch & such things, he gives to Charley, also his medical books, which if sold now, would bring a handsome sum. Except two—one of Woods the last edition[86] to Dr Hopkins & one to Dr Hoyt. His pony at Wm Fullers he gives to his sister Matilda. He wishes Ma to write a letter to Dr Hopkins, thanking him for his kindness, especially as he has been so much trouble. It will be appreciated.

I shall now close this letter. In the event of F's death, I wonder if Milton could meet Charley in Charleston at the proper time. But nothing can be arranged now. He is again a little wandering, but very still.

Your affect h.

Milton Maxcy Leverett to his mother

Fort Sumter, July 23$^{\underline{rd}}$ 1864

My dear mother,

I received your letter with Carrie's note inclosed just after I had sent mine. Always write those nice long letters, I never weary of them, always am delighted to receive them. We have been through a good deal since my last letter to you i.e in the way of bombardment, but it has slacked now somewhat. I didn't lay great stress on it to you as I did not wish to worry you needlessly. The enemy have fired on us near about five thousand shot and shell since the commencement of the bombardment and persons who have been through the different ones say that in damage to works and injury to men it has been the most severe. During one day and night they fired on us seven hundred (700) shot and shell. That is the most they ever fired on us in this bombardment in twenty-four hours. There has been more system displayed in this than any previous attacks. Foster brought his gun to bear on one point at a time, Gilmore fired indiscriminately. They have annoyed us excessively with mortar shells; the most destructive kind of shell to use, one a thirteen inch came through an insecurely stopped passage way, jumped over one man tearing off his coat collar without materially injuring him and pitched into the casemate crowded with men loafing around, lying down &^{c} &^{c} burst and wounded seven without killing one. Providential was it not? Foster missing his

---

86. George Bacon Wood, *Introductory Lectures and Addresses on Medical Subjects: Delivered Chiefly before the Medical Classes of the University of Pennsylvania* (Philadelphia: J. B. Lippincott, 1859).

queue on my main magazine has brought his guns to bear on another the position of which he was aware of, but although he may breach that he has been anticipated he won't find any powder to blow up there as I have got all safely stowed away somewhere else. He has not spared his incendiary shells, and not having succeeded in blowing up anything I think he feels disheartened and would be glad if he could draw out of the bombardment properly. Hence he has slackened his fire considerably and we begin to think he won't make any assault at all. I have seen a great many wounded and some few killed since being down here. One mortar shell dropped in a crowd of negroes working hitting one outright another died shortly after and wounding ten besides. Poor wretches they see a dreadful time of it, are worked very hard and are very much exposed. I feel very sorry for them, some of them their masters sending down here without any change of clothes for thirty days at a time. It seems to me I would rather pay a fine or stand a prosecution than send a negro of mine down here especially one I cared for. They are treated entirely too harshly. To be sure the answer would be if the negroes don't do the work the soldier will have to and the alternative is die negro or die soldier consequently the negro gets it, but taking that aside they are treated harshly by the overseers.

We have had a very severe loss in poor Capt. Mitchel. He was over with us in our battery chatting saying that he wanted to get out of the noise of the shells around his way but that he found them as bad over here. He was speaking of having a bad toothache said he must get a Yankee shell to cure it. Said he should go next day to Charleston to have it plugged. He was then sent for on some business over at the side of the Fort and five minutes after someone came over saying Capt. Mitchel was wounded. He had gone up on the parapet examining into the condition of things when the sentinel said "Lookout" and told him he had better dodge. He said he wouldn't dodge any of their shells when the shell (a mortar shell) exploded and sent a large fragment right through his thigh and hip mutilating and mangling it horribly taking out the bone clear. He lived about four hours after that. I staid at his head and fanned him with a hat until he died, then helped to cut off some curls to send his mother, assisted in laying him out and dressing him in his full uniform placing him in his coffin putting a large flag we had over him and then sending him off by boat to Charleston. He said he wished to be buried in Magnolia Cemetery without any 'row' quietly as possibly. His last message to his mother was quite peculiar. Says he, "Oh my poor mother when she hears of this," "Percy (speaking to Percy Elliott his adjutant) you must write to my mother, tell her I died like a <u>gentleman</u> at <u>my post</u> fighting gallantly in the same cause as my poor brother Willie only not as gallantly as he as I have screamed more than he." He spoke of screaming, he didn't scream he only groaned and half cried and fretted and justly so for his thigh was a mutilated mass of pulp so to speak. He said

he "had hoped to show the garrison how to die, but couldn't help it he was suffering so much pain." Sometimes he would get stupefied from the effects of the
anodynes given him and would speak of everything Ireland and its associations
then would speak French fluently but all pretty much disconnected and incon-
gruous. He seemed to be speaking in a cheering manner of France, speaking out
at one time "Vive la belle France," &c &c. He was quite disappointed at not
being made a Major before. When Capt. Johnson came in he said to him "ah
Captain <u>I am killed</u> and not made a Major." Capt. Johnson prayed for him with
his consent after which he seemed easier. He was a number one man and of
great intellectuality. Reminded me in some measure of brother i.e. in his great
ambition in his intellect and capabilities and also being a small frail delicate
man and in his high ideas and estimation of blood—his appreciation of the gentleman. As you know he was a thorough type of the Irish gentleman (don't imagine that he spoke a brogue, his language was pure English, you wouldn't have
known that he was an Irishman) and brave as Julius Caesar. My dear mother I
know that you can appreciate the state of things and the feelings which must be
excited when you see the life of a fine noble person ebbing away slowly but
surely before some fatal disease, but your feelings can hardly be so finely
wrought up as when you see such a person on his back on a surgeon's table with
a horrid wound and you see the very <u>life blood itself</u> and watch it saturating his
clothes and running down and dripping on the floor and feel and know that
every drop shortens his life—that the artery cannot be reached—and hear him
begging the doctor just to give him "one little dose of medicine and kill him and
all the pain will be over." But enough, I consider that I lost a good deal in him,
his name would have helped me considerably. I am anxious now to leave this
place that is after the assault if they make one. I don't feel as much interest now.
Tom Huguenin[87] is in command now and for that reason I am also anxious to
leave. Can you find out for me Ste Elliotts whereabouts. Do you think it advisable to write to Cos. Robert[88] after Stuart Barnwell's death. I will try and come
up about first part of August if possible. Where is Fred? I would like to write to
him. The <u>On dits</u> in Charleston about the condition of the fort are quite ludi-
crous, some say you can stand in the parade in the center of the fort and see all
over Morris Island, that the enemy has battered it down so—a perfect humbug—some that some of the works have fallen in and killed any number of persons, which is also perfectly false, besides many other foolish stories. The
enemy will never flog us. Has Anne gone yet. I wrote to have her shoes sent up

---

87.   Capt. Thomas Abram Huguenin of the First South Carolina Regulars succeeded Mitchel
      as commander of Fort Sumter.
88.   Robert Woodward Barnwell, father of James Stuart Barnwell.

to her, were they sent. I hope you are all getting on well, how is corn. Love to Pa and all the children.

Your aff<u>ct</u> son

Milton M. Leverett

Rev. Charles Edward Leverett to his son Milton

Richmond, Va. July 23, 1864

My dear Minny,

You will be grieved to hear that we have lost our dear Fred. He died this morning 20 minutes to 4 o/c. I reached here last Sunday night. Since day before yesterday, he has been wandering although had some clear intervals. He spoke of you very affectionately & said he wished to give you a start, that out of what he left, you should have 1/6 and that the rest should be divided among his sisters. To Charley he left his gold watch &c. & his medical books, which he said if sold now would bring a handsome sum. To Matilda he left his pony. He wished to be buried by the side of Edward & I shall go on, unless Charley should be in Columbia, with the body. I have written to Mr. W<u>m</u> Heyward to see about it. This is a terrible blow, especially as it was unexpected. Fred, however, died in full faith as a Christian, though he said, he acted more for the praise of men, he feared than the glory of God. He had me read to him every day & repeat hymns, such as Jesus, Saviour of My Soul, Rock of Ages, How firm a foundation &c, Inspirer and hearer of prayer. I had looked to Fred to take my place, but here I am left without such support. I am afraid it will come heavily upon Mamma & the girls as they all loved him dearly & he them. He has been treated very kindly particularly by Dr Hopkins, his friend, who tells me they were both sincerely attached to each other.

Fred told me yesterday, that he had the greatest affection for you. He would have been delighted to have seen you & it would have been perfect joy to him to have seen Mamma. He said he wished to see her more than all the world. Dr Hopkins, when he wrote advised me to bring on no lady on account of the difficulty of travelling & the great expenses here. At the South Caro. Home, a cheap place, a single meal is $5 & a bed $3. Poor F's death to him must be a glorious exchange, but a very sad thing to us. I hope God will sustain us. You must write a comforting letter to Ma. I shall hurry right on & not stop in Columbia for various reasons. So far as I can see, I will be in Columbia on Monday and at Pocotaligo Tuesday. But there may be detentions.

God Bless & protect you.

Your affectionate father C.

P.S.

I found so many obstacles in the way, that I was obliged to have poor Fred temporarily buried in Richmond. Charley has promised to see to his removal. It was best to have done so, as Mr. Heyward tells me he could not have been carried if as far, farther than this place. Charley did not get on in time, to his great regret. F. was very anxious to see him.

It is very hard getting on here for want of corn. The times are most dispiriting. The expense of living on almost nothing is so great, as to put one nearly in despair. If Mobile is taken, as it seems probable it will be, everything will be worse, as the Yankees will be more cheered to press on. I wish I could get some proper business that would help to pay—but it seems impossible. I was refused the place of chaplain applied for, as there were two already employed. Jervey I. one of these a fat, hearty, young man, ought to be in the army & not here.

I had a very bad fall, but I am greatly recovered from its effects. I hope by the end of this week to give up both crutch & cane. Where is Billy? Is he at Sumter? Your mother wanted me to send you Jake but I think the exposure for so valuable a servant is too great. I wish you could get a better place. But all are dangerous, field or fort. God can protect any where.

Rev. Charles Edward Leverett to his wife

Richmond, July 23, 1864

My dearest Mary,

My last letter has probably prepared you for the sad news of this. We have lost our dear Fred, but for him the exchange is a glorious one, as he died in full faith. It was pleasant to see that he had no alarm whatever. He was probably conscious of his sufferings last night as nearly all last night & yesterday afternoon he wandered though not greatly. All day yesterday, he was very still & slept a good deal. On one occasion, when waking up, he said, this is my last day on earth. Last night in some paroxym of pain or excitement, he said where is my bible, give me my bible, evidently looking at it as a protection. But he soon wandered. I kissed him when he was going for you and the children & myself & read the commendatory prayer. Early in the evening at his wish I prayed for him. I have just been in to take a look at him dressed in his military suit. He looks perfectly natural. The body will be obliged to be packed in charcoal. I do not think that I can stop at all in Columbia, but will be obliged to hurry on. I have written to Pocotaligo to ask some of the gentlemen there to receive him &c.

O, my dear Mary, what a dreadful loss we have all met with. I do not like to think about it. One thing however is glorious in regard to his death & that is he went without a particle of fear in the complete confidence of a believer. I had not a word to say to take from him any alarm. All he said was that he feared he had been more anxious for the praise of men than of God. But I told him even if it were so, the Saviour was all sufficient. He seemed fully satisfied & I don't think one could have scarcely had a more quiet end apart from his pains from his disease. Thank God, that he has simply gone before & that he is safe from all dangers forever and yet how I wish his life had been spared.

I shall read the funeral service, I think here. If Charley had come, some different arrangement could have been made, but I have made such arrangements as seemed most advisable under the circumstances. In regard to this loss, it seems, we should thank God, that the bringing up of our children is resulting, if not in training them for earth at least, in training them for heaven. That is the great thing after all. We have been greatly blessed in this.

So far as I can tell, we will reach Columbia Monday morning & Pocotaligo the next day, but there may be interruptions, so I cannot tell. If Charley had come, I would have stopped and not have gone on, but I shall be obliged to, I suppose.

I wish it had been so that you could have been here, but Dr Hopkins said there was no living here. I suppose it is all for the best, but for my sake, I wish you were here. This is & has been a sad journey. I hope I may stand up under it. Yesterday was a sad day to me, you may believe. Jake behaved very well. I have written to Charley and Minny. My best love to all of our dear children & with the same & more if possible.

I am dearest

yr. affect^{te} husband

P.S.

My plans are necessarily changed, as I find so many obstacles in the way of removing to S.C. the remains of our dear boy. On consultation with Dr Hopkins, he advises that he be temporarily interred here. It seems that the body might be several weeks on the road & being summer it is not certain that on all the line it can be conveyed. This is to my extreme regret. The place is Hollywood Cemetery about 1/2 mile from the city.[89] Mr. Barnwell had Stuart somewhere here. If possible, I shall leave to-morrow but doubt if I can, as I had a most dreadful fall on my hip this morning on the curb stone in the street. It was so severe, that I thought it must be a fracture, but Dr Campbell has examined & says it is not. I can however scarcely walk to-day & perhaps may be laid up for two or three days, but I trust not. I have been rubbing with Arnica but cannot say whether I shall be able to move to-morrow. It is however, I am glad to say only a most severe blow upon the muscles. It is very unfortunate. Look for me every day till I come.

yr aff husband

---

89. Fred was buried in Hollywood Cemetery, on the bluffs overlooking the James River in Richmond. His grave is listed as Grave 98, Section X, in *Register of the Confederate Dead, Interred in Hollywood Cemetery, Richmond, Va.* (Richmond: Gary, Clemmitt & Jones, Printers, 1869).

Anne Leverett DeSaussure to her brother Milton

July 24, 1864

Dear Minny,

We had a letter from Pa on last Friday, he writes in very bad spirits. Fred in no better and no worse. He had a bad earache which was critical. Charley came out here that very morning to see if we had heard & if Fred was better, would not go on as he himself was sick. We had heard from Pa that Fred was better but advised Charley when he went in to send to the Middletons & see if there was not a letter & found one accordingly, which determined him to go on immediately, that evening. I went to work & made six quarts of bread & cakes &c, ham & eggs for Pa & himself as the former is nearly starving. I made a plenty of biscuits for him but he had used them all & was then on short commons so we are in hopes it was only being in bad spirits made him write so. Charley is to telegram to us today and I dread getting the telegram, he says he will try his best to bring him on in a litter if at all possible. I do hope he will be able to, they had not heard from Charley & of course Fred must feel badly with only Pa who is no nurse and who would not know how to bring him on. Pa says Fred has grown so thin, his legs being no larger than Ma's arms and he has very little strength. Charley carried on some medicine we had got from Dr Chisolm for him to see if that would not check the disease. Ma is anxious about you too since we heard of Capt Mitchell's death, do try keep out of harms way, it would kill Ma if you were to get killed, it makes her miserable to hear how the Yankees are shelling Sumter on your account.

Annie Hanckel lost her little baby last Friday, she brought them out to see us only the Friday previous, it was so fat & a sweet pretty little thing. Ma walked all the way there on Saturday. She spent the day with Aunt Til who walked out here the day before & spent the day with us; neither party were tired after their jaunt.

The shoes came safely but Cos Cornelia's wont get near her feet, they are not much larger than mine & <u>maybe</u> I will be able to wear mine with the help of Ma's stretching them. Cos Cornelia will be awfully disappointed. She sent her love to you in her last letter to me. Corn is not be had scarcely here. Maybe you might get rice—rough—that will do. I am getting that at the Association for allowance but soon there will be none of that & everybody will make short crops this year, the drought is so bad. I am going to suggest it to Ma to write to Mr W Heyward for we must have help from some quarter 25 or 50 would be such a help at present. However no use worrying if you can't get it. Soon as we hear from Charley we will let you know.

Your affect—sister
Annie

Part of a letter from Milton Maxcy Leverett to his sister Julia

Fort Sumter July 15<u>th</u> /64[90]

My Dear dearest Julie

I grieve that I have not been able to answer your letters before, now I will. Your letter of the [illegible word] May was very interesting. I am sorry I did not answer it before. The Starvation Ball which you speak of is a good joke but too [illegible] for such times.

Willie Manigault wasn't lost in the Albemarle,[91] I've seen him down here since, he is now a Lieutenant.

July 25<u>th</u> 1864

My dear Julia,

My "cot beside the sea" is a great big brick and dirt fort with crowds of rats and fleas and therefore you must excuse any want of sentiment. Sentiment! ye gods and goddesses, it is impossible that there should be such an ethereal essence of the immortal part of our natures exhibited when the little villains "<u>thrample</u>" over you as if you were a road,—when a poor wretch rubs and scratches all night and no matter what part of the night and if he looks around will find some other poor brother sufferer looking gloomy and sitting up in his bed and scratching and cursing the fleas, then finally not being able to sleep himself gets up and walks over to the bunk of some other fellow whose miseries happen to be forgotten for the nonce in a troubled sleep and either pushes or calls him until he is awake then asks if he is asleep. The poor wretch awakes but to a hapless fate for he finds the fleas are gouging him and sleep no longer visits his eyelids, until tired of anathematizing and scratching he calls somebody else until finally the whole tea party is awake sitting up and scratching and cursing the fleas or jibing each other, having one grand scratching party or mayhap joining each other in a friendly scratch one goes and helps the other catch a whopper, vieing with each other in their success or running now and then to look at a whaler. Thus matters continue until the daylight appears when the miserable little wretches are less violent in their attacks and a sort of troubled slumber visits the agonized tea party. Your humble subscriber has suffered much in his country's cause and can show many a mark received from his enemies—the fleas. None of you can imagine what fleas are. Take it all in all this garrison has a hard time of it, quite a hard time of it.

---

90. This letter is a short note written on the same sheet of paper as the one dated 25 July 1864.

91. The C.S.S. *Albemarle,* an ironclad commissioned that spring, was badly damaged in a battle on 5 May with Union gunboats near the mouth of the Roanoke River, at Plymouth, North Carolina. On 28 October 1864 the *Albemarle,* anchored at Plymouth, was sunk by a spar torpedo placed under it by a raiding party commanded by Lt. William B. Cushing of the U.S. Navy.

Mary Maxcy Leverett to her son Milton

Monday morning, July 25, 1864

My beloved son, These are dark days to us. You will see from the enclosed letters, how desperately ill, alas, how far gone Fred, dear Fred is. Annie says she has told you of the letter from your father which came on Saturday. I now send a letter which has just come—Alas, for us all! I thought Fred would have sat by my dying bed. In another note which came with this (which I do not send, as it has a memorandum in it) your father says, he wonders whether you would be able to meet him in Charleston at the proper time, if the worst came to the worst,—in the event of Fred's death—do you think you could get leave? Could you receive a telegram at Sumter? I fear Charley did not get there in time. I hear Tom Huguenin is appointed to Sumter, & is spoken of very highly—he has now a chance to redeem the bad odour of his name. I hope you will be on good terms with him.

God bless you day & night, prays Yr aff mother
Mary

Do not lose this letter of your father's as I wish to read it again. Keep it safe, or send it back to me by mail.

Fred's state of mind is an unspeakable comfort to me. O my son, I pray if you are called hence (may God in his mercy compassionate me and spare you) you may have the same faith in an atoning Saviour.

In the memorandum which I have not sent, your father says, "Fred is quite calm & has been quite himself again. Speaking of Milton, just now, he said he had the deepest affection for him, & that he loved you all from the bottom of his heart." O, what do we not all lose in losing Fred!

Capt. Thomas Middleton Stuart Rhett to Milton Leverett

2 Gun Battery No 2 July 29th 1864[92]

My Dear Leverett:

You certainly are growing "dainty of" yourself when you wait for me to write to you with all the coyness of a bashful maiden; and prefer that you should receive no letter rather than one obtained at the sacrifice of your maiden modesty; Whence my friend such change conduct? Allow me to assure you that your virtue can remain still unblemished, even though you commit the serious indiscretion of

---

92.   Capt. Thomas Middleton Stuart Rhett of Company E, First South Carolina Artillery, commanded 2–Gun Battery No. 2 on Sullivan's Island near Charleston.

sometimes writing to me. I have not yet acquired such a reputation as may endanger your well known virtue.

I am now in command of a little two gun Battery, between Batteries Marshall & Beauregard; which so far still maintains its existence as a battery, notwithstanding the invidious efforts & implacable enmity of the over-topping sand hills, which in every high wind endeavor to bury the poor little place with all its frowning armament & grisly array of pikes & piles of cannon balls beneath clouds of driving dust. You can appreciate in their full force from this account the daily mortification my poor battery must undergo, and "the end is not yet" I fear. I endeavor to preserve it however from the unscrupulous prejudice of its enemies & maintain its identity by policing every morning, after the manner of that "chieftan trained to war" "whose gallant mien" etc—our former captain of the ever glorious BVA of antediluvian renown. Can you not pay George Stoney & myself a visit?[93] For he too has the grave responsibility of another two gun battery resting upon his shoulders; so you see as life advances cares increase & all becomes vanity of vanities—till I marry.

I have just received a letter from Heyward who makes the melancholy statement, ridiculous though it is, that Owens Tom Ellis & Henry Elliott of course, & others "have got the seven years itch" & "the Dr says it is bound to go through." You see, Leverett, one among the few disastrous consequences of our leaving that company; from the "seven years itch" having appeared in that camp, "We may draw a moral though not adorn a tale."[94] What pleasant little reunions the itch crowd will have consisting as they do of the hardest cases of the camp. How they will console themselves by saying "it is nothing; Nobody thinks anything of it," imagine too how rapidly the contagion will spread among peasant & prince, and perhaps it may even dim the glory of polished boots & bright buckles of a notable we wot of.

I hope for your sake, that you get on pleasantly with Capt Huguenin, who I must confess is not a man after my mind; he likes his toddy too well, & has not I fear a very high tone of character! but I may do him an injustice; you will soon be able to judge for yourself. Do tell me are the Parrotts seriously damaging the Fort or are they only occasioning serious inconvenience & annoyance in circumscribing your limits. Please be minute as regards the damage done. Alas I hear the watercloset has gone the way of all flesh. Poor Mitchell's death I really minded. I liked [him] so much. And close upon it follows the wounding of Capt Johnson.[95]

93. 2d Lt. George Mosse Stoney Jr. (1843–1865) of Company C, First South Carolina Regulars, commanded 2–Gun Battery No. 1 on Sullivan's Island; son of Sarah Woodward Barnwell and Dr. George Mosse Stoney.

94. Samuel Johnson, "Vanity of Human Wishes" (1749).

95. Capt. John Johnson was severely wounded in the head by a shell fragment while inspecting the fort on 28 July 1864 but recovered and became an Episcopal clergyman after the war.

"Stay low & keep dark," and you may yet escape unhurt. I hope so. Boag is now at Fort Moultrie, and I go down this evening to that port, where I hope to see him. Direct to Fort Moultrie.

Yours truly
T. M. S. Rhett

Mary Maxcy Leverett to her son Milton

The Farm, July 30<u>th</u> 1864

My beloved son

Night and day have I been looking to see you come up the path to the house, for I know you would wish to come to us in this extremity, that we may all mourn together over our sad loss in the death of our beloved Fred. O, to write that beloved name, and know that the dear owner of it will never again be seen coming up the path, excited and smiling, with the pleasure of getting home again, and the delight of seeing how delighted we were, to think that I will never again see him sit at that table, or hear his cheerful voice calling me, is a pang greater than I ever expected to be called to endure. It is, as if Edward had died over again, to me. But I bless God that he died without alarm or fear of any sort, with full trust in his Saviour as justifying him from all things, and I live in the full expectation of seeing him again with my dear Edward, as soon as I cast off this burden of the flesh. I sorrow not therefore as those without hope, but patiently await my appointed time.—We are all entirely of opinion with you, that we do not wish you to be under Tom Huguenin a moment longer than you can. <u>Resign</u>, if there is no other better step to take. You ask again Ste Elliott's direction, we do not know, neither does Mrs. Jas. Rhett know, but suppose any letter directed to <u>Richmond</u>, (Fred told me all letters go safe thus addressed) Army under Beauregard at Petersburg,—that they always know in Richmond in what direction to send them. But we do not wish you to go to Gen. Elliott. You have been under fire long enough and could with honor take a safer position. You may know what an effect Fred's death has had on your father, that he says now, that he wants you to come home, and get some position in the <u>Reserves</u>. Is there no chance of you passing the Ordnance Examination? have you given up all idea of it? I hope not. We all want you at home very much, and intend to inquire if no situation in any Government concern can be had for you, as a detail. But I fear not. Poor Fred has been taken, whom I was never half as uneasy about as you, thinking that as a Surgeon he had a safer position. He sacrificed himself as much as if he had died in battle; for he was very sick in camp, yet would not leave, as he said "until the campaign was over, as he thought this was the crisis of our country and that every man should remain at his post, and do his duty." And thus he remained until it was too late. The last time in camp he got on horseback it was to get his passport & furlough, he fatigued himself very much in doing it, & when done it was too late, the Yankees had cut the R. Road at Danville, and he could not come. He went then to Richmond to "recruit" he wrote us, but did not tell us he was really very ill, in fact his last two notes never mentioned any sickness, and only led us to conclude he was refreshing and recruiting himself on his way home. Alas! he only was unknowingly deceiving us as well as himself. He was too sick to move, but was vainly expecting each day to get well enough to leave, as you may see, by his not sending for Jacob from the camp to attend to him until just a week before his death when he was no longer able to help himself without assistance. I intend writing to D^r. Hopkins to thank him for writing to us without Fred's knowledge. Fred sent word by your father to ask me to write D^r. Hopkins to thank him for his kindness to him—poor fellow, he said D^r. H. would appreciate it. He kissed Fred constantly when he went into his room or came out, your father said he seemed to love Fred so much.

My dear Min, your letter with the account of the bombardment of Sumter & poor Capt. Mitchel's death was deeply interesting. I am glad you were with him & did what you could. Poor fellow! O will this cruel war never be over! It seems to me the Almighty will surely send some awful judgment on this execrable Yankee nation for their unjust, brutal cruel conduct during this war. Their women are a cold, hard, unfeeling set who will sell their very souls for fine clothes and fine furniture. I felt more than once at the North when travelling, a sort of shrinking feeling of aversion at their hard & grasping characters. Poor Capt. Mitchel, & oh, his poor mother!— since I commenced writing the Carolinian has come & I am still more shocked to see that Capt. Johnson is wounded in the head, it must be a dangerous wound! oh, my son, my beloved son, God protect and bless you. Oh Lord cover him with the shadow of thy wings til these perils be overpast, let no evil befal him, give him a strong trust and confidence in Jesus as Saviour, pardon his sins, blot out his iniquities and grant him the victory over all spiritual as well as temporal foes, for Christ's sake.

Dear child, I wish I could see you. You are passing thro' trying times night & day, & I can't help you.

I wish we had sent the box yesterday, but the girls were so sure you would come, that they thought I had better not.

Your aff$^{\underline{t}}$ Mother
Mary Leverett

Mary Bull Leverett to her brother Milton

Columbia, July, 30th 1864

My dearest Brother,

We have been looking out for you every day, please, if you can possibly get a furlough come home. I want you to come particularly on poor Mamma's account.

She feels so sadly, now that you are her last boy. We all long for you to get out of that post of danger, if anything were to happen to you it would kill her. Everything connected with Fred is of so bright & cheerful a character that I cannot realize his death. I will always consider that he died a martyr, in his country's cause. D^r. Hopkins says he tried his best to persuade him to come home in May, but he would not then, & when he did get his permit, the road was cut, so that he could not. In one of his last letters to Ma he said he did not think he ought to come, he saw so many men shirking their duties, he would not desert his post. If we only could have had the satisfaction of having him at home t'would be so much easier to bear. But we have a great [deal] to be thankful for in Papa's being allowed to get there in time, & also that he had so many kind friends around him, who were devoted in their attentions. He wanted for nothing. D^r. Hopkins says to show how kind ladies were, he had known them to go to <u>nine</u> different places to hunt up eggs, to make custard for him. Papa says two came to see Fred on Thursday, that he talked, & laughed with them, said the custard suited his taste exactly, they told him they were glad & would send some more. Although, it is so sad to know that he thought he would live to get home & wanted to & that last simple wish could not be gratified, it is very comforting that he died so happily. I think we were too much taken up with earthly things. We needed something to draw us to heaven. Oh! Minny let us strive to live better. I have to stop as Tony is going in now. Do come home.

Your affectionate sister
Mary Leverett

From the *Columbia Daily South Carolinian*, Wednesday, 3 August 1864

AND YET ANOTHER.

It is our painful task to add the name of another of South Carolina's best and bravest sons to the row of her martyred dead. A few weeks since an extract from a letter gave, in these columns, a grateful tribute to the memory of that true gentleman and hero, Gen. M. JENKINS, and now the writer of that eulogy comes, as one under the common fate, to be placed on a similar record. FREDERIC PERCIVAL LEVERETT, Surgeon of GREGG'S Texas Brigade, has been called away at a time when one of his professional accomplishments could ill be spared. Unwilling, though suffering from camp exposures in the campaign in Tennessee, and sick from heavy labors in Virginia during the late contests at Spotsylvania, to abandon his position, when the emergency of the hour required that every true man should be at his post, he actually sacrificed his life to a sense of duty. With the harness on he has passed from the din and turmoil of contending armies to join the illustrious dead of the Southern band.

The lamented subject of this brief paragraph was one of those born to make his mark upon the age, though altogether in that modest and unassuming manner which gives a very peculiar honor to its possessor. Graced with the very best literary and scientific education, which the country could afford, and that more expanded by study in France and Germany, his services, as one of the best physicians and surgeons in the Confederacy, were in requisition as soon as the Yankee war broke out. From that period to the date of his recent illness, Dr. LEVERETT, with a patriotic ardor and industry, not exceeded by the most devoted, has been steadily engaged. It was said, by a disinterested person, that of those who came under his observation he was prominent among those who knew and did their duty. That he was conscientious, every one could see; that he was skilful, is apparent from the fact that his services have been solicited for various fields of active duty; that he was honored and beloved, is the universal testimony; while that he was patriotic, his grave shows. It is very little to say of him that he was a young man of high and noble nature—a gentleman in every shape and way the term expresses—unselfish, humane, generous, courteous, affable, peaceable, pure, of marked integrity and kindliest sympathies. In him, also, were delicately blended the gentler virtues of a truly christian character. Throughout life he had nothing but words of affection and thoughtfulness of others. A professing christian from the date of his college connection, at Harvard, and a consistent member of the Episcopal Church, he was calm and undisturbed when the inexorable summons came. He went as a believer should, to join the great multitude who have washed their robes and made them white in the blood of the Lamb. His good example remains to comfort those who mourn his unexpected removal, and to inspire those who loved him to win, with him, the great prize for which earthly life was given.

> "Soldier of Christ, well done,
> Praise be thy new employ,
> And while eternal ages run
> Rest in thy Saviour's joy."

Rev. Charles Edward Leverett to his son Milton

Columbia, Aug. 9, 1864

My dear Minny,

I can scarcely realize the tremendous blow, which has been dealt upon us by the sudden and unlooked for death of our dear Fred. I can scarcely believe that we are never to see, on earth, the face of the dear, good fellow again or behold him hurrying about in his restless activity. Why one so worthy of living and so full of promise of usefulness not only as a moral and religious man, but as a skilful physician should be taken is beyond human ability to fathom. But it must be all right, though unintelligible to us, and all we have to do is to be glad that the infinitely wise and good is the author of events. After Edward, I had especially looked to Fred to take charge of the household and he had already seen after the general direction of affairs. His judgment was generally good and his interest in all that concerned us, was all that could be expressed by the most affectionate heart. His death, to be attributed to the odious and abominable Yankees, has added to my horror of that diabolical people. But for those, or even for that Virginia raid, which cutting the R. Road, prevented his return home, where he could have been especially cared for, and so far as we can see, he would have been spared to us longer. What infamous devils, the abolitionists and Northern people generally have shown themselves to be.

I was glad to have been with Fred a part of the time during his last illness. I wish your mother could have seen him, as he was extremely anxious to see her as well as Charley. It would have been a great comfort to him. I had no idea of his being so ill. I think, too, that he was not aware of being so near his end. Still he evidently thought it possible & was prepared for the contingency. It was pleasant to see how calm he was and how supremely he rested in the power of his Saviour to save him. One of the first hymns, I read to him was that which you may recollect. "Just as I am, without one plea," and when I had finished, he said, that is the very one I wished to see. Every day he asked me to repeat hymns to him & have prayers & read the Bible, the last, I believe, not long before his death, was "Jesus, Saviour of my soul" which I asked him to repeat over with me. He did, but was unable to keep up, & I told him to never mind, I would say it for him. Poor fellow! How I grieve for him. I am so sorry, now, that I did not do more for him, even in the way of writing to him oftener. But I never thought that he cared for my letters, when he could get those from Mamma and the girls. It is a great consolation to know, that we succeeded in making him so noble a character, and further in training him to the inheritance of immortality. Now, though he is lost to us, not only has he left a noble name behind, but he is safe in heaven & we may look to be joined together in that world, where there is neither sorrow nor death nor any more pain.

If God spare your life, my son, you will have to take his place. I trust you will try in every way to be worthy of the mantle, which now falls upon you. There is great incentive for you, for the character of the family so worthily represented by Edward & Fred, has to be sustained by you. That you may be able, imitate the excellences, which were preeminent in them & though you may naturally be unable, recollect, the grace of God, if truly sought can make you to be one of those, whom all will honor, and above all, whom God will bless.

I sent you a paper having a short notice of poor Fred. I hope you received it.

I hope God will protect you in yr. exposures to Yankee shot & shell. Our prayers are often offered that you may be shielded.

Mamma has not been very well lately, but is better. Anne & Lou have gone to Camden.

Your affect^{te} father
C. E. L.

P.S.

Rev. S. Elliott & S. E.'s wife passed thro' Columbia on their way to Rich^d last week. Have not heard how Ste is.[96]

Julia Blanche Leverett to her sister-in-law Mary Bull Leverett

Cheraw, August 12th, 18[64]

It was with deepest regret dear Mary, that I received the intelligence of your late sad bereavement & most sincerely do I sympathize with you & all of the family, in this your heavy affliction. In his death, I too have met with a great loss; for I know, I would have loved him just the same, as if he were my own brother, could I have become better acquainted with him. His manner towards me, when we met in Charleston, not long before I was married, was so kind & winning & all his letters since have been so affectionate, I could not, but feel the warmest regard for him. We both looked forward with so much pleasure to having him come & stay with us after the war. It makes me feel very sad, when I think that those hopes can never be realized.

Mr. Leverett's[97] health is much the same as usual, he comes back from school, every day very much worn out. I have been trying to persuade him to give the rest of this month holiday, but he says he will not, unless he finds himself, totally unable to continue. Mr. L. is extremly unpersuadable, as you must have found out, long since & when he says <u>no</u>, I generally let the matter rest, but I must not say any thing against the poor fellow now, when he has so much to trouble him. I am glad it is Friday, for he went off this morning feeling very badly. His Saturdays however are frequently taken up in hearing missed lessons. I tell him, he

---

96. Stephen Elliott Jr. was severely wounded in the battle of the Crater, near Petersburg, Virginia, on 30 July 1864. Federals detonated a mine with four tons of gunpowder under the lines occupied by his brigade, but after considerable confusion, a Confederate counter attack drove the Federals back.

97. Blanche's husband, Charles Hendee Leverett.

has grown <u>entirely</u> too soft hearted, he should administer the rod more frequently, & to abolish the going to school on Saturdays altogether. It is so provoking after a hard week's work to have him lose his only day of rest that I feel as if I could whip the refractory scholars well, myself, if I only had the power.

You have already heard, I believe, about our plans for the coming year; leaving Westmoreland for Miss Hawes'.[98] Mr. Leverett thinks that Miss Hawes will come up to her agreement & let us have possession of the house & premises in Novem. but it is impossible to tell. She is an <u>extremely</u> fickle person & does not know her own mind from one day to another. In short, she is perfectly unreliable & I fear we are depending on a broken stick. If we go, tell Julia, that she will have to come and pay a long visit, just as soon as we are comfortably settled. You also dear Mary, I shall expect. If you like that kind of work, I will give you a plenty to do, in the way of helping me to keep house & mind little Julie, but if not, you shall only do what you fancy, & be a perfect lady of leisure. When you are tired of Miss Hawes, I will carry you over to Westmoreland, where you will see more children & hear more noise (its two distinguishing characteristics) than ever before in your life. I am sure that my sister & you will be mutually pleased. We have had another addition to the household here, Aunt Eva (Mrs James La Roche)[99] has a little baby about two weeks old, her <u>tenth</u> child & <u>second</u> daughter. The last circumstance, I would suppose, must be the only thing that at all alleviates the first. Her other daughter is about twelve or thirteen years old, so this one stands a fair chance of being very much spoiled.

Mr. Leverett says about the middle of Sept he will try & pay you all a visit & also that he will write in a few days as soon as he feels a little better. How is your father? Mr. L. told [me] he had received several severe bruises from a fall in Richmond & was looking dreadfully. I hope that he has quite recovered by this time.—Your mother too, please assure her of my sincere sympathy. Write very soon, do not take four or five months to answer this letter as you did my last. Your affectionate sister

Blanche

P.S. Tell Lou Julie thanks her very much for the baby. She is delighted with it & her whole face lights up with smiles when after having hidden it away for two or three days, I bring it out & give it to her again as something new.

---

98. Miss M. J. Hawes of Cheraw, a farmer.
99. Mary Olivia Bailey LaRoche (1826–1869).

Mary Maxcy Leverett to her son Milton

Farm Sept. 16th 1864

My dear Son,

We read your letter to Gen. Martin,[100] and thought it a manly and well worded exposition of your position & a good and carefully expressed exposé of the state of affairs between yourself & T. H.[101] Your sister was very much pleased with it, being more manly and straight forward an explanation than T. H.'s letter to Gen Martin, which he gave your father to bring home and read; tho' of course, we did not think his impartial enough as he did not state at all as tho' he had made a "mistake"— (I still think it was on purpose) yet of course your father expressed himself satisfied, as is done on such occasions. T. H.'s letter was fluently written, much better as regards the matter as well as handwriting, than I expected. You must write carefully and incessantly to improve your hand and style—you are evidently improving now, we think, in these & other respects and I trust you will go on "conquering and to conquer" yourself as well as your enemies. You should always have a dictionary by you when writing a letter, not for the spelling in which you are usually accurate, but because you sometimes make use of words unsuitable, or which do not convey the meaning you intended by it. In fact I think education, as respects a free use of a variety of words is behind hand at the South, and as you were educated at home where there was seldom occasion to correspond with those at home all your boyhood (which is the time to acquire ease & quickness in writing) you find it more difficult to overcome faults which arose from those circumstances. I believe in public schools like Eton and Harrow in England, and wish there were such in the Confederacy. A boy is taught to be self-dependent early & acquires a degree of self confidence from being thrown on his own resources, which equally preserves him from over presumptions as from under-valuing himself. Yet, on the whole, principles remain sounder from home education, and if a boy does receive some hard knocks from the world about him from want of experience, yet on the whole it is made up for by the superiority of having right principles to guide one in difficult cases, & experience will come in time. Do you know I think all the disagreable circumstances you have been enduring, patiently or impatiently as it may be, for sometime past are forming your character gradually, and I trust and pray that God will make it all work together for your good temporal & spiritual. I have been quite relieved to find you have got well out of this hassle, & no harm's been done, but am not at all sorry your father spoke to Gen. Martin it has all turned out well. The Gen. is as kind as possible in all his intercourse with him, so much so, that at last your father dined with him last Sunday, after his coming into the Vestry

---

100. William Edward Martin of Beaufort, clerk of the South Carolina Senate.
101. Thomas A. Huguenin.

room (he having assisted Mr. P. at the Communion) and asking him. Claudia Rhett (Mr. Ben R. daughter)[102] was staying there, and Julius Heyward[103] came in with a bottle of Champagne for her and Sally Martin.[104] There was some talk of blockade runners, so this bottle may have been from the wreck of one.

Your conduct in all this matter has been pleasing to us all and especially to poor me, who am always so anxious about you. It would gratify me greatly for you to obtain a Lieutenancy but if you do not, I will not distress myself. "There are as good fish in the sea as ever came out of it."—Mrs. James Rhett stopt last week to see Annie—she gives a bad account of Gen Elliotts arm—it has been giving him such excruciating pain for sometime past that he could get no rest and has become very nervous—and the arm is as paralized as ever.

20$\underline{th}$ I have been too busy to finish my letter. We are all well and improving since Dr Fair came to see me & prescribed iron & quinine for Tillie & myself. I don't know however if any of us mentioned that after being so distressed about you after seeing Huguenin's note I couldn't sleep for several nights & it ended by palpitation & Dr Fair was sent for—said my heart was perfectly sound, but prescribed tonics for weakness & nervousness, which have really benefitted me. Dear Min I shall have a grudge against the Ord. Dpt. if they don't give you an appointment. You deserve it more than any that have applied. I see sharpshooters at Sumter are hurting the Yankees at Gregg. Success to them! My blood boils when today I have been reading of some of their atrocities in Virginia. We had better die than be in their hands. God grant us deliverance soon. I can't make up my mind to think of what your future course must be until your fate is determined. It is despicable to see how some young men are skulking in the Offices in this Town & I despise them for it. It would break me down for you to be killed, yet I would hate to see you act like these men who are so despised by all. Glover wrote to Jim that Stuart Rhett is wounded severely, but not seriously—Jim took tea with us Saturday night. Mary F. dined here Saturday.

The fall of Atlanta has made us all very uneasy, but it is impossible for me to believe that such horrible wickedness as is now being perpetuated by the enemies can in the end succeed.[105]

We hear there is yellow fever in Charleston, & that Gen. Jamison died of it.[106] Take care of yourself when you go to Town.

Your aff^{te} Mother
Mary Leverett

102. Claudia Smith Rhett (b. 1846), daughter of Benjamin Smith Rhett (1798–1868).
103. Julius Henry Heyward (1849–1923) of Colleton District.
104. Daughter of Eloise Mary Hayne and William Edward Martin.
105. Federal troops captured Atlanta on 2 September 1864.
106. David Flavel Jamison of Orangeburg and Barnwell Districts.

Do Minny see if you can't get my shoes from Mr F. I think if you paid him for the others he would do ours sooner.

P.S.

Why didn't you ask Capt. Minor[107] if Gen. Elliott did not write to them for you? it would be nothing wrong to say he had told you he would do so.

(Julie has been reading my letter over & says it is <u>horribly dull</u>—she evidently privately pities you for being obliged to read it)

Milton Maxcy Leverett to his father

Fort Sumter Sept. 28th /64

My dear father,

I went to the city yesterday thinking that I might be able to arrange matters for myself, at the same time that I attended to some Ordnance Duties relative to this post, but didn't succeed. Charlie Pinckney through whom I had heard of my failure to obtain my appointment, had asked me to call on him some day or other when I happened to be in town and he would have a talk with me about obtaining a position more suitable to me than the present. I had business at the Arsenal to attend to about scrap iron collected around this Fort and at the same time saw him, but it turned out to be nothing, he merely suggested my obtaining the same position that I now occupy somewhere near Richmond. Which of course does not suit me, I'd rather stay where I am than do that. In writing to me of the non success of my examination he said that "he was aware of the difficulties I had laboured under," i.e. in obtaining at such a late date as I did information on what I was to stand on. If he had written sooner <u>I am certain</u> there would have been a different tale to tell but as I have mentioned before I never obtained one of the books which I was to stand on until the night before the Examination, and Charlie Pinckney didn't write in answer to my letter until the very evening of the night I was coming down.

I have been meditating very seriously as to whether I should remain here or get a discharge, not from that reason, but from other reasons, the <u>pressure of red tape</u>, holding a position in which I am subject to the beck of Tom, Dick and Harry and yet not being considered on an equality with them, that is what "<u>riles me</u>" so to speak. But I can't come home now in the strait in which the country now is, unless I was sure it would put some skulker in the field, and besides not being wounded either. If Ma and yourself positively insist on it I <u>may</u>, as I will do anything to please you, but I am in doubt of the "multitude of counsellors"[108] now. If

---

107. Capt. C. L. C. Minor, chief ordnance officer of the Department of South Carolina, Georgia, and Florida.

108. Prov. 11:14.

I was home I could discuss it more satisfactorily. My faith has been almost staggered by the events of the last few months. A special Providence is what I wish to feel confident in not <u>that I don't believe</u> in a general dispensation of an Almighty Providence but I want to believe and <u>feel</u> a <u>belief</u> in a particular dispensation of a <u>special Providence</u>. I have been thrown back in the very path of life that I thought was meant for me and in which I thought I was directed and which certainly best suited me. But let the blank paper speak for itself. I am confused by doubt and hesitation and want guidance. Love to Ma and all, am well.

Your aff'<u>ct</u> son

Milton M. Leverett

P.S. Don't doubt my belief but only a sufficiency of belief, a belief of the interference of Providence in little matters, it requires an immense degree of faith.

Milton Maxcy Leverett to his mother

Fort Sumter Oct. 4th/64

My dear mother,

　　I have been and am very busy now making out my returns in which of course I am not very interested as it will not be in my line of life. I have already made out two Monthly Returns and have now three Quaterly <u>Returns</u> on hand which will annoy me as I have never made one out before—all of them,—duties in a great measure, of a commissioned officer. I am very glad my dear mother to have pleased you in my late difficulties, I will do anything to please Pa and yourself, I only wish I was a worthier son. You must not worry yourself so much about me, worry yourself so as to keep awake?, why that is <u>preposterous</u>; <u>I</u> sleep first rate myself. Fort Sumter is capital for that, sometimes it is near ten before I get up. If you get sick about me and my affairs I won't write and tell you anything of them. I don't think anyhow that I will ever take advice from any of you, again,—"a burnt child fears fire."[109] Don't you think now that in my late difficulties etc. my own counsel was the most appropriate?

　　I have received Sis', Pa's and your letters, and will write when I can get a chance. Don't mind about my disappointment it doesn't matter a great deal, I wouldn't be at all surprised if it was for the best. I am exceedingly obliged to Pa and yourself for your <u>tremendously</u> good opinion of me and make my best <u>devoirs</u> accordingly but feel very well satisfied at not entertaining the same opinion myself. "Depression" won't worry me much, my spirit is too buoyant, I wish things would make a deeper impress on my mind than they do.

---

109. John Heywood, *Proverbs* (1546).

I am very sorry indeed that Pa has opened a school and advertised for scholars. I don't like it at all, I thought he had done with it, it will just kill him up. There are other cogent reasons also. Tell him I'll try and recall "Cato's Dialogue" with the Yankee and write it out although I can't promise that after fifteen or sixteen months it will be perfectly correct. Tell sis I am much obliged for her letter which I will answer speedily. Julie's letter which she speaks of has not come to hand. As time presses my dear mother I must close. I had intended writing yesterday but was quite busy and forgot. There was a "Flag of Truce" yesterday, and one every now and then. Blockaders are also coming in every now & then.

Love to all

Your aff'<u>ct</u> son
M. M. Leverett

Rev. Charles Edward Leverett to his son Milton

Columbia, Wednesday, 12 Oct., 1864

My dear Minny,

I have just heard that there were to be some appointments in the Treas<u>y</u> Dept here, and I have just returned from seeing Major Jamison.[110] He says he shall make appointments early next week, & will take down names.

I write to ask if you would like to apply; if so, you must, Maj. J. says, obtain a certificate that you are entitled to exemption and write an application, simply to the purport that you apply for a vacancy in the Treas<u>y</u> Department, of the C.S.A. This certificate of exemption you can get from some surgeon, I should think without difficulty. Certificates of character, you can send, or they can be obtained here. Jamison says you are the kind of person, he should like, from my description. Jim says you had better apply. Jamison says, he wants those who are reliable. The salary Jim says, now is over $3000. I suppose it will be reduced by & by. I do not know what you will think about it, but I presume your chance will be as good as any & better than most. Jim will speak to Jamison whom he knows. I send this at once, as you will have to act at once. I give no counsel & you must decide for yrself. Ma & all are well. Write soon as you can & if you determine to apply & can't get the certificate at once, I suppose you can make the application, sending it a little later. I suppose in about a fortnights time the clerks chosen will enter on their duties.

yr. aff. f.

Write soon as the application must be handed in soon.
Jamison will not receive applications unless one means to accept if appointed.

---

110. Maj. Sanders G. Jamison, head of the Treasury Note Bureau in Columbia.

Mary Maxcy Leverett to her son Milton

The Farm Columbia, Oct. 20th
1864

Dearest Min

Your letter night before last to your father gave me great satisfaction. In fact I wished to have written before, so anxious was I for you to take advantage of the opportunity of getting out of so undesirable a position as you have in Fort Sumter, one, which must be intolerable, to any man of spirit and feeling, and which it is certain, no gentleman would willingly occupy, if there were means of escape from it. Major Jamison went to Richmond immediately after your father wrote you, and is to be back next week, when your father will again see him. I have little, if any doubt, you will be appointed, as he told your father he was afraid he would have some difficulty in filling the vacancies (a good many men were turned out) suitably, that is with men of the right sort, & when your father described your character, & cause of the exemption, he answered "That is just the man I want." However it is just as well not to feel too secure, & it is said that <u>ladies</u> are to be appointed in the place of most of the men turned out, & I know also that Eben Coffin has written to Mr Trenholm to try & get a place, as his salary is not large in Dr Chisolm's office, & their family have to pay $4000 a year <u>rent</u> to a man, who <u>bought</u> the house only two years ago for $3000. I can scarcely say I feel regret, at your father's commencing school-keeping again, it was so necessary that something should be done,—and yet I cannot bear that he should have the trouble. I think too, he may, and will do, a great deal of good in so doing. It is very pleasant to see that his school which commenced 1st Oct. has steadily increased, and today <u>fourteen</u> boys were here, & another is to come on Monday which will make $3000 a year for us, & has very much relieved our minds concerning the ways & means of getting on. Mrs. Arthur Middleton's two boys came today—she came to see us yesterday,[111] & asked your father from Mr Middleton, whether he would be willing to take it in corn, to which, of course, he assented, & it will be all the more convenient for us. We made much more corn this year than last, and a plenty of peas, but have not dug a potato yet for the hogs continually got into the first potatoes that were planted, & ruined them; ground-nuts are not dug yet, and the sugar cane did so badly that I don't think Annie made more than twelve gallons syrup which we are now using. Tillie intends getting her horse brought up from Wm Fullers, so you will have that to ride in to Town on, if you are fortunate enough

---

111.   Julia Emma Rhett Middleton, daughter of Charlotte Haskell and James Smith Rhett, and her sons Arthur (b. 1854) and James Smith (b. 1856).

to get the place. I had a letter from Charley—he says tell you he thanks you for your letter & will write when well enough. He has had a rising in the roof of his mouth, but it was better when he wrote last, yet he had diarrhea then. He really is never well. The baby was monstrous, he said, & quite well.

Saturday. Dear Min, Major Jamison has returned, & your letter to me with your exemption certificate has come just in the nick of time—your father will go in that evening to carry it to him—you ought to have sent in your application at the same time.—Aunt Til, Mary Heyward & Mary Fowles were all shocked this morning to find you had let so much time pass by without sending in your application in your own hand writing, they all want you to get it very much; Jim spoke to the Major for you this morning & your father also, & he (Jamison) says you must send it in at once. I hear they never will tell beforehand if they intend to appoint a man, until they have the application from himself in his hand. I have great hopes of your success. The salary is more than you think—Major Jamison says it is $3,700—so, you see it is worth trying for. A great many applications have been made. Otey Read is one who has been turned out, & he has succeeded in getting a Lieutenancy already under Lt. Col. Hardee. O. R. is a very undesirable somebody for a companion, by Jim's account.

I hope my dear boy, you will succeed & send you a form of application (from your father) which you must copy in your best handwriting & send up at once.

> Major Jamison
> Chief of Note Bureau
> Sir,
> I beg leave to offer myself as a candidate for a vacancy in your Department.
> Milton Leverett

Copy this, Min, and send it up in a letter to your father at once.

God bless you my dear child, and give you success—if it is good for you. I have prayed earnestly, while you were deliberating about this, & entreated, that you may be guided to a right decision by the Great Ruler of our affairs—so when your decision came, without my having done or said any thing to bias you (according to your father's desire) I took it as an answer to prayer, & trust it will so prove. Nevertheless, God's will be done, I will humbly say, if you do not succeed, & so must you.

In haste

Your ever aff^te mother
Mary Leverett

Rev. Charles Edward Leverett to his son Milton

Columbia Oct. 28 /64

My dear Minny,

 I have sent in your application, but I understand that Jamison says you will be required to resign first, before he can appoint you. He said to Jim that he had told me so. I did not understand him so you will therefore be obliged to resign, as he does not wish—or refuses to appoint any person in the service. That is reasonable. I hope it will not be too late for you. You had better resign at once, and telegraph me "resigned," and I will inform him. At all events, the resignation will relieve you of your present disagreeable position & if you do not get this, you can apply for service elsewhere. If you cannot telegraph, write at once that you have resigned or sent in your resignation or have obtained exemption. I presume the fact that you have obtained release, if there is no such thing as resignation allowed, would be sufficient. I trust if you write or send at once, it will be sufficiently early. Chas. Hanckle says you had better leave—Jim also.

 Nothing new. Charley was here one day this week. All well.

 In haste

Yr. aff father.

M. M. Leverett

Rev. Charles Edward Leverett to his son Milton

Col.ª 29 Oct. 1864

My dear Minny,

 I wrote you yesterday to resign, but I have just come to-day from seeing Jamison, & he says he has made his appointments, for the present from men out of the army over 50 years of age. I am so sorry to have you disappointed. It is a great disappointment to me, will be to your mother, when she hears it. But there is a higher director in these matters than man, & I trust it will prove for the best anyhow. If I were you I would resign and not remain in Sumter any longer. Come home & perhaps something may turn up. Don't be disheartened by this. All things are wisely ordered & I am sure this will so result. "In all your ways acknowledge Him & he shall direct your path."[112]

 I write from town in haste. In reply to my question Jamison said he had for "the present" made all of his appointments.

Very affy
yr. father

---

112. Prov. 3:6.

P.S.

I have just seen Capt. Ch. Hanckel of one of the same departments. He says you had better resign & come up here, & you will get a place in a week or two. He says you can get a better place even than one in the Dep[t] where you will be only a clerk. He tells me to advise you to come by all means. So resign and come.

Milton Maxcy Leverett to his mother

Fort Sumter Nov. 6th /64

My dear mother,

We are having a perfectly quiet state of things now, a truce is now pending, which is to last for some time i.e. until further orders, or until all the prisoners are exchanged. They have been exchanging today within a comparatively short distance of this fort, indeed I think that the Yankees crept a little nearer than they ought to have been allowed. We broke the truce yesterday unwillingly by firing over there from here with our sharpshooters and I believe killing a man, when they shelled us pretty sharply for awhile. We sent out a row boat afterwards and apologized for it as the Post had not been informed that the truce was to exist any longer than the day before. By their transferring the flag of truce from Savannah here evidently shows that that place is meant to be a point of attack at present, while this harbor escapes for awhile. We are now in a very critical state of the game and I am quite anxious as I think the result will prove whether the war will end shortly or last some time. I understand quite brisk fighting is going on at Grahamville in which my company is engaged and as usual are doing well. You cannot tell how I regret not being with them. I dislike their being in a fight and I not with them. I hardly think I can reconcile myself to leaving the army now, when we need all the force we can possibly obtain. But if the turn of the game will allow I will apply for a transfer to a cavalry company with a couple of months or so retirement home i.e. if you don't succeed in obtaining for me in Columbia the position I wrote of. Don't worry yourself about my being in a fight—I don't see any immediate chance of being in any and wish I could have been in the fight with my company.

Don't write to the Sec. of War or anybody else about anything else whatever.[113] Nothing of importance to mention. Love to all,

Your aff'[ct] son
Milton M. Leverett

---

113. Confederate Secretary of War James A. Seddon of Virginia.

Mary Maxcy Leverett to her son Milton

Farm, Columbia, Nov. 8th 1864

Dearest Min

You do not seem to be as much disappointed as I was at the termination of our late attempt to get you out of Sumter. Jim says you are entirely mistaken in supposing from any "Orders" that you would be liable to be sent to any Camp of Instruction, that it is no such thing. He wants you to come up and says you will get a place right off; and as it is thought by some that the whole Treasury Bureau will be stopped in January, (from already having Notes enough in circulation) so, he wants you and himself together to join in blockade-running. Miss Grimke writes Tillie that she hears that Fort Sumter has been represented to the Governor as being a "complete den of gamblers and drunkards." I have no doubt this is true, and do not doubt you could tell enough about it, if you choose to. Well, I do not like you to be there when the Fort has such a bad reputation, don't you think you had better come up at once? Nobody thinks the Fort is going to be attacked again, but that the Yankees will try all the energies of their fleet and army on Richmond, and content themselves with gradually destroying Charleston at a distance, as, in fact, they are now doing. If you were under a different Commander in the Fort, and also had been allowed a long furlough and had your boot repaired or a new one bought, I would not be so in earnest or if you had been promoted, I would say it would be well to stay to get you away, but really I think you are under too great disadvantages in your present case, and had better get a detail, or a discharge, or whatever other method you may be able to take, to get out of the Army. It is no honour to be in Sumter now, and I'm afraid some judgment from the Almighty, will come down on a place where so much wickedness is prevailing. Flee from Sodom like Lot, in time. I was so deeply interested in the account you gave of the mutiny, that I am very anxious to hear the conclusion. If they condemn those men to death, it will make me feel like writing to the Secretary of War to try to get them pardoned. It is reported that Ripley is giving way to his love for drink more and more openly, and I heard that Major Motte Pringle's sister[114] told Matilda Middleton privately that "her brother was her greatest trial and grief." Every body knows he is the "black sheep" of the family. What a shame to have such men in responsible situations.

If you had been in Columbia, <u>out of the army</u>, you would have got the place, but Jamison has orders <u>not</u> to take any out of the army, the way to do it, is, to get out <u>first</u>, then apply. However, you must do just as you please, and cut out your own path

---

114. Maj. Jacob Motte Alston Pringle's sisters were Susan (1829–1917) and Mary Frances (b. 1831).

for yourself in life. If you please yourself, you'll please me, so long as you do what is honorable and right, which, I have confidence in you to think, will be always.

I supposed your father told you he had fourteen scholars. A great relief to my mind it is, to see some sure means of having enough to live on. Last summer a year ago I felt often as if driven to my wits end to know how to get along with corn at $20, and not enough money coming in to half supply clothes & food for so large a family of people and yard full of servants. But now, we are much more comfortable, have supplied all the servants with clothes, and purchased a good deal for the family also. Having put off purchasing all we needed for three years, expecting each year the war would end, it was useless to delay any longer so, I have recently spent at least $300 on homespun, and probably will have to lay out as much again on the same article. Think of having to pay $90 to $100 on homespun, which before the war we gave $1 25cts for a whole piece! I wish you were getting as well provided with money, as we are beginning to be, when I have finished gradually buying all we need, I hope some will be left to send you, as I know you must need it. We have got shoes lately for several of the family, at 35, 50, & 70 dollars a pair, after awhile we will all have been "shod." I don't expect ever to hear anything more of Ficklings shoes—you must have offended him, somehow I suppose.

Did any of the children ever tell you that Jacob asked you to search Billy's things, as he had stolen articles from several of them when you last carried him down—a shirt from him, & a razor from Hercules, were some of the missing abstractions.

You will be sorry to hear, dear Minny, that poor old Ephraim is dead. He was sick a long time, off & on, not enough so to be in bed, except now & then, until toward the last. He spoke to me about taking Daphne for his wife some months ago, I told him I had no objections & he was pleased but he said Nanny worried him out of his life & complained also of Lindy & Molly. I tried to make them treat him better & finally got Annie to have Nanny punished, it did a little good, but you know they have ways & means of hurting each other which no owner can prevent. His hog was stolen, he told me he knew it was Nanny & that she worried her own mother Daphne to death also. Finally, on talking with him about it, he said he thought he would be more comfortable at the Saltpetre Works & I thought so too, and let Mr Gamewell[115] (who is extremely kind, & thought much of Ephraim) know & he sent a cart for him. He gradually got worse, the D^r said it was old age—he had every comfort, more indeed than we have in our house for ourselves, Mrs. Gamewell[116] sent him every day coffee, bread, chicken soup, milk, meat, until he told me he sent word to her himself that she mustn't send it, he couldn't eat it. Your father went several times to see him & prayed and talked with

---

115. Rev. Whatcoat Asbury Gamewell, a Methodist clergyman in Columbia.
116. Mary A. Gamewell of Columbia.

him, he asked after me, & sent "howdye" to all the children; I went to see him, made a worsted cap out of your old scarf to keep his head warm, & sent Daphne to stay altogether with him until he died, which was a fortnight after. It is very distressing to part with our servants when they die. Your father felt it very much. He was ailing in all about three months. He asked after you once, in the first part of his sickness. Your father told him he hoped to meet in heaven, he answered he hoped so. He said repeatedly he thought it was his last sickness.

You will be glad to hear the Townsend cow which we thought was killed, to the surprise of the whole establishment made her appearance the other day, looking very well. Where she had been for so long a time is a mystery, for Hercules went to Townsend's farm for her and she was not there. Since the fields are open, the cows are improving & Annie has made some beautiful butter twice lately. We have made almost no potatoes. They have almost finished digging groundnuts, made only a few. Fodder is the principal thing we have succeed in, of that we have more than we ever made before.

Do you know we actually have got a "Foreign Legion" in Columbia? Six hundred Germans, French &c. of our Yankee prisoners have taken the oath of allegiance and are now enrolled in our army. They will be set to do garrison duty. One Englishman told me that when they landed in N York often they were entrapped & made drunk, & when they came too found themselves enlisted, they were told. I am very glad, for they often don't care what side they are fighting on, & it will save our mens lives. Some people don't believe in them but I do.—All well here. Girls, as usual, say they haven't time to write, & your sister really has her hands full between teaching & the book-keeping.

yr. aff Mother
Mary Leverett

Rev. Charles Edward Leverett to his son Milton

Colª, Nov. 12, 1864.

My dear Minny,

I saw Mr. Hanckel today & he said so confidently about yr. getting a place, if here, that I write to you to come up. I am not satisfied with yr. being in yr. present position, and as you are our only son, I prefer to have you at home. If you don't succeed here, you certainly can get employment in the army again, but Mr. H. speaks in such a way that I would not hesitate any longer. I have been in town all day & am just going in again on business, so write only these few lines.

Yr. letter to your mamma came yesterday. Don't hesitate any longer but come.

In haste
yr. Aff. fr.

All well

Milton Maxcy Leverett to his father

Fort Sumter Nov. 15$\underline{th}$ /64

My dear father,

I received your letter last night. I will see what I can do. I may be able to get off but can't say. At any rate it will be some time before I can I expect. I am more disgusted than ever. Has Ste Elliott returned to Virginia? There is nothing of any importance transpiring. Love to all. I am well. Very sorry to hear of poor Daddy Ephraim's death but fully expected it when I was last home. Is sister going to send for her horse?

Your aff$\underline{ct}$ son
Milton M. Leverett

Julia Marcelline Leverett to her brother Milton

Nov. 16th Columbia

My dear Min,

I had intended writing to you last Saturday but I got hold of a novel and read it most the whole day. "Not that I love writing to Min less, but reading novels more." As to that letter of yours, the less you say about it the better. I am disgusted with it. What a "cute" invention to get letters that riddle of yours was but it failed most signally. Tillie's answer was "Because they stick to people." My opinion is that it is an ingenious but unsuccessful attempt to induce correspondence!! As to Mary I don't think she has considered the subject. I went to an oratorio at Christ Church (the same which Sister and Annie were invited to sing in) night before last. Mr. Pringle gave me a ticket. Some of the pieces were beautiful and others again I did not care much for. After we had taken our seats and before the music commenced we were surprised to see old Mr. Trescot enter the church look all about and finally call Jim out. Of course that set us on the "qui vive" thinking that the house was on fire and curious other things had happened. But what was our surprise when Jim returned and whispered to his mother that Newton had come. They all went out to see him and he came back with them. He is much improved in his looks. Has a thirty day furlough and is on parole so that it will be some time

I hope (not for unpatriotic motives but for his family's sake) before he goes into the army. He paid the surgeon of the place wherever it is, fifty dollars to let him come as hospital attendant or nurse or some thing. You do not know what nice block rings [illegible, paper torn] etc. the prisoners make. Newton showed us a set of studs he had made. They were very pretty indeed. We scolded him for not bringing us some. Dear Min, <u>why</u> don't you come up? We all want you to come and get this place, and then if it breaks up to commence blockade-running. Anyway you must not stay in Fort Sumter. I am afraid if the dear old fort remains any longer under its present commander its name will have to be changed to "Ichabod." Ma says must tell you that you must come up for she thinks that Mr. H. is keeping a place for you, and if so he has to do all the work himself until you come. He has to work until 7 o'clock P.M. The "other ways" that he said, of making money, we think means nothing more than going into the upper country buying bacon, lard etc cheap and then selling high. I would rather have you <u>almost</u> a private in Fort Sumter. I can't say <u>quite</u> however. So mind you <u>must</u> come up, for we are looking for you. I suppose Mame told you about Brother Charlie's coming here in Dec. and bringing little Julie with him. It is probable that I shall go back with him. Mame and the rest think that I have behaved shamefully in not giving my little god-daughter any thing, but what can I give. Really I have nothing—except my prayers, and besides I did give it a hat last summer. Tillie and Lila are in Pendleton but I suppose will be down pretty soon. Dont forget to bring that jacket with you. I have set my heart on having it.

Ever your sister
Julia

Matilda Leverett to her brother Milton

Columbia, Nov. 18th 1864

My dear Minny,

   It seems strange to see how averse you are to leave that drunken den—it looks as if you were becoming accustomed to it, and did not mind it any longer— The place is now notorious and I wish you were well out of it—we have not mentioned any-thing you wrote about, so that it is not through our means that it has gained its reputation. I suppose either Ma or Mame have told you what Miss Grimke said about it in a letter to me a few days ago—in all likelihood <u>all</u> of your friends are astonished at you. Jim says you could get a place in the Department in a minute if you only resigned and came up here—and Annie Hanckel says it is your duty to report the state of affairs down there—<u>it has been</u> reported to Gov. Bonham but as he is just going out of office, of course he will not take any notice of it—the President is the one who ought to be informed. Ma & Pa both dislike your remaining there exceedingly. Had you not better inquire all about the blockade running?—I mean your chances of being employed in it, though I understand that the danger of being captured is greater than ever. (Mr Lyons's son who was engaged in it was taken last May is still a prisoner at Point Lookout) but we all think that a great deal better, (I don't mean being a prisoner) than going either to Virginia or the West, which Ma won't hear of. Any how, come out of Fort Sumter.

Newton returned a few days ago from Point Lookout, having been there ever since last January—He looks very well and has improved in manners—is much graver and more like a man. He had to bribe the Yankee surgeon to say that he was sick—gave him $50. He was extremely ill for six weeks while there, but had recovered.

Seeing how much his mother is in need of money he is trying to persuade Jim to go blockading too—As it is very likely that from Mr. Trenholm's proposition, the Treasury appointments will not last very long. He, himself, has to return to the army in a few weeks time but seems sick of the very idea, having been a prisoner so long. Mrs. Hughes and the Markoes were very kind to him writing to him constantly and sending him things.—Poor Maxcy died in Texas[117]—it must have been a terrible blow to his mother, as he was her only child. Mrs. Markoe sent photographs of all her children to Newton—he brought them with him, but I have not seen them yet.

Annie heard from Cousin Cornelia last week—she said she was not coming for some time—We hear from Dr Ford that Cousin Julia is teaching in Dr. Snead's school in Raleigh, North Carolina.

All are well.

yr's truly & aff^{ec}

Matilda L

Mary Maxcy Leverett to her son Milton

Columbia, Nov. 26th 1864

My dear Min

Received your letter yesterday advising us to evacuate the premises if Sherman should come this way.[118] Well, we have talked it over several times, without coming to any determination,—it is too large a family to move; but Charley was to come in Dec. to see us, with his little Julie, and carry back our Julie with him;— if things look squally about then I may send Mary also back with him. I hope and

---

117. Maxcy G. Hughes.

118. Maj. Gen. William Tecumseh Sherman commanded the Federal army in the Western theater, which had embarked on its March to the Sea from Atlanta toward Savannah.

trust however that the cold-blooded wretch Sherman and his crew, may be over-taken by the vengeance of God, which though it may seem long to sleep, will, I firmly believe yet overwhelm and destroy them. It is true wickedness dwells in our land, and in Fort Sumter and other coast defenses probably is entirely in the ascendant, but God our good God, sometimes mercifully spares a place for the sake of a few therein who truly serve Him, and for His people's sake delivers a country. I see by todays Carolinian that there is a report of Gen. Ripley being removed, and the Charleston Delegation (Legislature) are passing Resolutions deploring it and requesting Government to retain him. Why, they must be fools, or perhaps they are drinking men themselves and have a fellow feeling. I feel strongly tempted to write to the Sec. of War, or the President, privately, either with, or without my name, and give them an insight into the state of things down there. I almost think it my duty to my country to do so. Evidently many persons know the state of affairs and wish them changed. Only a few days ago, a piece made its appearance in the paper, to say from Gov. Bonham, in answer to the anonymous communications addressed him, that he could not notice their account of the state of things in our coast defences, unless correspondents fur-nished him with the name of witnesses for him to proceed on. So, somebody has been enlightening him (not I). I heard that George Stoney had spoken of it, and others also.—You do not, my dear son, know, how deeply grateful I am to our God and Father for your preservation from contamination when in the midst of so much guilt and vice around. On receiving a letter from you not long ago which plainly portrayed the state of things, after getting into my chamber and thinking it all over, I was so struck with your remarkable preservation, kept in a hollow of a Father's hand and inwardly filled with disgust and abhorrence instead of being tempted to join in their orgies, that I was filled with wonder and adoration, and on my knees blessed and praised God for this great mercy to me and to you!—for Minny, nor you, nor I, nor any can withstand temptation in our own strength. If you do not feel it to be temptation but instead are inspired with a feeling of dis-gust and dislike, then bless God all the more, for He gave you that feeling. I tell you, Minny, I blessed God that night even for the afflictions I had endured, and told Him I willingly bore it all—cheerfully bore His not answering my prayers for the dear lives of those who are gone, now, that in this great thing He has answered my prayers! Yes! as exquisite as my agony has been, all goes for nothing, since I have the precious knowledge that my beloved, only remaining son, had been shielded from the evil around, as perfectly as the three men were in Nebuchad-nezzar's oven from the surrounding fire, so as they had not even the <u>smell of fire</u> on their garments when they came out.[119] I hope my darling, when you come out

---

119. Dan. 3:27.

of that trying furnace, Fort Sumter, that not even the "smell of fire" will be on your garments,—but that is, that your lips and your life and whole character will show you have come thro' the ordeal unscathed. I trust it may be more, and that your very trials and the hard knocks and cross accidents of life you meet with there may help to soften your disposition, keep down temper, and enable you to keep yourself with a bit and bridle, until you subdue yourself entirely.—

Monday. Dear Min. I feel exceedingly anxious about you as I see by the papers two hundred sail of Yankee vessels have arrived at Hilton Head, & this morning's paper says "it is rumored that the enemy are landing at Bulls Bay near Charleston, with a view to create a diversion in favor of Sherman, and to take our batteries on Sullivans Island in reverse." I don't know what that expression means unless it is to take them from the back or landside, or perhaps to take them after they have created the diversion for Sherman. Any how I feel it means danger to Fort Sumter, therefore to you. You appear to be delaying your departure so long that I suspect strongly that you are doing it on purpose to be in the fight, if there is one. The Mercury[120] seems to think Charleston is to be attacked. If you won't come out at once, suppose you let me write to the Secretary of War to promote you, & to Ste Elliott also? I'd just as lieve write to the General as not. His arm is just the same, wound well, but arm useless & often suffering intense pain, & is still in Camden. The members of the Legislature are arriving so I suppose he will soon be here. If I see him I will be sure to speak to him about you.

Newton was here this morning. He predicts you and Jim will be sure to see the inside of Point Lookout when you go blockade-running, & offers you both, letters of introduction! He looks well, but appears to be much sobered down. Persons here and there in Columbia seem to fear & expect an attack on Columbia, but at present nobody is thinking of moving, indeed people mostly could not move, & where to go to? nobody knows. People are coming here from all the Georgia towns, but where they stay I cannot imagine, for the town is crammed. Dr Parker is going to move into the Asylum with his family, & rent out his house for $10,000 to two families.—Dear Min I thank you for writing so regularly, do continue to do so. I feel so uneasy lest you be wounded or taken prisoner. God bless you, my dear boy, and preserve you from all evil accidents and bring you safe home to us all again.—I feel almost sure you are just diverting my attention by pretending you are coming home, and that in reality you are preparing for battle. God bless my child, and keep him safe from harm! but what can I expect under such commanders as Ripley & Co. I am much troubled about that. Men of such habits cannot have clear intellect, something somewhere will go amiss and betray defective judgment and muddy heads. Gen Johnston and Gen Lovell are both living in

---

120. The *Charleston Mercury,* one of two newspapers in Charleston.

Columbia. Soldiers from Va. are now going thro' to Georgia. Gen Hampton is on his way there also, tho I don't think he has arrived here yet. The Barnwells, who are at or near Graniteville, have taken the alarm & moved Sarah & Emily to Edgefield to their sister Mrs Ed. Walkers & Mrs. Robert Barnwell to Greenville,[121] I suppose to Mrs Dr Fuller Sen. They made nothing at that poor farm, & are hiring out their servants in different directions. Your father's school seems to be much liked, & people want him to go into Columbia.

Tillie Fowles is spending a few days with Julie.

yr aff Mother
Mary Leverett

J. D. Geddings to Rev. Charles Edward Leverett

Charleston Novr 28th 1864

Rev C. E. Leverett
Columbia S.C.

Dear Sir,

Your treatise on Written Arithmetic loaned me by a friend, was in my possession barely long enough for an <u>inspection</u> even of its contents—its plan and presentation of principles—the character of its examples for practice—the extent and methods of illustration &c yet I feel prepared to say that I regard it a work of great excellence, and, moreover, that when its mechanical execution shall be commensurate with its intrinsic merits it will prove one of the most attractive of books for pupils on the subject of Arithmetic

Yours truly
J. D. Geddings
St Philip St
Public School

Mary Bull Leverett to her brother Milton

Columbia, [November 1864]

My dear Minny,

Although the last to write to you it is not that you are least thought of or least loved by me, and my motto—"Better late than never" though a pretty sneaky one,

---

121. Sarah Bull Barnwell; Emily Howe Barnwell; Ann Bull Barnwell, wife of Rev. Edward Tabb Walker; and Eliza Barnwell, wife of Robert Woodward Barnwell, were sisters.

is a very good one, & if I only keep to it I will do very well. There is no use for me to make excuses, for no matter how good they are, you never believe them, besides when one is really wrong about anything I think it is very mean to make any excuses at all, therefore crying you mercy brother mine, I will strive to expiate my fault by sending you a weekly bulletin relating to the affairs & doings of the family at "Higeia." The reputation of the Fort is at so low an ebb now, that I cannot bear the idea of your being there, if you can possibly leave <u>please</u> do so. I want you to get a discharge so your leg can be fixed, & you know you could stay in office here until you made money enough to pay for it. I dare say Mamma has said enough on the subject therefore, I won't say any more.

I spent a week with Catherine Coffin[122] very quiet, but quite pleasant, the more I see of her, the more I like her. Eliza is spending her furlough in Greenville with her cousins, the Johnstone's, she is quite handsome. They are in great trouble about a house, the one they have has been sold over their heads, for $50,000 it has only five rooms too.

Did you hear about poor Col. A. Haskell' wound? that he may get over it but not only will lose his eye, but will probably be deaf, & some one said out of his mind. I think death in that case would be preferable. I am afraid it will all prove true, as when we last heard, they had not found the bullet, he has another bullet in his body also.[123] Mrs Arthur Middleton, his cousin, told us, he killed eleven Yankees in the fight, was surrounded by numbers, fought so splendidly, a General, at last took out a pistol & shot him, they really ought to promote him, even if he does not get well. Aunt Til & Annie Hanckle are coming to dine with us today, the latter has got rooms at the Seminary & will soon begin housekeeping. It is not very pleasant to go to Aunt Til now, she has so many people staying there. I have not dined or spent the night at her house for months. I do not suppose we will be alone long though as Annie has written to invite Cousin Cornelia here & Mamma thinks of having some boys here also, we ought not to mind it as it will enable Papa & Ma to live much more comfortable, & that's the principal thing. It seems to me that the winter would be so happy if I could only look forward to Fred's coming home. I cannot realize that I will never see him again.

Mrs. Wallace has just lost one of her little sons. The other Mrs. Wallace (Sally B.) wrote to ask the Middletons to leave their house, as she wanted it, luckily they had Dr Wallace' letter allowing them to keep the house for the war, for seven hundred a year, besides putting basement rooms &c. Miss Matilda just copied the letter & sent it to her, she was very vexed about it, said she could hire half of it for

---

122. Catherine Hume Coffin (1839–1886), sister of Eliza and Ebenezer.
123. Alexander Cheves Haskell was severely wounded and left for dead in a cavalry battle on the Darbytown Road near Richmond on 7 October 1864.

$4,000 a year & live in the other half & have one or two persons stay with her, who would pay board. Some one who was with her said "But Sallie if you made an agreement," she answered "Oh that was nothing." The Middletons, of course, feel very badly about it. It is not very pleasant to stay in anybody's house, even if you are paying rent, when they are wishing you out all the time.

I heard from Mary Seabrook a few days since, she says the deserters are getting very troublesome, as long as the soldiers were there, they gave no trouble, but latterly, & very unwisely I think, they have been removed, & the wretches have been robbing all of the uninhabited houses & it is expected they will soon begin the inhabited ones. In fact I believe they have already begun. Dr T. Means'[124] life was threatened if he did not leave, so Mr. Seabrook invited him to stay with him until he left, he was expected yesterday at Mrs. Rhetts. While little Annie Means[125] was writing to Mrs. R. she said the men were whooping under their windows, they expected an attack every moment. I hear they have given warning to everyone to leave or they will burn down their houses. When Mary wrote she said her father wished them to stay, as, if they left the house would be robbed & if they stayed she said there was some chance of their being killed, so they were "in a fix" as she expressed it. It would be very hard to me to leave my house at the order of such wretches. I would a great deal rather stay & fight it out. Government ought to send some help to the poor people up there, for of course everyone cannot leave, as so many have no where to go to.

Sister Mary Leverett

Mary Maxcy Leverett to her son Milton

Columbia, Dec 8th 1864

Come up at once, Min, what are you waiting for? Your letter yesterday evening informed me that the Board are willing to give you a recommendation to a Clerkship—why in the world did you not accept it and be thankful? You seem to think a Clerkship not the sort of thing that is "gentlemanly"—throw all such ideas overboard, old fellow, and come up to one in the Treas^y Dpt. at once. All the offices are "Clerkships," & the officers "clerks," but they are always designated in conversation and otherwise as "the gentlemen of the Treasury Dept." Do you expect an office to be thrust into your mouth? Without doubt you'll have one, and there are numbers of places to be had, but I don't know whether you would like them or not, all I can say is, <u>Come Up</u> & find out for yourself. Every body is doing something. Don't talk about coming up if you can "get a position agreable to you in

---

124. Dr. Thomas Means of Beaufort District, physician.
125. Anne Means (b. 1853), daughter of Ann Stuart Hanckel and Dr. Thomas Means.

Columbia"! nonsense, man,—how many positions are agreable in these days? Does
that sound like a man in earnest to make his way? It is ridiculous to tell us to ascertain and let you know if there is one that will be "decent and gentlemanly" enough
to suit you; a person can only find that out for himself. Twice have we had, I may
almost say, the promise of an office for you, if you had made an effort to come when
we first wrote on the subject you could have got it, but the first & probably the best
was filled in consequence of your delay in acting, and if you do not come at once
I daresay the second will be gone too—for you can't expect them to put off appointing someone, on your account. I actually cannot understand you. Here you are
writing to us to try for a place for you, when we have written to you over and over,
to come up at once and take one. Most men would have jumped at the prospect &
been on the spot in an instant, and here are you still waiting to know more. You can
know no more, and cannot even learn the salary unless you come to see yourself.
Your father has spoken for you repeatedly, & I really believe it is three weeks or a
month since he wrote you to come up, for Charles Hanckel said he would "guar-
antee you a place"; yet you are still delaying. Why, it was a great kindness in C H.
to say that much, for it is against the usage or custom to promise, or even allow you
to know if there is any prospect of getting appointed. Are you waiting like a bird to
be pushed off the roost? wait no longer, but come and strike out for yourself. Your
father on the receipt of your letter yesterday evening again went in to see Charles
Hanckel but could not find him,—he is acting as Clerk in the Legislature, as well
as being in the Treas^y, so must be making double. He did it to avoid being sent off
lately, for all are liable in the Dept I believe, as all belong to some regiment, & he
was an officer Major I think in the Reserves. Many have been sent to Hamburg or
to Georgia or Grahamville. I want you to come for another reason too. The Yankee
Officers (Prisoners) are to be put into the Men's Lunatic Asylum for safe keeping[126]
and are to be guarded by what is called the Foreign Legion, & the ladies & citizens
have no faith nor trust in them, & Dr Parker says they stole a cow from his brother
openly, to kill, the other day and what is worse, some of them robbed the Hamp-
tons of all their silver and jewelry to the amount of three hundred thousand dollars,
& wrote on the walls of the house that they had "sworn to exterminate the race of
Hampton" & many other abusive things. We are so near, that I am afraid we will
suffer. You must come.

In haste your aff. Mother.
Mary Leverett

---

126. Camp Asylum, a Confederate military prison for Federal officers in Columbia, was established in December 1864 to replace Camp Sorghum, an open prison camp with no real
facilities near the city. Camp Asylum operated until Sherman's troops approached the capital city in February 1865, when its prisoners were transferred to North Carolina.

Milton Maxcy Leverett to his mother

Fort Sumter Dec. 29th /64

My dearest Mother,

I arrived here last night safe, and find all things perfectly quiet in the harbour, no firing going on at all with either party. Tuesday night I spent at the Wayside Home, and on Wednesday morning went over to Mt. Pleasant, saw the Board and told them my chances of obtaining a detail were very slim and applied for either a discharge or a furlough of some months duration. All the members of the Board not being present no action could be taken and I will have to go there again next Wednesday, which I am perfectly tired of doing. The Board said they were not authorized to take action on anything except physical inability and would not be able to do as I wished as regarded a furlough or discharge except on these grounds. In answer I told them that they could <u>conscientiously</u> on those grounds. In answer they said that they were not able to decide as all the members were not present. (There was only one absent, three comprising a Board, and two of course a Quorum.) They then ordered the clerk to write me out another furlough, but I declined it,—told them I would rather come down to the Fort.—I had duties down here which it was necessary that I should perform as there was no one else that I knew of who could attend to them. I heard some rumour of the Fox having been captured and then again I heard she had been expected in for somedays.[127] If Jim leaves, the application can be made out and sent down to me. I told the board that I was not desirous of quitting the army but that it was necessary, and that it was my wish to rejoin a few months after.

I hope you all have been getting on well and that Mr. Dinkins or any other rascal has not been disturbing the quiet of the place. I heard that we had some twenty two thousand men on the C & S. R. R.[128] and that we intended falling back to Greenpond and making stand there.

Tell Mary and Julie and also Tillie Fowles I was much obliged to them for sitting up with me on Monday night, 'twas quite kind but the three poor 'creturs' all fell asleep <u>long</u> before two o'clock and were wishing all the time ''twas time for Minny to go.' I'll have to send Tillie Fowles a special note of thanks for her <u>gallantry.</u> My dear mother don't worry yourself about me. Fort Sumter is the safest place about and I am hale and hearty. I think I shall send Billy up in a day or so. Love to all.

Your affectionate son.
Milton M. Leverett

127. The *Fox* was a blockade runner built in 1864 in Liverpool, England, for Fraser, Trenholm and Company, which made eighteen successful runs between May 1864 and May 1865.
128. Charleston and Savannah Railroad.

Milton Maxcy Leverett to his mother

Fort Sumter Jan'y 20<u>th</u> 1865

My dear Mother,

I am still <u>waiting</u> here on the miserably slow procrastinating business men at Hd. Qrs., my papers not having yet returned. There is nothing at all of importance transpiring down here now, with the exception of four men having deserted from this post last night—supposed to have swam and waded across to Morris Island. It is very easily done at low water, not much swimming to be done especially when they get half way across they can easily hail the enemy's picket boat, which I suppose must have taken them up. Two were negroes—one a free negro and the other a slave. The other two were what is called galvanized soldiers, that is Yankees in our service who had been once in the Pen. They had joined us simply because of the hardships they had incurred in the Pen as they had told me themselves. Love to all my dear mother

Your aff'<u>ct</u>. son
Milton M. Leverett

On 1 February 1865 the combined Federal army commanded by Maj. Gen. William Tecumseh Sherman, containing some sixty thousand veterans, crossed the Savannah River in two large wings and advanced into South Carolina, a state they blamed for starting the war. "Here is where treason began, and, by God, here is where it will end!" a veteran of the Fifteenth Army Corps exclaimed. The Federals marched toward Columbia—though Sherman hoped to make the few Confederates defending the state believe that he might attempt to take Charleston instead—and were slowed only briefly by a small-scale battle at Rivers Bridge on the Salkehatchie River in Barnwell District. Pushing a small force of Confederates aside at the bridge on 2–3 February, Sherman's columns crossed the river and reached the outskirts of Columbia by 16 February. The Confederate defenders of the two Carolinas under the direction of Gen. P. G. T. Beauregard, evacuated the city the next day, leaving cotton bales smoldering and leaving large supplies of liquor intact.

After Mayor Thomas J. Goodwyn surrendered the city to Sherman gleeful Federal soldiers ransacked both the existing State House and the new State House, which had been under construction since 1855 and was still unfinished. They convened as the South Carolina Senate, repealed the Ordinance of Secession, and censured John C. Calhoun, adjourning to reconvene in the North Carolina State House. Many other soldiers roamed the streets of Columbia frightening and insulting the "secesh" citizens, looking for food and drink and often entering private houses either searching for valuables or simply destroying what they could.

That evening and into the night, high winds and excited or drunken Federals helped spread fires that had been left burning or started new ones; some men sang, "Hail Columbia, happy land, if I don't burn you, I'll be damned!" Most of Sherman's officers, however, tried to keep order, arresting the most conspicuous offenders, and numerous Federals helped Columbians save their homes and churches from the flames. About one-third of the city, some 450 buildings, burned on the night of 17–18 February.

Brig. Gen. John Wallace Fuller of Ohio, commander of the First Brigade, First Division, Seventeenth Army Corps, chose the Leveretts as his unwilling hosts and made their house his headquarters during the Federals' brief stay in Columbia.

Mary Maxcy Leverett to her son Milton

Farm, Columbia, Feb. 24. 1864[129]

My beloved son—The long week of agony is over. We are safe. Being uneasy about you I send Jacob to find you, if he can, and remain with you the rest of the war. We are entirely in the dark as to the situation of affairs at Charleston—some say it is evacuated others that it is to be defended—Hardee is abhorred and condemned by all. If Billy is still in statu quo, perhaps he had better have leave to go to see his wife at Robertville (where Dr H F.[130] left all of his negroes) and then come here. The fair city of Columbia is now a heap of ruins, little more than the outskirts remaining. We sent Annie & Lou, Mame & Julie, bedding, clothes & provisions, to the Asylum, where Dr Parker & his family were, who welcomed them heartily, & there they remained until all was over. If our men never fought before, tell them I say they must do it now: if they give up, or their knees shake, I won't count them as men, but as dogs who deserve to, deserve to die. When the fight first commenced it was near Granby where the enemy endeavored to throw across a pontoon bridge, Hampton stopt it, & the fight was kept up following the course of the river gradually until some got across on a bridge above Columbia & some just at the street which runs to the river, the fine bridge across was destroyed by Col. B Rutledge <u>without orders</u> (which ought to be a lesson to military men) and so spoilt a fine scheme of Beauregard's & he was very angry.[131] We had but eight thousand men & they forty thousand in reality, I believe, but they told me boastfully 60,000 another said 80,000 and a common soldier was fool enough to try and convince me they were 125,000. Beauregard holds them at 35,000, anyhow

129. The year was 1865.
130. Dr. Henry Middleton Fuller.
131. This action occurred on 16 February 1865, at Congaree Creek, in Lexington District across the Congaree River from Columbia.

they were four to one, but no negro soldiers, only a pioneer set. The Mayor surrendered the Town at 8 o'clock next morning. The girls saw the two flags of truce
meet in old Geiger's field & in no time they rushed in. Terms were, private property respected, women & children unmolested. Now hear how they were kept. I
forgot to say however they bombarded the Town, your sister (who stayed with us
to take care of Kate & Carrie who had measles) stood in the piazza and saw several as they burst over town, one fell on Nickersons,[132] fragments fell one in the
Coffins yard & Mrs. Keating's kitchen, two men were killed, but it did not last over
a day. The Asylum was untouched (yellow flag) & the Hospital at Campus[133] also,
but when the burning was commenced the Ladies Hospital was burnt. I must be
brief if possible for there is too much to say. In the shortest time you could suppose after the main body of their army entered (12 o'clock) & immediately after
our men filed out of town by our road, in rushed the wretches into our house to
pillage, smashed open desks (all of the Greggs & ours) broke open drawers with
axes, asked for keys to corn house & smoke house, & I laughed to myself to think
how nicely we had tricked they by, a few hours before, ripping open Cornelia's pil-
lows, empting the feathers & packing nearly all our meat & rice & flour, sent to
Asylum with the girls,—they found therefore but little to eat, but drank the few
bottles Champagne & eat Cornelias sweetmeats, drank my milk & took the bit of
butter. They went thro' every room and took every thing except our beds & bed
clothes & for the honour of human nature I will add, whenever they opened the
room where Tilly & the children were, she told them they were sick, & begged
them to go back, & they did. In my room they even crept under the bed & hunted
in every hole & corner & have not left me a second suit of underclothes, all your
shirts are gone, even the comb with which I comb my hair & your fathers hair
brush & his razor were taken, broke open my work box & stole my scissors, emptied my writing desk & carried that, as well as the little writing case of yours out
of my drawer. About one o'clock two officers came, looked around, said it was contrary to orders & a shame and left promising to send a guard to protect us; in the
buggy they came in, they showed me the old State House flag with a look of exultation[134] & one of them argued hotly with me to prove it all our own fault &c &c.
The rest of the day passed in the same riotous scenes, I was everywhere endeavoring to control the thieves, parry questions, lead them astray about everything
when I could & gleaning information in my turn. I kept your father out of the way

132. Nickerson's Hotel.
133. Of South Carolina College.
134. On 17 February 1865 Federal soldiers from the Thirteenth, Fifteenth, and Thirtieth Iowa
     Infantry regiments arrived on the grounds of the unfinished statehouse. The 18' x 36'
     South Carolina state flag was captured. The flag was presented to the Iowa Historical Soci-
     ety in 1910 and was loaned to the South Carolina State Museum in 1990.

as much as possible, for I was more uneasy about him than myself, finding I could manage them better, but he <u>would</u> come occasionally & show himself thinking to help me. I was on my feet all day, a tremor all over me (but I determined they should not see I was afraid) & often in the room with a crowd of armed men, &c &c about night time a polite & curteous young man Lieut. Farnhame came and let me know that Gen. Fuller would make it his Headquarters, which relieved me, for it made us safe for the night. The Gen. was very polite, so that your father absolutely conversed with him as if he was a friend & told him all he thought of them & that he was writing a History against them! What madness! I carried a cup of milk & putting it on the table told him I was sorry I had nothing better to offer, as his soldiers had taken everything. He politely asked me to take coffee, which I politely declined, telling him I had just taken a cup of tea sweetened with <u>syrup</u> & was quite accustomed to Confederate diet. In the meantime a horrible scene was going on in Town. They were robbing & setting on fire, drinking whiskey and acting like demons. As the houses burnt down one after another the terrified women & children rushed into the Asylum for safety surrounded by these yelling devils, who tore open their trunks & gave to negroes or tore to atoms. Poor Lizzie Logan as she ran in, threw herself into Annie's arms and cried "O Mrs. DeSaussure, <u>is</u> there a God in Heaven!" The fiends raged curseing, screaming up and down in front of the Asylum swearing they were going to blow up the Asylum that night. The poor ladies believed it and thought their last hour had come. One (old Mrs Henry) died of fright others were very ill & children the same, in all 500 ladies & children were there, and the scene was indescribable. Your Aunt Tils house is burnt down & she is at Mrs Pringle's, Mary H. & Annie H.[135] at the Seminary, they brought out their things themselves, Til saved very little. I invited all here, but as Mrs P. has a plenty of provisions Til said she'd stay there & the others saved provisions too. The Coffins[136] spent the whole night in the woods amid scenes of horror, and the wretches would say to them "Ladies, it is a very cold night, why don't you go into your city to warm yourselves?" Cold blooded wretches to taunt defenseless women & bid them warm by the flames of their burning homes! The Yankees intend to try and prove the fire was set by Negroes <u>but it was not</u>. The ladies saw the Yankees set different houses on fire. One lady saw a Yankee who seemed to be provided systematically with the means of doing so, he daubed grease all round the window frames, walls &c. then did the same with turpentine or terebene, then strewed matches on the floor & set fire. One lady had a baby only a <u>few minutes</u> old she was very ill & Dr Trezevant[137] who was with her, saw

---

135. Mary Heyward and Anne Heyward Hanckel.
136. Sarah Lewis Simons Coffin and her daughters Eliza and Catherine.
137. Dr. Daniel T. Trezevant of Columbia.

the Yankee soldiers take matches & deliberately set fire to the house she was in, <u>three</u> times & each time some more humane, put it out, and even prepared a litter to carry her out in case the others succeeded. I can't tell you half. If you are still in Sumter let all this be told in the papers, our men <u>must know</u> how we have been treated. There is not a cock to crow within miles—all our poultry killed, put in our wagon & carried off, mule gone, Quash & family except Lewis, gone. Sary & Hercules stuck to us & that & Jake together made Daphne's family stay. I can't tell you how kindly Sary behaved to us. One Yankee put a bayonet to your father threatening, one put a pistol to Mrs D. Hamilton's head & one shot at Mad. Sowsnowski, who jumped aside.[138] I conversed with a large number of officers of all grades, they regretted the burning of Columbia & said <u>we</u> caused it by giving the soldiers whiskey. I asked why didn't Sherman destroy the whiskey if he didn't wish them to get it? They seemed to think me a very notable rebel, and officers were all day coming to converse with me. I wish all I said could have been set down, for I felt as if inspired & repeatedly put them to silence. They are dreadfully afraid of our putting negro soldiers in the field & say, if we do they can't say <u>when</u> the war will end, but if we do not they will end it very soon, that our men do not fight with half the enthusiasm they once did.[139] They all long for peace and anxiously inquired my opinion and one after the other asked, & whether we had not been beaten enough to want peace, see their force how immense, see how they had destroyed our resources, railroads &c. I told them "we did want peace, but would agree to none but an honorable peace." Their countenances fell. They pointed to Columbia & referred to the wholesale destruction going on over the State, & asked if we were not ready to give up. I said "No! It would make us more determined & drive every man into the field with feelings more embittered & intense than ever. It was a <u>good thing</u> for us." Again they were disconcerted. Then said "the men would have to come home to take care of their families." I said "No, we would take care of ourselves, that I had suffered (pointing to our sacked house) but was willing to suffer. I could bear calamity. They referred to Georgia, how they had ruined her! "I said Georgia was recovering already, like an India rubber ball, and so would we." This is not half that passed. The ladies wish our men to know all about it & you had better let <u>some</u> Editor extract what they please.

God bless my dear Son
Mary Leverett

---

138. Rebecca Motte Middleton, wife of Daniel Heyward Hamilton, and Madame Sophie Sosnowski of Columbia, who succeeded Madame Acelie Togno as principal of the Barhamville Institute 1864–1865.

139. A vigorous debate over enlisting black Confederate soldiers, who would be offered their freedom in exchange for their service, was being waged in the Confederacy. Although the Confederate Congress passed a bill authorizing black Confederates on 13 March, the war ended before any units could be put in the field.

Catherine Hamilton Leverett died of measles at The Farm on 9 March 1865, at the age of fifteen.

Mary Maxcy Leverett to her cousin Caroline Pinckney Seabrook

The Farm, Columbia, March 18, 1865[140]

My dear Caroline,

When your letter arrived my poor little Kate was lying a corpse in the house, & [I] was in bed sick at heart and exhausted in body. When the Yankees came, Julia had just recovered, and Carrie and Kate were sick in bed with measles,—the three days terror did not seem to hurt them, as Tillie & myself always put on a cheerful look in their sick room, but my poor little lamb gave up her life in my arms, ten days after, from the <u>effects</u> of measles. Had you seen the grief in the house, you would have thought it was Fred or Edward for whom such tears were shed. I know that for her it was a glorious change—a most blessed relief—but reasoning cannot change nature, and even faith though it softens, and gives glorious glimpses of the future, cannot take away the pangs of parting from the present life. So I still grieve, yet chide myself for grieving.

You will wish to hear how we fared, & just think for a moment how you would feel, if you suddenly found what seemed to be hundreds of Yankees pouring through your house, breaking open drawers, destroying, stealing every thing to eat or to wear, often destroying what they could not, loading our own wagon with it all, making my own servants chop off the heads of about thirty head of ducks, turkeys, fowls, & guinea fowls & throw into the wagon, & I standing in the back piazza silently looking on! Luckily for us the day before we had determined to send Annie & Lou, Mame, and Julie to D[r] Parker's, who with his family were staying in the Female Lunatic Asylum which we were pretty sure would be respected (the yellow flag was hoisted). D[r] Parker is very friendly and not only took charge of them, but also of six or eight bags of provisions & buried Annie's silver for her and so we had that much off our minds. It is computed that about five hundred women, children with a few old men & boys, took refuge there the night of the fire.—All day the wretches were going through our house, broke open all the Gregg's drawers, stole their best blankets, Maxcy Gregg's gold headed cane (which had been presented to him) his gold epaulettes, (splendid but old fashioned things) they drove an axe into his Secretary burst it open & left nothing but his papers in it, stole his crimson sash, the pants he was killed in & in fact nothing is

140. This letter is in the collection of the South Caroliniana Library, University of South Carolina, and is included here with the permission of the library.

left but the coat he was killed in (off which they cut three buttons.) & his papers. Cornelia will be horrified when she sees her empty wardrobe &c. After a few hours such work two officers came to the door in a buggy, bringing with them our poor old State House flag, displaying it with evident exultation. Why they should have brought it to show me I can't imagine—they were evidently two representatives of the two corps who took possession of Columbia, the 15th & 17th.[141] They had heard we were being robbed and said they would send us a guard—the one of the 15th had a very bad expression and was hot against us for firing on the old flag at Sumter. They did not send a guard however but just before night Lieut. Farnham, Aid to Gen. Fuller's rode up, behaved very courteously, said the General would make it his Head Qtrs. and we would thus be protected. I was truly glad for I was exhausted with the events of the day, & feared that the night would be much worse. Had you seen the elaborate introduction which took place and General Fuller's very low bow as Lieut. Farnham presented him, you would have supposed we were great people & these peace times. I am sorry to say Mr Leverett appeared very insensible to the honour and did not remove his hat (he had just come up the entry) until I gave him a look & then merely nodded & asked the General into the parlour without shaking hands. Tillie & I greeted him more cordially with a pleasant bow & said I was glad to see him which was the truth for we would undoubtedly have had the roof burnt over our heads that night if he had not been here.

Oh, what a terrible sight it was to me that night to look out & see the watch fires of 25,000 men on our farm all around us up to our very doors! Ah, Caroline, think how Tillie & I felt as we saw this in front, and then looking out at the back door saw our neighbors houses all in flames, Capt. Adams's[142] (where all of Nat. Heywards wine was stored) Maj. Rhetts and Mr. Arthur Middleton's. The Middletons had taken refuge in Columbia (Mrs Girardeau with them) & Maj. Rhett had gone to parts unknown. They burned every house that no one was in on every road leading from Columbia towards N. Carolina. While this was going on out of doors, Mr. Leverett was in the parlour conversing with Gen Fuller, and telling him his opinions as plainly as if he was a friend, and even informing him of his intention, of publishing a History of this war which would be <u>fairly</u> written, that is, show off the North in its true colours. I went in several times to try and get him out, but he would not come—I knew it was madness to talk so to an enemy, even tho' the Gen took it pleasantly & courteously, and sure enough next day, Gen Meagher[143] came to the door & had his name, place of residence, college he was educated at &c all taken

141. The two Federal corps were commanded by Maj. Gen. John A. Logan and Maj. Gen. Francis Preston Blair Jr., respectively.
142. James Uriah Adams (1812–1871).
143. Brig. Gen. Thomas Francis Meagher, commanded a provisional division in the Federal Army of the Tennessee.

down in a book by his Orderly. If Sherman succeeds, I expect, & Mr. Leverett himself believes, that he will certainly be in a Northern prison & have his property confiscated, even if he is not hung. However, to go on with the "Evening's Entertainments," I carried in a cup of milk, & setting it on the table told the General I
was sorry (it went hard with me to say that much) I had nothing more to offer him,
as his men had completely cleared us out of everything. He smiled and said it
"seemed to have been the worse for him then, as well as myself that he did not
come sooner," he then asked me to take a cup of coffee with him. I declined,
adding I had just taken a cup of tea sweetened with syrup, that I was quite accustomed to Confederate diet, & then left the room. I must do him the justice to say
he was polite enough to offer to send his Orderly to my daughters at the Asylum,
for me, to let them know we were safe & see how they fared. So, I wrote a note
& received a reply the same night. His aid Lieut. Farnham procured a guard for
us next day & night & I think we are indebted to him for our safety as our neighbors son saw two men coming up to our house with torches the next night (when
Gen. F __ had left us), but the guard stopped them. Nothing can exceed the horror, the anguish, the sufferings of the people of Columbia the night of the fire &
the next day. My poor sister's house was burnt down—some houses were set afire,
& some caught—the latter was the case with hers, but a Captain of an Iowa company & his men were very kind, and assisted her, Mary Heyward & Annie Hanckel
in moving their things, that is provisions, bedding & clothes, but all of their furniture was burned. Charles Hanckel had hired half of Tils house, his & Mary Heyward's loss in furniture was very great. To add to the horrors of the night, the
wretches had cut the water pipes as well as destroyed the Gas, and Til says tho'
there was a horrible glare on one side of her house, the other side was so pitchy
dark, that having no candle (gas being in every room usually) she had to grope in
the dark even for her clothes, and consequently lost almost every thing. One of
these men gave her next day a number of yards of homespun of which she has
made a very nice dress. Some of these soldiers of Sherman were demons, others
were very humane, & even shed tears at the pitiful sights they saw, and denounced
the burning of the city. All that I saw endeavoured vehemently to prove that it was
not done by orders but that citizens would give the men liquor, & they became
maddened. That some gave liquor to propitiate them there is no doubt, but if
Sherman chose to he could have stopped that, for he is a severe disciplinarian &
they are afraid as death of him. Many ladies saw their houses fired. This army is
composed almost wholly of North Western men & they are a regularly educated
set of thieves, burglars, robbers & house burners—& are accomplished villains. If
the North does not rue the day they were sent to pillage the South, I am mistaken,
she will dearly reap the fruits of it when they are disbanded after the war. I conversed with a number of officers. They are evidently afraid of what the effect of

this great outrage—of firing a city, after its surrender, under an agreement declaring private property to be respected, will be in the eyes of the world. I pointed to the ruined town, while standing in my piazza speaking with them and asked if <u>this</u> was what <u>they</u> styled "civilized warfare"? & told them not a nation in Europe in the nineteenth century would be guilty of such an outrage. They did not deny it, but attempted to prove it was "accidental," the men got at liquor &c, but the last officer I conversed with, intends evidently to try and prove it <u>was done by the negroes</u>—(which is false)—said "the facts should be brought forward and would come to light one of these days, it could be proved." I told him it was not so, but even if he did succeed in proving a negroes' <u>hand</u> did it, it would prove nothing, for that <u>he</u> knew, and everybody knows, that negro could be induced by <u>bribing</u>, or by threat of a bayonet, to put fire to a house, and that "I should not in the least blame the negro's <u>hand</u> that did it, but the odium would fall on the head of those who <u>made</u> him do it." Tillie saved our silver & watches also, but they stole clothes belonging to Mr Leverett, myself & Minnie, & you imagine my feeling when one of these villains carried off Fred's dress sword (he never wore it) and rode off with his <u>handsome gold laced cap</u> on that guilty felon's head. It went to my heart. The only place they spared was the sick childrens chamber. One of them emptied my writing case (a handsome travelling Morocco one given to Edward by Gov. Wise' son, Rev. Henry Wise, & by him given to me) and took it as well as a smaller one & a valise of Mr Leveretts, forced open my work box & stole my scissors & black thread &c. Others broke some old china of the Greggs, swooped down Cornelia's sweetmeats & then smashed the glass jars, nay, they even emptied out all my okra seed Annie had put in a jar & then broke the jar! Can meanness go farther? But all this is a trifle to what was done in Col. in some houses. Ladies had their dresses violently torn open and were searched for their gold—negro women were carried into <u>ladies chambers</u> and ordered to flog them (I dont think it was actually done, however) & ladies rushed frantically away from these insults. As far as I could learn, no actual personal insult was inflicted on any lady, beyond the rude and violent attempts to search them for gold.

Almost every one lost watches & silver and from all accounts the silver alone they took in Columbia is beyond computation. "St Peters <u>Church</u>, Charleston" was on some of the silver—so an officer told a lady.

I stood or sat for hours in my piazza talking with officers of every grade. What betwixt a chilly east wind and intense excitement, during the whole three days in which there was a continual "cut and thrust" carried on between these officers and myself I trembled from head to foot and was so determined that they should see no signs of fear that to stop the tremor and prevent a tear being seen or a sob escaping, I had sometimes to compress my lips & bite them in the midst of a sentence, until I struggled off the emotion.—I hated so to let an enemy see he had it in his power to make me shed a tear. Oh! that some one could write with a pen of fire and tell the world, the history of the sufferings & agonies of those three days of Yankee rule. Oh that our men could hear & know all that passed that dismal night! It was like "hell let loose," in some parts of Columbia & will yet be heard of, this Mr. Sims, the Author who is about to issue a small paper for the purpose of letting our men know all that has occurred.[144]

I wish you would come and see me, it would cheer me up, and I sadly need it.

You ask how your uncle Ste[145] fared in Camden, he lost very little if anything, as the Yankees did not take that road. Cos. H. Stuart's house was spared from the first who got in finding poor Sarah Stuarts little boy laid out on the table in the room they entered.[146] The officer told them to tie crape on the door handle & orders should be given that no one should enter. So, they lost nothing, except Cousin Henry's horses. Bishop Davis' house was not entered at all, because when in Columbia a Lieut. McQueen[147] who worked hard and saved old Dr Reynolds'[148] house from burning, promised to protect to the utmost of his power, any one there, in whom Dr Reynolds was interested, & the Bishop, as well as others were mentioned by Dr R. & were not molested. Dr DeSaussure lost four negroes, his horses, & I believe his watch.

It would take hours to tell you all that occurred in and out of Columbia, and you as well as I, must now be heartily tired of so long a scrawl. God supported us most wonderfully, & not a finger was laid on one of us, tho' we were considered such notorious rebels that there was no end to the officers who came to argue, to persuade, or to—literally ask "if we had had enough"? The last thing that was done as this great army of ruffians filed along the road leading by us, was, to fire a parting shot at the house—we heard the sharp crack of the gun, and the ball as it struck— I went quickly out into the piazza and showed myself to them, to let them see I did not flinch, and stood some minutes looking at them. I expected every moment to have a ball put thro' me, & I think they felt sheepish, for they turned away their heads & walked on more quickly—those were some of the last stragglers.

---

144. William Gilmore Simms, *The Sack and Destruction of the City of Columbia*, S.C. (Columbia Power Press of *Daily Phoenix*, 1865).

145. Rev. Stephen Elliott (1804–1866).

146. Sarah Barnwell Stuart and her son John Barnwell (1860–1865), who were staying in Camden with her father-in-law, Henry Middleton Stuart Sr.

147. 1st Lt. John A. McQueen of Company K, Fifteenth Illinois Cavalry, who worked during the night to help protect homes in Columbia, remarked to Rev. Anthony Toomer Porter, an Episcopal clergyman from Charleston, "I do not wonder you have the worst opinion of every member of this army but we are not all like this—there are some gentlemen and Christians among them yet."

148. Dr. William Reynolds.

My heart is heavy—God's mercy never fails by his g. name.

Minnie arrived at home nearly a week ago, after incredible difficulties in get-ting from Fort Sumter to us here—he is in a hurry to get to the Army, but is wait-ing for Gen. Elliotts horse, which his wife sent to request him to carry on to the Gen, for her, just as Min was leaving [for] Camden. It has not yet arrived. Every-body is drawing rations & some pay, some do not.

Love to all of your circle,

Your aff.

Mary Leverett

Milton Maxcy Leverett to his mother

Camden in Box car.

April 1ˢᵗ 1865

My darling mother

I arrived here today about 11 oclock having travelled 20 miles last night, and putting up at a house on the road where we obtained a supper and beds for which we paid. We reached there about 9 o'clock and left at 3—arrived at the Ferry after 6—had to wait for about 3 hours when we got over and arrived here safe. My com-panions besides the driver (white) and Jacob were the Rev. Mr. Porter and Mr Wilkins nephew of Governeur Wilkins.[149] Had a tolerably pleasant trip. It seems as if there has been nothing but wait, wait, wait with me, for I now have to wait until Tuesday perhaps, before I can get off, one train of wagons having gone off and being compelled to wait for it, to return. One of the first persons I saw was cos. Henry. He told me all the news, it being very nearly what we already knew. Ste Elliott has returned home, his arm apparently failing from exposure, he will be assigned to some less active duty nearer home I believe, Ste Barnwell, I forgot to ask cos. Henry, but Mr. Haskell Rhett[150] told me yesterday had a rib broken by a glance shot, Frank Porcher[151] on Ste Elliott's staff had a contusion of the knee and has returned. Poor George Stoney so Haskell Rhett told me and cos. Henry the same was killed at Bentonsville. Our company buried him—another noble soldier, first rate officer, a large hearted man and just as brave (conspicuously so) a one as has ever breathed since this world was created. I do not think a man could be braver. I speak from self knowledge, having been an eye witness of his coolness under fire. He was a fellow of fine instincts and noble impulses. Henry

---

149. Rev. Anthony Toomer Porter and Gouverneur M. Wilkins of St. Luke's Parish, a planter.
150. Haskell Smith Rhett (1818–1868), brother of Albert Rhett, James Moore Rhett, and Roland Smith Rhett.
151. Francis Peyre Porcher.

Stuart poor fellow was killed dead the ball entering behind his left ear.[152] The man said to be killed in our company was Wilson Hall of Beaufort—it is not certain whether he was killed dead or not as we did not get his body.[153] Henry Stuart's body also we did not obtain.

Our army is in fine spirits and our cavalry in splendid condition, Wheeler's and Hampton's rivalling with each other in their prowess. Our army is not very large but what there is is good and I believe Sherman is feeling it to his cost.

Cos. Henry invited me to take dinner with him and spend the night which I would have done but I found out afterwards that I could not get off until Monday or Tuesday so I went to his house and excused myself having at first accepted. I would have liked to have taken dinner and spent one night but didn't like to stay as long as that which to be sure he had not asked me to do, and besides the Depot is about 3/4 of a mile off. I was also afraid I would fall in love with Sally[154] and didn't like to as I didn't know whether my Pa would approve of another daughter just about these hard times and besides I did not like to shake any firm intentions and fixed resolutions toward Annie Rhett and also my dear little Misses E. but I may go around to-night as he asked me. I saw the Bishop also today, he also asked me to call on him.

Don't be worried about me. I will get on very well, I found the driver had drawn two or three days rations for me yesterday and I have drawn since I have been here until Tuesday and with what Annie was so kind as to cook for me and the money you gave me will get on capitally. I may have to take charge of the transportation of this ammunition here until finished, but will try not, don't be troubled about me. God has always surprisingly taken care of me and I expect will continue so to do, besides my berth is not one of danger. I only hope and pray that he will take care of you and all the rest and let me meet you again all safe. I was very much surprised to find you all so much better off than I expected and believe that as he took care of you through all that trial, he will continue so to do. I try to believe in a Special Providence.

Goodbye

Your aff^{ct} son
Milton M. Leverett

The railroad is open to Cheraw I believe.

---

152. 1st Lt. Henry Middleton Stuart (b. 1841) of Company B, First South Carolina Artillery, killed at the battle of Averasboro, 17 March 1865, brother of Middleton, James Reeve, and Allan.

153. Pvt. Wilson E. Hall of the Beaufort Artillery was wounded at Averasboro and sent to Pettigrew General Hospital No. 13 in Raleigh, North Carolina, where he was captured on 13 April 1865.

154. Sarah Means Stuart.

I am sorry I have to write in pencil but I forgot to bring ink. Love to all. Will write all chances.

Sunday

I went to cos. Henry's and can say veni, vidi, vici i.e. I did not fall in love. Had a very good time, saw all the girls except Rosa & Belle.[155] I may go there again before I leave as cos H. has asked me especially.

Went to church today—communion—Parson Ste' and Genl. Ste both appeared glad to see me. Ste said he might get me with him sometime or other, he did write to Ex. Board but his letter was too late. Ste Barnwell did have his rib broken. Nenny Fuller is Sergt. Major of B. Rhett's battalion of artillery.[156] I wish I could have been there. We would both have been of the non-comissioned staff together. Willie Elliott has been also wounded in the rib, but not dangerously.[157] Nothing more to say. Love to all.

Your ever aff^{ct} son
Milton M. Leverett

I send this letter by Mr. McNamara the driver of the wagon. I'll write again before I leave.

---

155. Rosa and Isabel Stuart.

156. Henry Middleton Fuller and Maj. Andrew Burnet Rhett, son of Elizabeth Washington Burnet and Robert Barnwell Rhett.

157. Lt. Col. William Elliott (1838–1907), assistant adjutant general and son of Rev. Stephen Elliott (1804–1866), was wounded at the battle of Bentonville, North Carolina, 19–20 March 1865.

7

The Struggle of Reconstruction

July 1865–August 1868

I am afraid we shall never again look up.

—Rev. Charles Edward Leverett

When Rev. Charles Leverett reported his activities for the year ending in May 1865 to the diocese of South Carolina, he also expressed his views on the war. "The fierce and cruel war waged by the North has interrupted ecclesiastical as well as civil duties," he observed, pointing out that other than holding services at home and occasionally preaching or assisting the rectors of the Episcopal churches in Columbia, his major work was to perform the funeral service for one of his children and two of his slaves.[1]

With the Confederacy defeated, their land confiscated, and their slaves freed, the Leveretts spent the early postwar period attempting to recover Canaan and their Beaufort house and maintaining subsistence crops at The Farm with a few of their former slaves, now under contract as freedmen.

Caroline Pinckney Seabrook to her cousin Mary Maxcy Leverett

Hodges[2]—July 1st 1865.

My dear cousin

There had been such a hiatus in our correspondence that I scarcely know who wrote last, or whether I have even thanked you for your long & interesting

---

1.   Report of Rev. C. E. Leverett, in *Diocesan Records of the* A.D. *1865.* (Charleston: Walker, Evans and Cogswell, 1865).

2.   In Abbeville District.

account of "the Yankee Fury." A number of letters relating their exploits in <u>unde-</u>
<u>fended</u> towns & villages, I have preserved for my children—& among them yours
is conspicuous. <u>We</u> have been mercifully spared even the <u>sight</u> of one of these
wretches & none of our <u>near</u> relatives have been ill treated except Cotesworth,
who was captured near Anderson (while on a <u>preaching</u> trip)[3]—& horribly treated
by three Michiganders. They demanded his silver & gold, & being told he had
none, one searched him while another held a pistol to his head, declaring that if
he <u>lied</u> they "would blow his brains out." Jane Hume at whose house this happened, was first robbed of jewelry (<u>in</u> her pocket) & then turned out of the room,
& the door shut. C. said he felt very solemn, in spite of his violent indignation.
The main body had gone on & there was no sort of protection <u>but God's</u> against
these lagging ruffians. Indeed their whole conduct in Anderson was worse than
any where else that I heard of.

But I have wandered from the object of my letter, which is to tell you that we
have again had to part with one of our main ties to life. How strangely are private
sorrows mixed up with public disasters in these dreadful days. Our dear & venerated Father[4] bid adieu to the troubles of earth on the 9th June—after a decline of
four months during which his state of mind is best described in the hymn sung at
the funeral—"Thy children, <u>panting</u> to be gone" &c. He had recovered from his
first sickness so far as to ride out several times in the buggy, Mary driving him, but
in May he again declined,—lost appetite & strength, took to his room & then his
bed, & finally breathed out his life without either <u>disease</u> or <u>pain</u>—a fitting close
as Mary said, to a life of temperance & self denial.[5] I recollect that his Father died
much in the same way—a wearing out of nature, but he was 78[6]—Papa two years
younger. He was generally well enough to read during his long decline, & even to
write sometimes for a religious paper; & talked a great deal to Mary & myself
about his early life, telling us many things of which we were ignorant. He told me
that although he had joined the church in Charleston (some time after Mama
did)[7] he never understood the way of salvation until he heard M[r] Walker preach,
on his subsequent visits to Beaufort.[8] As a religious man, you know the stand he
took, & how truly he might say "I am not ashamed of the cross of Christ." D[r]
Capers[9] said he was the first <u>layman</u> who moved in the matter of religious instruc-

---

3. Rev. Charles Cotesworth Pinckney III (1812–1898).
4. Charles Cotesworth Pinckney II (1789–1865).
5. Mary Elliott Pinckney of Charleston, sister of Caroline Pinckney Seabrook.
6. Thomas Pinckney (1750–1828) of Charleston.
7. Phoebe Caroline Elliott Pinckney of Charleston.
8. Rev. Joseph Rogers Walker was rector of St. Helena's Church, Beaufort, from 1824 until his
   death in 1879, except for the years of the Federal occupation of Beaufort during the war.
9. Rev. William Capers of Charleston.

tion for negroes, & published a letter which Papa addressed him on the subject. I can recollect his "Address before the Agriculture Soc^y" of Charleston in '28 or 9[10]—in which he brought the subject before all his <u>old associates</u>—to their <u>great amazement</u>—so that one of them came up to him & said "Well Cotesworth, either you are crazy or I am." The only change I saw in him during his sickness was that he <u>showed</u> more plainly than ever before, his tenderness for us all. Mary & I were "my darling" & the boys "my little darlings"—so that what strangers might have thought <u>coldness</u> in him, but which we know to be only old fashioned gravity & reserve was gone—& this seemed to me the only thing wanting to complete his Christian Character. Cotesworth had paid him a long visit in the Spring, to his <u>extreme</u> enjoyment ("what a son I am blessed with!" he would say, when C. left the room, after praying or reading to him) & I must say C. <u>does</u> shine in the room of sickness & bereavement—but he did not arrive in time to see him at the last— there were disturbances in the neighborhood which made him unwilling to leave his daughters unprotected.[11] Tom & Charley were here;[12] the former got back from the army a week before—he was very severely injured in the ankle at Bentonville & is still lame, but recovering. We have laid my Father in a temporary grave here till the winter, when he will be removed to Pendleton, laid beside the faithful companion of more than fifty years of wedded life. A Methodist minister read the service in our parlour, & about a dozen gentlemen attended—what a contrast, I could not help thinking, to the burial of the last of the name! (We had preserved the newspaper account of Genl C. C. P's[13] funeral—which filled three or four columns).—Poor old cousin Harriott[14] still lives in Town—at one time, she was thankful for two loaves of bread per diem which a grateful baker sent her! She who has all her life been accustomed to dispense almost princely charities! Cotesworth has now gone to see her—also to see the condition of Grace Church, which we hear has sent to invite him back—the only Episcopal Church open in Town & consequently well filled.[15] (St Luke's given to the darkies.)[16] We have also

---

10. Charles Cotesworth Pinckney, *An Address Delivered in Charleston before the Agricultural Society of South Carolina at Its Anniversary Meeting on Thursday the 18th August, 1829* (Charleston: A. E. Miller, 1829).

11. Rev. Charles Cotesworth Pinckney's four youngest daughters were Elizabeth Anne (1848–1893), Maria Henrietta (1850–1939), Mary Barnwell (1857–1939), and Margaret Manigault (1860–1939).

12. Thomas Pinckney (1828–1915) and Charles Cotesworth Pinckney IV (1839–1909).

13. Charles Cotesworth Pinckney I (1746–1825) of Charleston.

14. Harriott Pinckney of Charleston.

15. Grace Episcopal Church in Charleston.

16. St. Luke's Episcopal Church closed in 1864 during the Federal bombardment of Charleston. After the war it was used by Federal occupation troops and as a school for freedmen until October 1865, when services resumed.

deputed C—<u>to take the oath</u> & save the Santee lands for the family—which as Executor, he must do, or leave us quite pennyless. Did ever such universal ruin descend on a people at one blow in the history of the world? With one stroke of a miscreant's pen 7 million are reduced to poverty.[17] And how cruel the treatment of our President & Cabinet—Tom (who knows Fort Pulaski) thinks the latter are sent there to die of fever. It was reported here lately that Jeff Davis was dead—but others say only dying from cruel treatment such as <u>heavy</u> <u>irons</u>, want of air &c.[18] I cannot trust myself to dwell on the subject—it makes me sick—so I try to employ myself in my daily duties—teaching the boys, gardening, feeding the chickens etc. & not thinking about "the times." "The Lord God omnipotent reigneth"[19] & to Him we must leave our fate, a great trial is to have a negro company at Abbeville C. H.[20]—where they are giving entertainments to their colour & making themselves odious generally. Numbers are flocking to them, whom they say will be sent back to their homes. None of our's have gone as yet. I am very anxious to go to F. R,[21] not only for health but to try and recover some of our furniture which has been <u>stolen</u> by <u>the country people</u>—(at Santee, it has been stolen by negroes—at Pocotaligo, burned I supposed by Yankees,) but I fear scarcity of food up there will prevent me. Mary P. has gone on a visit to Pendleton for a little change, she looked very badly after her long attendance in Papa's sick room. Margaret is there at school. Uncle George's[22] family in Cokesbury. Bet has 18 scholars—& they get on very well & make friends, in their cottage of <u>two rooms</u>. Mr S.[23] is pretty well, trying to make a crop here, but with indifferent prospects. Tom expects to move the negroes down to Santee in the Fall. Mary S. looks badly & is very lonely here—Caroline S. ditto, ditto. When we can make arrangements, we must sell out & move in a large body to some other country, where we will have a good government and make our own society. I scarcely think Mexico settled enough. Some people talk of Australia or New Zealand.[24] Our love to the girls & Mr L. Papa often spoke of his visit to you with pleasure—said you were all so kind to him—& liked Mary particularly. How my ties to earth are being broken—even

---

17. The Emancipation Proclamation.

18. Davis, captured by Federal troops near Irwinville, Georgia, on 10 May 1865. He was imprisoned in Fortress Monroe, at Hampton Roads, Virginia, and was released in May 1867; he was never tried. Davis was chained with leg irons for a few days but an outcry against such treatment persuaded authorities to stop the practice.

19. Rev. 19:6.

20. Courthouse.

21. Flat Rock, North Carolina.

22. George Parsons Elliott (1808–1871), brother of Phoebe Caroline Elliott Pinckney.

23. Archibald Hamilton Seabrook.

24. Many Confederates threatened to leave the country in 1865. Most exiles returned but some groups went to Latin America, the best known were the Confederados in Brazil.

my <u>local</u> ones. I saw a number of the "New South" yesterday—enough to make any Beaufort person crazy.[25] "Lord how long?"[26]

Aff Yr's

C. P. S.

Our poor fugitive President, passed thro' Cokesbury 1st May—Many persons called on him, In Abbeville he stayed with Mr Burt—said in No Ca people were afraid to recognize or receive him—but in So Ca it was very different that he was treated with words of sympathy & attachment from the moment he entered the state.[27] Mrs D. had spent some time in Abbe previously & Meta B. taught her children with Mr. Parkers'. Meta "wished she was a man to fight for him."[28]

P.S. <u>Monday 3d</u>

Your letter My dear Cousin, has just been received. Accept my thanks for it & for your sympathy & appreciation of our dear Father. You speak particularly of his humility which was indeed striking, a striving against <u>pride</u> was a daily exercise with him. Dr Fuller once said of him, "I know no one with so many <u>causes</u> for pride, so entirely free from it." But my dear Cousin, much as we miss him, I would not have kept him in this sad world a day longer. Life is hard enough on the middleaged & the young—it is too great a burden for the aged.

I am shocked to hear of so many persons being deserted by their house servants—<u>here</u> it is quite different—servants are generally afraid of being turned off—"put outside the gate" as they express it—without food or shelter. <u>No Yankees</u> have yet been here to demoralize them.

Cotesworth has just written us from Charleston, where he has seen George & Peg. The latter delighted to hear of us, & sends me some longcloth (what a present!) she has kept all through the war for me, & has an old set drawers also. How I wish I could send for them! I pine to have an attached, capable servant about me again. We know not what is to become of us, but I must try to get them back. C says his church has been <u>set up</u> by Naval Officers, who got an organ, choir &c & attend the services. <u>Rev. Jos Seabrook</u> & <u>Wm Whaley</u> fraternize extensively with

---

25. *The New South* was a Union newspaper established in 1862 during the Federal occupation of the sea islands; it moved to Beaufort in 1865 and ceased publication in 1867.

26. Isa. 6:11.

27. When Davis, the remnants of his cabinet, and several Confederate generals arrived in Abbeville on 2 May, the president stayed at the home of Armistead Burt, who served with Davis in the House of Representatives in the 1840s. That afternoon Davis held his last council of war in the house—which still stands on North Main Street—and though he initially clung to the hope of military success, the cabinet officials and generals persuaded him that further resistance was futile.

28. Margaret Harriet Barnwell of Beaufort District.

the Yanks. Cousin H.[29] is better, her old maid with her, & a small boy—but the Miss Rutledges do most of the work, & M[r] R. goes to the door.[30] Yet the yard is full of servants. Col. Hatch makes everything as disagreeable as possible to rebels.[31] Negro soldiers lined the road from Orangeburg to Charleston. I don't wish for commercial prosperity—it makes people love money too much.—Neither have I given up all hope of future independence. I think the Yankee nation is too corrupt—& that it will go to pieces after a while—& we shall escape as a bird out of the snare—God can easily bring it to pass after he has humbled us enough.

Rev. Charles Edward Leverett to Bvt. Maj. Gen. Rufus Saxton, U.S. Army, and Saxton's reply

Columbia, S.C., Sept. 1, 1865

General Saxton[32]

Sir:

I am the owner of a home in Beaufort—the 5th from the west end of the Bay—and a plantation on the Main, one mile from Garden's Corner on the lower road to Pocotaligo, on the right hand side across and bordering on the Huspa Creek. From the latter place, I was ordered by the Confederate authorities in 1862—My house was subsequently burned by the Confederate pickets. I have taken the oath required by the U.S. and now write to claim my property. Col. Ely[33] informed me that I was to address you and said there would not be the least difficulty in recovering the same. I am an Episcopal clergyman and have been in the exercise of my proper sacral engagements throughout the war at this place. Will you inform me in regard to the above. You are aware that we cannot on account of the climate return to our places until after frost, and then I do not know in consequence of what I hear of the carelessness of the negroes, if it would be possible at that time.

---

29. Harriott Pinckney.

30. Probably Eliza Lucas Rutledge, Elizabeth Rutledge, Rebecca Motte Lowndes Rutledge, and Frederick Rutledge, physician, of Charleston.

31. Bvt. Maj. Gen. John Porter Hatch, Federal officer who commanded occupation troops in the Northern District, Department of the South, with headquarters at Charleston.

32. Assistant commissioner, Bureau of Refugees, Freedmen, and Abandoned Lands (often referred to as the Freedmen's Bureau) for South Carolina, Georgia, and Florida, 1865–1866.

33. Bvt. Brig. Gen. Ralph Ely, acting assistant commissioner for the Freedmen's Bureau in Beaufort District.

You will oblige me, General, by addressing a letter to me stating if I can have my two homes &c. and am

Respectfully,

Your Obt. Svt.

Charles E. Leverett

Headquarters, Assistant Commissioner
Bureau Refugees, Freedmen and Abandoned Lands
South Carolina, Georgia and Florida
Beaufort, S.C.[34]
Sept 10 1865

E B 116 Asst Comr./SC & Ga./65

Respectfully returned with a copy of Cir No 13. If your land does not come under the head of "Abandoned" as defined therein it will be restored to you. Your house has been sold for unpaid taxes & the government has given al title to other parties & cannot now restore it to you.

R. Saxton

Brt. M. Gnl.

Between September 1865 and February 1866 the Leveretts succeeded in recovering Canaan, though the Beaufort house remained in the hands of two Northerners who had paid the delinquent property taxes on it. Milton was now a farmer planting subsistence crops with freedmen under contracts supervised and regulated by the Federal authorities in the Freedmen's Bureau.

Milton Maxcy Leverett to his mother

Sheldon Feby 3rd 1866

My dear Mother

I have deferred writing until I could be able to say that I was succeeding well but there is no use putting off any longer especially as I know you wish to hear from me and I from you. I have been trying my very best to drum up negroes all about but it is no go and I am almost in despair. They are such disgusting slow procrastinating wretches that they put off and put off and promise and promise until it will be too late to do anything. I have had several who concluded several times to contract with me but have each time dodged or failed to come up to the

---

34. A four-line printed heading pasted to the back of Rev. Charles Leverett's letter as an endorsement.

agreement. I have one man who seems perfectly willing and is putting up his camp on Canaan. He is trying to get others for me. I tried to get hands for wages and some agreed, but seeing perhaps something more advantageous elsewhere wouldn't conclude the bargain. I am trying now on shares, they to have a third, their food which I will supply, to come out of their share at the end of the year and they to assist in feeding my mules according to their proportions, and I will give them each a shoat and a couple of hens to start on, but no, nothing but half will satisfy them. In which case they bear half of the expenses. They have been injured down here by some of the planters planting on halves with them and others too lazy and unenergetic to come and work bravely have rented their lands at mere songs. This practice injures seriously those who have not a sufficiency of capital and who come with the intention of working cheerfully at the most difficult task the world has ever seen and one the whole world is looking at with curiosity and interest—the trial of free negro labour. If I furnished the capital myself I could plant on halves as there would be only two parties there to share but as I do not do that I cannot afford to plant thus, as the furnisher of the capital I wish to be suitably remunerated. If I had known what I know now I could have planted on halves as the Government will furnish rations on proper security, (and my chief trouble would have been mules then, but I would have managed without) as it is, I cannot do so, as I do not wish to break faith with McElroy having already made the bargain with him. Nat is in the same fix with myself. Nenny has about 30 hands (not their former ones) working on halves. Wm Fuller is doing the same. Henry Fuller is giving eight dollars a month and feeding them. Wm Jenkins next door has rented Chaplin's to the negroes for little or nothing. Dan'l Heyward has rented his to John. I am going to try hiring by the week, day, month and task until I do get hands so that I cannot be behind hand. I wish you could hire five or six hands about Columbia on my "<u>third</u> principle" then send them down to me. You could telegraph and let me know when to expect them. I dare say Government will pay their way down, it has been doing so. The negroes all put up camps to live in. You need not tell our negroes that I am not getting on well, you might only mention my "<u>third</u>" principle incidentally. I expect by next Monday to hire some hands by the <u>day</u>, <u>week</u> or <u>task</u>. Everybody is down here trying to plant but very few succeeding. Stuart Gibbes I expect will act as agent on Mrs. Fraser's place. I have not seen McElroy yet although I wrote to him sometime ago, to be sure though he must come slowly travelling by wagon route. Sheldon Church is not burnt down. It has been torn up inside somewhat but it could be repaired. A good many Beaufort people are living in Beaufort in any vacant house or story they can get, and I am surprised to see them so cheerful. Parson Ste[35] is

---

35. Rev. Stephen Elliott (1804–1866).

going to bring his family down. Mrs Ed. Rhett[36] and family are there also now I hear. Beaufort is not in near so bad a condition as we supposed. The Bay St. if anything looks better and our house and Mr Jno Smith's look neater than any I have seen, they have been recently painted with white. Our yard extends all the way back now, the old board is replaced by a nice looking whitewashed picked fence. The stable looks the same as does the kitchen and wash house. When I was on my way to Beaufort the man or rather one of them for two own it was on board and I took occasion to get acquainted with him. He offered it back to me for a thousand that they had already paid on it. They have yet to pay two thousand six hundred for it by March 1868. If I get it I will have to pay that instead of their doing it, but the Government may return the houses to their owners at <u>that</u> time. Collins one of the owners whom I saw afterwards said they all expected the original owners to get back their property.[37] I went into our house into the Drawing room, the one you used to occupy, it looked quite neat and I went all over the yard and was quite pleased to see how neat it had been kept. It had never been a hospital. Emery the other owner who showed me about said he supposed it was not in as good order as when we occupied it.[38] I did not at all undeceive him but left him I expect under that impression. One thing is certain to get back our house without going to law we will have to give something for repairs. If we pay them a thousand and the Government at the end of the time returns the houses it will of course return us what we paid for it and if we do not buy it and it is returned to us it will return to them what they paid for it. In either case whatever amt has been paid for it will of course be returned. If they do not pay by March 1868 the 2000 the Govt resumes possession of the house and in all probability will return it to us, we of course will have to pay for repairs. If we buy it at a thousand & do not pay the 2600 by Mar of 1868 the Govt resumes possession of the house because the price the Govt sold it for has not been paid up. It then resumes possession and and returns it in all likelihood to the original owners—ourselves—and then of course pays back what we have already paid on it i.e. the thousand. In this case we have the house two years earlier than we would otherwise get it, doing away at the same time with the chance of these fellows selling it to a third party. They have told me that they have already been offered by a third party 3700. I examined the town books kept by Brisbane[39]

36.   Mary Williamson Stuart Rhett.

37.   J. W. Collins, a lumber merchant in Beaufort and a native of Massachusetts.

38.   Moulton Emery, a native of Maine.

39.   Rev. William Henry Brisbane of South Carolina was a Baptist minister who sold his land and slaves and moved to Ohio in 1838. He became an abolitionist and bought the slaves back and emancipated them in the north. In October 1862 he returned to Beaufort District as chairman of the three-member United States Direct Tax Commission for South Carolina, which administered the land confiscated by the Federal government for the owners' failure to pay taxes.

& found that it had been sold for $3625.00 to be paid by March 1868 and 906.00 have already been paid on it.

Your aff^{ct} son
M. M. Leverett

Milton Maxcy Leverett to his mother

Feby 7th /66

My dear Mother,

How are all getting on? I hope Mame has entirely recovered. Write and let me know and tell her she must of course write to me, all the rest of course will also do the same having been always such capital correspondents—Julie I know will write, tell her I will never let her or anybody else pack up for me again. I didn't know where any thing was when I wanted it. Tell Sis the shirt fitted me exactly. I hope Anne is finding it easier in the housekeeping line. How is Pa? dull as ever? He ought not to be, I am sure I am having obstacles enough to encounter to give any-one the blues and certainly get them often enough. How is the planting interest, with all of those mules I could plough up the farm in less than a week. If I get started down here I can get ploughed all that I wish, even if I do not start until the first of March. How is the wagoning? has it gone up the spout, and my horse how is she? If you cannot keep any of the animals up there just send them down here I can easily dispose of them somehow or other. I have got up some hands since writing the first letter and am just anxiously awaiting McElroy who is to bring some of the mules and a wagon &^c down. I have been over to Canaan very often but there were no buildings; what fragments and sheds of them that had been left were carried off by the neighbouring negroes before I got there. I see fragments of Sheldon Church all about. Your grape vines (three of them) are there still having run about at a great rate—a good many of the fruit trees and several of the pecans are there still although the fire has hurt some of them. If our negroes wish to come down and work for a third they can do so with <u>one</u> or <u>two</u> excep-tions but will have to be very quick in their movements or I may get as many as I will want <u>but do not ask them to come</u> unless they say they wish to, at any rate they will have to stipulate beforehand that they are coming to work for me. How are my puppies thriving?

I minded leaving all of you very much—was almost homesick. I wish I could arrange so as to bring some of you down but it is impossible at present. Tell Pa he forgot to give me his usual goodbye kiss, something remarkable. I hope he is in good spirits and good health both, it don't do to be down in the mouth, and you my dear little mother, I hope you are still cheerful and well, I never saw anybody keep in such cheerful spirits for such disagreeable times. I believe I have mentioned pretty much every thing and having another letter to write as well as a contract to draw up must end, Your

affct son M. M. Leverett

Sarah Bull Barnwell to her cousin Mary Maxcy Leverett

Waynesboro' [Georgia]—21<u>st</u> Feb'y 1866

My dear cousin,—It is a very long time since I rec'd yr kind & welcome letter—tell Julia it was not a line too long—it was so interesting to us, as it contained news of many friends, & in these times when we cannot meet, letters from those we love are delightful to us—especially now that—we are in the country. I rec'd yr letter just before leaving Edgefield,[40] & fully intended answering it sooner, but our troublesome move here & finding much to occupy us, caused me continually to delay writing—I will not trouble you with any more excuses dear Cousin, as they are always very uninteresting. How glad you must all be that you settled yr'selves quietly for the war on a Farm, whilst so many other Beaufort families have been going from one place to another. We were sadly disappointed in not being able to join my dear Sister & her family at Greenville[41]—all our plans were frustrated & now we are still exiles & in Georgia—but we have a very comfortable & pleasant home for which we are very thankful. All the family here are very glad we are with them—as they wld' be otherwise very lonely—as there is scarcely any visiting in this neighborhood—at least not yet—& we have no Church to attend—tho' there are two little Churches in the Village, Presbyterian & Baptist—but, it is too inconvenient for us to go as it is a ride of 7 miles & we seldom have a good Sunday—we have had so much rain & cold. All the family here are quite well, but some of the children have the whooping cough & smallpox is in the neighbourhood too—all around us—but we hope to escape—it is said there are 2 thousand cases in Macon—but the disease is now of a very mild type. I rec'd a letter from Charlotte yesterday—she says her family are all quite well again, tho' <u>she had</u> the Varioloid, but her Physician said her case was the mildest he had ever attended. She was quite well again, visiting, & going to Church—& wrote to say that Bro' Stephen & herself expected to be here <u>to-morrow</u> on a visit to us—he will only remain two or 3 days, & in ten days time, on his return to Savannah will call for Charlotte.[42] We

---

40. Ann Bull Barnwell and her husband, Edward Tabb Walker, lived in Edgefield.
41. Eliza Barnwell; her husband, Robert Woodward Barnwell, was appointed professor and chairman of the faculty at South Carolina College; so they were moving to Columbia.
42. Sarah Bull Barnwell's sister Charlotte Bull Barnwell Elliott and her husband, Rt. Rev. Stephen Elliott (1806–1866), bishop of Georgia.

shall be delighted to see them, as it is a very long time since we have met—& we are almost weary seeing strangers. Do give my love to my dear Sister, should you see her, & tell her that I rec'd her letter of the 15th yesterday & will soon answer it. I hope you will see something of each other again, as in one of her Greenville letters, she said you were one she hoped to meet in Columbia. We think from her account that they must have quite a pleasant & comfortable home, & she mentioned having seen many friends & acquaintances—& among them Mr Leverett, Mary, & Julia. I hope since then that you & her have been able to meet. We were very glad to hear such good accounts from you of Cousin Matilda & her family, do when you write to her, give mine & Emily's love to her.[43] I heard a few days ago from Caroline Seabrook, she had been to Pendleton & wrote in excellent spirits, having enjoyed meeting many of her old friends there—she was there 6 weeks— said our dear old friend Mrs North was much worried by her freed negroes & shed tears in speaking of their ingratitude of her people—one of whom (a favorite house-servant) had gone to Anderson to inform against her to the Yankee Genl, that she had not clothed her servants, & that officier had written her an abusive letter—saying her treatment was so unchristian[44]—Mr Cornish very kindly undertook to explain the truth to the Yankee & then he wrote word 'reversed' on his letter—she had given the negroes as usual all the material for weaving—but they wld' not do the work. Caroline said she told her, she wld' have put the letter in the fire & not cared a straw about the Yankee Genl's opinion. Mrs North is now 83 yrs of age & I consider her one of the greatest Saints on the earth—dear old friend— she still corresponds with me, & I have just written to her as Caroline begged me to try & write a cheering letter to her. Edith & Emily Smith reside with her but suspect they are too young to manage for her—these young girls were washing their clothes, Caroline said. I hope yr daughters are not obliged to do that yet for themselves. Our servant Tena is still with us—& has behaved most admirable & kindly—more like a friend than a servant. Emma Stuart[45] rec'd a letter from some of her family yesterday, which said that <u>many</u> families were returning to Bluffton & that her brother James Stoney had procured <u>50</u> hands for planting,—ten of his former people & 40 were sent him by that <u>Delany</u>—the negro lawyer in Beaufort, who had promised them to him some time ago.[46] Delany says that he finds that the Southern gentleman are the <u>best</u> friends of the negroes & gives his people very good advice—so perhaps he may prove a good agent for us. The condition of

---

43. Emily Howe Barnwell of Beaufort District.
44. Eliza Elliott Drayton North of Pendleton and Brig. Gen. Charles Henry Van Wyck, the Federal officer who commanded occupation troops at Anderson.
45. Emma Barnwell Stoney Stuart of Beaufort District.
46. Maj. Martin Robinson Delany of the 104th United States Colored Troops, agent for the Freedmen's Bureau in Beaufort District.

things in Beaufort still seems very trying—Sarah Stuart writes word that life is horrid there, tho she still hopes on for better days—she had but one servant to cook & wash for her—she has a little girl to mind little Allan,[47] but she said as the girl went to school every day from 8 oclk' to 1—she had given her up—the servant you remember mentioning to me had left her, was formerly one of her own & she died of Pneumonia at the Ferry the week after she left Sara—her mamma was Charlotte. Hal had borrowed money to buy a Drug Store, as his practice did not pay well & they are now occupying the 1st floor in J. Johnson's house, being lent them by Cousin H. S.[48] Over 75 of the former inhabitants of Bft' had returned & among them—Mrs Edmund Rhett & family—but no one seemed to be in their own homes—our dear old home is desolated & desecrated—the negroes are now cutting our window sills for firewood. Cos. H. S. had kindly spoken to Brisbane about it—who said he wld prevent it but they say he is <u>afraid</u> of the negroes. My brother John[49] has made every effort to recover it, & offered to pay taxes—but it was refused—he says no more complete ruin has ever been visited by <u>heathen</u> conquerors upon a defeated people, than that which the people of Bft have suffered, & will continue to suffer under the <u>best</u> <u>Government</u>!—& it is indeed too true—as our Island homes & property are all given to our <u>former</u> <u>slaves</u> for 3 yrs & at the end of that time, our ruin will be complete. May God in his mercy help us all to bear our various trials as Christians should—& may He bless us dear Cousin with patient hearts & submissive wills. Mr Walker is again in Beaufort & preaching in the old Lecture rooms—& sometimes to a crowded congregation.[50] It makes me hope for better days in the dear old place again. Sister in her letter mentioned that yr' son Milton was at yr' place planting there again. We are so very glad—so many of our young men are reclaiming their places & planting again—& hope they will make the negroes feel that they are still the lords of the soil—. Are you to plant your Farm this year? I hope so as it will enable you all to live so comfortably. Middleton has 18 or 20 hands here—he works very hard indeed & has a great work before him & [I] only hope he may succeed.[51] Some of the negro women here, are ladies at ease—won't work for wages—but depend on their husbands labour—thus far all is going on very well & the people seem civil. Mary & Emily[52] both unite with me in love to you & in kind remembrances to Mr Leverett & all yr' daughters. I suppose Annie & her little girl are with you & little Lou a great pet still. We are so rejoiced that Bro' Robt's[53] & family are settled in Columbia & with as many

47.   Allan Stuart (b. 1864), son of Sarah Barnwell Stuart and Henry Middleton Stuart Jr.
48.   Henry Middleton Stuart Sr.
49.   John Gibbes Barnwell II.
50.   Rev. Joseph Rogers Walker.
51.   Middleton Stuart, nephew of Sarah Bull Barnwell.
52.   Mary Howe Barnwell Stuart and Emily Howe Barnwell sisters of Sarah Bull Barnwell.
53.   Robert Woodward Barnwell.

friends near them. I shall always be very glad to hear from you dear Cousin, & hope ere long you will send me another long letter & believe me as ever yr' aff^cte.

Cousin S. B. B.

Charles Hendee Leverett to his brother Milton

Cheraw, Feb. 23, '66

My dear Minny,

It's a long time since I have heard of, or from you. I suppose that, ere this, you have reached Columbia. Don't you want to go to Texas? I have just had a fine offer, which, very likely, I will accept. Can't Pa make arrangements to move out with the family. Bishop Gregg[54] has been here, for a few days, on a visit to his friends, & has offered me the position of Principal of a Church school which he is about to establish in San Antonio, Texas. He thinks that the school will require, at once, two teachers. Pa & myself might undertake it, & you carry on Stock-raising near the place. A capital of 2000 in a year or so can easily be doubled at the last named business.

Bishop Gregg gives glowering accounts of the condition of the State, not felt the war, a plenty on money &c—tuition very high, no good schools—Rev. Mr. Wagner is to be the Chaplain. In the course of the year, I will probably go out as Teacher or Stock raiser, if enough money can be raised. I want Pa to sell out & go also, it is practicable & do beg him to write to me at once on the subject. Free labor will fail here, & it will be years before this section becomes prosperous.

We might unite our capital to raise Stocks & teach together. What do you think of it? Let me hear at once as B'p G. is to write to me as soon as he arrives, about expense of going out &c. The school will commence operations in September.

I am getting on poorly here; my health is bad, suffering daily from intolerable headaches. I hope that you all are well, & making out to get along better than I.

We are looking out for some of you soon now, as Spring is here.

If money was not so scarce I would see you in less than 48 hours. With much love to all.

From your aff br
C. H. Leverett

P.S. Got a letter from Rev. J. B. S.[55] saying that he will not be able to pay me a cent in April, he has not paid the interest for two years.

---

54. Bishop Alexander Gregg of Texas.
55. Rev. Joseph Baynard Seabrook.

Milton Maxcy Leverett to his mother

Canaan April 4th 1866

My dear mother,

I have written to Sis, Pa and Julie, but have reserved all my domestic arrangement accounts for yourself. They can not be much of course, so you cannot look
out for a long letter. The first two have received my field narratives, explorations
adventures &^c of, the third my tète-a-tète talk, and now to you belongs my domestic chat, household arrangements &^c &^c. My house is very small consisting of but
one room and that filled up with a heterogeneous mass of all sorts of things for
plantation purposes. I occupy with my bedding, consisting of one blanket, one
overcoat and some hay, one corner of the room. Fortunately Stuart Gibbes has
some blankets and we get on very well. I go to bed generally about 11 or 12 oclock
and get up about 5, besides jumping up every now and then throughout the night
to run out and see if my mules are all right, or bawling out to my boy Plato loud
enough to wake up the whole plantation before I can wake him, about a dozen
times more or less, to go and count my mules, and see if any are hitched in their
ropes or otherwise in danger. Said boy being an <u>awfully</u> <u>handsome</u> boy i.e. black
as the chimney back, lazy as the old scratch and altogether ugly as the old boy. I
feed him for what work I can get out of him. Daddy Summer is another of my staff
acquisitions. He fishes for me and gardens and appears altogether well disposed
to work says he doesn't expect to live on me without doing anything in return. He
is just now occupied in planting watermelons, muskmelons and okra among the
ruins of our old house. In my garden I have green peas planted, of two different
kinds, just growing, almost ready to be stuck, besides turnips, radishes, cabbages
of different varieties, cucumbers, beets, lettuce, seewee beans, snap beans of different varieties, okra, water and muskmelons, a few onions, corn, a few beds of
Irish potatoes, besides some garden seeds sown broadcast, the names which I do
not know, having picked them out of some oats bought for planting purposes.
Most of my seeds have been late planted and are just coming up. Tomatoes I have
none as yet but will get some of the plants from Stuart Gibbes. Don't think I leave
all of my garden work to old Summer, I work there also although I make him do
the hoeing up portion. I have strawberry plants also in blossom. There are a great
many plants there. There are about six or seven pear and apple trees which I have
been trimming up and which appear as if about to blossom, one peach tree in
bloom, six quince trees in full bloom and three grapevines, for which I hope soon
to have some sort of trellis work. My negroes have all had garden seeds also which
have been planted and are coming up. The fig tree near the gate which I have
trimmed up has young figs on it, so that I hope I will get on well in the garden and
fruit line. In the orchard that was there are one or two peach trees that have

bloomed, and two or three pecan trees. There are a few plants in the half circle that was near the piazza. I saw some snowdrops in bloom and a blue hyacinth. The spice tree was broken down but is growing again very well. My corn that was planted all through the back part of the yard is coming up as well as that in the field. My oats in front is beginning to look very well although not as well as I could wish, having been planted during the last of February and the first of March, just in the commencement of a dry season. I haven't any poultry whatever, will not get any just yet. I have a cook—the daughter of my foreman—a little girl who cooks, does my washing and sewing and whatever housework I may have need of. I wish you would save me some darning thread as I want to make her darn some stockings for me. I wish to try and run up to Columbia in May if I can possibly do so and get all my things I have left up there. One thing I am in great need of is a clock or watch in order to keep the negroes from staying too long at their meals. I go as it is by guesswork. I have told you pretty much all my domestic arrangements. I haven't much to say as my family is quite small. I hope my dogs are well and that my mare and mule are doing good work. I wish I could supply you with corn for everything but I hope at the end of the year to help the family on. I don't know what will become of me if I do not succeed. Love to all and especially to yourself my dear mother.

Your aff<u>ct</u> son
M. M. Leverett

How is Mr Wilson's bill, has he sent it in—it worries me.

Milton Maxcy Leverett to his mother

Charleston May 31<u>st</u>,1866

My dear Mother,

I have some spare time so I write to you mindful of your wish and at the same time feeling like talking to you. I have been busy running all about the city and doing nothing. I have seen McElroy and talked over matters with him and we are on perfectly amicable terms. Although things had been written between us, enough I almost think to make two gentleman enemies if not fight yet everything passed off perfectly quiet between us. I never felt ruffled once, had a complete control over myself. I saw at the first glance that he was embarrassed and indeed I was a little. I told him I regretted the change that had occurred in the relations between us and found out that things that I had construed as insults and that anybody else would have also he did not mean as such, only couldn't express himself by letter properly e.g. his remark concerning the <u>leaf tobacco</u> and <u>cigars</u>. We talked the matter or matters over quite dispassionately calling to each other's notice different expressions and remarks that had displeased us. It is true our business matters are not yet settled and I ought not to say that the Ides of March have come until they are gone. But I am inclined to think that two persons can quarrel very easily when they want to and can keep out of a quarrel very easily when they wish to. He is willing to sell out but says he will "make all out of me he can." I on my side know how far I can go and will only pay him for his investment. He says he has sisters dependent on him. I tell him so have I. I doubt if we will come to any agreement on that point. I will just have to let him continue with me. I have tried to borrow money today but did not succeed there seems to be not much in Charleston. Went to Cohen & Hanckel,[56] Cohen didn't have any and he didn't think anybody else had or if they had the rate of interest would be very high. Saw Frederic Fraser, he thought the same thing.[57] I got some advice from him on matters between M^c—and myself. He said that M ought to sell out only for what he has invested and not require a percentage as the planting is still a matter of speculation and doubt, we do not know whether we will succeed or not. He said money was very hard to get and only at high rates of interest, he thought it best not to borrow for two years at such high rates 20 per ct for example. What I do I will be extremely careful about—doubt if I borrow on the mortgages—shall try and sell the farm in B if possible and also my tract.

I like Frederic Fraser would much prefer him for a factor than C. & H. but of course can make no arrangements of the sort now.

I leave tonight at 10 oclock the boat having put off her trip from this morning until that time.

I carried Pa's package to Mrs. Snowden's myself yesterday. Mrs Leland had arrived from Summerville then, was expected I believe last night. Mame had given Pa's other package to Mrs Snowden and is going around there again. Mame came to see me yesterday, she says she is better and stronger but there is room for improvement still. I will do my best to sell the farm and my tract. I returned Mame's visit this morning calling at the same time on Jim and his wife.[58] Aunt Til in the meantime had called on me so that I met her in the street. Nobody was at their house except Mame, Stephen and Mary Fowles who was sick in bed, and is so all the time pretty much now. Aunt Til wants her to go to Cheraw but she will not says Charlie has not invited her. Saw Newton somewhere in the streets yesterday and today as also Jim today. Saw Carrie Glover as I was leaving their house. Mame introduced us. She is prettier than I thought.

---

56. The firm of Cohen, Hanckel, and Company, cotton factors in Charleston, owned by Jacob and Joseph Cohen and Charles Francis Hanckel.

57. Frederic E. Fraser, principal in the firm of Fraser and Dill, cotton factors in Charleston, owned by Fraser and Joseph T. Dill.

58. James Henry Fowles and his wife, Caroline Glover.

I write bad enough anyhow but this pen is unmerciful.

Saw Billy dressed up in full uniform. Stopped him in streets talked to him he wishes he could get out of the army now. I told him I heard he had learnt to curse. He said all soldiers did. I told him if he didn't stop it, I would lick it out of him as soon as he got out of the army. He laughed. Says must tell all howdye.

M. M. L.

The little chickens are hearty.

Mary Maxcy Leverett to her daughter Anne Leverett DeSaussure

Farm Col. Feb. 18th 1867

My dear Annie,

If nothing hinders, the chessboard will go down tomorrow to you. I am afraid my dear children you all think us very neglectful of your requests,—if you could have known how extremely sick your father has been, and how entirely I had to devote myself to him night and day for <u>three weeks</u>, you would not be surprised at not receiving immediately what you write for. I often regretted, but could not possibly attend to anything but your father;—he was in bed suffering excruciating agony for nearly three weeks from an old chronic affection he was formerly liable to, and which chills and fever has again brought on worse than he ever had it before—he thought it would prove his death bed;—the doctors however said it was not dangerous. He had not been to church for two months, nor walked into town for six weeks. He is in the parlour at last, once more at his desk, but is not well yet. Really, I do not know how I got thro' with every thing & those bitter cold nights were terrible to get up in to light the fire, heat water, poultices &c; and I fully expected it would end in my being in bed, but I thank God! he is once more out, and I feel greatly relieved. Money troubles sink into insignificance at such times. But now I feel more for you three solitary ones at Canaan than for any thing else.

We sent the fowls, hope you received them safe? and your father sent $20 to Milton to buy Yates' cow,—hope you got it?[59] and the seed also. Did old Summer save no okra or other seed, whats become of him? don't let Minny's spirits sink, my dear Annie, he will weather it yet. Your father is straining every nerve to pay off Hanck. & Cohen the $230 he owes them, so that the $55 that were due on the Charleston Stk. in Jan. he paid over to them & hoped gradually to pay it off, but it straitens us, tho' it is such an insignificant debt. You ask if your father did not write to Dr Means[60]—No, he said it was useless <u>at present</u>—towards the Fall

---

59.   Thomas R. Yates, a planter.
60.   Dr. Thomas Means of St. Helena Parish, a physician.

when the D^r will have a crop coming on no doubt your father will write. You know, I suppose, that he & the Rev. Wm Hen. Hanckel[61] have hired <u>Albert Stuarts</u> <u>plantation</u> or farm, & are planting there & living together on the Wateree.[62] I am glad you are making a little from the cows to help yourself with—think you are right about raffling the brooch,—in <u>these</u> days, I really cannot think it wrong—only wish I had something to sell—your father won't hear of selling either the piano or my silver waiter. I want so much to help on Minny at Canaan & think it so important. Nat Barnwell was here last night—he says he has not been for so long because he minded the walk out here during this dreadful winter so much—that I have no idea how dreadfully keen & severe the weather was, he started several times to come, and gave up. He told us Rob was up week before last for <u>three days</u> <u>only</u>, they were shocked at his rheumatism—of which they were not aware, and his dreadfully low spirits, and above all the desperately bad condition of his affairs. Rob, he said, was in the greatest distress, because as he said, he had not only made no crop but actually got involved, & put the Bull's Point place in danger,— that being mortgaged for $2000, they spent another $1000, and in all are involved to the amount of $3,500, & the crop only amounted to $1000. It was all carried on in Rob's name, Nat says none of their family can do things together, each are obstinately bent on having their own way & won't give up, that it's the same case with himself—so John is to try to get other business. His father was so desperately cast down, not merely at their failure, but what was worse the involved state of affairs, that it made him sick in bed three days, in the most despairing spirits.[63]— So, let Min take courage, his affairs are nothing like that. You don't know how eagerly I look to go down, but when that will be I know not. Debts must be paid off first. Tillie made an application for Governess but has received no answer as yet. I received a long rigmarole of an answer from Wording & Co Tax Commissioners,[64] the conclusion of all only amounting to a few last sentences—that the house could not be got back except "by right of purchase," so, the only way evidently will be to buy out Collins, & next year when the house is put up for sale, it must be an understanding that he is not to bid. But where the money will come from I know not unless some great good luck happens to us, or some conscientious creditor fortunately pays us.—Tillie had a letter from A. Gibbes thanking her for her purchases & praising them & saying how much better she felt for her

---

61.   Rev. William Henry Hanckel of Richland District, Episcopal clergyman.
62.   Albert Rhett Stuart, served at Christ Episcopal Church, Lancaster, 1867–1869, as deacon and was ordained priest in August 1869.
63.   Nathaniel Bernes Barnwell, Robert Hayne Barnwell, and John Gibbes Barnwell (1831–1888) were the sons of Robert Woodward Barnwell.
64.   William E. Wording, served with William Brisbane and Judge Abram D. Smith of Wisconsin as the United States Direct Tax Commissioners for South Carolina.

Canaan visit. I wish you could ask any of your or Mary's friends to enliven your log hut, & could go over to B. yourselves.[65]

Whats become of Mr M?[66] Tillie threw us all into a commotion once or twice declaring you were going to accept & warning us <u>not</u> to disapprove—Pa was quite indignant—he has such a grand idea of his daughters, that only something very eligible seems to him to be good enough for them. I hate the idea of ever parting from one of you, but as that is very selfish, I can only answer your & Mary's query by saying, that I will object to no young man of good qualities, & the same standing in society as yourselves—but I wouldn't admire a widower with <u>a dozen children</u>—so, you have my answer.

I am deeply grateful to God that you all continue prayers, as indeed is your bounden duty to do, and I hope Minny will yet find the promise true, "those that honour me I will honour."[67] I can't bear to think of his bad spirits. I think Stuart Gibbes very fortunate & am very glad of it—do remember us to him.—I will send your pigeon peas soon—you know it is quite too early to plant them now. Minny ought to plant a quantity of oats, to last him the summer, now. Charley is just ploughing now for his. I wish I had fifty dollars to send you to buy corn & peas, they are so astonishingly cheap. Both are very high here.—I can't think of letting you spend the summer at Little Canaan—it would be too desolate, & too much endanger your & Mary's health, but I hope something will yet turn up favorable. If I was only with you I would feel more satisfied.

You & Mame ought to teach William and Sam to read & Sunday School too. I think Mrs old Edward B. quite right, & our people ought to teach the Negroes. Don't read Job always—the Psalms are a great comfort, and uphold one's faith as well as enliven one's hope. Sally Wallace lends me books now & then—I wish you could read "My farm of ten acres"[68] which she was delighted with & lent me—somebody showing how much they made by their strawberries &c. Sally is kind sometimes—sent your father two partridges when he was sick. Their house is at a stand still at present—the D^r paid the negro who was working there, in advance, he decamped & left the house just so—still unfinished, & they don't know when they will get in now. Sally is delighted and chuckles when she hears you feel like coming back to Columbia. I have never been sorry a moment that you left and think it was a duty we all owed Minny that some of us should go to him, Only wish 'twas I. Tillie has had fever again since she wrote you the other

---

65. Beaufort.

66. Mitchel.

67. From 1 Sam. 2:30.

68. Edmund Morris, *Ten Acres Enough: A Practical Experience, Showing How a Very Small Farm May Be Made to Keep a Very Large Family* (New York: J. Miller, 1864).

day and so has Carry who looks fat & rosy & yet has a sneaking mean chill fever every week for a day or so. She really ought to be down the country.

Some say Fanny Taber[69] jilted Green & some he ditto. I think it is "much of a muchness" he was dilatory in saying when they were to marry & she isn't a person to like waiting. <u>She</u> gives as a reason, her mother's distress at her marrying a Yankee.

I think Minny did surprisingly well this year, it was more than we made at C. except the last year & we never got the good of that. Considering the unsettled state of labour, & the dangerous circumstances in which he must have lived, it is strange he made anything. Charley half promised & offered to buy Min's land but says nothing of it lately. Tell Lou, Lena says she has not forgot, sends a plenty of love, & says Lou is the nicest playmate she ever had. Kiss the darling little body for me—tell Mame she must write too.

yr aff mother
Mary Leverett

Milton Maxcy Leverett to his sister Matilda

Canaan March 1st /67

My dear Sis,

I have not written home for a long time feeling so blue and disappointed about my last year's experience and the present year looking so dull. I was not the only one that failed last year almost every one down here did the same thing or just barely cleared expenses so that I cannot blame myself or the land either. The latter is perfectly good but principally needs draining. It is quite strong and every one down here will tell you the same thing. Plantations that formally brought 40, 80 or 100 bags have brought this year a dozen bags or so. The question of arbitration has not been decided as yet, the cotton not being sold, but there is no fear of might getting anything out of it to go to N. York as every bit will have to go to paying my debts and for which I have been dunned very often and which I do not see any chance of paying unless I get something <u>that way</u> or as I had hoped that possibly Pa might have been able to sell my land. And then my not being able to plant this year—I could not raise money without a mortgage and I really do not like mortgaging especially at the exorbitant rates of interest now exacted. I have been doing what I could since I found that I could not plant—been very busy gardening—expect to have a capital one—have laid it out in beds and walks, and have almost every kind of thing planted, fruit trees trimmed nicely, grapevines stuck up

---

69. Sarah F. Taber of Charleston.

and every thing getting on well a plenty of strawberries set out &^c &^c. Anne has helped me very much in it. The greatest difficulty is fences but I am having rails prepared for it and will also try and fence in the yard if I can. I have what I might call <u>one</u> contract <u>hand</u> and I am now preparing the ground to plant on shares with him 15 or so acres of corn, with some peas and potatoes, besides he does anything else I wish—I am learning to plough—expect to do a good deal of it, and if you could only take a peak down here some nice day you would see the <u>chivalry</u> wheeling his hoe in as vigorous and scientific manner as a good trencherman plies his knife and fork; and as I dig along I cannot help feeling grateful that I was not born a <u>nigger</u> or a mule, for I do hate this digging and delving when I am the party to do it. I have [a] store, quite a nice one built, and my partners are Nennie and William Fuller.[70] I expect we will open it in time for the Fall Cotton Trade which is an important season down here as every negro has cotton to sell then—I am very sorry Pa has been so sick and yourself besides and do wish all of you could have come to B. but rent is almost always $20 per month—Anne and Mary will stay here this summer with me. I think it is as healthy as up there. The reason <u>up there</u> is so sickly is I think on account of the pines in front of the house being cut down and thus exposes the house to the gases which rise out of the low ground, especially after the soil is turned up, and it being to the southerly part of the compass (the south wind being the prevalent wind in summer) you get the full benefit of its chills & fevers. I do hope all of the sickness will pass over and the next year will see us in better health spirits and circumstances—

Now to answering your questions—I have got a letter from McElroy stating that the cotton was in Duke's & Cos[71] hands and I have papers binding McElroy to conditions in which Duke is to sell the cotton and retain the money in his hands until the arbiters decide the affair. Jake when here built two outhouse chimneys for me ($3.) three dollars apiece and cleaned bricks for about three days I think, and I will allow but 50^{cts} per day and feed. I fed him but have not paid him any money but what Pa sent me. He was a great part of the time absent on his own affairs, and my [way] is almost always to pay by the job but not by the day or month. I consequently owe him ($7.50 cts) seven and a half dollars. Anne did receive the bundle sent by mail. The fowls came the other day 14 head all told—no letter has come stating how many were sent. No package of seeds came as Pa's letter intimates. I am glad to hear from him and hear he is up. The $20 enclosed in his letter came safe, but we have not bought any cow as yet with it. I have seen after our house in B. It will not be sold until the next year as that block was bought later in the war than others. March 1868 is the time when payment of the remain-

---

70.   William Hazzard Fuller.
71.   W. C. Dukes and Company, cotton factors in Charleston.

der of the purchase money by the present occupant falls due. I doubt if he will pay it as he has not payed it as yet. I wish Ma would not write to that contemptible old scoundrel Brisbane. I keep myself posted as much as possible on Beaufort affairs. I expect I will have to make Anne take Mr Mitchel as she is very fond of Edisto and he has gone there, besides it will come cheaper to have one less to feed. I cannot write any more at present as I am in a hurry to send it off. With much love to dear Mummer and Pa and all of you, I am

Your aff<u>ct</u> brother
Milton M. L.

Wish I could see all of you. If you can send us any writing paper etc. please do so.

We have all coming up more or less turnips, cabbages, carrots, tomatoes, onions, celery, peas, Irish potatoes, beets, cucumbers, salad, strawberries blossoming, green peas stuck, &^c &^c.

Mary Maxcy Leverett to her daughter Mary

The Farm, March 19th 1867

My dear Mame

Your delightful letter came two days ago and took a burden off my heart, as I really feared all sorts of evils from your and Annie's long continued silence. It created quite a commotion in the monotony of our daily life, all hands hurrying in to my chamber (I had not finished dressing when Charley Brown brought it) to hear it read, while your father (who is now well again) called out to me not to read it until I came into the parlour, so that he could hear, with which I, demurring, complied however. Why, my dear Mame, Tippy was sent with the other fowls, so she must have been stolen! What a pity! take the Dominica or any other you want of mine. We are very sorry. I thought I mentioned sending 17 head. The reason we did not mark the number was, we hadn't time. Charley is always in a tremendous hurry—we couldn't put the fowls in the coop until we knew what day he would take them in for us—after waiting a long time, he one day called to Tillie that he was going to town right off & would take them but she must hurry he couldn't wait. She had to fly out & with Carrie's help catch the fowls & put them in, and nailed down the coop herself; Charley wouldn't wait to have them marked, but promised to get them to mark the number in the Express Office & see them do it, when he came home, he said he hadn't time to wait to see it done, but they promised him to do it, and this is the consequence. However, I don't care about Tippy or any other little petty trials and grievances—you are well, and that makes up for everything—minor considerations are not worth thinking of. Remember too, Dolly is your cow, for your watch bought the horse, so console yourself for

Tippy. I am very glad to hear how well Minny is. Dr Wallace says <u>one</u> grain qui.[72] every morning is enough to prevent a return of chils & fever, if persevered in. Your father at last has lost his, yesterday was four weeks since his last attack. Dr Fair told me give him 10 grs. the day before, & the day he expected; so we gave him on the 13th & 14th, & again on the 20th & 21st, and lastly on the 27th & 28th & and at last he has missed it. Carrie still has uncertain returns of fever, but looks fat. I am very sorry at all of you not going over to Nancy B's wedding. Nat was here last Sunday night—said his brothers did not go for lack of clothes,—was that your reason also? Nat is now entertained in such inferior style to what it was when Annie was here, that I wonder at his coming at all. We are going without wheat flour at present, so he only gets corn bread & corn cake, & we do not have much milk now, as Charley is getting so many customers at 15 cts a qt. besides his contract with Dr Parker, that there is not much to spare. He has now seven cows (two are not giving milk yet.) What do you think of Tillie milking 30 qts a day? The more she milks, her muscles seem to strengthen the more, & she is up before the dawn, even in the worst weather. Charley intends to buy 30 cows in all.

March 21st. My dear Mary, I had written thus far when your & Minny's letters were brought over by Fanny. I was delighted at first, until your father's irritated and emphatic "I <u>wont</u> go down" set me all adrift. He dislikes Beaufort finds the minister unpleasant, says there is no library & no society for him. So, of course the project is gone, as the family & <u>myself</u> must do whatever he says. I am at a loss what plans to form for you all, but think with Minny the family ought to be together, especially in these times. Beaufort would be lonesome to you without us, & also you would be too unprotected. The negroes about here are so much more respectful & civil up here, & there are so few in comparison, that perhaps on the whole it would be best for you to return. Tillie thinks you & Annie ought to stay wherever Minny is, to make him comfortable and take care of him if he is sick. But I wouldn't exactly like your staying at Yemassee Bluff & I don't see the possibility of staying anywhere else without us—it would [be] like supporting three families. I don't like either, at all, your stay at Little Canaan alone now. What to do, I know not, & I know Minny must be very much bothered. Does he think George & Bill sufficiently sure pay? he ought to have a third advanced him. Why don't they stay there themselves & where in the world do they get the money? We heard they were to plant for Mr. Blake. What about Bluntville or McPhersonville? Tillie thought you might rent one or two rooms in somebody's house—perhaps with Mrs Fraser—but I don't think you'd find it pleasant. Your father won't hear of your staying at Canaan alone, so you'll <u>have</u> to come up at once. What to do

---

72. Quinine.

about the cows & Annie's furniture puzzles me. If the cows could be sold at a good price, we could buy others here. Charley has given your father one of his best pigs. He is succeeding with his experiment now, & probably will make handsomely. McKenzie will want 20 or thirty qts in summer he says. What will you do with the stove? If you all come back here we will send Hercules family down to the other house & make arrangements about doing up his house for you. I would much rather move into Town. I write hastily & in order to let you know your father won't hear of going down to Beaufort. <u>Why</u> does not Anne write?

yr aff^{te} Mother
Mary Leverett

Kiss my dear little Lou for me. Carrie misses her very much. Fanny is coming back to school to Tillie. Pity you couldn't get one of Minny's hands to sell your garden stuff in Beaufort for Annie. She must really be sorry to leave the garden. I really feel quite cut down at the idea of giving up Canaan. Minny is right however to do what he can for himself, if he is sure of the money. I rather fear his having anything to do with those hands of D^r DeSaussure's. They will probably give trouble still. I would not engage them.

The State is going [through] such a crisis now that one cannot make plans for the next fall yet. The gentlemen here are "taking the bull by the horns," and as universal suffrage is going to be a fixed fact, a number of them addressed a meeting of colored people a few days ago, Gen Hampton was one—& two freedmen also spoke. Beverly Nash was one.[73] The speeches were in the papers—Nash's was an excellent speech—in favour of <u>our</u> gentlemen & knows they are more the black man's friend than the Northern people are. I will send the paper.[74]

After Rev. Charles Leverett resigned as rector of Sheldon Church his principal intellectual pursuit was writing. Among his papers are a number of manuscripts, some of schoolbooks, but many on other subjects, such as a biography of his son Edward, sketches of birds, and sketches of rural life. His rural life sketches are set on a plantation called Liddesdale, but is actually Canaan. In an introduction to these sketches Charles Leverett wrote, "the following fragments relative to and descriptive of a South Carolina homestead, with some of the 'Black spirits and white,' figments in its scenic

---

73.   William Beverly Nash of Columbia, a former slave who represented Richland District in the South Carolina Senate, 1868–1877.

74.   On 18 March the freedmen of Richland District organized a mass meeting near Nickerson's Hotel concerning the question of black suffrage. Hampton told the crowd "it was to their interest to build up the South, for as the country prospered, so would they prosper," while Nash advocated universal suffrage, "believing that the driver of a one-horse cart was as much entitled to that right as the owner of a block of buildings." *Columbia Daily Phoenix*, 19 March 1867.

pageant, will be read South and North with a special degree of interest." The history of the Confederacy mentioned throughout these letters has not been found. What appears to be his most ambitious literary endeavor is a series of biographical sketches of prominent South Carolinians, including John C. Calhoun, Langdon Cheves, Chancellor Henry William DeSaussure, Bishop Stephen Elliott, James Gregg, Maxcy Gregg, Thomas S. Grimke, Robert Y. Hayne, Chancellor William Harper, Hugh S. Legaré, William Lowndes, George McDuffie, Jonathan Maxcy, and William C. Preston. With the exception of his Southern Confederacy Arithmetic, *none of these was ever published.*

Charles Leverett had been so long without a church of his own that his work on these biographies was perhaps his most enjoyable pursuit during the postwar period. "I am, in the words of Milton, in the category of those said by him also to serve, who only stand and wait," he observed in his annual report to the diocese of South Carolina for 1866–67.[75] He noted that he had proposed going back to Beaufort District as a missionary preaching among the freedmen rather than as rector of a parish church, but Bishop Thomas F. Davis regretfully declined his offer; he continued to hold occasional services at home and assisted the rectors of Columbia churches when asked.

Caroline Pinckney Seabrook to Rev. Charles Edward Leverett

[March-April 1867]

My dear Sir

There have been (I suspect) few public men whose private lives can bear examination like that of Mr Calhoun. I spent many summers in his neighbourhood & was intimate with his daughter, & can truly say that in all his domestic relations, whether as <u>husband, father</u> or <u>master</u>,* he was, so far as I knew, <u>blameless</u>. Especially was it pleasant to see the mutual affection & <u>admiration</u> which existed between himself & Anna, who as you know, resembled him most in mind & disposition. Whenever one was speaking, the other listened with an unconcealed delight that was really beautiful. Mrs North gave as the following account of his arrival at home after a long absence which will not do for publication, but will show <u>you</u> the family feeling.—She was passing through the Village on her way to Fort Hill[76] when she found Mr Calhoun there awaiting his carriage—(the stage was earlier than usual) Mrs N. offered a seat in her's, which he gladly accepted.

---

75. Report of Rev. Charles E. Leverett in *Journal of the Proceedings of the Seventy-seventh Annual Convention of the Protestant Episcopal Church in South Carolina, in Grace Church, Charleston, on the 8th, 9th, & 10th of May, 1867* (Columbia: W. W. Deane, 1867); the literary reference is to John Milton, "On His Blindness" (1652).

76. Calhoun's plantation near Pendleton, now a museum at Clemson University.

On rising a hill soon after leaving the Village, his three younger boys appeared on horseback, scampering along full speed to meet him. When near enough to see who was in the carriage with Mrs N. the one in front began to clap his hands, screaming "I saw him first! I saw him first." After a noisy greeting at the carriage window, they turned & escorted him home. Soon after this meeting, Andrew[77] the eldest son appeared in the carriage, going for his Father, who now left Mrs. North's vehicle for his own. But she went on. Anna was in bed, just recovering from a serious attack of fever—On seeing her Father enter the room, she sat up in bed—They put their arms around each other & <u>both</u> shed tears without speaking a word for some time. This was after one of those sessions of congress which had been protracted till Autumn & I <u>think</u> was in the year 1835.

As a neighbour & companion you know how delightful he was. Our society at Pendleton revolved as it were around him. "To meet Mr. Calhoun" was the form of invitation which made our little social dinners so attractive. The gentlemen generally took occasion to draw him out on some topic of general interest—& his manners were so simple & earnest, so <u>entirely</u> free from conceit or self importance that there was no drawback to the pleasure of listening. Where the conversation was not general, he had a peculiar tact which enabled him soon to find out the topics on which <u>you</u> could talk best, & on these he would converse, giving you entirely new views on subjects you had perhaps studied for months! His mind seemed to me like a ray of light let into a dark room & <u>bringing out</u> the object on which it happened to fall with a distinctness which was almost startling. When at Pendleton he was much interested in his farm & garden. His rich lands on the Seneca sometimes produced 60 or 70 bushels of corn to the acre. The house you recollect overlooked this valley. It was originally an ordinary one but a fine Portico in front gave it an imposing appearance & a wing added at the back made it quite sufficient for the free, but simple hospitality he exercised. [His sons were brought up in the most hardy manner—without flannel & even shoes & stockings, & I must say his idea that this would make them strong proved a <u>complete failure</u>, as all of them died before their mother. I well remember the contest Mama had with Tom[78] when leaving him at school in Pendleton for the winter, to make him adopt warmer clothing, & the whole secret of it was I firmly believe, that the Calhouns might laugh at him. Certainly, looking at results, Mama was <u>right</u>. Mrs Kinloch told me that she heard once the subject of shoes or no shoes for boys most admirably argued—Mr Bonaparte of Balt. <u>for shoes</u>—Mr Calhoun <u>against</u> them—& <u>she</u> thought M^r. Bonaparte had the best of it. Here again the result is against M^r C—for Mr Bonaparte's

---

77.   Andrew Pickens Calhoun.
78.   Thomas Pinckney (1828–1915).

only son is said to have an excellent constitution.[79] But all this is only <u>between ourselves</u>. Of course <u>climate</u> must be considered in the above matter—& Pendleton is you know a severe winter climate.][80]

Anna Clemson[81] told me that her ancestors settled first in V$^{\underline{a}}$ before going to Abbeville, whence her Father removed to Pendleton—& I <u>think</u> she said they formed a part of that Scotch-Irish Colony most of whom settled in this part of N$^{\underline{o}}$ C$^{\underline{a}}$. & the adjoining part of Tennessee. Her mother[82] had some Hugonot blood. Certain families came from the coast to Abbeville (whence the <u>name</u>) & from one of them named B—(I don't know how to spell it—but it sounds like Benneau), her mother was descended. Any information you may want I am sure Mrs Clemson would give you with pleasure. Address her as "Mrs Clemson, Pendleton, S.C." & tell her I advised you to write, & I promise you a favourable answer.

I think I have told you everything that could be of any use in your view of Mr Calhoun—except perhaps this—that he never omitted in his hurried & busy visits to Charleston, to call on my Aunt Lowndes,[83] in token of his undying attachment to her husband's memory. Oh my dear Sir! South Carolina once sent a <u>Lowndes</u>, a <u>Cheves</u>, & a <u>Calhoun</u> to Congress at the same time!![84] But even if we had them now, what could they do? I find it best not to <u>think</u> about politics at all—at least not more than I can help—In our political condition we can almost say that when we have reached "the lowest deepth" a "lower deep, still threatening to devour us, opens wide." Now that we are no longer <u>States</u> but military departments, & put <u>below</u> negroes in privileges, confiscation of our small amounts of property is threatened. What say you to a move to New Zealand? When it comes to the worst, shall I write & ask Charley Prioleau to send an English ship here to carry a colony to that fine soil & climate, (& English government)—& will <u>you all go</u>? The Episcopal Church is already established there you know. I wish you would send me yr piece when published—& if you can lend me the one on "the Barnwells" I will return it. Elliott has been asking me so many questions I have made many mistakes, wh[ich] you must excuse.

yrs
C. P. S.

79. Jérôme Napoléon Bonaparte-Patterson (1805–1870) of Baltimore, nephew of Napoléon I; and his son Jérôme Napoléon Bonaparte-Patterson Jr. (1830–1893).
80. Caroline Pinckney Seabrook's brackets in the original letter.
81. Anna Maria Calhoun married Thomas Green Clemson at Fort Hill 13 November 1838.
82. Floride Bonneau Colhoun Calhoun.
83. Elizabeth Brewton Pinckney Lowndes, wife of William Lowndes.
84. William Lowndes (1782–1822), Langdon Cheves (1776–1857), and John Caldwell Calhoun (1782–1850).

*When Anna was married, the whole plantation came up to wish her joy. She carried Mr. Clemson out into the piazza & introduced him to them. Mr. Calhoun built <u>stone</u> cottages for his negroes, but they proved not only very expensive but less healthy than the wooden buildings.[85]

Anna Calhoun Clemson to Rev. Charles Edward Leverett

Pendleton April 8<u>th</u>
1867

Dear sir,

Your letter of the 25th ult. should have been answered before this, but that I was not certain enough of your name, for an address, & on referring to a letter from M<u>rs</u> P. Hamilton, I found she had mentioned you, but strange to say, in her letter your name was so squeezed into a corner as to present the same difficulty. I wrote her the cause of the delay, but a few days after, received a note from her, enclosing your letter, to her, & my difficulty being thus removed, I hasten to reply.

I fear it will not be in my power to aid you, in the purpose you have in view not from want of inclination, for I should earnestly desire, to place before all, especially the young, the example of the best man I have ever known. Nor you will well understand, from want of interest in the theme. No day passes that my dear father is not present with me, & my heart is full of his memory, but my fathers actual life, except as connected with the history of the country, was singularly uneventful, & simple & unaffected goodness, & a daily discharge of every duty, tho presenting a rare & beautiful subject of contemplation, offers no salient points of interest, to the general reader. It is this which renders it so difficult, nay almost impossible to do the character of my father justice, in the eyes of those who knew, & loved him, as all did who knew him. His habits were simple, & regular, especially when at home. He practised a wise moderation in all things, mingling in due proportions intellectual effort, physical exertion, & relaxation, often saying that by so doing we preserved our capability of usefulness, & enjoyment, for a much longer time. He was peculiarly pleasant & cheerful in his every day intercourse. To say I never saw him angry, would but feebly express his rare equanimity. I never <u>saw him out of humour even</u>, or heard him use an expression, or do an action, I should not have been proud the whole world should hear or see. This may seem exaggerated, but it is simply the truth, & in him was plainly proved, that even in

---

85. Charles M. Wiltse described these slave dwellings as "a row of stone houses joined together to form a single barracklike structure, with gardens in the rear and a large open space in front." Wiltse, *John C. Calhoun: Nullifier, 1829–1839* (Indianapolis and New York: Bobbs-Merrill, 1949), 158.

this world virtue is its own reward, for as he was the best, so was he the most contented—I may even say the happiest person, (so far as happiness is possible in this
world), I ever knew. Not from stoicism did this proceed, for he had the tenderest
heart, & the readiest sympathy with all around him. He is commonly called a stern
man, but no one who saw the lovely smile which lit his countenance, when with
those he loved, or enjoyed the delight of daily intercourse with him, ever thought
him stern. In trouble or in joy all turned to him, certain of sympathy, & counsel.
He has been also called a stoic—"a cast iron man." This was equally untrue.
Where principle was involved, or duty required, no one was firmer or more self
reliant but no one enjoyed the simple pleasures of life more than he did, or was
more ready to promote the happiness of those around him. My earliest recollec-
tion, when he was Secretary of War,[86] are of the eagerness with which we children
listened for his return from the office, & the rush to be first to meet him & be
taken in his arms for our usual <u>game of romps</u>, & all who visited Ft Hill can tes-
tify to his geniality, & ready participation in all that was going on. He was very fond
of music, particularly songs, in which the words were expressive. Appreciated
highly <u>good</u> poetry, often repeating his favorite passages, & took intense delight in
the beauties of nature. He was early in life a keen sportsman, & a fine shot, &
often carried his gun when going around the plantation, but it is characteristic of
the man that as soon as his failing eye sight rendered him less certain, he laid
aside his gun & never used it again, tho always taking interest in the hunting
exploits of his sons.

Tho never humourous himself, he had a keen sense of humour, & laughed
readily & heartily when that sense was appealed to. I found him, one day, reading
The Pickwick Papers,[87] (then just out) to his eldest brother,[88] whose sight was bad &
both of them enjoying, with the greatest zest, Mr Pickwick's adventures. He was the
most affectionate husband, father, brother, & friend, & the kindest of masters. His
brothers were equally devoted to him, & no shade ever marred their intercourse.

I am aware this a disjointed, & meagre detail, & will probably be of no aid to
you. In conversation I might find many things that would interest you, & many of
those little personal incidents, & anecdotes, might be elicited, which seem scarce
worth writing. The sixteen years which have passed, since his death, & especially
the latter sad years, tho they have obliterated nothing connected with him, have
yet rendered less vivid individual incidents but if you will ask me questions, on
any particular point, I may thus be inabled to recal many things.

---

86. Calhoun was U.S. secretary of war, 1817–1825.
87. Charles Dickens, *The Posthumous Papers of the Pickwick Club,* first published in serial
    form in 1836–1837.
88. James Calhoun.

I am lothe to send this as doing neither the subject nor myself justice, but hope you will accept it as a proof of my sympathy in your purpose, & my desire to aid you. It is hastily written, & I would rewrite, & correct, had I time, but wishing to prevent further delay, I will send it as it is, hoping you will excuse all defects, & take the will for the deed.

Respectfully yours
Anna C. Clemson

Rev. C. E. Leverett

Anna Calhoun Clemson to Rev. Charles Edward Leverett

Pendleton April 22<u>d</u> 1867

Dear sir,

Yours was duly received, & I am pleased to find that my letter will be of some service to you. I send you two letters from my father, one to my mother, & one to my youngest brother,[89] which will give you some idea of his familiar style, but as he was never absent from home, save when he went to Washington, where being constantly occupied by his official duties, & overwhelmed by a numerous corre-spondence, his letters home were necessarily short, & limited to necessary details. I am sorry I have not with me, those written to Mr Clemson,[90] & myself while in Europe, as knowing how anxious we were for intelligence he always spared time, to write us more fully, but we are only here waiting events, & brought nothing, save our clothing, with us. Please return the letters sent, when you are done with them. I approach with some little delicacy the subject of my fathers religious belief, because he himself was always reserved as to the particular tenets of his belief. This was from no carelessness or indifference on the subject, which occu-pied much of his thoughts. Should their be any doubt on this subject, his answer when the Rev. Mr Butler of Washington,[91] called & sent up word (during his last illness) he wished to converse with him, on religion would be sufficient. He said, "tell Mr Butler I am too ill to see him, but I have not put off to my death bed, the consideration of a subject so important." He read, & studied the Bible constantly, & earnestly & conversed often, & beautifully about it, & his life was regulated, & governed, by an earnest & simple faith. His family was Presbyterian, but he always attended the Episcopalian Church, which was that of my mother, & grandmother, & all remarked, as you did, his reverential air during the services, but he never spoke of any particular form of worship, with preference, so far as I know, nor do

89.   William Lowndes Calhoun.

90.   Thomas Green Clemson.

91.   Rev. Clement Moore Butler, Episcopal clergyman and chaplain of the U.S. Senate, 1849–1853.

I believe he ever did, to any one, tho I know there has been an effort made to prove he was this, that, or the other. I enjoyed, I am proud to say his confidence, & to me he never broached the subject, tho we often conversed on religion.

I send you a pamphlet, written by Miss Mary Bates, which gives a pleasing & truthful picture of my father, as a private individual. Perhaps you have seen it, but I send it for the chance.[92] I have also obituary address, &c should you desire any thing of that sort. Mrs Elam Sharpe left here, with her family to join her husband this spring at a place he had purchased in Alabama I believe. I believe I can procure her address if you desire it, from her mother in law, who resides here.

Respectfully
Anna C. Clemson

Rev C. E. Leverett

Anna Calhoun Clemson to Rev Charles Edward Leverett

Pendleton May 20th 1867

Dear sir,

Yours of May 8th, was duly received with my father's letters. I have another of Miss Bates' pamphlets, & you can keep the copy you have. I am glad you can make use of it. I have no picture of Ft. Hill, nor do I believe there is one extant, but I send a Photo of my father, taken from a Daguerreotype in my possession, taken a few months before his death. It is not very good, but the best I have, & I am pleased to offer it to one who seems to appreciate my dear father, as I think his noble character merits.[93] I am sorry I am obliged always to disappoint you, but all my fathers papers were sent to Mr R. K. Cralle of Va, who published his Dissertation on Government[94]—his speeches &c and was to have written a Memoir, but the war came on, & during it Mr Cralle died, & his family dispersed. After much search, we got on the track of the trunk, & it is now in the charge of a friend of ours, in Va., till we can send for it. He writes it had been opened, & was in bad condition, & he thought some of the papers taken & I fear such will prove the case. This will account to you for there being none of my father's papers, except a few family letters here. I remember Mr Lowndes well, tho' but a child when he died. There was great intimacy in the families, & one

---

92. Mary Bates, *The Private Life of John C. Calhoun* (Charleston: Walker, Richards and Co., 1852).

93. A 2.5" x 4" carte-de-visite, inscribed on the reverse: "Hon. Jno. C. Calhoun taken a few months before his death. From Mrs. Clemson his daughter. May 1867."

94. After Calhoun's death in 1850 Richard K. Cralle edited Calhoun's *A Disquisition on Government* (Charleston: Press of Walker and James, 1851).

session, at least, if not more, they kept house together, in Washington. My youngest brother was named after him, & I have always heard my mother, & himself (my father) speak of Mr Lowndes, with great affection, & admiration of the purity of his character.

Respectfully

Anna C. Clemson

Milton Maxcy Leverett to his mother

Yemassee Bluff July 16$^{\underline{th}}$ /67

My darling mother,

I was very glad to get your letter as also Anne's and Mary's. Yours reached me before Anne's, Mary's a day or two ago. I cannot answer yours and Anne's in detail as I have mislaid them somewhere. I had a touch of fever when yours arrived but have been taking Quinine since and have not had it again but feel very well. I am sorry you have been unwell and hope that both Pa and yourself are now better—was very glad to hear that Pa had been able to walk into town.

17$^{\underline{th}}$ You and Anne needn't get scared about your letters. I've found them, after an indefatigable search, put away—as I usually do all my things—very nicely and snugly—in a volume of Spurgeons Sermons which I read every Sunday.[95]

Do hush about the Waight property, I'm sick of it—nobody I've come to the conclusion knows anything about it but the Leveretts. You needn't ask me to give your love to Mrs Gregorie for I couldn't think of it—its merely a subterfuge of yours to get off from writing—you always send that message to me, but I don't think I ever told it to her once. I left here the other day and paid Stuart a visit—the first time I've been away from here since the girls left—six weeks. The largest part of my crop here is quite handsome—with no grass—will have cotton open about the last of this month—have cotton bolls almost as large as hens eggs. Rains have retarded me very much. I am busy almost the whole day, from one week's end to another. Have exceedingly disagreeable business paying off hands. I work entirely with outside labour paying by the day week or month—haven't more than four contract hands—and am cultivating between 150 and 160 acres of short cotton. Bill comes down twice a week. I wish I could have as hopeful a view of the future as you have and think that this was the last hard year I am to have. I don't see much cause as yet for that hope. My debts will of course worry me until I have finished with them and in September or October I expect they will give me "par-

---

95.   Charles Haddon Spurgeon, *Sermons of the Rev. C. H. Spurgeon, of London* (New York: Sheldon, Blakeman and Co., 1858).

ticular ginger." I long to see you all very much. In the evening about dusk I get quite lonesome and very often think of you all—wish it was so that we could live together, however I expect that will come out so yet.

Minnie Elliott and Annie Rhett were married last week. Johnnie & Rosa Stuart are engaged.[96] Nothing else that I know of to speak of—have not been to Beaufort since the first of January. Wm Fuller lost another son, the youngest I believe—they are living in Buncombeville now—in the same yard with Mr Davis.

I haven't been to see the Tom Elliotts yet, but sent Pa's letter to him. I am much obliged to Mary and Anne for their letters. I miss them very much indeed especially when I am sickish and of an evening. I have not received the shirts but see by Mame's letter that they must be at the depot and will try & get them as soon as possible—am much obliged to Anne for them. I am sorry to hear she has been having headaches and Mame an attack of chill and fever—hope they will have no more. I daresay it was the fatigue and hot weather &^{c}. Do ask "Big Julie" if that "dreadful hat" still lives—get Mame to burn it up for me. Tell Anne I am afraid that she and Mary "are mistaken" about coming down next year—however we can't tell. Give my love to Sis and tell her I wish she could have been down here with us I expect she would have found it pleasant. I was quite interesting, was the life and soul of the house, except when I had the blues about money matters &^{c} and then I was decidedly uninteresting. Julie of course would never like coming down the country, she being of a decided house keeping turn.—By the bye I send her a recipe which I have been requested to send to her—for making doughnuts; tell Anne please give it to Julie to use whenever she has company. I would like myself to be one of the company, am really very fond of doughnuts, she makes them very nice—wish I had a bushel.

Tell Mame—enclosed—I send her a letter which I have had safely and carefully put aside in my trunk ever since she left about seven weeks; It is from Miss Catherine Coffin. She can tell Miss Catherine that I thought I would take good care of it and put it up—that I nobly admit that perhaps I was in the wrong, and that endeavoring to make all the amends in my power offer freely to write her a dozen letters or more as a set off to that one, if she would like it. Give my love to Pa and all and with much love to you, am

Your affectionate son
Milton M. Leverett

Whom do you think has turned up at last and is now with me—Billy—he came here today—evidently I think hunting me up so that I might help him on. I know he was quite sick and badly off sometime ago, and was living off Govt rations—

96. Middleton Stuart Elliott married Anne Stuart Rhett 9 July 1867, and his brother Rev. John Habersham Elliott married Rosa Stuart 12 March 1868.

he now looks very well, but I expect needs help as I hear the negroes on Beaufort Isld are in need. I shall find work for him—will put him to the plough tomorrow.

Julie must excuse the recipe being so much cut up and pasted but when I went to cut it out of the book which she had it printed in I made a mistake and cut it wrong. She'll observe that "Julias Doughnuts" being "very nice" are calculated to do a great deal, according to the recipe.

Rev. Joseph Henry Price to his sister-in-law Mary Maxcy Leverett

109 West 22^d St
New York[97]
Aug. 14, 1867

My dear Mrs L—

So far from being shocked at receiving a letter from you or rather in your handwriting, instead of Charles' I assure you I feel highly honored that in the midst of such cares & anxieties you should find time for one, deserving so little at your hands. Your letter has given me great pleasure and great pain; pleasure at hearing from you at all, & pain at hearing, for the first time, the painful details of your sufferings. You can have no idea of the confused state of things in which we live in New York. The rush of events & ideas from day to day drives out all [several words missing] calling Providences [several words missing] they begin to make the slightest [word missing] Charles' letter described your sufferings in such general terms, that I failed to grasp them. If I have appeared indifferent to your condition I hope you will forgive me & remember as an excuse for almost every thing, that I live in the city of New York.

I shall ship immediately to the address of Rev. Charles E. Leverett Columbia South Carolina a few trifles convenient in house-keeping, & you would oblige me by acknowledging the reciept that I may know if they come safely. The bill of lading will come with them, with which you can compare [missing word] if the two agree [missing word] inform me. The intention is that no excuse whatever shall come on you.

I hope you do not suppose that I enquired after Charles with my reference to the seventeen dollars for the shoes, paper, &c; but Charles has not written to me since the articles were sent & your letter is the first information I have had of their safe arrival in Columbia. Tell him to give himself no uneasiness about the $17 but forever dismiss it from his mind as I do.

---

97. Rev. Joseph Henry Price of New York, Episcopal clergyman, husband of Rev. Charles Leverett's sister Hannah Gray Leverett.

My principal regret is that I have not the ability to do more; but in order to set myself right on this score permit me to let you into my confidence. By great economy & [illegible] I contrived to get a lease & gradually to pay off all [several words missing] Hannah would have some [several words missing] assessments and taxes in this city [several words missing] keeping me in a trembling anxiety for the little I had. I was urged on all hands to sell, as property in our neighborhood was falling & if I waited my property would be valueless. I had for neighbors two old maids owning their house heavily mortgaged. They became frightened & an intimate friend of theirs in whom they confided frightened them still more. He represented the fall of property in prospect as perfectly ruinous to them. Now came along two Germans brothers desiring to buy the two houses mine & the two ladies but they must have both or none. The elder lady became fearful & excited. She came into my house [small piece missing] & raved, she cried & if she had not been a good Presbyterian should would have sworn, all because I would not sell. She at last over came me & I sold. Hannah always complaining of her lungs became worse. Leaving the house where we had been for twenty three years, depressed her. I had to complete my sale or forfeit five hundred dollars. I enquired for board & it was $60 per week—over $3000 dollars per year and my salary was $2000—I was distracted—sick wife growing worse &c. In the midst of this came Charles' letter—My Church was sold about the same time & we had only a small amount saved from the wreck. I found a house 109 West 22^d St & I just paid over what I recieved for another house & assumed besides a mortgage of $4000 & my present house costing more than the other though smaller & inferior every way. But the street is more fashionable. So you see we all have our troubles. Yet my people think I am rich. Now if under these circumstances I was able to afford you any c[several words torn off] it was a higher power than mine [missing words] my pen. [illegible]. If my dear sister we could only reduce our [word missing] to practice how much better and happier should we be. It is the Lord who afflicts us & not man. God through the instrumentality of nations much worse in every point of view than the Jews living near them for their sins & are we not in Israels place? Now though it does not excuse the wickedness of those who injure us yet it may well be to us an all powerful motive to submission—"It is the Lord let him do that seemeth to him good."[98] How this disarms all the malice of our enemies. While they intend evil are getting good. What they mean for punishment becomes "chastising" fitting us more & more for our heavenly inheritance. How calm, meek & humble this makes us. So that when we compromise no important principle nor sacrifice one [missing word] or manly feeling, we conciliate our persecutors by the moral elevation above them on which our submission to God pleases us. The secret of true nobility is in a real consistent Christian [word torn off]

---

98. From 1 Sam. 3:18.

We hardly know what to send you that won't be useful—would cloathes be acceptable?

I have been in the City all the summer unable on many accounts to leave it—The heat has been excessive—The air hard to breathe—Hannah is very poorly but keeps about—Give our love to all the family both yours & Charles'—God bless you & make all your sufferings conduce to your real good

Affectionately
yours
Joseph H Price

Mrs. Mary Leverett

Milton Maxcy Leverett to his mother

Sepr 4th /67 Yemassee Bluff

My dear Mother,

I received yours of Aug 19th about a week ago and hope now to answer it. I had already sent a letter, an answer to your preceding one about the same time. I suppose that you were about to send another one. I have sent more letters home than two. About the 17th of Aug I think I sent quite a voluminous double letter to Anne and Mary. I sent it to Beaufort by one of my hands (a sensible negro) and gave him a 25^{cts} to have it stamped and mailed. Not being able to get stamps he dropped it in the box and left it there, consequently I don't know whether it ever has or ever will get home. I wrote home long ago enclosing a letter of Miss Catherine Coffins to Mary but the receipt of it has never been acknowledged. One would suppose that I was not a good correspondent judging from the different letters received from home, but there are four letters—one of them a double letter, and this will make five that I will have sent home since the first of June. I am not so sure that I have not made a mistake and counted less than I ought to have, but however "least said soonest mended."

I shall now proceed to answer "all of your questions in a deliberate and detailed manner. I received the Quinine and the stamps safe. [torn] cooks for me—behaves very well—if he didn't I would "wallop" [torn] is disgustingly forgetful and although Anne and Mary think a [torn] of him I don't. They did all his work almost down here. I fare [torn] bacon and hominy—until I loath it—now and then manage to get a chicken or some eggs. Willie Cuthbert has sent me a piece of venison now and then but bacon & hominy is my staple article of diet morn, noon and night, unless I choose to starve in order to get an appetite—nothing else whatever—one week I had some tomatoes. In May I fared better but since then "hog and hominy."

I haven't seen the pamphlet you speak of—would like to see it—I have received the papers Pa sent and am always glad of them as I seldom have a chance of seeing any others.

I have a small lamp which I could read by at night, but generally the mosquitoes and sand flies are so bad that I am <u>generally</u> glad to take refuge under my pavilion and go to bed. <u>It</u> has been a real blessing to me. Speaking of sending a box direct to W. W. Elliott Esq. He is nearer the depot than W. Cuthbert and oftener in communication than the latter. The Railroad is now as far as Seller's but the depot is still at Saltketcher. I will be very glad indeed of the catsup, it is what I have been wishing for the whole summer. Seasoning I am quite fond of. But you couldn't pretend to send what I am "in want of" so I will not enumerate. Do tell Julie The "Depository" is <u>still here</u> but I am afraid it is going to play out. I have not seen any more of her cookery publications lately or I should have sent them to her. I am afraid anyhow as Lou says that they were all "old made up things." Sometimes I see white people but not very often. I am very glad that Dr Price has sent you a box.[99]

I would like to plant Canaan next year but cannot unless I am able raise the funds. Don't say anything to induce our negroes to come down—It doesn't matter at all. I think that the negroes [torn] must be the most injured and spoiled of any anywhere.

Some of my cotton stalks have as high as 121 bolls, not counting forms &c. I wouldn't be surprised if some had as high as 150.

Tuesday 10th Bellevue

My dear Mother

I put off sending this letter so that I could add more when I got here, but being quite busy now working the roads I am not able to write at length but must send this off immediately as I am ashamed not to have answered your letter before, but I deferred it chiefly on account of my coming over here. I shall write to Anne afterwards so this letter must go as it is. I've staid [here] and at Bull's Point since I have been here. Stuart begs to be remembered to all of you says he answered your letter but through some mistake it was not mailed, says he will reply to it soon. I dined at Willie Heyward's yesterday, I would like to plant Canaan next year but doubt if it can be done unless money is raised. Stuart says the country down here is much healthier than Columbia, says he has not been sick as yet. The crops at Canaan are "<u>so so</u>" like all negro crops. I think they all feel the need of being tacked on to a whiteman. Do ask Mary to look in her desk and see if a contract with Dr DeSaussure's hands is in it There has been tremendous stealing down here this year. That scoundrel [torn] with several others has broken open

---

99. Joseph Henry Price.

several store [torn] year and now he is in jail for only 2 months. Do send me a small piece of sweet soap (when you send down again) to shave with. Send me one or two stamps, if you have any to spare. Sorry I cannot write any more at present. Do send me two steel pens. I've got holders.

Your aff'<u>ct</u> son

M. M. Leverett

Love to Pa and all, hope all are well.

Part of a letter from Milton Maxcy Leverett to his father

U.S.

Christian Commission

"This is a faithful saying, and worthy of all acceptation, that Christ Jesus came into the world to save sinners; of whom I am chief."[100]

Who were the parties. I loaded my gun and fixed it in a convenient position as a trap to the intruder but he never would go in when it was fixed. I at last got tired waiting and watching, as it was evident I was watched as closely as I watched. I fixed my suspicions on one man of whom I was quite suspicious from his conduct, but couldn't prove it. I then tried another method and bribed one fellow of whom I was also a little suspicious. I found I was right to a great extent and at last determined to search his house or camp,—found nothing I could declare to. He behaved quite outrageously said I couldn't prove, spoke so improperly and was all the time so evidently guilty that I was quite provoked. We had a little struggle in his camp together. He was much the strongest and forced his way by me out of the camp. Then swore he was as good a man as I was, said he had never stolen from any damn man, rolled up his shirt sleeves and wanted to fight. I was in doubt what exactly to do. I didn't wish to fight him with my fists as I was pretty certain he would give me a beating. I didn't wish to use my dirk which I had in my pocket as I might kill him, besides I didn't want to strike first blow. I wished him to do it. However rather than be bullied by a negro before all my negroes I was going in and I knew that I should have used my dirk if I did and I expected to have killed him, although I should receive some bruises. As it was my foreman stepped between us and prevented any further collision. I determined to show him (as I couldn't prove positively then that he had any of my goods) that in the long run I was the best man. I left no stone unturned to bring proof against him. I took my time at it and never pushed the matter to extremes until I was ready. He in the

---

100. The beginning of this letter is missing, but it was written after the Leveretts recovered Canaan. This heading at the top of the printed stationery was written over.

meanwhile thought I was thwarted and together with his whole family which was large, were quite exultant and rode the high horse on the place. But I went quietly to work, gathered every item of intelligence, every look and sign I could, and by strategy and diplomacy as I flatter myself culminated my plans, and on a certain day when he was not dreaming of it all on a sudden slapped two Yankee guards on him had him pinioned tightly and had him off for Beaufort in an hour. I let him stay in jail three weeks then preferred charges against him, had him tried, appeared as a witness together with my other witnesses against him. He was convicted and sentenced to hard labour and imprisonment for two months—his imprisonment all together will be about three months and to pay cost of court ($5.00 cts.). A light punishment it is true but the furthest that court could inflict. Just before the trial I saw him he confessed what he had done, begged me to take him out of jail and wanted me to whip him. I told him the trial must go through and I would see what I could do for him but I think I will let him stay there his time out. He confessed to the court also, but said what I was pretty certain of that there were others concerned who they were &^{c} all of which I knew myself—said he didn't break open the house, told who it was (but the fellow whom I had carried as a witness, but did not use swore he didn't do it but that it was 'tother fellow so that I never expect to get that out. The real witness I had was one of the party and had turned states evidence. There were four concerned, one turned states evidence, one I had put in jail and the other two whom I did not carry to jail and against whom I did not prefer any charges, I required to give me a <u>written request</u> that I <u>should flog them in the old style</u>. I of course kindly accommodated them. I have things smoothed down admirably and have my hands under a perfect state of discipline. I of course will have the goods paid for out of their crops, if any cotton sufficient is made.

I have been off and on striving with some of my negroes for the mastery for the year and think that now, I have carried the day, having put one in jail and flogged two. If they do not do the work in the style or quantity I wish I cut down their allowance.

The fellow I had the difficulty with and whom I have in jail is named Peter at one time belonging to Louis and Anne. I told them I should let the Doctor[101] know of the family and of his conduct in order that he might not let them contract with him on his place. The whole family are terrible thieves.

I have had other troubles which I cannot now mention. I am very sorry you lost those coupons. I don't think you can be particular enough.

Mr Hamilton whose family and Dr Gibbes' are staying in B[102] told Stuart your farm was for sale. Have you advertised it? let me know immediately about the

---

101. **Louis McPherson DeSaussure Sr.**
102. **Beaufort.**

mortgage as I must positively raise the money on it. With it I intend to make arrangements that the family shall live comfortably down here and also enable me (should I not make enough cotton) to plant on my own hook. I intend to invest the money which I will borrow on the mortgage in such a manner that it may be turning all the time and at the same time supporting the family but I am not able to enter into details at present. I am very sorry you have all been so sick this summer. Wish I could run up and see you Love to all,

Your aff'<u>ct</u> son
M. M. Leverett

In the fall of 1867 Charles Hendee Leverett left South Carolina and went to Arkansas. The following year he moved with his wife, Blanche, and their children to Searcy, Arkansas, where Charles had accepted a position teaching high school.

Rev. Charles Edward Leverett to his son Milton

Col<u>a</u>, Oct. 26, 1867.

My dear Minny,

Your Letter acknowledging receipt of box came this week, and as you ask me to write a line about the proposition made to you to become a private tutor, I do so to say I question if it would be pleasant or profitable for you in this instance to do so. If I could have $1000 for the labor—that is if some other children could come in so as to bring in such an income, I myself would in these disjointed times take such position, but not you as it probably exists,—tho' you do not state particulars—I think I should decline, if there were any other work for me to do. I doubt if you would find it pleasant. Yr. Ma advises you against it. So do I. I have been sick again, but am better tho' I am scarcely ever well. Ma also has had another in turn & is in bed, but I think her better. Indeed some one of us is ever on the sick list, but sickness is by no means confined to our place. Columbia is an ailing town & for that matter the same is to be said of all places nearby, this season.

Miss Grimke is in Col<u>a</u> on her way with Mrs. Jno. Scriven down. Anne & Mame called to see her yesterday & I this morning. I would have been glad to have had her pay us a visit, but the house & every thing belonging to it, is in no condition to receive company. The fact is we are pretty hard up & do not have funds sufficient to keep going even poorly. I am tired out of being ever under such a pressure, but see no probability of relief. We are very much tired & nothing turns up that is cheering. Every little scrap of money we get goes to pay bills chiefly for articles in the flour line, for we don't venture much on meat. I am afraid we shall never again look up. I was in hopes that those who owed me & were planting would have been able to do something for us in our needs, but we hear only of lost crops. Miss G. thinks the Waight property is a myth, but tell George & Bill to <u>wait</u> & see. It may be something after all. I hope it will. Mr. W. Heyward is going to plant again & has engaged Geo. Martin. Charley has I see by a paper sent me, arrived at his destination. I suppose he will write us soon & tell us his prospects. Hercules is getting in the crops. I doubt if he makes in all more than 100 b. of corn & about 50 of peas & perhaps as many of potatoes. Dr Parker made 1200 bu. corn probably as many of peas &c. I suppose his products in this will be worth about $4000. How fortunate some persons are, how unfortunate others—& those who need. But its all right somehow. We shall be very glad to see you, but don't waste yr. money to come up. I wish I had some for you, but I have not. I pray that God will bless you & that we shall all see better & brighter days

yr aff. f.

Mary Maxcy Leverett to her son Milton

Farm Col. Feb 22. /68

My dear Min

After waiting in vain expectation of seeing your beloved phiz coming up the path once more, on receipt of your letter of the 20th last night to your father, I determined to write, as you are seemingly as resolute as ever in your intentions of sticking to old Prince William,[103] in spite of the brilliant (!) offer D H or any other. Have you received E. Coffin's letter?[104] I should have liked that, if we only had money to start you with. I think you are right in taking Screven's offer as it is impossible to expect any other to turn up, after such an unusual number to choose from—it seems singular that your first & last offers should have been that of teaching, so that you may consider it as a sort of pointing out the path you are to take. Perhaps you may get other children as well as J W's; if Screven offers $200 (you cannot expect more & you <u>may</u> have to take less) & you get the children too, and are at no expense in living, you may have a very decent salary; & it is something not to have to drive our beloved Sambo. Jos. Seabrook always said he would a great deal rather "drive boys than drive negroes." I shall be glad to have you in a healthy neighborhood, where other people are living, instead of on an isolated plantation, with no one to see after you if sick. Caroline's daughter Margaret is to teach in Capt Alfred Martin's family at Robertville—$100. up to the time they go

---

103. Prince William's Parish.
104. Ebenezer Coffin.

to Flat Rock. What is the reason you have not said a word about the Wm Fullers? What is the matter? Sarah Barnwell & Emily walked to the Asylum garden to meet me a few days ago & we had a pleasant meeting.—She said they had heard from Rob. they heard you are staying at Nenny's & thought you must have had something to do with the new Cotton Gin which they tell me Cousin H Stuart & Mr Ravenel have put up on Sheldons land. Is it near <u>your</u> store that was? I knew they were not going to give <u>you</u> any situation in it—people are not apt to think of others, so I told them I was sure <u>not</u>, as you hadn't said a word about it in your letters. They told me of Mr Trescot having hired Big Island to a rich friend of his, Mr Sanford, who is going to Europe as Minister to Belgium,[105] (he paid Mr T. $2000 in advance) & has Mid. Stuart[106] as manager at $1200 a year. Mr Sanford went with Mr T to see Big Id. & was quite shocked to find not a negro at work, when he expected with <u>free labor</u> to have seen every thing in fine order & a hundred negroes at work! I daresay he will be disgusted with his experiment.

Annie says tell you she will get to work at your clothes as soon as we get money. We are disappointed at not having you up here, tho' we think you very right to decide for yourself & make your own way.

Fraser Matthews murder has shocked us all very much. I hope Scipio won't escape.[107]—I hope you will have a horse to ride on—I was glad to hear of E. Means offer about the horse for food.

Dont trouble yourself about my health, dear child, I am surprising myself even, being so much improved in health & strength—am taking quinine & <u>red</u> pepper pills every day, a lately discovered antidote to chills & fever, & Tillie gives me tincture of iron three times a day, & besides the girls bought me a few bottles of porter & some Sherry wine also, & between all this, I have improved wonderfully, so that the girls themselves are relieved & pleased. And your father has come on remarkably he is extremely well & walked in to Town five days in succession last week—he has gone in now. We have planted a bushel of oats only, so far, and a peck of Irish potatoes but hope soon to plant more. The peas you planted are all up very prettily—so are the Dutch turnips Annie planted. She fixed a small frame over a hot bed & put a sash over we took out of the corn

---

105. William Henry Trescot's wife, Eliza Natalie Cuthbert, inherited Big Island from her mother. Henry Shelton Sanford (1813–1891) was United States minister to Belgium, 1861–1869.

106. Middleton Stuart.

107. On 4 February 1868 J. Fraser Mathewes of Coosaw plantation went to Dr. Louis McPherson DeSaussure Sr.'s plantation with an arrest warrant for Peter Holmes, a freedman suspected of stealing Mathewes's mules. After Mathewes fired a shot to intimidate the freedmen, Holmes and two others overpowered Mathewes, and Holmes shot him in the head. "The Murder of J. Fraser Mathewes," *Charleston Courier,* 10 February 1868.

house, & have some Cabbage seed come up in it beautifully—they are said to be Mammoth Cabbages—got the seed from a bad place tho'—<u>Massachusetts</u>.

Hercules & Sary have moved into the corn house—Quash' house we have put the fodder & hay in, & he has gone to live with Lucretia.

Lumber from Mr Douglas has just this moment come into the yard, for the fence. Your sister has planted an arbor in my old garden down the walk, & we knocked those water troughs to pieces & used them for the slats for it. Bought the vines from Mrs Hiller, Madeira, Lenoir & Scuppernong. This looks very much as if we were going to live here—don't it? Tillie has received a letter from Blanche— Charleys school doing well—Trustees all approving him, but he isn't satisfied— has a dreadful headache once a week, & as soon as he makes a plenty of money, "means to <u>come back to South Carolina</u>." Likes a few people only, the generality are the sharpest, closest, keenest set he ever saw. He asks what your plans are for the next year, & wants you to write to him, says if he ever has time again, he will write to you.

Old Mr Guignard is dead—appoplexy I believe—found dead in the road— his mule grazing quietly by him.[108]

And now I will wind up with a piece of good news—<u>Pa's bought a horse</u>, a nice, strong dark bay, nine years old & in good order, for $87. gentle & will plough & wagon both but it don't look like a riding nag—too strong & may be clumsy, but we are all delighted. I think he got such a good one at last because he made such a fuss & difficulty in choosing, that the whole town seems to know at last that he was about buying a horse,—at least a dozen have been out here for him to look at, & between Dr Smith & himself, they must have examined at least fifty—so he had a variety to choose from. The man asked $100 for this, but Dr S. told Pa it was fully worth $75 & had some years good service in him still, so it was compromised to $87. We are delighted, as it is very good looking.

Dr Parker paid Mame to day too, $40 & we will have something good to live on for some time—for a month past we have been faring hard, as we did not wish to go into debt, & now we feel rewarded.

You had better get Mr Screven to pay you quarterly. If I was you, I'd <u>sell</u> Bills note to whoever would buy it.

Your father says if you come to the conclusion that you will come up, you had best not bring up the horse E M.[109] offered you, on account of our now owning one, as it would be difficult to feed two.

Your Affectionate Mother
Mary Leverett

---

108. James Sanders Guignard Jr. of Columbia died 19 February 1868.
109. Edward Means.

Julia Marcelline Leverett to her brother Milton

Columbia, March 10th [1868]

My dear Minny,

Your letter has just been received. It is a great shame in you to have taken so long to write it. Where have you been all this time and what have you been doing and haven't you been sick? Don't tell a story Minny, you know you have. Now do be sure and take quinine before your next attack and don't behave as you always do. I am very glad you have got with such kind people as Mr. & Mrs. Gregorie who will be sure to take good care of you when you are sick. Do be pleasant as you can. I think you have a pretty good offer for this year and hope that next year if nothing happens you will be able to make some business arrangements with Mr. Eben Coffin. By the way did you ever get his letter? You did not mention. Newton who came to see this evening, seemed to think it would have been a very good thing. What a pity he hadn't written earlier because you could have got things so cheap in December, but I hope, if it be God's will that you will be able to come back and stay with us next year. Newton was passing through on his way up the country. I think he has turned out very well. It is so funny to hear him talk about his mother borrowing money from him and promising to return it, but he dont seem to expect to get it back. It is strange how much they always seem to want money always but I expect Aunt Til gives away too. It is a great thing to have a good mother, and Newton was saying that was what had kept him from dissipation and I expect it is true.

Sure enough, Minny, Pa is "down again." He has been gradually feeling worse and last Saturday took to his bed, but I think perhaps his attack has not been so bad as usual.

Friday.

He is better today and out in the parlor. He says must tell you he is up again but still sick. He is one of the hardest persons to make acknowledge he is better. Ma has had a rising behind her ear, but it has gone down a great deal by the use of iodine, and as she expressed it this morning when her breakfast was carried to her is "right sharp" again. Newton shocked us by telling us the doctor said poor Miss Ford cannot live. She has been sick a very long time, had an attack of pneumonia. Mame has been sending her milk every day for about a month if not more. Poor Miss Ford! I think when you look at what self denying life she has led, one might call her a noble woman, and I believe she will receive a reward. I think those two sisters must have had a sad life.

Our horse is a splendid one and though I dont think it fell off "the next morning" yet it, of course does not get the same feed, Mr. McIntosh gave it, but I think it looks very well indeed. It is a horse just suited for us. Things do turn out for the best for people Minny. Now though we had to wait so long, and be disappointed so often yet here we got a horse almost as if it had been picked out for us. McIntosh only paid $2.50 and sold it for $87.50 a pretty good gain. He bought at a Government sale, that is to say a soldier who owed him $5.00 let him have it and another one for the debt as they both had distemper. McIntosh took them and cured them, and now values the other at $150. Hercules thinks ours a very fine horse only he says it is scary. He and Tom are busy at the fence, doing the side next to Jake's house. Pa is inexorable on the subject of cutting down the trees in front to make a garden. We have also had an arbor made in the old garden and planted vines from the fence down. We might as well try and make ourselves comfortable up here for I am afraid there is little chance of our going to the low country very soon again. I do hope next year if nothing happens you will be able to come and live with us. How is it possible that you could be so forgetful as not to send the children word what the Fuller children said about their presents. Do Minny dont be too hard on those boys and dont "kill any poor little child." Do write a nice letter soon, dont wait to get news but write anything just as if you were talking to us. You see I have followed that plan and the consequence is lo! what a nice long letter. But you don't care for us Minny and that's the reason you wont take the trouble to write. Now clear yourself of such an imputation as soon as you receive this favor.

Mrs. Darby[110] has been busying herself with getting up some tableaux for the Ladies Association, and almost all the girls are to act. Seppie Parker is to be "Catherine of Arragon." Emma a queen in the "Morte d'Arthur" of Tennyson.[111] Miss Shelton "Joan of Arc," Sallie Le Conte a Bride. The Popes, Mrs Anna Heyward Taylor,[112] Mrs. Darby, Miss Preston, & Mrs Waring[113] are also to act and a good many of the students among them Mr. Townsend so I hear. Mr. Barnwell and Mr. Walker wont let their daughters act. I expect they will make a good deal by it. There was a concert not long ago, also for the same object, which did very well, although, there were only three lady performers. The Yankees also have a theatrical association which gives public performances. One of the Miss Prestons was married a day or two ago to Mr. Rollins Lowndes but it was a very private affair, they were to be married at 3 o'clock in the day.[114]

---

110. Mary Cantey Preston Darby of Columbia.
111. Alfred, Lord Tennyson, *Idylls of the King* (1859).
112. Mary Anna Heyward Taylor of Columbia.
113. Malvina Sarah Black Waring of Columbia.
114. Sarah Buchanan Preston married Rawlins Lowndes 10 March 1868 in her parents' home in Columbia, now known as the Hampton-Preston Mansion, which is open to the public.

Pa says must tell you he does not know what books to recommend as he is not well enough yet to go in town to look at any, but says you had better send down to Dawson or Holmes and ask them to send you a sample which you will either return to them or keep and Sister says there is none better than Cornell's Geography which is what they used at Barhamville when I was there and which is excellent. Davies' Arithmetic is very good too, and Davies' Algebra, and I wish I could remember of the history too which we used but I cant and Carroll's I think it is Catechism on Common Things is what the other class used and a Scholar's Companion.[115] But if you are one of those unbelievers in "Madame"[116] of course, you will think nothing of my recommendations.

O, I have at last had my chicken pen made and a very nice place too, but I have lost 8 chickens since, but have two left which are fine little things. I hope to do better next time though. Sister's chickens are a very fine looking set, except little Baldy, whose head however has feathers on it at last and who has improved. Two of them have beautiful rose combs, both roosters, and one is a very pretty little Dominica. I suppose somebody has told you of the four pigs dying. I think, perhaps, there were too many for the cowhouse. Now I believe I have told you the principal things of interest in the farmyard at "Ravenswold" as I happened to see written in Pa's prayerbook as the name of this little rural retreat. My cow is as usual illtreated in regard to food, not having what it ought, but I heard some one the family remarking on its skin looking sleek. Minny, that's a fine cow, no doubt.

Newton mentioned having taken Anne Elliott to the theater. Tell her, if you see her, that I would have come to see her but when I asked about her, found she was gone. Eldred Fickling[117] and his little wife were at church on Sunday. I did not see them but heard Mame or Annie talking about them. They said he had on his police uniform, and, she only reached up to the buttons at the back. Her name was Bessie Edwards. What is the reason Mr. Fuller left the Mercury. His name is not there now. Mary Smith was to have acted too but is prevented by the death of her aunt. Miss Tabor is here on a visit to Miss Crawford, which seems to be an extensive one, as I think she has been here about a month pretty near, & is singing at Trinity, again. <u>Now</u> write soon Minny.

With much love believe me
Your dear sister Julie

---

115. Either Sarah S. Cornell, *Cornell's Primary Geography,* or *Cornell's First Steps in Geography* (New York: D. Appleton and Co., 1857 and 1858); and Charles Davies, *Arithmetic, Designed for Academies and Schools* (New York: A. S. Barnes & Co., 1852), Charles Davies, *Elementary Algebra* (New York: A. S. Barnes & Burr, 1852) and [Henry Butter], *The Scholar's Companion* (Philadelphia: Perkins & Purves, 1842).

116. Madame Acelie Togno.

117. Eldred S. Fickling of Columbia.

Ann Sarah Maxcy Hughes to her cousin Mary Maxcy Leverett

Tulip Hill[118] March 18th 1868

Since writing you dearest Coz I've been the busiest <u>little body</u> & I trust with some effect for the South. Your letter did a great amount of good, as I copied parts of it, & showed to my most intimate friends, as the <u>real</u> suffering down there was not known, & people wd. say to me "it has been three years since the war & we thought they were getting on." You know how unreflecting country people are, & many do not take <u>the gazette</u>[119] which is the only paper which published the sad letter from Carolina. As if to help me in our good work, just at the opportune moment strengthening the effect of your letter came one from near Beaufort from the Father of the Rev.nd. Mr. Harris (our pastor who left us last year & who was at the Seminary with your dear boy. Not a gentleman <u>originally</u> but a man of a most lovely spirit & greatly beloved in this neighborhood. Do you know the family? Poor but respectable people before the War.) Well! he writes <u>his Son</u>, his whole family wd Starve, unless he could send him money to buy corn, till corn came again—They made a subscription up for him & these two letters set the people to work, & I have collected quite a good box full of half <u>worn garments</u> for you to distribute after selecting any thing you may want—& think good enough.— & I am going to Baltimore Saturday when, if it is full, I shall send off, without delay not waiting for the children's offering after Easter. We've had a good deal of corn promised & Sister[120] got for me 50 bags, a donation from Baltimore, as many farmers will give a bushel of corn who won't give bags—We are doing all we can, & Sister since she recovered is working in B.[121] She was instrumental in selling most of yr. silver & most fortunately had two pieces of yrs. in her pocket trying to sell, the very night the Depository was broken in by Robbers, & much silver taken. (See how God took care of you that day!) Now dear Cousin don't be surprised to find in the box a good many <u>common</u> things. The people here are generally straitened & give much away. We used to make splendid wheat crops. They have failed now <u>9 years</u>, & that, & losing servants, high taxes, has plunged every one, more or less in debt. No body now here has any thing they can do without—& it is not a rich neighborhood but warm <u>Christian</u> hearts—I have placed in the box a division, separating the things I thought useful <u>to you</u>, & the others it will gladden yr heart to give to the poor around you, <u>after</u> taking any thing you want for your family.—

118. Near Annapolis, Maryland, formerly the home of her great-grandfather, Samuel Galloway, and her parents, Mary Galloway and Virgil Maxcy.
119. The *Baltimore Gazette,* one of several newspapers in Baltimore.
120. Mary Maxcy Markoe.
121. Baltimore.

I shall pack the box tomorrow with a happy feeling & prayer to God it may reach you in Safety & do good to some weary Spirit. Many things are for winter but they will put away til fall & then be comfortable. Write me after Easter collection, if I shall send you any of the bags of corn—& mention particularly what you want as if they have it I will select for you, as being instrumental in getting this up, I shall have that privilege. Most of these articles will go to Baltimore to be sent South by the Relief association but they would send any where I requested. George[122] has just come from Annapolis. One of his objects was, to try to get a bill passed in the Legislature to send money South. He dont know yet, if they will do it as the state treasury is empty—One thing, we have observed in Md. dear cousin that Rich Southerners, do not seem to help each other as much as people do here. I know many families who curtail their expenses so as to send South. Why is this—It seems unnatural to me, except I hear those who made money out of the War were—Union—How does Mr. Hayward get on? I heard his wife was dead[123]—You need not take the trouble to write me the letter you suggested as I made extracts from yours which serve my purpose. There are some really conscientious Union people with us, who were kind & considerate during the war, & really helped when they were stealing horses & searching houses &c &c with the authorities when they were so rabid against those of So. sentiments, tho this may seem strange to you.—It is hard to forgive those who have ruined us, and as in my case, snatched from me, my hearts chief treasure. He was born in Brussels, the delight of his parents on St. Patricks day (yesterday would have been 27) Oh! When these days come around, how I remember the joy of his Grandparents at his birth & ours, & now contrast our desolation. But blessed Spirit safe in his heavenly home. Why should I murmur or mourn!—Dear Coz. nothing but God's grace can help us to forgive our enemies, it is not in the natural man, & I often pray to be helped to do it and am helped by Him, who was crucified. And oh! What a state now the country is in, ruled by Scepters, blasphemers, & drunkards, truly when bad men are exalted the wicked abound on every side. I feel as if I had no country, but Heaven, & no Ruler but the King of Kings—but God reigneth & we will rejoice for He alone can bring good out of all this evil.

Dear Cousin I have in Phila a dear friend Mrs McCall, who was Miss Mercer niece of the celebrated Miss Margaret Mercer who kept a school & was so good & intellectual. [illegible]

Remember the box is entirely at yr disposal & to give away what you do not want. I would have got more at Christmas but we all empty our wardrobes then of everything we can do without but I hope you'll find much in the box that is useful. Write at once to me in Baltre, 52 Franklin Street.

---

122. George Wurtz Hughes, husband of Ann Sarah Maxcy, served as a representative from Maryland in Congress, 1859–1861.

123. Elizabeth Barnwell Rhett Heyward, Daniel Heyward's second wife, died 27 July 1865.

Julia Marcelline Leverett to her brother Milton

Columbia July 4th [1868]

My dear young brother Min,

I will celebrate the "glorious 4th" by writing you one of my interesting home letters, so prepare now, settle yourself comfortably in your chair and let us have a nice talk like those you and I used to have sitting out in the piazza with your head in my lap, "O scratch my head for me Julie." The Yankees have been celebrating, by firing off 38 guns so I suppose we are now back in the "glorious Union forever." Pic-nics and barbecues seem to be the order of the day. The "quality" are going to a barbecue in the Park and a pic-nic at Barhamville, where two of the rooms which formerly held the august presence of "Madame" are to be open to our cook Lucy and her fellows. Quelle horreur. I wish we were so situated that we could have little parties and picnics, how nice it would be.

Your last letter was, I may say, the best I have ever received from you, unusually interesting, and I hope your next may be still better. Even Pa thought it was pretty good. Minny what is it the sign of when a young gentleman sends word to his sister of how beautifully, some young ladies sing, and when he is so particular about his dress as to carry two cravats on a ride. Now I would like to know how you would look with your horses standing still in the middle of the road, Mr Leverett discovered putting on his cravat, while t'other lies in the bottom of the buggy and Miss—A or P. looks on with lively interest. If such a thing happens I would advise you to give her t'other as a souvenir. O yes sir Mrs Fuller has been advising us of your carryings on, and of your personal appearance etc—Well Minny, please yourself, but do not attempt to hide it from your family, for be sure we will hear it.

Mr. Fred Brown was married on Thursday to a Miss Murphy of Charleston.[124] None of the family went down to it. They will live over the store which Mr. Brown sr says is the only part of the whole arrangement, he likes, as his son will be able to attend to the business and live there. Charlie and Dick used to call her the "little speckle face Catholic" so we fancy they didn't like it much. You know Charlie, and Fannie and Lena are on at the North. Fannie has been very anxious to come back home. I think her relations laughed at some of her clothes, a sack, and that quite vexed Fannie. Mr. Brown also went on and stayed a month till the elections were over. You know he was registrar and people called him a Radical, though he is not, and we think he must have heard it, for Mrs. Brown told us he said if he was only forgiven this time he'd never be caught in such a scrape again. He was made commissioner too at the same time with the "Honourable, Judge Bevely

---

124. Fred J. Brown of Columbia married Margaret Murphy of Charleston. His father, James Brown, a native of England, owned a painting and wallpaper business.

Nash." The truth is he said he had lost so much money by the Yankees, he wanted to make some money out of them so he accepted the Registrar office, but he has done it at the expense of his reputation.

We have gathered in our wheat, but have not been able to thresh but a part. It is a very nice grain, but I am afraid we won't make more than 15 bushels. The rice is looking very nicely, and Hercules has been working it the second time. We have had a man helping him, but he has left us and we have to try and get some one else because it needs the working so badly. You see they all want ready money which we haven't got. The cows ate up your cotton plants and some okra. They are a great bother.

Dr. Parker has cut off our supply of milk to 5 quarts at 10 cent per qt, but we make butter with the rest, so it makes us more comfortable that way, though it isn't much. If the Charleston stock would only pay, it would help so much. I believe it has gone up some, but no pay yet.

We heard from Brother Charlie last week, and would you believe it, he has another son? He says it is the finest of any and I think his letter is rather more cheerful, but his health is still bad, and he says the doctor tells him, he is killing himself teaching school. He says he thinks he could make a hennery, and sheep-raising pay, and says he will raise 200 chickens this year. Says little Julie every evening meets him at the door with "Pa I have fed the chickens, and given them water and now they are all gone to bed." She will be very capable, but I am afraid unless he gets well off, she will have a hard time poor little soul.

Columbia at length rejoices in Mayor Guenther, Yankee, and Aldermen Joe Taylor, Simons, and Wilder negroes. We heard that Mayor Stark did not know what to do.[125] Just to think that you can go to New York and back for this month for 29 dollars. Cousin Cornelia, and Mr & Mrs. William Wallace went to Canada this week. What a chance it would be for Pa if he had the money. He is not very well. Dr Smith has been giving him morphine, and we are to let him know at the end of a month so he may decide on what to do. They have been most kind friends to us, and we are glad to have let them have some of the things which came in the boxes. Annie says must set the table so I must "haul up" for the present.

Pa says must tell you he would have written but he is sick all the time, that tomorrow will make 6 Sundays since he has been to church. Poor Pa, there's so much to worry him and you know he always took life hard and besides he does suffer. The thing is, when he gets better, he takes a long walk which is not good for him. He needs change of air and everything. Some people think that you ought

125. On 19 June 1868 United States military authorities in Columbia replaced Mayor Theodore Stark and five city aldermen, naming Col. Francis L. Guenther as mayor and appointing six new city aldermen, including freedmen Joseph Taylor, William Simons, and Charles M. Wilder.

not to write to those away about your troubles, but I don't know about that, for it is a comfort to us to write to you & it is a comfort to you to write to us about yours. Not that I am in favor of writing gloomy letters, but I hope this is not one.

Mame had an attack on Sunday, but is much better, and is going to Mrs. Wallace's[126] with Annie this evening.

God bless the people of Maryland. I don't know Minny what we would have done without what they have done for us. We are living on the corn they gave us, the frock and petticoat—I am now wearing is what they have sent. Besides what we have given away, Cousin Sallie[127] had been trying to get up some sort of affair, and says some one has given her two hams for us. She says Ma's letters have done much good, speaks in the highest terms of them & said Mrs. Howard the President I believe said if she had had Ma's letter when she went to the Legislature, she could have got $5,000 more to the $20,000 which was appropriated. But that has fallen through or something because they left out "Be it enacted" or some such phrase. Aunt Til has been staying with us for a week, but is gone up to Pendleton. They are all going to Flat Rock next week. I expect Cousin Mary Heyward will stay with us about a week sometime in fall or summer.

Good bye old Minny, don't get sick and if you do take quinine and pepper.

From your <u>dear</u> sister
Julie

Ma says she is very glad to find through Mrs F's letter that you are enjoying yourself riding about etc. says she has not given up hopes of spending her next winter with you at Canaan. I hope you'll be with us somehow.

Goodbye
Julie

We got Dr. Smith to come out today, & we are to give Pa things which he said. He seemed tolerable today. I expect that will do him good. Anyhow be sure that it's all right and keep up heart. Julie

Mary Bull Leverett to her brother Milton

The Farm, July 30th, 1868

My Dear Minny,

You needn't try too hide your being sick at any time from us, as we hear from both Mrs. Fuller & Annie Gibbes all about you. How I wish I could be with you to take care of you, do make William fan & wait, make poultices & do everything

---

126. Sarah Burroughs Wallace.
127. Ann Sarah Maxcy Hughes.

else thats necessary, tell him how-dye for me & that he must take good care of you & I will bring him something good when we come down in the fall. All of our plans point to that event, since we have come back & talked to them all, even Papa has changed, & is willing to go down, if we can only get the money. Mr. Nicols has asked Pa to let him know this week what he will take for this place, so if he will only buy it, look out for us! & then you will be able to plant on your own hook, it will be so nice. It is dreadful to hear so much of politics, things do not look bright for us in that line. The Phoenix, the only paper up here now, has turned Radical.[128] The negroes & low white people & Black Republicans are having what they call, Union meetings. General Burton[129] the commander of the post here, & who had charge of Davis & was so kind to him, does not countenance these meetings at all

31st I am trying each night to write a few lines to you, my time is so fully taken up during the day, you will be astonished to hear that I am <u>out</u> by <u>five</u> o'clock every morning seeing about the cow, the pig, & the chickens. You will laugh & say Pshaw she will soon give it up! but I have been doing it now for weeks, & like it very much, I churn every other day, & make the yellowest kind of butter. We are all pleased with the cow, the hens are not as accomodating, they held a Convention the other day, but the results of it, was, only a few eggs.

Sept. 7th My dear old fellow,

Now that I have a little breathing space, I will finish off this old letter, thinking it is much better late than not at all. Tillie & I have just finished off 15 yards, each, of embroidery, & feel quite proud of our handiwork, mine will help me pay for a cow that I have bought from Charley. I find, that although it is only giving between five & six quarts a day, I can make about (5$) five dollars a week, pretty good, don't you think so? So look out soon for a box, only <u>be sure</u> in your next letter to say how we must send it or rather how to direct it. Our efforts at making money are at last beginning to tell. Cousin Sallie Hughes sent on 21 dollars two days ago, for some of the articles, we had sent on to the Depository, in Baltimore, had been sold. Annie is as busy as a bee preserving oranges &c. (We sent to Annie Gibbes to buy some for us). All are trying their hands at carving, as those sell very high, & we have some engaged to a southern lady, who is living in New York. Cousin Emily & Sarah Barnwell are both hard at work sewing & preserving also, say they find making money is not easy work. Nat has gone to keep school, has a very good place, will board with Mr. Car Michael.[130] He took tea with us before he

---

128. The *Columbia Daily Phoenix*, published from March 1865 through December 1875.
129. Bvt. Brig. Gen. Henry Stanton Burton.
130. Nathaniel Berners Barnwell left the University of South Carolina and went to Georgia to live with his cousin Elizabeth Barnwell Elliott and her husband, William Paul Carmichael, near Savannah; he tutored the Carmichael children for a year but returned to Columbia in 1869.

left, seemed quite provoked with his brothers for not writing, said no matter what they send, clothes, boxes, &c they never answer. That reminds me that you have not yet said, if you had received the shirts. I have been so worried about your being sick, wish so much that I could be with you to take care of you, do write oftener. Charley expects to leave for Arkansas next week, he received the offer of an excellent school in Searcy in Ar., is trying to settle up all of his business this week. I don't know how he will manage about the crop. The baby is pitiful looking, she has been sick for some time. I shall be sorry for it to go away. I am afraid it will be very much neglected.

Hercules & Sary are so unfortunate with their children, little Sallie is very sick with dropsy, we are trying our utmost, but I afraid their is no hope. They, all of them behaved remarkably well. Lewis is as polite as possible, is very obliging about bringing out things out of town. All are very well, do for pity sake write more regularly. I am going right in so will end.

Your affec.
sister Mary

Julia Marcelline Leverett to her brother Milton

"Ravenswold"[131] Aug 12th—68

My dear Minny,

I was sorry to perceive by your last effort to me that you are not one of the few human beings that can stand praise. Your former letter was well written. Your latter was—stuff. Excuse my plainness, my dear sir, but "faithful are the wounds of a friend."[132] Take warning, therefore, and let your next letter be worthy of yourself and me.

Wherefore is it, O my brother, that in your last letter was no mention made of those syrens, that dwell at the Elysian Fields yclept "Millwood"? Of what color is your "courting" coat, and how many times a week dost thou don it. Come Minny, make a confidante of thy sister, if thou hast any confidence in her and any confidence to give. Ma has been giving it as her opinion "I declare I think Minny must be engaged." Come, now tell us the truth for I fancy, you have been flying round pretty extensively from what I hear. Do be sure though about it before you venture on the last step. We want you to be happy and we will resign your graces [torn] when the time comes, We hear that Mr. Marion Hutson is deeply [torn] also, is it true?[133]

---

131. The Farm.

132. Prov. 27:6.

133. Probably Marion Martin Hutson of Prince William's Parish.

Cousin Sallie sent us on Saturday two boxes, one with 3 hams and 20 pounds of [torn] and the other with clothes and some tea, so we are going to send you [torn] a box. And the other day we had from the Bishop a present of $50 and some dresses, but the 50 went like nothing, principally in paying debts, which is a great help however. We have had a good deal of money on the whole, and yet Minny, we live hard nearly all the time, but it takes so much to live even in the plainest manner, and there are so many debts, but by the help of God I think we'll win through. I am glad you have such a good position, for it is a good one though the salary is not high, and I wish you would not speak or think of its being menial for it is no such thing, far less so than planting for any one, and having all the dirty work to do with the negros, having them abusing you and all that sort of thing. You all ought to be organizing into clubs, down there as they are doing up here. Our convention met last week, and Col Haskell is to stump this district I believe.[134] From what the different delegates say the negroes are arming, and drilling all over the state, instigated by General Scott in one place.[135] When election day comes you ought to frighten them something about K.K.K. They say that at some of the elections up here, the Democrats voted one negro ten times. Walter was appointed to over look the books and see that all was right. When he found any radical negro's name who had not voted he would step to the door and tell Radcliffe and one or two others and they would march up this negro and vote him under that name, and then they would march him to the lower box and vote him there, at last they were found out and they hid themselves in some hogsheads in Hope's store till it was over. We went to the procession that the Democrats had. I thought it was beautiful. Then we went to Carolina Hall and heard the Generals or rather Hampton, for we couldn't hear the others speak.[136] I fell deeply in love with Hampton and was so anxious to be introduced to him. He was much lionized when in New York. Some of the Federal Generals were talking about making him next President after Seymour, and his tailor made him a present of [a] new suit. We spent the night at the Reynolds' where Gens. Kershaw & Chesnut[137] were staying and then what part of my heart I could spare from Hampton I gave to Kershaw. Pretty good for one night to fall in love with two generals and both of them grand [torn]. When we went upstairs I said I had fallen in love with Hampton and

---

134. Alexander Cheves Haskell.

135. Brig. Gen. Robert Kingston Scott, assistant commissioner for the Freedmen's Bureau in South Carolina, 1866–1868, Republican candidate for governor in 1868.

136. On 28 July 1868 a Democratic Party meeting was held in Columbia at Carolina Hall. Hampton, Confederate Brig. Gen. Joseph Brevard Kershaw (1822–1894) of Camden, and others gave campaign speeches. On 29 July 1868 the *Columbia Daily Phoenix* reported that Hampton said "he wanted restoration on the basis of truth, harmony and justice, and he firmly believed we would have it in November, by the triumph of the Democratic party."

137. Confederate Brig. Gen. James Chesnut Jr. (1815–1885) of Camden.

a little girl who was staying there said "But, he is married.[torn] It sounded so innocent and funny.

John Maxcy came over to see us on Sunday at [torn] and stayed until 11
oclock at night. You know all this time he has had nothing to do with us at all, but
this is the second time he has been over in about eight days, and invited us to go
over and get fruit, so if nothing prevents we are going this evening. We thought
that Cousin Julia must have sent word to him to come and make up. She has been
very ill, almost died and was only saved by a Miss Scott. John says he does not
expect she has had it all as she wanted or she would have said something about
[it]. She has given up trying to establish the Asylum and gone to teach in the vernacular schools. Cousin Cornelia went on a Jaunt with Mr. and Mrs. Wallace during the time that you could go to New York on the excursion ticket for $29. We
have not seen her since she has come back. I must stop now for the present. My
hand is tied up and the pen is poor and the ink black and I am ashamed of my
writing, but still

"My pen is poor, my ink is bad
My — — — — —

Thursday, Installment—No. 2. Well we went to the Maxcy's and got plenty of
peaches. O they have such loads. Mame is busy making peach leather. She hopes
to sell it at the Association as Mrs. Fickling sent word to her to send it as none
had been there, since Margaret S.' and there had been constant inquiries for it,
and she is going to make some for you too. Annie is going to preserve some for
home use (so called) and I am going to make a jar for Dr. Fair. I so wish we could
get Pa well and out of bed. It is a sore trial, both on him, poor Pa, and on us. I
don't know how a person can stand so much agony as he seems to have. I think
perhaps on the whole he is better since the operation sometimes he seems a great
deal better, but then again he seems to feel so badly. Now, he slept well last night,
and a good breakfast this morning but he has been groaning ever since almost &
made Ma give him morphine, though only a little and then he said I must come
and write off his will for him, but I told him no I wouldn't and no more I will, but
I carried him Blanche's letter to read and then he spoke about "those rascally
[torn] crossed letters" You know he detests them, so what is one to think when he
speaks always as if he wants to die and all that sort of thing [torn] do hope he may
be slowly improving, though he is always confined to his bed. The doctors Fair and
Smith will perform the operation I believe, and we must hope and pray for the
best. I hope by the next letter you get he may be much better.

Minny these blots look shamefully, don't they, but I am writing with a quill
and every now and then I dip it in and take it out to write and plump goes a drop
right where the word [ink blot] & now look there! The Parkers asked me when

they came back from paying Anna a visit, to come in and play croquet with them, so if nothing happens I am in hopes of having that pleasure this winter. Is Sallie Stuart engaged and to whom? I heard she was. I do not think it likely that Carrie and I will go on to that school for we have not heard anything of it for sometime, so I dare say Dr. Wharton has not got the funds, though he published a circular which was in the kindest manner so I heard. I would like much to take singing and music for I believe I have got a tolerable voice, and I have had so little teaching in any thing. When you think of it Minny my education is very superficial, for the only teaching in public was only one quarter at Mr Well's, and six months at Mad. Togno's; for the teaching at home is a humbug unless there is more than one child. and of course I don't count when I was a little bit of a girl at Mrs. Colcock's. I would like to take French and German too. I never practice now. I don't feel like it when Pa is sick all the time.

I believe I am pretty well pumped out now Minny. When next you come up I hope you will come prepared to do the sundry little jobs you left unfinished such as silling the parlor, digging out the well, etc. Does your engagement extend to the end of the year? Brother Charlie says little Screven was head and shoulders above the others in viciousness. I hope you will give a different report. His address is Searcy Ark. The little one is not named for you so dont be afraid. It is named Storer Leverett, after Mrs. Storer who has been so kind to them. The trustees invited Brother Charlie to take the school again, as he is the only teacher, the boys have not overridden. He has 50 scholars and an assistant. If they miss, he makes them come before school, if that dont do he makes them come on Saturday, and if that dont do he marches them through the streets to his house in the evening. He is a born teacher. He is negotiating for eight acres near Searcy which he is going to improve. He has 70 pullets, 25 hens and 22 guinea fowls. Now Minny write to him and us. You know we always want to hear from you, and don't be in the blues, it is foolish, and I think you had better take a <u>blue</u> pill.

With much love old Minny, I am your dear sister
Julie

Rev. Charles Leverett died at The Farm on 30 November 1868, three days before his sixty-third birthday, leaving an estate that was primarily real property—The Farm and another farm near Columbia; Canaan, his plantation in Beaufort District; and a claim on his former home, which the U.S. government had seized in Beaufort. The appraised value of his personal property, which consisted only of his household furnishings and his horse and cow, was $691.50.[138]

---

138. Estate of C. E. Leverett, Richland County Inventories, Appraisals, and Sales, Volume B: 1862–1870, South Carolina Department of Archives and History, Columbia.

Bishop Davis's address to the annual convention of the Protestant Episcopal Church in South Carolina, at St. Philip's Church, Charleston, the following May included this tribute to Charles Leverett's career as an Episcopal clergyman:

Our brother Leverett was not a native of this State, but came early in life to Edisto Island as a teacher. Some time after he became a candidate for orders, and being subsequently ordained, united the office of his ministry with his school duties. He was successful in both, and Edisto has always remembered him as a faithful instructor, and a vigorous and efficient preacher of the gospel. He removed thence to Sheldon Church, and thence to the neighborhood of Columbia, about the commencement of the war. At its close, he was reduced in circumstances and broken in constitution. He soon fell into a painful and certain decline; so distressing was his illness finally, that under the influence of the sufferings of the earth, and the clear and sustaining hope of heaven and immortal life, he earnestly longed to depart and be with Christ. He was a scholar, a man of practical understanding, and of perfectly honest and unflinching purposes, he was a true christian, and his last days threw out a strong light of sustaining faith uniting with the prospective joys of heaven.[139]

---

139. *Journal of the Proceedings of the Seventy-ninth Annual Convention of the Protestant Episcopal Church in South Carolina, in St. Philip's Church, Charleston, on the 12th, 13th, & 14th of May, 1869* (Charleston: n.p., 1869).

Epilogue

After his father's death on 30 November 1868 Milton was left to take care of his mother and five sisters—Anne, who was widowed with one child, and Matilda, Mary, Julia, and Caroline. Although Rev. Charles Leverett recovered all his land after the war and Mary Maxcy Leverett finally had their home in Beaufort restored to her some years after his death, the family never really recovered from the effects of the war. Milton farmed, both at Canaan and at The Farm near Columbia, but the family struggled and never regained the life they had enjoyed in prior years.

In Julia's letter to Milton dated 12 August 1868 she writes of her father "then he said I must come and write off his will for him, but I told him no I wouldn't and no more I will." But someone wrote it for him. A will dated 18 November 1868, about two weeks before his death, is part of this collection. It is neatly written on a single large sheet of paper and signed by him, and witnessed by Selena Brown and Amanda Garner. The executors were to be his son Milton and three others: Thomas Middleton Hanckel of Charleston, Archibald Hamilton Seabrook, and James Henry Fowles. By it he leaves all of his property to his wife and gives instructions as to his burial. For some reason it must not have been considered a legal will as it was never probated and it is hard to believe his family did not know of it since it was written less than two weeks before his death.

Also in this collection is a partition deed drawn up in 1881 and signed on various dates in December of 1881 and January of 1882 in which Rev. Charles Leverett's real estate is divided among his heirs. By this deed, which states that he died intestate, Mary Maxcy Leverett received the house in Beaufort, Milton was given Canaan, the plantation in Beaufort County, and also a farm of seventy acres near Columbia. The five daughters, jointly, got The Farm, the sixty-four-acre farm, and home near Columbia. This deed was recorded in Richland County on 29 January 1887 and in Beaufort County on 4 April 1905.

Milton never married, nor did Matilda, Mary, or Julia. Caroline married James Ironsides Adams on 30 March 1875 and moved to his plantation in the lower part of Richland County about twenty miles from Columbia. Caroline and James had fourteen children, ten of whom lived to an old age, and many grandchildren, so that Rev. Charles Leverett has many descendants but none with the family name Leverett.

When Rev. Charles Leverett died, his adopted son Charles, son of Rev. Charles Leverett's brother, Frederic Percival Leverett Sr., had already moved to Arkansas to take charge of an academy in Searcy. In the fall of 1869 he moved to Washington County to teach at the Ozark Institute near Fayetteville and when the University of Arkansas was founded in 1871 he was elected to the chair of ancient languages. Professor Leverett remained at the university until all faculty members were forced to resign in 1885 but was recalled in 1888 as adjunct professor of ancient languages. Shortly afterward he was made full professor, a position he held until his death on 12 November 1897. He adapted quite well to the postwar reconstruction environment and was successful not only as a teacher but also in his business ventures, and acquired considerable property. His wife, Julia Blanche Jenkins, lived until 3 March 1916. Charles was survived by eleven children.

About the time Caroline married and moved away Mary Maxcy Leverett succeeded in having her home on the bay in Beaufort restored to her by the U.S. government, and Anne and her daughter, Louise Isabel DeSaussure, moved there to live. Louise married Henry Middleton Stuart (1859–1933) and lived in Beaufort until her death at age 102 in 1961. The house at 1301 Bay Street, though no longer belonging to anyone related to the Leverett family, is still standing and is known as the Leverett House. The Farm near Columbia was the principal residence for the remainder of the family for the rest of their lives. The city grew around them and parts of the farm were sold but the section near the home remained in the family. Caroline and her husband built a house across the road just opposite the old house. When Caroline's children grew up several of them built houses on this road, which first became known as Leverett Street and later Adams Grove. The old residence was occupied by several of Caroline's daughters long after the Leveretts were gone. Her youngest daughter moved out to enter a nursing home in 1985, 123 years after the Leveretts first moved there and 120 years after it was occupied by Gen. Fuller of Sherman's army in 1865.

Julia died on 26 February 1887 and is buried at Saint Helena's Episcopal Church in Beaufort. Matilda died on 29 November 1894 and Mary Maxcy Leverett on 30 January 1897; Milton lived until 19 December 1908. The graves of all three are at Trinity Episcopal Cathedral in Columbia. Caroline, her husband, and her sister Mary died in a span of two months in 1913—James Ironsides Adams on 28 August, Caroline on 12 September, and Mary on 17 October. Caroline and her husband are buried with the Adams family at Saint John's Episcopal Church, Congaree, about twenty miles from Columbia. Mary is buried at Trinity Cathedral. The grave of Anne, who died on 8 June 1916, and those of Louise DeSaussure Stuart and her husband are at Saint Helena's Church. Charles Hendee Leverett and Blanche are buried in Evergreen Cemetery in Fayetteville, Arkansas.

Of the Leverett children who died prior to 1870, Edward died on 21 December 1861 and is buried at Sheldon Episcopal Church near Beaufort. Only the walls of this old church remain, but the graveyard is still there. Their adopted son Frederic died on 23 July 1864 in Richmond, Virginia, and his grave is in the officers' section in Hollywood Cemetery. There is also a stone marker for him in the churchyard at Saint Helena's Church in Beaufort. Catherine, who died at age fifteen on 9 March 1865, about three weeks after Sherman burned Columbia, is buried at Trinity Cathedral. There were several Leverett children who died in infancy; one is buried at Sheldon Church and three at Trinity Church on Edisto Island.

The graves of Rev. Charles Leverett and his wife are side by side in the churchyard at Trinity Cathedral, near those of four of their children and it seems fitting to end this—to lay Charles and Mary to rest—by quoting the epitaphs on their grave stones.

Rev. Charles Edward
Son of
Benjamin & Comfort
Marshall Leverett
Born at Boston, Mass.
for many years a
Minister of the
Protestant Episcopal
Church
Died—1868
Aged 62 yrs.
Nothing to glory in
but Jesus, the Rock of
Ages and atonement of
the world

Mary Bull
Daughter of
Mary Bull &
Milton Maxcy
Wife of
Rev. Charles Edward
Leverett
Rector of Sheldon Church.
Died Jan. 30, 1897
Aged 88 yrs.
A Christian of exalted piety:
A woman of superior intellect:
A daughter, wife, mother and friend
of deep devotedness;
Her memory is to be fondly cherished;
Her virtues, and worth and walk
with God, closely imitated.

Appendix
The Leveretts and Their Contemporaries

The Leverett Household

Adams, Caroline Pinckney Leverett (1853–1913), "Carrie"; wife of James Ironside Adams (1850–1913); youngest daughter of Mary Maxcy and Rev. Charles Edward Leverett.

Billy (fl. 1887), a slave; purchased by Rev. Charles Edward Leverett before 1855; as a freedman after the war he served as a soldier in the United States Colored Troops in 1866–67 and later worked for Milton Maxcy Leverett at Canaan.

DeSaussure, Anne Heyward Leverett (1836–1916), "Annie," "Nan"; wife of Louis McPherson DeSaussure Jr.; daughter of Mary Maxcy and Rev. Charles Edward Leverett.

DeSaussure, Louis McPherson, Jr. (1836–1858), husband of Anne Heyward Leverett; son of Isabella Harper Means and Dr. Louis McPherson DeSaussure Sr.

DeSaussure, Louise Isabel, see Stuart, Louise Isabel DeSaussure.

Ephraim (ca. 1802–1864), "Ephy," "Eph"; a slave purchased by Rev. Charles Leverett from W. T. Watkins in 1839 for $675.

Hercules (fl. 1887), a slave; husband of Sary; purchased by Rev. Charles Edward Leverett from Mary M. Webb and the estate of Rev. Benjamin C. Webb in 1856 for $950; after the war he lived on The Farm near Columbia and later at Canaan.

Jenkins, Julia Blanche, see Leverett, Julia Blanche Jenkins.

Leverett, Anne Heyward, see DeSaussure, Anne Heyward Leverett.

Leverett, Caroline Pinckney, see Adams, Caroline Pinckney Leverett.

Leverett, Catherine Hamilton (1850–1865), "Kate"; daughter of Mary Maxcy and Rev. Charles Edward Leverett.

Leverett, Rev. Charles Edward (1805–1868), husband of Mary Maxcy Leverett; son of Comfort Marshall and Benjamin Leverett.

Leverett, Charles Edward, Jr. (1833–1861), "Edward," "Ed"; son of Mary Maxcy and Rev. Charles Edward Leverett.

Leverett, Charles Hendee (1833–1897), "Charles," "Charley," "Charly"; son of Matilda Gorham (1813–1834) and Frederic Percival Leverett Sr. (1803–1836); adopted son of Mary Maxcy and Rev. Charles Edward Leverett; husband of Julia Blanche Jenkins; they lived in Fayetteville, Arkansas, after the war; had eight children by 1878: Julia Blanche, Frederic Percival, Mary Maxcy, Storer, Amarinthia, Charles Jenkins, Abby Matilda Gorham, and Rosa Catherine Elizabeth.

Leverett, Frederic Percival (1831–1864), "Fred"; son of Matilda Gorham (1813–1834) and Frederic Percival Leverett Sr. (1803–1836); adopted son of Mary Maxcy and Rev. Charles Edward Leverett.

Leverett, Julia Blanche (b. 1863), daughter of Julia Blanche Jenkins and Charles Hendee Leverett; born in South Carolina and grew up in Fayetteville, Arkansas.

Leverett, Julia Blanche Jenkins (1845–1916), daughter of Mary Amarinthia LaRoche (1822–1888) and Richard Henry Jenkins (1812–1868); wife of Charles Hendee Leverett.

Leverett, Julia Marcelline (1846–1888), "Julia," "Julie"; daughter of Mary Maxcy and Rev. Charles Edward Leverett.

Leverett, Mary Bull (1840–1913), "Mame"; daughter of Mary Maxcy and Rev. Charles Edward Leverett.

Leverett, Mary Maxcy (1808/9–1897), daughter of Mary Bull and Milton Maxcy; wife of Rev. Charles Edward Leverett.

Leverett, Matilda (1835–1894), "Sister," "Tilly"; daughter of Mary Maxcy and Rev. Charles Edward Leverett.

Leverett, Milton Maxcy (1838–1908), "Minnie," "Minny," "Min"; son of Mary Maxcy and Rev. Charles Edward Leverett.

Leverett, Storer (b. 1868), son of Julia Blanche Jenkins and Charles Hendee Leverett; born in South Carolina and grew up in Fayetteville, Arkansas.

Lewis (fl. 1868), a slave purchased by Rev. Charles Edward Leverett before 1856; as a freedman after the war he lived on The Farm near Columbia.

Nancy, a slave belonging to Anne Leverett DeSaussure

Nancy (1799–1859), a slave purchased by Rev. Charles Edward Leverett before 1856.

Sarah, "Sary"; a slave purchased by Rev. Charles Edward Leverett from Ann E. Stevens in 1846 for $275; the bill of sale noted that Sary was "warranted sound except having but one eye." She was the wife of Hercules.

Stuart, Louise Isabel DeSaussure (1858–1961), "Lou"; only child of Anne Heyward Leverett and Louis McPherson DeSaussure Jr.; granddaughter of Mary Maxcy and Rev. Charles Edward Leverett; wife of Dr. Henry Middleton Stuart III (1859–1933).

Contemporaries

Adams, James Hopkins (1812–1861), of Richland District; a general in the state militia; state senator and representative; governor of South Carolina, 1854–1856; delegate to the Secession Convention.

Adams, Lawrence A., of Charleston; physician; private in Capt. W. L. Trenholm's Company A, Rutledge Mounted Riflemen, later Company B, Seventh South Carolina Cavalry.

Adams, Nathalie Heyward (1841–1913), of White Hall plantation in St. Bartholomew's Parish; daughter of Elizabeth Barnwell Smith and Nathaniel Barnwell Heyward; married Warren Adams (1838–1881) of Columbia after the war.

Ancrum, James K. Douglas (1844–1864), "Jemmy," of Camden; private in the Kirkwood Rangers, an independent South Carolina cavalry company, and later in the Second South Carolina Cavalry; he died of disease at Charleston 20 June 1864.

Axson, Rev. Samuel Edward (1836–1884), of Beaufort District; pastor of Stoney Creek Presbyterian Church, McPhersonville 1861–1862, chaplain in the First Georgia Infantry.

Ayer, Lewis Malone, Jr. (1821–1895), of Barnwell District; a planter; state representative; general in the militia; delegate to the Secession Convention; served in the Confederate Congress; was a Baptist minister and teacher after the war.

Bailey, Mary Olivia, see LaRoche, Mary Olivia Bailey.

Baker, Isabella Field Jenkins Chaplin Fields (1785–1863), of Beaufort District; daughter of Elizabeth Perry and John Cato Field; she married four times: Daniel Jenkins, Saxby Chaplin Sr., Rev. John Fields, and Robert Little Baker.

Barnwell, Ann Bull, see Walker, Ann Bull Barnwell.

Barnwell, Anne Heyward (1838–1864), daughter of Margaret Manigault (1818–1864) and Edward Barnwell (1813–1885).

Barnwell, Charlotte Bull, see Elliott, Charlotte Bull Barnwell.

Barnwell, Edward H. (1832–1908), of Charleston; a merchant; son of Catherine Osborn Barnwell and Rev. William Hazzard Wigg Barnwell (1806–1863); first lieutenant on the staff of Brig. Gen. William S. Walker; captain, assistant adjutant general, and inspector general for the Third Military District of South Carolina in the Department of South Carolina, Georgia, and Florida.

Barnwell, Eliza (1807–1891), daughter of Sarah Bull (1782–1862) and John Gibbes Barnwell I; wife of Robert Woodward Barnwell; first cousin of Mary Maxcy Leverett.

Barnwell, Elizabeth (1837–1916), "Bet"; daughter of Catherine Osborn Barnwell and Rev. William Hazzard Wigg Barnwell (1806–1863).

Barnwell, Emily Howe (1820–1894), of Beaufort District; daughter of Sarah Bull (1782–1862) and John Gibbes Barnwell I; first cousin of Mary Maxcy Leverett.

Barnwell, Helen, see Geiger, Helen Barnwell.

Barnwell, Isabella Elliott, see Elliott, Isabella Elliott Barnwell.

Barnwell, James Stuart (1845–1864), "Stuart," of Beaufort District; son of Eliza Barnwell and Robert Woodward Barnwell; twin brother of Nathaniel Berners Barnwell; a Confederate private in the Rutledge Mounted Rifles, later Company B, Seventh South Carolina Cavalry; died of typhoid fever at Richmond, 9 July 1864.

Barnwell, John Gibbes, II (1816–1905), of Beaufort District; son of Sarah Bull (1782–1862) and John Gibbes Barnwell I (1778–1828); first cousin of Mary Maxcy Leverett; a planter at Coosaw, The Retreat, and three other plantations; captain in the Beaufort Volunteer Artillery, 1839–1860; Confederate staff officer under Gen. P. G. T. Beauregard and Brig. Gen. James Heyward Trapier, inspecting artillery in the Department of South Carolina, Georgia, and Florida.

Barnwell, John Gibbes (1831–1888), son of Eliza Barnwell and Robert Woodward Barnwell.

Barnwell, Margaret Harriet (1822–1900), "Meta," of Beaufort District; daughter of Elizabeth Osborn Barnwell and Capt. Edward Barnwell.

Barnwell, Nathaniel Berners (1845–1883), "Nat," of Beaufort District; son of Eliza Barnwell and Robert Woodward Barnwell; twin brother of James Stuart Barnwell; private in the Rutledge Mounted Rifles, later Company B, Seventh South Carolina Cavalry, and later aide-de-camp to Col. Hilary P. Jones, chief of artillery of the IV Corps, Army of Northern Virginia; lawyer; secretary and treasurer of the Board of Trustees of the University of South Carolina after the war.

Barnwell, Nathaniel Heyward (1844–1910), of Beaufort District; son of Catherine Osborn Barnwell (1809–1886) and Rev. William Hazzard Wigg Barnwell (1806–1863); corporal and 3d sergeant in the Beaufort Artillery; planter in South Carolina and Georgia after the war; married Mary Richardson Barnwell (d. 1895).

Barnwell, Robert Woodward (1801–1882), of St. Helena's Parish; husband of Eliza Barnwell; son of Elizabeth Hayne Wigg (1775–1823) and Robert Gibbes Barnwell (1761–1814); planter at Woodward plantation; U.S. senator and congressman; state representative; president of South Carolina College; delegate to the Secession Convention; member of the Confederate Senate.

Barnwell, Robert Woodward (1831–1863), husband of Mary Carter Singleton (1837–1863); son of Catherine Osborn Barnwell and Rev. William Hazzard Wigg Barnwell; nephew of Robert Woodward Barnwell (1801–1882); deacon in charge of Zion Church, Eastover; professor of history and political economy, chair of literature and moral philosophy, and chaplain at South Carolina College; served as army chaplain and chairman of the executive committee of the South Carolina Hospital Association; died of typhoid fever.

Barnwell, Sarah Bull (1814–1881), daughter of Sarah Bull (1782–1862) and John Gibbes Barnwell (1778–1828); first cousin of Mary Maxcy Leverett.

Barnwell, Stephen Elliott (1842–1890), "Ste," of Beaufort District; son of Emma Gibbes Elliott (1817–1894) and Maj. John Gibbes Barnwell II (1816–1905); sergeant in the Beaufort Artillery, the Corps of Engineers, and Barnwell's Georgia Battery; Episcopal priest in Georgia and Kentucky after the war.

Barnwell, Woodward (1838–1927), "Woodie," of Beaufort District; son of Eliza Zubly Smith and Capt. Edward Barnwell; private in Company D, Hampton Legion Cavalry, and later a sergeant in Company H, Second South Carolina

Infantry; an independent scout in the Third Military District, Department of South Carolina, Georgia, and Florida.

Bedon, Josiah (d. 1864), of Walterboro; lawyer; first captain of the Summerville Guards, Company C, Ninth (later Eleventh) South Carolina; he was later a lieutenant in the Second South Carolina Battalion, then a private in the Charleston Light Dragoons, Company K, Fourth South Carolina Cavalry; he was either killed or mortally wounded and captured at Haw's Shop, Virginia, 28 May 1864.

Bedon, William Z., of Colleton District and Mississippi; physician; assistant surgeon and surgeon of the Palmetto Sharpshooters.

Bonaparte-Patterson, Jérôme Napoléon (1805–1870), of Baltimore; son of Elizabeth Patterson (1785–1879) and Jérôme Bonaparte (1784–1860); nephew of Napoléon I; father of Jérôme Bonaparte-Patterson Jr. (1830–1893).

Bonham, Milledge Luke (1813–1890), of Edgefield District; lawyer; officer in the Mexican War; state representative; Confederate brigadier general in the Army of the Potomac; Confederate congressman; governor of South Carolina, 1862–1864; state representative and railroad commissioner after the war.

Branch, W. S., of Beaufort District; Confederate private in the Beaufort Artillery.

Brannon, Barney (b. 1820), native of Ireland; private in Company G, Eighteenth South Carolina Infantry and on detached service as a carpenter in the Engineer Corps.

Brisbane, Rev. William Henry (1806–1878), of South Carolina; Baptist clergyman; an abolitionist who sold his slaves and moved to Ohio in 1838; he returned to South Carolina, repurchased the slaves, and took them north and set them free around 1840; returned to the sea islands during the war as a Federal official, serving as chairman of the United States Direct Tax Commission for South Carolina, 1862–1876.

Brown, Fred J., of Columbia; clerk in his father's painting and wallpaper business.

Brown, James, of Columbia; native of Great Britain; owned a painting and wallpaper business.

Brown, Margaret Murphy, of Columbia; wife of Fred J. Brown.

Brown, Samuel G., of Sumter District; Confederate private in Company E of the Palmetto Sharpshooters.

Bull, Mary, see Maxcy, Mary Bull.

Burnet, Andrew William (1840–1894), assistant surgeon of the Ninth South Carolina Volunteers (later the Eleventh South Carolina Infantry).

Burton, Henry Stanton (d. 1869), Federal artillery officer in the Army of the Potomac and the Army of the James; after the war he was a brigadier general and second in command of Fortress Monroe; commander of Federal troops in Columbia during Reconstruction.

Butler, Rev. Clement Moore (1810–1890), rector of Trinity Episcopal Church, Washington, D.C., 1849–1861; chaplain of the United States Senate, 1849–1853.

Butler, Matthew Calbraith (1836–1909), of Edgefield; lawyer; state representative; captain and major in the Hampton Legion (Cavalry); colonel of the Second South Carolina Cavalry; commanded a South Carolina cavalry brigade as brigadier general; commanded a cavalry division in the Army of Northern Virginia as major general; after the war he was a United States senator; major general of United States volunteers during the Spanish-American War.

Calhoun, Andrew Pickens (1811–1865), of Fort Hill plantation in Pendleton District; son of Floride Bonneau Colhoun and John Caldwell Calhoun.

Calhoun, Anna Maria, see Clemson, Anna Maria Calhoun.

Calhoun, Floride Bonneau Colhoun (1792–1866), of Fort Hill plantation in Pendleton District; daughter of Floride Bonneau and John Ewing Colhoun; wife of John Caldwell Calhoun.

Calhoun, James (1779–1843), of Pendleton District; brother of John Caldwell Calhoun.

Calhoun, John Caldwell (1782–1850), of Fort Hill plantation in Pendleton District; United States vice president; South Carolina state representative 1808–9; United States congressman and senator; United States secretary of war.

Calhoun, William Lowndes (1829–1858), of Fort Hill plantation in Pendleton District; son of Floride Bonneau Colhoun and John Caldwell Calhoun.

Campbell, Daniel P. (1842–1862), of Charleston District; graduate of the South Carolina Military Academy (The Citadel); private in Company I, Eleventh South Carolina Infantry; killed at Pocotaligo 22 October 1862.

Campbell, Robert (1838–1876), of Charleston; lawyer; lieutenant colonel of the Ninth South Carolina Volunteers from its creation until its reorganization in May 1862; a private in the Third South Carolina Cavalry; lieutenant in Company I, Eleventh South Carolina Infantry.

Capers, Bishop William (1790–1855), of Charleston; Methodist Episcopal clergyman noted for his religious instruction of slaves; superintendent of missions to the Creek Indians; secretary of the Southern Missionary Department of the Church; bishop of the Methodist Episcopal Church, South, from 1846 until his death.

Carmichael, Elizabeth Barnwell Elliott (1829–1890), of Georgia; daughter of Mary Gibbes Barnwell and Rt. Rev. Stephen Elliott (1806–1866); wife of William Paul Carmichael.

Carmichael, William Paul (1826–1866), of Georgia; husband of Elizabeth Barnwell Elliott.

Carrington, William A., of Virginia; Confederate surgeon in charge of General Hospital No. 10; medical director of all Confederate general hospitals in Virginia.

Chaplin, Martha Fripp (b. 1788), of Prince William's Parish; wife of Archibald Chaplin (1783–1849).

Chaplin, Washington A., of St. Helena's Parish; planter; private in the Beaufort Artillery.

Cheves, Langdon (1776–1857), of Charleston and Abbeville District; planter; judge; state representative; United States congressman; president of the Bank of the United States.

Chisolm, Alexander Robert (1834–1910), of Prince William's Parish; planter on Coosaw Island; staff officer under Gen. P. G. T. Beauregard in the Department of South Carolina, Georgia, and Florida.

Chisolm, Julian John (1830–1903), of Charleston and Columbia; physician; surgeon at Wayside Hospital, Columbia; author of *A Manual of Military Surgery*, the official manual for Confederate surgeons; dean of the Medical University of South Carolina; dean of the Medical School at the University of Maryland; physician in Baltimore after the war.

Chisolm, Mary Edings (d. 1903), of Charleston and Columbia; wife of Dr. Julian John Chisolm.

Chisolm, Robert, of Charleston and Birmingham, Alabama; captain in Company A of the First Battalion South Carolina Sharpshooters (later Company E, Twenty-seventh South Carolina Infantry).

Claiborne, Charles Harrison (b. 1841), second lieutenant of Company K, First South Carolina Regulars, on detached engineering service at Fort Sumter.

Clark, Henry M., a Confederate adjutant and inspector general on the staff of Maj. Gen. Sterling Price in the Department of Mississippi and East Louisiana.

Clemson, Anna Maria Calhoun (1817–1875), of Fort Hill plantation in Pendleton District; daughter of Floride Bonneau Colhoun and John Caldwell Calhoun; wife of Thomas Green Clemson (1807–1888).

Codding, Elisha (b. 1799), of Prince William's Parish; an overseer.

Coffin, Catherine Hume (1839–1886), of Charleston; daughter of Sarah Lewis Simons and George Mathews Coffin.

Coffin, Ebenezer (1842–1910), of Charleston; son of Sarah Lewis Simons and George Mathews Coffin; Confederate private and 4th sergeant in Company A, Hampton Legion (Infantry).

Coffin, Eliza Mathews, see Taylor, Eliza Mathews Coffin.

Coffin, George Mathews (1808–1862), of Charleston; son of Mary Mathews (1771–1813) and Ebenezer Coffin (1765–1817); a cotton factor with James Reid Pringle in the firm Coffin & Pringle.

Coffin, Sarah Lewis Simons (1817–1881), of Charleston; daughter of Catherine Hume (1787–1872) and Thomas Grange Simons (1789–1863); wife of George Mathews Coffin.

Colcock, Charles Jones (1820-1891), of Prince William's Parish; a planter; owned three plantations on Foote Point, Bonnie Doon, Okatie River, and The Camp; Colonel Third South Carolina Cavalry; married first Mary Caroline Heyward (1822–1848), second Lucy Frances Horton (d. 1862).

Collins, J. W., native of Massachusetts; a lumber merchant; during Reconstruction Collins and Moulton Emery owned Mary Maxcy and Rev. Charles Edward Leverett's house on Bay Street in Beaufort.

Cornish, Rev. John Hamilton (1815–1878), rector of St. Thaddeus Episcopal Church, Aiken, 1846–1869.

Cornish, Martha Sarah Jenkins (1821–1864), "Mattie"; wife of Rev. John Hamilton Cornish.

Creighton, James (d. 1862), of Charleston; planter; private in the Charleston Light Dragoons, Company K, Fourth South Carolina Cavalry; died of disease at McPhersonville on September 15, 1862.

Crowell, Nathaniel S., Confederate surgeon and medical director of the Department of Mississippi and East Louisiana and later the Department of South Carolina, Georgia, and Florida.

Cuthbert, Edward Barnwell (1828–1878), of Beaufort District; a planter; husband of Ophelia Juliet Lasak; son of Charlotte Barnwell (1808–1841) and George Cuthbert (1802–1835); private in the Beaufort Artillery.

Cuthbert, James, Jr. (1819–1852), of Prince William's Parish; a planter at Richfield plantation.

Cuthbert, Lucius, Sr. (1798–1860), of St. Helena's Parish; a planter; married Ann Barnwell (1801–1820); after her death he married Charlotte Bull Fuller (b. 1802).

Cuthbert, Rev. Lucius, Jr. (1833–1906), of St. Helena's Parish; son of Charlotte Bull Fuller and Lucius Cuthbert Sr.; graduated from South Carolina College with Edward Leverett in the Class of 1853; he became a Baptist clergyman, was appointed pastor of Aiken First Baptist Church in 1856, and served the church on three separate occasions over the next twenty years; husband of Susan Margaret Mikell.

Cuthbert, Thomas Fuller (b. 1834), son of Charlotte Bull Fuller and Lucius Cuthbert.

Cuthbert, William Henry, Jr. (1842–1887), of St. Helena's Parish; son of Susan Caroline Porcher and William Henry Cuthbert (b. 1814).

Davidge, Sally D. Martin (b. 1845), daughter of Eloise Mary Hayne and William Edward Martin; married Robert Cunningham Davidge.

Davis, Rt. Rev. Thomas Frederick (1804–1871), of Camden; succeeded Rt. Rev. Christopher Edwards Gadsden (1785–1852) as Episcopal bishop of the diocese of South Carolina 1853–71.

DeFontaine, Felix Gregory (1834–1896), of Massachusetts; married a South Carolinian and moved to Columbia in 1860; editor with the *Columbia Daily South Carolinian* when the war began; went to Virginia with the First South Carolina Infantry as a war correspondent with the pen name of "Personne"; his dispatches were published in the *Daily South Carolinian*, the *Charleston Courier*, and other Confederate newspapers.

Delany, Martin Robinson (1812–1885), of Pennsylvania; a free black physician, ethnologist, abolitionist, and newspaper editor; major of the 104th United States Colored Troops; after the war he was an agent for the Freedmen's Bureau in Beaufort District; customs house inspector; judge in Charleston.

DeSaussure, Charles Alfred (1846–1935), of Woodstock plantation in St. Helena's Parish; son of Jane Hay Hutson and Louis McPherson DeSaussure Sr.; private in the Beaufort Artillery.

DeSaussure, Henry Alexander (1788–1865), brother of Dr. Louis McPherson DeSaussure Sr.; practiced law in Charleston; member of the South Carolina House of Representatives, 1826–1831; husband of Susan Boone.

DeSaussure, Isabella Harper Means (1809–1844), of Woodstock plantation in St. Helena's Parish; first wife of Louis McPherson DeSaussure Sr.; mother of Louis McPherson DeSaussure Jr.; daughter of Mary Hutson Barnwell (1781–1851) and Robert Means (1774–1832).

DeSaussure, Jane Hay Hutson (1809–1887), of Woodstock plantation in St. Helena's Parish; daughter of Martha Hay and William Maine Hutson (1777–1835); second wife of Louis McPherson DeSaussure Sr.

DeSaussure, Louis McPherson, Sr. (1804–1870), of Woodstock plantation in St. Helena's Parish; physician and planter; son of Elizabeth Ford (d. 1822) and Henry William DeSaussure (1763–1839); first married Isabella Harper Means (1809–1844), then Jane Hay Hutson (1809–1887).

DeSaussure, William Ford (1792–1870), brother of Dr. Louis McPherson DeSaussure Sr.; practiced law in Charleston and Columbia; member of the South Carolina House of Representatives in 1846; filled vacancy caused by the resignation of Robert Barnwell Rhett in the U.S. Senate, 1852–1853.

DeTreville, John L., "Johnny," of Beaufort District; private in the Beaufort Artillery.

Dorman, James Baldwin (1825–1893), of Virginia; major of the Third Virginia Artillery, Local Defense Troops; commander of the camp of instruction at Dublin, Virginia.

Drayton, Thomas Fenwick (1808–1891), of St. Luke's Parish; a planter at Rephaim plantation; state senator; brigadier general in command of the Second Military District in the Department of South Carolina and Georgia; commanded a South Carolina brigade in the Army of Northern Virginia; on administrative duty in the Trans-Mississippi Department.

Dunovant, Richard Gill Mills (1821–1898), of Edgefield District; planter; delegate to the Secession Convention; Confederate officer of the Twelfth South Carolina Infantry from its organization until April 1862.

Dunwody, Ellen Galt Martin (1823–1857), of Beaufort District; second wife of Rev. James Bulloch Dunwody.

Dunwody, Rev. James Bulloch (1816–1902), of Beaufort District; pastor of Stoney Creek Presbyterian Church, McPhersonville, 1843–1856 and 1873 until his death.

Dunwody, Laleah Georgiana Wood Pratt (1823–1853), of Alabama; first wife of Rev. James Bulloch Dunwody.

Durban, Egbert E., of St. Helena's Parish; a student in 1860; Confederate private in the Beaufort Artillery.

Elliott, Anne (b. 1822), of St. Helena's Parish; daughter of Ann Hutchinson Smith (1802–1877) and William Elliott Sr. (1788–1863).

Elliott, Anne Barnwell (1842–1926), of St. Helena's Parish; daughter of Ann Hutson Habersham and Rev. Stephen Elliott (1804–1866).

Elliott, Ann Hutson Habersham (1813–1843), first wife of Rev. Stephen Elliott (1804–1866); daughter of Anne Middleton Barnwell (1783–1840) and John Habersham (d. 1821).

Elliott, Ann Stuart Rhett (1846–1918), of Beaufort; daughter of Mary Williamson Stuart and Edmund Rhett; wife of Middleton Stuart Elliott (1841–1921).

Elliott, Caroline (1842–1894), of Savannah and Rome, Georgia, and San Antonio; daughter of Margaret Couper Mackay and Dr. Ralph Emms Elliott (1797–1853); wife of Rt. Rev. Robert Woodward Barnwell Elliott.

Elliott, Charlotte Bull Barnwell (1810–1895), of Savannah; daughter of Sarah Bull (1782–1862) and John Gibbes Barnwell I; first cousin of Mary Maxcy Leverett; second wife of Rt. Rev. Stephen Elliott (1806–1866), bishop of Georgia.

Elliott, Charlotte Stuart (1833–1868), daughter of Ann Hutson Means and Henry Middleton Stuart Sr.; wife of Stephen Elliott Jr. (1830–1866).

Elliott, George Parsons (1807–1871), of Prince William's Parish; son of Phoebe Waight (1772–1855) and William Elliott (1761–1808); husband of Mary Bower Barnwell; a planter at Yemassee plantation; captain in the Beaufort Volunteer Artillery company in the state militia; state representative; Confederate staff officer under Brig. Gen. William S. Walker in the Department of South Carolina, Georgia, and Florida.

Elliott, Henry DeSaussure (1848–1906), of Beaufort District; son of Sarah Gibbes DeSaussure and Rev. Stephen Elliott (1804–1907); Confederate private in the Beaufort Artillery; after the war he married Mary Amarinthia Lowndes (1850–1913); planter; master of tugboats for Port Royal Sound.

Elliott, Isabella Elliott Barnwell (1841–1867), daughter of Emma Gibbes Elliott (1817–1894) and Maj. John Gibbes Barnwell II (1816–1905); first wife of Col. William Elliott (1838–1907).

Elliott, Rev. James Habersham (1819–1877), son of Esther Wylly Habersham and Stephen Elliott (1771–1830); assistant rector of St. Michael's Episcopal Church, Charleston; coeditor of the *Southern Episcopalian*, the journal of the diocese of South Carolina; married Harriet Barnwell Fuller (1818–1854); his second wife was Catherine Ann Sadler, widow of Rev. Joseph A. Shanklin.

Elliott, Rev. John Habersham (1832–1906), of Beaufort District; son of Ann Hutson Habersham and Rev. Stephen Elliott (1804–1866); was ordained an Episcopal clergyman in 1861; after the war was rector of the Church of the Ascension in Washington, D.C.

Elliott, Mary Barnwell Fuller (1835–1862), first wife of Rev. John Habersham Elliott; daughter of Elizabeth Barnwell and Dr. Thomas Fuller (1788–1862).

Elliott, Middleton Stuart (1841–1921), "Minnie"; of Beaufort District; son of Ann Hutson Habersham and Rev. Stephen Elliott (1804–1866); private in the Beaufort Artillery and on detached service as an engineer; lieutenant in the Engineer Corps; staff officer in the Army of Northern Virginia; after the war was deputy collector of customs for Beaufort; married Ann Stuart Rhett (d. 1918).

Elliott, Percival (1840–1865), of Savannah; son of Margaret Couper Mackay and Dr. Ralph Emms Elliott (1797–1853); lieutenant in the Savannah Volunteer Guards, Company B, Eighteenth Georgia Battalion; on detached service in the Signal Corps as adjutant at Fort Sumter and with the Eighteenth Georgia Battalion in the Army of Northern Virginia until he was mortally wounded at Sayler's Creek, Virginia, 6 April 1865; he died a prisoner in Washington, D.C., 30 May.

Elliott, Phoebe Caroline, see Pinckney, Phoebe Caroline Elliott.

Elliott, Ralph Emms (1834–1864), of St. Helena's Parish; physician; son of Ann Hutson Habersham and Rev. Stephen Elliott (1804–1866); captain in Company I, Second South Carolina Infantry; mortally wounded at Cold Harbor, Virginia, 1 June 1864 and died five days later.

Elliott, Rt. Rev. Robert Woodward Barnwell (1840–1887), son of Sarah Bull Barnwell and Rt. Rev. Stephen Elliott (1806–1866); husband of Caroline Elliott (1842–1894); first lieutenant in the Savannah Volunteer Guards, Company B, Eighteenth Georgia Battalion, aide-de-camp on the staff of Brig. Gen. Alexander R. Lawton, captain on the staff of Maj. Gen. Lafayette McLaws and major on the staff of Brig. Gen. John Doby Kennedy, all in the Army of Northern Virginia; Episcopal clergyman in Georgia after the war; first missionary bishop of West Texas.

Elliott, Rosa Stuart (1843–1926), daughter of Ann Hutson Means and Henry Middleton Stuart Sr.; second wife of Rev. John Habersham Elliott.

Elliott, Sarah Gibbes DeSaussure (1811–1891), second wife of Rev. Stephen Elliott (1804–1866); daughter of Susan Boone and Henry Alexander DeSaussure; her first husband was Alexander L. Barron.

Elliott, Sarah Means Stuart (1846–1939), daughter of Ann Hutson Means and Henry Middleton Stuart Sr.; second wife of Col. William Elliott (1838–1907).

Elliott, Rev. Stephen (1804–1866), of Beaufort District; son of Phoebe Waight and William Elliott (1761–1808); preceded Rev. Charles Leverett as rector of Sheldon Church, 1833–47; ministered to the slaves in Prince William's Parish; chaplain in the Third Military District, Department of South Carolina and Georgia.

Elliott, Rt. Rev. Stephen (1806–1866), of Savannah; bishop of Georgia; son of Esther Wylly Habersham (d. 1836) and Stephen Elliott (1771–1830); married first Mary Gibbes Barnwell (d. 1837); his second wife was Charlotte Bull Barnwell (1810–1895).

Elliott, Stephen, Jr. (1830–1866), of Beaufort District; son of Ann Hutson Habersham and Rev. Stephen Elliott (1804–1866); husband of Charlotte Stuart Elliott; a planter; state representative; captain in the Beaufort Artillery at the beginning of the war; major and chief of artillery, Third Military District, Department of South Carolina and Georgia; lieutenant colonel and commander of Fort Sumter, as colonel of Holcombe's Legion; brigadier general in command of a South Carolina brigade in the Department of North Carolina and Southern Virginia, the Army of Northern Virginia, and the Army of Tennessee.

Elliott, Thomas Rhett Smith (b. 1819), of Prince William's Parish; planter; son of Ann Hutchinson Smith and William Elliott (1788–1863); husband of Mary Cuthbert; staff officer under Brig. Gen. Thomas Fenwick Drayton in the Department of South Carolina and Georgia.

Elliott, William (1838–1907), son of Ann Hutson Habersham and Rev. Stephen Elliott (1804–1866); husband of Isabella Elliott Barnwell (1841–1867); second wife was Sarah Means Stuart (1846–1939); colonel in the confederacy; after war practiced law in Beaufort; member of the South Carolina House of Representatives in 1866; member of Congress for more than thirteen years, between 1887 and 1903; appointed commissioner of the United States to mark the graves of the Confederate dead in the North.

Elliott, William Waight (1831–1884), "Bill," of Beaufort District; son of Mary Bower Barnwell and George Parsons Elliott; husband of Elizabeth Gregorie (d. 1920); captain in Company F, Ninth South Carolina Volunteers until the regiment's reorganization in May 1862; first lieutenant and ordnance officer of the Third Military District, Department of South Carolina, Georgia, and Florida.

Ellis, Daniel Hix (1824–1873), of Prince William's Parish; a planter; son of Rebecca Larisey DeLoach and Isaac Ellis; husband of Emily Caroline Searson; state representative; colonel of the Eleventh South Carolina Infantry from its reorganization in May 1862 until his resignation in November 1862; state senator; magistrate; commissioner of roads and tax collector for Beaufort District 1863–1864.

Ely, Ralph (d. 1883), of Michigan; a Federal colonel of the Eighth Michigan Infantry and commander of a brigade in the Department of the South; after the war he was brevet brigadier general and acting assistant commissioner for the Freedmen's Bureau in Beaufort.

Emery, Moulton, of Maine; school commissioner, co-owner of Mary Maxcy and Rev. Charles Edward Leverett's Bay Street house in Beaufort during Reconstruction.

Eustis, Patience Wise Blackett Izard (1786–1860), of Tomotley plantation in Prince William's Parish; wife of Brig. Gen. Abraham Eustis (1786–1843).

Evans, Nathan George (1824–1868), adjutant general of South Carolina state troops; Confederate colonel who commanded a South Carolina brigade in the Army of the Potomac; commanded a brigade in the Army of Northern Virginia and the Army of Tennessee as brigadier general; he was court-martialed for intemperance and disobedience but was acquitted and subsequently removed from command.

Ezell, Landrum C., of Spartanburg District; son of John S. Ezell; sergeant in Company H of the Palmetto Sharpshooters.

Fair, Samuel (1805–1870), of Columbia; physician; taught medical courses on a private basis before the war; shared a practice with Dr. Louis V. Huot; chief surgeon at the Soldiers' Hospital at the old State Fair Grounds, Columbia, 1861–1862.

Fickling, Eldred S., of Beaufort District; resident of St. Luke's Parish in 1860; Confederate private in Company H, Hampton Legion (Cavalry); a brevet second lieutenant and first lieutenant in Company D, First South Carolina Artillery; policeman in Columbia after the war.

Fielding, Rev. John, of Beaufort and Columbia; Roman Catholic priest; principal of Beaufort College before the war.

Foster, John Cantzon (b. 1832), of Lancaster District; a planter; Confederate orderly sergeant in the Fourth South Carolina Cavalry, then first lieutenant and captain of Company H.

Fowles, Caroline Lydia Glover (b. 1841), of Orangeburg; daughter of Caroline Elizabeth Jamison and Thomas Worth Glover; wife of James Henry Fowles (1843–1913).

Fowles, Eliza Yallowley (d. 1892), "Lila," of Columbia; daughter of Matilda Maxcy and Rev. James Henry Fowles; niece of Mary Maxcy Leverett.

Fowles, Rev. James Henry (1812–1854), rector of Christ Episcopal Church, Wilton, Adams Run; rector of the Church of the Epiphany in Philadelphia from 1845 to his death; his wife, Matilda Miltonia Maxcy, was Mary Maxcy Leverett's sister.

Fowles, James Henry (1843–1913), "Jim," "Jimmy," of Columbia, Orangeburg, and Birmingham, Alabama; son of Matilda Maxcy and Rev. James Henry Fowles; nephew of Mary Maxcy Leverett; private in Company D, Hampton Legion (Cavalry); a private and first sergeant in Company H, Second South Carolina Cavalry; farmer, real estate salesman, and insurance salesman after the war.

Fowles, John Newton (1840–1913), "Newton," of Columbia, Charleston, and Newberry; son of Matilda Maxcy and Rev. James Henry Fowles; nephew of Mary Maxcy Leverett; private in Company A, Hampton Legion (Cavalry) and Company I, Second South Carolina Cavalry, and scout for Brig. Gen. Matthew C. Butler's South Carolina brigade in the Army of Northern Virginia; owned several sawmills after the war.

Fowles, Mary Ann (d. 1907), of Columbia; Madison, Florida; and Tuscaloosa, Alabama; daughter of Matilda Maxcy and Rev. James Henry Fowles; niece of Mary Maxcy Leverett.

Fowles, Matilda Maxcy, see Glover, Matilda Maxcy Fowles.

Fowles, Matilda Miltonia Maxcy (1811–1879), "Aunt Til"; wife of Rev. James Henry Fowles (1812–1854), sister of Mary Maxcy Leverett.

Fowles, Stephen Bull (d. 1890), "Stevy," "Ste," of Columbia and Beaufort; son of Matilda Maxcy and Rev. James Henry Fowles; nephew of Mary Maxcy Leverett.

Fripp, Edgar (1806–1860), of Beaufort District; a planter at Tidalholm plantation in Beaufort and Seaside plantation on St. Helena Island; married Eliza Fripp (1811–1861).

Fripp, J. Edmund (d. 1862), of St. Luke's Parish; a planter; private in the Beaufort Artillery; mortally wounded at Pocotaligo 22 October 1862 and died the next day.

Fuller, Elizabeth Barnwell (1797–1872), of Beaufort; second wife of Dr. Thomas Fuller (1788–1862); sister of Robert Woodward Barnwell (1801–1882).

Fuller, Harriet Barnwell (1791–1864), of Beaufort; daughter of Elizabeth Middleton (d. 1833) and Thomas Fuller (1760–1830); sister of Rev. Richard Fuller, Baptist clergyman; taught the slaves in Sunday school at Beaufort Baptist Church; lived with her brother Dr. Henry Middleton Fuller and his family and was with them at Robertville when she died.

Fuller, Henrietta Potter Hamilton (1840–1922), of Beaufort; was the daughter of Catharine Amarinthia Percy and Paul Hamilton; wife of Robert Barnwell Fuller.

Fuller, Henry Middleton (1807–1871), of Beaufort; physician and planter in St. Helena's Parish; son of Elizabeth Middleton and Thomas Fuller (1760–1830); husband of Mary Barnwell Means (d. 1878); his mother was the half sister of Mary Bull Maxcy; member of the Board of Trustees of Beaufort College.

Fuller, Henry Middleton (1842–1904), "Nenny," "Nennie"; son of Mary Barnwell Means and Henry Middleton Fuller.

Fuller, John Wallace (1827–1891), born in Great Britain, moved to New York as a child, and settled in Ohio shortly before the war; a Federal colonel of the Twenty-seventh Ohio Infantry, then colonel and brigadier general commanding a brigade in the Army of the Tennessee; commanded the First Brigade, First Division, XVII Army Corps of that army in the March to the Sea of 1864 and the Carolinas Campaign of 1865; businessman and customs collector in Toledo, Ohio, after the war.

Fuller, Josephine Rogers Walker, daughter of Mariana Smith and Rev. Joseph Rogers Walker; wife of Robert Means Fuller (1839–1893).

Fuller, Mary Barnwell, see Elliott, Mary Barnwell Fuller.

Fuller, Mary Barnwell Means (1811–1878), of Beaufort; wife of Henry Middleton Fuller (1807–1871).

Fuller, Nathaniel Barnwell (1837–1910), "Nat," of Beaufort District; son of Elizabeth Barnwell and Dr. Thomas Fuller (1788–1862); corporal and third sergeant of the Beaufort Artillery; became an Episcopal minister in South Carolina, Texas, and Florida after the war.

Fuller, Robert Barnwell (1830–1895), "Barney," "Rob," of Beaufort District; husband of Henrietta Potter Hamilton; son of Elizabeth Barnwell and Dr. Thomas

Fuller (1788–1862); a planter; sergeant and later second lieutenant of the Beaufort Artillery; treasurer of Beaufort County after the war.

Fuller, Robert Means (1839–1893), of Beaufort District; husband of Josephine Rogers Walker; son of Sarah Barnwell Means and Thomas Fuller (1813–1845); lieutenant of the Beaufort Artillery.

Fuller, Sarah Barnwell Means, see Stuart, Sarah Barnwell Means Fuller.

Fuller, Thomas (1788–1862), of Beaufort; a physician and planter; son of Elizabeth Middleton and Thomas Fuller (1760–1830); his mother was the half sister of Mary Bull Maxcy; married first Phoebe Louisa Waight; married second Elizabeth Barnwell.

Fuller, William Hazzard (1829–1902), of Prince William's Parish; physician and planter; a Confederate second lieutenant in Company F, Ninth South Carolina Volunteers (later the Eleventh South Carolina Infantry); physician in Barnwell District during the war.

Gamewell, Mary A., of Columbia; wife of Rev. Whatcoat Asbury Gamewell.

Gamewell, Rev. Whatcoat Asbury (1814–1869), of Columbia; Methodist clergyman.

Gantt, Frederick Hay (1833–1885), of Barnwell District; lieutenant of Company K, Ninth South Carolina Volunteers until the regiment's reorganization in May 1862; lieutenant colonel of the Eleventh South Carolina Infantry for the rest of the war; state solicitor of South Carolina after the war.

Geddings, J. D., of Connecticut; teacher at the St. Philip Street Public School, Charleston in 1864; assistant United States treasurer during Reconstruction.

Geiger, Helen Barnwell (1839–1879), of Beaufort District; daughter of Eliza Zubly Smith and Capt. Edward Barnwell; married Dr. Charles Atwood Geiger of Roswell, Georgia, during the war.

Gibbes, Ann Reeve (1835–1889), "Annie," of Beaufort; daughter of Phoebe Sarah Campbell and Arthur Smith Gibbes.

Gibbes, Arthur Smith (1807–1885), of Beaufort; physician and planter.

Gibbes, James Stuart (1833–1867), "Stuart," of Beaufort; son of Phoebe Sarah Campbell and Arthur Smith Gibbes; corporal and chief of caisson of the Beaufort Artillery; on detached duty superintending boats and as engineer in the Department of South Carolina, Georgia, and Florida.

Gibbes, John Barnwell Campbell (1839–1886), "Campbell," of Beaufort; son of Phoebe Sarah Campbell and Arthur Smith Gibbes; taught school in Florida; a private, first in the Second Florida Infantry and later in Company A, Twenty-fifth South Carolina Infantry.

Gibbes, Phoebe Sarah Campbell (1813–1852), of Beaufort; wife of Arthur Smith Gibbes.

Gibbes, Robert M. (1846–1924), private in the Beaufort Artillery.

Gibbes, Robert Reeve (1836–1877), of Beaufort; son of Phoebe Sarah Campbell and Arthur Smith Gibbes; listed as a surgeon in the U.S. Navy in the 1860 census; assistant surgeon in the Confederate navy aboard the C.S.S. *Savannah,* C.S.S. *Sampson,* C.S.S. *Atlanta,* and C.S.S. *Chicora.*

Glover, Caroline Lydia, see Fowles, Caroline Lydia Glover.

Glover, Matilda Maxcy Fowles, "Tilly," of Columbia and Orangeburg; daughter of Matilda Maxcy and Rev. James Henry Fowles; wife of Mortimer Glover (1838–1921); niece of Mary Maxcy Leverett.

Goddard, Peter Cuttino (1827–1862), of Charleston; physician; Confederate private in Capt. W. L. Trenholm's Company A of the Rutledge Mounted Riflemen; he was killed at Pocotaligo 29 May 1862.

Goodwyn, Thomas Jefferson (1800–1877), of Orangeburg District and Columbia; physician; state senator; delegate to the Secession Convention; mayor of Columbia 1863–65 who surrendered the city to Federal troops commanded by Maj. Gen. William T. Sherman on 17 February 1865.

Gould, Benjamin Apthorp (1787–1859), of Boston; schoolmaster and merchant; preceded Frederic Percival Leverett Sr. (1803–1836) as principal of the Public Latin School, Boston, 1814–1828.

Gregg, Rt. Rev. Alexander (d. 1893), first Episcopal bishop of Texas.

Gregg, Cornelia Manning (1826–1896), of Columbia; daughter of Cornelia Manning Maxcy and James Gregg; sister of Maxcy Gregg; first cousin once removed of Mary Maxcy Leverett.

Gregg, Cornelia Manning Maxcy (1792–1862), of Columbia; daughter of Susan Hopkins and Jonathan Maxcy; wife of Col. James Gregg (1787–1852); first cousin of Mary Maxcy Leverett; mother of Maxcy Gregg.

Gregg, Julia deBerniere (1823–1893), of Columbia; daughter of Cornelia Manning Maxcy and James Gregg; sister of Maxcy Gregg; first cousin once removed of Mary Maxcy Leverett.

Gregg, Maxcy (1815–1862), of Columbia; lawyer; son of Cornelia Manning Maxcy and James Gregg; first cousin once removed of Mary Maxcy Leverett; volunteer officer in the Mexican War; delegate to the Secession Convention; first colonel of the First South Carolina Infantry (Gregg's) and later brigadier general of a South Carolina brigade in the Army of Northern Virginia; mortally wounded at Fredericksburg, Virginia, 13 December 1862 and died two days later.

Gregg, Thomas Edwards (1836–1911), of Marion District; first lieutenant and captain of the McQueen Light Artillery, an independent South Carolina artillery battery, later Company C, Manigault's Battalion, South Carolina Artillery (Siege Train) and still later Capt. Gregg's Company, South Carolina Artillery, in the Army of Northern Virginia.

Gregorie, Alexander Fraser (1824–1904), of Prince William's Parish; a planter.

Gregorie, Isaac McPherson (b. ca. 1826), of Prince William's Parish; a planter.

Gregorie, James (1798–1874), of Prince William's Parish; a planter.

Gregorie, John White (1829–1887), of Prince William's Parish; a planter at Richfield plantation; Confederate first lieutenant and captain in the South Carolina state troops; first lieutenant and captain in the Confederate Corps of Engineers in charge of several fortifications in the Department of South Carolina, Georgia, and Florida; captain of engineers in the Army of Tennessee.

Gregorie, Martha McPherson (d. 1884), of Beaufort District; wife of James Gregorie.

Gregorie, Sarah Eliza Baker (d. 1912), of Richfield plantation in Prince William's Parish; wife of John White Gregorie.

Grimké, Mary Augusta Secunda (1826–1895), of Buckfield and Spotsylvania plantations in Prince William's Parish; daughter of Mary Augusta Barron and Benjamin Secundus Grimké; stepdaughter of Capt. William Heyward (1800–1871).

Guerard, Jacob J. (d. 1864), Confederate second lieutenant and first lieutenant, often in command of the company, of Company C, Ninth South Carolina Volunteers (later the Eleventh South Carolina Infantry) until he was captured at Swift Creek, Virginia, 9 May 1864; he died in prison at Fort Delaware, Delaware, 14 September 1864.

Guignard, James Sanders, Jr. (1803–1868), of Columbia; a planter in Richland and Lexington Districts; son of Caroline Richardson and James Sanders Guignard; first married Elizabeth Richardson, then Mrs. Anna Margaret Coffin Edwards.

Guild, Lafayette (1825–1870), of Alabama; Confederate surgeon; inspector of hospitals; medical director of the Army of Northern Virginia.

Habersham, Ann Hutson, see Elliott, Ann Hutson Habersham.

Hall, Wilson E. (b. 1845), of Beaufort; Confederate private in the Beaufort Artillery.

Hamilton, Catharine Amarinthia Percy (1818–1877), of Winterdale plantation in St. Helena's Parish; wife of Paul Hamilton (1816–1899).

Hamilton, Henrietta Potter, see Fuller, Henrietta Potter Hamilton.

Hamilton, Henry C. (b. 1831), of St. Luke's Parish; a planter; private in Company H; Third South Carolina Cavalry detached as a clerk at Pocotaligo.

Hamilton, Paul (1816–1899), of Beaufort District; a planter at Winterdale plantation in St. Helena's Parish and in Beaufort; husband of Catharine Amarinthia Percy.

Hamilton, Paul A. (1842–1862), of Winterdale plantation in St. Helena's Parish; son of Paul and Catharine Percy Hamilton; Confederate staff officer under Brig. Gen. Stephen D. Lee in the Army of Tennessee; killed at Chickasaw Bayou, Mississippi, 29 December 1862.

Hamilton, Rebecca Motte Middleton (b. 1818), of Charleston and Columbia; daughter of Mary Burroughs and John Middleton (1784–1826); wife of Daniel Heyward Hamilton Sr. (1816–1868).

Hampton, Wade, III (1818–1902), of Richland District; a planter; the first colonel of the Hampton Legion and later brigadier general and major general in the Army of Northern Virginia and lieutenant general in the Department of South Carolina, Georgia, and Florida and the Army of Tennessee; governor of South Carolina 1876–80; United States senator.

Hanckel, Allan Stuart, son of Ann Stuart (1786–1840) and Rev. Christian Hanckel (1789–1870); husband of Charlotte Bull Heyward.

Hanckel, Anne Matilda Heyward (b. 1833), "Annie," of Charleston; daughter of Daniel and Anne Maxcy Heyward; wife of Charles Francis Hanckel; niece of Mary Maxcy Leverett.

Hanckel, Charles Francis (1829–1898), of Charleston; merchant; attorney; son of Ann Stuart (1786–1840) and Rev. Christian Hanckel (1789–1870); private in the First South Carolina Rifles, captain and brigade commissary, then major and brigade commissary on the staffs of Brig. Gen. Thomas F. Drayton and Brig. Gen. Paul J. Semmes, before resigning in 1863 to become a superintendent of the Confederate States Treasury Bureau in Columbia.

Hanckel, Charlotte Bull Heyward (1838–1860), of Heyward Hall plantation, Prince William's Parish; daughter of Daniel and Anne Maxcy Heyward; wife of Allan Stuart Hanckel; niece of Mary Maxcy Leverett.

Hanckel, Middleton Stuart (1827–1904), of Beaufort District; physician; son of Ann Stuart (1786–1840) and Rev. Christian Hanckel (1789–1870); husband of Augusta Berkley Heyward (b. 1830); Confederate captain and quartermaster in the Third Military District at Pocotaligo.

Hanckel, Sarah Thomas Heyward, of Prince William's Parish; wife of Thomas Middleton Hanckel; daughter of Charity Wilson (1802–1829) and Thomas Heyward (1805–1828).

Hanckel, Thomas Middleton (1822–1888), of Prince William's Parish; attorney and planter; son of Ann Stuart (1786–1840) and Rev. Christian Hanckel (1789–1870).

Hanckel, Rev. William Henry (1824–1892), son of Ann Stuart (1786–1840) and Rev. Christian Hanckel (1789–1870); rector of St. John's Episcopal Church, Congaree, 1859–1871.

Harrison, John J. (1832–1862), of Beaufort District; a farmer; captain in Company D, Ninth South Carolina Volunteers until the regiment's reorganization in May 1862; major of the Eleventh South Carolina Infantry; he was killed at Pocotaligo 22 October 1862.

Haskell, Alexander Cheves (1839–1910), of Abbeville District; Confederate officer on the staff of Brig. Gen. Maxcy Gregg and later as lieutenant colonel of the Seventh South Carolina Cavalry.

Haskell, John Cheves (1841–1906), of Abbeville District and Columbia; Confederate lieutenant in the First South Carolina Artillery; captain on the staffs of Maj. Gen. G. W. Smith and Brig. Gen. David R. Jones; major and staff officer with Maj. M. W. Henry's Battalion; major and later lieutenant colonel in command of Haskell's Battalion, First Corps Artillery, Army of Northern Virginia.

Haskell, Rebecca Coles Singleton (1839–1862), of Abbeville District and Columbia; wife of Alexander Cheves Haskell; daughter of Mary Lewis Carter and John Coles Singleton.

Haskell, Rebecca Singleton (b. 1862), of Abbeville District and Columbia; daughter of Rebecca Singleton and Alexander Cheves Haskell.

Haskell, William Thomson (1837–1863), of Abbeville District; captain of Company H, First South Carolina Infantry (Gregg's); killed at Gettysburg, Pennsylvania, 2 July 1863.

Haven, Charles Chauncy (b. 1787), of Massachusetts; lawyer; half brother of Rev. Charles Leverett's mother, Comfort Marshall.

Hazzard, Emily St. Pierre Trenholm (1839–1901), of Charleston; daughter of Anna Helen Holmes and George Alfred Trenholm; wife of William Miles Hazzard.

Hazzard, William Miles (d. 1903), of St. Simons Island, Georgia; a Confederate private and sergeant in Company A, Twenty-sixth Georgia Infantry; captain of Hazzard's Company, Third Battalion Georgia Cavalry; captain of Company B, Fourth Georgia Cavalry (Clinch's) and a cavalry scout; planter in Georgetown District after the war.

Henning, Robert, of Columbia; harness maker and owner of a shoe store.

Heyward, Anne Bull Maxcy (1813–1851), of Beaufort District; sister of Mary Maxcy Leverett; first wife of Daniel Heyward.

Heyward, Anne Matilda, see Hanckel, Anne Matilda Heyward.

Heyward, Charlotte Bull, see Hanckel, Charlotte Bull Heyward.

Heyward, Daniel (1810–1888), of Prince William's Parish; planter at Heyward Hall plantation; son of Charlotte Mivillepontoux and William Miles Heyward; brother-in-law of Mary Maxcy Leverett; vestryman at Sheldon Church.

Heyward, Daniel Cuthbert (1836–1871), "Dan," of Heyward Hall plantation in Prince William's Parish, and Columbia; son of Anne Maxcy and Daniel Heyward; nephew of Mary Maxcy Leverett.

Heyward, Eliza Barnwell (b. 1848), "Lila," of Heyward Hall plantation in Prince William's Parish; daughter of Anne Maxcy and Daniel Heyward; niece of Mary Maxcy Leverett.

Heyward, Elizabeth Barnwell Rhett (1828–1865), of Heyward Hall plantation in Prince William's Parish; daughter of Caroline Barnwell and Thomas Moore Rhett; second wife of Daniel Heyward.

Heyward, Julius Henry (1849–1923), son of Eliza Barnwell Smith (1815–1887) and Nathaniel Barnwell Heyward (1816–1891); first married Elizabeth Smith Middleton, then Anne Louise Heyward.

Heyward, Mary Bull (1835–1898), of Heyward Hall plantation in Prince William's Parish; daughter of Anne Maxcy and Daniel Heyward; niece of Mary Maxcy Leverett.

Heyward, Nathalie, see Adams, Nathalie Heyward.

Heyward, William (1800–1871), of Prince William's Parish; a planter at Buckfield and Spotsylvania plantations; son of Charlotte M. Villepontoux and William Miles Heyward; brother of Daniel Heyward; his wife was Mary Augusta Barron, widow of Benjamin Secundus Grimké.

Heyward, William Cruger (1808–1863), of Charleston; a planter at Cypress plantation on the Combahee River; son of Sarah Cruger and William Heyward (1779–1845); first colonel of the Ninth South Carolina Volunteers and commander of Fort Walker, on Hilton Head Island; died of yellow fever.

Heyward, William Henry (1817–1889), of Prince William's Parish; a planter at Clay Hall plantation; son of Susan Hayne Simmons and William Manigault Heyward (1788–1820); married Esther Barnwell Heyward; state representative; vestryman at Sheldon Church.

Heyward, William Milton (1842–1871), "Willie"; son of Anne Maxcy and Daniel Heyward; nephew of Mary Maxcy Leverett; private and corporal in Company C, Third South Carolina Cavalry, and in the signal corps.

Hitt, Virginius G., of Georgia; private in Company D, First Georgia Infantry (Ramsey's), corporal in Company A, Twelfth Battalion Georgia Light Artillery and Company A, Sixty-third Georgia Infantry; assistant surgeon on duty at the General Hospital, Petersburg, Virginia, and assistant surgeon of the Ninth Battalion Georgia Light Artillery.

Horsey, Lizzie F., see Huot, Lizzie F. Horsey.

Howe, Rev. George (1802–1883), of Columbia; professor at the Columbia Theological Seminary, 1831–1883; pastor of the First Presbyterian Church, Columbia, 1865–1866.

Howe, William (1842–1862), of Columbia; son of Rev. George Howe; Confederate private and orderly sergeant of the Columbia Grays, Company C, Second South Carolina Infantry; died of typhoid pneumonia in Richmond, 2 February 1862.

Hoyt, William D., surgeon in the Seventeenth Georgia Infantry 1863–1864; surgeon in charge of General Hospital No. 13 in Richmond, 1864–1865.

Hughes, Ann Sarah Maxcy, "Sallie," of Maryland; wife of Col. George Wurtz Hughes; daughter of Mary Galloway and Virgil Maxcy (1785–1844); first cousin of Mary Maxcy Leverett.

Hughes, G. C., of Charleston; private in Capt. W. L. Trenholm's Company A, Rutledge Mounted Riflemen, later Company B, Seventh South Carolina Cavalry.

Hughes, George Wurtz (1806–1870), born in Elmira, New York; son of Anna Konkle and John Hughes; civil engineer in New York City; topographical engineer in the U.S. Army in 1838; president of the Baltimore and Susquehanna Railroad; quartermaster general of Maryland in 1857; member of U.S. Congress, 1859–1861; lived at Tulip Hill in West River, Maryland.

Hughes, Henry Thomas, of Union; Confederate first lieutenant and ensign of the Palmetto Sharpshooters.

Hughes, Maxcy G. (d. 1863), of Baltimore; son of Ann Sarah Maxcy and George Wurtz Hughes; first cousin once removed of Mary Maxcy Leverett; Confederate private in the First Maryland Infantry; second lieutenant and first lieutenant and assistant ordnance officer in the District of Texas, New Mexico, and Arizona until his death at Houston, Texas, 12 November 1863.

Huguenin, Julius Gillison (1806–1862), of St. Luke's Parish; a planter at Point Comfort and Roseland plantations on the Coosawhatchie River and at McPhersonville.

Huguenin, Thomas Abram (1839–1897), of Charleston; professor at the South Carolina Military Academy (The Citadel) 1859–1861; first lieutenant and captain of Company A, First South Carolina Infantry (Regulars), (Third South Carolina Artillery); commander of Battery Beauregard, Sullivan's Island, September 1863; the last commander of Fort Sumter, July 1864–February 1865; after the war he was superintendent of streets in Charleston.

Huot, Lizzie F. Horsey, of Charleston; wife of Dr. Louis V. Huot.

Huot, Louis V. (b. 1831), of France; physician; partner of Samuel Fair in Columbia.

Hutson, Charles Woodward (1840–1936), "Charley," of Laurium plantation in Prince William's Parish; son of Sophronia Lucia Palmer and William Ferguson Hutson; graduated from South Carolina College in the Class of 1860; private in Company A, Hampton Legion (Infantry); private in the Beaufort Artillery; professor at the University of South Carolina and several other Southern state universities after the war.

Hutson, Eliza Ferguson (1859–1862), of Beaufort District; daughter of Eliza Ferguson Bacot and Thomas Woodward Hutson.

Hutson, Eliza Ferguson Bacot, of Beaufort District; second wife of Thomas Woodward Hutson.

Hutson, Louis DeSaussure (1856–1862), of Beaufort District; son of Eliza Ferguson Bacot and Thomas Woodward Hutson.

Hutson, Marion Martin (b. 1844), of Jericho plantation in Prince William's Parish; husband of Mary Bower Elliott; son of Sarah Mikell McLeod and Richard Woodward Hutson Sr. (1788–1866); private in Company H, First South Carolina Infantry (McCreary's), then Company A, Eleventh South Carolina Infantry (Ninth Volunteers), and in the Beaufort Artillery.

Hutson, Richard Woodward, Jr. (1836–1857), son of Sarah Mikell McLeod and Richard Woodward Hutson Sr. (1788–1866).

Hutson, Sophronia Lucia Palmer (d. 1873), of Laurium plantation in Prince William's Parish; wife of William Ferguson Hutson; daughter of Sarah Bunce and Rev. Edward Palmer.

Hutson, Thomas Woodward (b. 1803), of Prince William's Parish; a physician and planter.

Hutson, William Ferguson (1815–1881), "Ferguson," of Prince William's Parish; a planter at Laurium plantation; lawyer; son of Martha O'Reily Ferguson (1794–1816) and Richard Woodward Hutson Sr. (1788–1866); state representative; delegate to the Secession Convention; officer in the South Carolina Reserves during the war.

Ingraham, N. Duncan (1802–1891), of South Carolina; an antebellum career officer in the U.S. Navy; Confederate naval captain and flag officer in command of the naval defenses of South Carolina, with headquarters at Charleston, 1861–1863.

Izard, Allen Cadwallader (1834–1901), of Walterboro, Colleton District; son of Mary Cadwallader Green and Walter Izard; husband of Julia Davie Bedon; antebellum officer in the U.S. Navy; Confederate captain in Company I, Eleventh South Carolina Infantry; major and lieutenant colonel until his resignation in December 1864; postmaster of Walterboro after the war.

Izard, Ella Elizabeth (b. 1840), daughter of Rosetta Ella Pinckney and Ralph Stead Izard; moved to Baltimore after the war.

Izard, Rosetta Ella Pinckney (d. 1872), daughter of Elizabeth Izard (1784–1862) and Thomas Pinckney (1780–1842); wife of Ralph Stead Izard (1815–1858).

James, Joseph Allston (b. 1829), of Georgetown; surgeon of the Fifteenth South Carolina Infantry; surgeon of Maj. Gen. Joseph B. Kershaw's division in the Army of Northern Virginia.

Jamison, David Flavel (1810–1864), of Orangeburg and Barnwell Districts; planter; state representative; president of the Secession Convention; general in the South Carolina militia; Confederate judge advocate of the military court in the Department of South Carolina, Georgia, and Florida; died of yellow fever at Charleston, 14 September 1864.

Jenkins, Caroline Harper Jamison (1837–1902), of York District; daughter of Elizabeth Ann Carmichael Rumph and David Flavel Jamison; wife of Micah Jenkins (1835–1864).

Jenkins, Martha (1797–1857), of Beaufort District; wife of Micah Jenkins (b. 1796).

Jenkins, Micah (b. 1796), of Prince William's Parish; a planter; vestryman and warden at Sheldon Church.

Jenkins, Micah (1835–1864), of York District; son of Elizabeth Clark and John Jenkins (1794–1854); first colonel of the Fifth South Carolina Infantry; commander of a South Carolina brigade in the Confederate Army of the Potomac; colonel of the Palmetto Sharpshooters; as brigadier general he commanded a South Carolina brigade in the Army of Northern Virginia; accidentally wounded by Confederate fire at the Wilderness, Virginia, 6 May 1864, and died later that day.

Jenkins, Richard Henry (1812–1868), of Charleston District; son of Phoebe Waight Jenkins and Richard Jenkins; husband of Mary Amarinthia LaRoche; father of Julia Blance Jenkins Leverett.

Johnson, John (1829–1907), of Charleston; civil engineer, Confederate officer and the engineer in charge of the defenses of Fort Sumter; became an Episcopal clergyman after the war; rector of St. Philip's Church, Charleston; author of *The Defense of Charleston, including Fort Sumter and the Adjacent Islands, 1863–1865*, published in 1889.

Johnson, Rev. Richard, Episcopal clergyman; before the war was the rector of St. Mathew's Parish, Orangeburg District; during the war he was a priest in the diocese of Georgia.

Johnson, Rev. William H. (1811–1892), of Beaufort District; rector of St. Helena's Episcopal Church, St. Helena Island, 1856–1858, preceding Rev. Charles Leverett.

Johnstone, Andrew (1805–1864), of Annandale plantation in Prince George Winyah Parish, Georgetown District, and Beaumont plantation in Flat Rock, North Carolina; a planter; first married Sophie Beaumont Clarkson, then Mary Barnwell Elliott; murdered at Beaumont 10 June 1864.

Johnstone, William Clarkson (1829–1893), son of Sophie Beaumont Clarkson (d. 1845) and Andrew Johnstone (1805–1864); husband of Alice Louise Fraser.

Johnstone, William Elliott (1849–1871), son of Mary Barnwell Elliott (1824–1909) and Andrew Johnstone (1805–1864).

Keitt, Lawrence Massillon (1824–1864), of St. Matthews, Orangeburg District; lawyer; state representative; United States congressman; delegate to the Secession Convention; first colonel of the Twentieth South Carolina Infantry; last commander of Battery Wagner on Morris Island; temporary commander of Kershaw's old South Carolina brigade in the Army of Northern Virginia when his regiment was transferred to Virginia; mortally wounded at Cold Harbor on 1 June 1864 and died the next day.

Kerrison, Edwin Lane, of Columbia; a lawyer; during the war operated a warehouse that furnished clothing and other necessities to South Carolina Confederate soldiers through the efforts of local organizations such as the Soldiers' Clothing Association and the Central Association for the Relief of South Carolina Soldiers.

Kollock, Cornelius (1824–1897), of Chesterfield District; physician in Cheraw.

LaBorde, Maximilian (1804–1873), of Edgefield and Columbia; physician; newspaper editor; secretary of state of South Carolina; chairman of the Central Association for the Relief of South Carolina Soldiers during the war; professor at South Carolina College, serving as chairman of the faculty briefly during the war; unofficial president after the college became the University of South Carolina, 1865–1873.

LaRoche, James (1823–1899), of Charleston District; son of Martha Seabrook Jenkins and Richard Jenkins LaRoche; married first Mary Olivia Bailey, second Henrietta Sams; uncle of Julia Blanche Jenkins Leverett.

LaRoche, Mary Olivia Bailey (1828–1869), first wife of James LaRoche.

Lawton, J. Charles (ca. 1842–1865), of Charleston; Confederate private in Capt. W. L. Trenholm's Company A, Rutledge Mounted Riflemen, later Company B, Seventh South Carolina Cavalry; killed at Farmville, Virginia, 6 April 1865.

LeConte, John (1818–1891), professor at the University of Georgia; professor of physics at South Carolina College, 1855–1869; superintendent of the Niter and Mining District No. 6 1/2 of the Confederate States Niter and Mining Bureau during the war; professor at the University of California, Berkeley, after the war.

LeConte, Joseph (1823–1901), physician; professor at Oglethorpe University in Georgia, the University of Georgia, and professor and chair of geology at South Carolina College, 1857–1862; a chemist for Niter and Mining District No 6 1/2 of the Confederate States Niter and Mining Bureau during the war; professor at South Carolina College and the University of California, Berkeley, after the war.

Leverett, Frederic Percival, Sr. (1803–1836), of Boston; brother of Rev. Charles Edward Leverett; husband of Matilda Gorham (1813–1834); father of Frederic Percival Leverett and Charles Hendee Leverett; head of the Public Latin School, Boston; author of *Lexicon of the Latin Language*.

Leverett, Hannah Gray, see Price, Hannah Gray Leverett.

Leverett, Matilda Gorham (1813–1834), born in Cuba; wife of Frederic Percival Leverett Sr.; mother of Frederic Percival Leverett and Charles Hendee Leverett.

Lowndes, Elizabeth Brewton Pinckney (d. 1857), of Charleston and St. Bartholomew's Parish; daughter of Elizabeth Motte and Thomas Pinckney (1750–1828); wife of William Lowndes.

Lowndes, Rawlins (1838–1919), of Oakland plantation in St. Bartholomew's Parish and Charleston; Confederate captain on the staff of Brig. Gen. Roswell S. Ripley; husband of Sarah Buchanan Preston.

Lowndes, Sarah Buchanan Preston (1842–1880), of Columbia; daughter of Caroline M. Hampton and John Smith Preston; wife of Rawlins Lowndes.

Lowndes, Thomas Pinckney (1839–1899), of Charleston; corporal in the Marion Artillery and later on detached service to the Signal Corps in the Department of South Carolina, Georgia, and Florida.

Lowndes, William (1782–1822), of Charleston and St. Bartholomew's Parish; a planter; state representative; United States congressman.

Mackay, Isabella Fripp (bapt. 1840), of Mackay's Point plantation in Prince William's Parish; daughter of George C. Mackay Sr.

Manning, John Laurence (1816–1889), of Clarendon District; state representative; senator; governor of South Carolina, 1852–1854; staff officer under Gen. P. G. T. Beauregard in the Department of South Carolina, Georgia, and Florida.

Markoe, Francis, Jr., "Frank," of Baltimore; son of Mary Maxcy and Francis Markoe Sr; first cousin once removed of Mary Maxcy Leverett; lieutenant in the Signal Corps in the Department of South Carolina, Georgia, and Florida; signal officer and aide-de-camp on the staff of Maj. Gen. John B. Gordon in the Army of Northern Virginia.

Markoe, Mary Maxcy, of Baltimore; first cousin of Mary Maxcy Leverett; wife of Francis Markoe Sr.; daughter of Mary Galloway and Virgil Maxcy (1785–1844).

Markoe, Maxcy, of Baltimore; son of Mary Maxcy and Francis Markoe Sr.; first cousin once removed of Mary Maxcy Leverett.

Martin, Sally D., see Davidge, Sally D. Martin.

Martin, William Edward (1815–1869), of Beaufort; lawyer; husband of Eloise Mary Hayne (b. 1818); son of Harrietta Williamson and William Dickinson Martin; brigadier general in the South Carolina militia before the war; state representative; clerk of the South Carolina Senate, 1840–1866 with the exception of 1860–1861, when he served as colonel in the First South Carolina Mounted Militia; director for the Charleston and Savannah Railroad, 1857–1860; secretary and treasurer for the Episcopal state convention, 1860–1861.

Martin, William Heyward (1841–1862), of Bindon plantation in Prince William's Parish; son of William Galt Martin; graduated from South Carolina College in the class of 1860; private in Company H, First South Carolina Infantry (Gregg's); died of typhoid fever at Richmond 15 July 1862.

Mason, Julien Jacquelin, of Virginia; private in Company C, Ninth Virginia Cavalry, later major and commissary of Field's Division, First Corps, Army of Northern Virginia.

Mason, Wiley Roy, Jr., of Virginia; first lieutenant and aide-de-camp on the staff of Brig. Gen. Charles W. Field, in the Bureau of Conscription in Richmond and on Field's staff after Field's promotion to major general.

Maury, Richard B., of Mississippi; Confederate surgeon in charge of the General Hospital in Brookhaven, Mississippi.

Maxcy, Anne Bull, see Heyward, Anne Bull Maxcy.

Maxcy, Ann Sarah, see Hughes, Ann Sarah Maxcy.

Maxcy, Mary, see Markoe, Mary Maxcy.

Maxcy, Mary Bull (1776–1857), of Beaufort; wife of Milton Maxcy (1782–1817); daughter of Ann Barnwell and Gen. Stephen Bull; first husband was Nathaniel Barnwell (1772–1801); from her first marriage, she was the mother of Eliza Natalia Barnwell Cuthbert (1801–1831) and by her second marriage Matilda Miltonia Maxcy Fowles (1811–1879), Anne Bull Maxcy Heyward (1813–1851), and Mary Maxcy Leverett (1808/9–1897).

McCay, Charles Francis (1810–1889), of Columbia; professor of mathematics at the University of Georgia; successor to James Henley Thornwell as president of South Carolina College, 1855–1857.

McDowell, Rev. James, Presbyterian clergyman; Confederate chaplain of the Palmetto Sharpshooters.

McElheran, Rev. David (1793–1875), of Beaufort District; rector of St. Helena's Episcopal Church, St. Helena Island, 1831–1856; principal of a school at St. Helenaville, the planters' village on St. Helena Island.

McFall, James M. (1843–1875), of Anderson; clerk; Confederate adjutant of the Palmetto Sharpshooters.

McKee, Henry (1811–1875), of St. Helena's Parish; planter at Ashdale plantation; steward of the Confederate Hospital on the campus of South Carolina College, 1862–1865.

McKee, Jane Monroe Bold (1819–1904), wife of Henry McKee.

McKenna, Anne Randolph, see Pinckney, Anne Randolph McKenna.

McLure, John William (1831–1916), of Limestone Springs; lieutenant in Company G, Fifth South Carolina Infantry; regimental quartermaster of the Palmetto Sharpshooters; division quartermaster of Field's Division, First Corps, Army of Northern Virginia.

Means, Anne (b. 1853), of St. Helena's Parish; daughter of Ann Stuart Hanckel and Dr. Thomas Means.

Means, Edward Barnwell (1821–1898), of Beaufort District; a planter; husband of Henrietta Aiken Martin (1831–1883); son of Mary Hutson Barnwell (1781–1851) and Robert Means (1774–1832); after the war he lived in Charleston.

Means, Isabella Harper, see DeSaussure, Isabella Harper Means.

Means, John Hugh (1812–1862), of Fairfield District; brigadier general in the state militia; governor of South Carolina, 1850–1852; delegate to the Secession Convention; first colonel of the Seventeenth South Carolina Infantry; wounded at Second Manassas, Virginia, 30 August 1862, and died two days later.

Means, Sarah Barnwell, see Stuart, Sarah Barnwell Means Fuller.

Means, Thomas (1812–1876), of St. Helena's Parish; physician and planter; husband of Ann Stuart Hanckel (1813–1899); son of Mary Hutson Barnwell and Robert Means.

Melton, George W., major and quartermaster of the Second Military District of South Carolina.

Memminger, Christopher Gustavus (1803–1888), of Charleston; member of the Board of Trustees of South Carolina College; state representative; commissioner of Charleston schools; delegate to the Secession Convention; and first Confederate secretary of the Treasury.

Michel, William Middleton (1822–1894), of Charleston; physician; medical professor; surgeon in charge of the South Carolina Hospital and of General Hospital No. 21 in Richmond; was at the South Carolina Hospital in Petersburg; edited the *Confederate States Medical and Surgical Journal,* 1863–1864.

Mickler, John H. (b. ca. 1830), of St. Luke's Parish; steamboat captain; Confederate first lieutenant and then captain of the Hamilton Guards, Company E of the Eleventh South Carolina Infantry.

Middleton, Eleanor Maria, see Rutledge, Eleanor Maria Middleton.

Middleton, John Izard, Sr. (1800–1877), of Crowfield, on the Waccamaw River in All Saints' Parish, Georgetown District; state representative and senator; member of the Board of Trustees of South Carolina College; delegate to the Secession Convention.

Middleton, John Izard, Jr. (1834–1907), of Crowfield plantation in All Saints' Parish, Georgetown District; son of Sarah McPherson Alston and John Izard Middleton (1800–1877); graduated first in the Class of 1853 at South Carolina College; officer on the staff of Brig. Gen. Thomas F. Drayton in the Department of South Carolina and Georgia; captain and assistant quartermaster of the Fifteenth South Carolina Infantry; chief quartermaster, major of the First Corps Artillery in the Army of Northern Virginia.

Middleton, Julia Emma Rhett (b. 1835), of Charleston; daughter of Charlotte Haskell and James Smith Rhett; wife of Arthur Middleton (b. 1832).

Middleton, Oliver Hering, Jr. (1845–1864), of Charleston; son of Susan Matilda Harriet Chisolm and Oliver Hering Middleton Sr.; private in the Charleston Light Dragoons, Company K, Fourth South Carolina Cavalry; wounded at Haw's Shop, Virginia, 28 May 1864, and died three days later.

Middleton, Rebecca Motte, see Hamilton, Rebecca Motte Middleton.

Middleton, Susan Matilda (1830–1880), of Charleston and Colleton Districts; daughter of Susan Matilda Harriet Chisolm and Oliver Hering Middleton Sr.

Middleton, Susan Matilda Harriet Chisolm (1807–1865), of Charleston and Colleton Districts; daughter of Dr. Robert Trail Chisolm; wife of Oliver Hering Middleton Sr.

Mitchel, John C., Jr. (1839–1864), of Ireland and Charleston; engineer; captain in the First South Carolina Artillery; commander of Fort Sumter from mid-May 1864 until he was wounded and died 20 July 1864.

Moore, Henry Woodbury (1831–1902), of St. Luke's Parish; physician; Confederate assistant surgeon of the Hampton Legion (Cavalry).

Moore, Samuel Preston (1813–1889), of South Carolina; an antebellum assistant surgeon and surgeon in the U.S. Army; Confederate officer; surgeon general; commanded the medical department from mid-1861 to the end of the war.

Morris, Caspar (1805–1884), of Philadelphia; physician; member of the Board of Managers of the Hospital of the Protestant Episcopal Church in Philadelphia from 1851 until his death.

Murray, Phillip P., of Beaufort District; a wheelwright; private in the Beaufort Artillery until his one-year term of enlistment expired in April 1862.

North, Eliza Elliott Drayton (d. 1866), of Pendleton; wife of John Laurens North (1782–1848) of Rusticello plantation.

Norton, R. W., Baptist clergyman; private in the Beaufort Artillery; chaplain of the Nineteenth Tennessee Infantry in the Army of Tennessee.

Nowell, Lionel Chalmers (1836–1896), of Charleston; husband of Anne Heyward Barnwell (1838–1864); son of Harriet Sarah Wigfall and John Lascelles Nowell; first lieutenant in command of the Charleston Light Dragoons, later Company K, Fourth South Carolina Cavalry; captured at Cold Harbor on 30 May 1864.

Ogier, Thomas Lewis (1810–1900), of Charleston; physician and Confederate surgeon in the Department of South Carolina, Georgia, and Florida.

O'Neall, John Belton (1793–1863), of Newberry; president of the South Carolina court of appeals; state representative; Speaker of the House; chief justice of the state supreme court.

Palmer, Rev. Benjamin Morgan (1818–1902), of New Orleans; minister of First Presbyterian Church, Columbia, 1843–1854; professor of the Columbia Theological Seminary, 1854–1856; minister of the First Presbyterian Church, New Orleans, 1858–1902.

Palmer, Sophronia Lucia, see Hutson, Sophronia Lucia Palmer.

Parker, Francis LeJau (1836–1913), of Charleston; physician; surgeon, assistant surgeon, and surgeon of general hospitals in Virginia; surgeon of the Hampton Legion (Infantry); chief surgeon of Field's Division, First Corps, Army of Northern Virginia; dean of the faculty at the Medical University of South Carolina after the war.

Parker, John W. (1803–1882), of Columbia; physician; superintendent of the South Carolina Lunatic Asylum, 1836–1856; superintendent and chief medical officer 1856–1870; assistant physician, 1876–1882.

Paterson, James T. (d. 1870), of Virginia; jeweler, printer, and publisher; moved to Columbia and then to Augusta, Georgia, during the war; printed Confederate treasury notes and published works including Rev. Charles Leverett's *Southern Confederacy Arithmetic*.

Patton, John G. (d. 1862), captain of Company F, First Georgia Regulars; killed at Second Manassas, Virginia, 30 August 1862.

Peake, Henry T., of Charleston; superintendent of the South Carolina Railroad during and immediately after the war.

Pelham, Charles P. (1816–1877), professor at South Carolina College, 1846–1857; editor of *The Southern Guardian*, a Columbia newspaper.

Pemberton, John Clifford (1814–1881), of Pennsylvania; married a Virginian; a Confederate brigadier general in the Department of South Carolina and Georgia; a major general commanding the department; a lieutenant general commanding the Department of Mississippi and Eastern Louisiana, including Vicksburg, which he surrendered to Maj. Gen. Ulysses S. Grant in July 1863.

Pickens, Francis Wilkinson (1805–1869), of Edgefield District; a planter; U.S. congressman; state senator; U.S. minister to Russia; governor of South Carolina, 1860–1862, elected just before the state seceded.

Pinckney, Anne Randolph McKenna (d. 1839), of Virginia; first wife of Rev. Charles Cotesworth Pinckney (1812–1898).

Pinckney, Charles Cotesworth, II (1789–1865), of Beaufort and Abbeville Districts; a planter; son of Elizabeth Motte and Thomas Pinckney; husband of Phoebe Elliott; father of Phoebe Caroline Pinckney Seabrook.

Pinckney, Rev. Charles Cotesworth, III (1812–1898), of Charleston; son of Phoebe Caroline Elliott and Charles Cotesworth Pinckney II; husband of Esther Heyward Barnwell; first wife, Anne Randolph McKenna (d. 1839); rector of Grace Episcopal Church, Charleston, 1854–1864.

Pinckney, Charles Cotesworth, IV (1839–1909), of Charleston; son of Anne Randolph McKenna and Rev. Charles Cotesworth Pinckney III; private in the Marion Artillery; an independent South Carolina artillery battery; captain and ordnance officer of the First Military District of South Carolina; assigned to the Charleston Arsenal.

Pinckney, Harriott (1776–1866), of Charleston; daughter of Sarah Middleton and Charles Cotesworth Pinckney I.

Pinckney, Mary Elliott (1833–1912), of Beaufort and Charleston; daughter of Phoebe Caroline Elliott and Charles Cotesworth Pinckney II.

Pinckney, Phoebe Caroline, see Seabrook, Phoebe Caroline Pinckney.

Pinckney, Phoebe Caroline Elliott (1794–1864), of Abbeville; daughter of Phoebe Waight and William Elliott (1761–1808); wife of Charles Cotesworth Pinckney II; mother of Phoebe Caroline Pinckney Seabrook; second cousin of Mary Maxcy Leverett.

Pinckney, Thomas (1828–1915), of Charleston; son of Phoebe Caroline Elliott and Charles Cotesworth Pinckney II; married first Mary Stewart and second Camilla Scott; captain and staff officer in the Department of South Carolina, Georgia, and Florida, primarily with the Bureau of Conscription at Columbia; captured at Hawe Shop, Virginia, May 1864 and exchanged in December.

Porcher, Francis Peyre (1824–1895), "Frank," "Peyre," of Charleston; physician; medical professor; botanist; assistant surgeon of Holcombe's Legion and on the staff of Brig. Gen. Stephen Elliott Jr.; surgeon in charge of the South Carolina Hospital at Petersburg, Virginia.

Porteous, John Fuller, Jr., of Beaufort District; private in the Beaufort Artillery; second lieutenant of artillery at the Charleston Arsenal.

Porter, Rev. Anthony Toomer (1828–1902), of Charleston and Columbia; Episcopal clergyman; rector of the Church of the Holy Communion in Charleston; founder of Porter Military Academy.

Potter, Rt. Rev. Horatio (1802–1887), provisional Episcopal bishop of New York 1854–61; bishop of New York, 1861–1884.

Potter, Rev. William T. (d. 1879), of Beaufort District; preceded Rev. Charles Leverett as rector of Sheldon Episcopal Church, serving January–May 1846.

Prentiss, Christopher Jenkins (1835–1885), of Colleton District; physician; son of Mary Sarah Jenkins (1819–1848) and Rev. William Otis Prentiss; student at South Carolina College in 1853, a year ahead of Edward Leverett, but left school and did not graduate with the class of 1855; assistant surgeon of the First (later Second) South Carolina Artillery, and later the Palmetto (Third) Battalion South Carolina Light Artillery.

Prentiss, Rev. William Otis (1814–1897), of Colleton District; Episcopal clergyman; planter at Buzzard Roost plantation in St. Bartholomew's Parish.

Preston, John Smith (1809–1881), of Columbia; state senator; member of the Board of Trustees of South Carolina College; officer on the staff of Gen. P. G. T. Beauregard in the Department of South Carolina, Georgia, and Florida; in command of Confederate prisons and conscript camps; brigadier general and superintendent of the Bureau of Conscription in Richmond.

Preston, Sarah Campbell Buchanan, see Lowndes, Sarah Campbell Buchanan Preston.

Preston, William Campbell (1794–1860), of Columbia; state representative; U.S. senator; president of South Carolina College, 1845–1851.

Price, Hannah Gray Leverett, of New York; wife of Rev. Joseph Henry Price; sister of Rev. Charles Edward Leverett; her first husband was Nathaniel Dowse Nicholson.

Price, Rev. Joseph Henry, rector of St. Stephen's Episcopal Church, New York City; husband of Hannah Gray Leverett.

Pringle, Maj. Jacob Motte Alston (1827–1886), "Motte"; son of Mary Motte Alston and William Bull Pringle; husband of Gabriella Ravenel (b. 1827); quartermaster at Charleston.

Pringle, Rev. James Maxwell (1822–1905), rector of Christ Episcopal Church, Columbia; son of Sarah McKewn Maxwell and Robert Alexander Pringle; served Zion Episcopal Church in lower Richland District, 1847–1855.

Pringle, James Reid (1813–1884), of Charleston; husband of Sarah Gilmer Ladson; son of Elizabeth McPherson and James Reid Pringle (1782–1840); cotton factor and partner in the firm Coffin & Pringle.

Pringle, Jane Edwards Ford (1829–1866), wife of Rev. James Maxwell Pringle; daughter of Sarah Amelia Edwards and Gen. Malachi Ford (d. 1840).

Pringle, Sarah Gilmer Ladson (1824–1877), of Charleston; wife of James Reid Pringle.

Prioleau, Charles E. (b. ca. 1840), of Prioli plantation in St. John's, Berkeley, Parish, in Charleston District; son of Mary Hutson Ford and Thomas Grimball Prioleau; private and corporal in Company K, Fourth South Carolina Cavalry.

Proctor, James T., second lieutenant of Company C, First South Carolina Infantry (Gregg's); acting assistant adjutant general to Col. Oliver E. Edwards of the Thirteenth South Carolina Infantry until he was severely wounded in the right leg at Chancellorsville, Virginia, 3 May 1863; later an ordnance officer with heavy artillery in the Department of South Carolina, Georgia, and Florida.

Raoul, Alfred (1815–1885), physician and planter in Prince William's Parish and in Charleston District; Confederate surgeon in the Department of South Carolina, Georgia, and Florida.

Raoul, Cornelia McPherson Smith (1823–1891), of Charleston District; second wife of Alfred Raoul.

Raoul, Eliza B. (1814–1852), of Beaufort District; first wife of Alfred Raoul.

Read, Benjamin Huger (1823–1887), physician and planter at Rice Hope plantation in Berkeley District; captain and assistant adjutant general on the staff of Brig. Gen. Roswell S. Ripley in the Department of South Carolina, Georgia, and Florida.

Read, Mary Julia Middleton (1828–1904), of Charleston; wife of Dr. Benjamin Huger Read; daughter of Susan Matilda Harriet Chisolm and Oliver Hering Middleton Sr.

Reynolds, Richard M. (d. 1863), of Beaufort; Confederate private in the Beaufort Artillery for only two days before he was accidentally killed in camp near McPhersonville on 5 October 1863.

Reynolds, Sallie (d. 1863), of Beaufort; teacher; died in Spartanburg during the war.

Rhett, Albert (1833–1895), son of Charlotte Haskell and James Smith Rhett; corporal in the Beaufort Artillery; married Frances Emma Jessie (1844–1874) of Virginia after the war.

Rhett, Albert Moore (1834–1911), of Charleston; son of Caroline Barnwell (1805–1867) and Thomas Moore Rhett (1794–1860); husband of Martha Goodwin (1835–1912); Confederate major and assistant quartermaster in Richmond and Columbia.

Rhett, Alfred Moore (1829–1889), of Charleston District; a planter on the Ashepoo River; son of Elizabeth Washington Burnet and Robert Barnwell Rhett Sr.; colonel of the First South Carolina Artillery; commander of Fort Sumter from April to October 1863; married Marie Alice Sparks after the war.

Rhett, Andrew Burnet (1831–1879), son of Elizabeth Washington Burnet and Robert Barnwell Rhett Sr.; husband of Henrietta Aiken; major, chief of artillery for the second military district of South Carolina; commanded a battalion of artillery composed of Le Gardeur's Light Artillery and the Beaufort Volunteer Artillery.

Rhett, Anne Stuart, see Elliott, Anne Stuart Rhett.

Rhett, Benjamin Smith (1798–1868), of Charleston; born Benjamin Smith; planter and merchant; son of Mariana Gough and James Harvey Smith (1761–1835); husband of Mary Pauline Haskell.

Rhett, Charlotte Haskell (1794–1871), of Beaufort District and Columbia; wife of James Smith Rhett (1797–1855).

Rhett, Claudia Smith (b. 1846), of Charleston; daughter of Mary Pauline Haskell and Benjamin Smith Rhett (1798–1868).

Rhett, Edmund (1808–1863), of Beaufort; born Edmund Smith; son of Mariana Gough and James Harvey Smith (1761–1835); husband of Mary Williamson Stuart (1821–1874); state representative and senator from St. Helena's Parish.

Rhett, Elizabeth Barnwell, see Heyward, Elizabeth Barnwell Rhett.

Rhett, Haskell Smith (1818–1868), of Colleton District and Beaufort; born Elnathan Haskell Smith; son of Charlotte Haskell and James Smith Rhett; husband of Rebecca Rosa Means (1823–1913); owned Smiley Plantation.

Rhett, James Moore (1820–1888), son of Charlotte Haskell and James Smith Rhett; husband of Eliza Martha Means (1818–1900).

Rhett, Julia Emma, see Middleton, Julia Emma Rhett.

Rhett, Mary Williamson Stuart (1821–1874), of Beaufort District; wife of

Edmund Rhett; daughter of Mary Anne Williamson (d. 1862) and Dr. Thomas Middleton Stuart (b. 1794).

Rhett, Robert Barnwell, Sr. (1800–1876), of Colleton District; born Robert Smith; son of Mariana Gough and James Harvey Smith (1761–1835); husband of Elizabeth Washington Burnet (1809–1852); lawyer; state representative; attorney general of South Carolina; U.S. congressman and senator; helped draft the Confederate States constitution; ran unsuccessfully for the Confederate Congress; was an outspoken critic of Jefferson Davis.

Rhett, Robert Barnwell, Jr. (1828–1901), of Charleston; lawyer; son of Elizabeth Washington Burnet and Robert Barnwell Rhett Sr.; husband of Josephine Horton (1830–1860); married second Harriet Moore; became editor of the *Charleston Mercury* in 1857; state senator; colonel on the staff of Gov. Francis W. Pickens during the war; joined his father in criticizing Jefferson Davis through the editorial pages of the *Mercury*; editor of the *New Orleans Times-Picayune* after the war.

Rhett, Roland Smith (1830–1898), of Charleston; son of Charlotte Haskell and James Smith Rhett; husband of Julia Lowndes Brisbane (b. 1833); a clerk and broker; Confederate captain and post quartermaster of Columbia.

Rhett, Thomas Middleton Stuart (b. 1844), "Stuart," of Beaufort; son of Mary Williamson Stuart and Edmund Rhett; nephew of Robert Barnwell Rhett Sr.; private in the Beaufort Artillery and later a second lieutenant in Companies E and F, First South Carolina Artillery; lawyer in Colorado after the war.

Rhodes, John Jenkins (b. 1829), of Beaufort District; first lieutenant of the Beaufort Artillery.

Ripley, Roswell Sabine (1823–1887), of Ohio; second husband of Alicia Middleton (1824–1898) of Charleston; lieutenant colonel of South Carolina state forces; Confederate brigadier general; commanded the Department of South Carolina in the fall of 1861 and later a South Carolina brigade in the Army of Northern Virginia, a district in the Department of South Carolina, Georgia, and Florida, and a South Carolina brigade in the Army of Tennessee.

Rivers, William James (1822–1909), of Columbia; professor at South Carolina College, 1856–1862; professor at the reopened University of South Carolina, 1865–1873; president of Washington College in Maryland.

Rivers, William James, Jr. (d. 1862), of Columbia; son of William James Rivers.

Rose, Arthur Barnwell (1824–1892), of Charleston; physician and planter.

Rowan, Sallie (b. 1832), of Columbia; the wife of William Rowan, a clerk.

Rutledge, Benjamin Huger (1829–1893), of Charleston; lawyer; son of Alice Ann Weston (1798–1862) and Benjamin Huger Rutledge (bapt. 1798–1832); delegate to the Secession Convention; captain of the Charleston Light Dragoons, an independent cavalry company, later Company K of the Fourth South Carolina Cavalry; colonel of the Fourth South Carolina Cavalry.

Rutledge, Eleanor Maria Middleton (1831–1905), daughter of Susan Matilda Harriet Chisolm and Oliver Hering Middleton Sr.; wife of Benjamin Huger Rutledge.

Rutledge, Eliza Lucas (1810–1893), of Charleston; daughter of Harriett Pinckney Horry (d. 1858) and Frederick Rutledge (1768–1821).

Rutledge, Elizabeth (1830–1912), of Charleston; daughter of Rebecca Motte Lowndes (1810–1893) and Edward Cotesworth Rutledge (1798–1860); niece of Eliza Lucas Rutledge and Frederick Rutledge (1800–1884).

Rutledge, Frederick (1800–1884), of Charleston; a physician and planter at Waterhorn plantation in St. James, Santee Parish; son of Harriett Pinckney Horry (1770–1858) and Frederick Rutledge (1768–1821).

Rutledge, Julia Rose (1841–1899), of Charleston and Columbia; daughter of Maria Rose (1801–1881) and John Rutledge (1792–1864).

Rutledge, Maria (1834–1912), of Charleston and Columbia; daughter of Maria Rose (1801–1881) and John Rutledge (1792–1864).

Rutledge, Rebecca Motte Lowndes (1810–1893), of Charleston; wife of Edward Cotesworth Rutledge (1798–1860); daughter of Elizabeth Pinckney and William Lowndes.

Sams, Melvin Melius (1815–1900), of Beaufort District; physician and planter; husband of Margaret Black (1817–1899); son of Elizabeth Hamm Fripp (1795–1831) and Dr. Berners Barnwell Sams (1787–1855).

Saxton, Rufus (1824–1908), of Massachusetts; Federal brigadier general in the Department of the South, primarily on the South Carolina sea islands, where he was instrumental in the enlistment of free blacks and former slaves into the United States Army; after the war he was assistant commissioner for the Freedmen's Bureau in South Carolina, Georgia, and Florida.

Scott, Robert Kingston (1826–1900), of Ohio; Federal colonel of the Sixty-eighth Ohio Infantry; brigadier general in the Army of the Tennessee; after the war he was assistant commissioner for the Freedmen's Bureau in South Carolina, Georgia, and Florida; governor of South Carolina, 1868–1872.

Screven, John Henry (1823–1903), of Prince William's Parish; a planter at Old Brass and Castle Hill plantations; a lawyer; Confederate major and quartermaster at Pocotaligo.

Seabrook, Archibald Hamilton (1816–1894), "Archy," of St. Helena's Parish; a planter at Rest Park plantation; husband of Phoebe Caroline Pinckney Seabrook; son of Margaret Wilkinson Hamilton and Whitmarsh Benjamin Seabrook; vestryman at Sheldon Church and St. Helena's Church, Beaufort.

Seabrook, Cotesworth Pinckney (1839–1863), "Pinckney"; son of Caroline Pinckney and Archibald Hamilton Seabrook; second lieutenant in Company H, First South Carolina Infantry (Gregg's); he was killed at Chancellorsville, Virginia, 3 May 1863.

Seabrook, Rev. Joseph Baynard (1809–1877), of Edisto Island, Charleston District; Episcopal clergyman and schoolteacher who ministered primarily among the slaves and ran a classical and mathematical school at Bluffton; the first rector of St. Mark's Church, Charleston, a black Episcopal church established in April 1865, where he served until his death.

Seabrook, Margaret Hamiton (1849–1925), daughter of Caroline Pinckney and Archibald Hamilton Seabrook; married Henry Middleton Rutledge.

Seabrook, Mary E. (b. ca. 1843), of Rest Park plantation in St. Helena's Parish; daughter of Caroline Pinckney and Archibald Hamilton Seabrook.

Seabrook, Phoebe Caroline (1846–1864), "Carrie"; daughter of Archibald Hamilton Seabrook and Caroline Pinckney Seabrook.

Seabrook, Phoebe Caroline Pinckney (1816–1892), "Caroline," of Rest Park plantation in St. Helena's Parish; daughter of Phoebe Caroline Elliott and Charles Cotesworth Pinckney II; wife of Archibald Hamilton Seabrook.

Shand, Rev. Peter Johnson (1800–1886), of Columbia; rector of Trinity Episcopal Church, 1834–1886.

Sigourney, Lydia Howard Huntley (1791–1865), of Connecticut; most popular American poet of the nineteenth century; published many volumes of prose and contributed hundreds of articles to various literary periodicals.

Singleton, Rebecca Coles, see Haskell, Rebecca Coles Singleton.

Sitton, Augustus John, of Pendleton; a coachmaker; Confederate quartermaster sergeant of the Palmetto Sharpshooters.

Smalls, Robert (1839–1915), of Beaufort District; a slave impressed into Confederate service on the crew of the *Planter*; after he captured the vessel in May 1862 and turned it over to the South Atlantic Blockading Squadron of the U.S. Navy, Smalls became a pilot on the U.S.S. *Keokuk*, then captain of the *Planter* for the remainder of the war; after the war Smalls was a delegate to the South Carolina constitutional convention, state representative, and senator, and United States congressman.

Smith, Benjamin Burgh, Jr. (1835–1904), of Charleston; physician; major of the Ninth South Carolina Volunteers from its creation until its reorganization in May 1862; major of the Second Battalion South Carolina Sharpshooters; on the staff of Brig. Gen. States Rights Gist and as commander of the Sixteenth and Twenty-fourth South Carolina Infantry (Consolidated).

Smith, Clifton Hewitt, of Virginia; Confederate aide-de-camp to Gen. P. G. T. Beauregard in Virginia, Tennessee, and South Carolina; on the staff of Brig. Gen. Dabney H. Maury in Alabama.

Smith, LaRoche Jacquelin, of Virginia; Confederate second lieutenant and first lieutenant of artillery at the Augusta Arsenal; captain and assistant chief of ordnance in the Department of South Carolina, Georgia, and Florida; captain and ordnance officer of the District of Georgia.

Smith, William Duncan (1825–1862), of Georgia; Confederate colonel of the Twentieth Georgia Infantry; brigadier general in command of a district in the Department of South Carolina, Georgia, and Florida; died of yellow fever at Charleston on 4 October 1862.

Sosnowski, Sophie Wentz (1809–1899), of Germany; wife of Josef Stanislaus Sosnowski; principal of the South Carolina Female Collegiate Institute (Barhamville Institute), near Columbia, from the fall of 1864 to the burning of Columbia in February 1865.

Stewart, Rev. Kinsey Johns, of Virginia; chaplain of the Sixth North Carolina Infantry.

Stoney, Emma Barnwell, see Stuart, Emma Barnwell Stoney.

Stoney, George Mosse, Jr. (1843–1865), of Beaufort; son of Dr. George Mosse Stoney and Sarah Woodward Barnwell Stoney; private and sergeant in the Beaufort Artillery; commanded a two-gun battery on Sullivan's Island as second lieutenant of Company C, First South Carolina Regulars; wounded at Bentonville, North Carolina, 19 March 1865, and died the same day.

Storer, David Humphreys (1804–1891), of Boston; a physician, professor, and naturalist; a founder of the Tremont Street Medical School, established in 1838 as a summer school affiliated with the Harvard University Medical School; professor of obstetrics and jurisprudence at Harvard, 1854–1868.

Stuart, Rev. Albert Rhett (1846–1902), of Richland District; son of Claudia Smith and John Allan Stuart; married Sophia Clarkson (b. 1844); Confederate private in the Marion Light Artillery; Episcopal clergyman in South Carolina, Ohio, and the District of Columbia after the war.

Stuart, Allan (1835–1864), of Beaufort District; a planter; son of Mary Howe Barnwell and Middleton Stuart; officer in the Beaufort Artillery and a second lieutenant of ordnance in the Department of South Carolina, Georgia, and Florida and under Brig. Gen. James Cantey in Confederate Department No. 2, in Alabama; died in Aiken on 1 January 1864 of wounds received at Port Royal on 7 November 1861.

Stuart, Ann Hutson Means (1808–1862), of Page's Point plantation in Beaufort District; wife of Henry Middleton Stuart Sr.; daughter of Mary Hutson Barnwell and Robert Means.

Stuart, Ann Means (1827–1905), daughter of Ann Hutson Means and Henry Middleton Stuart Sr. (1803–1872).

Stuart, Benjamin Rhett (1835–1904), "Ben," of Beaufort District; husband of Emma Virginia Thompson (1834–1904); son of Claudia Smith (d. 1875) and John Allan Stuart (d. 1852); ran a school in Charleston before the war and in Columbia during the war.

Stuart, Charlotte, see Elliott, Charlotte Stuart.

Stuart, Emma Barnwell Stoney (1837–1914), of Beaufort District; daughter of Sarah Woodward Barnwell and Dr. George Mosse Stoney; wife of Middleton Stuart.

Stuart, Henry Middleton, Sr. (1803–1872), of Page's Point plantation in Beaufort District; a planter; son of Anne Middleton and Dr. James Stuart Sr.; married first Ann Hutson Means (1808–1862), and after her death married her sister Sarah Barnwell Means (1816–1879), widow of Thomas Fuller (1813–1845); his mother was the half sister of Mary Bull Maxcy.

Stuart, Henry Middleton (1841–1865), "Henry," of Beaufort District; son of Mary Howe Barnwell and Col. Middleton Stuart; private in the Beaufort Artillery; a drill master in the Engineer Corps; second lieutenant and first lieutenant of Company B, First South Carolina Artillery; he was killed at Averasboro, North Carolina, 16 March 1865.

Stuart, Henry Middleton, Jr. (1835–1915), "Hal," of Beaufort District; a physician; son of Ann Hutson Means and Henry Middleton Stuart Sr.; husband of Sarah Barnwell Stuart; second lieutenant, first lieutenant, and captain of the Beaufort Artillery and chief of artillery for the Third Military District in the Department of South Carolina, Georgia, and Florida.

Stuart, Isabel (1831–1873), "Bell," of Page's Point plantation in Beaufort District; daughter of Ann Hutson Means and Henry Middleton Stuart Sr.

Stuart, James Reeve (1834–1915), of Beaufort District; artist; son of Mary Howe Barnwell and Col. Middleton Stuart; corporal and ordnance sergeant in the Beaufort Artillery; professor of art at the University of Wisconsin after the war.

Stuart, Mary Howe Barnwell (1812–1876), of Beaufort District; wife of Col. Middleton Stuart (1806–1840).

Stuart, Mary Williamson, see Rhett, Mary Williamson Stuart.

Stuart, Middleton (1831–1920), "Minny," of Beaufort District; husband of Emma Barnwell Stoney; son of Mary Howe Barnwell and Col. Middleton Stuart; Confederate captain of the Hamilton Guards, Company E, Ninth South Carolina Volunteers (later the Eleventh South Carolina Infantry); plantation manager in South Carolina and Texas after the war.

Stuart, Rosa, see Elliott, Rosa Stuart.

Stuart, Sarah Barnwell Means Fuller (1816–1879), of Beaufort District; daughter of Mary Hutson Barnwell and Robert Means; wife of Thomas Fuller (1813–1845); second husband was Henry Middleton Stuart Sr. (1803–1872).

Stuart, Sarah Barnwell Stuart (1838–1918), of Beaufort District; daughter of Mary Howe Barnwell and Col. Middleton Stuart; wife of Henry Middleton Stuart Jr.

Stuart, Sarah Means, see Elliott, Sarah Means Stuart.

Stuart, Thomas Middleton (1830–1873), of Charleston; a physician; a Confederate assistant surgeon; son of Claudia Smith (d. 1875) and John Allan Stuart (d. 1852); husband of Josephine Maria Clay.

Taber, Sarah Frances (1847–1869), "Fanny," of Charleston; daughter of Emma Smith and William Robinson Taber.

Talbird, Franklin, of Beaufort District; a builder; private in the Beaufort Artillery.

Taylor, Mary Anna Heyward (1844–1907), of Beaufort District and Columbia; daughter of Elizabeth Barnwell Smith and Nathaniel Barnwell Heyward; wife of Benjamin Walter Taylor.

Taylor, Benjamin Walter (1834–1905), of Columbia; a physician; Confederate assistant surgeon and medical director of the Cavalry Corps, Army of Northern Virginia.

Taylor, Eliza Mathews Coffin (1843–1919), of Charleston; daughter of Sarah Lewis Simons and George Mathews Coffin; worked in the Columbia branch of the Confederate Treasury Note Bureau during the war; married John Taylor (1842–1912) of Columbia in 1870.

Taylor, William Hayne (1838–1862), of Columbia; son of Sarah Martha Hayne and Alexander Ross Taylor (1812–1888); first lieutenant and adjutant of the Hampton Legion; died of disease at Petersburg, Virginia, 18 April 1862.

Thom, William Alexander, of Virginia; Confederate surgeon in charge of General Hospital No. 12 in Richmond and surgeon in charge of the Fourth Division, Jackson Hospital, Richmond.

Thomas, David L., of Beaufort District; private and gunner's corporal in the Beaufort Artillery and on detached service with the Commissary Department in the Department of South Carolina, Georgia, and Florida.

Thomas, Rev. Edward (1800–1840), of Charleston; rector of Trinity Protestant Episcopal Church, Edisto Island, Charleston District, from 1827 to 1835 and of St. John's Parish, Berkeley District, from 1836 to his death.

Thomson, William, of St. Helena's Parish; a student in 1860; corporal and later sergeant in the Beaufort Artillery.

Thornwell, Gillespie Robbins (1844–1863), of Columbia; the son of Rev. James Henley Thornwell; private in Company D, Hampton Legion (Cavalry), then in Company H, Second South Carolina Cavalry; wounded and captured at Warrenton Junction, Virginia, 2 May 1863; died two days later.

Thornwell, Rev. James Henley (1812–1862), president of South Carolina College, 1851–1855; professor of theology at the Columbia Theological Seminary; minister of First Presbyterian Church, Columbia.

Timrod, Henry (1828–1867), of Charleston; poet; associate editor of the *Columbia Daily South Carolinian,* 1864–1865; popular in the South for his Confederate poems.

Togno, Rosalie Acelie Guillou, "Madame," of Charleston and Columbia; wife of Dr. Joseph Togno (d. 1859); an educator and wartime principal of the South Carolina Female Collegiate Institute (Barhamville Institute or Barhamville Academy), near Columbia from June 1862 to the fall of 1864.

Torriani, Eugenio, of Italy; an opera singer stranded in the South at the beginning of the war; professor of music at the Barhamville Institute in 1863.

Trenholm, Emily St. Pierre, see Hazzard, Emily St. Pierre Trenholm.

Trenholm, George Alfred (1807–1876), of Charleston; a banker and businessman; state representative; partner in Fraser, Trenholm and Company, the Liverpool branch of the Charleston cotton shipping firm of John Fraser and Company, which regularly ran the Federal blockade of Confederate ports; Confederate secretary of the Treasury.

Trescot, Edward Boquet, of Beaufort District; son of Eliza Natalie Cuthbert and William Henry Trescot; private in the Beaufort Artillery until he was severely wounded at Pocotaligo on 22 October 1862; midshipman in the Confederate navy in 1864–1865.

Trescot, Eliza, of Beaufort District; resident of St. Helena's Parish; sister of Edward Boquet Trescot.

Trescot, Eliza Natalie Cuthbert (1827–1910), of Charleston and Beaufort Districts; wife of William Henry Trescot; daughter of Eliza Natalia Barnwell (1801–1831) and Thomas Heyward Cuthbert (1798–1840); granddaughter of Mary Bull Maxcy.

Trescot, William Henry (1822–1898), of Charleston and Beaufort Districts; a planter on Barnwell Island in the Savannah River; attorney; assistant U.S. secretary of state in 1860; secretary of U.S. legation in London in 1852.

Tucker, Daniel, assistant surgeon of the Eleventh South Carolina Infantry.

Tyng, Rev. Stephen Higginson (1800–1885), of New York; Episcopal clergyman; preceded Rev. James H. Fowles as rector of the Church of the Epiphany in Philadelphia; served over thirty years as rector of St. George's Church, New York City.

Van Wyck, Charles Henry (1824–1895), of New York; Federal colonel of the Fifty-sixth New York Infantry; commander of a brigade in the Department of the South; after the war was brigadier general in command of occupation troops in Anderson.

Walker, Ann Bull Barnwell (1818–1807), wife of Rev. Edward Tabb Walker; daughter of Sarah Bull (1782–1862) and Capt. John Gibbes Barnwell (1778–1828); first cousin of Mary Maxcy Leverett.

Walker, Edmund Rhett (1836–1891), of Beaufort; physician; son of Mariana Smith and Rev. Joseph Rogers Walker; Confederate surgeon in charge of the South Carolina Hospital at Petersburg, Virginia; husband of Jane Lewis Perkins of Virginia.

Walker, Rev. Edward Tabb (1818–1896), of St. Helena's Parish; son of Elizabeth Rogers and Zadock Walker; husband of Ann Bull Barnwell; a planter; Episcopal clergyman who ministered among the slaves near Beaufort with Rev. Charles Leverett, 1856–1860; rector of St. Helena's Parish Chapel of Ease on St. Helena Island; rector of Trinity Protestant Episcopal Church in Edgefield, 1863–1866.

Walker, Joseph (1835–1902), of Spartanburg; captain in Company K, Fifth South Carolina; lieutenant colonel and colonel of the Palmetto Sharpshooters for most of the war; state representative in 1864; bank president; mayor of Spartanburg after the war.

Walker, Rev. Joseph Rogers (1796–1879), born in Pennsylvania; son of Elizabeth Rogers and Zadock Walker; rector of St. Helena's Church, Beaufort, 1824–1879; husband of Mariana Smith.

Walker, Josephine Rogers, see Fuller, Josephine Rogers Walker.

Walker, William Stephen (1822–1899), of Florida; Confederate colonel and acting inspector general; colonel and brigadier general in command of districts in the Department of South Carolina, Georgia, and Florida; South Carolina brigade in the Department of North Carolina and Southern Virginia.

Wallace, Alfred (1835–1890), of Columbia; physician; son of Sarah Clifton Patrick and Andrew Wallace (1783–1862); husband of Sarah Davie Burroughs; served at Wayside Hospital periodically during the war.

Wallace, Sarah Davie Burroughs, of Columbia; daughter of Ella DeSaussure and Henry Burroughs; wife of Dr. Alfred Wallace.

Wallace, Victoria C. McLemore (d. 1873), of Columbia; wife of William Wallace; daughter of John McLemore.

Wallace, William (1824–1902), of Columbia; a planter and a lawyer; son of Sarah Clifton Patrick and Andrew Wallace (1783–1862); husband of Victoria C. McLemore; colonel of the Second South Carolina Infantry; state representative and state senator after the war.

Waring, Malvina Sarah Black (1842–1930), of Columbia; wife of Clark Waring.

Washburn, Emory (1800–1877), governor of Massachusetts, 1854–1855.

Washburn, Minnie, of Boston; daughter of Gov. Emory Washburn (1800–1877).

Webb, Rev. Benjamin C. (d. 1855), of Prince William's Parish; planter and Episcopal clergyman who ministered among the slaves, 1837–1855.

Webb, Mary M., of Beaufort District; wife of Rev. Benjamin C. Webb.

Whitehead, Stephen, of St. Peter's Parish; a planter.

Wilkie, Joseph B., "Joe," of Charleston; merchant; private in Company B, Third South Carolina Cavalry; in the Beaufort Artillery; a clerk to the assistant quartermaster in the Third Military District, Department of South Carolina, Georgia, and Florida.

Wilkins, Gouverneur M., of St. Luke's Parish; a planter.

Willcox, Charles H., of St. Helena's Parish; a native of Massachusetts; merchant; quartermaster sergeant of the Beaufort Artillery.

Williams, George Walton (1820–1903), of Charleston; a banker and merchant; president of George W. Williams and Company; director of the Bank of South Carolina; city alderman of Charleston.

Wyman, Benjamin Franklin (b. 1839), of Beaufort District; medical student in 1860; Confederate sergeant, orderly, and captain of Company F, Ninth South Carolina Volunteers (later the Eleventh South Carolina Infantry); physician in Columbia after the war.

Wyman, Mary N. Edwards (b. 1835), of Beaufort District; wife of Benjamin Franklin Wyman.

Yates, Thomas R. (b. 1826), of Prince William's Parish; a planter.

Bibliographical Essay

A complete bibliography of sources consulted in editing the Leverett papers would be of little interest to most readers of this volume and not as useful as a brief discussion of the major sources consulted, arranged by type.

Federal, state, and local governmental records, including the United States Census for South Carolina with components such as the Population Schedules for 1850, 1860, and 1870, the Slave Schedules for 1850 and 1860, and the Agricultural Schedules for 1850, 1860, and 1870, were very useful in identifying persons, places, events, and other terms. Also vital were Confederate military records, such as "Compiled Service Records of Confederate Soldiers Who Served in Organizations from the State of South Carolina" and "Compiled Service Records of Confederate General and Staff Officers and Nonregimental Enlisted Men." Land and property records, such as the Beaufort County and Richland County deeds; the Richland County inventories, appraisements, and sales; and "Claims for Property Loss Due to the Enemy" were also helpful. All these records were consulted on microfilm or as original records at the South Carolina Department of Archives and History in Columbia. Another significant unpublished source is the four-volume set of "University of South Carolina Alumni Questionnaires" at the South Caroliniana Library in Columbia.

Significant nineteenth-century periodicals consulted include newspapers such as the *Columbia Daily South Carolinian, Columbia Daily Southern Guardian, Columbia Daily Phoenix, Charleston Mercury, and Charleston Courier* and, to a more limited extent, the *New York Times* and *New York Herald*. Also useful were the *Southern Episcopalian*—the monthly magazine of the diocese of South Carolina—and the annual *Journal of the Proceedings of the . . . Annual Convention of the Protestant Episcopal Church in South Carolina,* as well as the published city directories for Charleston and Columbia for most of the period. The dozens of South Carolina genealogies published in the *South Carolina Historical and Genealogical Magazine* and its successor, the *South Carolina Historical Magazine*, were also of considerable value in identifying persons and establishing birth and death dates.

Standard biographical directories consulted include *Appleton's Cyclopëdia of American Biography*, revised edition (1898) and the *Dictionary of American Biography*, as well as more specialized biographical directories such as Richard J. Côté, *Dictionary of South Carolina Biography*; Ezra J. Warner, *Generals in Blue* and *Generals in Gray*; and Robert K. Krick, *Lee's Colonels*. Other significant reference works consulted include Albert Sidney Thomas, *A Historical Account of the Protestant Episcopal Church in South Carolina*; Patricia L. Faust, ed., *The Historical Times Illustrated Encyclopedia of the Civil War*; E. B. Long, *The Civil War Day By Day*; and the massive documentary sets *The War of the Rebellion: Official Records of the Union and Confederate Armies* and *Official Records of the Union and Confederate Navies*.

Charles Edward Leverett, *A Memoir, Biographical and Genealogical, of Sir John Leverett, Knt., Governor of Massachusetts, 1673–9; of Hon. John Leverett, F.R.S., Judge of the Supreme Court, and President of Harvard College; and of the Family Generally* (1856) was helpful in identifying the relatives of Rev. Charles Edward Leverett. Stephen B. Barnwell, *The Story of an American Family* (1969), was particularly useful in identifying and determining the relationships among the various people mentioned in the letters, most of whom were Mary Maxcy Leverett's relatives whose families had lived in the South Carolina lowcountry for generations.

Index